To Katherine —

Going to miss you.
Hope you get a chance to
read this and as you
do that the Lord Himself Him
will draw your heart to Him
Billy Graham is one of my
many favorites & has been a faithful
servant of the Lord.

Karen

BILLY GRAHAM

BILLY GRAHAM

THE INSPIRATIONAL WRITINGS

Peace With God

The Secret of Happiness

Answers to Life's Problems

Inspirational Press · New York

First Inspirational Press edition published in 1995.

Inspirational Press
A division of BBS Publishing Corporation
450 Raritan Center Parkway
Edison, NJ 08837

Inspirational Press is a registered trademark of BBS Publishing Corporation.

Published by arrangement with Word Publishing, a division of Thomas Nelson,
Inc.

Distributed by World Publishing
Nashville, TN 37214
www.worldpublishing.com

Library of Congress Control Number: 95-77764

ISBN: 0-88486-357-3

Printed in the United States of America.

Contents

Peace With God

Therefore being justified by faith, we have peace with God through our Lord Jesus Christ. ROMANS 5 :1

CONTENTS

PREFACE

IN THE THREE decades since *Peace with God* was originally written, an embattled world seems to have permanently lost its fragile grasp on serenity. For the first time in history, an entire generation of young people lives in fear that time, in the form of a nuclear holocaust, will run out before they can grow up, which may explain in part why tragic numbers of them at the peak of youthful promise find various ways to drop out of life. We have become a generation of escape artists. As I write these words, armed conflicts are raging in many places around the globe and the streets of more than one great city ring with gunfire. An American President was assassinated since the book was written, as were an Attorney General, a civil rights leader, an Egyptian President and a famous rock star. Another President was the victim of an attempted assassination. Hostages have been in many places and a Korean passenger jet shot down. Many wars have been fought. Nor can we turn to the security of our homes to find inner peace, for many of our homes simply aren't there anymore as nearly half of all new marriages now end in divorce. This strife that runs rampant in the world at large is but a reflection of the conflict storming individual hearts.

Millions have read this book in its original version. It has been translated into more than thirty languages. Thousands have written to tell how their own lives or the lives of someone else have been transformed and affected. We have been told that it is the most read and distributed religious book in the Eastern world. A customs official in one of these areas came across a copy of *Peace with God* in the luggage of a Christian visiting his country. The tourist said he would happily give it to him, but he had promised it to a friend in that country.

"Then will you wait while I read it?" the official asked. So our friend waited— half an hour, an hour, two hours. Finally, without comment, the book was returned to the suitcase and our friend was waved through. In revising it, I was amazed to find how relevant the original was, yet some details needed updating.

This revised edition, as did the original *Peace with God*, points the way, the *only* way, to authentic personal peace in a world in crisis. Since its publication thirty-one years ago, millions of readers here and in other lands have followed its clear, simple steps and discovered for themselves the revolutionary new life offered by a once unknown Galilean. These include men writing on Death Row and even one of my sons-in-law.

One of the reporters who covered our Crusade in Bristol, England, was asked if she had been involved in a church before coming to Bristol and she replied, "O yes, I'm a Christian. I was converted through Billy Graham in 1954." As a ten-year-old girl, away at boarding school, she had gone to a "jumble sale" (similar to our garage sales). On the table were a number of books. She noticed a copy of *Peace with God* and was immediately drawn to it. She paid sixpence for it—

all the money she had at the moment—and stayed up all night reading it by flashlight in her room back at the school. She accepted Christ as a result of reading that book. Although she had grown up in the church, she had never had anyone explain the simple message of the gospel and how she could respond to Christ.

It is my prayer that this revised edition will find its way into the hands and hearts of a lost, confused and searching world, for I sense that now, even more than when the book was first written, men, women and young people everywhere thirst for peace with God.

I am deeply grateful to all those who have counseled with me in the preparation of this new edition. Special thanks are due to my wife, Ruth, who worked many hours on its revision; my oldest daughter, GiGi Tchividjian; and my secretary, Stephanie Wills. May God use this book to touch the lives of millions more in this new generation.

BILLY GRAHAM

I
ASSESSING
THE SITUATION

1

The Great Quest

And ye shall seek me, and find me, when ye shall search for me with all your heart.
JEREMIAH 29:13

YOU STARTED ON the Great Quest the moment you were born. It was many years perhaps before you realized it, before it became apparent that you were constantly searching—searching for something you never had—searching for something that was more important than anything in life. Sometimes you have tried to forget about it. Sometimes you have attempted to lose yourself in other things so there could be time and thought for nothing but the business at hand. Sometimes you may even have felt that you were freed from the need to go on seeking this nameless thing. At moments you have almost been able to dismiss the quest completely. But always you have been caught up in it again—always you have had to come back to your search.

At the loneliest moments in your life you have looked at other men and women and wondered if they too were seeking—something they couldn't describe but knew they wanted and needed. Some of them seemed to have found fulfillment in marriage and family living. Others went off to achieve fame and fortune in other parts of the world. Still others stayed at home and prospered, and looking at them you may have thought: "These people are not on the Great Quest. These people have found their way. They knew what they wanted and have been able to grasp it. It is only I who travel this path that leads to nowhere. It is only I who goes asking, seeking, stumbling along this dark and despairing road that has no guideposts."

The Cry of Mankind

But you are not alone. All mankind is traveling with you, for all mankind is on this same quest. All humanity is seeking the answer to the confusion, the moral sickness, the spiritual emptiness that oppresses the world. All mankind is crying out for guidance, for comfort, for peace.

We are told that we live in the "age of anxiety." Historians point out that there have been few times in all history when man has been subject to so much fear and uncertainty. All the familiar props seem to have been swept away. We talk of peace but are confronted by war at every turn. We devise elaborate schemes for security but have not found it. We grasp at every passing straw and even as we clutch, it disappears.

For generations we have been running like frightened children, up first one blind alley and then another. Each time we have told ourselves: "This path is the right one, this one will take us where we want to go." But each time we have been wrong.

The Path of Political Freedom

One of the first paths we chose was labeled "political freedom." Give everyone political freedom, we said, and the world will become a happy place. Let us select our own government leaders and we shall have the kind of government that will make life worth living. So we achieved political freedom, but we did not achieve our better world. Our daily newspapers give us reports of corruption in high places, of favoritism, of exploitation, of hypocrisy equal to and sometimes surpassing the despotism of ancient kings. Political freedom is a precious and important thing, but it alone cannot give us the kind of world we long for.

There was another very hopeful path marked "education," and many put their whole faith in it. Political freedom coupled with education will do the trick, they said, and we all rushed madly along the educational path. It seemed a bright, well-lighted, sensible path for a long time, and we traveled it with eager, expectant feet, but where has it led us? You know the answer. We are the most informed people in the history of civilization—and yet the most confused. Our high school students know more about the physical laws of the universe than the greatest scientist in the days of Aristotle. But though our heads are crammed with knowledge, our hearts are empty.

The brightest, most inviting path of all was the one marked "higher standards of living." Almost everyone felt he could trust this one to carry him automatically into that better and more joyful world. This was felt to be the sure route. This was the "press the button and you're there" route! This was the path that led through the beautiful full-color magazine advertisements, past all the shining new cars, past the gleaming rows of electric refrigerators and automatic washing machines, past all the fat chickens cooking in brand-new copper-bottomed pots. We knew we'd hit the jackpot this time! The other paths might have been false leads, but this time we had it!

All right, look around you right this minute. At this very moment in history you see in America a country that has political freedom to an extent undreamed of in many parts of the civilized world. You see the greatest and most far-reaching public education system that man has ever created, and we are eulogized at home and abroad for our high standard of living. "The American way of life" we like to call this fully electrified, fully automatic, chrome-plated economy of ours—but has it made us happy? Has it brought us the joy and satisfaction and the reason for living that we were seeking?

No. As we stand here feeling smug and proud that we have accomplished so much that generations before us only dreamed about; as we span our oceans in hours instead of months; as we produce miracle drugs that wipe out some of man's most dread diseases; as we erect buildings that make the Tower of Babel seem an anthill; as we learn more and more of the mysterious secrets that lie in the depths of the sea, and probe further and further into outer space, do we lose one iota of that empty feeling within us? Do all these modern wonders bring us a sense of fulfillment, do they help to explain why we are here, do they point out what we are supposed to learn?

Or does that awful hollow feeling persist? Does every further discovery of the magnitude of the universe comfort us or make us feel more alone and helpless than ever? Does the antidote for human fear and hatred and corruption lie in some laboratory test tube, or in an astronomer's telescope?

The Seduction of Science

We cannot deny that science has given man many things he thought he wanted. But this same science has now presented us the most dreaded gift ever bestowed upon humanity. The life and future of every living being on this planet is affected by this gift of science. It stands like a somber shadow behind our waking thoughts. It stalks like a specter of horror through our children's dreams. We pretend it isn't there. We try to pretend that we haven't received this gift, that it's all a joke, and that some morning we'll wake up and find that we haven't conquered outer space and that nuclear weaponry has never been perfected— but our morning newspaper tells us a different story.

There are other paths, of course, and many are traveling them this very moment. There are the paths of fame and fortune, of pleasure and power. None of them leads anywhere but deeper into the mire. We are ensnared in the web of our own thinking, trapped so cleverly and so completely that we can no longer see either the cause or the cure of the disease that is inflicting such deadly pain.

If it is true that "for every illness there is a cure," then we must make haste to find it. The sand in civilization's hourglass is rapidly falling away, and if there is a path that leads to the light, if there is a way back to spiritual health, we must not lose an hour!

The Search for Solutions

Many are floundering in this time of crisis and finding that their efforts are leading them not up but only further down into the pit.

The suicide rate has sky-rocketed in the '80s. For children 10–14 the suicide rate has tripled in the last ten years. *Leadership* magazine estimates that half a million people attempt suicide annually—and 50,000 succeed. In 1981 more people died by suicide than by homicide.

Last year thousands of Americans, many of them teenagers, who couldn't find even the wrong answers, took their own lives in preference to wandering any further in this man-made jungle we call civilization.

Over the past couple of decades our divorce rates have soared, even within the church with one out of two marriages ending in divorce. The divorce rate has increased 100 percent since 1900!

We spend a fortune to "adopt" cute cabbage patch dolls, while our children are caught up in child abuse or subjected to the horrible atrocities of "kiddy-porn." We hear about abortion on demand, surrogate motherhood, sperm banks and so on. Our families are riddled with all kinds of abuses and aberrations.

So "Where are we?" you ask. "Where are we now and where are we going?" Let me tell you *where* we are and *what* we are. We are a nation of empty people. Our heads are crammed full of knowledge, but within our souls is a spiritual vacuum.

We complained in the past that the youth of this country had lost its drive, its push, its willingness to work and to get ahead. Every day I heard parents say that they didn't understand why their children didn't want to work but just wanted everything handed to them. Parents didn't seem to realize that their well-educated, carefully brought up children were actually empty inside. They weren't filled with the spirit that makes work a joy. They weren't filled with the determination that makes pushing ahead a pleasure. And why were they so empty? Because they didn't know where they had come from, why they were here, or where they were going!

Today our young people are asking for direction and perspective. They are looking for models to follow, for patterns of purpose.

They are like rows of beautiful new automobiles, perfect in every detail but with no gasoline in the tanks. The exteriors are fine, but there's nothing inside to give them power. And so they just sit and rust—with boredom.

The Breadth of Boredom

America is said to have the highest per capita boredom of any spot on earth! We know that because we have the greatest variety and greatest number of artificial amusements of any country. People have become so empty that they can't even entertain themselves. They have to pay other people to amuse them, to make them laugh, to try to make them feel warm and happy and comfortable for a few minutes, to try to lose that awful, frightening, hollow feeling—that terrible, dreaded feeling of being lost and alone.

You may think that boredom is a minor matter. Everyone gets bored sometimes, it's only natural. But let me tell you something about boredom, and this dangerous apathy that is creeping over the land and over the minds and hearts of the people. Man is the only one of God's creatures who is capable of being bored, although I've seen animals in a zoo that *look* very bored! No other living thing except man can ever be bored with itself or its surroundings. This is very significant, for the Creator never does anything without a purpose, and if He gave man the capacity for boredom, He did it for a purpose.

Boredom is one of the sure ways to measure your own inner emptiness! It's as accurate as a thermometer for telling just how hollow your inner spirit really is. The person who is thoroughly bored is living and working in a vacuum. His inner self is a vacuum, and there is nothing that nature resents more than a vacuum. It is one of the unfailing rules of this universe that all vacuums must be filled, and filled immediately.

A Nation of Empty People

We do not have to go back to ancient times to see what happens to a nation of empty people. We need look no further than the recent history of Germany or Italy to see with what deadly speed nature fills up the vacuums that occur within us. Nazism in Germany and fascism in Italy could find no place in the heart and soul of a person who was filled with the Spirit of God, but false ideologies flood with the greatest ease into the minds and hearts of those who are empty and waiting. Nature abhors a vacuum, but it is up to us as individuals to determine with what our inner vacuums shall be filled.

So that is where we stand today—nations of empty people. We have tried to fill ourselves with science and education, with better living and pleasure, with the many other things we thought we wanted. We have increasingly decadent capitalism at one extreme, and godless communism at the other. But we are still empty. Why are we empty? Because the Creator made us for Himself; and we shall never find completeness and fullness apart from fellowship with Him.

In a recent interview in the *Presbyterian Journal* (2 November 1983) the eminent Catholic columnist, Michael Novak, says of our situation: "Socialism is a system for saints, . . . democratic capitalism . . . is a system for sinners." That's why he feels socialism won't work in this world.

Jesus told us long ago that "Man shall not live by bread alone" (Luke 4:4), but we have paid no heed. We have tried to do just that.

We cannot stand the terrible emptiness of ourselves, we cannot look at the lonely, desolate road that lies ahead. We are desperately weary of the hatred and greed and lust that we know are within us, but we are helpless to be rid of them and be filled with something better.

"Time and tide wait for no man," said Sir Walter Scott. The tools of total annihilation have been placed within our reach. We cannot scurry up any more false paths, we cannot explore any more unknown roads, we cannot afford to be trapped in any more blind alleys. We don't have that much time! For our generation has accomplished what other generations only *tried* to do, or dreamed of doing in their most insane moments of power and ruthlessness! We have achieved the weapons of total destruction. We are witnessing the climax of man's madness—the impending nuclear holocaust.

How the demons must have laughed as some of the most brilliant men on earth worked furiously for years to achieve this horror! The atom cleaved! Divide and conquer! Split apart, destroy, shatter, crush, crumble! The great deceiver has done his work, and men have been eager to aid him. We see before us Satan's masterpiece, his clever counterfeit of the cloven tongues of divine fire. For this satanic fire and the pentecostal flames both fall from above, both are cloven, both illuminate, both instantly transform everything they touch—but with such a difference. The difference of heaven and hell!

A Topsy-turvy World

We are living in a topsy-turvy world, where all is confusion. But you may be sure that it is confusion with a plan—Satan's plan! The Bible tells us that Satan is the great deceiver and he has devoted himself to the cause of our great self-deception and to the deceptions that lie between nations all over this world. He has led us to believe that things were getting better, when they are really getting worse.

We all recognize that the world has changed radically since the beginning of this century. We are aware of its increased tempo, of the spirit of revolution that is sweeping away the established landmarks and traditions, of the speed with which language, fashions, customs, housing, and our ways of living and thinking are being altered and changed.

Only a few years ago children were delighted at the prospect of a trip to the train station to watch the trains come in. Today they are blasé about the space shuttle. How many know when the next shuttle flight takes off, or who will be aboard? We who once marveled at the telegraph, now take the far greater miracle of television for granted. Not so long ago many of man's physical diseases were termed hopeless and incurable. Today, we have drugs so effective that many age-old diseases are disappearing. We have accomplished much, of that there is no doubt.

But with all this progress, man has not solved the basic problem of the human race. We can build the highest buildings, the fastest planes, the longest bridges. We have successfully probed the far reaches of space and conquered the unknown. But we still can't govern ourselves or live together in equality and peace!

We may create great new schools of art and music, we may discover newer and better vitamins, but there is nothing new about our troubles. They are the same old ones that man has always had, only they seem magnified and more abundant. They may come upon us in new ways, they may seem to give sharper pain and deeper anguish; but fundamentally we are facing the same temptations, the same trials, the same testings that have always confronted mankind.

Forever since that tragic moment in the Garden of Eden, when man gave up God's will for his own will, man has been plagued by the same problems. Their cause is stated in the third chapter of Genesis. The terrible conditions that produced them are related in the first chapter of Romans. And the gospel of Jesus Christ gives us their remedy.

It is man's depraved and sinful nature that fills him with hate, envy, greed, and jealousy. The curse of sin is upon his body and he is forever haunted by the fear of death. His inventive genius has enabled him to change everything but himself. For man, in spite of the loudly acclaimed "progress" of our times, remains just as he was in the beginning.

Sin Is Still the Same

Sin, too, has remained unchanged, although man has done his best to alter it. We've tried to dress it up with other names. We've put new labels on the same old bottle of poison. We've tried to whitewash the rotting building and pretend it was sound (or new).

We've tried calling sin "errors" or "mistakes" or "poor judgment," but sin itself has stayed the same. No matter how we try to salve our conscience, we've known all along that men are still sinners; and the results of sin are still disease, disappointment, disillusionment, despair, and death.

Sorrow hasn't changed, either. It began when Adam and Eve looked with broken hearts upon the lifeless body of their murdered son Abel and knew the crushing weight of grief. It has gone on, until today sorrow is the universal language of man. No one escapes it, everyone experiences it. It even seemed to one of Job's comforters that it was the aim of life, for he said, "Yet man is born unto trouble, as the sparks fly upward" (Job 5:7).

Death is also still the same. Men have tried to change its appearance. We have changed the word "undertaker" to "mortician." We place bodies in "caskets" now instead of "coffins." We have "funeral homes" instead of "undertaking parlors" and "memorial parks" instead of "graveyards." We try to soften the starkness of the last rites; but regardless of what we call it, or how lifelike we make the corpse through make-up, the cold, hard, cruel reality of death has not changed throughout all of man's history. A friend, struggling with terminal cancer, recently wrote: "It has dawned on me that cancer is not terminal—life is!"

These three facts constitute the true story of man: his past is filled with sin; his present is overflowing with sorrow; and the certainty of death faces him in the future.

The Bible says, "It is appointed unto men once to die . . ." (Hebrews 9:27), and to the average person this seems a stark and hopeless situation. Hundreds of philosophies and scores of religions have been invented by men in their efforts to circumvent the Word of God. Modern philosophers and psychologists are still trying to make it appear that there is some way out other than the path of Jesus. But man has tried them all and none of them leads anywhere but down.

Christ came to give us the answers to the three enduring problems of sin, sorrow, and death. It is Jesus Christ, and He alone, who is also enduring and unchanging, "the same yesterday, and today and forever" (Hebrews 13:8). As the hymnwriter, Henry F. Lyte, wrote: "Change and decay in all around I see; O Thou who changest not, abide with me."

All other things may change, but Christ remains unchangeable. In the restless sea of human passions, Christ stands steadfast and calm, ready to welcome all who will turn to Him and accept the blessings of safety and peace. For we are living in an age of grace, in which God promises that whosoever will may come and receive His Son. But this period of grace will not go on indefinitely. We are even now living on borrowed time.

2

The Indestructible Bible

Heaven and earth shall pass away, but my words shall not pass away. MATTHEW 24:35

TIME IS RUNNING out. The seconds are ticking away toward midnight. The human race is about to take the fatal plunge. Have we just been placed here by some unknown creator or force without any clue as to where we came from, why we are here, and where we are going? Which way shall we turn? Is there any authority left? Is there a path we can follow? Is there any light penetrating the inky darkness? Can we find a codebook that will give us the key to our dilemmas? Is there any source of authority to which we can turn?

The answer to the first question is, No. The answer to all the rest is, Yes. We do have a codebook. We do have a key. We do have authoritative source material. It is found in the ancient and historic Book we call the Bible. This Book has come down to us through the ages. It has passed through so many hands, appeared in so many forms—and survived attack of every kind. Neither barbaric vandalism nor civilized scholarship has touched it. Neither the burning of fire nor the laughter of skepticism has accomplished its annihilation. Through the many dark ages of man, its glorious promises have survived unchanged. It is interesting to note that while Bible reading has been outlawed in our public schools it is required reading in the Catholic schools of communist Poland.

The British and Foreign Bible Society was on Jerusalem Street, one of the main streets of Old Warsaw in World War II. When the Germans began bombing the city, the wife of the director went to the storeroom and carried some 2,000 Bibles down to the basement. She was trapped by the bombing and later captured by the Germans and put in a prison camp. She managed to escape, and after the war was over was able to get to those 2,000 Bibles and distribute them to people in need. Warsaw was flattened, but on Jerusalem Street one wall of the old British and Foreign Bible Society remained standing. On it were these words, painted in large letters: "HEAVEN AND EARTH SHALL PASS AWAY, BUT MY WORDS SHALL NOT PASS AWAY."

Now, as we approach what appears to be another decisive hour in world history, let us re-examine this indestructible Book of wisdom and prophecy; let us

find out why this particular volume has endured and been man's unfailing source
of faith and spiritual strength.

The Bible Is More Than Just Great Literature

There are those who regard the Bible principally as the history of Israel. Others
admit that it sets forth the soundest ethics ever enunciated. But these things,
important as they are, are only incidental to the real theme of the Bible, which
is the story of God's redemption as it exists in Jesus Christ. In an editorial which
appeared 30 June 1983 the *International Herald Tribune* recommended that the
Bible should be read as literature because it is "The English language at its best."
Those who read the Scriptures as magnificent literature, breath-taking poetry
or history, and overlook the story of salvation, miss the Bible's real meaning
and message.

God caused the Bible to be written for the express purpose of revealing to man
God's plan for his redemption. God caused this Book to be written that He might
make His everlasting laws clear to His children, and that they might have His
great wisdom to guide them and His great love to comfort them as they make
their way through life. For without the Bible, this world would indeed be a dark
and frightening place, without signpost or beacon.

The Bible easily qualifies as the only Book in which is God's revelation. There
are many bibles of different religions; there is the Muslim Koran, the Buddhist
Canon of Sacred Scripture, the Zoroastrian Zend-Avesta, and the Brahman
Vedas. All of these have been made accessible to us by reliable translations.
Anyone can read them, comparing them with the Bible, and judge for themselves. It is soon discovered that all these non-Christian bibles have parts of
truth in them, but they are all developments ultimately in the wrong direction.
They all begin with some flashes of true light, and end in utter darkness. Even
the most casual observer soon discovers that the Bible is radically different. It
is the only Book that offers man a redemption and points the way out of his
dilemmas. It is our one sure guide in an unsure world.

Sixteen hundred years were needed to complete the writing of the Bible. It is
the work of more than thirty authors, each of whom acted as a scribe of God.
Those men, many of whom lived generations apart, did not set down merely
what they thought or hoped. They acted as channels for God's revelation; they
wrote as He directed them; and under His divine inspiration they were able to
see the great and enduring truths, and to record them that other men might see
and know them too.

During these sixteen hundred years, the sixty-six books of the Bible were
written by men of different languages, living in different times, and in different countries; but the message they wrote was one. God spoke to each man in
his own language, in his own time, but His message basically in each case was

the same. When the great scholars gathered together the many ancient manuscripts written in Hebrew, Aramaic and Greek, and translated them into a single modern tongue, they found that God's promises remain unchanged, His great message to man had not varied. As we read these ageless words today, we find that the rules of conduct set forth by the ancient scribes are as fresh and meaningful to this generation as they were to the people of Jesus' time. John Ruskin said: "The Bible is the one Book to which any thoughtful man may go with any honest question of life or destiny and find the answer of God by honest searching."

The World's Best Seller!

It is small wonder, then, that the Bible has always been the world's best seller! No other book can touch its profound wisdom, its poetic beauty, or the accuracy of its history and prophecy. Its critics, who claimed it to be filled with forgery, fiction, and unfilled promises, are finding that the difficulties lie with themselves, and not the Bible. Greater and more careful scholarship has shown that apparent contradictions were caused by incorrect translations rather than divine inconsistencies. It was man and not the Bible who needed correcting. Someone has said, "The Bible does not have to be rewritten, but reread."

And yet—in many homes and among so-called educated people—it has become fashionable to joke about the Bible and to regard it more as a dust catcher than as the living Word of God. When asked by her minister if she knew what was in the Bible, one little girl proudly replied that she knew everything that was in it, and proceeded to list "the picture of her sister's boyfriend, the coupon for mother's favorite hand lotion, a lock of baby brother's hair, and the ticket for Pa's watch!" That was all she knew about the family Bible. Too many families have used the Bible as a safe storage place for old letters and pressed flowers, and have overlooked entirely the help and assurance that God intended this Book to give them.

This attitude is changing now, and changing fast! Life is being stripped of its artificialities, its meaningless trimmings. The false promises that man has made to man are standing forth now as the glaring errors they are. As we cast our frightened eyes around for something that is real and true and enduring, we are turning once more to this ancient Book that has given consolation, comfort, and salvation to millions in the centuries past. My wife Ruth once said, "If our children have the background of a godly, happy home and this unshakeable faith that the Bible is indeed the Word of God, they will have a foundation that the forces of hell cannot shake." I thank God for her godly influence in the lives of our children.

Yes, people are "discovering" the Bible again! They are dusting off their old copies or buying new ones. They are finding that the familiar but almost forgotten phrases ring with a current meaning that makes them seem to have been written only yesterday. This is because the Bible embodies all the knowledge man needs to fill the longing of his soul and solve all his problems. It is the blueprint of the Master Architect, and only by following its directions can we build the life we are seeking.

Here in America we have another great document that we value and respect. It was written some 200 years ago by a number of men who labored long and debated even longer over its many provisions, and finally sent it to the thirteen federated states for ratification. The men who framed our Constitution knew they were writing the basic document for a government of free men; they recognized that men could live as free and independent beings only if each one knew and understood the law. They were to know their rights, their privileges, and their limitations. They were to stand as equals before the court of law and few judges could be unfair; for the judge, too, was bound by the same law and required to try each case accordingly.

The Truth Shall Set Us Free!

While the rest of the world watched this great human experiment, men found that if they knew the law and lived according to it, they could, in truth, be free! A man could know just where he stood. He had his Constitutional rights and he also had his Constitutional responsibilities. If he neglected one, the other would suffer—as so many negligent voters who came later were to discover when they found themselves saddled with governmental restrictions they didn't like!

Just as America has grown and prospered within the framework of our Constitution, so Christianity has flourished and spread according to the laws set forth in the Bible. Just as the Constitution was intended to apply equally to all men living under it, without special favor or interpretation, so the Bible stands as the supreme Constitution for all mankind, its laws applying equally to all who live under its domain, without exception or special interpretation.

As the Constitution is the highest law of the land, so the Bible is the highest law of God. For it is in the Bible that God sets forth His spiritual laws. It is in the Bible that God makes His enduring promises. It is in the Bible that God reveals the plan of redemption for the human race.

In the wonders of nature we see God's laws in operation. Who has not looked up at the stars on a cloudless night, and marveled in silent awe at the glory of God's handiwork? Even our astronauts have lauded the Lord as Creator of the vastness of space and the intricacies of our universe which we are just now beginning to explore. If we could not depend on His laws, we could not make these excursions into space. Who has not felt his heart lifted in the spring of the year, as he sees all creation bursting with new life and vigor? In the beauty and abundance around us we see the magnitude of God's power and the infinite detail of His planning; but nature tells us nothing of God's love or God's grace. We do not find the promise of our personal salvation in nature.

Conscience tells us in our innermost being of the presence of God and of the moral difference between good and evil; but this is a fragmentary message, in no way as distinct and comprehensive as the lessons of the Bible. It is only in its pages that we find the clear and unmistakable message upon which all true Christianity is based.

The laws of our land find their genesis in the Ten Commandments. And Sir William Blackstone, the great English jurist, wrote: "The Bible has always been regarded as part of the Common Law of England."

Christianity finds all its doctrines stated in the Bible, and Christianity denies no part, nor attempts to add anything to the Word of God. While the Constitution of the United States may be amended from time to time, no amendment is ever necessary for the Bible. We truly believe that the men who wrote the Bible were guided by the Holy Spirit, both in the thoughts they expressed and in their choice of words. As Peter said, "For the prophecy came not in old time by the will of man: but holy men of God spake as they were moved by the Holy Ghost" (2 Peter 1:21).

Paul tells us that "All scripture is given by inspiration of God, and is profitable for doctrine, for reproof, for correction, for instruction in righteousness: That the man of God may be perfect, thoroughly furnished unto all good works" (2 Timothy 3:16–17).

In setting down their forthright messages, biblical scribes have never attempted to gloss over the realities of life. The sins of the great and small are freely admitted, the weaknesses of human nature are acknowledged, and life in biblical times is recorded as it was lived. The startling thing is that the lives and motivations of these people who lived so long ago have such a modern flavor! As we read, the pages seem like mirrors held up before our own minds and hearts, reflecting our own prides and prejudices, our own failures and humiliations, our own sins and sorrows.

Truth is timeless. Truth does not differ from one age to another, from one people to another, from one geographical location to another. Men's ideas may differ, men's customs may change, men's moral codes may vary, but the great all-prevailing Truth stands for time and eternity.

The message of Jesus Christ, our Savior, is the story of the Bible—it is the story of salvation. Profound students of the Bible have traced the story of Jesus Christ from the beginning of the Old Testament, for He is the true theme of the Old as well as the New Testament.

The fact of Jesus Christ is the eternal message of the Bible. It is the story of life, peace, eternity, and heaven. The Bible has no hidden purpose. It has no need for special interpretation. It has a single, clear, bold message for every living being—the message of Christ and His offer of peace with God.

One day upon a mountain near Capernaum Jesus sat with His disciples. They gathered before Him—perhaps Peter on one side and John on the other. Jesus may have looked quietly and tenderly at each of these devoted disciples, looked at them the way a loving parent looks at the members of his family—loving each child separately, loving each one for a special reason, loving them in such a way that each child feels singled out and individually embraced. That is how Jesus must have loved His disciples.

The little group must have become very reverent under His serene and loving gaze. They must have become very still within themselves with the feeling that something momentous was about to be said, something they must remember, something they must be able to transmit to others all over the world who were not privileged, as they were, to hear these words from the Master's own lips.

For there, on the mountain, standing perhaps under the silvery gray-green leaves of an olive tree, Jesus preached the greatest sermon that human ears have ever heard. He explained the essence of Christian living. When He was through and a holy hush had settled on His wide-eyed listeners, they "were astonished at his doctrine: for he taught them as one having authority, and not as the scribes" (Matthew 7:28, 29).

Indeed He did teach with authority, the authority of God Himself; and the rules He set forth were God's own rules, the ones which every Christian with the hope of salvation in his heart must follow.

You and the Bible

If you do not have a Bible in your home, go out and get one now—get the one that suits you best, get the size that is most comfortable for you to handle, get the kind of type that is most pleasant for you to read, and then settle down and find out for yourself why this one Book has endured. Don't be afraid to invest in the best Bible you can afford—for that is what you are making: an investment. We spend our money for expensive clothing which perishes but hesitate to buy the best in Bibles which is an investment in eternity. Find out for yourself why it answers every human need, why it supplies the faith and strength that keeps humanity marching forward.

If you and the Bible have had a long absence from each other, it might be well for you to renew your acquaintance by reading again the Gospel of John. While this is considered one of the most profound books in the Bible, it is also the clearest and most readily understood. It was written for the very purpose of showing the how and the why of man's salvation, so that the questions of the mind as well as the gropings of the heart might be satisfied.

After reading the Book of John, you might acquaint yourself with the Gospel as taught by Mark, Luke, and Matthew, noting how these men of widely different personalities and writing styles set forth the eternal story of redemption through Jesus. You will become aware of the powerful, universal truth that underlies all gospel teaching and be impressed anew with what the biblical writer meant when he said, "Jesus Christ the same yesterday, and today, and forever" (Hebrews 13:8).

When you have read each of the Gospels individually, start in at the beginning of the New Testament and read straight through all the books in order. When you have done that, you will have developed such a taste for Bible reading, you will have found it such a fountain of inspiration, such a practical counselor and guide, such a treasure chest of sound advice, that you will make Bible reading a part of your daily life.

A knowledge of the Bible is essential to a rich and meaningful life. For the words of this Book have a way of filling in the missing pieces, of bridging the gaps, of turning the tarnished colors of our life to jewel-like brilliance. Learn to take your every problem to the Bible. Within its pages you will find the correct answer.

But most of all, the Bible is a revelation of the nature of God. The philosophers of the centuries have struggled with the problem of a Supreme Being. Who is He? What is He? Where is He? If there is such a Person, is He interested in me? If so, how can I know Him? These and a thousand other questions about God are revealed in this Holy Book we call the Bible.

A Christian once asked, "Do you know a book that you are willing to put under your head for a pillow when you are dying? Very well," Joseph Cook went on, "that is the Book you want to study when you are living. There is only one such Book in the world!"

3

What Is God Like?

Canst thou by searching find out God? Job 11:7

WHO IS GOD? What is He like? How can we be sure He exists? When did He begin? Can we know Him?

Everyone has asked these questions either aloud or to himself, for we cannot look at the world around us and not wonder about its creation. We are daily faced with the miracle of life and the mystery of death, of the glory of flowering trees, the magnificence of the star-filled sky, the magnitude of mountains and of sea. Who made all this? Who conceived the law of gravity by which everything is held in its proper place? Who ordered the day and the night and the regular procession of the seasons? What about the infinity of the universe? Can we honestly believe (as someone has written), "This is all there is or was or ever will be"?

The only possible answer is that all these things and many more are the work of a Supreme Creator. As a watch must have a designer, so our precision-like universe has a Great Designer. We call Him God. His is a name with whom the whole human race is familiar. From earliest childhood we have breathed His name. The Bible declares that the God we talk about, the God we sing about, the God "from whom all blessings flow!" is the God who created this world and placed us in it. Our exploration of space would be impossible in a universe ungoverned by the laws of God.

No less a wise man than Benjamin Franklin said, "I have lived a long time and the longer I live the more convincing proofs I see that God governs in the affairs of men." Another wise man, Blaise Pascal, wrote: "If a man is not made for God, why is he happy only in God? If man is made for God, why is he opposed to God?" This is our dilemma.

But "Who is He?" you ask. "Where is He?" We know that He exists. We call upon Him in our hours of greatest difficulty and trial. Some try to let the thought of Him fill every waking moment. Others say they don't believe in Him, that He doesn't exist. And still others say, "Explain Him to me and maybe I'll accept God."

For those who, at this crucial point in world history, are wondering "What is God like?" it has been simply stated: God is like Jesus Christ. Just as Jesus came to make God visible to mankind and to become our Redeemer, even so, on His return to Heaven, He sent the Holy Spirit to indwell believers and enable them to live so as to make Christ visible to an unbelieving world.

If that is how you feel, if all your life you have been hearing about God and talking about God, but waiting for someone to explain God to you before you could put your faith in Him, and Him alone, let us see just how concrete a description the Bible can give us.

What Is God Like?

At this crucial point in world history, everyone should be seeking an answer to the question, "What is God like?" Everyone should ask it, and everyone should make very sure of the answer. Everyone should know beyond a shadow of a doubt exactly who God is and what He is capable of accomplishing. The Bible says, "Because that which may be known of God is manifest in them; for God hath shewed it unto them" (Romans 1:19).

It is the absence of the knowledge of God and man's refusal to obey Him that lie at the root of every problem which besets us. It is man's confusion about God's plan that has the world in chaos. It is man's unwillingness to learn and to obey God's laws that has laid such a heavy burden on our souls. So let us learn all that we can about Him.

Where shall we go for this knowledge? Who among us can tell us the truth? Are we not all finite creatures here together? Has God designated any one person here on earth to speak with final authority about Him? No—the one Man who could do that lived two thousand years ago, and we crucified Him! How then, are we to find out?

We can ask the learned scholars, and they may tell us that God is the expression of everything in nature and life, that all living beings are one with God, that life itself is an expression of His Divine Being. They will tell you that you can see God in the tiniest drop of water and in the great arch of the sky above.

Ask a philosopher, and he will tell you that God is the original and immutable force behind all creation, that He is the Master Dynamo who keeps all the worlds in motion—that He is the Power without beginning or end. The philosopher will say that every bit of life and beauty we see is a manifestation of this power which flows in an unending current out from the Dynamo and back again.

Ask still further and you may be told that God is absolute, that He is All in All, and that no one can possibly know any more about Him. There are many differing definitions for God. Dr. Akbar Haqq says that *originally* all people were monotheistic in their concept of God. Every country, every race of people, every family, every individual has tried to explain the Great Being behind the universe. Men of all ages have tried to discover the Creator whose work they saw, but whom they did not know. Which of these varied explanations is right? Which of these many theories are we to accept? By which of these self-appointed authorities are we to be guided?

As we have already seen in our previous chapter, God has revealed Himself in the Book called the Bible. In the Bible we have a revelation of God—and based on it our minds can be satisfied and our hearts filled. We can rest assured that we have the correct answer, that we are on our way to knowing and understanding the true nature of God.

God reveals Himself in hundreds of ways in the Bible, and if we read the Bible as carefully and as regularly as we read the daily papers, we would be as familiar with and as well informed about God as we are about our favorite player's batting average during baseball season!

As a diamond has many facets, so there are innumerable aspects of God's revelation of Himself which would take volumes to fill. Suffice it to say, with our limited space we can cover four aspects of God's revelation of Himself which seem to be the most significant, and which we should carry with us always.

'God Is Spirit'

First: the Bible declares God to be *Spirit.* Jesus talking to the woman at the Well of Sychar made this straightforward statement about God: "God is Spirit" (John 4:24).

What do you think of when you hear the word *spirit?* What mental image does it bring to your mind? Do you think of a wisp of vapor drifting across the sky? Does *spirit* mean the sort of thing that frightens children on Halloween? Is *spirit* just a formless nothingness to you? Do you think that was what Jesus meant when He said, "God is Spirit"?

To discover what "spirit" really is, and what Jesus meant when He used that particular word, we must turn again in the Bible to the scene where Christ after His resurrection says: "Handle me, and see; for a spirit hath not flesh and bones, as ye see me have" (Luke 24:39). Therefore we can be sure that spirit is *without* body. It is the *opposite* of body. Yet it has being and power. This is difficult for us to understand because we are trying to understand it with our limited, finite minds.

As human beings deprived of the unlimited vision that God originally intended His creatures to have, we cannot comprehend the glory and the magnitude of the Spirit that lies so far outside ourselves. When we hear the word "spirit," we immediately try to reduce it to our puny size, to make it fit within the scope of our small minds. It is like trying to explain the sweep and majesty and awe-inspiring grandeur of the ocean to a person who has never seen a body of water larger than a mud puddle! How can such a person envision the boundless sea? How can such a person, looking into a shallow, murky pool, fathom the bottomless depths, the mysterious life, the surging power, the ceaseless roll, the terrible ruthlessness of ocean storm or the all-surpassing beauty of ocean calm? How could anyone who had looked only into a mud puddle know what you were talking about? What words could you use to describe the mighty sea convincingly? How could you make a person believe that such a wonder really exists?

How infinitely more difficult it is for us to grasp what Jesus meant when He said: "God is Spirit." Jesus knew! His mind was not limited as our minds are limited. His eyes were not focused on the mud puddle of life. He knew full well the borderless reaches of the Spirit, and He came to try to give us some understanding of its wonders, its comfort, and its peace.

We do know that the spirit is not something bound in a body. Spirit is not wearable as a body. Spirit is not changeable as a body. The Bible declares that God is a Spirit—that He is not limited to body; He is not limited to shape; He is not limited to boundaries or bonds; He is absolutely immeasurable and undiscernible by eyes that can see only physical things. The Bible tells us that because He has no such limitations He can be everywhere at once—that He can hear all, see all, and know all.

We can't do any of that, and so we try to limit God as we are limited. We try to deny God the power to do things we can't do. We try to say that because we can't be everywhere at once, God can't be, either! We are rather like the person who, having heard about the ocean, finally makes his way to the beach one day and going down to the edge of the water, scoops up a few drops and holds them in his hands.

"Ah," he exclaims, "at last I have made the ocean mine! I hold the ocean in my hands, I possess it!" True, he does have a part of the ocean, but at the same moment other people on a thousand other shores may be reaching down and claiming a few drops of the ocean for themselves. The world's millions could come down to the beach and reach out their hands to be filled with sea water. They could each take as much as they wanted, as much as they needed—and still the ocean would remain unchanged. Its mightiness and power would be the same, the life in its unfathomable depths would continue unaltered, although it had supplied the needs of every single person standing with outstretched hands along its many shores.

So it is with God. He can be everywhere at once, heeding the prayers of all who call out in the name of Christ; performing the mighty miracles that keep the stars in their places and the plants bursting up through the earth and the fish swimming in the sea. There is no limit to God. There is no limit to His wisdom. There is no limit to His power. There is no limit to His love. There is no limit to His mercy.

If you have been trying to limit God—stop it! Don't try to confine Him or His works to any single place or sphere. You wouldn't try to limit the ocean. You cannot limit the universe. You wouldn't be bold enough to try to change the course of the moon, or to stop the earth as it turns on its axis! How everlastingly more foolish it is to try to limit the God who created and controls all these wonders!

I am eternally grateful to my mother for many things, but one of the most enduring blessings she brought into my life was to teach me in the Catechism at the age of ten that "God is a Spirit. infinite, eternal, and unchangeable in His being, wisdom, power, holiness, justice, goodness, and truth." That definition of God has been with me all my life, and when a man knows in his heart that God is an infinite, eternal, and unchangeable Spirit, it helps to overcome the temptation to limit Him. It helps to overcome all doubt about His ability to accomplish things that we can't do ourselves!

Some who doubt that the Bible is the true Word of God, doubt it because they are unwilling to ascribe to God anything they cannot themselves achieve. If you have any uncertainty about the inspiration of the Bible, go back and look at it again. Look at it in the light of a person who has been staring at a mud puddle all his life, and who is confronted for the first time by a view of the ocean! Perhaps you are only now catching your first glimpse of God's unlimited power. Perhaps you are only now beginning to understand Him for what He actually is. For if God is the Spirit that Jesus declares Him to be, there is no problem of providence, there is no problem of His sovereignty in the affairs of men, there is no problem of His inspiration of the men who wrote the Bible. Everything fits into place once you understand who and what God really is.

God Is a Person

Second: the Bible reveals Him as a *Person*. All through the Bible it says: "God loves," "God says," "God does." Everything that we attribute to a person is attributed to God. A person is one who feels, thinks, wishes, desires, and has all the expressions of personality.

Here on earth we confine personality to the body. Our finite minds cannot envision personality that is not manifested through flesh and bones. We know that our own personalities will not always be clothed in the bodies they now inhabit. We know that at the moment of death our personalities will leave our bodies and go on to the destinations that await them. We know all this—yet it is difficult for us to accept it.

What a revelation if we could all realize that personality does not have to be identified with a physical being. God is not bound by a body, yet He is a Person. He feels, He thinks, He loves, He forgives, He sympathizes with the problems and sorrows that we face.

God Is Holy and Righteous

Third: the Bible states that God is not only a Spirit and a Person, but God is also a *Holy and Righteous Being* From Genesis to Revelation, God reveals Himself as a Holy God. He is utterly perfect and absolute in every detail. He is too holy to tolerate sinful man, too holy to endure sinful living.

If we could envision the true picture of His majestic righteousness, what a difference it would make in the way we live as individuals and as nations! If we could but realize the tremendous gulf that separates unrighteous man from God's perfect righteousness! The Scripture declares Him to be the Light in whom there is no darkness at all—the one Supreme Being without flaw or blemish.

Here again is a difficult concept for imperfect man to understand. We, whose faults and weaknesses are everywhere apparent, can scarcely imagine the overwhelming holiness of God—but we must recognize it if we are to understand and benefit from the Bible.

The chasm that separates imperfect man from perfect God is emphasized all through the Scriptures. We see it in the division of the Old Testament Tabernacle and the New Testament Temple into the Holy and Most Holy places. It is pointed out in the prescribed offering that must be brought if a sinner would approach God. It is underscored by a special priesthood to mediate between God and the people. It is emphasized by the laws concerning impurity in the Book of Leviticus. We see it in the many feasts of Israel, by the isolation of Israel in Palestine. The Holiness of God regulates all other principles of God.

The Scripture declares that His throne is established on the basis of His holiness. It is because God is holy and man is unholy that so wide a rift exists between God and the unrepentant sinner. The Bible tells us that our iniquities have separated us from God—separated us so completely that His face is hidden from us and He will not hear us when we call. "If I regard iniquity in my heart," says the psalmist, "the Lord will not hear me" (Psalm 66:18). On the other hand, the psalmist says, "The eyes of the Lord are upon the righteous, and his ears are open unto their cry. . . . The Lord . . . will fulfill the desire of them that fear him: he also will hear their cry, and will save them" (Psalms 34:15; 145:18, 19).

God is too pure to look with approval upon evil, which means that He is too holy to have any dealings with sin. Before sin entered into the human race, God and man had fellowship with each other. Now that fellowship is broken, and all communication between God and man is lost outside of Jesus Christ. It is only through Jesus Christ that man can ever again re-establish his fellowship with God. There are those who say that all roads lead to God. But Jesus said, "I am *the way, the truth, and the life,* no man cometh unto the Father but by me" (John 14:6). He also said, "I am the door: by me if any man enter in, he shall be saved, and shall go in and out, and find pasture" (John 10:9).

Man is a sinner, powerless to change his position, powerless to reach the pure ear of God unless he cries out for mercy sincerely. Man would have remained forever lost if God in His infinite mercy had not sent His Son to earth to bridge this gulf.

It is in God's holiness that we find the reason for the death of Christ. Jesus was the only one good enough, pure enough, strong enough, to bear the sins of the whole world. God's holiness demanded the most exacting penalty for sin, and His love provided Jesus Christ to pay this penalty and provide man with salvation. Because the God we worship is a pure God, a holy God, a just and righteous God, He sent us His only begotten Son to make it possible for us to have access to Him. But if we ignore the help He has sent, if we fail to obey the laws He has set forth, we cannot cry out to Him for mercy when the punishment we deserve falls upon us!

'God Is Love'

Fourth: *God is Love.* But as with the other attributes of God, many persons who do not read their Bibles fail to recognize what is meant when the Scriptures say: "God is love" (1 John 4:8).

We aren't always sure ourselves what we mean when we use the term love. That word has become one of the most widely misused words in our language. We use the word love to describe the basest as well as the most exalted of human relationships. We say we "love" to travel; we "love" to eat chocolate cake; we "love" our new car, or the pattern in the wallpaper in our home. Why, we even say we "love" our neighbors—but most of us don't do much more than just say it and let it go at that! No wonder we don't have a very clear idea of what the Bible means when it says: "God is Love."

Don't make the mistake of thinking that because God is Love that everything is going to be sweet, beautiful, and happy and that no one will be punished for his sins. God's holiness demands that all sin be punished, but God's love provides the plan and way of redemption for sinful man. God's love provided the cross of Jesus, by which man can have forgiveness and cleansing. It was the love of God that sent Jesus Christ to the cross!

Never question God's great love, for it is as unchangeable a part of God as is His holiness. No matter how terrible your sins, God loves you. Were it not for the love of God, none of us would ever have a chance in the future life. But God is Love! And His love for us is everlasting! "But God commendeth his love toward us, in that while we were yet sinners, Christ died for us" (Romans 5:8).

The promises of God's love and forgiveness are as real, as sure, as positive as human words can make them. But like describing the ocean, its total beauty cannot be understood until it is actually seen. It is the same with God's love. Until you actually accept it, until you actually experience it, until you actually possess true peace with God, no one can describe its wonders to you.

It is not something that you do with your mind. Your finite mind is not capable of dealing with anything as great as the love of God. Your mind might have difficulty explaining how a black cow can eat green grass and give white milk—but you drink the milk and are nourished by it. Your mind can't reason through all the intricate processes that take place when you plant a small flat seed that produces a huge vine bearing luscious red and green watermelons—but you eat them and enjoy them! You can't understand radio, but you listen. Your mind can't explain the electricity that may be creating the light by which you are reading at this very moment—but you know that it's there and that it is making it possible for you to read!

You have to receive God by faith—by faith in His Son, the Lord Jesus Christ. And when that happens, there isn't any room for doubt. You don't have to question whether or not God is in your heart, you can know it.

Whenever anyone asks me how I can be so certain about who and what God really is, I am reminded of the story of the little boy who was out flying a kite. It was a fine day for kite flying, the wind was brisk and large billowy clouds were blowing across the sky. The kite went up and up until it was entirely hidden by the clouds.

"What are you doing?" a man asked the little boy.

"I'm flying a kite," he replied.

"Flying a kite, are you?" the man said. "How can you be sure? You can't see your kite."

"No," said the boy, "I can't see it, but every little while I feel a tug, so I know for sure that it's there!"

Don't take anyone else's word for God. Find Him for yourself, and then you too will know by the wonderful, warm tug on your heartstrings that He is there *for sure.*

4

The Terrible Fact
of Sin

For all have sinned, and come short of the glory of God. ROMANS 3:23

IF GOD IS a righteous and loving Being, why then is there so much wickedness, suffering and sorrow? How did all this hatred come to be? Why have we created false idols? Why do we worship at the shrines of greed, self-interest, and war? How did the human race, which God made in His own image, sink so deep into depravity that the Ten Commandments had to be set forth with the demand that they be kept? Why did God have to send His own Son to save us? How did God's creatures become so filled with lust and evil?

To understand it, to see clearly why nation is pitted against nation, why families are divided, why every newspaper is filled with reports of violent, insane acts of brutality and hatred, we must go back to the very beginning. We must go back to the story of Adam in the Garden, back to the first chapter of Genesis.

Some people say that this familiar story of creation is only a myth. They say it is but a simple way to explain an unanswerable question to children. But this is not so. The Bible tells us exactly what happened in the beginning and why man has moved steadily along the path of his own destruction ever since.

For God created this world as a perfect whole. He created the beautiful, harmonious world that man threw away—the perfect world that we are longing to find again, the world for which we are all searching.

In this perfect world God placed a perfect man. Adam was perfect because nothing that God does can ever be less than perfect, and upon this perfect man God bestowed not only the most precious gift of all—the gift of life eternal. He also gave him the gift of freedom. God gave to man the freedom of choice.

A friend of ours, Dr. M. L. Scott, the great black preacher, tells about a friend of his. The friend's son had gone away to the university for study, and returned home for a visit, filled with his newly acquired knowledge.

"Dad," he said one evening with vast importance, "now that I've been to university, I'm no longer sure I can go along with your simple, childlike faith in the Bible."

The friend sat there studying his son with unblinking eyes. Finally he said, "Son, that is your freedom—your terrible freedom." That is what God gave to Adam—his freedom to choose. His terrible freedom.

The first man was no cave dweller—no gibbering, grunting, growling creature of the forest trying to subdue the perils of the jungle and the beasts of the field. Adam was created full-grown with every mental and physical faculty developed. He walked with God and had fellowship with Him. He was intended to be as a king on earth, ruling by the will of God.

This, then, was Adam's position as he stood in the Garden, the perfect man, the first man, with his priceless, if terrible gift of freedom. Adam had *total* freedom—freedom to choose or to reject, freedom to obey God's commands or to go contrary to them, freedom to make himself happy or miserable. For it is not the mere possession of freedom that makes life satisfying—it is what we choose to *do* with our freedom that determines whether or not we shall find peace with God and with ourselves.

The Heart of the Problem

This is the real heart of the problem, for the moment a man is given freedom he is faced by two paths. Freedom is meaningless if there is only one possible path to follow. Freedom implies the right to choose, to select, to determine one's individual course of action.

We all know men and women who are honest, not so much from free choice, but because they have no opportunity to be dishonest. Dr. Manfred Gutzke has said, "You old people, don't think you are becoming better just because you are becoming deader." We all know people who pride themselves on being good, when it is actually their surroundings and way of life that keep them from being bad. We cannot take credit for resisting temptation if no temptation is placed before us!

God gave Adam no such handicap. He granted him freedom of choice and He gave him every opportunity to exercise it. Because God could do nothing that was less than perfect, He provided Adam with the perfect setting in which to prove whether or not he would serve God.

As Adam stood there in the Garden he was without sin, his innocence was without blemish. The whole universe lay before him. The as yet unwritten history of the human race stretched like a great sheet of purest parchment beneath his hand, waiting for him to write the opening chapter—waiting for him to determine which road future generations would take.

God had completed His work. He had created an earthly garden, rich in everything that man might need. He had created a perfect man in His own likeness. He had endowed this man with a mind and a soul, and given him complete freedom to use his mind and to dispose of his soul as he saw fit. Then, like the wise Parent that He was, God waited to see what choice this child of His would make.

The Choice Man Made

This was the test! This was the moment when Adam would use his free will to choose the right path or the wrong path—choose it because he wanted to, and not because there was only one path open to him!

Adam made his choice. He suffered the consequences of it, and he set the pattern that all humanity was to follow. "Therefore, as by the offence of one, judgment came upon all men to condemnation" (Romans 5:18). Paul also says, "Wherefore, as by one man sin entered into the world, and death by sin; and so death passed upon all men, for that all have sinned" (Romans 5:12).

For Adam was the fountainhead of the human race. He sprang like a crystal-clear spring from the ground, and was permitted to choose whether he would become a river running through pleasant and productive green pastures, or a muddy torrent forever dashing against rocks and churning between deep, sunless cliffs—cold and miserable in itself, and unable to bring joy and fruitfulness to the surrounding land.

God is not to blame for the tragic snarl in which the world has so long found itself. The fault lies squarely with Adam—Adam who was given his choice and who chose to listen to the lies of the Tempter rather than to the truth of God! The history of the human race from that day to this has been the story of man's futile effort to gain back the position that was lost by Adam's fall, and, failing that, to reverse the curse.

"But this is unfair!" you may say. "Why should we suffer today, because the first man sinned away back in the furthest reaches of time? Why hasn't mankind recovered during the intervening years? Why should we go on being punished every day of our lives?" There is a thought current today that it is possible to improve man by improving his environment. Isn't it strange to recognize that the first sin was committed in the perfect environment?

Let us turn again to the story of the river—the cold, dark river that runs at the bottom of the deep, dreary gorge. Why doesn't this river make its way back up to the warm, pleasant fields that lie above it? Why doesn't it leave its mournful route and become the happy, bubbling stream it was when it burst spontaneously from the earth?

It doesn't, because it *can't*. It has no power within itself to do other than it has always done. Once it has plunged down the steep banks into darkness, it cannot lift itself again to the bright, sunny land above. The means by which it could be lifted exists, the way is at hand, but the river does not understand how to make use of it. This reminds me of the Yangtze River in China (now called the Chiang Jiang). This river spews its mud for miles out to sea, turning the blue-green waters of the ocean to a murky yellow. It is helpless to do otherwise.

A miracle stands ever ready to bring the river of humanity out of its misery and to place it once more in the warm valley of peace, but the river doesn't see or heed it. It feels that it can do nothing but continue on its tortuous way until it finally loses itself in the sea of destruction.

The story of the river is the story of man since the time of Adam, winding, twisting, plunging ever deeper into the frightening darkness. Though we lift up our voices and cry out for help, still we deliberately choose—as Adam did—the wrong way. In our despair we turn against God and blame Him for our dilemma. We question His wisdom and judgment. We find fault with His mercy and love.

We forget that Adam was the head of the human race, even as in this country our President is the head of our government. When the President acts, it is really the American people acting through him. When the President makes a decision, that decision stands as the decision of the entire people.

Adam stands as the federal head of the human race. He is also our first forefather. Just as we inherit characteristics, such as intellect, coloring, body size, temperament, etc., from our parents and grandparents, mankind inherited its fallen, corrupt nature from Adam. When he failed, when he succumbed to temptation and fell, the generations yet unborn fell with him, for the Bible states very clearly that the results of Adam's sin shall be visited upon every one of his descendants. We know all too well the bitter truth of those passages in Genesis 3:17–19 which describe the tragedy that Adam's act brought upon us all: "Cursed is the ground for thy sake; in sorrow shalt thou eat of it all the days of thy life; Thorns also and thistles shall it bring forth to thee; and thou shalt eat the herb of the field; In the sweat of thy face shalt thou eat bread, till thou return unto the ground; for out of it wast thou taken: for dust thou art, and unto dust shalt thou return."

And to Eve, God said: "I will greatly multiply thy sorrow and thy conception; in sorrow thou shalt bring forth children; and thy desire shall be to thy husband, and he shall rule over thee" (Genesis 3:16).

In other words, because of Adam's original sin, the ground which once bore only beautiful and nourishing plants now produces both good and bad alike. Man, who once had but to walk in the Garden and reach out his hand for food, who had no need for clothing or for shelter, must now toil all the days of his life to provide these necessities for himself and his family. Woman, once the most carefree of creatures, is now burdened with sorrow and pain; and both man and woman are under penalty of spiritual and physical death. Death is a threefold circumstance: 1) immediate spiritual death; 2) the beginning of physical death (the minute we are born, we begin to die); and 3) ultimate eternal death.

Sin Makes Its Entry

Sin entered the human race through Adam, and the human race has been trying without success to get rid of it ever since. And, short of that, mankind has been seeking in vain to reverse the curse. The Bible teaches that God warned Adam before he sinned that if he ate of the tree of knowledge he would surely die. The Bible also tells us that God instructed Adam and Eve to be fruitful and to multiply and to replenish the earth. But although they had been created in the image of God, after the Fall Adam and Eve gave birth to children after their own likeness and image. Consequently Cain and Abel were infected with the death-dealing disease of sin, which they inherited from their parents and which has been passed on to every generation since. We are all sinners by inheritance, and try as we will, we cannot escape our birthright.

We have resorted to every means to win back the position that Adam lost. We have tried through education, through philosophy, through religion, through governments to throw off our yoke of depravity and sin. We have sought to accomplish with our sin-limited minds the things that God intended to do with the clear vision that can come only from on high. Our motives have been good and some of our attempts have been commendable, but they have all fallen far, far short of the goal. All our knowledge, all our inventions, all our developments and ambitious plans move us ahead only a very little before we drop back again to the point from which we started. For we are still making the same mistake that Adam made—we are still trying to be king in our own right, and with our own power, instead of obeying God's laws.

Before we label God as unjust or unreasonable for permitting sin to envelop the world, let us look at the situation more carefully. God in His infinite compassion sent His Son to show us the way out of our difficulties. He sent His Son to experience the same temptations that were set before Adam and to triumph over them. Satan tempted Jesus, just as he tempted Adam. Satan offered Jesus power and glory if He would forsake God, just as he offered it to Adam through Eve.

The Choice Christ Made

The great difference was that Jesus Christ resisted the temptation! When the devil showed Him all the kingdoms of the world and promised Him all the glory of them if He would but follow Satan instead of God, our blessed Lord said: "Get thee hence, Satan: for it is written, Thou shalt worship the Lord thy God and him only shalt thou serve" (Matthew 4:10). He completely triumphed over the Tempter to reveal to all peoples of all succeeding generations His sinless character. He is our victory!

In our weakness and because of our depraved nature we have proved to be the true sons of Adam and have followed faithfully in his steps. We may deplore Adam's choice but we still imitate him!

There is not a single day that we do not face the same test that was set before Adam. There is not a day that we do not have a chance to choose between the devil's clever promises and God's sure Word.

We long for the day to come when disappointment, disease, and death will vanish—but there is no possibility of this dream coming true as long as we are the unregenerate sons of Adam. Something must be done about our sins. In succeeding chapters we will see that God has done something about this basic problem of the human race.

From the beginning of time until the present moment, man's ungodly quest for power, his determination to use his gift of free choice for his own selfish ends, has brought him to the brink of doom. The rubble and ruins of many civilizations lie scattered over the earth's surface—mute testimony to man's inability to build a lasting world without God. New rubble, new misery is being created daily, and yet man plunges on his pernicious way.

God, meanwhile, in His infinite understanding and mercy, has looked on, waiting with a patience and compassion that passes all understanding. He waits to offer individual salvation and peace to the ones who will come to His mercy. The same two paths that God set before Adam still lie before us. We are still free to choose. We are living in a period of grace while God withholds the eternal punishment we so justly deserve.

It is the presence of sin that prevents man from being truly happy. It is because of sin that man has never been able to obtain the utopia of which he dreams. Every project, every civilization that he builds ultimately fails and falls into oblivion because man's works are all wrought in unrighteousness. The ruins around us at this moment are eloquent witness to the sin that fills the world.

Cause and Effect

Man seems to have lost sight of the ever-present law of cause and effect that operates on every level of this universe. The effects are plain enough, but the deep-seated, all-prevailing cause seems to be less distinct. Perhaps it is the blight of the modern-day philosophy of "progress" that dims man's vision. Perhaps it is because man is so enamored of this foolish, man-created theory that he clings to the belief the race is advancing slowly but surely toward ultimate perfection.

Many philosophers will even argue that the present world tragedy is but an incident in the upward march, and they point to other periods in human history when the prospect seemed as bleak and the outcome as hopeless. Philosophers would try to say that the sad conditions through which we are now living are but the birth pangs of a better day! That men are still children groping and stumbling along in the kindergarten of existence, still a long, long way from the mature and sensible beings that they will become centuries hence!

But the Bible makes plain what natural science seems so unwilling to admit—that nature reveals both a Creator and a corrupter. Man blames the Creator for the work of the corrupter. Man forgets that our world is not as God made it. God made the world good. Sin corrupted it. God made man innocent, but sin entered and made him selfish. Every manifestation of evil is the result of basic sin—sin that has remained unchanged since the moment it first entered the human race. It may manifest itself in different ways, but fundamentally it is the same sin that causes an African savage to skulk along a jungle trail awaiting his victim with spear in hand, and a well-trained, educated pilot to fly a jet plane over the same jungle ready to bomb an unsuspecting village.

The two men are separated by centuries of culture. One can be said to be much further "progressed" than the other, one has all the advantages of man-made civilization; while the other is still in the "primitive" state—and yet, are they really so different? Are they not both motivated by fear and distrust of their fellow men? Are both not selfishly bent on achieving their own goals at any cost to their brothers? Is a bomb any less savage or brutal, or more civilized than a naked spear? Can we hope to find a solution to our problems so long as both the most "primitive" and the most "progressive" among us are more eager to kill than to love our neighbors?

All the sorrow, all the bitterness, all the violence, tragedy, heartache and shame of man's history are summed up in that one little word—sin. Today, the general reaction is "so what?" In fact. there is a definite attempt to popularize and glamorize sin. Our most popular T.V. series are concerned with the *decadent* rich. Our magazine covers frequently feature the immoral, the perverted, the psychologically sick. Sin is "in."

People don't like to be told they are sinners, even as their parents and grandparents were sinners before them! Yet the Bible declares, "There is no difference: for all have sinned, and come short of the glory of God" (Romans 3:22–23). The Bible declares that every person on earth is a sinner in the sight of God; and whenever I hear anyone take exception to so strong a statement I am reminded of the story of the church officer who came to talk to the minister one day about sin.

He said to the minister, "Doctor, we of the congregation wish you wouldn't talk quite so much or so plainly about sin. We feel that if our boys and girls hear you discuss the subject so much they will all the more easily become sinners. Why don't you call it a 'mistake' or say that our young people are often guilty of using 'poor judgment'—but please don't talk so openly about sin."

The minister walked over and took down a bottle of poison from a high shelf and showed it to his visitor. The bottle was plainly marked in big red letters, "Poison! Do not touch!" "What would you have me do?" asked the minister.

"Do you feel it would be wise for me to remove this label and put on one that reads 'Essence of Peppermint'? Don't you see that the milder you make the label, the more dangerous you make the poison?"

Sin—plain, old-fashioned sin, the selfsame sin which caused Adam's downfall—is what we are all suffering from today, and it will do us far more harm than good to try to dress it up with a fancy, more attractive label. We don't need a new word for it. What we need is to find out what the word we already have means! Because, although sin is certainly prevalent in the world today, however popularized, however glamorized, there are multitudes of people who are wholly ignorant of its real meaning. It is the misguided, shortsighted view of sin that stands in the way of conversion for many men and women. It is the lack of real understanding of sin that keeps many Christans from living the true life of Christ.

The old spiritual says. "Everybody talkin' 'bout heaven, ain't going there," and the same thing is true of sin. Everybody who talks about sin doesn't have a clear realization of what it means, and it is of supreme importance that we become familiar with how God looks at sin.

We may try to take a light view of sin and to refer to it as "human weakness." We may try to call it a trifle, but God calls it a tragedy. We would pass it off as an accident, but God declares it is an abomination. Man seeks to excuse himself of sin, but God seeks to convict him of it and to save him from it. Sin is no amusing toy—it is a terror to be shunned! Learn, then, what constitutes sin in the eyes of God!

Dr. Richard Beal gives us five words for sin.

First: sin is *lawlessness*, the transgression of the law of God (1 John 3:4). God established the boundary line between good and evil, and whenever we overstep that boundary, whenever we are guilty of intrusion into the forbidden area of evil, we are breaking the law. Whenever we fail to live up to the Ten Commandments, whenever we go contrary to the precepts of the Sermon on the Mount, we have transgressed the law of God and are guilty of sin.

If you look at the Ten Commandments one by one, you will note how today mankind is deliberately, it seems, not only breaking them, but glamorizing the breaking! From idolatry, which is anything we put before God, to remembering the Sabbath day to keep it holy (where would professional baseball and football be if Christians refused to watch them on Sunday?), to honoring parents (books like *Mommie Dearest* that expose the sins of parents), to covetousness to adultery—it appears there has been a concerted effort to deliberately break each Commandment. And not only that, but there seems to be a deliberate attempt to make it attractive to do so!

James made it plain that we are all guilty when he said: "But every man is tempted, when he is drawn away of his own lust, and enticed. Then when lust hath conceived, it bringeth forth sin: and sin, when it is finished, bringeth forth death" (James 1:14–15). It is because we have all broken God's laws, all transgressed His commands that we are all classified as sinners.

Second: the Bible describes sin as *iniquity*. Iniquity is the deviation from right, whether or not the particular act has been expressly forbidden. Iniquity has to do with our inner motivations, the very things that we so often try to keep hidden from the eyes of men and God. They are the wrongs which spring from our own corrupt nature rather than the evil acts which force of circumstances sometimes causes us to commit.

Jesus described this inner corruptness when He said: "From within, out of the heart of men proceed evil thoughts, adulteries, fornications, murders, thefts, covetousness, wickedness, deceit, lasciviousness, an evil eye, blasphemy, pride, foolishness: All these evil things come from within, and defile the man" (Mark 7:21-23).

Third: the Bible defines sin as *missing the mark*, falling short of the goal that has been set. God's goal is Christ. The object and end-purpose of all of life is to live up to the life of Christ. He came to show us what it is possible for man to achieve here on earth; and when we fail to follow His example, we miss the mark and fall short of the divine standard.

Fourth: sin is a form of *trespass*. It is the intrusion of self-will into the sphere of divine authority. Sin is not merely a negative thing, it is not just the absence of love for God. Sin is the making of a positive choice, the preference for self instead of God. It is the centering of affection in one's own being instead of reaching out with all one's heart to embrace God. Egoism and selfishness are the marks of sin as surely as are theft and murder. Perhaps this is the most subtle and destructive form of sin, for in this form it is so easy to overlook the label on the bottle of poison. Those who cling to themselves, those who center their entire attention on their own beings, those who regard only their own interests and fight to protect only their own rights—these are sinners as much as the drunkard or harlot.

Jesus said: "What shall it profit a man, if he shall gain the whole world, and lose his own soul?" (Mark 8:36). Translated into modern terms, could we not say, "What shall it profit a man to build a vast industrial empire if he is eaten away by ulcers and can enjoy nothing of life? What shall it profit a dictator though he conquer a hemisphere if he must live in constant fear of an avenger's bullet or an assassin's knife? What shall it profit a parent to bring up children with harsh domination if he is rejected by them later and left to a lonely old age?" Without question, the sin of self is a deadly sin.

Fifth: sin is *unbelief*. Unbelief is a sin because it is an insult to the truthfulness of God. "He that believeth on the Son of God hath the witness in himself. He that believeth not God hath made him a liar because he believeth not the record that God gave of his Son" (1 John 5:10).

It is unbelief that shuts the door to heaven and opens it to hell. It is unbelief that rejects the Word of God and refuses Christ as Savior. It is unbelief that causes men to turn a deaf ear to the gospel and to deny the miracles of Christ.

Sin incurs the penalty of death, and no man has the ability in himself to save himself from sin's penalty or to cleanse his own heart of its corruption. Angels and men cannot atone for sin. It is only in Christ that the remedy for sin can be found. It is only Christ who can save the sinner from the fate that surely awaits him. "For the wages of sin is death" (Romans 6:23). "The soul that sinneth, it shall die" (Ezekiel 18:4). "None of them can by any means redeem his brother, nor give to God a ransom for him" (Psalm 49:7). "Neither their silver nor their gold shall be able to deliver them in the day of the Lord's wrath" (Zephaniah 1:18).

The Only Remedy

Man's only salvation from sin stands on a lonely, barren, skull-shaped hill; a thief hangs on one cross, a murderer on another, and between them, a Man with a crown of thorns. Blood flows from His hands and feet, it pours from His side, it drops down His face—while those who stand looking on sneer and mock Him.

And who is this tortured figure, who is this Man whom other men seek to humiliate and kill? He is the Son of God, the Prince of Peace, heaven's own appointed Messenger to the sin-ridden earth. This is He, before whom angels fall down and veil their faces. And yet He hangs bleeding and forsaken upon the cross.

What brought Him to this place of horrors? Who inflicted this hideous torture upon the Man who came to teach us love? You did and I did, for it was for your sin and my sin that Jesus was nailed to the cross. In this immortal moment the human race experienced the darkest reaches of sin, it sank to its lowest depths, it touched its foulest limits. No wonder that the sun could not endure and veiled its face!

As Charles Wesley writes:

> And can it be that I should gain
> An interest in the Savior's blood?
> Died He for me, who caused His pain? . . .
>
> Amazing love! how can it be
> That Thou, my God, shouldst die for me?

But sin overreached itself on the cross. Man's hideous injustice that crucified Christ became the means that opened the way for man to become free. Sin's masterpiece of shame and hate became God's masterpiece of mercy and forgiveness. Through the death of Christ upon the cross, sin itself was crucified for those who believe in Him. Sin was conquered on the cross. His death is the foundation of our hope, the promise of our triumph! Christ bore in His own body on the tree the sins that shackle us. He died for us and rose again. He proved the truth of all God's promises to man; and if you will accept Christ by faith today, you, too, can be forgiven for your sins. You can stand secure and free in the knowledge that through the love of Christ your soul is cleansed of sin and saved from damnation.

5

Dealing With the Devil

For we wrestle not against flesh and blood, but against principalities, against powers, against rulers of the darkness of this world, against spiritual wickedness in high places.
EPHESIANS 6:12

THERE IS A satanic principle involved in all that is happening today. The Bible describes "that old serpent, called the Devil and Satan, which deceiveth the whole world" (Revelation 12:9) and we know him to be at work confusing all peoples and all nations. His handiwork is to be seen at every turn.

While we would like to take hope that universal peace is drawing closer, it appears instead that we are standing on the brink of Armageddon. We are told that there were hundreds of "little" wars between 1945 and 1979 which caused between twelve and thirteen million deaths. For Satan is determined that the dark, joyless river of humanity shall continue on its tormented way until the end of time. He won over Adam in the Garden, and he is convinced that he can claim the souls of Adam's descendants for himself.

There is not a thinking person in the world today who has not wondered many times about the existence of the devil. That he *does* exist, there is no doubt. We see his power and influence everywhere. The question is not is there a devil, but *how* and *why* did the devil come to be?

We know from the story of Adam and Eve that the devil was already present on earth before God made the first man. Evil already existed, else God would not have made a tree whose fruit gave the awareness of good and bad. There would have been no necessity for such a tree, no possibility of it, if evil had not already been present and man been in need of protection from it.

Did God Create Evil?

Here we face the greatest of all mysteries, the most significant of all secrets, the most unanswerable of all questions. How could God—who is all-powerful, all-holy and all-loving—have created evil, or permitted the devil to create it? Why did Adam have to be tempted? Why didn't God strike the devil dead when he entered the body of the serpent to whisper evil thoughts to Eve?

The Bible gives us a few hints as to what the answer may be. But the Bible also makes it very clear that man is not supposed to know the full answer until God has allowed the devil and all his designs to help work out His own great plan.

Before the fall of Adam, long before Adam even existed, it would appear that God's universe was divided into spheres of influence, each of which was under the supervision and control of an angel or heavenly prince, all of whom were responsible directly to God. Paul tells us of "thrones, governments, princedoms, and authorities" in both the visible and the invisible world (Colossians 1:16; Ephesians 1:21). The Bible makes frequent mention of angels and archangels, showing that there was established order among them, some being more powerful than others.

The devil must have been just such a powerful, heavenly prince, having the earth assigned to him, perhaps, as his special province. Known as Lucifer, the "lightbearer," he must have stood very close to God—so close, in fact, that ambition entered his heart and he determined not to be God's beloved prince, but to place himself on an equal footing with God Himself! Lucifer was not the counterpart of God, but the counterpart of Michael or Gabriel; he was not a fallen god, but a fallen angel.

It was at this moment that the breach appeared in the cosmos. It was at this moment that the universe—which had been all good and all harmonious to God's will—split, and a portion of it set itself in opposition to God. Just as there are today regimes and sects that deny the existence of God or defy His authority, the devil defied God and attempted to set up his own authority. He abandoned his own position in the government of God and descended into the lower heavens and cried out that he would be like the Most High God. He had been set by God as the prince of this world; and God has not yet removed him from that position, though the righteous basis for that removal has been laid by the death of Christ. Ever since that moment, the devil has been contesting God on earth.

The Devil's Kingdom

As a mighty prince, with hosts of angels at his command, he has set up his kingdom on earth. His power and position here are the very reasons that the Scriptures came to be written. Had Satan not defied God and attempted to rival His power and authority, the story of Adam in the Garden would have been very different. Had Satan not set himself in opposition to God, there would have been no need to give mankind the Ten Commandments, there would have been no need for God to send His Son to the cross.

Jesus and His apostles were well aware of the devil. Matthew records an actual conversation between Jesus and the devil (Matthew 4:1–10). The devil was very real to the Pharisees—so real, in fact, that they accused Jesus of being the devil himself (Matthew 12:24)! There was no doubt in Jesus' mind of the existence of the devil, nor of the power that he wields here on earth.

The devil's strength is clearly demonstrated in the passage from Jude 9 which relates: "Yet Michael the archangel, when contending with the devil he disputed about the body of Moses, durst not bring against him a railing accusation, but said, The Lord rebuke thee."

Modern confusion about the personality of the devil has resulted in large measure from the caricatures of him which became popular during the Middle Ages. To allay their fear of the devil, people tried to laugh at him, and pictured him as a foolish, grotesque creature with horns and a long tail. They put a pitchfork in his hand, and a feeble-minded leer on his face, and then said to themselves, "Who's afraid of a ridiculous figure like this?"

The truth is that the devil is a creature of vastly superior intelligence, a mighty and gifted spirit of infinite resourcefulness. We forget that the devil was perhaps the greatest and most exalted of all God's angels. He was a sublime figure, who decided to use his divine endowments for his own aims instead of God's. His reasoning is brilliant, his plans ingenious, his logic well nigh irrefutable. God's mighty adversary is no bungling creature with horns and tail—he is a prince of lofty stature, of unlimited craft and cunning, able to take advantage of every opportunity that presents itself, able to turn every situation to his own advantage. He is unrelenting and cruel. He is not, however, all-powerful, omniscient or omnipresent.

The devil is quite capable of bringing forth the false prophet of which the Bible warns. Upon the wreckage of disbelief and faltering faith the devil will set his masterpiece, the counterfeit king. He will create a religion without a Redeemer. He will build a church without a Christ. He will call for worship without the Word of God.

The Apostle Paul predicted this when he said: "But I fear, lest by any means, as the serpent beguiled Eve through his subtlety, so your minds should be corrupted from the simplicity that is Christ. For if he that cometh preacheth another Jesus, whom we have not preached, or if ye receive another spirit, which ye have not received, or another gospel, which ye have not accepted, ye might well bear with him . . . For such are false apostles, deceitful workers, transforming themselves into the apostles of Christ" (2 Corinthians 11:3, 4, 13).

The Devil and the Anti-Christ

We know that the anti-Christ will appear and try to ensnare the minds and hearts of men. The time draws close, the stage is set—confusion, panic, and fear are abroad. The signs of the false prophet are everywhere at hand, and many may be the living witnesses of the awesome moment when the final act of this age-old drama begins. It may well come in our time, for the tempo is speeding up, events move more swiftly, and on every side we see men and women consciously or unconsciously choosing up sides—aligning themselves with the devil or with God.

It will be a battle to the death, in the truest meaning of that word—a battle that will give no quarter, that will make no allowances or exceptions. The human phase of this battle started in the Garden of Eden when the devil seduced mankind from God, making it possible for there to be billions of warring wills, every man turning to his own way. "All we like sheep have gone astray; we have turned every one to his own way; and the Lord hath laid on him [Christ] the iniquity of us all" (Isaiah 53:6). It will continue until the end of time, until one or the other of these two mighty forces—the force of good or evil—triumphs and places the True King or the false king on the throne.

At this moment in history, two mighty trinities stand face to face: the Trinity of God (the Father, Son, and Holy Ghost) and the false trinity that Satan would have us worship in its place. The trinity of evil (the devil, anti-Christ, and false prophet) is described in the Book of Revelation: "And I saw three unclean spirits like frogs come out of the dragon, and out of the mouth of the beast, and out of the mouth of the false prophet" (Revelation 16:13).

Never for a second of your waking or sleeping life are you without the influence of these two powerful forces, never is there a moment when you cannot deliberately choose to go with one or the other. Always the devil is standing at your side tempting, coaxing, threatening, cajoling. And always on your other side stands Jesus, the all-loving, the all-forgiving, waiting for you to turn to Him and ask His aid, waiting to give you supernatural power to resist the Evil one. You belong to one or the other. There isn't a no-man's land in between where you can hide.

In moments of your greatest fear and anxiety, in moments when you feel yourself helpless in the grip of events you cannot control, when despair and disappointment overwhelm you—in these moments many times it is the devil who is trying to catch you at your weakest point and push you further along the path that Adam took.

In these perilous moments remember that Christ has not deserted you. He has not left you defenseless. As He triumphed over Satan in His hour of temptation and trial, so He has promised that you, too, can have daily victory over the Tempter. Remember: "Ye are of God . . . and have overcome them: because greater is he that is in you, than he that is in the world" (1 John 4:4).

The same Book that tells us over and over again of God's love, warns us constantly of the devil who would come between us and God, the devil who is ever waiting to ensnare men's souls. "Be sober, be vigilant; because your adversary the devil, as a roaring lion, walketh about, seeking whom he may devour" (1 Peter 5:8). The Bible describes a personal devil who controls a host of demon spirits that attempt to dominate and control all human activity, "The prince of

the power of the air, the spirit that now worketh in the children of disobedience" (Ephesians 2:2).

Don't Doubt the Devil

Don't doubt for a moment the existence of the devil! He is very personal and
he is very real! And he is extremely clever! Perhaps the cleverest thing that he
has ever done is to convince people he does not exist. Look again at the front
page of today's newspaper if you have any question about the personality of the
devil. Switch on your local radio or television news commentator. Note the local
theater listings, glance at the magazine stands, and book racks—in short, just
look around you if you feel you need concrete evidence!

Would sane, thinking men and women behave in this way if they were not
in the grip of evil? Could hearts filled only with God's love and God's goodness
conceive and carry out the acts of violence and malice that are reported to us
every day? Could men of education, intelligence, and honest intent gather
around a world conference table and fail so completely to understand each
other's needs and goals if their thinking was not being deliberately clouded and
corrupted?

Whenever I hear an "enlightened" person of our time take issue with the
plausibility of a personal, individualized devil in command of a host of evil
spirits, I am reminded of this poem by Alfred J. Hough:

Men don't believe in the Devil now, as their fathers used to do;
They've forced the door of the broadest creed to let his majesty through.
There isn't a print of his cloven foot or fiery dart from his brow
To be found on earth or air today, for the world has voted it so.
Who dogs the steps of the toiling saint and digs the pits for his feet?
Who sows the tares in the fields of time whenever God sows the wheat?
The Devil is voted not to be, and of course, the thing is true;
But who is doing the kind of work that the Devil alone can do?
We are told that he doesn't go about as a roaring lion now;
But whom shall we hold responsible for the everlasting row
To be heard in home, in church and state, to the earth's remotest bound,
If the Devil by unanimous vote is nowhere to be found?
Won't someone step to the front forthwith and make their bow and show
How the frauds and crimes of a single day spring up? We want to know!
The Devil was fairly voted out, and of course, the Devil's gone;
But simple people would like to know who carries the business on.

Who, indeed, is responsible for the infamy, terror, and agony that we see all
around us? How can we account for the sufferings that we all experience if evil

is not a potent force? Modern education has, in truth, impeded our minds. Because of allegedly scientific findings, some have lost their belief in the supernatural powers of Satan, while others worship him.

George Galloway summed up this dubious contribution of current education when he said: "The theory that there is in the universe a power or principle, personal or otherwise, in eternal opposition to God is generally discarded by the modern mind."

The modern mind may discard it, but that doesn't cause the evil principle itself to disappear! Once asked how he overcame the devil, Martin Luther replied, "Well, when he comes knocking upon the door of my heart and asks, 'Who lives here?' the dear Lord Jesus goes to the door and says, 'Martin Luther used to live here but he has moved out. Now I live here.' The Devil, seeing the nail-prints in His hands, and the pierced side, takes flight immediately."

The Certainty of Sin

Sin is certainly a grim fact! It stands like a titanic force, contesting all the good that men may try to accomplish. It stands like a dark shadow, ever ready to blot out whatever light may reach us from on high. We all know this. We all see it. We all are conscious of it in every move we make. Call it what we may, we know of its very real existence. "For we wrestle not against flesh and blood, but against principalities, against powers, against the rulers of the darkness of this world, against spiritual wickedness in high places" (Ephesians 6:12).

How do those who deny the devil and his minions account for the speed with which evil spreads? How do they explain the endless stumbling blocks that are placed in the path of the righteous? How can they reason away the fact that destruction and disaster are but the work of seconds, while construction and rehabilitation are often agonizingly slow?

Breathe a lie into the air, let loose a slanderous tongue—and the words are carried as by magic to the farthest corners. Speak a truth, perform a generous and honest act—and unseen powers will be at work at once to try to hide this tiny ray of light and hope.

When this book was first written thirty years ago no one built churches to the devil, no one constructed pulpits to preach his word. And yet today they do. His word is everywhere, and all too often his word is translated into desperate deeds. If no unseen power is at work corrupting men's hearts and distorting men's thoughts, how can you explain humanity's eagerness to listen to the base and vulgar and vile, while it turns a deaf ear to the good and clean and pure? One has only to listen to the blasphemous words of punk rock to realize that Satan is alive and well on earth.

Would one single person among us ever pass up a piece of ripe delicious fruit to select a rotten piece that was crawling with worms and reeking with decay, if we were not driven to this dreadful choice by a great and sinister power? Yet that is exactly what we all do over and over again. We constantly pass up the rich and beautiful and ennobling experiences and seek out the tawdry, the cheap, and the degrading. These are the works of the devil, and they flourish on every side!

The Struggle Between Good and Evil

What we see happening here on earth is but a reflection of the far greater struggles between good and evil in the unseen realm. We like to think that our planet is the center of the universe, and we attach too much importance to earthly events. In our foolish pride we see with human eyes. But a struggle of infinitely greater magnitude is being waged in the world we cannot see!

The wise men of old knew this. They knew that there is much that the human eye fails to discern and much to which the human ear is deaf. Modern man likes to feel that he "created" radio, television, and computers, that he made it possible to send audible sounds and visible images through space, and to make and record impossible amounts of data. The truth is, of course, that these waves, unknown to man, have always existed, and that far greater wonders exist in outer space, of which man may never gain the slightest knowledge. That these wonders were there, the ancient prophets knew—but even they had but a suggestion of their magnitude, even they could catch but the faintest echoes of the mighty battle of the spheres.

One of the many prices Adam paid for listening to the devil was to lose the vision of spiritual dimensions. He lost for himself and all of humanity the capacity for seeing and hearing and understanding anything that was not basely material. Adam closed himself off from the eternal wonders and splendors of the unseen world. He lost the power of true prophecy, the ability to look ahead, and by so doing to better understand and perform the work of the present. He lost his sense of continuity. He became literally "dead in trespasses and sins." He had alienated himself from God.

G. Campbell Morgan says: "Our distance from God is that of inability to know and apprehend the near. It is the distance of the blind man from the glory of the picture in front of him. The distance of the deaf man from the beauty of the symphony sounding round about him. It is the distance of the sensate man from all the movement of life in the midst of which he lives."

But let tragedy or sickness come to us, let us suffer the consequences of our own sins, and we immediately blame God for it! We may be somewhat patient and understanding with our television sets when they do not give us what we want, but we are quick to rail against God and His universe when we get a distorted picture of it.

Let someone get the business promotion we wanted, let someone we consider less deserving succeed where we have failed, and we cry out against God's injustice. We demand to know why God permits such inequalities! We lose sight of the fact that God, like a great master television station, is sending out a perfect image of love and righteousness all the time, and that the faulty reception lies with us!

The Evil in Our Eyesight

It is the evil and distortion within ourselves that keeps us from seeing and experiencing God's perfect world. It is our own sin that blurs the image, that keeps us from being God's pure children instead of the children of evil. Paul spoke for all of us when he said: "For the good that I would I do not, but the evil which I would not, that I do" (Romans 7:19). Paul recognized the dreaded enemy, the powerful foe of all mankind, and cried out, "O wretched man that I am! who shall deliver me from the body of this death? I thank God through Jesus Christ our Lord. So then with the mind I myself serve the law of God; but with the flesh the law of sin" (Romans 7:24–25).

Two overwhelming adversaries were clearly apparent to Paul and he was acutely aware of being torn between their mighty magnetisms. The power of good was pulling his mind and heart toward God, while the power of evil was trying to drag his body down into death and destruction. Two books on demon possession and the rise of the cults might be of interest to you: *Demon Possession* by John L. Nevivus (published by Kregel) and *Unholy Devotion: Why Cults Lure Christians*, by Harold L. Bussell (copyright 1983 by The Zondervan Corporation).

You are caught between these same two forces: life and death! Choose God's way, and there is life. Choose Satan's way, and it is death!

6

The Despair of Loneliness

I am forgotten as a dead man out of mind. I am like a broken vessel. PSALM 31:12

AFTER THE DEATH of her husband, Queen Victoria said, "There is no one left to call me Victoria." Even though she was a queen, she knew what it meant to be lonely.

H. G. Wells said on his sixty-fifth birthday, "I am sixty-five, and I am lonely and have never found peace."

Isadora Duncan, the great ballet dancer who danced before the royalty of Europe and was considered one of the greatest ballet dancers of all time, said, "I have never been alone but that my heart did ache, my eyes fill with tears, and my hands tremble for a peace and a joy that I never found." She went on to say that in the midst of millions of admirers, she was actually a very lonely woman.

A few years ago, a beautiful young Hollywood star with apparently everything a girl could want, ended her life. In the brief note that she left was an incredibly simple explanation—she was unbearably lonely.

The psalmist said, "I am like a pelican of the wilderness: I am like an owl of the desert. I watch, and am as a sparrow alone upon the house top" (Psalm 102:6).

Again the psalmist said, "Reproach hath broken my heart; and I am full of heaviness: and I looked for some to take pity, but there was none; and for comforters, but I found none" (Psalm 69:20).

The Loneliness of Solitude

First, there is the *Loneliness of Solitude*. I have felt the loneliness of the ocean where there is never a sound except the booming of the surf along rock-strewn shores. I have felt the loneliness of the prairie with only the occasional mournful howl of the coyote. I have felt the loneliness of the mountains broken only by the sighing of the wind.

The sentry standing duty alone at an outpost, the thousands in mental institutions, and those in solitary confinement in prisons and concentration camps know the meaning of the loneliness of solitude.

Louis Zamperini, the great Olympic track star, has told of the terrible lone-liness of solitude on a life-raft where he spent forty-eight days during the sec-ond World War.

In his fascinating book, *Alone,* Admiral Richard E. Byrd told about the time he spent in bewildering and soul-shattering darkness. He lived alone in a shack that was literally buried in the great glacial icecap that covers the South Pole. He spent five months there. The days were as black as the nights. No living creature of any kind existed within a hundred miles. The cold was so intense that he could hear his breath freeze and crystallize as the wind blew it past his ears.

"At night," he says, "before blowing out the lantern, I formed the habit of planning the morrow's work." He had to, in order to preserve his sanity. "It was wonderful," he continues, "to be able to dole out time in this way. It brought me an extraordinary sense of command over myself; and without constant activity, the days would have been without purpose; and without purpose, they would have ended—as such days always end—in disintegration."

The Loneliness of Society

Probably you think that in that frozen wasteland, Richard Byrd was of all people most lonely. But the *Loneliness of Society* is far worse than the loneli-ness of solitude, for there is loneliness in great cities far worse than his.

That poor creature living in the dingy tenement who never receives a letter, who never hears one word of encouragement, who never experiences the hand-clasp of a friend—that wealthy society leader whose money has bought every-thing but love and happiness—each knows a loneliness few can understand.

There is the loneliness of the street people living in doorways or cardboard boxes, scrounging food in garbage cans—a unique loneliness.

A recent television program showed the demoralizing loneliness of some of our neglected and forgotten old people in dilapidated institutions. The aimless sitting, the vacant eyes, haunted me. They are the living dead. Yet in the back-ground an old derelict, with one finger, was picking out on an equally derelict piano, "What a friend we have in Jesus."

In John 5 we read about Jesus as He made His way through the narrow streets of Jerusalem. When He reached the sheep-gate by the pool of Bethesda, He observed the great multitudes plagued with various infirmities, waiting to be moved into the water. Suddenly He noticed a poor creature who seemed more needy than all the rest, and tenderly He asked, "Wilt thou be made whole?"

The helpless paralytic looked up and answered, "Sir, I have no man, when the water is troubled, to put me into the pool." Think of it, thirty-eight long, weary years, this bundle of pain had been buffeted by the surging human tide of Jerusalem, and after all these years, he must say to Jesus, "Sir, I have no man." He was absolutely friendless.

You can have a friend who sticks closer than a brother. Jesus Christ can make life joyful, satisfying and glorious to you. All over the world are millions of men and women who love and serve Jesus Christ. The moment you accept Him, you are closer to them than you are to your own blood relatives.

There is not a city in the United States that does not have a warm church to which you could go and meet the most wonderful people in America. There is a giant network of true Christians in every community of America. The moment you clasp their hands, you know that you have friends.

But first, you must repent, surrender and commit your heart and life to Christ. Let Him forgive your past sins, and He will take you into His family; He will bring you to the hearth, and you will feel the warmth of the fire. If you are lonely today, I beg you, come to Christ and know the fellowship that He brings.

The Loneliness of Suffering

Third, there is the *Loneliness of Suffering*. Some years ago we received a letter from a radio listener who for five years had been crippled into a sitting position by arthritis. For five long, weary, painful years she was unable to stretch out or to lie down, yet she wrote, "I have spent many a day alone, but never a lonely day." Why? It was Christ who made the difference. With Christ as your Savior and constant Companion, you too, although alone, need never be lonely.

You today who are lying on a hospital bed enduring the loneliness of suffering can rest assured that Christ can give you His grace and strength. While you lie there, you can be useful to Him. You can know something of the ministry of intercession, the greatest ministry on earth, as you pray for others.

The Loneliness of Sorrow

Fourth, there is the *Loneliness of Sorrow*. In the eleventh chapter of John we read of Mary and Martha. Their brother Lazarus was dead. Jesus had not yet come. They stood beside the body of their brother and wept.

For you, too, perhaps the world has become a vast cemetery containing but one grave. You have stood in the sick room and watched the one dearer than all the world to you slip beyond your reach. You crave fellowship.

You want someone to come along with a strong hand to help wipe the tears away and put the smile back on your face, and give you joy through the sorrow.

Jesus can do just that. The Bible says, "Casting all your care upon him, for he careth for you" (1 Peter 5:7). God loves His children. If you are willing to trust Him and give yourself to Him, He can carry your sorrow.

The Loneliness of Sin

Fifth, there is the *Loneliness of Sin.* In John 13 we find the story of the Last Supper. Jesus prophesied the betrayal of Judas. In amazement the innocent disciples looked at one another. John asked, "Lord, who is it?" And Jesus said, "He it is, to whom I shall give bread when I have dipped it." And when He had dipped the bread, He gave it to Judas Iscariot, the son of Simon; and then we are told that Satan entered into Judas. Immediately Jesus said, "That thou doest, do quickly." And the Bible says, "He then, having received the bread, went immediately out, and it was night." He went out—out from the presence of Christ—and it was night.

Perhaps you at one time thought you knew the joy and peace of being born into God's family. You experienced the sweet fellowship of God's people. You tasted the complete happiness and satisfaction of Christ's presence with you, but you sinned. You went out from the presence of Christ, and you have found that it is night. You have neither the fellowship of Christians nor the fellowship of sinners, and certainly you no longer have the fellowship of Christ. Perhaps there is no loneliness quite so bitter as the loneliness of a backslidden Christian.

Yet there is forgiveness for you. As you confess and forsake your sins, your fellowship with Christ will be restored. "If we confess our sins, he is faithful and just to forgive us our sins, and to cleanse us from all unrighteousness" (1 John 1:9).

Perhaps you say you are having a pretty good time sinning—and you well may. The Bible says there is a certain pleasure in sin. However, it is short lived and fatal. Perhaps you have read Dr. Kinsey's report or some other survey and are finding a certain satisfaction in knowing how many sinners there are who are as bad as—or worse than—you. You're not alone. No. You're in the vast majority. Where then, you ask, does the loneliness of sin come in? You may be one of a crowd now, but the day is *coming* when each one of you must stand *alone* before Almighty God and be judged. That will be for you the climax of all the loneliness of earth, and but the preview of the loneliness of hell.

For all of these who travel the pathway of sin, there is an engulfing pall of night that isolates them from all good and true fellowship. Sin always has been darkness. Sin always will be darkness. Judas was lonely because of his sin. God says in Hosea 4:17: "Ephraim is joined to idols, let him alone." Because of the covetousness and idolatry of the people of Ephraim, God had said, "Have no fellowship with him, let him completely alone." "All we like sheep have gone astray; we have turned every one to his own way" (Isaiah 53:6). Here again we find the loneliness of sin.

One hour before his fatal duel with Alexander Hamilton, Aaron Burr, sitting in his library at Richmond Hill in New York, wrote to his daughter, "Some very wise man has said, 'O fools, who think it solitude to be alone.'" Already, even before the fatal shot was fired and the bloody deed was done, he felt the loneliness of his sin. In a few hours he was to be a fugitive from the sudden and deep abhorrence of his fellow citizens. His political career was gone forever, and his great ambitions were wrecked.

There are thousands of lonely people in the city and in the country, who carry heavy and difficult burdens of grief, anxiety, pain and disappointment; but the loneliest soul of all is the man whose life is steeped in sin.

I want to tell you that every sin you deliberately cling to is a mighty power in making you lonely. The older you get, the lonelier you will be. I beg you, come to the foot of the cross and confess that you are a sinner, forsake your sins.

Christ can give you power to overcome every sin and habit in your life. He can break the ropes, fetters and chains of sin; but you must repent, confess, commit and surrender yourself to Him first. Right now, it can be settled, and you can know the peace, joy and fellowship of Christ.

The Loneliness of the Savior

Last, there is the *Loneliness of the Savior*. Thousands of human beings were swarming around Him. There was great joy at the Passover season everywhere, but Jesus was "despised and rejected of men; a man of sorrows and acquainted with grief: and we hid as it were our faces from him; he was despised, and we esteemed him not. Surely he hath borne our griefs, and carried our sorrows: yet we did esteem him stricken, smitten of God, and afflicted. But he was wounded for our transgressions, he was bruised for our iniquities: the chastisement of our peace was upon him; and with his stripes we are healed. All we like sheep have gone astray; we have turned every one to his own way; and the Lord hath laid on him the iniquity of us all" (Isaiah 53: 3–6).

Jesus was *alone*. He had come to His own, and His own received Him not. "But all this was done, that the Scriptures of the prophets might be fulfilled. Then all the disciples forsook him, and fled" (Matthew 26:56). The crowds who had so recently shouted, "Hosanna," had that very day shouted, "Crucify him. Crucify him." Now even His loyal twelve had left.

And at last we hear Him cry out, "My God, my God, why hast thou forsaken me?" (Mark 15:34). Not only had He been forsaken by His human companions, but now in that desperate and lonely hour, He—because He was bearing our sins in His own body on the cross—had been forsaken by God as well. Jesus was enduring the suffering and judgment of hell for you and me.

Hell, essentially, is separation from God. Hell is the loneliest place in the universe. Jesus suffered its agony for you, in your place. Now God says, Repent, believe on Christ, receive Christ, and you will never know the sorrow, the loneliness and the agony of hell.

"Whosoever shall call upon the name of the Lord shall be saved" (Romans 10:13).

7

After Death—What?

There is but a step between me and death. 1 SAMUEL 20:3

IT HAS BEEN said that all of life is but a preparation for death.

The psalmist said: "What man is he that liveth, and shall not see death?" (Psalm 89:48).

This is supposed to be a free-thinking age of radical experiment. We have sought to change the world and the laws which govern it through knowledge, science, invention, discovery, philosophy, and materialistic thinking. We have tried to enthrone the false gods of money, fame, and human intelligence; but however we try, the end is always the same: "It is appointed unto men once to die" (Hebrews 9:27).

In the midst of life, we see death on every hand. The wail of the ambulance, the illuminated mortuary signs, the graveyards we so frequently pass, and the sight of a hearse threading its way through traffic, all remind us that the Grim Reaper may call for us at any moment. None of us can be sure when that exact moment will be, but we are well aware that it may come at any time.

Someone has said, "The only certain thing about life is death." Oscar Wilde said, "One can survive everything nowadays—except death!" Books on death and dying have proliferated in recent days—as have books by those who claim to have experienced death and come back to tell about it. Rather than looking for a way to make our peace with God, the world has instead come up with classes on dying and how to face death—accepting it as a normal part of living. Actually, all mankind is sitting on Death Row. How we die or when is not the main issue, but where do we go after death.

Each year hundreds of Americans step into their automobiles little realizing this is to be their last ride. In 1980 53,200 Americans died in automobile accidents. In spite of all the increased safety measures, another 46,900 persons were killed in accidents at home, when all thought of death was far from their minds. For death stalks mankind relentlessly, and although medical science and safety engineers wage a constant war against it, in the end, death is always the victor.

Because of this long-fought scientific battle, we now have the advantage of a few years more of life, but death is still standing at the end of the road, and the life span of the average person does not far exceed the biblical three score years and ten.

Heart diseases still cut down far too many of our citizens in the prime of life. Cancer still presses its pain into the bodies of thousands. Blood disorders take their toll, although medical research has greatly decreased their annual number. Herpes and AIDS (acquired immune deficiency syndrome) are the illnesses of the '80s. They are on the rise around the world and have been reported on all the major continents. But however optimistic the statistical surveys, however much our life span has been increased since 1900, whatever the figures may show on murder, suicide, and other forms of violent death, the inevitable fact of death remains unchanged—it is still our ultimate experience on earth!

A Lifelong Battle

From the moment a child is born, the death process, and the fight against it, begins. The mother devotes years of attention to protecting the life of her child. She watches the food, the clothes, the environment, the medical checkups and inoculations, but in spite of her loving care, the child has already begun to die.

Before many years the tangible signs of weakness will be obvious. The dentist will check the decay of our teeth. Glasses will be needed to help improve our fading vision. Skin will wrinkle and sag as time passes, and our shoulders will droop and our step become slower and less sure. The brittleness of our bones will increase as our energy lessens. Almost without realizing it we have begun to move closer to death.

Health insurance and hospitalization will be used to help us cushion the blow. Life insurance will be purchased to cover our final expenses and obligations, and we shall suddenly see our whole life as a great and never-ending battle with death. We shall see that we are all running a race in which the most we can hope for is a little more time, and outwit our opponent as we may, in the end we know that death will always win!

What a mysterious thing is this enemy of ours—as mysterious as life itself. For the life that we see so plentifully around us in plants and animals, as well as in human beings, cannot be reproduced by us, or even explained. Death is also without explanation, although we are as aware of its presence as we are of life. How little we like to talk about it, however, or consider its importance! When life comes, and a child is born, we rejoice. When life goes, and a man dies, we try to dismiss the thought as quickly as possible.

Today there are something like three billion people living on this planet. Almost all of them will be dead in a hundred years. Their bodies will be without feeling. But what about their souls—the essential and eternal part of life?

Here is the mystery. What is missing when a man dies? Where does that missing thing go?

Why Do Men Reject God?

Some years ago a newspaper columnist died in Denver, Colorado. The mourners listened to his recorded voice at the funeral when he said, "This is my funeral. I am an atheist and have been for many years. I have the utmost contempt for theological nonsense. Clergymen are moral cowards. Miracles are the product of the imagination. If any four reporters were sent to an execution and got their facts as twisted as the apostles in the Bible report, they would be fired forthwith. I want no religious songs. This is going to be a perfectly rational funeral."

Contrast this to the beautiful description of death pictured by Alfred Lord Tennyson, in his poem, *In Memoriam:* "God's finger touched him, and he slept."

Every age has produced men who in their hatred of God have attempted to heap ridicule and abuse upon the church, the Scriptures, and Jesus Christ. Without presenting evidence they cry out against the voice of God. History testifies of the George Bernard Shaws, the Robert Ingersolls, the B. F. Skinners and many other philosophers who strove, by argument, to destroy the fear of death.

Listen to the anthropologist tell of death in the jungle. There is no "theological nonsense" there, for they have not heard of Jesus Christ. What of death there? In some tribes the old are turned into the bush so that the wild animals might attack them and death need not be faced by the young. In another tribe the clothes are stripped off and the bodies of the mourners painted with white. Hour after hour the moans and screams of the women tell the world that a soul is about to leave a body. Death outside of Christian influence is filled with horror and despair—or, at best, resignation and indifference. Among the Moslems, for instance, death is looked forward to in anticipation, for Moslems believe that great pleasures await the faithful—if they die while killing infidels or fighting for their faith.

Compare this to the death of the Christian. When Christ came He gave a new approach to death. Man had always looked upon death as an enemy, but Jesus said that He had conquered death and taken the very sting out of death. Jesus Christ was the Master Realist when He urged men to prepare for death, which was certain to come. Do not worry, said the Lord Jesus, about the death of the body, but rather concern yourself with the eternal death of the soul.

I think of Helen Morken who, as she lay dying, was surrounded by her husband and children singing hymns for hours each day. Literally, she was sung into the presence of the Lord. And I think of those saints of God described by Alexander Smellie in his book, *Men of the Covenant.* He tells of the great men of faith who died during those "killing times" in Scotland when executions were anything but pleasant. There were no electric chairs, firing squads, lethal injections to make death as painless as possible. It was a time of torture—thumb screws, the boot, of being hanged and then quartered. For this reason, each man described by Smellie had a horror of death. Yet, each one, when he came to the actual point of dying, died in an ectasy of joy!

The Bible indicates that there are actually two deaths: one is *physical death* and the other is *eternal death.* Jesus warned that we are to fear the *second death* far more than the *first death.* He described the *second death* as hell, which is eternal separation from God. He indicated that the death of your body is nothing compared to the conscious everlasting banishment of a soul from God.

The Death of a Saint

The last statements of dying men provide an excellent study for those who are looking for realism in the face of death.

Matthew Henry—"Sin is bitter. I bless God I have inward supports."

Martin Luther—"Our God is the God from whom cometh salvation: God is the Lord by whom we escape death."

John Knox—"Live in Christ, live in Christ, and the flesh need not fear death."

John Wesley—"The best of all is, God is with us. Farewell! Farewell!"

Richard Baxter—"I have pain; but I have peace. I have peace."

William Carey, the missionary—"When I am gone, speak less of Dr. Carey and more of Dr. Carey's Savior."

Adoniram Judson—"I am not tired of my work, neither am I tired of the world; yet when Christ calls me home, I shall go with the gladness of a boy bounding away from school."

How different is the story of the Christian who has confessed his sin and by faith received Jesus Christ as his personal Savior!

For many years Dr. Effie Jane Wheeler taught English and literature where I attended college. Dr. Wheeler was noted for her piety as well as for her knowledge of the subjects she taught. In May of 1949, on Memorial Day, Dr. Wheeler wrote the following letter to Dr. Edman, then president of the college, her colleagues, and former students:

"I greatly appreciate the moment in chapel that may be given to reading this, for before you leave for the summer I should like to have you know the truth about me as I learned it myself only last Friday. My doctor at last has given what has been his real diagnosis of my illness for weeks—an inoperable case of cancer. Now if he had been a Christian he wouldn't have been so dilatory or shaken, for he would have known, as you and I do, that life or death is equally welcome when we live in the will and presence of the Lord. If the Lord has chosen me to go to Him soon, I go gladly. Please do not give a moment's grief for me. I do not say a cold goodbye but rather a warm Auf Wiedersehen till I see you again—in the blessed land where I may be allowed to draw aside a curtain when you enter. With a heart full of love for every individual of you. (Signed) Effie Jane Wheeler."

Just two weeks after writing this letter, Dr. Wheeler entered the presence of her Savior, who had kept His promise to take the sting out of death.

While we were writing this chapter, in one mail we received four letters. One was from a ninety-four-year-old saint, eager to be with her Lord; one from a woman on Death Row who, since becoming a Christian six years ago, can now look beyond her approaching execution to the glory that lies ahead; and two letters from women whose husbands had just died after many years of marriage (one just short of their forty-ninth wedding anniversary). Each is looking beyond death to the glory that lies ahead.

The great Dwight L. Moody on his deathbed said: "This is my triumph; this is my coronation day! It is glorious!"

The Bible teaches that you are an immortal soul. Your soul is eternal and will live forever. In other words, the real you—the part of you that thinks, feels, dreams, aspires; the ego, the personality—will never die. The Bible teaches that your soul will live forever in one of two places—heaven or hell. If you are not a Christian and you have never been born again, then the Bible teaches that your soul goes immediately to a place Jesus called Hades, where you will await the judgment of God.

An Unpopular Subject

I am conscious of the fact that the subject of hell is not a very pleasant one. It is very unpopular, controversial, and misunderstood. In my crusades across the country, however, I usually devote one evening to the discussion of this subject. Following my discussion many letters to the editors of newspapers appear for days as people argue the pros and cons, for the Bible has almost as much to say about this subject as any other. In student discussions on many campuses of America I am continually asked the question, "What about hell? Is there fire in hell?" and similar questions. As a minister I must deal with it. I cannot ignore it, even though it makes people uncomfortable and anxious. I grant that it is the hardest of all teachings of Christianity to receive.

There are those who teach that everybody eventually will be saved, that God is a God of love and He will never send anyone to hell. They believe that the words *eternal* or *everlasting* do not actually mean forever. However, the same word which speaks of eternal banishment from God is also used for the eternity of heaven. Someone has said that "fairness demands that we make the joy of the righteous and the punishment of the wicked both qualify, as they are the same Greek word and of the same duration."

There are others who teach that after death those who have refused to receive God's plan of redemption are annihilated, they cease to exist. In searching the Bible from cover to cover I cannot find one shred of evidence to support this view. The Bible teaches that whether we are saved or lost, there is conscious and everlasting existence of the soul and personality.

There are others who teach that after death there is still a possibility of salvation, that God will offer a second chance. If this is true, the Bible gives no hint of it because the Bible is continually warning that "now is the accepted time; behold, now is the day of salvation" (2 Corinthians 6:2).

What the Bible Says

Scores of passages of Scripture could be quoted to support the fact that the Bible does teach there is hell for every man who willingly and knowingly rejects Christ as Lord and Savior:

"I am tormented in this flame" (Luke 16:24).

"Whosoever shall say, Thou fool, shall be in danger of hell fire" (Matthew 5:22).

"The Son of Man shall send forth his angels, and they shall gather out of his kingdom all things that offend, and them which do iniquity; and shall cast them into a furnace of fire: there shall be wailing and gnashing of teeth" (Matthew 13:41–42).

"So shall it be at the end of the world: the angels shall come forth, and sever the wicked from among the just, and shall cast them into the furnace of fire: there shall be wailing and gnashing of teeth" (Matthew 13:49–50).

"Then shall he say also unto them on the left hand, Depart from me, ye cursed, into everlasting fire, prepared for the devil and his angels" (Matthew 25:41).

"But he will burn up the chaff with unquenchable fire" (Matthew 3:12).

"In flaming fire taking vengeance on them that know not God, and that obey not the gospel of our Lord Jesus Christ: Who shall be punished with everlasting destruction from the presence of the Lord, and from the glory of his power" (2 Thessalonians 1:8–9).

"The same shall drink of the wine of the wrath of God, which is poured out without mixture into the cup of his indignation; and he shall be tormented with fire and brimstone in the presence of the holy angels, and in the presence of the Lamb: and the smoke of their torment ascendeth up for ever and ever: and they have no rest day nor night" (Revelation 14:10–11).

"And death and hell were cast into the lake of fire. This is the second death. And whosoever was not found written in the Book of Life was cast into the lake of fire" (Revelation 20:14–15).

"But the fearful, and unbelieving, and the abominable, and murderers, and whoremongers, and sorcerers, and idolators, and all liars, shall have their part in the lake which burneth with fire and brimstone: which is the second death" (Revelation 21:8).

But I hear someone say, "I don't believe in hell. My religion is the Sermon on the Mount."

Well, let's listen to a passage from the Sermon on the Mount: "And if thy right eye offend thee, pluck it out, and cast it from thee: for it is profitable for thee that one of thy members should perish, and not that thy whole body should be cast into hell. And if thy right hand offend thee, cut it off, and cast it from thee: for it is profitable for thee that one of thy members should perish, and not that thy whole body should be cast into hell" (Matthew 5:29–30).

Here we have the distinct teaching of Jesus that there is a hell. In fact, Jesus told stories and gave illustrations on the subject and warned men time after time about the folly of living a sinful and hypocritical life here on earth.

Hell on Earth

There is no doubt that wicked men suffer a certain hell here on earth. The Bible says, "Be sure your sin will find you out" (Numbers 32:23). Again the Bible says, "Whatsoever a man soweth, that shall he also reap" (Galatians 6:7). However, there is evidence all around us to show that some wicked men seem to prosper and the righteous suffer for their righteousness. The Bible teaches that there is going to be a time of equalization when justice shall be done. Someone has said that "we are not punished for our sins but by them." Both are true.

Will a loving God send a man to hell? The answer is—yes, because He is just. But He does not send him willingly. Man condemns himself by his refusal of God's way of salvation. In love and mercy, God is offering to men and women a way of escape, a way of salvation, a hope and anticipation of better things. Man in his blindness, stupidity, stubbornness, egotism, and love of sinful pleasure refuses God's simple method of escaping the pangs of eternal banishment.

Suppose I am sick and call a doctor, who comes and gives me a prescription. But after thinking it over I decide to ignore his advice and to refuse the medicine. When he returns a few days later he might find my condition much worse. Could I blame the doctor, could I hold him responsible? He gave me the prescription. He prescribed the remedy. But I refused it!

Just so, God prescribes the remedy for the ills of the human race. That remedy is personal faith and commitment to Jesus Christ. The remedy is to be born again, as we will discuss in another chapter. If we deliberately refuse it, then we must suffer the consequence; and we cannot blame God. Is it God's fault because we refuse the remedy?

The man who refuses to believe in life after death, in heaven to gain or hell to shun, the man who refuses to believe what God says in His Word about heaven and hell awakes in the next life to find that he has been wrong, he has lost everything. In *People* magazine, one of the nation's leading gamblers, Lem Banker, has been quoted as saying, "Never bet what you want to win, only what you can afford to lose." Can you afford to lose your eternal soul?

There are others who ask, "What is the nature of hell?" There are four words that have been translated in our Bible as "hell." One word is *Sheol*, which is translated thirty-one times as "hell" in the Old Testament. It means an "unseen state." The words of *sorrow*, *pain*, and *destruction* are used in connection with it.

The second word is *Hades*, which is translated from the Greek and used ten times in the New Testament. It means the same as *Sheol* in the Old Testament. Judgment and suffering are always connected with it.

The third word is *Tartarus*, used only once in 2 Peter 2:4, where it says that disobedient angels are cast into Tartarus. It indicates a place of judgment, such as a prison, or dungeon, where there is intense darkness.

The fourth word is *Gehenna*, used eleven times, and translated as "hell" in the New Testament. It is the illustration that Jesus used of the Valley of Hinnon, a place outside Jerusalem where rubbish and debris were burned continually.

Others ask, "Does the Bible teach literal fire in hell?" If it is not literal fire, it is something worse. Jesus would not have exaggerated. There is no doubt that the Bible many times uses the word fire figuratively. However, God does have a fire that burns and yet does not consume.

When Moses saw the bush of fire, he was amazed to find that the bush was not consumed. The three Hebrew children were put in a fiery furnace, but they were not consumed; in fact, not a hair of their heads was singed.

On the other hand, the Bible talks about our tongues being "set on fire of hell" (James 3:6) every time we speak evil about our neighbors. That does not mean that literal combustion takes place every time we say something against our neighbors. But whether it be literal or figurative does not affect its reality. If there is no fire, then God is using symbolic language to indicate something that could be far worse.

Separation from God

Essentially, hell is separation from God. It is the second death, which is described as the eternal conscious banishment from the presence of all that is light, joyous, good, righteous, and happy. The Bible has many fearful descriptions concerning this awful condition in which the soul will find itself one minute after death.

It is strange that men will prepare for everything except death. We prepare for education. We prepare for business. We prepare for our careers. We prepare for marriage. We prepare for old age. We prepare for everything except the moment we are to die. And yet the Bible says it is appointed unto all of us once to die.

Death is an occurrence that to each man seems unnatural when related to himself, but natural when related to others. Death reduces all men to the same rank. It strips the rich of his millions and the poor man of his rags. It cools avarice and stills the fires of passion. All would like to ignore death, and yet all must face it—the prince and the peasant, the fool and the philosopher, the murderer and the saint alike. Death knows no age limits, no partiality. It is a thing that all men fear.

Toward the end of his life, Daniel Webster related how once he attended a church service in a quiet country village. The clergyman was a simple-hearted, pious old man. After the opening exercises he arose and pronounced his text, and then with the utmost simplicity and earnestness said, "My friends, we can die but once."

Daniel Webster, commenting on this sermon, later said, "Frigid and weak as these words might seem, at once they were to me among the most impressive and awakening I ever heard."

An Appointment with Death

It is easy to think of others having to keep this appointment with death, but difficult for us to remember that we, too, must keep this same appointment. When we see soldiers going to the front or read of a condemned prisoner or visit a dying friend, we are conscious of a certain solemnity which gathers about such persons. Death is appointed for all, and the question of its occurrence is merely a matter of time. Other appointments in life—the appointment of pleasure— we can neglect or break and take the consequence, but here is an appointment that no man can ignore, no man can break. He can meet it only *once*, but meet it he must!

If physical death were the only consequence of a life lived apart from God, we would not have so much to fear, but the Bible warns that there is the second death, which is the eternal banishment from God.

However, there is a brighter side. As the Bible pronounces hell for the sinner, it also promises heaven for the saint. A saint has been described as a sinner who has been forgiven. The subject of heaven is much easier to accept than the subject of hell. And yet the Bible teaches both.

If you are moving to a new home, you want to know all about the community to which you are going. If you are transferring to another city, you want to know all about the city—its railroads, industries, parks, lakes, schools, etc. And since we are going to spend eternity someplace, we ought to know something about it. The information concerning heaven is found in the Bible. It is right that we should think about it and talk about it. In talking about heaven, earth grows shabby by comparison. Our sorrows and problems here seem so much less when we have keen anticipation of the future. In a certain sense the Christian has heaven here on earth. He has peace of soul, peace of conscience, and peace with God. In the midst of troubles and difficulties he has an inner peace and joy, not dependent on circumstances.

There Is a Heaven

But the Bible also promises the Christian a heaven in the life hereafter. Someone asked John Quincy Adams at the age of ninety-four how he felt one morning. He said, "Quite well. Quite well. But the house I live in is not so good." Even though the house we live in may be sick and weak, we can actually feel strong and sure if we are Christians. Jesus taught there is a heaven.

There are a number of passages that could be quoted, but the most descriptive is found in John 14:2: "In my Father's house are many rooms; if it were not so, would I have told you that I go to prepare a place for you? And when I go and prepare a place for you, I will come again and receive you to myself, that where I am there you may be also" (RSV). Paul was so certain of heaven that he could say, "We are confident, I say, and willing rather to be absent from the body and to be present with the Lord" (2 Corinthians 5:8).

How different is the anticipation of the Christian and that of the agnostic Bob Ingersoll, who said at the grave of his brother, "Life is a narrow veil between the cold and barren peaks of two eternities. We strive in vain to look beyond the heights. We cry aloud and the only answer is the echo of our wailing cry."

The Apostle Paul said time after time, "We know," "We are confident," "We are always confident." The Bible says that Abraham "looked for a city which hath foundations, whose builder and maker is God."

Many people say, "Do you believe that heaven is a literal place?" Yes! Jesus said, "I go to prepare a place for you." The Bible teaches that Enoch and Elijah ascended in a literal body to a literal place that is just as real as Hawaii, Switzerland, the Virgin Islands, or more so!

Many people have asked, "Where is heaven?" We are not told in the Scripture where heaven is. Nor does it matter. It will be heaven and Christ will be there to welcome us home.

A Place of Beauty

The Bible teaches that this country will be a place of beauty. It is described in the Bible as "a building of God"—"a city"—"a better country"—"an inheritance"—"a glory."

You may ask, "Will we know each other in heaven?" The Bible indicates in a number of places that it will be a time of grand reunion with those who have gone on before.

Others say, "Do you believe that children will be saved?" Yes. The Bible indicates that God does not hold a child accountable for his or her sins until he reaches the age of accountability. There seems to be plenty of indication that the atonement covers their sin until they reach an age at which they are responsible for their own right and wrong actions.

The Bible also indicates that heaven will be a place of great understanding and knowledge of things that we never learned down here.

Sir Isaac Newton, when an old man, said to one who praised his wisdom, "I am as a child on the seashore picking up a pebble here and a shell there, but the great ocean of truth still lies before me."

And Thomas Edison once said, "I do not know one millionth part of one percent about anything."

Many of the mysteries of God, the heartaches, trials, disappointments, tragedies, and the silence of God in the midst of suffering will be revealed there. Eli Wiessel said that eternity is ". . . the place where questions and answers become one." And in John 16:23 Jesus says, "And in that day ye shall ask me nothing." All our questions will be answered!

Many people ask. "Well, what will we do in heaven? Just sit down and enjoy the luxuries of life?" No. The Bible indicates that we will serve God. There will be work to do for God. Our very beings will praise God. The Bible says, "And there shall be no more curse; but the throne of God and of the Lamb shall be in it; and his servants shall serve him" (Revelation 22:3).

It will be a time of total joy, service, laughter, singing, and praise to God. Imagine serving Him forever and never growing tired!

Into the Presence of Christ

Now the Bible teaches to be absent from the body is to be present with the Lord. The moment a Christian dies, he goes immediately into the presence of Christ. There his soul awaits the resurrection, when the soul and body will be rejoined.

Many people ask, "How can the bodies that have decayed or been cremated be raised?" God knows. But the new body that we will have will be a glorious body like the body of Christ. It will be an eternal body. It will never know tears, heartache, tragedy, disease, suffering, death, or fatigue. It will be a renewed body, but still recognizable.

Here we have a picture of two eternal worlds floating out into space. Every son of Adam will be on one or the other. There is a great deal of mystery surrounding both of them, but there are enough hints and implications in the Bible to give us light that one will be a world of tragedy and suffering and the other will be one of light and glory.

We have now seen the problems of the human race. Superficially, they are complex; basically, they are simple. We have seen that they could probably be summed up in one word—sin. We have seen that man's future is hopeless without God. But just to analyze our problems and have an intellectual understanding of God's plan is not enough. If God is to help man, then man must meet certain conditions. In the next few chapters we will survey these conditions.

II

ADVANCING

THE SOLUTION

8

Why Jesus Came

The Son of man is come to seek and to save that which was lost. Luke 19:10

WE HAVE SEEN that the most terrible, the most devastating fact in the universe is sin. The cause of all trouble, the root of all sorrow, the dread of every man lies in this one small word—sin. It has crippled the nature of man. It has destroyed the inner harmony of man's life. It has robbed him of his nobility. It has caused man to be caught in the devil's trap.

All mental disorders, all sicknesses, all perversions, all destruction, all wars find their *original* root in sin. It causes madness in the brain, and poison in the heart. It is described in the Bible as a fatal disease that demands a radical cure. It is a tornado on the loose. It is a volcano gone wild. It is a madman escaped from the asylum. It is a gangster on the prowl. It is a roaring lion seeking its prey. It is a streak of lightning heading toward the earth. It is quicksand sucking man under. It is a deadly cancer eating its way into the souls of men. It is a raging torrent that sweeps everything before it. It is a cesspool of corruption contaminating every area of life.

But, as someone has said, "Sin can keep you from the Bible—or the Bible can keep you from sin."

For ages men were lost in spiritual darkness, blinded by the disease of sin, made to grope—searching, questing, seeking some way out. Man needed someone who could lead him out of the mental confusion and moral labyrinth, someone who could unlock the prison doors and redeem him from the devil's prison. Men with hungry hearts, thirsty minds, and broken spirits stood hopelessly with searching eyes and listening ears. Meanwhile the devil gloated over his mighty victory in the Garden of Eden.

From the primitive man in the jungle through the mighty civilizations of Egypt, Greece, and Rome, bewildered men were all asking the same question, "How can I get out? How can I be better? What can I do? Which way can I turn? How can I get rid of this terrible disease? How can I stop this onrushing torrent? How can I get out of the mess in which I find myself? If there is a way, how can I find it?"

The Bible's Answer

We have already seen how the Bible teaches that God was a God of love. He wanted to do something for man. He wanted to save man. He wanted to free man from the curse of sin. How could He do it? God was a just God. He was righteous and holy. He had warned man from the beginning that if he obeyed the devil and disobeyed God, he would die physically and spiritually. Man deliberately disobeyed God. Man had to die or God would have been a liar, for God could not break His word. His very nature would not allow Him to lie. His word had to be kept. Therefore, when man deliberately disobeyed Him, he was banished from the presence of God. He deliberately chose to go the devil's way.

There had to be some other way, for man was hopelessly involved and helplessly lost. Man's very nature was inverted. He opposed God. Many even denied that God existed, so blinded were they by the disease from which they suffered.

But even in the Garden of Eden, God gave a hint that He was going to do something about it. He warned the devil and promised man, "And I will put enmity between thee and the woman, and between thy seed and her seed; it shall bruise thy head, and thou shalt bruise his heel" (Genesis 3:15). "And thou shalt bruise his heel"—here was a brilliant flash of light from heaven. The head refers to a total permanent wound; the heel refers to a temporary injury. Here was a promise. Here was something that man could hold on to. God was promising that some day a Redeemer would come, a Deliverer would come. God gave man hope. Down through the centuries man held on to that one bit of hope!

That was not all. There were other occasions through the thousands of years of history when other flashes of light came from heaven. All through the Old Testament, God gave man the promise of salvation if by faith he would believe in the coming Redeemer. Therefore God began to teach His people that man could only be saved by substitution. Someone else would have to pay the penalty for man's redemption.

Go Back to Eden

Go back again with me in your imagination to Eden for a moment. God said, "In the day that thou eatest thereof thou shalt surely die." Man did eat of it. He died.

Suppose that God had said, "Adam, you must have made a mistake, that was a slight error on your part. You are forgiven. Please don't do it again." God would have been a liar. He would not have been holy, neither would He have been just. He was forced by His very nature to keep His word. God's justice was at stake. Man had to die spiritually and physically. His iniquities had separated him from his God. Thus man had to suffer. He had to pay for his own sins. As we have seen, Adam was the federal head of the human race. When Adam sinned, we all sinned. "Wherefore, as by one man sin entered into the world, and death by sin; and so death passed upon all men, for that all have sinned" (Romans 5:12).

The burning question became "How can God be just and still justify the sinner?" It must be remembered that the word justify means the "clearance of the soul from guilt." Justification is far more than just forgiveness. Sin must be put away and made as though it had never been. Man must be restored so that there shall be no spot or blemish or stain. In other words, man must be taken back to the position he had before he fell from grace.

For centuries men in their blindness have been trying to get back to Eden—but they have never been able to reach their goal. They have tried many paths, but they have all failed. C. S. Lewis says that "All religions are either a preview or a perversion of Christianity."

Education is important, but education will not bring a man back to God. False religions are an opiate which attempt to keep men from present misery while promising future glory, hut they will never bring man to the place of his goal. The United Nations may be a practical necessity in a world of men at war, and we are thankful for every step that can be taken in the field of international relations to settle disputes without recourse to war; but if the United Nations could bring lasting peace, man could say to God, "We do not need You any more. We have brought peace on earth and have organized humanity in righteousness." All of these schemes are patchwork remedies that a sick and dying world must use while waiting for the Great Physician. Back in history we know that the first attempt of united man ended with the confusion of tongues at the Tower of Babel. Men have failed on every other occasion when they have tried to work without God, and they will continue to be doomed to such failures.

The question remains "How can God be just—that is, true to Himself in nature and true to Himself in holiness, and yet justify the sinner?" Because each man had to bear his own sins, all mankind was excluded from helping, since each was contaminated with the same disease.

The only solution was for an innocent party to volunteer to die physically and spiritually as a substitution before God. This innocent party would have to take man's judgment, penalty, and death. But where was such an individual? Certainly there was none perfect on earth, for the Bible says, "All have sinned" (Romans 3:23). There was only one possibility. God's own Son was the only personality in the universe who had the capacity to bear in His own body the sins of the whole world. Certainly Gabriel or Michael the archangel might possibly have come and died for one, but only God's Son was infinite and thus able to die for all.

God in Three Persons

The Bible teaches that God is actually three Persons. This is a mystery that we will never be able to understand. The Bible does not teach that there are three Gods—but that there is one God. This one God, however, is expressed in three Persons. There is God the Father, God the Son, and God the Holy Spirit.

The Second Person of this Trinity is God's Son, Jesus Christ. He is co-equal with God the Father. He was not *a* Son of God but *the* Son of God. He is the Eternal Son of God—the Second Person of the Holy Trinity, God manifested in the flesh, the living Savior.

The Bible teaches that Jesus Christ had no beginning. He was never created. The Bible teaches that the heavens were created by Him (John 1:1–3). All the myriads of stars and flaming suns were created by Him. The earth was flung from His flaming fingertip. The birth of Jesus Christ that we celebrate at Christmas time was not His beginning. His origin is shrouded in that same mystery that baffles us when we inquire into the beginning of God. The Bible only tells us, "In the beginning was the Word, and the Word was with God, and the Word was God" (John 1:1).

About Christ, the Bible teaches us, "Who is the image of the invisible God, the firstborn of every creature: For by him were all things created, that are in heaven, and that are in earth, visible and invisible, whether they be thrones, or dominions, or principalities, or powers: all things were created by him, and for him: And he is before all things, and by him all things consist" (Colossians 1:15–17).

That last phrase indicates that He holds all things together. In other words, the entire universe would smash into billions of atoms were it not for the cohesive power of Jesus Christ. The Bible again says, "And, thou, Lord, in the beginning has laid the foundation of the earth; and the heavens are the works of thine hands: They shall perish; but thou remainest; and they all shall wax old as doth a garment; And as a vesture shalt thou fold them up, and they shall be changed: but thou art the same, and thy years shall not fail" (Hebrews 1:10–12).

Jesus Christ, the Redeemer

Again Jesus said of Himself, "I am Alpha and Omega, the beginning and the end." He, and He alone, had the power and capacity to bring man back to God. But would He? If He did, He would have to come to earth. He would have to take the form of a servant. He would have to be made in the likeness of men. He would have to humble Himself and become obedient unto death. He would have to grapple with sin. He would have to meet and overcome Satan, the enemy of man's souls. He would have to redeem sinners out of the slave market of sin. He would have to loose the bonds and set the prisoners free by paying a price—that price would be His own life. He would have to be despised and rejected of men, a man of sorrows and acquainted with grief. He would have to be smitten of God and separated from God. He would have to be wounded for the transgressions of men and bruised for their iniquities, His blood shed to atone for man's sin. He would have to reconcile God and man. He would be the great Mediator of history. He would have to be a substitute. He would have to die in the place of sinful man. All this would have to be done—voluntarily.

And that is exactly what happened! Looking down over the battlements of heaven He saw this planet swinging in space—doomed, damned, crushed, and bound for hell. He saw you and me struggling beneath our load of sin and bound in the chains and ropes of sin. He made His decision in the council halls of God. The angelic hosts bowed in humility and awe as heaven's Prince of Princes and Lord of Lords, who could speak worlds into space, got into His jeweled chariot, went through pearly gates, across the steep of the skies, and on a black Judean night, while the stars sang together and the escorting angels chanted His praises, stepped out of the chariot, threw off His robes, and became man!

It was as though I, while walking along a road, stepped on an ant hill. I might look down and say to the ants, "I am terribly sorry that I've stepped on your ant hill. I've disrupted your home. Everything is in confusion. I wish I could tell you that I care, that I did not mean to do it, that I would like to help you."

But you say, "That's absurd, that's impossible, ants cannot understand your language!" That's just it! How wonderful it would be if I could only become an ant for a few moments and in their own language tell them of my concern for them!

That, in effect, is what Christ did. He came to reveal God to men. He it is who told us that God loves us and is interested in our lives. He it is who told us of the mercy and long-suffering and grace of God. He it is who promised life everlasting.

But more than that, Jesus Christ partook of flesh and blood in order that He might die (Hebrews 2:14). "He was manifested to take away our sins" (1 John 3:5). The very purpose of Christ's coming into the world was that He might offer up His life as a sacrifice for the sins of men. He came to die. The shadow of His death hung like a pall over all of His thirty-three years.

The night Jesus was born Satan trembled. He sought to slay Him before He was born, and tried to slay Him as soon as He was born. When the decree went forth from Herod ordering the slaughter of all the children, its one purpose was to make certain of the death of Jesus.

The Sinless Son

All the days of His life on earth He never once committed a sin. He is the only man who ever lived who was sinless. He could stand in front of men and ask, "Which of you convinceth me of sin?" (John 8:46). He was hounded by the enemy day and night, but they never found any sin in Him. He was without spot or blemish.

Jesus lived a humble life. He made Himself of no reputation. He received no honor of men. He was born in a stable. He was reared in the insignificant village of Nazareth. He was a carpenter. He gathered around Him a humble group of fishermen as His followers. He walked among men as a man. He was one of the people. He humbled Himself as no other man has ever humbled himself.

Jesus taught with such authority that the people of His day said, "Never man spake like this man" (John 7:46). Every word that He spoke was historically true. Every word that He spoke was scientifically true. Every word that He spoke was ethically true. There were no loopholes in the moral conceptions and statements of Jesus Christ. His ethical vision was wholly correct, correct in the age in which He lived and correct in every age that has followed it.

The words of this blessed Person were prophetically true. He prophesied many things that are even yet in the future. Lawyers tried to catch Him with test questions, but they could never confuse Him. His answers to His opponents were clear and clean-cut. There were no question marks about His statements, no deception in His meaning, no hesitancy in His words. He knew, and therefore spoke with quiet authority. He spoke with such simplicity that the common people heard Him gladly. Though His words were profound, they were plain. His words were weighty, yet they shone with a luster and simplicity of statement that staggered His enemies. He dealt with the great questions of the day in such a way that, from simple to sophisticated, man had no difficulty in understanding Him.

The Lord Jesus cured the sick, the lame, the halt, and the blind. He healed the leper and raised the dead. He cast out demons. He quieted the elements. He stilled storms. He brought peace, joy, and hope to the thousands to whom He ministered.

He showed no sign of fear. He was never in a hurry. He met with no accidents. He moved with perfect coordination and precision. He had supreme poise of bearing. He did not waver or worry about His work. Though He did not heal all the sick, raise all the dead, open the eyes of all the blind, or feed all the hungry, yet at the end of His life He could say, "I have finished the work thou gavest me to do."

He stood before Pilate and quietly said, "Thou couldst have no power at all against me, except it were given thee from above" (John 9:11). He told the frightened people that angelic legions were at His command.

He approached His cross with dignity and calmness, with an assurance and a set purpose that fulfilled the prophecy written about Him eight hundred years earlier: "He is brought as a lamb to the slaughter, and as a sheep before her shearers is dumb, so he openeth not his mouth" (Isaiah 53:7).

Defeating the Devil

He moved supremely, gloriously, and with great anticipation toward the mission that He had come to accomplish. He had come to save sinful men. He had come to appease the wrath of God. He had come to defeat the devil forever. He had come to conquer hell and the grave. There was only one way that He could do it. There was only one course set before Him.

His death had been prophesied thousands of years before. First, as we have seen, in Eden's Garden; and then in sermon, story, and prophecy the death of Christ was set forth in the ages past. Abraham foresaw His death as the lamb was slain. The children of Israel symbolized His death in the slaughtered lamb. Every time blood was shed on a Jewish altar it represented the Lamb of God who was someday to come and take away sin. David prophesied His death in detail in more than one prophetic Psalm. Isaiah devoted whole chapters to predicting the details of His death.

Jesus Christ said that He had power to lay down His life when He said, "The good shepherd giveth his life for the sheep" (John 10:11). He said again, "Even so must the Son of man be lifted up: That whosoever believeth in him should not perish" (John 3:14, 15). Jesus Christ had faced the possibility of the cross far back in eternity. During all the ages which preceded His birth, He knew that the day of His death was hastening on. When He was born of a virgin, He was born with the cross darkening His pathway. He had taken on a human body in order that He might die. From the cradle to the cross, His purpose was to die.

Someone has described how He suffered as no man has ever suffered: "The night watches in Gethsemane, lighted by the flaming torches, the kiss of the traitor, the arrest, the trial before the high priest, the hour of waiting, the palace of the Roman governor, the journey to the palace of Herod, the rough handling by Herod's brutal soldiers, the awesome scenes while Pilate tried to save Him as priests and people clamored for His blood, the scourging, the howling multitudes, the path from Jerusalem to Golgotha, the nails in His hands, the spike through His feet, the crown of thorns upon His brow, the sarcastic and mocking cries of the two thieves on either side, 'You have saved others, now save yourself.'"

Sometimes people have asked me why Christ died so quickly, in six hours, on the cross, while other victims have agonized on the cross for two and three days—and longer. He was weak and exhausted when He came there. He had been scourged, He was physically depleted. But when Christ died, He died voluntarily. He chose the exact moment when He expired.

There He hung between heaven and earth. Having suffered unspeakably, He voiced neither complaint nor appeal but simply a statement by which He let us know in two words something of the terrible physical pain He suffered when He said, "I thirst."

Some unknown poet has put it this way:

> But more than pains wracked Him there
> Was the deep longing thirst divine
> That thirsted for the souls of men,
> Dear Lord—and one was mine!

Sinner or Substitute

God demands death, either for the sinner or a substitute. Christ was the substitute! Gabriel and ten legions of angels hovered on the rim of the universe, their swords unsheathed. One look from His blessed face and they would have swept the angry, shouting multitudes into hell. The spikes never held Him—it was the cords of love that bound tighter than any nails that men could mold. "But God commendeth his love toward us, in that, while we were yet sinners, Christ died for us" (Romans 5:8).

For you! For me! He bore our sins in His body upon the tree. As someone has said, "Behold Him on the Cross, bending His sacred head, and gathering into His heart in the awful isolation of separation from God the issue of the sin of the world, and see how out of that acceptance of the issue of sin He creates that which He does not require for Himself that He may distribute to those whose place He has taken." Standing overwhelmed in the presence of this suffering, feeling our own inability to understand or explain, and with a great sense of might and majesty overwhelming us, we hear the next words that pass His lips, "It is finished."

But the physical suffering of Jesus Christ was not the real suffering. Many men before Him had died. Others had hung on a cross longer than He did. Many men had become martyrs. The awful suffering of Jesus Christ was His spiritual death. He reached the final issue of sin, fathomed the deepest sorrow, when He cried, "My God, why hast thou forsaken me?" This cry was proof that Christ, becoming sin for us, had died physically, and with it He lost all sense of the Father's presence at that moment in time. Alone in the supreme hour of mankind's history Christ uttered these words! Light blazed forth to give us a glimpse of what He was enduring, but the light was so blinding, as G. Campbell Morgan says, "that no eye could bear to gaze." The words were uttered, as Dr. Morgan has so well expressed it, "that we men may know how much there is that may not be known."

He who knew no sin was made to be sin on our behalf that we might become the righteousness of God in Him (Galatians 3:13; Mark 15:34; 2 Corinthians 5:21). On the cross He was made sin. He was God-forsaken. Because He knew no sin there is a value beyond comprehension in the penalty He bore, a penalty that He did not need for Himself. If in bearing sin in His own body He created a value that He did not need for Himself, for whom was the value created?

How it was accomplished in the depth of the darkness man will never know. I know only one thing—He bore my sins in His body upon the tree. He hung where I should have hung. The pains of hell that were my portion were heaped on Him, and I am able to go to heaven and merit that which is not my own, but is His by every right. All the types, the offerings, the shadows, and the symbols of the Old Testament were now fulfilled. No longer do the priests have to enter once a year into the Holiest Place. The sacrifice was complete.

Now that the ground of redemption has been laid, all the guilty sinner has to do is believe on the Son, and he can have peace with God. "For God so loved the world, that he gave his only begotten Son, that whosoever believeth in him should not perish, but have everlasting life" (John 3:16).

Three Things in the Cross

In the cross of Christ I see three things: First, a description of the depth of *man's sin*. Do not blame the people of that day for hanging Christ on the cross. You and I are just as guilty. It was not the people or the Roman soldiers who put Him to the cross—it was your sins and my sins that made it necessary for Him to volunteer this death.

Second, in the cross I see the overwhelming *love of God*. If ever you should doubt the love of God, take a long, deep look at the cross, for in the cross you find the expression of God's love.

Third, in the cross is the only *way of salvation*. Jesus said, "I am the way, the truth and the life: no man cometh unto the Father but by me" (John 14:6). There is no possibility of being saved from sin and hell, except by identifying yourself with the Christ of the cross. If there had been any other way to save you, He would have found it. If reformation, or living a good moral and ethical life would have saved you, Jesus never would have died. A substitute had to take your place. Men do not like to talk about it. They do not like to hear about it because it injures their pride. It takes all self out.

Many people say, "Can I not be saved by living by the Golden Rule? Or following the precepts of Jesus? Or living the ethical life that Jesus taught?" Even if we could be saved by living the life that Jesus taught, we still would be sinners. We still would fail, because not one of us has ever lived the life that Jesus taught from the time we were born till the time we die. We have failed. We have transgressed. We have disobeyed. We have sinned. Therefore, what are we going to do about that sin? There is only one thing to do and that is to bring it to the cross and find forgiveness.

Years ago King Charles V was loaned a large sum of money by a merchant in

Antwerp. The note came due, but the King was bankrupt and unable to pay. The merchant gave a great banquet for the King. When all the guests were seated and before the food was brought in, the merchant had a large platter placed on the table before him and a fire lighted on it. Then, taking the note out of his pocket, he held it in the flames until it was burned to ashes.

Just so, we have all been mortgaged to God. The debt was due, but we were unable to pay. Two thousand years ago God invited a morally corrupt world to the foot of the cross. There God held your sins and mine to the flames until every last vestige of our guilt was consumed.

The Bible says, "Without shedding of blood is no remission" (Hebrews 9:22). Many people have said to me, "How repulsive! You don't mean to tell us that you believe in a slaughterhouse religion!" Others have wondered, "I do not understand why God demands blood." Many people have wondered, "I cannot understand why Christ had to die for me." Today the idea of the shed blood of Christ is becoming old-fashioned and out of date in a lot of preaching. It is in the Bible. It is the very heart of Christianity. The distinctive feature of Christianity is blood atonement. Without it we cannot be saved. Blood is actually a symbol of the death of Christ.

Recently I was standing at the admissions desk at Mayo Clinic in Rochester, Minnesota. There, in a little box, were a number of folders entitled "A Gift of Blood" lettered in red forming a large drop of blood. My first reaction was that this must be a gospel tract, but on looking more closely I saw that it was a challenge to people to assist in the blood program. Blood could mean the difference between life and death for someone ill in the hospital. No one who has ever had to receive a blood transfusion will look upon that blood with anything but gratitude. Some might say that blood taken is somewhat revolting, but blood given is a blessing!

The fact remains that blood represents life, as Leviticus 17:11 says, "For the life of the flesh is in the blood and I have given it for you . . . to make atonement for your soul." So the blood sacrifice runs throughout the Old Testament— a foreshadowing or a symbol of Christ's perfect sacrifice.

Five Things Blood Brings

The Bible teaches that it first of all *redeems*. "Forasmuch as ye know that ye were not redeemed with corruptible things, as silver and gold, from your vain conversation received by tradition from your fathers; But with the precious blood of Christ, as of a lamb without blemish and without spot" (1 Peter 1:18–19). Not only are we redeemed from the hands of the devil, but from the hands of the law handed down by God through Moses. Christ's death on the cross brings me out from under the law. The law condemned me, but Christ satisfied every claim. All the gold and silver and the precious stones of earth could never have bought me. What they could not do, the death of Christ did. Redemption means "buying back." We had been sold for nothing to the devil, but Christ redeemed us and brought us back.

Second, it *brings us nigh*. "But now in Christ Jesus ye who sometimes were far off are made nigh by the blood of Christ" (Ephesians 2:13). When we were "aliens from the commonwealth of Israel, and strangers from the covenants of promise, having no hope, and without God in the world," Jesus Christ brought us nigh unto God. "There is therefore now no condemnation [judgment] to them which are in Christ Jesus" (Romans 8:1). The redeemed sinner will never have to face the judgment of Almighty God. Christ has already taken his judgment.

Third, it *makes peace*. "And, having made peace through the blood of his cross, by him to reconcile all things unto himself; by him, I say, whether they be things in earth, or things in heaven" (Colossians 1:20). The world will never know peace until it finds it in the cross of Jesus Christ. You will never know the peace with God, peace of conscience, peace of mind, and peace of soul until you stand at the foot of the cross and identify yourself with Christ by faith. There is the secret of peace. This is peace with God.

Fourth, it *justifies*. "Much more then, being now justified by his blood, we shall be saved from wrath through him" (Romans 5:9). It changes men's standing before God. It is a change from guilt and condemnation to pardon and forgiveness. The forgiven sinner is not like the discharged prisoner who has served out his term and is discharged but with no further rights of citizenship. The repentant sinner, pardoned through the blood of Jesus Christ, regains his full citizenship. "Who shall lay any thing to the charge of God's elect? It is God that justifieth. Who is he that condemneth? It is Christ that died, yea rather, that is risen again, who is even at the right hand of God, who also maketh intercession for us" (Romans 8:33–34).

Fifth, it *cleanses*. "But if we walk in the light, as he is in the light, we have fellowship one with another, and the blood of Jesus Christ his Son cleanseth us from all sin" (1 John 1:7). The key word in this verse is *all*. Not part of our sins, but *all* of them. Every lie you ever told, every mean, low-down dirty thing that you ever did, your hypocrisy, your lustful thoughts—all are cleansed by the death of Christ.

"Just As I Am"

The story has often been told that years ago, in London, there was a large gathering of noted people, and among the invited guests was a famous preacher of his day, Caesar Milan. A young lady played and sang charmingly and everyone was delighted. Very graciously, tactfully, and yet boldly the preacher went up to her after the music had ceased and said, "I thought as I listened to you tonight, how tremendously the cause of Christ would be benefited if your talents were dedicated to His cause. You know, young lady, you are as much a sinner in the sight of God as a drunkard in the ditch or a harlot on scarlet street. But I'm glad to tell you that the blood of Jesus Christ, His Son, can cleanse from all sin."

The young woman snapped out a rebuke for his presumption, to which he replied, "Lady, I mean no offense. I pray God's Spirit will convict you."

They all returned to their homes. The young woman retired but could not sleep. The face of the preacher appeared before her and his words rang through her mind. At two o'clock in the morning she sprang from her bed, took a pencil and paper, and with tears streaming down her face, Charlotte Elliott wrote her famous poem:

> Just as I am, without one plea,
> But that Thy blood was shed for me,
> And that Thou bidd'st me come to Thee,
> O Lamb of God, I come! I come!
>
> Just as I am, and waiting not
> To rid my soul of one dark blot,
> To Thee, whose blood can cleanse each spot,
> O Lamb of God, I come! I come!

But this is not the end. We do not leave Christ hanging on a cross with blood streaming down from His hands, His side, and His feet. He is taken down and laid carefully away in a tomb. A big stone is rolled against the entrance of the tomb. Soldiers are set to guard it. All day Saturday, His followers sit gloomily and sadly in the upper room. Two have already started toward Emmaus. Fear has gripped them all. Early on that first Easter morning, Mary, Mary Magdalene, and Salome make their way to the tomb to anoint the dead body. When they arrive, they are startled to find the tomb empty. As Alfred Edersheim, the Jewish scholar, writes, "There was no sign of haste, but all was orderly, leaving the impression of One Who had leisurely divested Himself of what no longer befitted Him." An angel is standing at the head of the tomb and asks, "Whom do you seek?" And they reply, "We seek Jesus of Nazareth." And then the angel gives the greatest, most glorious news that human ear has ever heard, "He is not here, He is risen."

The Fact of the Resurrection

Upon that great fact hangs the entire plan of the redemptive program of God. Without the resurrection there could be no salvation. Christ predicted His resurrection many times. He said on one occasion, "For as Jonah was three days and three nights in the whale's belly; so shall the Son of man be three days and three nights in the heart of the earth" (Matthew 12:40). As He predicted, He rose!

There are certain laws of evidence which hold in the establishment of any historic event. There must be documentation of the event in question made by reliable contemporary witnesses. There is more evidence that Jesus rose from the dead than there is that Julius Caesar ever lived or that Alexander the Great died at the age of thirty-three. It is strange that historians will accept thousands of facts for which they can produce only shreds of evidence. But in the face of the overwhelming evidence of the resurrection of Jesus Christ they cast a skeptical eye and hold intellectual doubts. The trouble with these people is that they do not want to believe. Their spiritual vision is so blinded and they are so completely prejudiced that they cannot accept the glorious fact of the resurrection of Christ on Bible testimony alone.

The resurrection meant, first, that Christ was undeniably God. He was what He claimed to be. Christ was Deity in the flesh.

Second, it meant that God had accepted His atoning work on the cross, which was necessary to our salvation. "Who was delivered for our offenses, and was raised again for our justification" (Romans 4:25).

Third, it assures mankind of a righteous judgment. "For as by one man's disobedience many were made sinners, so by the obedience of one shall many be made righteous" (Romans 5:19).

Fourth, it guarantees that our bodies also will be raised in the end. "But now is Christ risen from the dead, and become the firstfruits of them that slept" (1 Corinthians 15:20). The Scripture teaches that as Christians, our bodies may go to the grave but they are going to be raised on the great resurrection morning. Then will death be swallowed up in victory. As a result of the resurrection of Christ the sting of death is gone and Christ Himself holds the keys. He says, "I am he that liveth, and was dead; and, behold, I am alive forevermore, Amen; and have the keys of hell and death" (Revelation 1:18). And Christ promises that "Because I live, ye shall live also."

And, fifth, it means that death will ultimately be abolished. The power of death has been broken and death's fear has been removed. Now we can say with the Psalmist, "Yea, though I walk through the valley of the shadow of death, I will fear no evil: for thou art with me; Thy rod and thy staff they comfort me" (Psalm 23:4).

Paul looked forward to death with great anticipation as a result of the resurrection of Christ. He said, "For to me to live is Christ, and to die is gain" (Philippians 1:21). As Velma Barfield on Death Row in North Carolina said: "I love Him so much I can hardly wait to see Him."

Without the resurrection of Christ there could be no hope for the future. The Bible promises that someday we are going to stand face to face with the resurrected Christ, and we are going to have bodies like unto His own body.

Face to face with Christ my Savior,
Face to face, what will it be?
When with rapture I behold Hirn,
Iesus Christ who died for me?

Face to face I shall behold Him,
Far beyond the starry sky;
Face to face in all His glory
I shall see Him by and by.

Carrie E. Breck

9

How and
Where to Begin

Except ye be converted, and become as little children, ye shall not enter into the king-dom of heaven. MATTHEW 18:3

WE NOW RECOGNIZE that there is a natural principle which pulls us down to the animal plane—blinding reason, searing conscience, paralyzing will. It is the pull of spiritual gravity. We stand condemned by our own deeds.

God is a holy and righteous God. He cannot tolerate sin. Sin separates from God. It brings the wrath of God upon the human soul. Man has lost his moral, intellectual, and spiritual sense of God because he has lost God. He will not find God until he finds the way back to God.

The way back to God is not an intellectual way. It is not a moral way. You cannot *think* your way back to God because human thought-life will not coordinate with divine thought-life, for the carnal mind is at enmity with God. You cannot *worship* your way back *to* God because man is a spiritual rebel from God's presence. You cannot *moralize* your way back to God because character is flawed with sin.

The Way Back to God

The natural questions come to you—What shall I do? Where shall I start? Where do I begin? What is my road back to God? There is only *one way* back to God. Jesus said, "Except ye be converted, and become as little children, ye shall not enter into the kingdom of heaven" (Matthew 18:3). It is significant that Jesus did not tell the little children to become as His disciples, but His disciples to become as little children. By childlike faith, *everyone* has a chance, from feeble-minded to intellectuals. Thus Jesus demanded a conversion. This is how to begin! This is where it starts! You must be converted!

There are many people who confuse conversion with the keeping of the law. The law of Moses is set forth in specific terms in the Bible and the purpose of the law is made very clear. It was not offered at any time as a panacea for the world's ills. Rather, it was given as a diagnosis of the world's ills; it outlines the reason for our trouble, not the cure. The Bible says, "Now we know that what things soever the law saith, it saith to them who are under the law: that every mouth may be stopped, and all the world may become guilty before God" (Romans 3:19). The law has given a revelation of man's unrighteousness, and the Bible says, "By the deeds of the law there shall no flesh be justified in his sight" (Romans 3:20). It is impossible to be converted by the keeping of the law. The Bible says, "By the law is the knowledge of sin." The law is a moral mirror, the gauge by which man can see how far he has fallen. It condemns but does not convert. It challenges but does not change. It points the finger but does not offer mercy. There is no life in the law. There is only death, for the pronouncement of the law was, "Thou shalt die." It is the "straight stick" beside which the crookedness of human nature is obvious.

There are many people who say that their religion is the Sermon on the Mount, but the man or woman is yet to be born who has ever lived up to the Sermon on the Mount. The Bible says that all have sinned and come short of His glory.

Examine your own motives before you decide that you are above reproach and living a life that absolves you from all need of conversion. Look into your own heart fearlessly and honestly before you say religious conversion is all right for some but you certainly don't stand to benefit from it.

The Universal Question

When I was preaching in Hollywood, a group of movie people asked me to talk to them about religious experiences. After my address we had a discussion period and the very first question asked was, "What is conversion?"

Some time later it was my privilege to address a group of political leaders in Washington. When the discussion period started, the first question again was, "What is conversion?"

In almost every university and college group where I have led discussions, this same question is invariably asked, "What do you mean by born again?" In my book, How to Be Born Again (Word, 1976), I described the process this way:

> This new birth happens in all kinds of ways. It may seem to happen over a period of time or in a moment. The paths which people take to reach that point of decision may be very direct or very circuitous. Whatever the path, we always find Christ at the end to welcome us. And that encounter with Christ, that new birth, is the beginning of a whole new path in life under His control. Lives can be remarkably changed, marriages excitingly improved, societies influenced for good—all by the simple, sweeping surge of individuals knowing what it is to be born again.

In today's economy we hear about "born again" cars, businesses, and fashions—but that is not what I'm talking about here. Probably the simplest way to state what it means to be "born again" is to refer to it as being born into God's family.

Probably there are more different answers to this query than to almost any other pertaining to religion. What is conversion? What is involved in it? How is it accomplished? What are its effects? Why must you be converted in order to get to heaven?

The idea of conversion is certainly not unusual in our society. Any good salesman knows that he must *convert* the prospect to his particular product or way of thinking. The chief business of advertising is to *convert* the buying public from one brand to another. We speak of political leaders being *converted* from their original political philosophy and adopting a different one. During the last war, we heard a great deal about peacetime industries *converting* to war production, and most of the oil furnaces in private homes were *converted* to coal, and more recently converting from coal back to gas. We also talk about *converting* our money into foreign currency.

Actually the word *conversion* means "to turn around," "to change one's mind," "to turn back," or "to return." In the realm of religion it has been variously explained as "to repent," "to be regenerated," "to receive grace," "to experience religion," "to gain assurance."

I remember one confirmed alcoholic who came to one of the opening meetings of a crusade and said to me, "Mr. Graham, I'm not sure there's a word of truth in what you're saying, but I'm going to give your Christ a trial, and if He works even a little bit the way you say He will, I'll come back and sign up for life!"

Weeks later he told me that he didn't quite understand it, but every time he started to take a drink it seemed as though something or someone stopped him. Christ had given him victory over his vicious habit. He returned to his family, and is now living his life for Christ. In other words, he turned around, he changed his direction, he changed his way of thinking—he had been converted!

The Nature of Conversion

Conversion can take many different forms. The way it is accomplished depends largely upon the individual—his temperament, his emotional balance, his environment, and his previous conditioning and way of life. Conversion may follow a great crisis in a person's life; or it could come after all former values have been swept away, when great disappointment has been experienced, when one has lost one's sense of power through material possessions, or lost the object of one's affections. A man or woman who has been focusing all attention on financial gains, business or social prestige, or centering all affection on some one person experiences a devastating sense of loss when denied the thing that has given life its meaning.

In these tragic moments, as the individual stands stripped of all his worldly power, when the loved one is gone beyond recall, he recognizes how terribly and completely alone he really is. In that moment, the Holy Spirit may cause the spiritual bandages to fall from his eyes and he sees clearly for the first time. He recognizes that God is the only source of real power, and the only enduring fountainhead of love and companionship.

Or again, conversion may take place at the very height of personal power or prosperity—when all things are going well and the bountiful mercies of God have been bestowed generously upon you. The very goodness of God can drive you to a recognition that you owe all to God; thus, the very goodness of God leads you to repentance (Romans 2:4).

Conversion at such a moment can be as sudden and dramatic as the conversion of Paul on the road to Damascus.

Not all conversions come as a sudden, brilliant flash of soul illumination that we call a crisis conversion. There are many others that are accomplished only after a long and difficult conflict with inner motives of the person. With others, conversion comes at the climactic moment of a long period of gradual conviction of their need and revelation of the plan of salvation. This prolonged process results in conscious acceptance of Christ as personal Savior and in the yielding of life to Him.

In his spiritual autobiography, C. S. Lewis describes his conversion experience:

> You must picture me alone in that room in Magdalen, night after night, feeling, whenever my mind lifted even for a second from my work, the steady, unrelenting approach of Him whom I so earnestly desired not to meet. That which I greatly feared had at last come upon me. In the Trinity Term of 1929 I gave in, and admitted that God was God, and knelt and prayed: perhaps, that night, the most dejected and reluctant convert in all England. I do not then see what is now the most shining and obvious thing; the Divine humility which will accept a convert even on such terms. The Prodigal Son at least walked home on his own feet. But who can duly adore that Love which will open the high gates to a prodigal who is brought in kicking, struggling, resentful, and darting his eyes in every direction for a chance of escape? The words *compelle intrare,* "compel them to come in," have been so abused by wicked men that we shudder at them; but, properly understood, they plumb the depth of the Divine mercy. The hardness of God is kinder than the softness of men, and His compulsion is our liberation.*

We may say, therefore, that conversion can be an instantaneous event, a crisis in which the person receives a clear revelation of the love of God; or it can be a gradual unfolding accompanied by a climactic moment at the time the line is crossed between darkness and light, between death and life everlasting.

It does not always happen in exactly this way. My wife, for example, cannot remember the exact day or hour when she became a Christian, but she is certain that there was such a moment in her life, a moment when she actually

*From *Surprised by Joy: The Shape of My Early Life,* copyright 1966 by Harcourt, Brace, Jovanovich, pp. 228–229.

crossed the line. Many young people who have grown up in Christian homes and had the benefit of Christian training are unaware of the time when they committed their lives to Christ. Someone has said we may not know the exact moment when the sun rises—but we most certainly know once it has risen. Others remember very clearly when they made their public confession of faith. The reports of conversions in the New Testament indicate that most of them were the dramatic, crisis type.

Psychology Looks at Conversion

For many years, psychology left conversion and religious experience alone. In the last fifty years, however, psychologists have studied the whole process of conversion. They have pointed out that conversion is not only a Christian experience but is also found in other religions, and that it is not necessarily a religious phenomenon but also occurs in nonreligious spheres. Students of psychology have agreed that there are three steps in conversion: First, a sense of perplexity and uneasiness; second, a climax and turning point; and, third, a relaxation marked by rest and joy.

In an article entitled "Why It's Good to Feel So Bad," *The New York Times* (29 November 1983) pointed out, "Guilt, the sense of anguish that we have fallen short of our own standards, is the guardian of our goodness. It is necessary to the development of conscience in children and to the avoidance of antisocial behavior." The article goes on to explain, "In early childhood, good behavior is enforced mainly through parental introduction of guilty fear, the fear of punishment for violating a code of behavior. But as the child grows up, an 'ego ideal'—a form of father figure—becomes internalized as a model of correct behavior . . . and by adulthood, people seek to punish themselves when they betray that model. Dr. Gaylin sees the lack of appropriate role models or father figures as one cause of the growing rash of guiltless antisocial behavior among young people today." It is this feeling of guilt that creates the hunger for something better—to be found only in a right relationship to Christ.

Psychologists say that there are two kinds of conversion. One is accompanied by a violent sense of sin, and the other by a feeling of incompleteness, a struggle after a larger life and a desire for spiritual illumination.

The value of psychological studies of conversion has been underestimated. We cannot brush them aside and ignore them. Psychologists shed a great deal of light, but most of them are unwilling to accept the biblical conversion as a supernatural experience.

Actually, biblical conversion involves three steps—two of them active and one passive. In active conversion, repentance and faith are involved. Repentance is conversion viewed from its starting point, the turning from the former life. Faith indicates the objective point of conversion, the turning to God. The third, which is passive, we may call the new birth, or regeneration, commonly called being "born again," which literally means being born into God's family.

Now in order to get to heaven, Jesus said that you must be converted. I didn't say it—Jesus said it! This is not man's opinion—this is God's opinion! Jesus said, "Except ye be converted, and become as little children, ye shall not enter into the kingdom of heaven" (Matthew 18:3).

True conversion will involve the mind, the affection, and the will. There have been thousands of people who have been intellectually converted to Christ. They believe the entire Bible. They believe all about Jesus, but they have never been really converted to Him. The Bible tells us "even the devils believe and tremble" (James 2:19).

The Difference Between Intellectual Belief and Conversion

In John there is a description of the hundreds of people who were following Jesus early in His ministry. The Bible says that "many believed in his name when they saw the miracles which he did. But Jesus did not commit himself unto them" (John 2:23–24) because He knew the hearts of all men. Why would Jesus not commit Himself to them? He knew that they believed with their heads and not with their hearts.

There is a vast difference between intellectual belief and the total conversion that saves the soul. To be sure, there must be a change in our thinking and intellectual acceptance of Christ.

There are thousands of people who have had some form of emotional experience that they refer to as conversion but who have never been truly converted to Christ. Christ demands a change in the way you live—and if your life does not conform to your experience, then you have every reason to doubt your experience! Certainly there will be a change in the elements that make up emotion when you come to Christ—hate and love will be involved, because you will begin to hate sin and love righteousness. Your affections will undergo a revolutionary change. Your devotion to Him will know no bounds. Your love for Him cannot be described.

But even if you have an intellectual acceptance of Christ, and an emotional experience—that still is not enough. There must be the conversion of the will! There must be that determination to obey and follow Christ. Your will must be bent to the will of God. Self must be nailed to the cross. Many of us can identify with the young woman who wrote us regarding this: "But I don't hang easy." None of us do, yet. Our main desire must be to please Him. It is a total commitment.

In conversion as you stand at the foot of the cross, the Holy Spirit makes you realize that you are a sinner. He directs your faith to the Christ who died in your place. You must open your heart and let Him come in. At that precise moment the Holy Spirit performs the miracle of the new birth. You actually become a new moral creature. There comes the implantation of the divine nature. You become a partaker of God's own life. Jesus Christ, through the Spirit of God, takes up residence in your heart.

Conversion is so simple that the smallest child can be converted, but it is also so profound that theologians throughout history have pondered the depth of its meaning. God has made the way of salvation so plain that "the wayfaring men, though fools, shall not err therein" (Isaiah 35:8). No person will ever be barred from the kingdom of God because he did not have the capacity to understand. The rich and the poor, the sophisticated and the simple—all can be converted.

To sum it up, conversion simply means "to change." When a person is converted he may continue to love objects which he loved before, but there will be a change of reasons for loving them. A converted person may forsake former objects of affection. He may even withdraw from his previous companions, not because he dislikes them, for many of them will be decent and amiable, but because there is more attraction for him in the fellowship of other Christians of like mind.

The converted person will love the good he once hated, and hate the sin he once loved. There will even be a change of heart about God. Where he once may have been careless about God, living in constant fear, dread, and antagonism to God, he now finds himself in a state of complete reverence, confidence, obedience, and devotion. There will be a reverential fear of God, a constant gratitude to God, a dependence upon God, and a new loyalty to Him. Before conversion there may have been gratification of the flesh. Cultural and intellectual pursuits or the making of money may have been of first and supreme importance. Now, righteousness and holiness of heart, and living the Christian life will be placed above all other concerns, for pleasing Christ will be the only goal of real importance. In other words, conversion means a complete change in the life of an individual.

A Case of Conversion

I remember so vividly a young New York career girl who came out to Los Angeles to be married. She and her fiance had met when they were both working in a high-powered New York advertising agency, and their courtship had been conducted against a background of cocktail parties and night clubs. Filled with ambition and "on his way up," he had himself transferred to the California office, with the understanding that the girl would follow him in six months and they would be married.

About a week after she had arrived in Los Angeles, expecting to take up a joyous new life, she discovered that the man had fallen in love with a movie starlet and lacked the courage to write her about it before she left New York!

Here she was, alone in a city where she knew no one—all her plans in ruins, her pride crushed, and the future stretching ahead, bleak and empty. Her family had not been religious, and in this hour of extreme need she knew of nowhere to turn for comfort, advice, or guidance.

As she walked along the unfamiliar streets, trying to overcome her shock and humiliation, she came upon the "canvas cathedral" in which we were conducting our crusade in 1949. She said she was never sure what made her come inside, but she did, and sat glumly through the entire service. The next night she came again, and every night for the whole week, until through the cloud of bitterness and misery that surrounded her, God made His voice heard, and she came forward to confess her need of salvation.

With the burden of guilt and rejection lifted from her through faith in the Lord Jesus Christ, she came to see that the love she had lost was but a stepping stone to a far greater and much richer love. The sense of humiliation that prevented her from returning to her former New York job vanished, and rather than life being finished, she found upon her return that it was fuller than ever. Only instead of wasting her brains and organizational ability on an endless round of cocktail parties, she became extremely active walking with God and serving others.

The imagination she formerly devoted to entertaining the "office crowd" now goes into making Bible stories come alive for the young people. Her training as a fund-raiser is now being put to good use in the service of the Lord, and her minister says her ideas have been invaluable in increasing regular church attendance. Far from being rejected and unwanted, she is sought after constantly by her fellow church members. But, most important of all, her sense of loneliness has vanished, for she knows now that Jesus Christ is ever by her side, ready to comfort, to guide, and to protect her.

All this had come as a result of her conversion—her turning away from the bleak, empty, worldly road she was traveling so unhappily—to her Lord and Savior, Jesus Christ! She had found peace with God.

10

What Is Repentance?

Joy shall be in heaven over one sinner that repenteth, more than over ninety and nine just persons which need no repentance. Luke 15:7

WE HAVE NOW seen that Jesus demanded conversion. We have also seen that the three elements of conversion are repentance, faith, and regeneration. It may be debatable in which order these three should come, but it is generally agreed that they probably happen at the same time. Whether you are conscious or unconscious of it, in that critical moment of conversion these three take place simultaneously.

If repentance could be described in two words, I would use the words "turning around." Turn around from what? you ask. The answer can be given in one word—"sin." The Bible teaches, as we have already seen, that sin is a transgression of the law. Sin is the rejection of all authority and the denial of all obligation to God. Sin is that evil principle which came into the Garden of Eden when Adam and Eve were tempted and fell. Ever since the disaster in Eden this evil poison has affected all men so that "all have sinned," and "there is none righteous, no, not one." Sin has destroyed our relationship with God, and as a consequence it has disturbed our relationship with each other, and even with ourselves.

We cannot possibly have peace with God or peace with each other in the world or even peace within ourselves until something is done about that "abominable thing which God hates." Not only are we told that we must renounce or turn our backs on sin, but we are also told to renounce *sins*—plural. We are to renounce the evil influence of the world, the flesh, and the devil. There can be no parleying, bargaining, compromise, or hesitation. Christ demands total loyalty.

Repentance and Faith

But here again the principle of love is involved, because when you fall in love completely and absolutely with Jesus Christ you will not want to do the things that He hates and abhors. You will automatically renounce all the sins of your life when you surrender by faith to Him. Therefore repentance and faith go hand in hand. You cannot have genuine repentance without saving faith, and you cannot have saving faith without genuine repentance.

The word *repentance is* sadly missing today from the average pulpit. It is a very unpopular word. The first sermon Jesus ever preached was "Repent: for the kingdom of heaven is at hand" (Matthew 4:17). This was God speaking through His Son. Jesus had come with a heart filled with love and compassion, but He immediately began to press home man's guilt and sins. He called upon men to acknowledge their guilt and to turn from their ungodliness. He said repentance must come before He could pour out His love, grace, and mercy upon men. Jesus refused to gloss over iniquity. He insisted upon self-judgment, upon a complete right about-face. He insisted upon a new attitude before He would reveal the love of God.

The people came to Jesus one day and told Him of certain Galileans whose blood Pilate had mingled with sacrifices as his Roman legions quelled the Jewish uprising. They reported, too, how the falling of a tower in Siloam had killed many. In answer Jesus declared, "Suppose ye that these Galileans were sinners above all the Galileans . . . I tell you, Nay: but, except ye repent, ye shall all likewise perish" (Luke 13:3). In other words, Jesus said whether men are taken away by violence, by accident, or by natural death, their doom is the same unless they have turned to God in repentance. Until this is done, faith is absolutely impossible. This does not limit the grace of God, but repentance makes way for the grace of God.

Repentance and the Grace of God

We know that salvation is based entirely upon the grace of God. The Bible says that no man is justified by the law in the sight of God, and it also says, "The just shall live by his faith" (Romans 9:17). Salvation, forgiveness, and justification are based entirely upon the atoning work of Christ. However, if the sacrifice of Christ on the cross is to be made effectual for any individual of any age, that individual must repent of sin and accept Christ by faith.

Jonah preached repentance in Nineveh until Nineveh repented. Ezekiel preached repentance when he said, "Therefore I will judge you, O house of Israel, every one according to his ways, saith the Lord God. Repent, and turn yourselves from all your transgressions; so iniquity shall not be your ruin" (Ezekiel 18:30).

The great message of John the Baptist was repentance when he said, "Repent ye: for the kingdom of heaven is at hand" (Matthew 3:2).

Repentance is mentioned seventy times in the New Testament. Jesus said, "Except ye repent, ye shall all likewise perish." The sermon that Peter preached on the Day of Pentecost was, "Repent, and be baptized every one of you in the name of Jesus Christ for the remission of sins" (Acts 2:38). Paul preached it when he said that he "testified both to the Jews, and also to the Greeks, repentance toward God, and faith toward our Lord Jesus Christ" (Acts 20:21). The Bible says God commands repentance, "And the times of this ignorance God winked at; but now commandeth all men everywhere to repent" (Acts 17:30). It is a command. It is an imperative. God says. "Repent! Or perish!" Have you repented? Are you sure of it?

There are many biblical examples of false repentance. For example, Pharaoh said to the children of Israel who were seeking to leave Egypt for the promised land, "I have sinned . . ." (Exodus 9:27). Obviously it was an expression of regret or remorse but not an expression of true repentance. Saul did the same thing in 1 Samuel 15:24, 30 and 26:21. But when David said to the prophet Nathan, "I have sinned" in 2 Samuel 12:13 and 20:10, 17, he was truly repentant (see Psalm 51).

Jesus' Definition of Repentance

What did Jesus mean by the word *repent?* Why does it appear over and over throughout the Bible? If you look in a modern dictionary you will find that repent means "to feel sorry for, or to regret." But the original words that Jesus spoke meant a great deal more than that. They meant a great deal more than just regretting and feeling sorry about sin. The biblical word *repent* means "to change, or to turn." It is a word of power and action. It is a word that signifies a complete turnabout in the individual. When the Bible calls upon us to repent of sin, it means that we should turn away from sin, that we should do an about-face and walk in the opposite direction from sin and all that it implies.

Jesus told the parable of the Prodigal Son to dramatize what He meant by the word *repent.* When the Prodigal Son repented he didn't just sit still and feel sorry about all his sins. He wasn't passive and limp about it. He didn't stay where he was, surrounded by the swine. He got up and left! He turned his feet in the other direction. He sought out his father and humbled himself before him, and then he was forgiven.

Too many modern Christians have lost sight of what the Bible means when it talks about repentance. They think that repentance is little more than shaking their heads over their sins and saying, "My, but I'm sorry I did that!" and then continuing to live just as they have lived before.

True repentance means "to change, to turn away from, to go in a new direction." To be sorry is not enough in repentance. Judas was sorry enough to hang himself. It was an admission of guilt without true repentance. Even reformation is not enough. There is no torture that you can give your body, no trials you can set for your mind that will be pleasing to Almighty God. Our sins were atoned for by Christ on the cross. There He suffered sin's penalty. No suffering that we can undergo will lead us to repentance.

Repentance Is Not Mere Emotion

When I speak of repentance I am not speaking of the old-time mourners' bench. Many people have taught that to repent you must mourn for a stated time in order to be ready for salvation. One man told me the night he found Christ he went forward in an old-fashioned camp meeting some years ago. While he was kneeling at the altar trying to find God, some dear sister came and slapped him on the back and said, "Hold on, brother! If you want God, you'll have to hold on." A few minutes later a church officer came up and slapped him across the back and said, "Brother, turn loose!" Then another sister came up a few minutes later and said, "The night I was converted a big light hit me in the face and knocked me cold." He said, "I tried to turn loose and hold on at the same time while looking for the light. I almost never made it in the confusion!"

A very intelligent Christian leader once told me that at the time he was converted the demonstration of emotion expected of him by the preacher and congregation almost kept him from coming to God.

Falsely produced emotionalism in some revival meetings has been a stumbling block to many a sincere, searching soul. But the type of repentance I'm talking about is true biblical repentance, which involves three things: it involves the *intellect*, the *emotion*, and the *will*.

Three Aspects of Repentance

First, there must be a *knowledge* of sin. The Bible says, "All have sinned, and come short of the glory of God" (Romans 3:23). When Isaiah was convicted of his sins he said, "Woe is me! . . . I am a man of unclean lips" (Isaiah 6:5). When Job got a glimpse of God's holiness he said, "I abhor myself" (Job 42:6). When Peter was convicted of his sins he said, "I am a sinful man" (Luke 5:8). When Paul was convicted of his sins he called himself "the chief of sinners" (1 Timothy 1:15).

It is the Holy Spirit who brings about this conviction. Actually, repentance cannot take place unless first there is a movement of the Holy Spirit in the heart and mind. The Holy Spirit may use a mother's prayers, a pastor's sermon, a Christian radio program, the sight of a church steeple, or the death of a loved one to bring about this necessary conviction. However, I have seen men in some of our meetings stand trembling under conviction and still not repent of their sins. It is possible to be convicted of sin and know you are a sinner and even shed tears over your sins, and yet not repent.

Second, the *emotions* are involved in repentance, just as they are in all genuine experiences. Paul said there is a godly sorrow that worketh toward repentance. Someone has said, "Many people abhor all emotion, and some critics are suspicious of any conversion that does not take place in a refrigerator. There are many dangers in false emotionalism, produced for its own effect, but that does not rule out true emotion and depth of feeling."

As Dr. W. E. Sangster, the great British Methodist preacher, says in his book, *Let Me Commend*, "The man who screams at a football or baseball game but is distressed when he hears of a sinner weeping at the cross and murmurs something about the dangers of emotionalism hardly merits intelligent respect."

Horace Walpole once accused John Wesley of acting out very ugly emotionalism in his preaching, yet Wesley turned thousands to God.

Third, repentance involves the *will*

It is only when we come to the *will* that we find the very heart of repentance. There must be that determination to forsake sin—to change one's attitudes toward self, toward sin, and toward God; to change one's feeling; to change one's will, disposition, and purpose.

Only the Spirit of God can give you the determination necessary for true repentance. It means more than the little girl who prayed, "Make me good—not real good, but good enough so I won't get whipped."

There are thousands of people in America who have their names on church rolls. They go to church when it is convenient. They give their money to the church and support its activities. They shake hands with the minister after the service and tell him what a splendid sermon he preached. They may talk the language of the Christian and many of them can quote a fair amount of Scripture, but they have never really experienced true repentance. They have a sort of "I can take-it-or-leave-it-alone" attitude toward religion. They turn to God and pray when they get in a tight place, but the rest of the time they do not give God very much thought. The Bible teaches that when a person comes to Christ a change takes place that is reflected in everything he does.

Repentance Demands Surrender

There is not one verse of Scripture that indicates you can be a Christian and live any kind of a life you want to. When Christ enters into the human heart, He expects to be Lord and Master. He commands complete surrender. He demands control of your intellectual processes. He requires that your body be subject to Him. He expects you to surrender your talents and abilities to Him. He expects nothing less than that all your work and labor will be performed in His name.

Too many of today's professing Christians would give up going to church before they would give up getting a new refrigerator. Given a choice between making the down payment on a new car or contributing to the building of a new Sunday school, it is easy to guess what the decision of many would be. Thousands of so-called Christians are putting money and the things that make up our high standard of living ahead of the teachings of Christ. We can find time for the movies, baseball, or football games, but we can't find time for God. We can save toward a new home or a bigger television set, but we feel we no longer can afford to tithe. This is idolatry.

A change must take place! We point our fingers at the heathen and at the idol worshipers of old, but the only difference is that our graven images are made of gleaming chromium and steel and have thermostats and defrosting devices instead of jeweled eyes! Instead of gold, their surfaces are covered with easy-to-clean lifetime porcelain, but we worship them just the same, and feel that our lives would be impossible without them. We have come to worship things, status, fame, popularity, money, security. Anything that comes between God and ourselves is idolatry.

Jesus demands Lordship over all such things. He wants you to yield everything concerning your social life, your family life, your business life to Him. He must have first place in everything you do or think or say, for when you truly repent you turn toward God in everything.

We have the warning of Christ that He will not receive us into His kingdom until we are ready to give up all, until we are ready to turn from all sin in our lives. Don't try to do it part way. Don't say, "I'll give up some of my sins and hang on to some others. I'll live part of my life for Jesus and part for my own desires." Jesus expects one hundred percent surrender, and when that is accomplished He rewards a thousandfold. But don't expect Jesus to hand out any five hundred percent awards for fifty percent surrenders! God doesn't work that way. He demands all. When you have determined that you are renouncing sin, forsaking sin, and yielding all to Christ, you have taken another step toward peace with God.

The repentant thief on the cross said to Jesus, "Lord, remember me . . ." (Luke 23:42). His use of the word, "Lord," implied his total submission to Jesus Christ. It implied his total surrender and true conversion. This is the result of true repentance.

With the hymnwriter, the repentant sinner says:

All to Jesus I surrender, All to Him I freely give;
I will ever love and trust Him, in His presence daily live.
All to Jesus I surrender, make me, Savior, wholly Thine.
Let me feel the Holy Spirit, Truly know that Thou art mine.

11

What Is Faith?

For by grace are ye saved through faith; and that not of yourselves: it is the gift of God: not of works, lest any man should boast. EPHESIANS 2:8, 9

WE ARE NOW ready to take up the next step in finding peace with God. You are now ready to forsake your past sinful life. You are determined that this change is going to take place in your life. You are no longer headed away from God, but you are moving toward His love and mercy and protection. You have made your decision. You have repented; you have chosen the right road, even though it may be a difficult one. You have chosen the road that Moses took almost 3,500 years ago when he renounced his right to the throne of Egypt and decided in favor of God!

Moses was forty years old when he fled Egypt for fear of his life. Forty years later he came back to lead the Israelites out of Egypt. What had changed? He had made his great decision. He concluded that faith and truth in company with agony and hardship were better than wealth and fame and the absence of God's love. Few men in history have been called upon to make a more difficult decision than his.

A Man of Faith

Moses was a man of education and culture, a man of wealth and prominence. As the son of Pharaoh's daughter he had been accustomed to every honor, every luxury, and every privilege. The throne of Egypt, richest, most powerful, most spectacularly successful country of its time, was within his grasp.

Yet the Bible records that "By faith Moses, when he was come to years, refused to be called the son of Pharaoh's daughter; Choosing rather to suffer affliction with the people of God, than to enjoy the pleasures of sin for a season; Esteeming the reproach of Christ greater riches than the treasures in Egypt: for he had respect unto the recompense of the reward. By faith he forsook Egypt, not fearing the wrath of the king: for he endured, as seeing him who is invisible" (Hebrews 11:24–27). This passage was referring to Moses after his forty years in the wilderness with God—not the fiery young murderer who fled from Pharaoh in fear of his life.

Notice, it says that he "refused" and he "forsook"—this is true repentance. And then it says he did it "by faith"! This is the next step—*faith*. Moses made this decision not in a moment of overt emotionalism that some psychologists insist is necessary for religious experience. He was not motivated by frustration. He was not a hopeless misfit or an unfulfilled man. Moses was not choosing the path of God as a compensation for the rewards that he felt life had withheld from him, nor was he turning to the religious life out of boredom and apathy. He did not want for interest, entertainment, and amusement.

A Matter of Choice

None of these arguments, or the many others so often advanced as reasons for seeking life with God, were valid in the case of Moses. He was not forced to run from the flesh and the devil. He did it from choice. Moses was certainly neither weak-minded nor weak-willed. He was not a child clinging to the security of an established order. He was not a nonentity seeking recognition and prestige. He was not any of the things that those who mock religion say one must be to feel the need of salvation. Moses had even more than the dreams to which most men would aspire; and yet out of his mature judgment in the prime of life he turned his back on wealth, position, and esteem and chose instead faith in God.

Every time I hear it said that only the hopeless and helpless, only the maladjusted need the comfort of "religion," I think of Moses.

It has been my privilege to talk to many men and women concerning their spiritual problems. I have learned that when men and women of sound judgment reject Christ as their Lord and Master, they do it not because they find Christian doctrines intellectually distasteful, but because they seek to avoid the responsibilities and obligations that the Christian life demands. Their faint hearts rather than their brilliant minds stand between them and Christ. They are not willing to submit themselves and surrender everything to Christ.

It is interesting to note that the two men most used of God in the Bible (one in the Old Testament and one in the New) were also the two best educated: Moses and Paul.

Moses considered the claims and obligations of God carefully. At forty he fled, a murderer. At eighty, he returned—a leader. He realized that if he was to embrace God he would have to do it at the sacrifice of the things that men usually hold most dear. He made no hasty examination. He came to no half-considered conclusions under sudden impulse or emotional reaction. He knew how much was at stake and he arrived at his decision with the full use of his well-trained and superior mental faculties. His final choice was not in the nature of a temporary experiment. He did not select faith as a tentative measure. It was a mature conviction with an unalterable purpose, a conviction not to be shaken by changes of fortune or the trials of long-endured privation. He carefully burned all the bridges and ships that might have made retreat possible from his new position. When Moses had his great crisis moment at the age of eighty, he committed himself totally and without reservation for all time and under all circumstances to God and His commands.

How different was the quality of Moses' decision from that of the famous biographer Gamaliel Bradford, who as he neared the end of his life said, "I do not dare read the New Testament for fear of awakening a storm of anxiety and doubt and dread, of having taken the wrong path, of having been a traitor to the plain and simple God."

Moses had no such fear. And neither should you fear if you turn yourself wholeheartedly to Christ now and forever *by faith*. Don't turn to Him saying, "I'll try Christianity for a while. If it works I'll go on with it, but if it doesn't I still have time to choose another way of life." When you come to Christ, every bridge has to be burned behind you, with no thought of ever turning back.

They Turned Back on Their Boats

Years ago, when the wings of the fierce Roman eagle cast an ominous shadow over the world, those audacious warriors whom Caesar led set out to conquer Britain. As the enemy vessels appeared on the horizon, thousands of Englishmen bravely gathered on the heights to defend their homeland. To their amazement, the tides and the sea destroyed most of the Roman ships. Thus the only avenue of retreat was cut off for the daring invaders. They fought with wild abandon, their escape route cut off. With such an indomitable spirit, how could they fail to conquer! Little wonder the petty village on the banks of the Tiber became the Mistress of the world!

Just so, Christ will accept nothing less than complete surrender and absolute devotion. "And Jesus said unto him, No man, having put his hand to the plow, and looking back, is fit for the kingdom of God" (Luke 9:62).

Moses made his soul-shaking choice as he stood at the fork of life's highway. His judicial mind weighed all the facts that bore upon his decision. He looked long and carefully down each road to its termination. He considered all the pros and cons and only then did he decide to put his trust and faith in God.

Moses Burned His Bridges

First he looked down the broad road, the bright road filled with power and luxury, filled with gaiety and wine, rich in the things the world counts as pleasure. It was a familiar road. He knew it well. He had traveled it for forty years and he knew that it ended in destruction, knew that it could only lead to hell.

Then Moses looked down the other road, the narrow road, the more difficult road. He saw the suffering, the affliction, the humiliation and disappointment. He saw the hardships and the trials, the sorrows and the pains, but by *faith* he saw also the triumphs and the reward of eternal life.

A man of lesser judgment, a man of lesser experience than Moses. might have been tempted to take the first road. Egypt was then the greatest power on earth. It held command of the fertile Nile valley, the granary of the world. Its armies were invincible, its colleges and universities were setting the pattern that other centuries would follow.

Few of us are ever asked to give up as much for God as Moses did. Few of us are ever shown temptation in such abundance and variety and asked to withstand it. Few of us have such earthly delights and pleasures spread before our eyes, and even the Scriptures admit that there is pleasure in sin, if only for a season. The pleasure is fleeting and leaves no comfort in its wake.

In choosing God, Moses made a great sacrifice, but he also won a great reward. Great fortunes were rare in Moses' time, and few men indeed had the opportunity that he had to become the wealthiest man on earth.

The Wealth of the World

Today, many men can amass great fortunes. In 1923 (when fortune gathering was this country's major interest) a group of the world's most successful financiers gathered at the Edgewater Beach Hotel in Chicago. Even in the fabulous twenties, the meeting was an impressive array of wealth and power. Seated at a single table were the president of the world's largest independent steel company, the president of the largest utility company, the president of the New York Stock Exchange, a member of the cabinet of the President of the United States, the president of the Bank of International Settlements, the man who was known as the biggest trader on Wall Street, and another who headed the world's most powerful monopoly. Together, these men controlled more wealth than the United States Treasury! Their success stories were known to every schoolboy. They were the models whom other men tried to copy. They were the financial and industrial giants of America!

In 1923 the widely publicized stories of these men were glamorous and exciting. They fired the imagination! They kindled envy! They inspired other men to try to be as they were! But in 1923 their stories were only half told—the closing chapters were yet to be written.

At the time these seven men sat down together at the hotel in Chicago they were each at the place in their individual lives where Moses had been when he stood at the crossroads. These men were at the crossroads also, and two paths stretched out before each of them. Perhaps they were paths they could not see, paths about which they did not care. Certainly they were paths they didn't choose to follow, and today their stories are complete. Today we know those final chapters. We can review their lives, just as we can review the life of Moses, and see which seems the wisest and the best.

Charles Schwab, president of the steel company, lived the last years of his life on borrowed money and died penniless. Arthur Cutten, greatest of the wheat speculators, died abroad insolvent. Richard Whitney, president of the New York Stock Exchange, served a term in Sing-Sing Penitentiary. Albert Fall, the cabinet member, was pardoned from prison so he could die at home. Jessie Livermore, the "bear" of Wall Street; Leon Frazer, president of the Bank of International Settlements; and Ivon Kreuger, head of the world's largest monopoly, all committed suicide!

These men all had money, power, fame, prestige, intelligence, and education—but every one of them lacked the one attribute that gives life its real meaning and purpose. They lacked the one attribute that is essential to the Christian creed and conduct—the attribute that makes conversion possible, that makes regeneration real. They refused to believe! Compare their lives with those of missionaries who have left all to follow Christ. They may die penniless and in pain, but they have died *for* something!

These wealthy men had no faith, or if they did have faith, they refused to act upon it. How different the closing chapters of their lives would have been if they had been able to count faith in Christ among their treasuries.

Moses Turned His Back on the World's Wealth

Notice it was through *faith* that Moses renounced the wealth of Egypt. It was his *faith* that made him know that even though he might suffer privation and humiliation all the rest of his life on earth, in the end he would receive the greatest of rewards—eternal life.

Men like Cutten and Schwab might have thought Moses a fool. They would have said, "A bird in the hand is worth far more than two in the bush." They would have said, "Look, you know what you have in Egypt. You know what a man of your brains can do to manipulate this wealth and power. Play your cards right and Egypt will control the world. You can put all the lesser countries out of business. You can get rid of all the competition and run things your own way." That's what they would have said, because that's the way they thought, that's the way they operated, that's the way many of them amassed their fortunes. They would have laughed at a person who said he believed God or had faith in Christ. They would have said, "Faith isn't good business. It isn't smart."

The Bible teaches that faith is the only approach to God. "For he that cometh to God must believe that he is, and that he is a rewarder of them that diligently seek him" (Hebrews 11:6). The Bible also teaches that faith pleases God more than anything else. "Without faith it is impossible to please him" (Hebrews 11:6).

People all over the world torture themselves, clothe themselves in strange garments, disfigure their bodies, deny themselves the necessities of life, spend much time in prayer and self-sacrifice in an effort to make themselves acceptable in God's sight. This may be all well and good, but the greatest thing we can do to please God is to believe Him.

I might go to a friend and flatter him, but, if after all my flowery phrases I were to tell him I did not believe him, every flattering thing I said would have been in vain. I would have built him up only to let him down.

Belief Is Essential

The greatest way we can please God is to *believe* His Word. It would seem that Christ was almost pleading for faith on the part of His hearers when He said, "Believe me that I am in the Father, and the Father in me: or else believe me for the very works' sake" (John 14:11).

The Bible declares that *faith* is absolutely essential. You ask, "Well, if faith is so important, what is faith? What do you mean by faith? What is a definition of faith? How can I know if I have proper faith? How much faith must I have?"

Wait just a minute—not so many questions at a time! I'll try to answer them as we go along.

The Bible teaches, time and time again, that we can have salvation only through faith:

"*Believe* on the Lord Jesus Christ, and thou shalt be saved, and thy house" (Acts 16:31).

"But as many as received him, to them gave he power to become the sons of God, even to them that *believe* on his name" (John 1:12).

"And by him all that *believe* are justified from all things, from which ye could not be justified by the law of Moses" (Acts 13:29).

"But to him that worketh not, but *believeth* on him that justifieth the ungodly, his faith is counted for righteousness" (Romans 4:5).

"Therefore being justified by *faith*, we have peace with God through our Lord Jesus Christ" (Romans 5:1).

"But we are not of them who draw back unto perdition; but of them that *believe* to the saving of the soul" (Hebrews 10:39).

"For by grace are ye saved through *faith*; and that not of yourselves: it is the gift of God" (Ephesians 2:8).

The Nature of Faith

Are we actually saved by faith? No, we're saved by grace *through faith*. Faith is simply the channel through which God's grace to us is received. It is the hand that reaches out and receives the gift of His love. In Hebrews 11:1, we read, "Now faith is the substance of things hoped for, the evidence of things not seen." Weymouth has translated it this way, which makes it easier to understand, "Now faith is a confident assurance of that for which we hope, a conviction of the reality of things which we do not see." Faith literally means "to give up, surrender, or commit." Faith is complete confidence.

I have never been to the North Pole, and yet I believe there is a North Pole. How do I know? I know because somebody told me. I read about it in a history book, I saw a map in a geography book and I believe the men who wrote those books. I accept it by faith.

The Bible says, "Faith cometh by hearing, and hearing by the word of God" (Romans 10:17). We believe what God has to say about salvation. We accept it without question.

Martin Luther has translated Hebrews 11:27 this way, "For he held on to Him whom he saw not just as though he saw Him."

It is not some peculiar, mysterious quality for which we must strive. Jesus said we must become as little children, and just as little children trust their parents, so we must trust God.

Suppose I were driving along the road at fifty miles an hour and I came to the crest of a hill. Would I immediately slam on my brakes, stop my car, get out, walk up to the top of the hill, and look over to see if the road continues? No, I wouldn't do that. I would trust the highway department of the particular state in which I was driving. I would continue at my normal rate of speed, secure in the knowledge that the road continued on ahead even though I couldn't see it. I would accept it on faith. So it is with saving faith in Christ!

Three Aspects of Faith

Again, as in repentance, there are three things involved in faith. First, there must be a *knowledge* of what God has said. That's why it's so important for you to read the Bible. That's why it's important for you to know something of the teaching of the Bible concerning the salvation of the soul. Just to know that you are a sinner and that Christ died for you is enough knowledge. Knowing no more than John 3:16 could be enough knowledge. Many have been converted on less. But on anything as important as this you should be as well informed as possible and the only place to learn about salvation is in the Bible!

Many people say, "But I cannot understand much of the Bible, therefore I don't try to read it." That is not the wise attitude. There are many things in the Bible that I do not understand. My finite mind will never understand all about the infinite. I do not understand all about television, but I do not refuse to turn on my television set. I accept it by faith.

But God does not ask the impossible. He does not ask you to take a leap in the dark concerning conversion. Believing in Christ is based on the best evidence in the world, the Bible. Even though you do not understand it all, you can accept it at face value because God said it. One of the first attacks the devil makes on man is to get him to doubt the Word of God: "Yea, hath God said?" (Genesis 3:1). If you begin doubting and putting question marks over God's Word, then you're in trouble. There must be a knowledge that you are a sinner. You must have the knowledge that Christ died for your sins and that He rose again for your justification. The death, burial, and resurrection of Jesus Christ is the very heart of the Gospel. That must be believed and accepted as a minimum for conversion.

Second, the *emotions* again are involved. The Bible says, "The fear of the Lord is the beginning of wisdom" (Proverbs 1:7). Paul said, "The love of Christ constraineth us" (2 Corinthians 5:14). Desire, love, fear—all are emotions. Emotion cannot be cut out of life. No intelligent person would think of saying, "Let's do away with all emotion." To remove all personality from deep feeling is impossible. We cannot imagine life without the warm overtones of feeling. Suppose we had a family where everyone acted only from a cold sense of duty. Suppose I asked my wife to marry me after I had explained to her first of all that I had no feelings for her at all.

As Dr. Sangster says, "Carry the same principle over into religion. Require that the Herald of God announce the offer of His King, freely to pardon and fully to bless, but firmly forbid that any transport of joy should accompany either the announcement of the news or its glad reception, and you ask the impossible."

There is going to be a tug at the heart. Emotion may vary in religious experience. Some people are stoical and others are demonstrative, but the feeling will be there.

When Churchill gave his masterful speeches to the British people during the war, he appealed to logic, but at the same time he made his audience *feel*. I remember hearing him one time in Glasgow. He challenged my thinking, but he made me feel like standing up and shouting and waving a flag! When you fall in love with Jesus Christ your emotions are bound to be stirred.

Third, and most important of all, is the *will*. It's like three little men—one is named "Intellect," the second is named "Emotion," and the third is named "Will." Intellect says that the gospel is logical. Emotion puts pressure upon Will and says, "I feel love for Christ," or "I feel fear of judgment." And then the middleman, called Will, is the referee. He sits there with his hand on his chin, in deep thought, trying to make up his mind. It is actually the *will* that makes the final and lasting decision. It is possible to have the intellectual conviction and the emotional feeling and still not be properly converted to Christ. Faith has legs. "Faith without works is dead" (James 2:20).

An Example of Faith

I heard about a man some years ago who was rolling a wheelbarrow back and forth across Niagara River on a tightrope. Thousands of people were shouting him on. He put a two-hundred-pound sack of dirt in the wheelbarrow and rolled it over, and then he rolled it back. Then he turned to the crowd and said, "How many of you believe that I can roll a man across?"

Everybody shouted! One man in the front row was very excited in his professed belief. The man pointed to this excited professor and said, "You're next!"

You couldn't see that man for dust! He actually didn't believe it. He said he believed it, he thought he believed it—but he was not willing to get in the wheelbarrow.

Just so with Christ. There are many people who say they believe on Him, who say they will follow Him. But they never have gotten into the wheelbarrow. They actually never have committed and surrendered themselves wholly, one hundred percent to Christ.

There are many people who ask, "Well, how much faith does it take?" Jesus said only the faith as of "a grain of mustard seed."

Others ask, "What kind of faith?" It is not a matter of any special kind of faith. There is only one kind, really. It is the *object* of the faith that counts. What is the object of your faith? The object of your faith must be Christ. Not faith in ritual, not faith in sacrifices, not faith in morals, not faith in yourself—not faith in anything but Christ!

Now the Bible teaches that faith will manifest itself in three ways. It will manifest itself in doctrine—in what you believe. It will manifest itself in worship—your communion with God and the fellowship of the church. It will manifest itself in morality—in the way you live and behave, which we will discuss in other chapters.

The Bible also teaches that faith does not end with trust in Christ for your salvation. Faith continues. Faith grows. It may be weak at first, but it will become stronger as you begin to read the Bible, pray, go to church, and experience God's faithfulness in your Christian life. After you have repented of sins and accepted Him by faith, then you must trust Him to keep you, strengthen you, enable you, sustain you. You will learn more and more how to rely on Christ for every need, in meeting every circumstance, and every trial. You will learn to say with Paul, "I am crucified with Christ; nevertheless I live; yet not I, but Christ liveth in me: and the life which I now live in the flesh I live by the faith of the Son of God, who loved me, and gave himself for me" (Galatians 2:20).

When you have saving faith in Jesus Christ, you have taken an additional step toward having peace with God.

12

The Old
and the New

Except a man be born again, he cannot see the kingdom of God. John 3:3

IF I COULD come and have a heart-to-heart chat with you in your living room, you perhaps would turn to me and confess, "I am perplexed, confused, and mixed up. I have transgressed God's laws. I have lived contrary to His commandments. I thought I could get along without God's help. I have tried to make up my own rules and I've failed. The bitter lessons that I've learned have come through suffering and tragic experience. What wouldn't I give to be born again! What wouldn't I give to be able to go back and start all over—what a different road I'd travel if I could!"

If those words strike a familiar chord in your heart, if they echo the thoughts that have been moving through your mind, I want to tell you some glorious news. Jesus said you can be born anew! You can have the fresh and better start for which you've prayed. You can lose your despised and sinful self and step forth a new person, a clean and peaceful being from whom sin has been washed away.

A Way Out

No matter how soiled your past, no matter how snarled your present, no matter how hopeless your future seems to be—there is a way out. There is a sure, safe, everlasting way out—but there is only one! You have only one choice to make. You have only one path to follow, other than the torturous, unrewarding path you've been treading.

You can go on being miserable, discontented, frightened, unhappy, and disgusted with yourself and your life; or you can decide right now that you want to be born again. You can decide right now to wipe out your sinful past and make a new start, a fresh start, a right start. You can decide now to become the person that Jesus promised you could be.

How Do I Find It?

The next logical question that you may ask is, "How can I have this rebirth? How can I be born again? How can I start afresh?"

This is the question that Nicodemus asked Jesus that night two thousand years ago under an Oriental sky. Being born again, however, means a great deal more than just a fresh start, or turning over a new leaf, or reforming. As we have already seen, the Bible teaches that you were born the first time into the physical world but your spiritual nature was born in sin. The Bible declares that you are "dead in trespasses and sins" (Ephesians 2:1).

The Bible teaches that there is nothing in your dead and sinful nature that can originate life. Being dead in sin, you cannot produce a life of righteousness. Many people are trying to produce a good, holy and righteous life without being born again, but they can do nothing but fail. A corpse cannot reproduce. The Bible teaches that "sin, when it is finished, bringeth forth death" (James 1:15). All of us are dead spiritually.

Your old nature cannot serve God. The Bible says, "The natural man receiveth not the things of the Spirit of God . . . neither can he know them" (1 Corinthians 2:14). In our natural state we are actually at enmity with God. We are not subject to the laws of God, neither indeed can we be, according to Romans 8:7.

The Bible also teaches that our old nature is totally corrupt. From its head to its feet "there is no soundness in it"; it is full of "wounds, and bruises, and putrifying sores" (Isaiah 1:6). Its heart is "deceitful above all things, and desperately wicked" (Jeremiah 17:9). It is corrupt, subject to deceitful lust.

The Bible also teaches that our old nature is a self-nature. It is incapable of being renovated. The Bible teaches that when we are born again, we put off the old man—we do not patch him up. The old self is to be crucified, not cultivated. Jesus said the cleansing of the outside of the cup and the platter leaves the inside just as dirty as before.

You Must Be Born Again!

The Bible also teaches that unless we have experienced this new birth we cannot get into the kingdom of heaven. Jesus made it even stronger. He said, "Ye *must* be born again" (John 3:7). There is nothing indefinite, nothing optional about that. He who would enter the kingdom of God must be born again.

Salvation is not just repairing the original self. It is a new self created of God in righteousness and true holiness. Regeneration is not even a change of nature, or a change of heart. Being born again is not a change—it is a regeneration, a new generation. It is a second birth. "Ye must be born again."

There is nothing about the old nature that God will accept. There is no soundness in it. The old nature is too weak to follow Christ. Paul said, "Ye cannot do the things that ye would" (Galatians 5:17). Those who are in the flesh cannot serve God. "Doth a fountain send forth at the same place sweet water and bitter? Can the fig tree, my brethren, bear olive berries?" asked James (James 3:11, 12).

The old man is described in Romans as "Their throat is an open sepulchre; with their tongues they have used deceit; the poison of asps is under their lips: Whose mouth is full of cursing and bitterness: Their feet are swift to shed blood: Destruction and misery are in their ways: . . . There is no fear of God before their eyes" (Romans 3:13–18).

How are you going to reform or patch up or change such throats and tongues and lips and feet and eyes as these? It is impossible. Jesus, knowing that it was impossible to change, patch up, and reform, said you must have a total new birth, "Ye must be born again." Jesus said, "That which is born of the flesh is flesh." On another occasion the Bible says, "Can the Ethiopian change his skin, or the leopard change his spots?" (Jeremiah 13:23). Again in Romans the Bible says, "They that are in the flesh cannot please God." "In me (that is, in my flesh) dwelleth no good thing" (Romans 7:18). Again the Bible says, "Without holiness no man shall see the Lord" (Hebrews 12:14).

The life that comes from the new birth cannot be obtained by natural development or self-effort. Man does not by nature have this holiness that God requires for heaven. In the new birth alone is the beginning of such a life to be found. To live the life of God we must have the nature of God.

What God Does

The whole matter of receiving new life is like a coin. A coin has two sides. The receiving of new life has a divine side and a human side. We have seen the human side in our chapter on conversion, we have seen what we must do. Now let's see what God does.

Being born again is altogether a work of the Holy Spirit. There is nothing we can do to obtain this new birth. The Bible says, "But as many as received him, to them gave he power to become the sons of God, even to them that believed on his name: Which were born, not of blood, nor of the will of the flesh, nor of the will of man, but of God" (John 1:12–13). In other words, we cannot be born of blood; that means we cannot inherit the new birth. God has no grandchildren.

We cannot inherit Christianity. We might have had a Christian father and mother, but that does not necessarily produce a Christian child. I could be born in a garage, but that doesn't make me an automobile! God has no grandchildren.

We cannot be born of the will of the flesh, the Scripture says. In other words, there is nothing we can do about it. The unbeliever is dead. A dead man has no life to do anything.

Nor can one be born of the will of man. This new birth cannot be produced by human devices or schemes. Many people think they are automatically born again when they join a church or go through some religious ritual or make some New Year's resolution or give a large gift to an outstanding charitable institution. All of these are fine and right, but they do not produce the new birth.

A Divine Work

Jesus told us we must *be* born again. The infinitive *be* is passive. It shows that it is something that must be done for us. No man can "born" himself. He must *be* born. The new birth is wholly foreign to our will. In other words, the new birth is a divine work—we are born of God.

Nicodemus could not understand how he could be born the second time. In perplexity he asked twice, "How?"

Even though the new birth seems mysterious, that does not make it untrue. We may not understand the how of electricity, but we know that it lights our homes, runs our television and radio sets. We do not understand how the sheep grows wool, the cow grows hair, or the fowl grows feathers—but we know they do. We do not understand many mysteries, but we accept by faith the fact that at the moment we repent of sin and turn by faith to Jesus Christ we are born again.

It is the infusion of divine life into the human soul. It is the implantation or impartation of divine nature into the human soul whereby we become the children of God. We receive the breath of God. Christ through the Holy Spirit takes up residence in our hearts. We are attached to God for eternity. That means that if you have been born again you will live as long as God lives, because you are now sharing His very life. The long lost fellowship man had with God in the Garden of Eden has been restored.

The Results of the New Birth

When you are born again several results follow: First, it will increase your vision and *understanding*. The Bible says, "God, who commanded the light to shine out of darkness, hath shined in our hearts, to give the light of the knowledge of the glory of God in the face of Jesus Christ" (2 Corinthians 4:6). Again the Bible says, "The eyes of your understanding being enlightened" (Ephesians 1:18). Things that you used to laugh at as foolishness you now accept by faith. Your whole mental process is changed. God becomes the hub of your intellectual thinking. He becomes the center. The ego has been dethroned.

Second, your *heart* undergoes a revolution. The Bible says, "A new spirit will I put within you: and I will take away the stony heart out of your flesh, and I will give you an heart of flesh" (Ezekiel 36:26).

Your affections have undergone a radical change. Your new nature loves God and the things pertaining to God. You love the finest and highest things in life. You reject the lower and baser. You discover a new appreciation for the social problems around you. Your heart beats with compassion for those who are less fortunate.

Third, your *will* undergoes a tremendous change. Your determinations are different. Your motives are changed. The Bible says, "Now the God of Peace . . . make you perfect in every good work to do his will, working in you that which is well-pleasing in his sight" (Hebrews 13:20, 21).

This new nature that you receive from God is bent to the will of God. You will want to do only His will. You are utterly and completely devoted to Him. There is a new self-determination, inclination, disposition, a new principle of living, new choices. You seek to glorify God. You seek fellowship with other Christians in the church. You love the Bible. You love to spend time in prayer with God. Your whole disposition is changed. Whereas your life once was filled with unbelief, the root and foundation of all sin, and you once doubted God, now you believe Him. Now you have utmost confidence and faith in God and His Word.

There may have been a time when pride was the very center of your life. You had ambitious thoughts of yourself, your powers, desires, and aims; but now that will begin to change. There may have been a time when there was hatred in your life. Envy, discontent, and malice filled your thoughts toward others. That, too, will gradually change.

There was a time when you could easily tell a lie. There were falsehoods and hypocrisies in many of your thoughts, words, and deeds. That is now all changed. There was a time when you gave in to the lust of the flesh. That is now changed. You have been born again. You may stumble into some of these traps that the devil puts out for you, but immediately you will be sorry, confess your sins, and ask forgiveness, because you have been born again. Your very nature has changed.

The Pig and the Lamb

There is an old story about the pig and the lamb. The farmer brought the pig into the house. He gave him a bath, polished his hoofs, put some Chanel No. 5 on him, tied a ribbon around his neck, and placed him in the living room. The pig looked fine. He almost seemed to be acceptable to society and to friends who might come in, he was so fresh and clean. He made a very nice and companionable pet for a few minutes. But as soon as the door was opened, the pig left the living room and jumped into the first mud puddle he could find. Why? Because he was still a pig at heart. His nature had not been changed. He had been changed outwardly but not inwardly.

Take a lamb, on the other hand. Put a lamb in a living room and then turn him out into the yard, and he will try his best to avoid all mud puddles. Why? Because his nature is that of a lamb.

You can take a man—dress him up, put him in the front row in church, and he almost looks like a saint. He may fool even his best friends for a while, but then put him in his office the next day, or put him at home or put him in the club on Saturday night, and you will see his true nature come out again. Why does he act that way? Because his nature has not been changed. He has not been born again.

The Meaning of Justification

Now the moment you receive the new birth, the moment you are born again, the moment you receive this divine impartation of a new nature, you are justified in the sight of God. By being justified is meant "just-as-if-I'd" never sinned. Justification is that act of God whereby He declares an ungodly man to be perfect while he is still ungodly. God places you before Him as though you had never committed a sin.

As Paul says, "Who shall lay anything to the charge of God's elect? It is God that justifieth" (Romans 8:33). Your sins have been forgiven. God has buried them in the depths of the sea and placed them behind His back of forgetfulness. Every sin is completely wiped out. You stand before God as a debtor, and you have received your discharge, you have become reconciled to God. You were actually an enemy of God before. The Bible says, "And all things are of God, who hath reconciled us to himself by Jesus Christ, and hath given to us the ministry of reconciliation" (2 Corinthians 5:18).

But more than all of that, you have been adopted into the family of God. You are now a child of God. "Having predestinated us unto the adoption of children by Jesus Christ to himself, according to the good pleasure of his will" (Ephesians 1:5). You are now a member of the royal family of heaven. You have royal blood in your veins. You are a child of the King. Even your friends will begin to notice the change that has taken place in your life. You have now been born again.

The Old and the New

Certain changes will take place once you have been born again. First, there will be a different attitude toward sin. You will learn to hate sin as God hates it. You will detest it and abhor it.

Down in Houston, Texas, a man was born again in one of our meetings. He owned a liquor store. The next morning he had a sign on the front of his door saying, "Out of business."

I heard about a man some time ago who had been born again in an evangelistic service. He was known as the city drunk. He was called "Old John." Somebody spoke to him the next morning on the street and said, "Good morning, Old John."

He said, "Who are you talking to? My name is not Old John. I'm *new* John." A complete revolution had taken place in his life.

Second, you will know that you have been born again because you will want to obey God. "And hereby we do know that we know him, if we keep his commandments" (1 John 2:3).

Third, you will be separated from the world. The Bible says, "Love not the world, neither the things that are in the world. If any man love the world, the love of the Father is not in him" (1 John 2:15). An unknown poet explains it this way:

> All the water in the world,
> However hard it tried,
> Could never sink a ship
> Unless it got inside.
>
> All the evil in the world,
> The wickedness and sin,
> Could never sink the soul's craft
> Unless it got inside.

Fourth, there will be a new love in your heart for other people. The Bible says, "We know that we have passed from death unto life, because we love the brethren" (1 John 3:14).

Fifth, we will not practice sin. The Bible says, "We know that whosoever is born of God sinneth not" (1 John 5:18). We will not engage in sinful practices.

In Texas they tell a story about a man who used to hitch his horse every morning in front of the saloon. One morning the saloon-keeper came out and found that the horse was hitched in front of the Methodist Church. He saw the man walking down the street and called out, "Say, why is your horse hitched in front of the Methodist Church this morning?"

The man turned around and said, "Well, last night I was converted in the revival meeting, and I've changed hitching posts."

That's what it means to be born again. That's what it means to be converted. That's what it means to be separated from the world. It means that you change hitching posts.

13

How to Be Sure

These things have I written unto you that believe on the name of the Son of God; that ye may know that ye have eternal life, and that ye may believe on the name of the Son of God. 1 John 5:13

EVERY WEEK I receive scores of letters from those who say they have doubts and uncertainties concerning the Christian life. Many come from genuine Christians who seem to have none of the joy of Christian faith, or the assurance, because they have failed to understand a basic truth of Christian experience. Even though the Bible says, "But these [the Bible] are written that ye might believe that Jesus is the Christ, the Son of God; and that believing ye might have life through his name" (John 20:31), many are unsure.

Now let's use this chapter to *sum up* what has happened to us. We have seen what it means to repent, to have faith, and to be born again. Now, how can I be certain, how can I be sure that all of this has happened to me? Many people with whom I talk have repented and have believed and have been born again, but they often lack the assurance of their conversion. Let's go over a few things that we've learned. First of all, becoming a Christian can be a crisis experience in your life, or it can be a process with a climactic moment of which you may or may not be conscious. Do not misunderstand me; you do not become a Christian as a result of a process of education. Some years ago a great preacher said, "We must so educate and train our youth in the Christian way of life that they will never know when they were not Christians." Much of the philosophy of religious education has been based upon this premise, and perhaps many have missed the essence of Christian experience because nothing more than religious training took its place. No change took place in the heart.

At the turn of the century, Professor Starbuck, a leading thinker in the field of psychology, observed that Christian workers generally were recruited from the ranks of those who had had a vital experience of conversion. He also observed that those who had a clear concept of what it means to be converted were mainly those who had come out of rural areas where in the early days they had had either little or no carefully planned religious training.

This is not a criticism of religious training, but it may be taken as a warning of the dangers involved in improper use of religious training that becomes a substitute for the experience of the new birth.

Religion Is Not Rebirth

To Nicodemus, one of the most religious men of his times, Jesus said, "Except a man be born again, he cannot see the kingdom of God" (John 3:3). Nicodemus could not substitute his profound knowledge of religion for spiritual rebirth, and we have not progressed beyond this point in our generation.

The ugly larva in its cocoon spends much time in almost unnoticeable growth and change. But no matter how slow that growth may be, the moment comes when it passes through a crisis and emerges a beautiful butterfly. The weeks of silent growth are important, but they cannot take the place of that experience when the old and the ugly are left behind and the new and the beautiful come into being.

It is true that thousands of Christians do not know the exact day or hour that they came to know Christ. Their faith and lives testify that consciously or unconsciously they have been converted to Christ. Whether they can remember it or not, there was a moment when they did cross over the line from death to life.

Probably everyone has had doubts and uncertainties at times in his religious experience. When Moses went up on Mount Sinai to receive the tables of the law from the hand of God, he was lost for some time to the sight of the Hebrews who stood anxiously waiting his return. They finally became doubtful and said among themselves, "As for this Moses, the man that brought us up out of the land of Egypt, we wot not what is become of him" (Exodus 32:1). Their defection was a result of their doubting and uncertainty.

The dreadful uncertainty that haunts the souls of multitudes grows out of a misunderstanding of what constitutes true Christian experience. Many do not seem to understand the nature of Christian experience, while others have been misinformed and are seeking something for which we are not warranted by Scripture to expect.

More than three hundred times the word *faith* is mentioned in the New Testament with reference to man's salvation, and many more times it is implied. The writer of the Book of Hebrews said, "He that cometh to God must believe that he is, and that he is a rewarder of them that diligently seek him." And again he said that "Without faith it is impossible to please him" (Hebrews 11:6).

It is because we have confused *faith* with *feeling* that many experience the difficulty and uncertainty that is so common among professing Christians today.

Faith always implies an object—that is, when we believe, we must believe something. That something I call the *fact*. Let me give you, then, three words, three words that must always be kept in the same order and never rearranged. Let me give you these three words that will point the way, for you, out of uncertainty to a confident Christian life. These three words are *fact, faith,* and *feeling.* They come in this order and the order is essential. If you confuse them, eliminate one, or add one, you will end up in the mire of despair and continue to grope about in semidarkness, without the joy and confidence of one who can sav. "I know him in whom I have believed" (2 Timothy 1:12).

Fact

If you are saved from sin at all, you are saved through a personal faith in the gospel of Christ as defined in the Scriptures. Though it may at first seem dogmatic and narrow to you, the fact remains that there is no other way. The Bible says, "I delivered unto you first of all that which I also received, how that Christ died for our sins according to the Scriptures; and that he was buried, and that he arose again the third day according to the Scriptures" (1 Corinthians 15:3, 4). The Bible says that we are saved when our faith is in this objective fact. The work of Christ is a fact, His cross is a fact, His tomb is a fact, and His resurrection is a fact.

It is impossible to believe anything into existence. The gospel did not come into being because men believed it. The tomb was not emptied of its deposit that first Easter because some faithful persons believed it. The fact always preceded the faith. We are psychologically incapable of believing without an object of our faith.

The Bible does not call upon you to believe something that is not credible, but to believe in the fact of history that in reality transcends all history. The Bible calls upon you to believe that this work of Christ, done for sin and for sinners, is effective in all who will risk their souls with Him. Trusting in Him for your eternal salvation is trusting in a fact.

Faith

Faith is second in this order of three words. Faith is rationally impossible where there is nothing to believe. Faith must have an object. The object of Christian faith is Christ. Faith means more than an intellectual assent to the claims of Christ. Faith involves the will. It is volitional. Faith demands action. If we actually believe, then we will live. Faith without works is dead. Faith actually means surrender and commitment to the claims of Christ. It means an acknowledgment of sin and a turning to Christ. We do not know Christ through the five physical senses, but we know Him through the sixth sense that God has given every man—which is the ability to believe.

The Experience of Faith

In reading carefully through the New Testament to see just what kind of an experience you can expect, I find that the New Testament sets forth only one. There is just one experience for which you can look—only one feeling you can expect—and that is the experience of faith. Believing is an experience as real as any experience, yet many are looking for something more—some dramatic sensation that will bring a physical thrill, while others look for some spectacular manifestation. Many have been told to look for such sensations, but the Bible says that a man is "justified by faith" and not by feeling. A man is saved by trusting in the finished work of Christ on the cross and not by physical excitement or religious ecstasy.

But you may say to me, "What about feeling? Is there no place in saving faith for any feeling?" Certainly there is room for feeling in saving faith, but we are not saved by it. Whatever feeling there may be is only the result of saving faith, but it in itself is not what does the saving!

Feeling

Feeling is the last of the three words, and is the least important. I believe that much religious unrest and uncertainty is caused by earnest, honest seekers after salvation who have a predetermined idea that they must be in some kind of an emotional state before they can experience conversion.

Those who are seeking salvation as it is presented through the Scriptures will want to know what kind of an experience the Bible leads you to expect. I speak to those who have gone often to an altar, or to an inquiry room, or perhaps have knelt beside a radio or television set when an invitation has been given to receive Christ. You have heard the message, you have known that you were a sinner in need of the Savior, you have recognized that your life is a spiritual wreck, you have tried every man-made scheme for self-improvement and for reformation but they all failed. In your lost and hopeless condition you looked to Christ for salvation. You believed that He could and would save you. You have often read His invitation to sinners when He said, "Come unto me, all ye that labor and are heavy laden, and I will give you rest" (Matthew 11:28). You have read the promise that says, "Him that cometh unto me, I will in no wise cast out" (John 6:37). You have read how He said, "If any man thirst, let him come unto me and drink" (John 7:37).

Feeling Comes After Faith

When I understand something of Christ's love for me as a sinner, I respond with a love for Christ—and love has feeling. But love for Christ is a love that is above human love, though there is a similarity. It is a love that frees us from self. In marriage there is commitment. There is also feeling. But feelings come and go. Commitment stays. We who have committed ourselves to Christ have feelings that come and go—joy, love, gratitude, and so on. But the commitment remains unchanged. Feelings are important, but not essential. The Bible says, "Perfect love casteth out fear" (1 John 4:18). And those who love Christ have that confidence in Him that raises them above fear. Psychologists tell us there is destructive fear and healthy fear. Healthy fear is *instructive,* causing us to care for our bodies and our loved ones—Jesus told us to *fear* Satan.

When I understand that Christ in His death gained a decisive victory over death and over sin, then I lose the fear of death. The Bible says that "He also himself likewise took part of the same that through death he might destroy him that had the power of death, that is, the devil; And deliver them who through fear of death were all their lifetime subject to bondage" (Hebrews 2:14, 15). Surely this also is a feeling. Fear is a kind of feeling, and to overcome fear with boldness and confidence in the very face of death is feeling and experience. But again I say, it is not the feeling of boldness and confidence that saves us, but it is our faith that saves us, and boldness and confidence result from our having trusted in Christ. From Genesis to Revelation we are told to fear the Lord. It is the fear of the Lord that puts all other fears in proper perspective.

The Part Guilt Plays

To have a guilty conscience is an experience. Psychologists may define it as a guilt experience, and may seek to rationalize away the sense of guilt; but once this has been awakened through the application of the law of God, no explanation will quiet the insistent voice of conscience. Many a criminal has finally given himself over to the authorities because the accusations of a guilty conscience were worse than prison bars.

In an article on guilt which appeared in *The New York Times* (29 November 1983) Dr. Helen Block Lewis, a psychoanalyst and psychologist at Yale University, described guilt as a feeling that "helps people stay connected" to their fellow human beings. "Guilt is one of the cements that binds us together and keeps us human," she explained. "If it occurs to you that you've done something to injure someone else, guilt compels you to do something to fix it, to repair the bond."

Samuel Rutherford said to "Pray for a strong and lively sense of sin; the greater the sense of sin, the less sin." A sense of sin and guilt is the same thing. It not only tells you when you are in trouble, but like the sense of pain it can keep you out of it. Without a sense of pain one could put his hand on a hot stove and feel nothing. The vital part that a sense of pain plays in keeping us healthy is explored in the book, *Fearfully and Wonderfully Made,* by Paul Brand and Philip Yancey. They explain that it is not the disease of leprosy itself which causes the deformation so common among lepers. It is the absence of a sense of pain when the extremities are injured (for instance, the hand in a fire) which causes the horrible mutilation associated with leprosy.

The Bible teaches that Christ cleanses the conscience. The Bible says, "For if the blood of bulls and of goats and the ashes of an heifer sprinkling the unclean sanctifieth to the purifying of the flesh: How much more shall the blood of Christ, who through the eternal Spirit offered himself without spot to God, purge your conscience from dead works to serve the living God?" (Hebrews 9:13, 14).

To have a guilty conscience cleansed, and to be free from its constant accusation is an experience, but it is not the cleansing of the conscience that saves you; it is faith in Christ that saves, and a cleansed conscience is the *result* of having come into a right relationship with God.

Joy is a feeling. Inward peace is a feeling. Love for others is a feeling. Concern for the lost is a feeling.

Finally, someone may say, "I believe the historic facts of the gospel, but still I am not saved." Perhaps so, for the faith that saves has one distinguishing quality—saving faith is a faith that produces obedience, it is a faith that brings about a way of life. Some have quite successfully imitated this way of life for a time, but for those who trust Christ for salvation, that faith brings about in them a desire to live out that inward experience of faith. It is a power that results in godly living and surrender.

Let that intellectual faith, that historical faith that you may now have, yield itself to Christ in full surrender, earnestly desiring His salvation, and upon the authority of the Word of God you become a child of God. "But as many as received him, to them gave he the right to become the sons of God, even to them that believe on his name" (John 1:12).

III

APPLYING

THE ANTIDOTE

14

Enemies
of the Christian

For we wrestle not against flesh and blood, but against principalities, against powers, against the rulers of darkness of this world, against spiritual wickedness in high places.
Ephesians 6:12

Now that you have made your decision—now that you have been born again—now that you have been converted—now that you have been justified—now that you are a child of God—what next? Is that all there is to it? Just one moment of decision and then it is all over? "Do I have any more responsibilities?" you ask.

Ah, yes, you have just begun the Christian life. You have just been born into a new world—the spiritual world. Everything is brand new. You are actually a spiritual baby. You need tenderness, love, care, nurture. You need to be fed. You need protection. That is one of the reasons why Christ established the church. It is nearly impossible to live the Christian life alone. Most of us need help and fellowship.

The newborn Christian is like a newborn baby in his need for love. While revising this book my wife and I took an island vacation with our oldest daughter, her husband, and their seventh child, little three-month-old Anthony—our sixteenth grandchild. In the week we were together he cried only twice. Why? He was surrounded by tenderness, love, care, nurture. All he did was eat, sleep, and smile. Ideally, at the outset of their spiritual experience, "baby" Christians need this kind of nurture, but unfortunately our world is not geared to that kind of beginning for the Christian life. The church is the place where that beginning takes place, in the plan and purpose of God.

Possibly you have already found that you have enemies. These are dangerous, vicious enemies who will use any method to defeat you in your Christian life. Within minutes after you made your decision you found these enemies already at work: either you were tempted to commit some sin, or you had a moment of depression and discouragement. To be sure, everything is exciting and thrilling just after you have made your decision for Christ! But it is also natural to have doubts, problems, questions, temptations, discouragements, and even difficulties.

The Bible teaches that you have three enemies which will be warring against you as long as you live. You must be prepared. They must be warded off.

First, let's look at these enemies whom we must face. Let's unmask them and see what they are, and who they are, and how they operate.

The Devil

First—*the devil*. We have already seen that the devil is a mighty being who opposes God and tempts God's people. We have found that even though he was beaten at the cross by Christ he still has power to influence men for evil. The Bible calls him "the wicked one," "the devil," "a murderer," "a liar, and the father of lies," "an adversary" who seeks to devour, "that old serpent" and "accuser of our brethren" (Matthew 13:19; Luke 4:33; John 8:44; 1 Peter 5:8; Revelation 12:9–10).

The moment you made your decision for Christ Satan suffered a tremendous defeat. He is angry now. From now on he is going to tempt you and try to lead you into sin. Don't be alarmed. He cannot rob you of your salvation, and he need not rob you of your assurance and victory. He will do everything in his power to sow seeds of doubt in your mind as to whether your conversion is a reality or not. You cannot argue with him for he is the greatest debater of all time.

The moment of test has come with the first temptation. Remember to refuse any reliance upon your feelings; they will change like a weather vane in a whirlwind. His next approach probably will be to make you feel proud and important—to make you confident of your own powers, ambitions, desires, and aims. On another occasion he will put hatred in your heart. He will tempt you to say unkind and ungenerous things about others. He will put envy, discontent, and malice in your heart. Then on another occasion he will tempt you to lie, and you could easily find yourself being a hypocrite. Lying is one of the worst of all sins and can be committed by a thought, word, or deed. Anything that is intended to deceive another person is lying. The devil will do his best to make a liar of you. He also will try to get you to work for him to tempt others to sin— to try to lead other Christian friends astray. If you are not careful you will find yourself actually in the employ of the devil. He is powerful, slick, crafty, wily, and subtle. He is called the "god of this world," "the prince of this world," "the prince and power of the air" (2 Corinthians 4:4; John 12:31; Ephesians 2:2).

The devil will try to discourage you, to divert you; he will seek to dilute your testimony; he will attempt anything to destroy your relationship to Christ and your influence upon others.

You ask "How can I overcome him? What can I do? Which way can I turn? Is there any escape?"

"There hath no temptation taken you but such as is common to man: but God is faithful, who will not suffer you to be tempted above that ye are able; but will with the temptation also make a way to escape, that ye may be able to bear it" (1 Corinthians 10:13).

Years ago I heard my friend J. Edwin Orr compare the Christian attacked by Satan to a mouse being attacked by a housewife wielding a broom. The mouse does not sit there contemplating the housewife or the broom, he is busy looking for a hole—a way to escape. So we Christians under satanic attack should look for our "way of escape."

God says in this verse that He has made a way of escape. Now remember this: temptation of the devil is not a sign that your life is not right with God. It is actually a sign that you are right with God. Temptation is not sin. Also remember that God never tempts His own children. He never causes His children to doubt. All doubts and temptations come from the devil. Remember also that Satan can only tempt. He can never compel you to yield to the temptation. Remember also that Satan has already been conquered by Christ. His power is made inoperative in the life of a fully trusting and yielded Christian who is completely dependent upon God.

The poet put it this way:

> The devil trembles when he sees
> the weakest saint upon his knees.

To say that Satan will be defeated when we read or quote Scripture and will run like a scalded dog when we resist him is an oversimplification. But we can depend upon the blood of Christ when we are under attack. There are times when we simply must hide behind the Person of Christ and ask Him to handle our problems. Jude says, "Yet Michael the archangel, when contending with the devil he disputed about the body of Moses, durst not bring against him a railing accusation, but said, The Lord rebuke thee" (v. 9). That's what we need to do—call upon God.

Now the Bible says that we are to "resist the devil and he will flee" from us (James 4:7). But before that, God says "Submit yourselves . . . to God." If you have fully submitted, one hundred percent yielded and surrendered yourself to Christ, then you can "resist the devil," and the Bible promises he will flee from you. The devil will tremble when you pray. He will be defeated when you quote or read a passage of Scripture to him, and will leave you when you resist him.

The World

Your second enemy is *the world*. The world means the cosmos, this world system. The world has a tendency to lead us into sin—evil companions, pleasures, fashions, opinions, and aims.

You will find in your born-again experience that your pleasures have been lifted into an entirely new and glorious realm. Many non-Christians have accused the Christian life as being a set of rules, taboos, vetos, and prohibitions.

This is another lie of the devil. It is not a series of "don'ts," but a series of "dos." You become so busy in the work of Christ and so completely satisfied with the things of Christ that you do not have time for the things of the world.

Suppose someone should offer me a hamburger after I had eaten a T-bone steak. I would say, "No, thank you, I am already satisfied."

Young Christian, that is the secret. You are so filled with the things of Christ, so enamored of the things of God, that you do not have time or taste for sinful pleasures of this world. The Bible says, "The full soul loatheth an honeycomb; but to the hungry soul every bitter thing is sweet" (Proverbs 27:7).

Worldliness, however, has been vastly misunderstood on the part of thousands of Christians. It needs a little clarification. It is probably one of the greatest difficulties that meets a young and inexperienced Christian.

Dr. W. H. Griffith Thomas has said, "There are certain elements of daily life which are not sinful in themselves, but which have a tendency to lead to sin if they are abused. Abuse literally means extreme use, and in many instances overuse of things lawful becomes sin. Pleasure is lawful in use but unlawful in its overuse. Ambition is an essential part of true character, but it must be fixed on lawful objects and exercised in proper proportion. Our daily occupation, reading, dress, friendships and other similar phases of. life are all legitimate and necessary, but can easily become illegitimate, unnecessary and harmful. Thought about the necessities of life is absolutely essential, but this can easily degenerate into anxiety, and then as Christ reminds us in the parable, the cares of this life choke the spiritual seed in the heart. Making of money is necessary for daily living, but money-making is apt to degenerate into money-loving and then the deceitfulness of riches enters into and spoils our spiritual life. Worldliness is thus not confined to any particular rank, walk, or circumstance of life so that we cannot separate this class from that and call one worldly and the other unworldly . . . one spiritual and the other unspiritual. Worldliness is a spirit, an atmosphere, an influence permeating the whole of life and human society, and it needs to be guarded against constantly and strenuously."

The Bible says, "Love not the world, neither the things that are in the world" (1 John 2:15). The Bible also warns that the world and the "lust thereof" shall pass away, "but he that doeth the will of God abideth forever" (1 John 2:17).

However, under certain conditions these can become perplexing problems in our modern-day living. Many young people come to me and ask, "Is this wrong?" or "Is that wrong?" "Is this sinful?" or "Is that sinful?" One simple question, earnestly and prayerfully asked, will settle about ninety percent of your problems along this line. Just ask this question to yourself every time, "What would Christ have me to do?" Another question you can ask is, "Can I ask His blessing upon this particular thing for me?" "What would Christ think about my amusements, recreation, books, companions, and television programs?" "Could I ask Christ to go along with me to this particular event?" Being omnipotent, He'll be there anyway. The point is, should you?

It does not mean that in society we are snobs or have a superiority complex, lest we be in danger of spiritual pride—which would be far worse than any worldliness. But today there are so many professing Christians who are walking hand in hand with the world that you cannot tell the difference between the Christian and the unbeliever. This should never be.

The Christian should stand out like a sparkling diamond against a rough background. He should be more wholesome than anyone else. He should be poised, cultured, courteous, gracious, but firm in the things that he does and does not do. He should laugh and be radiant, but he should refuse to allow the world to pull him down to its level.

The Bible says that "whatsoever is not of faith is sin" (Romans 14:23), and the Bible again says that he who doubts is condemned if he does it. In other words, we are never to do anything of which we are not perfectly clear and certain. If you have a doubt about that particular thing that is bothering you, as to whether it is worldly or not, the best policy is "don't do it."

The Flesh

The third enemy that you will face immediately is *the lust of the flesh*. The flesh is that evil tendency of your inward self. Even after you are converted, sometimes your old, sinful cravings will return. You become startled and wonder where they come from. The Bible teaches that the old nature, with all its corruption, is still there and that these evil temptations come from nowhere else. In other words, "a traitor is living within." "That wretched bent toward sin is ever present to drag you down." War has been declared! You now have two natures in conflict, and each one is striving for dominance.

The Bible teaches "the flesh lusteth against the Spirit, and the Spirit against the flesh" (Galatians 5:17). It is the battle of the self-life and the Christ-life. This old nature cannot please God. It cannot be converted, or even patched up. Thank God, when Jesus died He took you with Him, and the old nature can be made inoperative and you can "reckon ye also yourselves to be dead indeed unto sin" (Romans 6:11). This is done by faith.

However, you must distinguish very carefully again between use and abuse—between that which is lawful and that which is unlawful. Some of these things that will be cropping up may be sinful lusts, or they may not be.

As Dr. W. H. Griffith Thomas says, "The original meaning of the word lust is 'strong desire' and not necessarily a sinful desire, since there are certain desires of our physical nature—such as hunger and thirst—which we have in common with the animal world and which, in themselves, are natural and not sinful. It is only their abuse that is evil. Hunger is a natural lust. Gluttony is a sinful lust. Thirst is a natural lust. Intemperance is a sinful lust. Sloth should not be confused with exhaustion or illness. Marriage is according to the will of God and the dictates of human nature, physical, mental and social. Adultery is a sin and is opposed to the will of God and to all that is pure in body, mind and heart. But there are other lusts of the flesh which are sensually and inherently sinful. Such as, for instance, the desire to gratify at all cost our hatred and revenge. We must, therefore, distinguish carefully between the lust which is simply a strong desire, and the same lust as a sinful desire. Sins of the flesh are in some respects the most terrible of all because they represent the yearnings of the nature to do evil. Neither the devil nor the world, nor even our own evil heart can compel us to sin. It must be by our consent and will and it is at this point that our evil nature comes in with its awful power and possibility of evil."

Paul said he had no confidence in the flesh. On another occasion he said, "I make no provision for the flesh" (Romans 13:14). On another occasion he said, "I keep my body under" (1 Corinthians 9:27). We are so to re-yield and re-surrender ourselves to God that we can, by faith, reckon the old nature dead indeed unto sin.

Fighting Our Foes

These then, are our three foes: the devil, the world, and the flesh. Our attitude toward them as Christians can be summed up in one word—*renounce*. There can be no bargaining, compromise, or hesitation. Abiding in Christ, as taught in John 15, is the only possible course for the Christian who has to be "in" the world but does not want to be "of" it. Someone has said that the apostle Paul was dealing with this dilemma when he wrote to the Ephesians, "Paul, an apostle of Jesus Christ . . . to the saints . . . at Ephesus and to the faithful in Christ Jesus" (Ephesians 1:1). Ephesus was their business address, but "in Christ" was their home address! In relation to the devil, we resist him only as we submit ourselves to God. In relation to the world, the Bible says, "This is the victory that overcometh the world, even our faith" (1 John 5:4). In relation to the flesh, the Bible says, "Walk in the Spirit, and ye shall not fulfill the lust of the flesh" (Galatians 5:16).

Here is glorious news to you who have already been fighting these battles and temptations. You are not asked to fight the battle alone. The Bible says in Romans 8:13 that you, *by the Spirit*, shall put to death the deeds of the body. Remember, Jesus promised that He would never leave us, or forsake us. Remember Jesus promised us that after He left the earth He would send Another—the Third Person of the Trinity—the Holy Spirit, who is called a Comforter (which actually means "one who comes alongside to help") that He may abide with us forever (John 14:16). Jesus said, "I am not going to leave you alone. I will come to you in the person of the Holy Spirit." Jesus is the vine and believers are the branches is the way Jesus put it (see John 15).

The Holy Spirit is the most powerful Being in the world today. The time of the Old Testament was an age of God the Father. During the time that Jesus was on earth it was an age of God the Son. Now we are living, since Pentecost, in the age of God the Holy Spirit. The Bible says, "Be filled with the Spirit" (Ephesians 5:18) which reads literally, "Be *being* filled. . . ." It's a continuous and ongoing process. Just as Christ came to make God visible and redeem mankind, so the Holy Spirit came to make Christ visible in the life of the believer and enable the individual Christian to offer Christ's redemption to a lost and dying world.

The Bible says that the moment you accepted Christ as Savior the Holy Spirit took up residence in your heart. Your body is now "the temple of the Holy Ghost *which is in you*" (1 Corinthians 6:19). Paul even warned that if any man has not the Spirit of Christ he is none of His.

You say, "But I don't feel anything down in my heart. I don't feel the Spirit of God in me."

Faith Is a Fact

Disregard feelings. You're not saved by feeling, and you may or may not feel the Spirit. Accept Him by faith as a fact. He lives within you right now to help you live the Christian life. He is living in you in order to magnify, glorify, and exalt Christ in you so that you can live a happy, victorious, radiant, Christ-honoring life.

The Bible commands, "Be filled with the Spirit" (Ephesians 5:18). If you are filled with the Spirit, then you are going to produce the fruit of the Spirit, which is "love, joy, peace, longsuffering, gentleness, goodness, faith, meekness, temperance" (Galatians 5:22–23). To be filled with the Spirit is not optional. It is a command to be obeyed—a duty to be done.

How do you know that you are filled? And how can you be filled? Is it some emotional experience through which you must pass? Not necessarily. When you give all you know of yourself to all that you know of Him, then you can accept by faith that you are filled with the Spirit of God. That means that He can have all of you. Commitment actually is surrender—total, absolute, unconditional, irreversible surrender. "I beseech you, therefore, brethren, by the mercies of God, that ye present your bodies a living sacrifice, holy, acceptable unto God, which is your reasonable service" (Romans 12:1).

It is only the consecrated, Spirit-filled Christian who can have victory over the world, the flesh, and the devil. It is the Holy Spirit who will do the fighting for you. "We wrestle not against flesh and blood, but against principalities, against powers, against the rulers of darkness" (Ephesians 6:12). This is a spiritual warfare. You cannot fight against these three enemies with normal weapons. Only as we become channels and let the Holy Spirit do the fighting through us are we going to get complete victory. Don't hold back anything from Christ. Let Him be completely the Lord and Master of your life. He said, "Ye call me Master and Lord: and ye say well; for so I am" (John 13:13).

I believe unself-consciousness is characteristic of the fruit of the Holy Spirit. The person who says, "I am Spirit-filled" sets himself up for some pretty uncomfortable scrutiny. Did any apostle or disciple say of himself, "I am filled with the Holy Spirit"? But of many it was said, "They were filled with the Holy Spirit." The person who is self-consciously loving, self-consciously joyful, self-consciously peaceful, has about him the odor of self. And as one Christian sanely observed, "Self is spiritual B.O."

A little child playing one day with a very valuable vase put his hand into it and could not withdraw it. His father, too, tried his best, but all in vain. They were thinking of breaking the vase when the father said, "Now, my son, make one more try. Open your hand and hold your fingers out straight as you see me doing, and then pull."

To their astonishment the little fellow said, "O no, father. I couldn't put my fingers out like that, because if I did I would drop my penny."

Smile, if you will—but thousands of us are like that little boy, so busy holding on to the world's worthless penny that we cannot accept liberation. I beg you to drop that trifle in your heart. Surrender! Let go, and let God have His way in your life.

Now, after you have given yourself completely to Christ in consecration, remember that God has accepted what you have presented. "Him that cometh unto me I will in no wise cast out" (John 6:37). You have come to Him; now He has received you. And He will in no wise cast you out!

The Fruit of the Spirit

Not only will you have boldness, but you will produce the fruit of the Spirit. Keep in mind that these fruits of the Spirit are *of* the Spirit. One does not produce them himself. They are supernatural in origin. The first is, according to Galatians 5, love, and from this root will grow all the others. Jesus said, "This is my commandment, that ye love one another, as I have loved you. . . . If ye keep my commandments ye shall abide in my love; even as I have kept my Father's commandments, and abide in his love" (John 15:12, 10). We must differentiate between the *gifts* of the Spirit and the *fruit* of the Spirit. Gifts are *given*—fruits are *grown*. To grow something there must be a close, intimate, personal relationship between the vine and the branch. A person must be rooted and grounded in Christ.

As we pointed out earlier, one of the characteristics of the Holy Spirit is unself-consciousness. Whenever a person is self-conscious of spiritual fruit there goes up the odor of self.

Another fruit of the Spirit is joy. One of the characteristics of the Christian is an inward joy that does not depend upon circumstances. Nehemiah says, "For the joy of the Lord is your strength" (8:12). S. D. Gordon, the well-known devotional writer of a past generation, said of joy: "Joy is distinctly a Christian word and a Christian thing. It is the reverse of happiness. Happiness is the result of what happens of an agreeable sort. Joy has its springs deep down inside. And that spring never runs dry, no matter what happens. Only Jesus gives that joy. He had joy, singing its music within, even under the shadow of the cross. It is an unknown word and thing except as He has sway within."

"Real joy comes not from ease or riches or . . . the praise of men, but from doing something worthwhile," said the missionary, Sir Wilfred Grenfell. And Alexander MacLaren said, "To pursue joy is to lose it. The only way to get it is to follow steadily the path of duty, without thinking of joy, and then, like sheep, it comes most surely, unsought, and we 'being in the way' the angel of God, fair-haired joy, is sure to meet us."

There will be peace. Paul said, "Troubled on every side, yet not distressed; we are perplexed, but not in despair; persecuted, but not forsaken; cast down, but not destroyed" (2 Corinthians 4:8–9). We could go through all the rest of the supernatural list—longsuffering, gentleness, goodness, faith, meekness, and temperance and see how all of this fruit flourishes in the lives of those who are truly yielded and Spirit-filled.

The victory is yours. Claim it! It is your birthright. Browning said, "The best is yet to be." This doesn't mean the Christian can never suffer defeat or experience low periods in life. But it does mean that the Savior goes with you no matter the problem. The peace comes in the midst of problems and in spite of them.

15

Guidelines for
Christian Living

And as ye would that men should do to you, do ye also to them likewise. Luke 6:31

WHETHER WE ARE playing a game, driving a car, or baking a cake, there are certain rules that must be followed for our safety as well as our success.

I well recall what happened near my home in Montreat, North Carolina, some years ago. The road between Black Mountain and Asheville was being widened from two lanes to four. For several weeks during the construction period there were no lane markers. One night there was a tragic head-on collision and five people were killed—because the "road rules" had not been clearly marked.

The Bible teaches that the Christian life is one of constant growth. When you were born again, you were born into God's family. My wife Ruth and I now have sixteen grandchildren. And each of them is precious to us. Each is an accepted, treasured member of our family. And that's the way God feels about you. It is God's purpose that you will grow into full stature and become mature in Christ. It would be against the law of God and nature if you were to remain a baby and thus become a spiritual dwarf. In 2 Peter 3:18, the Bible says that we are to grow. This implies steady development, constant enlargement, increasing wisdom.

Read the Bible Daily

For one to grow properly certain rules must be observed for good spiritual health. First: you should *read your Bible daily*. It is one of your greatest privileges. Your spiritual life needs food. What kind of food? Spiritual food. Where do you find this spiritual food? In the Bible, the Word of God. The Bible reveals Christ, who is the Bread of Life for your hungry soul, and the Water of Life for your thirsty heart. If you fail to partake of daily spiritual nourishment, you will starve and lose your spiritual vitality. The Bible says, "Desire the sincere milk of the Word, that ye may grow thereby" (1 Peter 2:2). Read it, study it, meditate on it, memorize it. Ninety-five percent of the difficulties you will experience as a Christian can be traced to a lack of Bible study and reading.

Suppose an archaeologist discovered the original diary of Genghis Khan, or Alexander the Great, or the love letters of Cleopatra? Or what if our astronauts had discovered a mysterious manuscript during their moon walk? Imagine the stampede into the bookstores across America to get copies of such books. Yet we have here a Book that God Himself has written for mankind—and think how it is either ignored or attacked by many so-called civilized people.

Some parts of our world do not enjoy the freedom we have to read the Bible and study it together with fellow Christians. In most of the world, in fact, there's a veritable famine for the Word of God! I recall the story of a Chinese musician in the Peoples Republic of China. He was converted and strengthened spiritually through the reading of individual pages of the Scripture torn from a Bible and slipped to him by an unknown friend. There are other stories of prisoners who survived twenty to thirty years at hard labor—and sometimes terrible torture—and came out with their minds intact, totally lacking in bitterness toward their captors.

One more story of the Bible's power comes from a mental hospital here in this country. A young man, an inmate of the hospital, wrote to our organization requesting a copy of the Bible. His recovery and subsequent complete rehabilitation date back to his receipt of that Bible—and his reading of its pages. Today he is married and self-supporting!

Do not be content to skim through a chapter merely to satisfy your conscience. Hide the Word of God in your heart. A little portion well digested is of greater spiritual value to your soul than a lengthy portion scanned hurriedly. Do not be discouraged because you cannot understand it all. Some excuse themselves saying, "It's too hard to understand." Any book is difficult to understand if you don't read it! Read simple portions of the Bible first. You do not feed a baby beefsteak the first day—you give him milk.

I would suggest that you start by reading the Gospel of John. As you read, the Holy Spirit will enlighten the passages for you. He will illuminate the difficult words and make obscure meanings clear. Even though you cannot remember all you have read, or understand it all, go on reading. The very practice of reading in itself will have a purifying effect upon your mind and heart. Let nothing take the place of this daily exercise.

Scripture memorized can come to mind when you do not have your Bible with you—on sleepless nights, when driving a car, traveling, when having to make an instantaneous important decision. It comforts, guides, corrects, encourages— all we need is there. Memorize as much as you can.

Learn to Pray

Second: *learn the secret of prayer.* Your prayers may falter at first. You may be awkward and inarticulate. But the Holy Spirit who lives within you will help you and teach you. Every prayer that you pray will be answered. Sometimes the answer may be "Yes" and sometimes "No," and sometimes it is "Wait," but nevertheless it will be answered.

Prayer is communicating. A baby's first response is to his parents. He isn't asking for anything. He is simply smiling back when his parents smile, cooing when they talk to him. What a thrill his first response brings to the entire family! In the same way, can you imagine the joy our first response to Him brings to God?

Your petitions should always be conditioned by "Thy will be done." "Delight thyself also in the Lord and he shall give thee the desires of thine heart" (Psalm 37:4). But the delighting of oneself in Him precedes the fulfillment of our desires. Delighting ourselves in Him will direct our desires, so God *can answer* our petitions.

Remember that you can pray any time, anywhere. Washing dishes, digging ditches, working in the office, in the shop, on the athletic field—even in prison—you can pray and know God hears! We have a friend on Death Row who prays for us every morning between four and six. How often this fact has encouraged and cheered us on.

Try to have a systematic method of prayer. Prayer combined with Bible study makes for a healthy Christian life. The Bible says, "Pray without ceasing." If you have special prayer periods that you set aside during the day, your unconscious life will be saturated with prayer between the prayer periods. It is not enough for you to get out of bed in the morning and just bow your knee and repeat a few sentences. There should be stated periods in which you slip apart with God. For the overworked mother or one living under extremely busy circumstances, this may be impossible. But here is where "prayer without ceasing" comes in. We pray as we work. As we have said, we pray everywhere, any time.

The devil will fight you every step of the way. He will cause the baby to cry, the telephone to ring, someone to knock at the door—there will be many interruptions, but keep at it! Don't be discouraged. Soon you will find that these periods of prayer are the greatest delight of your life. You will look forward to them with more anticipation than to anything else. Without constant, daily, systematic prayer your life will seem barren, discouraging, and fruitless. Without constant prayer you never can know the inner peace that God wants to give you.

Rely on the Holy Spirit

Third: *rely constantly on the Holy Spirit*. Remember that Christ dwells in you through the Holy Spirit. Your body is now the dwelling place of the Third Person of the Trinity. Do not ask Him to help you as you would a servant.

Ask Him to come in and do it all. Ask Him to take over in your life. Tell Him how weak, helpless, unstable, and unreliable you are. Stand aside and let Him take over in all the choices and decisions of your life. We know that the Holy Spirit prays for us (Romans 8), and what a comfort that should be to the weakest of us.

It is impossible for you to hold out in your Christian life—but He can hold you. It is very difficult for Him to hold you if you are struggling, fighting, and striving. Just relax and rest in the Lord. Let go all those inner tensions and complexes. Rely completely on Him. Do not fret and worry about important decisions—let Him make them for you. Do not worry about tomorrow—He is the God of tomorrow, He sees the end from the beginning. Do not worry about the necessities of life—He is there to supply and provide. A true victorious Christian is one who, in spite of worries, inner conflicts, and tensions, is confident that God is in control and will be victorious in the end. In reliance on the Holy Spirit, you will find that many of your physical and mental ailments will disappear along with many worries, inner conflicts and tensions. Whatever our difficulties, whatever our circumstances, we must remember, as Corrie ten Boom used to say, "Jesus is victor!"

Attend Church Regularly

Fourth: *attend church regularly.* Christianity is a religion of fellowship. Following Christ means love, righteousness, service; and these can only be achieved and expressed through social relations. These social relationships are to be found in the church.

There is a visible church and there is an invisible church. The invisible church is made up of true believers down through the centuries and the world over. The visible church is made up of both Catholic and Protestant—the latter with its various denominations. But we are told in the Scriptures, "Forsaking (not) the assembling of ourselves together . . ." (Hebrews 10:25). Christians need fellowship—the fellowship of fellow believers.

The visible church is Christ's organization upon earth. It is a place where we gather to worship God, learn from His Word, and fellowship with other Christians. The Bible calls the church "a holy nation," "God's own people," "the household of God," "a holy temple in the Lord," "a dwelling place of God in the Spirit," "the body of Christ." These are all figures of speech, symbols, or pictures used to indicate the spiritual reality of the church.

Nothing can take the place of church attendance. If you are a true follower of Christ you will scorn such flimsy excuses as the weather being too hot or too cold, rain or snow, as unworthy of a true follower of Christ. There are many people who say they can stay at home on Sunday morning and worship God in their own minds. The person who does only this fails to give God the complete worship to which He has a right, for God is the Creator of our bodies, no less than of our minds and souls; therefore both the mind and the body should participate in rendering to God a complete act of worship.

In certain countries today, however, church gatherings are not encouraged. For years people have been forced to meet privately in homes, perhaps just a single family or perhaps a few Christian friends gathering together. In the Peoples Republic of China, for example, the government has reopened some of the old churches. The packed buildings prove that what I have said above is true. Christians need one another, we need to gather together to worship God and nothing can take the place of church attendance.

At the same time I think we should be grateful for the electronic church. There are many in hospitals, institutions, like old people's homes, or even prisons where the only way they have to attend a church service is by television or even radio.

On the other hand, there are many who claim they can stay at home and listen to a sermon on the radio or television and that this takes the place of a church service. That is not enough. You do not go to church to hear a sermon. You go to church to worship God and to serve Him in the fellowship of other Christians. You cannot be a successful and happy Christian without being faithful in church. In the church you will find your place of service. We are saved to serve. The happy Christian is the serving Christian.

Be a Witnessing Christian

Fifth: *be a witnessing Christian.* If you are faithfully practicing the four preceding rules this one will take care of itself—just as it follows naturally that if a cup is being filled continually it is bound to overflow.

Sometime ago I came across the question, which is more important, to witness by one's life or to witness by the Word? And the answer was, "Which is more important, the left or right wing of an airplane?" Thinking this very clever, I repeated it one day in a car as I was driving some missionaries out to lunch. One of them spoke up and said, "That's very clever. But it's just not true." Surprised, I asked what she meant. "All the way through the Scriptures," she replied, "God has promised to bless His Word, not our lives: 'My Word shall not return unto me void but shall accomplish . . . He that hath my word let him preach my word faithfully, for what are the tares to the wheat, saith the Lord.'" I realized she was speaking the truth. We are responsible to God for the way in which we live but it is His Word that He has promised to bless and this explains why a musician in a communist country can pick up a page torn from the Bible and be converted. That is why a surgeon general in Portugal, returning home on a muddy day and finding a piece of paper stuck to his shoe, can pull it off and read a portion of the Word of God and be converted.

We Christians are now duly appointed and commissioned ambassadors of the King of kings. We are to let our flag fly high over our embassy. Suppose our ambassador to Russia should order the American flag pulled down because it is not popular in Russia—we would soon call him home! He would not deserve to represent the United States.

If we are not willing to let our flags fly in the home, in the office, in the shop, on the campus—then we are not worthy to be ambassadors for Christ! We are to take our stand and let all those around us know that we are Christians. We are to bear witness for Christ.

We witness in two ways: by life and by word—and the two, where possible, should go hand in hand. God's purpose for you and me after we have been converted is that we be witnesses to His saving grace and power. We are to be commandos for Christ. We are to be minute-men for Him.

Christ said, "Whoever therefore shall confess me before men, him will I confess also before my Father which is in heaven" (Matthew 10:32). Acts 28:23 presents a thrilling scene. Paul, held in bonds at Rome, persuaded men concerning Jesus, from morning to evening. Concerning each of us it should be said every day, "Behold a sower went forth to sow."

Very little originality is permitted a Western Union messenger boy. His sole obligation is to carry the message he receives from the office to the person to whom it is addressed. He may not like to carry that message. It may contain bad news or distressing news for the person to whom he carries it. He cannot stop on the way, open the envelope, and change the wording of the telegram. His duty is to take the message.

We Christians have the Word of God. Our Great Commander has said, "Go, and take this message to a dying world." Some are neglecting it. Some are tearing up the message and substituting one of their own. Some are taking out a part of it. Some are telling the people that the Lord does not mean what He says. Others are saying that He really did not write the message but that it was written by ordinary men who are mistaken about the meaning of it.

Let us remember that the apostle Paul exhorted the Christians centuries ago to teach only the Word. Remember we are sowing seed. Some indeed may fall on beaten paths and some among thorns, but it is our business to keep on sowing. We are not to stop sowing because some of the soil looks unpromising.

We are holding a light. We are to let it shine! Though it may seem but a twinkling candle in a world of blackness, it is our business to let it shine.

We are blowing a trumpet. In the din and noise of battle the sound of our little trumpet may seem to be lost, but we must keep sounding the alarm to those who are in danger.

We are kindling a fire. In this cold world full of hatred and selfishness our little blaze may seem to be unavailing, but we must keep our fire burning.

We are striking with a hammer. The blows may seem only to jar our hands as we strike, but we are to keep on hammering. Amy Carmichael of India once asked a stonecutter which blow broke the stone. "The first one and the last," he replied, "and every one in between."

We have bread for a hungry world. The people may seem to be so busy feeding on other things that they will not accept the Bread of Life, but we must keep on giving it, offering it to the souls of men.

We have water for famishing people. We must keep standing and crying out, "Ho, every one that thirsteth, come ye to the waters." Sometimes they can't come and we must carry it to them.

We must persevere. We must never give up. Keep using the Word!

Jesus said that much of our seed will find good soil and spring up and bear fruit. We must be faithful witnesses. The most thrilling experience known to man is to win another to Jesus Christ. It has been my privilege to win others to a saving knowledge of Christ. I never cease to thrill at hearing of one who has listened, accepted Christ, and been transformed by His grace. This is worth more than all the money in all the world. There is no happiness, no experience, no romantic adventure comparable to the thrill of winning another person to Christ.

The Bible says, "He that winneth souls is wise" (Proverbs 11:30). "And they that be wise shall shine as the brightness of the firmament; and they that turn many to righteousness as the stars for ever and ever" (Daniel 12:3).

"Ye are the salt of the earth" (Matthew 5:13). Salt makes one thirsty. Does your life make others thirsty for the water of life?

Let Us Love

Sixth: *let love be the ruling principle of your life. Be ruled by love.* Jesus said to those who followed Him, "By this shall all men know that ye are my disciples, if ye have love one to another." In another part of the Bible we find the same thing stated: "Beloved, let us love one another, for love is of God; and every one that loveth is born of God, and knoweth God. He that loveth not knoweth not God, for God is love. In this was manifested the love of God toward us, because that God sent his only begotten Son into the world, that we might live through him. Herein is love, not that we loved God, but that he loved us, and sent his Son to be the propitiation for our sins" (1 John 4:7–10). Love does not necessarily imply approval of the one loved. If God had waited until He could approve of us before He sent His Son to redeem us, where would we be?

Of all the gifts God offers His children, love is the greatest. Of all the fruits of the Holy Spirit, love is the first.

The Bible declares that we who follow Christ should love one another as God loved us when He sent His Son to die on the cross. The Bible says that the moment we come to Christ He gives us supernatural love, and that His love is shed abroad in our hearts by the Holy Spirit. The greatest demonstration of the fact that we are Christians is that we love one another. If we learn this secret of God early in our Christian experience, we will have gone a long way toward a mature, happy Christian life.

Be an Obedient Christian

Seventh: *be an obedient Christian.* Let Christ have first place in all the choices of your life. Make Him Lord and Master.

Learn How to Meet Temptation

Eighth: *learn how to meet temptation.* As we have already learned, temptation is natural. Temptation is not sin. It is *yielding* that is sin. God never brings temptation to us. He allows it to test us. It is the work of the devil. Recognize it as such. One way to meet temptation is to quote a verse of Scripture at the Tempter—he will always run, for he cannot stand the Word of God.

When Jesus was tempted in the wilderness, the only resource that He had was the Word of God. He said three times, "It is written."

Say to the devil, "Thus saith the Lord," and he will flee. At the same time let Christ through the Holy Spirit do the fighting for you. Be like the little girl who said, "Every time I hear the devil knock, I send Jesus to the door."

Everyone has temptations but some folks entertain them. They seem to enjoy being tempted. Chase a mouse with a broom and you will notice that he isn't eyeing the broom. He is looking for a hole. Get your eyes off the temptation and onto Christ!

I once asked an army officer which he would rather have on the field of battle—courage or obedience. He flashed right back, "Obedience!"

God would rather have your obedience than anything else. In order to be obedient you must know His commands. That is another reason for the necessity of studying and reading the Bible. The Bible is your compass and rule book. Obey what God tells you.

Be a Wholesome Christian

Ninth: *be a wholesome Christian.* It has been well said that "Some Christians are so heavenly minded they are no earthly good."

Certainly the Bible teaches separation from sin, but the Bible says nowhere that we are to be peculiar or unnatural. We are to be radiant. We should be chivalrous, courteous, clean of body, pure of mind, poised, and gracious. Silly flirtations, unhealthy gossip, shady conversations, suggestive amusements should be avoided like rattlesnakes. We should be neat in appearance, clean, attractive, and as much as possible in style, with good taste. Extremes should be avoided. Our lives and appearance should commend the gospel and make it attractive to others. As the late Dr. Barnhouse once said, "Men may not read the gospel in sealskin, or the gospel in morocco, or the gospel in cloth covers; but they can't get away from the gospel in shoe leather."

Live Above Your Circumstances

Tenth: *live above your circumstances*. God made you as you are! He placed you where you are! So you can best serve and glorify Him just as you are, where you are. Some people are always looking on the other side of the fence because they think the grass is greener. They spend so much time wishing things were different, and thinking up alibis for why they are not, that they overlook all the advantages and opportunities open to them right where they are.

Be as the apostle Paul when he said, "But none of these things move me" (Acts 20:24). Paul said he had learned how to abound and how to be abased. He had learned to be every inch a Christian even in prison. Don't let your circumstances get you down. Learn to live graciously within them, realizing the Lord Himself is with you.

These principles and suggestions may seem simple—but keep them—they work. I have seen them tested in the lives of thousands. I have tested them in my own life. Properly and faithfully kept, they will give you peace of soul, happiness, peace of mind, and pleasure, and you will have learned the secret of living life with satisfaction.

16

The Christian
and the Church

In whom ye also are builded together for an habitation of God through the Spirit.
EPHESIANS 2:22

MAN IS A social animal, gregarious by nature, and finds his greatest sense of security and satisfaction in the company of others who share his interests and attitudes. Of all the many groups into which humans have collected themselves, of all the many tribes, clans, organizations, and societies throughout history, none has been so powerful, so far-reaching, or more universal than the church.

In primitive times, men gathered together for mutual protection, and at a far later date they learned to join together for mutual benefit and pleasure. With more advanced civilization, secret societies came into being, to give their members a sense of belonging, a feeling of being "set apart" and therefore distinguished from nonmembers. Special oaths, rituals, and codes were established and given great significance.

Racial and national groups were established with membership restricted to those of similar place of origin, or with allegiance to a common flag. Country clubs, college fraternities, lodges, literary societies, political parties, military organizations—all of these, from the most select "gentlemen's club" to the high school "gang," represent man's need to find comfort and reassurance in the company of others who approve of his way of life, because their own way of life is similar.

Nowhere, however, has man found this comfort, this reassurance, this peace to the extent that he has found it in the church, for all other groups are obviously man-inspired. They draw artificial boundaries and set up only the illusion of protection; while the church provides a living, vibrant organism that draws its power from God Himself, instead of relying upon outside sources to give it meaning and vitality.

Origin of the Church

The word *church* is an English translation of the Greek word *ecclesia*, which means "the called-out ones," or an assembly of people. Although *church* soon became a distinctively Christian word, it has a pre-Christian history. Throughout the Greek world the word *church* was the designation of the regular assembly of the whole body of citizens in a free city-state. A group of the citizens would be called out by the herald for the discussion and decision of public business. This same word *church* was also the Hebrew equivalent in the Old Testament and is translated in English as "congregation" or "community" of Israel in which members were designated as the called-out people of God. Thus we find Stephen in the Book of Acts using it when he describes Moses as "he that was in the church in the wilderness" (Acts 7:38). In the first century, therefore, the word *church* would suggest to the Greek a self-governing, democratic society; to the Jew, a theocratic society whose members were the subjects of God.

The word *church* as applied to the Christian society was first used by Jesus Himself when He told Peter, "Upon this rock I will build my church, and the gates of hell shall not prevail against it" (Matthew 16:18). Thus Jesus Christ Himself founded the church. He is the great cornerstone upon which the church is built. He is the foundation of all Christian experience, and the church is founded upon Him. "For other foundation can no man lay than that is laid, which is Jesus Christ" (1 Corinthians 3:11). Jesus proclaimed Himself to be the founder of the church, the builder of the church, and the church belongs to Him and to Him alone. He has promised to live with, and in, all those who are members of His church. Here is not only an organization but an organism which is completely unlike anything else that the world has ever known: God Himself living with, and in, ordinary men and women who are members of His church.

Jesus Christ Its Head

The New Testament teaches that while there is actually only one universal church there can be any number of local churches formed into various denominations and societies or councils. These local churches and denominational groups may be divided along national and theological lines, or according to the temperament of their members. However, the New Testament teaches that even though there may be many cleavages and divisions within the structure of the church, yet we have only "one Lord." As the hymn puts it, "The church's one foundation is Jesus Christ her Lord."

Jesus Christ is the head of this great universal church. From Him must spring all the activities and teachings of the church, for He is the fountainhead of all Christian experience.

In this day of electronics it is easy to draw a comparison with a far-flung communications system in which there is one central station toward which all light or sound waves converge and from which all connections are made. In a railroad system there is always one central office from which orders governing the operations of all trains originate. In the army, one commanding general issues orders to the many groups under his jurisdiction. His various subordinates may interpret his orders in slightly different ways, but his orders still remain the basis for their conduct.

In relation to the church, Jesus Christ stands in the position of the commanding general. It is upon His orders that the church has its existence. Its very power comes directly from Him, and it is up to every church group to follow His commands as closely as possible. Just as the commanding general expects to have his orders carried out faithfully, so does Jesus expect every branch of the church to abide by His teachings to the fullest.

The church has been widely criticized for many internal squabbles, much hair-splitting and apparent lack of unity. These, however, are superficial things; these are the conflicts that come from the slightly varying interpretations of the general's orders and in no way reflect upon the wisdom of the general or His absolute authority in issuing His orders!

Study the underlying beliefs of the various denominations and you will find that basically and historically they are almost identical. They may differ widely in ritual, they may seem to lock horns over theological technicalities; but fundamentally they all recognize Jesus Christ as God incarnate, who died upon the cross and rose again that man might have salvation—and that is the all-important fact to all humanity.

The Church—or Churches?

Now that you have accepted Christ as your Savior and put your trust and confidence in Him, you have already become a member of the great church invisible. You are a member of the household of faith. You are a part of the body of Christ. Now you are called upon to obey Christ, and if you obey Christ, you will follow His example of joining with others in the worship of God. "Not forsaking the assembling of ourselves together, as the manner of some is" (Hebrews 10:25).

It is true that we are now talking about the local church, the one in your own community, of whose many imperfections and shortcomings you may be well aware. But we must remember that perfection does not exist among human beings, and the institutions they create to the greater glory of God are filled with these self-same flaws. Jesus is the only perfect Man who ever lived. The rest of us are at best but repentant sinners, try as we may to follow His magnificent example; and the church is but turning a blind eye toward itself when it claims infallibility or perfection for itself or any of its members.

Samuel Rutherford at one point received a complaint from some church members who were unhappy with their pastor and the local church situation. He wrote them a very stern reply, telling them that they were not responsible for the life of their pastor. But they were responsible to pray for him, and to remain in the church, and to work for the Lord. And that the Lord would honor and bless them for it.

The Tabernacle under Eli had degenerated so terribly that the people despised the sacrifice of the Lord because Eli's "sons made themselves vile, and he restrained them not" (1 Samuel 3:13). But little Samuel was left in that environment and grew up to be a great prophet.

In the New Testament, it was the Temple leaders who had Christ crucified, yet after His resurrection and ascension, the disciples were "continually in the temple, praising and blessing God" (Luke 24:53).

When Jesus founded the church, He intended His followers to join it and remain faithful to it. Today, if you are among the more than fifty percent of the population of this country who have no active formal church affiliation, you may stand in bewilderment before the number whose membership is open to you. In selecting one you may well have a natural tendency to return to the church of your childhood, or you may feel you want to make a choice based on your more spiritually mature judgment. A church affiliation is not something to be entered into lightly, for if the church is to be of the greatest service to you, and even more important, if it is to give you the greatest possible opportunity to be of service to others, you must prayerfully select the one where you feel you can be of the most service to God.

A Church for Everyone

Some people find it easier to draw closer to God in magnificent buildings and with some form of ritual. Others find they can seek God only in stark simplicity. Some people find themselves more comfortable with formality, others feel more at home with informality. The important thing is not *how* we do it, but the sincerity and depth of purpose *with which* we do it, and we should each find and join the church in which as individuals we can best accomplish this.

Do not make the mistake of attaching yourself to a particular minister rather than to the body of the church itself. The ministry may change—it is healthy and stimulating that it should—but the tenets of the church remain the same, and it is to the church and its Christ that you owe allegiance. A stable church is built up when the members of the congregation recognize that it is their mutual love of Jesus Christ and the sincere desire to follow in His steps that hold them together.

The true Christian goes to church not only for what he gets out of it, but also for what he can put into it. He goes to add his prayers to those of others, he goes to add his voice to the other voices raised in praise of the Lord, he goes to add his strength in beseeching the Lord's blessing, he goes to add his weight of testimony to the possibility of salvation through the Lord Jesus Christ. He goes to join with others in the worship of God, in the contemplation of His boundless mercy and love. He also goes for the necessary companionship of fellow believers.

Christians who are not actively involved in the life of a local church remind me of what happens when a burning coal is removed from the fire. You've seen it happen. The coal gradually cools and its flame dies, once it is removed from the bed of glowing coals.

In the far west, when the wolves attack a flock of sheep, the first thing they do is try to scatter them, and then they close in for the kill on one of the isolated sheep.

The Church Is a Channel

The church should be the means of channeling your funds for Christian work and the needs of fellow Christians. The Bible teaches tithing. A tithe is one tenth of your net income. That one tenth of your income belongs to the Lord. In addition to your tithe, you should give as the Lord has prospered you. Giving is a Christian grace that should be woven into the fabric of our daily lives until it becomes a part no longer distinguishable from the rest. Generosity should motivate us in all things.

Christ said, "It is more blessed to give than to receive" (Acts 20:35). He knew how giving warms the heart and satisfies the soul. He coveted for you that particular blessing. Selfishness is caused by fear—and a Christian should stand forth unafraid. Jesus stood always with hands that were open—not with hands that were clenched tight with selfishness and greed. As far as possible, one should give inconspicuously and quietly. Jesus also said that when we are giving, ". . . let not thy left hand know what thy right hand doeth" (Matthew 6:3).

Giving cannot be measured in dollars and cents, it cannot be measured in boxes of old clothes. Sometimes the greatest gift is the gift of friendship and neighborliness. A kind word, a friendly greeting, an evening spent with someone who is lonely can reap rich harvest for the kingdom of God. It is impossible for you to become a soul winner unless you are prepared to give something of yourself. Not only your money, but your time, your talents, your very self—everything is to be given to the service of Christ.

The giving of your offering which is above the tithe should not be limited by set rules or organized methods. It should be governed by the need that is brought to your attention according to the rules set down by Christ in Matthew 6:1–4. It might be a neighbor, the newsboy who brings the daily paper, or someone in far-off Africa or South America. Our giving is the expression of our love for God. We give back to Him in return for the great love He has bestowed on us, and in that way we spread His love abroad.

The Christian should also share in community responsibilities as time and money allow. The people to whom the money is given should know that you are giving it in the name of Christ. The letter accompanying the financial gift to the social or charitable organization should say something like, "As a Christian, believing the Lord would have me assist my community as I am able, I send this gift. God bless your efforts."

Be careful that you do not become guilty of the sin of robbing God. The Bible says, "Bring ye all the tithes into the storehouse, that there may be meat in mine house, and prove me now herewith, saith the Lord of hosts, if I will not open you the windows of heaven, and pour you out a blessing, that there shall not be room enough to receive it" (Malachi 3:10).

Dr. Louis Evans has said, "The gospel is free, but it costs money to provide the pails in which to carry the water of salvation."

The act of giving is just as much an act of worship as praying or singing. The United States Government now allows individuals to give up to fifty percent of adjusted gross income to charitable institutions and/or religious organizations. It is deductible from our income tax, and yet it is estimated that less than ten percent of the American people take advantage of this. Corporations are allowed to give up to ten percent and yet only about fifteen percent of them are taking advantage of this provision of the government. Yet even if our government made no such allowance, ten percent still *belongs* to God.

The Church Spreads the Gospel

The church is for the spreading of the gospel. The church is commanded to "Go ye into all the world, and preach the gospel," and to baptize those who believe. The basic and primary mission of the church is to proclaim Christ to the lost. The need of the world today is sending forth its S.O.S., asking the church to come to its help. The world is being overwhelmed by social, moral, and economic problems. Its people are going down, swept under the waves of crime and shame. The world needs Christ. The mission of the church is to throw the lifeline to the perishing sinners everywhere.

Jesus said, "Ye shall receive power, after that the Holy Ghost is come upon you: and ye shall be witnesses unto me" (Acts 1:8). With the power of the Holy Spirit we can join hands with other Christians to win people to Christ. Sixty-five percent of the world has yet to hear the gospel of Jesus Christ. In this generation we have failed miserably to fulfill our mission to evangelize the world. According to the Wycliffe Bible translators, there are still more than three thousand languages and dialects into which the Bible has not been translated.

The early church had no Bibles, no seminaries, no printing presses, no literature, no educational institutions, no radio, no television, no automobiles, no airplanes; and yet within one generation the gospel had been spread to most of the known world. The secret of the spread of this gospel was the power of the Holy Spirit.

Today in the face of vastly improved methods of communication the power of the Holy Spirit is the same. We need not do things in our own strength, and as a result, fail.

Today the only feet that Christ has are our feet. The only hands, our hands. The only tongues, our tongues. We must use every talent, facility, and method possible to win men to Christ. This is the great mission of the church. Our methods may vary. We may use visitation evangelism, educational evangelism, preaching missions, industrial evangelism, cell evangelism, radio-television evangelism, movie evangelism, or so-called mass evangelism.

I am aware today that in many parts of the world the church is outlawed, discredited, and at times virtually destroyed. Yet again and again it has been proven "The blood of the martyrs is the seed of the church." And God's church is a Bible-centered church, and it grows strong under persecution. "Where two or three are gathered, there am I in the midst of them" has become literally true in some parts of the world. In such places where believers in Christ live in abject poverty, they still tithe. And when one member suffers, the others come to that one's aid. Unable to preach openly, they look for opportunities to witness by life. So, for instance, when one is punished harshly for some unjust reason and bears it cheerfully, a curious observer will slip up to him and say, "I saw that. It was unfair. And yet you remain cheerful." And the Christian has the opportunity to share his faith in Christ.

So even where Christ's church suffers, she grows. What a challenge to us to do likewise!

17

Am I My Brother's Keeper?

And forgive us our debts, as we forgive our debtors. MATTHEW 6:12

SINCE YOU HAVE made your decision for Christ and have begun studying the Bible, you find yourself confronted with various social obligations and problems. You have made your peace with God. You are no longer at war and at enmity with God. Sin has been forgiven. You have new horizons for your thinking—new perspectives for your life. The whole world has changed. You now begin to see others through the eyes of Jesus. Old ideas and ideals have changed. Prejudices that you once held are beginning to slip away. Selfishness that was once characteristic of you in many areas of your life has now disappeared. Suddenly you understand what the little story means: Someone asked, "Am I my brother's keeper?" And the reply came, "No, I am my brother's *brother.*"

Many people have refused the Christian life because it has been presented to them in its negative rather than its positive aspect. They say that Christian conduct is against everything pleasant and profitable. They say Christians are like the woman who complained that everything worth doing in this life was either immoral, illegal, or fattening!

Contrary to worldly belief, being a true Christian does not mean the forfeiting of all real pleasure. Only sinful pleasure that has been forbidden by God is to be given up. The full acceptance of Christ and the determination to be guided by God's will draws you almost immediately to the source of the only true pleasure—which is fellowship with Christ. To you who have *not* been born again this may seem a far cry from pleasure, but those who have actually experienced daily fellowship with Christ know that it surpasses all worldly activities.

In his introduction to his anthology on George MacDonald, C. S. Lewis writes, "He seems to have been a . . . playful man, deeply appreciative of all the really beautiful and delicious things that money can buy and no less deeply content to do without them."

George MacDonald himself wrote: "I would, if I may, be ever greeted in my study in winter by a glowing hearth, and in the summer by a bowl of flowers. But if not, then let me think how nice they would have been and let me bury myself in my work. I do not think that contentment lies in despising what you have not got."

Even as the psalmist says, "They shall be abundantly satisfied with the fatness of thy house; and thou shalt make them drink of the river of thy pleasures" (Psalm 36:8). God has also said, "No good thing will he withhold from them that walk uprightly" (Psalm 84:11). Paul said that "[God has] given us richly all things to enjoy" (1 Timothy 6:17).

The fact that we have daily fellowship with Christ should enable us to live realistically. Christ's way of life does not require that a man renounce legitimate interests or ambitions. Though the Scriptures may teach that Christ may return at any time, the Scripture also exhorts us to carry on business as usual until He comes.

For example, there was nothing wrong about the eating, drinking, marrying, and giving in marriage in Noah's day except that the people had become totally preoccupied with these activities to the neglect of the spiritual dimension of life (Luke 17:27). Nor was there anything wrong about the buying, selling, planning, and building in Lot's day except that they were carried on by sinful methods (Luke 17:28). What seems to have been fundamentally wrong in the days of Noah and Lot was that men made these the sole interest of their lives. They thought of nothing but their personal pleasures, their personal property, and the material profits they were amassing. They became so absorbed in the things of this life that they had no time for God. This was displeasing to God and He visited the offenders with judgment.

As someone has said, "The Bible was not written to encourage people to take an interest in the affairs of this life. It *assumes* that they already have more than their share of interest in that. The Bible aims to encourage man to see his worldly affairs in the light of the greater importance and value of spiritual things."

The Bible teaches that we are to perform our daily tasks and that we are to take pride in performing them well. We were put here on earth and given certain work to do, and those who claim to be Christians are taught not only to labor but to labor to the best of their ability.

The Bible speaks approvingly of Bezaleel as a worker in metals, stone, and wood. He was filled with the Holy Spirit for *craftsmanship:* "And I have filled him with the spirit of God, in wisdom, and in understanding, and in knowledge, and in all manner of workmanship . . . to work in gold, and in silver, and in brass, and in cutting of stones, to set them, and in carving of timber, to work all manner of workmanship" (Exodus 31:3–5). Jacob and his sons were shepherds. Joseph was a prime minister. Daniel was a statesman. Both Joseph and Jesus were carpenters, and some of the disciples were fishermen. We are told of the Ethiopian eunuch who was treasurer under Candace; of Lydia, the seller of purple; of Paul, Priscilla, and Aquila who were tentmakers; and Luke, the beloved physician.

The Christian ideal certainly does not demand that a person renounce all interest in the affairs of this life; but rather that we seek God's guidance in performing our daily work to the best of our ability, and that we keep both our work and our ambitions in subordination to the Lord at all times. Thus we find that Christ offers positive help in our daily living here on earth. He inspires us in our gifts, helps us in our work, and blesses us in our pleasure.

In one of his delightful essays, F. W. Boreham, quoting Isaiah, goes on to recount how the carpenter of Nazareth has encouraged the goldsmiths of the ages. The world's greatest writers have been inspired by Jesus of Nazareth, the greatest artists, musicians, and sculptors have also been illumined by Him.

He also helps in facing the social problems that confront us and it is here that we may become confused. For it is in our daily tasks and in the way we face the social problems around us that the world will see Christ in us.

As my father-in-law, the late Dr. L. Nelson Bell, once wrote in the *Southern Presbyterian Journal*, "If you are in church on Sunday the people who see you there may *presume* that you are a Christian. But what about the people with whom you come in contact during the week on the street, in your office, in your store, and the multiple places where you make these inevitable daily contacts? Orthodox Christian profession has its place. Attendance at, and active participation in, the program and activities of the church are an inescapable part of Christian living. But as we all know, the business of making a living, the responsibilities of a home, the daily routine all combine to test the reality of our Christian experience and faith. In these daily contacts what do others see? Can our week-day associates tell that we are Christians? Do casual acquaintances see anything in us to suggest that we are different from those who do not know Christ? Certainly one of the real tests of Christian character is to be found in the lives we live from day to day.

"The reality of our Christian profession is shown in many ways: the things we say, as well as the things we do not say; the things we do, as well as the things we do not do. For while Christianity is not primarily a matter of externals, nevertheless it does find expression in conversation, habits, recreation, emphasis, and ambitions to be noted in our daily life. Does our conversation honor Christ? Are our habits those of which He approves? Are our sources of recreation those in which His presence can be a part? Do we bow our heads in a word of thanks when eating in a public place? Can people tell from the emphasis we attach to material things whether we have set our affection on things above, or whether we are primarily attached to this world? Do people see in us an ambition for place and position out of accord with that of a Christian? We should ask ourselves these and many other questions, for in such things men judge whether we are Christians or not."

Some time after my father-in-law's death, my wife hired a man to help with some road work on our mountain property. One day, on the way to town, she stopped to speak to him. Suddenly he asked, "Is you Dr. Bell's daughter?" She admitted she was, whereupon the man exclaimed with deep appreciation, "Law! He was the awfullest Christian I ever knowed!"

What is our attitude toward those of other races? What is our attitude toward sex? What is our attitude toward the labor-management problems? What is our attitude toward the abortion issue, sexual deviation as an acceptable alternate lifestyle, drug and alcohol abuse and the problems inherent in them? All of these are very real and practical questions that must be answered, interpreted, and lived before our fellow men.

The guiding principle of our relation to the world about us should be, as Jesus said, "And as ye would that men should do to you, do ye also to them likewise" (Luke 6:31).

Many people have criticized the so-called "social gospel," but Jesus taught that we are to take the gospel to the world. Actually there is no such thing as a "social gospel." It is a misnomer. There is only one gospel. "If any man preach any other gospel to you, let him be accursed" (Galatians 1:9). At the same time, in 1 Timothy 5:8 we are told, "If any provide not for his own, and especially for those of his own house, he hath denied the faith, and is worse than an infidel." What a relief to the federal government if Christians made themselves responsible for the needs of their own!

My son, Franklin, is deeply involved in social work, heading up a Christian relief agency. In a recent interview he was quoted as saying that "proclaiming the gospel must always have priority." He urged evangelical relief and development agencies not to lose sight of the need to reach people for Christ. "The gospel—not development—is the Christian's mandate," he said.

The cup of cold water comes *after* and sometimes *before* rather than *instead of* the gospel. Christians, above all others, should be concerned with social problems and social injustices. Down through the centuries the church has contributed more than any other single agency in lifting social standards to new heights. Child labor has been outlawed. Slavery has been abolished in Britain, the U.S.A., and some other parts of the world. The status of women has been lifted to heights unparalleled in history, and many other reforms have taken place primarily as a result of the influence of the teachings of Jesus Christ. The Christian is to take his place in society with moral courage to stand up for that which is right, just, and honorable.

Be a Good Citizen

First: *the Christian should be a good citizen.* The Bible teaches that the Christian should be law-abiding. The Bible also teaches loyalty to country. A loyalty and love of country does not mean that we cannot criticize unjust laws. The Bible says that God is no respecter of persons. All should have equal opportunities. The government of God should be our model.

The Bible also teaches that we are to cooperate with the government. The apostle Paul exhorted Timothy to "... supplications, prayers, intercessions ... for all men; for kings, and for all that are in authority ..." (1 Timothy 2:1, 2). Jesus was asked, "Is it lawful to give tribute?" Then He set the example forever by paying taxes. It takes money to run a government and to maintain law and order. The tax dodger is a civic parasite and an actual thief. No true Christian will be a tax dodger. Jesus said, we are to "render to Caesar the things that are Caesar's" (Mark 12:17). We ought to be more than taxpayers. To be simply law-abiding is not enough. We ought to seek and work for the good of our country. Sometimes we may be called upon to die for it. We are to be conscientious in our work as good citizens.

We should be generous and give to those who are in need and to those organizations who are faithfully and honestly ministering to those in need. We should enter into various activities such as the Red Cross, the Salvation Army, World Vision, Samaritan's Purse, the Tear Fund, and other good, constructive, and helping-hand organizations. At the same time, as responsible stewards we are to check our various organizations for trustworthiness and honesty, and also to find if the relief given certain governments is given where designated.

Christians should be interested in orphanages, hospitals, asylums, prisons, and all social institutions. Jesus said, "Love thy neighbor as thyself" (Matthew 22:39). Think of a country without any philanthropic enterprises whatever! No one would want to live in it.

I recall visiting a country in which there were both government and Christian homes for the elderly. In the Christian home we saw love in action, but in the government home the care was impersonal and perfunctory. The doctor who served both homes said that the people in the Christian home were not only happier but lived longer. We want to live where neighborly love prevails. We are to take our place in the community. Those in positions of responsibility are entitled to respect, support, and cooperation. "Let every soul be subject unto the higher powers. For there is no power but of God: the powers that be are ordained of God" (Romans 13:1).

Be Hospitable

Second: *Christians should he "given to hospitality"* (1 Timothy 3:2). The Bible teaches that our homes should be hospitable and that those who come in and out of our homes should sense the presence of Christ. The happiest Christian homes I know are those given to hospitality, where neighbors feel at home, where young people are welcome, where the elderly are respected, where children are loved. That which God has given to us should be shared with others. In doing so God will bless and prosper our homes.

A Proper View of Sex

Third: *we should have the Christian attitude toward sex.* Nowhere does the Bible teach that sex in itself is a sin, although many interpreters of the Bible would try to make it appear so. The Bible teaches that the *wrong use* of sex is sinful. For sex, the act by which all life on this earth is created, should be a wonderful, meaningful, and satisfying human experience.

Man, with his vile, self-destructive nature, however, has taken what was intended to be the most glorious and complete act of love between two people and made of it something low and cheap and filthy. Sex, stripped of total commitment, of mutual love, respect, and the sincere desire to give joy and fulfillment to the other person, becomes simply an animal act, about which the Bible warns us in no uncertain terms!

It is significant that the Bible is one of the world's most outspoken books on the subject of sex. It does not try to gloss over sex in either its right or wrong aspects. The sly, secret, embarrassed, "let's-pretend-it-doesn't-exist" attitude about sex is purely man-made.

In trying to overcome the mysterious, "let's-not-talk-about-it" approach to sex, our present civilization has put far too much emphasis on the mechanics of it, and far too little insistence on the spiritual atmosphere in which this overwhelming expression of human love must have its origin.

Our divorce courts bear tragic testimony to the inability of men and women to achieve this lasting and ever more beautiful relationship without a firm foundation of spiritual values.

Sex is a part of life that we cannot abolish, even if we would, for without it all life would cease. For sex, the act by which all life on this earth is perpetuated, should be a wonderful and meaningful human experience. Used rightly it can bring joy into the home. Used wrongly it can make it a hell. Use it wisely and it will become a wonderful servant. Use it wrongly and it will be a terrible taskmaster.

Christians feel a sense of outrage, a sense of violation, when they see sex emblazoned in newspaper headlines, exploited in advertisements, and used as a cheap lure outside theaters. They blush for their fellowmen that they can be so stupid, so gross, so indecent as to defile and distort the act by which all God-given life is bestowed.

A Christian View of Marriage

Fourth: it follows naturally that *those who take a Christian view of sex will take a Christian view of marriage.* Before you enter into a marriage, consider the real spiritual implications that make an earthly marriage binding in heaven. Little by little as we grow toward maturity, we learn to love, first our parents and our friends, and later the one person who is to share our life. We have already seen how difficult this process is, for it is passion and not love that comes naturally to the unregenerate sinner.

Many have the terrible misfortune of selecting their mates while they are still in the toils of the world, the flesh, and the devil, and while the man or woman they select is also still in the same condition. Is it any wonder then that so many marriages contracted by two spiritually ignorant souls, who most of the time are incapable of real and lasting love, end up in the divorce courts?

Marriage is a holy bond because it permits two people to help each other work out their spiritual destinies. God declared marriage to be good because He knew that man needed a helpmate and woman needed a protector. He desires that husbands and wives never lose sight of the original purpose of marriage. It is woman's role to love and help and reassure her husband in every way she can, and it is man's role to love and protect and provide for his wife and the children she bears, so that the home may be filled with God's peace and harmony. They are to submit to each other—to love each other.

Marriages entered into with a clear understanding of God's purpose and God's laws have no need for divorce courts. Marriages that fall short of this ideal (and it is appalling how many of them do) should first seek to learn what God expects of the husband and the wife, and then pray for God's help and guidance in carrying out His commands.

A Christian Approach to Labor Management Problems

Fifth: *we are to take the Christian attitude in labor-management relationships.* The Bible says, "Whatever you do, put your whole heart and soul into it, as into work done for God, and not merely for men—knowing that your real reward, a heavenly one, will come from God, since you are actually employed by Christ, and not just by your earthly master. But the slacker and the thief will be judged by God Himself, Who naturally has no distinction to make between master and man. Remember, then, you employers, that your responsibility is to be fair and just towards those whom you employ, never forgetting that you yourselves have a Heavenly Employer" (Colossians 3:22–4:1, PHILLIPS).

If Christ could prevail in all labor-management relations we would rarely have strikes. There would not be these long drawn-out arguments in which both sides are unwilling to concede the rights of the other. Management would treat employees with generosity, and employees would be eager to put in a full day's work for their hire or what their contract calls for—for they would be working not only for wages. We can learn from the attitude of both employer and employees in Japan toward one another in this regard.

The Bible teaches that all honest work is honorable, and the Christian should be the most faithful, the most willing and efficient worker of all. He should stand out in a factory or shop as one who wants justice, but one who would not stoop to take unfair advantage.

By the same token, the Christian employer should treat his employees with a respect and generosity that will become an example for other employers. A man of real Christian concepts cannot help being concerned about safety precautions, good working conditions, and the well-being of those in his employ. He will not only see his workers as "man power," but also as human beings.

Both management and labor should remember that the improved conditions and better understanding they now enjoy had their beginnings as the result of a great spiritual revival. The heritage of labor unions comes from the church and the mighty Wesleyan revivals of the eighteenth century. Social liberty for the working classes began when a Christian leader, Lord Shaftesbury, in the face of bitter family opposition, led a lifelong crusade for better working conditions, shorter hours, more pay, and fair treatment for the working man.

Had it not been for the spiritual revival of the eighteenth century, the gains that labor has made might not have been achieved, or might have been delayed until much later in our history. When some labor leaders talk of outlawing religion, disregarding God, the Bible, and the church, they should remember how much of what they have today is due to the power of the gospel of Christ.

Some labor leaders, as well as industrialists, have grown haughty, proud, rich, self-satisfied, and power-seeking. All of them should humble themselves before God, seek to recognize the needs of each other, their extreme dependence on each other, and above all, try to apply the Golden Rule in its most practical and realistic sense.

A Christian View of Other Races

Sixth: *the Christian looks through the eyes of Christ at the race question* and admits that the church has only partially solved this great human problem. We have let the sports world, the entertainment field, politics, the armed forces, education and industry outstrip us. The church should have been the pace-setter. The church should voluntarily be doing what the federal courts in America are doing by pressure and compulsion. But in the final analysis the only real solution will be found at the foot of the cross where we come together in brotherly love. The closer the people of all races get to Christ and His cross, the closer they will get to one another.

The Bible says in Christ there is neither Jew nor Gentile, there is neither male nor female, neither Greek nor barbarian, neither rich nor poor. The Bible indicates that we are all one in Christ. The ground is level at the foot of the cross. When Christ opens our spiritual eyes we behold not color, nor class, nor condition, but simply human beings with the same longings, fears, needs, and aspirations as our own. We begin to see people through the Master's eyes. Become friends—invite them to your home.

A Christian View of Materialism

Seventh: *the Christian attitude should prevail in the matter of economics.* Jesus said a man's life does not consist in the abundance of the things which he possesses. Money is a good slave but a bad master. Property is to be used, enjoyed, shared, given, but not hoarded. Paul said that the *love* of money was the "root of all evil" (1 Timothy 6:10). Wealth has its place and its power, but it is not entitled to occupy the throne or swing the scepter. Covetousness puts money above manhood. It shackles its devotee and makes him its victim. It hardens the heart and deadens the noble impulses and destroys the vital qualities of life.

Beware of covetousness in every phase and form! All of us should keep ourselves from it through vigilance, prayer, self-control, and discipline. Life is not a matter of dollars and cents, houses and lands, earning capacity and financial achievement. Greed must not be allowed to make man the slave of wealth.

When Jesus was asked to settle an inheritance dispute between two brothers, He declined with a word of warning and with one of the magnificent parables with which He so frequently pointed out the earthly applications of heavenly messages. He told the story of the wealthy landowner, who in the midst of prosperity, envisioned even greater wealth and made long-range plans which would fill his life with all the physical comforts and personal glory that he held most dear. Apparently he was talented, economical, industrious, prudent, honest, and moral in all his dealings—but he was the victim of ambition and self-interest, as are so many others.

He measured his success in broad fields and full barns, and fed his soul on human vanities. His life was wrapped up in his riches and centered in himself, and he made his plans without thought of God or the uncertainty of life.

But God spoke the final word, and the plans that extended for years ahead were cut short by sudden death. The property he had amassed so painstakingly slipped through his cold fingers to be divided, scattered, and squandered by others, while he was left to stand before God with nothing to show for the life he had led on earth.

The Christian, above all others, should realize that we come into life with empty hands—and it is with empty hands that we leave it. Actually we can possess nothing—no property and no person—along the way. It is God who owns everything, and we are but stewards of His property during the brief time we are on earth. Everything that we see about us that we count as our possessions only comprises a loan from God, and it is when we lose sight of this all-pervading truth that we become greedy and covetous.

When we clutch an object or a person and say, "This thing is mine," when we look with envious eyes at what another person has and plan to "get it by fair means or foul," we are forgetting that no matter what we get, we can't take it with us when we go to make our final accounting before the seat of judgment.

This does not mean that earthly riches in themselves are a sin—the Bible does not say that. The Bible makes it clear that God expects us to do the best we can with the talents, the abilities, the situations with which life endows us. But there is a right way and a wrong way to acquire money and a right way and a wrong way to achieve power. Too many Christians have misunderstood this and taken a most sinful and damaging spiritual pride in being poverty-stricken, in standing by helplessly and saying, "God's will be done," as their children suffered and went untended. The apostle Paul said, "But if any provide not for his own, and especially for those of his own house, he hath denied the faith, and is worse than an infidel" (1 Timothy 5:8).

Jesus told one of His most revealing parables to illustrate this very point when He recited the story of the rich man who gave each of his servants a certain amount of money to invest while he was away in a far land. When he returned he found that some servants had made wise investments and his money was multiplied, and he praised them for their sound judgment and prudence; but the frightened, unimaginative servant who could think of nothing to do with the money but to hide it from thieves, he condemned.

Earn your money, as much as you can, according to God's laws, and spend it to carry out His commands. Give one tenth of it to the Lord, the firstfruits (Proverbs 3:9), tithe faithfully, for the Bible says that this is right and just. After you have given a tithe—gifts and offerings. Whenever you have any doubts about material values, get out your Bible and read what Jesus taught about money, read what He had to say about the earning of money and the use and distribution of wealth. Just ask yourself, "What would Jesus have done in this situation?" and be guided by that and that alone.

It was my privilege at one time to have among my close friends an extremely wealthy industrialist. One day as we were lunching together he calmly announced that the day before he had sold a certain product, his family clearing $13,000,000 on the deal. "But let me tell you what I discovered in the Scriptures this morning!" he exclaimed, changing the subject abruptly to his deepest interests. This man had his priorities in order.

A Christian View of Those Who Suffer

Eighth: *a Christian will be concerned about suffering humanity around him.* The great slum areas of your own country will become a burden to you. The poverty and suffering of thousands of people in your own neighborhood will become a concern to you. You will join with organizations and associations to help alleviate the suffering of humanity around you. Many people spend so much time in lofty enterprises that they make no contribution to suffering immediately at hand. Who is our neighbor? Whoever is closest to us. It could be a wife, a husband, a child, or those living next door. Our neighbor is that one closest to us—then in our city or country—then the world.

The Bible says, the common people heard Jesus gladly. Wherever He went, He healed the sick. He comforted the sorrowful, He gave practical encouragement. Years ago, an Anglican bishop told me that he could think of no social organization in England which did not have its roots in some evangelical awakening (including the SPCA!). The Christian will be interested in helping build and develop hospitals, orphanages, old people's homes, and other charitable institutions that are trying to help the less fortunate. The Christian will be interested in doing his part to help share the great wealth of this country with the needy in other parts of the world. He will be a supporter of reputable national or international social organizations helping the unfortunate of the world. A word of caution here. When we're giving God's money to an organization, it behooves us as good stewards to check out how this money is being spent. There are many responsible, worthwhile charitable ministries who deserve our support and prayers—there are others we should not support.

Nowhere in the Bible does it teach that we are to withdraw ourselves from society. Rather, it teaches quite the contrary. We are to join with others who are working to good purpose to help lift the unfortunate. God needs social workers, prison guards, policemen, doctors, hospital attendants, nurses, charity workers, and many other types of people who can help alleviate human suffering.

The motto of the Rotary Club is "Service above self." The motto of the Kiwanis Club is "We build." The motto of the Lions Club is "Liberty, intelligence, our nation's safety." All of these ideas originated in Christianity. Lots of the pagan religions never had a service club. All of these organizations are really by-products of Christianity even when some of their members are not Christians. The perfume of Christ is in the fragrance of any and all social service.

Love for the Brethren

Ninth: *the Christian has a special obligation to fellow Christians.* Fellow Christians are in a special class. We are to have *supernatural love* for them. "We know that we have passed from death unto life, because we love the brethren. He that loveth not his brother abideth in death" (1 John 3:14).

We are to love our enemies. We are even to love those who persecute us and say "all manner of evil against us, falsely" (Matthew 5:11).

But the greatest of our human love is for those other believers. Jesus said, "This is my commandment, that ye love one another, as I have loved you" (John 15:12).

We are told *to serve* one another, "Brethren, through love be servants of one another."

> Lord, help me to live from day to day
> In such a self-forgetful way
> That even when I kneel to pray
> My prayers shall be for others.
>
> Help me in all the work I do
> Ever to be sincere and true,
> And know that all I do for Thee
> Must needs be done for others.
>
> Others, Lord; yes, others.
> Let this my motto be.
> Let me live for others
> That I may live like Thee.

> *C. D. Meigs*

The Bible says that our obligation to each other as Christians is such that we should be examples to each other. Paul said, "Be thou an example of the believers, in word, in conversation, in charity, in spirit, in faith, in purity" (1 Timothy 4:12). This is not a suggestion—it is a command! It is not a recommendation, but an obligation. We are to be model Christians.

The Bible also says we are to *forgive* one another. "And be ye kind one to another, tenderhearted, forgiving one another, even as God for Christ's sake hath forgiven you" (Ephesians 4:32). Jesus said that if you will not forgive, neither will your Father which is in heaven forgive your sins. He also said, "When ye stand praying, forgive, if you have ought against any; that your Father also may forgive you" (Mark 11:25).

We are told as Christians *not to judge* one another, but rather decide never to put a stumbling block or hindrance in the way of a brother.

The Bible says that we are *to be subject* one to another; we are to clothe ourselves with humility toward each other. We are to be "in honor, preferring one another." We are to put others first, and ourselves last.

During the last six years of her life my mother-in-law was confined to a wheelchair as a result of a stroke. My father-in-law, Dr. L. Nelson Bell, who had been an extremely active athlete, physician, missionary, and writer (for the last year of his life he also served as moderator of the Southern Presbyterian

Church before its union), devoted himself totally and lovingly to her care. One day he said to my wife, "You know, these are the happiest days of our lives! Taking care of your mother is the greatest privilege of my life." And those of us who watched him care for her knew that he meant it.

As Christians we are *to bear one another's burdens.* There are burdens which every man must bear for himself for no one can do it for him, and if he neglects them they will not be borne. However, there are other burdens that our friends can help us bear, such as sorrow, misfortune, trials, loneliness, family cares, spiritual difficulties, a son or daughter on drugs or in prison—or a child who has disappeared. But we are not to worry about our burdens. We are to roll them onto God's shoulders, looking to Him for power to sustain and strengthen us. However, it is our duty to help our fellow man bear his own burden.

The Bible says as Christians also we are *to be generous* with each other. God says it is our duty as Christians to take care of widows and orphans, and to help the poor within the Christian society. The Bible says: contribute to the needs of the saints . . . practice hospitality . . . lodge strangers . . . wash the saints' feet . . . relieve the afflicted . . . be not forgetful to entertain strangers. And Jesus said, "Inasmuch as ye have done it unto one of the least of these my brethren, ye have done it unto me. . . . It is more blessed to give than to receive." "God loveth a cheerful giver." All of these are our social obligations one to another as Christians.

Grace in Action

Lastly, Christians ought *to be gracious,* and this is one of the most important of Christian virtues—and one of the greatest. The very power of our conviction sometimes inclines us toward feeling that we are right and that all other people are wrong. This is well and good when our convictions are based upon the "Thou shalts" and the "Thou shalt nots" of Scripture rather than our own ideas. The many different and frequently warring factions within the church emphasize the terrible human tendency to gather into select little groups, built upon profound convictions on trivial matters, each insisting that they and they alone have the right answer.

As the late Dr. Harry Ironside once said: "Beware lest we mistake our prejudices for our convictions."

To be sure we must deplore wickedness, evil and wrongdoing, but our commendable intolerance of sin too often develops into a deplorable intolerance of sinners. Jesus hates sin but loves the sinner.

I was amused and shocked to hear a man of considerable religious background declare on television not long ago that "you didn't catch Jesus associating with questionable people or those whose basic ideas and attitudes were at variance with what Jesus knew to be honorable and right!"

Such a man should have known that Jesus wasn't afraid to associate with anyone! One of the things which the scribes and Pharisees criticized most bitterly was His willingness to help and talk to and exchange ideas with anyone, be they publicans, thieves, learned professors or prostitutes, rich or poor! Even His own followers decried some of the people with whom He was seen in public, but this did not lessen the compassion that Jesus felt for all the members of poor, blinded, struggling humanity.

Jesus had the most open and all-encompassing mind that this world has ever seen. His own inner conviction was so strong, so firm, so unswerving that He could afford to mingle with any group, secure in the knowledge that He would not be contaminated. It is fear that makes us unwilling to listen to another's point of view, fear that our own ideas may be attacked. Jesus had no such fear, no such pettiness of viewpoint, no need to fence himself off for His own protection. He knew the difference between graciousness and compromise and we would do well to learn of Him. He set for us the most magnificent and glowing example of truth combined with mercy of all time, and in departing said: "Go ye and do likewise" (Luke 10:37).

These are just a few of the scores of things that could be mentioned that are the social obligations of the Christian. He cannot withdraw himself as a hermit and live a solitary life. He is a member of society. Therefore, the teachings of Jesus deal frequently with our attitudes toward our fellow men.

Study the Bible, read it—and then live by it. Only then can you demonstrate to a confused world the transforming power of the indwelling Christ.

18

Hope for the Future

For the Lord himself shall descend from heaven with a shout, with the voice of the archangel, and with the trump of God: and the dead in Christ shall rise first: then we which are alive and remain shall be caught up together with them in the clouds, to meet the Lord in the air: and so shall we ever be with the Lord. Wherefore comfort one another with these words. 1 THESSALONIANS 4:16–18

SOME TIME AGO the book review section of one of the great newspapers of America ran an article entitled, "The Literature of Doom." In it, they listed all the titles of books today that are dealing with the end of the world. Also a number of movies are coming out today that are called "Armageddon" movies. This concern about the last days has dramatically invaded the entertainment world. People are wondering whether there's going to be a world of tomorrow or not. There is concern about what is going to happen by the year 2000—or if we'll even reach that landmark year. Because of the armament race and the tension in the world, the turmoil on almost every continent, some world leaders doubt we will survive beyond the year 2000—we seem to be getting worse and worse every day.

Some people ask the question, "When is Jesus Christ coming back?" He told us not to speculate about a certain day, but He did leave some signs that we'll discuss later. The coming again of Jesus Christ is mentioned in the Scripture more than 300 times in the New Testament alone. This shows that the Holy Spirit, who directed the writing of the Bible, puts tremendous stress on the fact that Christ is coming back to this earth again.

C. S. Lewis, the great Cambridge and Oxford professor, once said that there are three things which keep people from believing in the coming of Christ. First, he said Jesus didn't come when they expected Him to come in that first century. So people say, "Well, things are going on just as they have always gone, and He hasn't come. Why hasn't He come?" The second reason, he said, was the theory of evolution—the idea that we are making progress on our own, and we really don't need Christ. We're doing it ourselves! And the third reason, Lewis added, is that the coming of Christ cuts across our materialism and our good times—all the things that we like the most in this world. Even though he has been dead for some years now, Lewis saw our day with a perceptive eye.

Just a few days before president-elect John F. Kennedy was to be inaugurated, I was invited to join him and Senator George Smathers in Florida for a golf game and an evening visit at the Kennedy compound in Palm Beach. As we were driving back from the golf course, President Kennedy parked the car, turned to me and asked, "Do you believe Jesus Christ is coming back to earth again?" I was dumbfounded at his question. For one thing, I never dreamed that Mr. Kennedy would ask a question like that, and for another, I wasn't even sure that he knew Jesus was supposed to come back! Having only been with him a few times prior to that incident I had no grasp of his religious knowledge. "Yes, sir, I do," I replied.

"All right," he said. "Explain it to me." So for several minutes I had the opportunity to talk to him about the second coming of Jesus Christ. I have often wondered why he asked that question, and I think part of the answer came a thousand days later when he was assassinated. Cardinal Cushing read the verses I've quoted at the beginning of this chapter at President Kennedy's funeral, and millions of people watched and heard the services around the world.

That statement in verse 17 especially stands out: we who are alive on that day will be caught up together with those who have gone before to meet the Lord in the air. That phrase, "caught up," is the translation of a Greek word which means to snatch away. The day is fast approaching when Jesus Christ will come back to "snatch away" His followers from all the graveyards of the world, and those of us who are alive and remain will join them in the great escape! That is the hope of the future for the Christian.

Because of the Promises of the Old Testament

Why is Christ going to come? There are five reasons why Christ *has* to come back to this earth. First, He must come back because of the promises of the Old Testament that have yet to be fulfilled. Scores of prophecies were fulfilled concerned His first coming. But some prophecies still remain to be fulfilled. For example, the Scripture says, "For unto us a child is born, unto us a son is given: and the government shall be upon his shoulder: and his name shall be called Wonderful, Counselor, The mighty God, The everlasting Father, The Prince of Peace. Of the increase of *his* government and peace there shall be no end, upon the throne of David and upon his Kingdom, to order it and to establish it with judgment and justice from henceforth even forever" (Isaiah 9:6, 7). Someone has said, "When our government is upon His shoulder, of its increase and of our peace there shall be no end."

That portion has not been fulfilled to completion. A child was born. A Son was given. But the government is not upon His shoulder. He did not bring world peace in that first coming, nor did He bring world justice at His first coming. But He's going to bring it the second time, because the Scripture teaches that all of these prophecies are going to be fulfilled. In Micah the prophet says, "He shall judge among many people, and rebuke strong nations afar off; and they shall beat their swords into plowshares, and their spears into pruning hooks: nation shall not lift up sword against nation, neither shall they learn war any more" (4:3). But consider the wars that are being fought right now. Look at the armament race that is escalating. Some day, however, men *are* going to make spears into pruning hooks; and some day, nation will not lift up sword against nation. Why? Because the Prince of Peace is coming back—He's going to be the world ruler.

Because of His Own Statements

Second, Christ has to return because of His own statements. He is absolute truth. Matthew 24 and 25 are entirely given over to statements about His coming again. For example, Matthew 24:27, "For as the lightning cometh out of the east, and shineth even unto the west; so shall also the coming of the Son of man be." The Bible again says in Matthew 25:31–32, "When the Son of man shall come in his glory, and all the holy angels with him, then shall he sit upon the throne of his glory: and before him shall be gathered all nations. . . ." This prophecy has yet to be fulfilled, but He said it and I believe it will be.

Jesus didn't lie to us. He said, "I go to prepare a place for you. And if I go and prepare a place for you, I will come again, and receive you unto myself; that where I am, there ye may be also" (John 14:2, 3). He's going to come back in person. The Lord Jesus is coming back Himself! That's how much He loves us. The plan of salvation is not only to satisfy us in this world and give us a new life here, but He has a great plan for the future. For eternity!

The Bible says we are going to reign with Him. We're joint heirs with the Lord Jesus Christ, and we're going to spend eternity with Him! What is He doing now? He's preparing a home for us! It's been nearly two thousand years. What a home it must be! Eye cannot see nor ear hear, nor hath entered into the heart of man, what God has prepared for those who love Him!

Because of the Present Position of Satan

There is a third reason why Christ must come: the present position of Satan. The most powerful being in all the world today, outside of God Himself, is the devil. And the Bible says, strangely enough, that he has access to heaven itself—to the throne of God. The Bible says that he's the accuser of the brethren, night and day. He's called the anointed cherub—he's called the roaring lion—he's called the king of beasts. He's going about seeking whom he may devour. And at the temptation he showed Jesus all the kingdoms of the world, and he said in effect, "I will give you all of these if you will bow down and worship me" (Matthew 4:9). Jesus did not dispute him. Satan had the power to give Jesus the cosmos, the world system of evil. But, thank God, our Lord quoted Scripture, and that's one thing the devil can't stand! The Scripture defeats him every time.

In 2 Corinthians 4:4 he's also called, "the god of this age." That means that he's the director of the false religions and philosophies of the world. The Bible says the whole cosmos (world) is under his control. What's going to transpire if something doesn't happen to Satan? Who's going to dispose of evil? Who's going to dispose of Satan? Humanity is helpless before him. Man is unable to chain him. The church cannot dethrone him. Legislation is impotent. The United Nations does not know how to handle him. They don't even understand that they're dealing with a spiritual power—an enormous power of evil in the world today.

Let's not forget one fact, however. There is One who is more powerful than Satan! This One defeated him two thousand years ago on the cross. The devil didn't want Jesus Christ to go to the cross, because he was afraid of what Christ would do on the cross. He knew that when Christ died on the cross, He was bearing the sins of the whole world. And God was saying to mankind from the cross, "I love you. I want to forgive you of all of your sins. I want you to be My child, and one day to join Me in heaven." And if Jesus had come down from the cross, we couldn't be saved. We couldn't go to heaven. That's why the devil didn't want him on the cross. That's why they taunted Him, "If thou be the Son of God, come down from the cross." Satan suffered his greatest defeat at the cross, and in the resurrection of the Lord Jesus Christ.

But the devil is still loose, still in charge of the cosmos, the evil that is in the world. All the injustices, all the wars in the world, the devil is promoting—all the crime, all the wickedness, all the terrible things that are going on. In his supernatural power, he has a supernatural plan, even to try to dethrone God.

There's only one person in heaven or earth who can deal with the devil, and He's coming back to deal with him. He's going to throw Satan into the bottomless pit, and ultimately into the lake of fire. Then there will be no devil anymore. We're going to be freed from this terrible pull of evil, and the satanic power that has controlled the hearts of men for so many centuries. That's why Christ has to come. He's the only One who can do it. The world right now is looking for a deliverer, as I read in one of our magazines the other day: "Oh, that the world had a deliverer."

Because of the Present Chaos in the World

And then fourth, Jesus must return because of the present chaos in the world— a world everywhere racked with pain, suffering, hunger, war, murder, lust, greed, hate, fraud, and corruption. Every possible form of human government seems to be failing. Each new one seems to be unsuccessful in dealing with our problems. The world is becoming more helpless and more hopeless as we enter this terribly involved and complicated computerized technological age. The Scripture says, "Say to them that are of a fearful heart, Be strong, fear not; behold your God will come with vengeance, even God with a recompence; he will come and save you" (Isaiah 35:4). Jesus Christ is going to save us from ourselves. There are many sociologists and scientists today who believe we have the capability to destroy ourselves. And we can. The human race has the power right now to destroy itself. But Christ is going to come. And just as man is ready to hurl those bombs at each other, He's going to come to set up His kingdom of righteousness and glory and peace and justice. What a world that's going to be!

Will you be ready?

Because of the Dead in Christ

The fifth reason Christ must come is the dead in Christ—those people who died believing in God and trusting Him. When I saw the film, "The Holocaust," I thought of all those people who were murdered by Hitler—many of them true believers. Thousands of people have suffered injustice, and killings, and all that has gone on in history, as believers in Christ and wondered why they had to die. Many must have wondered why they had to suffer for their faith. Jesus is coming back and there's going to be a great resurrection. Believers are going to be raised from the dead! And then those who are alive and remain shall be caught up in the air, and so shall we ever be with the Lord. When is that going to take place? We don't know the exact day, but I believe it's drawing near. It's certainly two thousand years nearer than when He made the prediction.

Jesus left some signs behind for us to watch for. He said, first of all, there will be intellectual and mental confusion and disturbances throughout the world: "Upon the earth distress of nations, with perplexity . . ." (Luke 21:25). That word "distress" means tossed from all sides. And that word "perplexity" means no way out. We as a human race are going to reach a point where there's no way out.

The Way Out

Jean-Paul Sartre wrote a book entitled *No Exit*, and he told us there is no exit from the human dilemma. No way out. I tell you, there *is* a way out. And that way is the Lord Jesus Christ.

Jesus also said there would be a collapse of morals just before He comes back. Jesus said, "Likewise, also as it was in the days of Lot; they did eat, they drank, they bought, they sold, they planted, they builded; but the same day that Lot went out of Sodom it rained fire and brimstone from heaven, and destroyed them all" (Luke 17:28, 29). Then He said, "Even thus shall it be in the day when the Son of man is revealed" (v. 30). "As it was in the days of Noah, so shall it be in the days of the coming of the Son of man" (Luke 17:26). In both instances, in Lot's day and in Noah's day, morals had collapsed, and moral fiber is collapsing all around us right now. The world is on an immoral binge such as it's never known in history. Jesus said just before He returns that will be the condition of the human race.

Third, Jesus also said there will be a falling away. That means that people who were believers will be falling away individually or collectively. And "many false prophets shall rise, and shall deceive many." Look at the false prophets we have today. Now "the Spirit speaketh expressly that in the latter times, some shall depart from the faith, giving heed to seducing spirits and doctrines of devils" (1 Timothy 4:1). There will be a falling away from true faith. Many have a false idea of God and see a caricature of Christianity. They are not really true disciples of Jesus Christ. They have already unwittingly fallen away—maybe not intellectually. They may still believe, but they've fallen away in the way they live. Your life justifies what you believe. Jesus says, "By their fruits ye shall know them." And the devil is still coming around and saying, "Yea, hath God said?" trying to make us doubt His holy Word. A lot of false prophets are coming around today and saying, "This cannot be trusted." I tell you, the Bible was inspired by God from cover to cover. It is God's holy Word. And there are those who are telling us, "Jesus Christ was a mere man," that He was not God. He is a God-man. Equally God and equally man. Filled with love for us, so much that He died for us.

A fourth point: Jesus indicated there would be an increase in lawlessness. He said that as lawlessness spread, men's love for one another will grow cold (Matthew 24:12). Newspapers are filled with these accounts right now. Have you ever heard of such terrorism all over the world? Terrorist activities are increasing in almost every country. Because of modern technology, people don't know how to cope with it. Jesus said in Luke 21:9, "Ye shall hear of wars and commotions," and that word "commotions" carries with it the idea of rebellion against all authority. We're seeing that in many parts of the world. Jesus said that would be one of the signs. And then He said there will be peace conferences. Paul wrote, "For when they shall say Peace and safety; then sudden destruction cometh upon them" (1 Thessalonians 5:3). The prophet Isaiah wrote, "There is no peace, saith the Lord, unto the wicked" (48:22). Never before have we had so many people seeking peace. The United Nations goes into one emergency session after another. The Congresses and the Parliaments of the world are searching for peace. The leaders of the world—our Secretary of State goes back and forth around the world seeking peace, trying to patch this little place here, and this place there. By the time he gets back to Washington, trouble has broken out somewhere else. Jesus said it would be like that: "Except those days be shortened, there should no flesh be saved: but for the elect's sake those days shall be shortened" (Matthew 24:22).

Then Jesus said something else: there would be a worldwide emphasis on evangelism, and the proclamation of the gospel before He came back. "And this gospel of the kingdom shall be preached in all the world for a witness unto all nations; then shall the end come." For the *first* time in history, the gospel is now being heard all over the world. By radio, by television, by literature, by satellite in every part of the world. There's not a place that they could not hear the gospel. For the first time.

Now, what are we to do? How do we face this? First, we purify ourselves. The Scripture says, "Every man that hath this hope in him purifies himself." Do you have the hope of the coming again of the Lord Jesus Christ? Then you should live it—a pure life, a godly life, a surrendered life, a consecrated life. There's a sense in which we're sanctified when we receive Christ. There's a sense in which we grow in the grace and knowledge of Christ in progressive sanctification. But one day we shall see Jesus face to face, and total sanctification is when we're perfect, as He is perfect. We shall see Him as He is.

Second, we are to wait with patience. I know sometimes we get a little anxious and wonder if Jesus is really going to come back. The Scripture says, "For you have need of patience, for yet a little while, and he that shall come will come, and will not tarry" (Hebrews 10:37). He has appointed a day. God knows the day. It's all set. He will be back right on time—He won't be an hour late or an hour early.

The third thing we're to do is to watch. That word "watch" means that we are to desire His coming. We are to be constantly thinking about His coming. At the beginning of this chapter I quoted the verse, "Looking for that blessed hope and glorious appearing."

The fourth thing is that we're to work. People say, "Well, Christ is coming back—let's quit all these activities that we're involved in." No! He may not come for a hundred years, or a thousand years. He may not come in our lifetime. Let's do our best to help reach our fellow man for Christ. His return should be our incentive toward work.

The last point: we're to be prepared. Are you prepared? "Be ye therefore ready also: for the Son of man cometh at an hour when ye think not" (Luke 12:40). The Scripture says, "By faith Noah being warned of God of things not seen as yet, moved with fear, prepared an ark to the saving of his house." That word "fear" means terrified. Yes! Some people are drawn into the kingdom of God by love and some come into it in terror. We have a right to be terrified. Because for those who know not Jesus Christ as their Lord and Savior, it means judgment, it means hell. We must come to Christ while we can.

19

Peace at Last

And God shall wipe all tears from their eyes; and there shall be no more death, neither sorrow, nor crying, neither shall there be any more pain. . . . REVELATION 21:4

IN THIS BOOK we have been looking at what it means to be at peace with God. We now know what it means to be a Christian. We know the price that was paid to get this illusive thing called peace and happiness. I know men who would write a check for a million dollars if they could find peace. Millions are searching for it. Every time they get close to finding the peace found only in Christ, Satan steers them away. He blinds them. He throws up a smoke screen. He bluffs them. And they miss it! But we Christians have found it! It is ours now forever. We have found the secret of life.

The word "peace" has been used often in the last forty or fifty years. We talk about peace, and we have many peace conferences; yet at the moment it seems that the world is heading toward anything but peace.

"The way of peace have they not known," the apostle Paul says concerning the human race (Romans 3:17). As we look around, we find that there is little personal, domestic, social, economic or political peace anywhere. Why? Because we all have the seeds of suspicion and violence, of hatred and destruction within us.

Jesus said, "Blessed are the peacemakers" (Matthew 5:9). We are to try for peace. This does not mean pacifism. We are to work for peace. But Jesus also predicted: "Ye shall hear of wars and rumors of wars: see that ye be not troubled: for all these things must come to pass, but the end is not yet. For nation shall rise against nation, and kingdom against kingdom" (Matthew 24:6–7).

Peace can be experienced only when we have received divine pardon—when we have been reconciled to God and when we have harmony within, with our fellow man and especially with God. "There is no peace, saith my God, to the wicked" (Isaiah 57:21). But through the blood of the cross, Christ has made peace with God for us and is Himself our peace. If by faith we accept Him, we are justified by God and can realize the inner serenity that can come to man through no other means. When Christ enters our hearts, we are freed of that haunting sense of sin. Cleansed of all feeling of contamination and unfitness, we can lift up our heads secure in the knowledge that we can look with confidence into the face of our fellow men. "When a man's ways please the Lord he maketh even his enemies to be at peace with him" (Proverbs 16:7). Even more important, we know that we can stand before God in the hour of our death with this same feeling of peace and security.

In the Bible Jesus told us there is going to be war until the end of the age. He knew that human nature is not going to change without a spiritual new birth. He knew that the vast majority of the human race were never going to be converted to Him. The vast majority of the people of the world today are not "born again." So we always have the potential that violence will break out in a home, in a community, in the world.

There are three kinds of peace described in the Bible.

Peace with God

First, peace *with* God. "Therefore being justified by faith, we have peace with God through our Lord Jesus Christ" (Romans 5:1). "Having made peace through the blood of his cross . . ." (Colossians 1:20). There is a peace that you can have immediately—peace with God.

The greatest warfare going on in the world today is between mankind and God. People may not realize that they're at war with God. But if they don't know Jesus Christ as Savior, and if they haven't surrendered to Him as Lord, God considers them to be at war with Him. That chasm has been caused by sin. The Bible says that all have "sinned and come short of the glory of God" (Romans 3:23). "Oh," people say, "I have joined the church. I have been baptized." But has Jesus come to live in their hearts? Not only as Savior, but as Lord?

It would be the greatest tragedy if I didn't tell you that unless you repent of your sins and receive Christ as your Savior, you are going to be lost.

"For God so loved the world, that he gave his only begotten Son, that whosoever [that "whosoever" is you] believeth in him should not perish, but have everlasting life" (John 3:16). It's not just head-belief. It's heart-belief too. It's total trust, total commitment. We bring everything to the cross where the Lord Jesus Christ died for our sins. He made peace with God by His death on the cross. If we turn our backs on Him, and don't commit our lives to Him, we will have no hope in the future.

For one to have peace with God, it cost the blood of His Son. "With the precious blood of Christ, as of a lamb without blemish and without spot," said Peter (1 Peter 1:19). If I were the only person in all the world, Jesus would have died for me, because He loves me. And He loves you! His love is pouring out from the cross.

"Meet Me in Heaven"

I read a biography of Queen Victoria, and I learned that the queen would sometimes go to the slums of London. She went into one home to have tea with an older lady, and when the queen rose to leave, she asked, "Is there anything I can do for you?" And the woman said, "Yes, ma'am, Your Majesty, you can meet me in heaven." The queen turned to her and said softly, "Yes. I'll be there, but only because of the blood that was shed on the cross for you and for me." Queen Victoria, in her day the most powerful woman in the world, had to depend on the blood of Christ for her salvation. And so do we. The Bible says that God is the Author of peace (1 Corinthians 14:33). God provided salvation through the cross. He made peace by the shedding of His blood. The war that exists between you and God can be over quickly, and the peace treaty is signed in the blood of His Son Jesus Christ.

Are you at peace with God? Or do the sins of your heart separate you from God?

The Peace of God

The second peace spoken of in the Bible is the peace *of* God. Everyone who knows the Lord Jesus Christ can go through any problem, and face death, and still have the peace of God in his heart. When your spouse dies, or your children get sick, or you lose your job, you can have a peace that you don't understand. You may have tears at a graveside, but you can have an abiding peace, a quietness.

A psychiatrist was quoted in the newspaper as saying that he could not improve upon the Apostle Paul's prescription for human worry. Paul said, "Be [anxious] for nothing; but in every thing by prayer and supplication with thanksgiving let your requests be made known to God. And the peace of God, which passeth all understanding, shall keep your hearts and minds through Christ Jesus" (Philippians 4:6–7). Be anxious for nothing. How many times do you and I fret and turn, looking for a little peace? God's peace can be in our hearts—right now.

Colossians 3:15 says, "Let the peace of God rule in your hearts." Some of you believe that you know Jesus Christ as your Savior, but you haven't really made Him your Lord. You're missing the peace of God in your struggles and turmoils and trials and pressures of life. Is the peace of God in your heart?

We are all familiar with the transformation that took place in Saul on the road to Damascus, when Christ entered his heart and changed him from one of His most destructive enemies to one of His mightiest advocates. Many equally dramatic changes in human personalities are taking place today, and they are being brought about by the self-same means that transformed Saul into Paul—birth again through Jesus Christ!

There is no human philosophy that can achieve such changes or provide such strength. This mighty strength stands ready to be available at your beck and call at all times. God said, "Fear thou not; for I am with thee: be not dismayed; for I am thy God: I will strengthen thee; yea, I will help thee; yea, I will uphold thee with the right hand of my righteousness" (Isaiah 41:10).

Whatever the circumstances, whatever the call, whatever the duty, whatever the price, whatever the sacrifice—His strength will be your strength in your hour of need.

There are physical benefits that accrue from Christian living. Sin and the sense of inner unworthiness impair physical and mental well-being. The sense of physical impurity and physical immorality, the sense of hatred directed toward our fellow men, the awareness of our own inadequacy and frustration and our inability to achieve the goals to which we aspire—these are the real reasons for physical and mental illness. The sense of guilt and sin that natural man carries within himself renders him unfit for the performance of his duties, renders him sick in both mind and body. It was no accident that Jesus combined healing with His preaching and teaching when He was on earth. There is a very real relationship between the life of the spirit and the health of the body and mind.

Peace with God and the peace of God in a man's heart and the joy of fellowship with Christ have in themselves a beneficial effect upon the body and mind and will lead to the development and preservation of physical and mental power. Thus, Christ promotes the best interest of the body and mind as well as of the spirit, in addition to inward peace, the development of spiritual life, the joy and fellowship with Christ, and the new strength that comes with being born again.

There are certain special privileges that only the true Christian can enjoy. There is, for example, the privilege of *having divine wisdom and guidance continually.* The Bible says, "If any of you lack wisdom, let him ask of God, that giveth to all men liberally, and upbraideth not; and it shall be given him" (James 1:5).

Also the Christian has a sense of *true optimism,* the assurance that according to divine revelation everything will turn out well in the end.

The Christian also has a *world view.* This world view sets forth God's purpose and the end toward which all are proceeding. It assures us that in spite of men's war upon each other and in spite of the destructive forces of nature which seem to hold us in their grip, God is still on the throne and in command of everything. Satan himself is held back by God's power and given an opportunity to exercise his evil influence only as God sees fit and only as long as God sees fit to let him do it. The Scriptures teach us that God has a definite plan for each period of history, for every nation and for every individual. The Scripture discloses God's plan for the return of Christ when His kingdom shall be established, as we have already seen. Thus, for the Christian, life has a plan and an assurance that God will ultimately triumph over all unrighteousness.

In summing up the superiority of the Christian life over all other ways of living we cannot overlook the advantage that the Christian will have for all eternity. Job said, "If a man die, shall he live again?" (14:14). He answered his own question when he said, "For I know that my Redeemer liveth and that he will stand at the latter day upon the earth" (Job 19:25).

What a prospect! What a future! What a hope! What a life! I would not change places with the wealthiest and most influential person in the world. I would rather be a child of the King, a joint-heir with Christ, a member of the Royal Family of heaven!

I know where I've come from, I know why I'm here, I know where I'm going—and I have peace in my heart. His peace floods my heart and overwhelms my soul!

The storm was raging. The sea was beating against the rocks in huge, dashing waves. The lightning was flashing, the thunder was roaring, the wind was blowing; but the little bird was asleep in the crevice of the rock, its head serenely under its wing, sound asleep. That is peace: to be able to rest serenely in the storm!

In Christ we are relaxed and at peace in the midst of the confusions, bewilderments, and perplexities of this life. The storm rages, but our hearts are at rest. We have found peace—at last!

Future Peace

The third peace the Scriptures mention is *future* peace. The Bible promises that there will be a time when the whole world is going to have peace. It seems that the world is heading toward Armageddon. In Revelation 6:4 John the beloved apostle says there's a red horse, "and power was given to him that sat thereon to take peace from the earth." We're not going to have peace—permanent peace—until the Prince of Peace comes.

And He is coming. One of these days the sky is going to break open and the Lord Jesus Christ will come back. He will set up His reign upon this planet, and we're going to have peace and social justice. What a wonderful time that's going to be!

Isaiah predicted, "The government shall be upon his shoulder: and his name shall be called Wonderful, Counselor, The mighty God, The everlasting Father, The Prince of Peace. Of the increase of his government and peace there shall be no end" (Isaiah 9:6–7). Think of it: no fighting, no war, no hatred, no violence. It will all be peace.

To Be with Christ

Do you know Christ? Are you sure He's in your heart? Perhaps you have been thinking, "I want to be sure I have peace with God. I want to be sure that I'm ready for death. I want my sins forgiven. I want my guilt removed. I want to be with Christ when He comes and sets up His Kingdom."

It's all yours, and it's free. You don't have to work for it. "For by grace are ye saved through faith; and that not of yourselves: it is the gift of God: not of works" (Ephesians 2:8–9).

Give your heart and life to Christ now. Do not put it off.

20

The Day After

It is appointed unto men once to die, but after this the judgment. HEBREWS 9:27

THIS PAST YEAR, one of the television networks aired a program called "The Day After." At the end, it was as if the entire earth was a cemetery littered with corpses. For millions, this picture was a disturbing and traumatic experience.

If imagining such a possible nuclear winter experience would cause millions to think of their future, how much more so should the fact that however the end may come for them, the real "day after" for those who reject Christ is not this grim oblivion but *even worse* judgment and eternal hell, which would make the T.V. portrayal seem like a picnic in comparison!

But your future does not hinge on the world situation, however grim it might become. It depends on what happened 2,000 years ago at the cross, and your acceptance or rejection of the Prince of Peace.

In updating this book, it has been our prayer that you will not delay finding the end of your Quest a moment longer. The time is far shorter than it was when this manuscript was originally written. Few of us know for certain when death will come for us. Make your *Peace with God* today.

O God, I am a sinner; I am sorry for my sin; I am willing to turn from my sin. I receive Christ as Savior; I confess Him as Lord, I want to follow Him, and serve Him and others in the fellowship of His church. In Christ's Name, Amen.

The Secret of Happiness

To my Mother and Father,

whose dedicated lives
taught me *The Secret of Happiness*

CONTENTS

PREFACE

I SAT DOWN to write a book on "The Greatest Sermon Ever Preached"—the Sermon on the Mount—but I got no further than the eight Beatitudes. The more I read them, meditated on them and studied them, the more I realized that Christ was giving a formula for personal happiness that applied to anyone, no matter what his race, geographical situation, age or circumstance! I have based my comments on the beautiful and beloved King James Version of the Beatitudes, although I follow the suggestion of scholars and many modern Bible translations who use the word "happy" for "blessed" since it suggests joy in the midst of real life.

When trying to put these thoughts on paper, I consulted with other writers. In these few statements Jesus shares almost the whole depth and scope of His teaching. As someone has said, "The character which we find in the Beatitudes is beyond all question, nothing less than our Lord's own character put into words. It is a description set side by side with an example."

The Beatitudes are revolutionary! Startling! Deeply profound, and yet amazingly simple! If applied on a universal scale, they could transform the world in which we live. If you apply these simple formulae in your own personal life, you can never be the same!

As I have restudied the Beatitudes to prepare for this revised edition I have been amazed again at the timelessness and universal nature of these teachings of Jesus. I have sensed afresh the depth and challenge of these brief words of our Lord. In this revised edition I have made numerous minor changes to bring the book up to date and make it practical. I also have included some additional insights which I have gathered since the first edition was published in 1955. But the Word of God does not change, nor does its power to change our lives. Just as Christ brought hope and new life to those who first gathered in Galilee to hear the Sermon on the Mount, so He can bring hope and new life to us today as we understand His truth, commit ourselves to it, and live each day in its light.

In the first edition, my friend and assistant Lee Fisher was a tremendous help. In this revised edition, my wife Ruth, my daughter Gigi Tchividjian, my able research assistant Dr. John Akers, and Word editor Al Bryant have been indispensable. I am deeply grateful also to my administrative assistant Stephanie Wills for her invaluable counsel, advice, and for keeping us on track.

It is my prayer that as you read this book, and as you meditate on the Beatitudes themselves, you will realize that these ancient truths are as modern as tomorrow. They can change your life and point the way to true and lasting happiness—because they will point you to Christ and His timeless principles for living.

One final note: I have used the word "man" in this book, along with the appropriate pronouns that follow it, in the generic sense of the term, to mean the human race in its most inclusive sense.

August, 1985   —Billy Graham
Montreat, NC

1

The Search for Happiness

Blessed—happy, to be envied, and spiritually prosperous that is, with life-joy and satisfaction in God's favor and salvation, regardless of their outward conditions—are the poor in spirit. . . . MATTHEW 5:3, AMP

A FRENCH PHILOSOPHER once said, "The whole world is on a mad quest for security and happiness." A former president of Harvard University observed, "The world is searching for a creed to believe and a song to sing."

A Texas millionaire confided, "I thought money could buy happiness—I have been miserably disillusioned." A famous film star broke down: "I have money, beauty, glamor and popularity. I should be the happiest woman in the world, but I am miserable. Why?" One of Britain's top social leaders said, "I have lost all desire to live, yet I have everything to live for. What is the matter?"

The poet, Amy Wilson Carmichael, wrote:

> The lonely, dreary road he trod.
> "Enter into my joy," said God.
> The sad ascetic shook his head,
> "I've lost all taste for joy," he said.

A man went to see a psychiatrist. He said, "Doctor, I am lonely, despondent, and miserable. Can you help me?" The psychiatrist suggested that he go to a circus and see a famous clown who was said to make even the most despondent laugh with merriment. His patient said, "I am that clown."

A college senior said, "I am twenty-three. I have lived through enough experiences to be old, and I am already fed up with life."

A famous Grecian dancer of a generation ago once said, "I have never been alone but what my hands trembled, my eyes filled with tears, and my heart ached for a peace and happiness I have never found."

One of the world's great statesmen said to me, "I am an old man. Life has lost all meaning. I am ready to take a fateful leap into the unknown. Young man, can you give me a ray of hope?"

The Christian, on the other hand, has a different perspective on the meaning of happiness. C. S. Lewis said, "Joy is the serious business of heaven." He added, "All his biddings are joys." Mother Teresa of Calcutta says, "True holiness consists of doing the will of God with a smile."

Jesus declared, "I am come that they might have life, and that they might have it more abundantly" (John 10:10). Or again He stated, "These things have I spoken unto you, that my joy might remain in you, and that your joy might be full" (John 15:11).

Searching for Happiness in the Wrong Places

Over 2500 years ago the prophet Isaiah looked out on a people who longed for happiness and security but were looking for it in the wrong places. They were running to the marketplace and to places of amusement, spending their money madly for things which brought them no permanent satisfaction.

He stood before them one day and gave them the Word of God: "Ho, every one that thirsteth, come ye to the waters, and he that hath no money; come ye, buy, and eat; yea, come, buy wine and milk without money and without price. Wherefore do ye spend money for that which is not bread? And your labor for that which satisfieth not? Hearken diligently unto me, and eat ye that which is good, and let your soul delight itself in fatness" (Isaiah 55:1, 2).

Isaiah didn't speak negatively and berate them for their sins in this particular sermon. He didn't grab the bottle from the drunkard's hand, he didn't lecture them about the evils of gluttony, he didn't shame them for their immoral practices. He overlooked that for the moment. He simply asked them: "Are you getting what you want out of life? Why do you spend your money for that which is not bread and your labor for that which does not satisfy?"

If Isaiah were living today he would probably stand at Forty-second and Broadway in New York, in the Loop in Chicago, or on Market Street in San Francisco, and simply ask the milling, restless throngs: "Are you getting what you want? Are you finding satisfaction?"

He would ask the actress, surfeited with fame and fortune, but peering out on life hungrily: "Are you getting what you want?" He would say to the eminently successful financier who commands his fleets and controls his industries: "Are you getting what you want?"

He would say to the laborers and workmen of America who are enjoying the highest standard of living in history: "Are you getting what you want?" He would ask the youth of America: "Are you getting what you want?"

He would say to the consumers of America who have the best homes, the most comfortable furniture, the finest food, the cleverest gadgets, and the smoothest, most powerful automobiles: "Are you getting what you want?"

God Has the Answer

Isaiah did not leave them with an unanswered question. He went on to tell them that there is a satisfying way of life, if they would seek it. He exhorted them to abandon their vain searching for pots of gold at the end of mythical rainbows, and to start searching for happiness where it is really found, in a right relationship with God.

Our materialistic world rushes on with its eternal quest for the fountain of happiness! The more knowledge we acquire, the less wisdom we seem to have. The more economic security we gain, the more bored and insecure we become. The more worldly pleasure we enjoy, the less satisfied and contented we are with life. We are like a restless sea, finding a little peace here and a little pleasure there, but nothing permanent and satisfying. So the search continues! Men will kill, lie, cheat, steal, and go to war to satisfy their quest for power, pleasure, and wealth, thinking thereby to gain for themselves and their particular group peace, security, contentment, and happiness, and yet in vain.

Yet inside us a little voice keeps saying, "We were not meant to be this way—we were meant for better things." We have a mysterious feeling that there is a fountain somewhere that contains the happiness which makes life worthwhile. We keep saying to ourselves that somewhere, sometime we will stumble onto the secret. Sometimes we feel that we have obtained it—only to find it illusive, leaving us disillusioned, bewildered, unhappy, and still searching.

There are, we need to realize, two kinds of happiness. One kind of happiness comes to us when our circumstances are pleasant and we are relatively free from troubles. The problem, however, is that this kind of happiness is fleeting and superficial. When circumstances change—as they inevitably do—then this kind of happiness evaporates like the early morning fog in the heat of the sun. In addition, even when our outward circumstances are seemingly ideal, we still may be troubled inside by a nagging hunger or longing for something we cannot identify. We say we are "happy"—but down inside we know it is only temporary and shallow at best. Yes, from time to time we may think we have found a degree of happiness, but sooner or later it will vanish. Our search for happiness remains unfulfilled.

But there is another kind of happiness—the kind for which we all long. This second kind of happiness is a lasting, inner joy and peace which survives in any circumstances. It is a happiness which endures no matter what comes our way—and even may grow stronger in adversity. This is the kind of happiness to which Jesus summons us in the Beatitudes. It is happiness which can only come from God. He alone has the answer to our search for lasting happiness.

The happiness which brings enduring worth to life is not the superficial happiness that is dependent on circumstances. It is the happiness and contentment that fills the soul even in the midst of the most distressing of circumstances and the most adverse environment. It is the kind of happiness that survives when things go wrong and smiles through the tears. The happiness for which our souls ache is one undisturbed by success or failure, one which dwells deep within us and gives inward relaxation, peace, and contentment, no matter what the surface problems may be. That kind of happiness stands in need of no outward stimulus.

Near my home is a spring that never varies its flow at any season of the year. Floods may rage nearby, but it will not increase its flow. A long summer's drought may come, but it will not decrease. It is perennially and always the same. Such is the type of happiness for which we yearn.

The Three Things We Search For

First, we search for peace. As we have just seen, the whole human race is consumed with a search for inner peace, happiness, and joy.

The peace we seek is not merely a nondescript, so-called peace of mind which is blind to reality or comes and goes according to our moods or circumstances. The peace every man and woman seeks is one which will free them from the anxiety and frustrations of life's distracting conflicts and problems. It is a peace of soul which permeates one's entire being, a peace that operates through the trials and burdens of life.

Second, we search for purpose. Man is confused and perplexed, wondering where he came from, why he is here, and where he is going. He wants to know if there is truth in this universe—truth which will be like a polar star to guide him and give him meaning.

Some speculate that humanity is an accident on this planet. According to their views, man was not put here for a purpose—he just happened. The existentialist philosopher declares that man has no God-given purpose, and is left to make up his own purpose and meaning in life if he can. But down inside we yearn for something more certain. Even the skeptic searches for truth, for man needs truth as the animals do not—not just the truth of the physical sciences and mathematics, but the truths about his being and why he is here.

Third, we search for a relationship with God. Even when men vehemently deny God's existence, they still are searching for something to fill the vacuum in their souls. But it is a vacuum God, our Creator, placed there—and only He can fill it.

Man was created in the image of God. At first, Adam and Eve had perfect fellowship with God. But they turned their backs on God, substituting themselves at the center of their lives instead of God their Creator. Now man is a lost and lonely wanderer upon the earth apart from God. To have a vague knowledge that He exists is not enough. Man yearns to know that he is not alone in this universe, that there is a Higher Power guiding his destiny. He yearns for a relationship with his Creator—even if he does not admit it.

The Beatitudes: God's Key to Man's Search

Yes, every human being ever born yearns for peace, purpose, and God Himself. But can we know these? Can our search be ended? Will our quest for true happiness ever be satisfied? The Bible declares a resounding "Yes!" And in these eight Beatitudes Jesus points the way.

In each one of the Beatitudes—which someone has called the "beautiful attitudes"—Jesus used the word *blessed*. This word *blessed is* actually a very difficult word to translate into modern English, because in the original Greek language of the New Testament it has a far richer meaning than the everyday content of our English word. As we noted at the beginning of this chapter, the Amplified Version of the New Testament defines it as "happy, to be envied, and spiritually prosperous . . . with life-joy and satisfaction. . . ." But perhaps the word "happy" comes as close as any single English word to conveying the idea of "blessed" to us today, and that is the word we will use for the most part through this book. But let us never forget that the "blessedness" of which Jesus speaks is far, far deeper than any superficial happiness which comes and goes according to circumstances. That is why the word "blessed" guards well against its reduction and perversion.

Jesus' first words were: "Happy are ye." In those three words He was telling us that there *is* an answer to our search! We can know peace. We can know the truth about our lives. We can know God. And because of that, we can be blessed!

But is that possible, or is Jesus simply speaking some high-sounding words which have no substance? To answer that, look first of all at Jesus Himself. Certainly if anyone had genuine happiness and blessedness, it was Jesus—in spite of the controversy, abuse, and eventual injustice of His death. He knew the secret of true happiness, and in these Beatitudes He unveils it to us.

Who Was This Jesus?

The Beatitudes are not the whole of Jesus' teaching, nor is even the Sermon on the Mount. (You can read the entire Sermon on the Mount in chapters five through seven of the Gospel of Matthew.) There is much else that Jesus taught during the three short years of His public ministry. But Jesus was more than a great teacher. Who was this man Jesus, who never traveled outside His native Palestine and yet changed the entire course of human history?

Some have said that Jesus' main role was as a social reformer, coming to change society and liberate people who were bound by injustice and oppression. Others have said He came merely as an example, showing us by His acts of love how we should live. Still others have dismissed Him as a misguided religious reformer with no relevance to a modern, scientific age.

But none of these is adequate to explain Jesus Christ as we see Him clearly pictured in the New Testament. The Bible, in fact, makes a startling assertion: Jesus was not only a man, but He was God Himself, come down from the glory of Heaven to walk on this earth and show us what God is like. Christ "is the image of the invisible God" (Colossians 1:15). More than that, He is the divinely appointed Savior who died for sinners, bearing their transgressions upon the cross. He died to save all who had disobeyed God and who were slandering Him in their unregenerate natures. And He demonstrated beyond all doubt that He was the Divine Savior and Lord by being raised from the dead. The gospel is the good news of God "concerning his Son Jesus Christ our Lord, which was made of the seed of David according to the flesh; And declared to be the Son of God with power, according to the spirit of holiness, by the resurrection from the dead" (Romans 1:3–4).

The best modern scholarship is discovering once again that even the Sermon on the Mount, and the Beatitudes as well, cannot be isolated from the fact of Jesus' saviorhood. The Old Testament had taught that the Christ was to be meek. He was to turn mourning into joy; righteousness was to be His meat and drink; even upon the cross it was His deepest hunger and thirst.

He also was the One who would show God's mercy to those who were separated from God and in need. He likewise would be pure and without sin. Most of all, He would not flee the persecution that would come His way, but would bring peace—peace with God, peace within the human heart, and peace on earth.

This is another way of saying that, in reality, Jesus Christ is the perfect fulfillment, example and demonstration of the Beatitudes. He alone, in the history of the human race, experienced fully what He tells us about the happiness and blessedness of life. What He tells us, He tells us as the Savior who has redeemed us and who is teaching His followers. But more than that, He is the One who gives us the power to live according to His teachings.

Christ's message when He was upon the earth was revolutionizing and understandable. His words were simple yet profound. And they shook people. His words provoked either happy acceptance or violent rejection. People were never the same after listening to Him. They were invariably better or worse—better if they accepted Him, worse if they rejected Him. They either followed Him in love or turned away in anger and indignation. There was a magic in His gospel which prompted men and women to decisive action. As He clearly said, "He that is not with me is against me."

Men Right Side Up in an Upside-down World

The people who followed Him were unique in their generation. They turned the world upside down because their hearts had been turned right side up. The world has never been the same. History took a sharp turn for the better. People began to behave like human beings. Dignity, nobility, and honor followed in the wake of Christianity. Art, music, and science—sparked by this new interpretation of life's meaning—began to progress and develop. Mankind began at long last to resemble again the "image of God" in which he was created. Society began to feel the impact of the Christian influence. Injustice, inhumanity, and intolerance were dislodged by the tidal wave of spiritual power which was released by Christ. As F. W. Boreham once said, "The Carpenter of Nazareth has encouraged the goldsmiths of the ages." Virtually every significant social movement in Western Civilization—from the abolition of slavery to child labor laws—owes its origin to the influence of Jesus Christ.

Centuries have rolled by since that initial surge of spiritual life. The stream of Christianity has flowed unceasingly, sometimes at flood tide but more often at ebb tide.

At times the church has been gloriously renewed and used of God. Emboldened by the Holy Spirit, and stirred by the truth of the Word of God, men and women throughout the centuries have continued to turn the world upside down for Christ. At other times, however, manmade tributaries have flowed into it, polluting and adulterating it. Deism, Pantheism, and, of late, Humanism and blatant Naturalism have flowed like muddy currents into the mainstream of Christian thought, so that the world has had difficulty in distinguishing the real from the false. In some parts of the world armies have fought and killed supposedly in the name of Christ—and yet by their actions showing they understood little of His spirit of forgiveness and love.

Yes, Christians are imperfect, and some who have claimed most loudly to follow Him have been the furthest from His teaching. But don't let that divert you or keep you from Christ Himself. At times people have said to me, "Christians are all hypocrites—I don't want anything to do with Christ!" But that is an excuse to keep from having to face the truth that is in Christ. Instead, understand His teaching and examine His life. And if you know Christ and have committed your life to Him, learn from Him and live a consistent life for Him. Do others see something of Christ—His love, His joy, His peace—in your life?

True Christians are supposed to be happy! Our generation has become well versed in Christian terminology, but is remiss in the actual practice of Christ's principles and teachings. Hence, our greatest need today is not more Christianity but more true Christians.

The Impact of Christlike Living

The world may argue against Christianity as an institution, but there is no convincing argument against a person who through the Spirit of God has been made Christlike. Such a one is a living rebuke to the selfishness, rationalism, and materialism of the day. Too often we have debated with the world on the letter of the law when we should have been living oracles of God, seen and read of all people.

It is time that we retrace our steps to the source and realize afresh the transforming power of Jesus Christ.

Jesus said to the woman at Jacob's well: "Whosoever drinketh of the water that I shall give him shall never thirst" (John 4:14). This sinsick, disillusioned woman was the symbol of the whole race. Her longings were our longings! Her heart-cry was our heart-cry! Her disillusionment was our disillusionment! Her sin was our sin! But her Savior can be our Savior! Her forgiveness can be our forgiveness! Her joy can be our joy!

An Invitation to a Journey

I invite you to go with me on a thrilling, adventuresome journey. The object of our search? The secret of happiness. The place? Galilee! Let us roll back the pages of time almost two thousand years.

It's a hot, sultry day with the sweltering wind spinning little dust whirls and carrying them swiftly down the winding road by the Sea of Galilee. There is an air of expectancy in the atmosphere we breathe. The wind skips happily across the surface of the ancient sea. We hear voices raised in an excited, feverish pitch as friend calls a greeting to friend. Along every trail leading to Galilee little groups of people begin to gather. The word has spread abroad that Jesus is returning to Galilee.

Suddenly He and His little band of followers emerge over the brow of a hill on the road to Capernaum, and immediately in their wake follows a vast multitude of people from Galilee, Decapolis, Jerusalem, Judea, and from beyond the Jordan River.

Quickly the word spreads from mouth to mouth: "Jesus is coming!" Other multitudes from Tiberias, Bethsaida, and Capernaum soon appear and join the others. Together they follow thirteen robed men. As they reach the summit of the hill where the gentle winds from the plains sweep over them, affording relief from the sun, Jesus stops and motions for them to sit down and rest.

The air is tense. It is a moment to be captured and held for eternity. The crowd hushes as Jesus climbs atop a large rock and is seated. In the valley on the deserted road, a lone camel rider wends his way along the trail toward Tiberias. A quiet falls upon the multitude as their faces gaze expectantly at Jesus. Then He begins to speak.

What He said there on that Mount of Beatitudes in faraway Palestine was to go down in history as the most profound, sublime words ever spoken! There in reverent, measured, simple words He revealed the secret of happiness—not a superficial happiness of time and space, but a happiness which would last forever.

His first word was "happy." Immediately His listeners must have pricked up their ears, as we are prone to do. In the pages to follow it is my prayer that you will do even more: prick up your ears . . . open your heart . . . surrender your will. Then you will begin living life with a capital *L*, find a contentment and joy that crowd the futility and vanity out of the daily walk, and discover the secret of happiness!

2

Happiness through Poverty

Blessed are the poor in spirit: for theirs is the kingdom of heaven. MATTHEW 5:3

TODAY, THROUGH THE media, we have all been made aware of the abject, hopeless poverty in much of the world. We have seen the starving in Africa, the displaced persons of southeast Asia.

I myself have traveled in more than sixty countries of the world, many of them hopelessly buried in poverty. I have returned from cities like Calcutta with a heavy heart, wondering if anything can ever be done to alleviate their suffering.

Throughout the world I have found many Mother Teresas. Still, the poverty is virtually untouched. We have sent our own contributions through reliable relief organizations.

Yet under the filth, the starvation, the abject poverty I have sensed an even greater poverty—the poverty of the soul.

A French leader has said that if the whole world had enough to eat, money to spend, and security from the cradle to the grave they would ask for nothing more. And that is something to think about. I have on occasion visited places where the wealthy gather to relax, escape bad weather, or just play—and I have discovered that wealth can be anesthetizing. It is, as Jesus said, easier for a camel to go through the eye of a needle than for a wealthy person to enter the kingdom of heaven (see Matthew 19:24). Surely one reason is that wealth tends to preoccupy a person and dull his sensitivity to his spiritual needs.

I have often asked myself the question: would wealth make people happy? And I have answered it just as quickly by saying an emphatic "No!" I know too many rich people who are miserable. There are people with everything that money can buy who are tormented, confused, bewildered, and miserable! Yet how many times I have heard people say, "If only I had a little security, I could be happy." Or, "If only I could have a fine home, a new car, and a winter condominium in Florida, I would be content."

There is nothing inherently wrong with being rich. I have been privileged to know some very wealthy people across the years who were humble and generous, seeing their wealth as a God-given means to help others. The Bible, however, warns that riches easily overwhelm a person, distorting his values, making him proud and arrogant, and making him think he does not need God. "But they that will be rich fall into temptation and a snare, and into many foolish and hurtful lusts, which drown men in destruction and perdition. For the love of money is the root of all evil" (1 Timothy 6:9–10). For others, wealth only leads to boredom. King Solomon was unquestionably one of the wealthiest men who ever lived. In his search for happiness he tried everything—possessions, music, sex, great building projects, knowledge—but in the end he declared about them, "I have seen all the works that are done under the sun; and, behold, all is vanity and vexation of spirit" (Ecclesiastes 1:14). Only God could satisfy his deepest longings and give him true happiness.

On the other hand, many great people stay poor all their lives, either through choice (such as a missionary or a person who chooses to live modestly and give away money to help others) or through unavoidable circumstances. There are others, however, who go through life filled with resentment, jealousy, and bitterness because they want "just a little bit more." They may have enough to satisfy their legitimate needs, but instead of being thankful for what they have— which would make them unimaginably wealthy in the eyes of those in poorer nations—they are consumed by a desire for riches. They believe the key to happiness would be found in greater wealth.

But Jesus made it plain that happiness and contentment are not found in possessions or money. He stated that material things and riches do not in themselves bring happiness and peace to the soul.

Happy is that person who has learned the secret of being content with whatever life brings him, and has learned to rejoice in the simple and beautiful things around him.

In his Introduction to his *Anthology* on George MacDonald, C. S. Lewis says of MacDonald: "His resignation to poverty was at the opposite pole from that of a stoic. He appears to have been a sunny, playful man, deeply appreciative of all really beautiful and delicious things that money can buy, and no less deeply content to do without them." In *Annals of a Quiet Neighborhood* MacDonald said of himself, "Let me, if I may, be ever welcomed to my room in winter by a glowing hearth, in summer by a vase of flowers; if I may not, let me then think how nice they would be, and bury myself in my work. I do not think that the road to contentment lies in despising what we have not got. Let us acknowledge all good, all delight that the world holds, and be content without it."

An Unforgettable Day

On that day almost two thousand years ago there were undoubtedly many in that great throng who believed as many today believe—that the key to happiness is to be found in wealth and possessions. As they gathered to listen to Jesus, perhaps they wondered if His words could actually make any difference to them in their search for happiness—as you may wonder. It was soon clear to them, however, that His message was unique, for He was pointing another way to happiness—God's way. And it was a message which applied to every person.

The Sermon on the Mount was delivered to two distinct groups of people: the *multitude* and the *disciples of Christ.* We can therefore assume that it contains significance and meaning for both the disciples and the multitude, else Jesus would not have addressed it to both.

It gave the *disciples* a glimpse into the lofty spiritual Promised Land in which they were to live as the followers of Christ. It revealed the high ethical plane on which they were to live. It showed that to be a Christian was no mere child's play.

As for the *multitude,* the Sermon was an unveiling of what it actually meant to be a follower of Christ. Up to that time Jesus had been to them a fascinating and intriguing miracle worker. His person was magnetic, His manner winsome, His voice compelling. His entire being marked Him as a man of unusual power. He was a master teacher, a formidable debater, a compassionate healer—the gentlest and the sternest of men. Never had they heard anyone like Him.

These people, whose lives were monotonously humdrum in that unromantic faraway land, responded to this Galilean. To spend a day following Him through the villages where He healed the sick, blessed little children, and talked about the kingdom of God was a never-to-be-forgotten experience.

But on this particular day many who followed Him were to be surprised. Religion to them had been little more than superstition and meaningless ceremony. It little occurred to them that there was any relevance between religion and life. They had given up ever being happy; and if they ever knew the meaning of the word *happy,* they had forgotten it.

But Jesus was to put the words *blessed, joyful,* and *happy* back into their vocabularies—and even better, He was to put the words into their very hearts and lives. As Henry van Dyke's grand old hymn puts it: "Joyful, joyful, we adore Thee."

When Jesus opened His mouth, the first word to fall from His lips was "happy." This word means "blessed, contented, or highly favored." *Happy!* Could any word have been more incongruous? Those who listened that day were far from being blessed or happy. Subdued by the Roman Empire, they were conquered. Poor, dejected, ill-clad, and pawns of an alien government, their lives were without hope and expectation. Happy? How could the meager existence of their lives be highly favored, blessed, and contented?

The Nature of Poverty

Quickly on the heels of that first word followed five others: "Happy are the poor in spirit." If Jesus had omitted the last two words, they would have all rejoiced, for they were all poor—even if they would have been puzzled at how their grinding poverty could possibly make them happy. But Jesus said "the poor in spirit."

Wondering, they listened as He went on. Hidden in these seemingly cryptic words was the first foundational secret of happiness. At first it sounds like a contradiction. We usually think of people who are poor as being unhappy. But Jesus teaches that happiness can be found in spite of poverty.

What kind of poverty did Jesus have in mind? Did He mean those who had very little of this world's goods? No! Certainly they were included. But Jesus was speaking to persons of every type—rich or poor, sick or well, educated or uneducated, young or old. God is concerned about every person on this planet, and Jesus' words were addressed to all persons, in every circumstance, and in every generation. They are addressed to you and me today.

The True Meaning of Spiritual Poverty

What did Jesus mean by being "poor in spirit"? There are at least four dimensions to this crucial question.

FIRST: If we are to be poor in spirit, *we must be aware of our spiritual poverty.*

No man is more pathetic than he who is in great need and is not aware of it. Remember Samson? Standing there in the valley of Sorek, surrounded by the lords of the Philistines, ". . . he wist not that the Lord was departed from him" (Judges 16:20).

The pitiable thing about the Pharisees was not so much their hypocrisy as it was their utter lack of knowledge of how poor they actually were in the sight of God.

Jesus told a dramatic story about a man who had mistaken ideas concerning poverty and riches. This man, in a self-satisfied soliloquy, one night said: "Soul, thou hast much goods laid up for many years; take thine ease, eat, drink, and be merry" (Luke 12:19).

It had never occurred to him that the soul cannot subsist on goods and that the heart cannot be nourished by wine and food. Because of his stupidity and his attaching an undue importance to material things, God said: "Thou fool" (Luke 12:20). And to all those of every age who are tempted to reason falsely as he did, God said: "So is he that layeth up treasure for himself, and is not rich toward God" (Luke 12:21).

Each of us has a body with eyes, ears, nose, hands, and feet. This body has certain legitimate desires and appetites: the appetite for food and drink, the appetite for sex, and the appetite for fellowship. Each of these has been given to us by God, to be used as He intended. At the same time, they can be distorted and misused, eventually bringing sorrow and ruin to our lives.

But the Bible teaches that a person is more than just a body—each of us is actually a living soul! Our souls are created in the image of God. Just as our bodies have certain characteristics and appetites, so do our souls. The characteristics of the soul are personality, intelligence, conscience, and memory. The human soul or spirit longs for peace, contentment, and happiness. Most of all, the soul has an appetite for God—a yearning to be reconciled to its Creator and to have fellowship with Him forever.

In the world in which we live, we give most attention to satisfying the appetites of the body and practically none to the soul. Consequently we are one-sided. We become fat physically and materially, while spiritually we are lean, weak, and anemic. Or we spend enormous amounts of time and money on fad diets, expensive exercise machines, and health clubs. For many people, these things only demonstrate their preoccupation with the physical side of life. To be sure, our bodies have been given us by God, and we are to take care of them in every way possible. But even more important is taking care of our souls. The apostle Paul told Timothy, "Train yourself in godliness; for while bodily training is of some value, godliness is of value in every way, as it holds promise for the present life and also the life to come" (1 Timothy 4:7–8, RSV).

The soul, created in the image of God, cannot be fully satisfied until it knows God in the proper way. Only God can resolve the deepest longings, desires, and appetites of the soul.

I may have the glamor of a movie queen or I may have the riches of a Texas millionaire and still not find happiness, peace, and contentment. Why? Simply because I have given attention to the body but not to the soul.

The soul actually demands as much attention as the body. It demands fellowship and communion with God. It demands worship, quietness, and meditation. Unless the soul is fed and exercised daily, it becomes weak and shriveled. It remains discontented, confused, restless.

Many people turn to alcohol or drugs to try to drown the cryings and longings of the soul. Some turn to a new sex experience. Others attempt to quiet the longings of their souls in other ways. But nothing but God ever completely satisfies, because the soul was made for God, and without God it is restless and in secret torment.

The First Step

The first step to God is a realization of our spiritual poverty. The poor in spirit do not measure the worth of life in earthly possessions, which fade away, but in terms of eternal realities, which endure forever. Wise is the man who openly confesses his lack of spiritual wealth and in humility of heart cries, "God, be merciful unto me, a sinner."

In God's economy, emptying comes before filling, confession before forgiveness, and poverty before riches. Christ said there is a happiness in that acknowledgment of spiritual poverty which lets God come into our souls.

Now, the Bible teaches that our souls have a disease. It is worse than any dreaded cancer or heart disease. It is the plague that causes all the troubles and difficulties in the world. It causes all the troubles, confusions, and disillusion-ments in our own lives. The name of the disease is an ugly word. We don't like to use it. But it's a word that the psychiatrists are beginning to use once again. In our desire to be modern, we had almost forgotten it, but once again we are beginning to realize that it is the root of all man's troubles. It is *sin*.

We have sinned against our Creator. God is holy, righteous, and just. He can-not allow sin to enter His presence. Consequently, sin has come between God and us.

Now, there must be a confession that we have broken His laws and are will-ing to renounce our sins. We must acknowledge that without His fellowship life has no real meaning. This is not easy! All of us have pride, though it may be expressed in various ways. We do not like to confess that we are wrong or that we have failed. But God says: "All have sinned, and come short of the glory of God" (Romans 3:23). We must confess our sin as the first step to happiness, peace, and contentment!

This generation, encouraged by many second-rate philosophies, has tried in vain to live oblivious to God. The current resurgence of religion in the world is a mass confession that Humanism has failed. Like the Laodiceans of old, we have said, "I am rich, and increased with goods, and have need of nothing" (Revelation 3:17); but we have discovered that our riches, like our beauty, are only skin-deep and not sufficient to satisfy our eternal souls.

Let us face this fact: We came into the world with nothing, and we will leave it with nothing.

Where do we get the notion that our idea of success and God's are the same? You have written a book; you are a clever manager and promoter; you are a talented artist; you are independently wealthy; you have achieved fame and fortune. Without the gifts of intelligence, imagination, personality, and physi-cal energy—which are all endowed by God—where would you be?

Are we not born poor? Do we not die poor? And would we not be poor indeed without God's infinite mercy and love? We came out of nothing; and if we are anything, it is because God is everything. If He were to withhold His power for one brief instant from us, if He were to hold in check the breath of life for one moment, our physical existence would shrivel into nothingness and our souls would be whisked away into an endless eternity.

Those who are poor in spirit recognize their creatureliness and their sinful-ness—but more, they are ready to confess their sins and renounce them.

The Cure for Our Spiritual Disease

We have seen that the first dimension of "poor in spirit" is a realization of our spiritual poverty. But can our poverty be overcome? Yes! And that leads us to the second dimension of what Jesus meant by being "poor in spirit."

Second: If we are to be poor in spirit, *we must receive the riches that Christ has provided by His death and resurrection.*

Would it not be wonderful if we could find an absolute cure for the troubles of human nature? Suppose we could give a shot in the arm to the whole human race that would fill us with love instead of hate, with contentment instead of greed. This would immediately solve all the problems that the world faces at this moment.

Many years ago two Americans were crossing the Atlantic and on a Sunday night they were singing the hymn, "Jesus, Lover of My Soul." They were joined by a third party who had a very rich tenor voice. When the music stopped one of the Americans turned to the third party to ask if he had been in the Civil War. The man replied that he had been a Confederate soldier. Then he was asked if he was at a certain place on a certain night and the man replied, "Yes." And he said that a curious thing had happened that night. This hymn recalled it to his mind. "I was on sentry duty at the edge of the wood. It was dark and very cold. I was frightened because the enemy was supposed to be near. I felt home-sick and miserable. About midnight, when everything was still, I was begin-ning to feel so weary I thought I could comfort myself by singing a hymn and I remembered this hymn. 'All my trust on Thee is stayed,/all my help from Thee I bring./Cover my defenseless head/with the shadow of Thy wing.' After I had sung those words, a strange peace came on me and through the long night I felt no fear."

"Well," said one of the men, "listen to my story. I was a Union soldier and I was in the woods that night with a party of scouts. I saw you standing in the woods. My men focused their rifles on you but when you began to sing, we lis-tened. We could not fire and I told them to put down their rifles. 'We'll go home,' I said."

Our daily papers and television newscasts record discontentment and unhap-piness all over the world. They are the result of greed, ambition, lust, preju-dice, and evil desire. If people could only be content in whatever state they find themselves; if they could love their fellow men regardless of the color of the skin or their station in life; if those who "have" would show compassion on the "have-nots"; if the greedy would give up their unholy ambition for power— would not this world be a different place in which to live?

Suppose, also, a cure could be found for the past mistakes, failures and sins of mankind. Suppose by some miracle all the past could be straightened out, all of life's tangles could be unraveled and the broken strings of life could be repaired. Such a cure would cause a world-wide stampede!

The most thrilling news in all the world is the fact that there is a cure! A medicine has been provided! People can be forgiven of all sin! The cobwebs that have collected in our lives can be removed!

The sin, confusion, and disillusionment of life can be replaced by righteous-ness, joy, contentment, and happiness. A peace can be imparted to the soul that is not dependent on outward circumstances. This cure was provided by Jesus Christ two thousand years ago on the cross of Calvary.

The cross has become a symbol in much of the Western world, misused by many rock stars and others who do not comprehend its significance.

The death of Christ on that first Good Friday was no mere accident. It was an act of a loving God to reconcile people to Himself. Sin had come between us and God. We could not be happy and contented apart from God. Therefore, in loving grace God sent His Son to bear our sins and to take the penalty and judgment that we deserved.

However, God requires something of *us*. We must confess our spiritual poverty, renounce our sins, and turn by faith to His Son, Jesus Christ. When we do that, we are born again. He gives us a new nature. He puts a little bit of heaven down in our souls. Our lives change. Contentment, peace. and happiness come into our souls for the first time.

In my travels I have watched for lastingly contented and happy people. I have found such people only where Christ has been personally and decisively received. There is only one permanent way to have peace of soul that wells up in joy, contentment, and happiness, and that is by repentance of sin and personal faith in Jesus Christ as Savior.

Has such a moment come to your life? Have you had the experience of receiving Christ? It is not simply an emotional experience. It is a simple surrender of the will to Christ. Do you really want happiness? Then you will have to pay the price of humbling yourself at the foot of the cross and receiving Christ as Savior.

Our Dependence on God

We must know our spiritual poverty . . . we must turn to Christ in repentance and faith to receive His riches . . . but there is still more if we are to grasp the true meaning of being "poor in spirit."

THIRD: If we are to be poor in spirit, *we must be conscious of our dependence on God,* our spiritual bankruptcy.

Jesus said we must become like children before we can enter the kingdom of heaven. Children are dependents. That is to say, they depend upon their parents for protection and care. Because of their relationship and position they are not poor; but if it were not for their established relationship with their parents, they could be helpless and poor indeed.

When we come to Christ, a wonderful thing immediately happens to us: We become children of God! We become part of His family, as His sons and daughters! "As many as received him, to them gave he power to become the sons of God, even to them that believe on his name: Which were born, not of blood, nor of the will of the flesh, nor of the will of man, but of God" (John 1:12–13).

In fact, the Bible uses the idea of "adoption" to illustrate this great fact. At one time we were alienated from God, with no rights or privileges. But in Christ we were adopted into His family (Ephesians 1:5–6). "For ye are all the children of God by faith in Christ Jesus" (Galatians 3:26).

As God's children, we are His dependents. The Bible says: "Like as a father pitieth his children, so the Lord pitieth them that fear him" (Psalm 103:13).

Dependent children spend little time worrying about meals, clothing, and shelter. They assume, and they have a right to, that all will be provided by their parents.

Jesus said: "Take no thought, saying, What shall we eat? or, What shall we drink? or, Wherewithal shall we be clothed? . . . But seek ye first the kingdom of God . . . and all these things shall be added unto you" (Matthew 6:31, 33).

Because God is responsible for our welfare, we are told to cast all our care upon Him, for He cares for us (1 Peter 5:7). Because we are dependent upon God, Jesus said: "Let not your heart be troubled" (John 14:1). God says, "I'll take the burden—don't give it a thought—leave it to Me."

Dependent children are not backward about asking for things. They would not be normal if they did not boldly make their needs known.

God has said to His dependent children: "Therefore come boldly unto the throne of grace, that we may obtain mercy, and find grace to help in time of need" (Hebrews 4:16). God is keenly aware that we are dependent upon Him for life's necessities. It was for that reason that Jesus said: "Ask, and it shall be given you; seek, and ye shall find; knock, and it shall be opened unto you" (Matthew 7:7).

What is troubling you today? Is your heart burdened because of some problem which threatens to overcome you? Are you filled with anxiety and worry about some problem, wondering what will happen? Listen: as a child of God through faith in Christ, you can turn these over to Christ, knowing that He loves you and He is able to help you. At times He may take the problem away; other times He may give you strength to bear it. But you can rest in Him. "Have no anxiety about anything, but in everything by prayer and supplication with thanksgiving let your requests be made known to God. And the peace of God, which passes all understanding, will keep your hearts and your minds in Christ Jesus" (Philippians 4:6–7, RSV).

Happy is the person who has learned the secret of coming to God daily in prayer. Fifteen minutes alone with God every morning before one starts the day can change our outlooks and recharge our batteries.

But all of this happiness and all of these unlimited benefits which flow from the storehouse of heaven are contingent upon our relationship to God. Absolute dependency and absolute yieldedness are the conditions of being His child. Only His children are entitled to receive those things that lend themselves to happiness; and in order to be His child, there must be the surrender of the will to Him.

We must admit we are poor before we can be made rich. We must admit we are destitute before we can become children by adoption.

When we realize that all our own goodness is as filthy rags in God's sight and become aware of the destructive power of our stubborn wills, when we realize our absolute dependence upon the grace of God through faith and nothing more, then we have started on the road to happiness.

We do not come to know God through works—we come to know Him by faith through grace. We cannot work our way toward happiness and heaven; we cannot moralize our way, we cannot reform our way, we cannot buy our way. Salvation comes as a gift of God through Christ.

Serving Christ

As God's children we are not just meant to sit back and selfishly enjoy our privileges. Instead, God wants to use us to serve Him and help others. But before we can do that something else must happen in our hearts if we are truly to know the full meaning of Jesus' words: "Happy are the poor in spirit."

FOURTH: If we are to be poor in spirit, *we must willingly deny ourselves that we might better serve Christ.*

The poor in spirit are those who are willing to sell out their stock in themselves and to do as Jesus said: "Deny himself, and take up his cross, and follow me" (Matthew 16:24).

Our modern philosophy of self-reliance and self-sufficiency has caused many to believe that man can make the grade without God. "Religion," they argue, "may be all right for certain emotional people, but you can't beat a man who believes in himself." For example, the Austrian neurologist and founder of psychoanalysis, Dr. Sigmund Freud, said that religion was the universal obsessional neurosis.

But alas, this self-confident generation has produced more alcoholics, more drug addicts, more criminals, more wars, more broken homes, more assaults, more embezzlements, more murders, and more suicides than any other generation that ever lived. It is time all of us, from the intellectuals on down, began to take stock of our failures, blunders, and costly mistakes. It is about time that we placed less confidence in ourselves and more trust and faith in God.

The rich young ruler who came to Jesus was so filled with his piety, his riches, and his greed that he revolted when Jesus informed him that the price of eternal life was to "sell out" and come and follow Him. He went away sorrowfully, the Bible says, because he could not detach himself from himself. He found it impossible to become "poor in spirit" because he had such a lofty estimate of his own importance.

All around us are arrogance, pride, and selfishness: these are the results of sin. From the heavens comes a voice speaking to a tormented, bankrupt world: "I counsel thee to buy of me gold tried in the fire, that thou mayest be rich; and white raiment, that thou mayest be clothed, and that the shame of thy nakedness do not appear; and anoint thine eyes with eye-salve, that thou mayest see. . . . Behold, I stand at the door, and knock: if any man hear my voice, and open the door, I will come in to him, and will sup with him, and he with me" (Revelation 3:18, 20).

Heaven in this life and heaven in the life to come are not on a monetary standard. Nor can flesh and blood find the door to the kingdom of heaven with its contentment, peace, joy, and happiness. Only those who are poor in spirit and are rich toward God shall be accounted worthy to enter there, because they come not in their own merit but in the righteousness of the Redeemer.

Someone has said, "A man's wealth consists not in the abundance of his possessions, but in the fewness of his wants." "The first link between my soul and Christ," said C. H. Spurgeon, "is not my goodness but my badness, not my merit but my misery, not my riches but my need."

"Happy are the poor in spirit: for theirs is the kingdom of heaven!"

3

Happiness while Mourning

Blessed are they that mourn: for they shall be comforted. MATTHEW 5:4

THERE COMES A time in our lives when good-natured, well-meant encouragement like "Hang in there, pal" and "Cheer up, friend" fail to hoist us out of the doldrums. Because our needs are deeper than psychological, such suggestions only seem to make keener our feeling of helplessness.

The truth is: Regardless of our cleverness, our achievements and our gadgets, we are spiritual paupers without God.

Christ's message was directed to one specific group—to the "poor," the poor in spirit. Christ said: "The Spirit of the Lord is upon me, because he hath anointed me to preach the gospel to the poor" (Luke 4:18). This did not mean that Christ's message was only for the financially poor, the socially poor, or the intellectually poor. It meant that it was for those who recognized their spiritual poverty. That was the first Beatitude. It was the dominant note upon which this celestial anthem of truth was composed. Of the Macedonian Christians Paul wrote, ". . . in a great trial of affliction the abundance of their joy and their deep poverty abounded unto the riches of their liberality" (2 Corinthians 8:2).

If we would find genuine happiness, we must begin where Jesus began. If we would have meaningful lives, we must live by the Beatitudes.

This second Beatitude, "Happy are they that mourn," at first seems paradoxical. Do crying and joy go together? How can we possibly be happy while we are in the throes of mourning? How can one extract the perfume of gladness from the gall of sorrow?

But rest assured that there is deep and hidden significance here, for remember, Jesus was speaking to all people of all beliefs and of all ages and was revealing to them the secret of happiness.

The Shallowness of Our Lives

This present age is definitely not an age of mourning. Instead, people deliberately turn away from anything unpleasant, determined to fill their lives with those things which will divert their minds from anything serious. In their preoccupation with momentary pleasures and diversions, people settle for shallow and empty substitutes for reality. Millions give more thought to what programs they will watch tonight on TV or what videotape they will rent for the weekend than they do to the things of eternity.

This century could well go down in history not so much as a century of progress but as "the century of superficiality." The popular exclamation "So what!" aptly describes the attitude of many toward life. Many think that so long as we have sleek automobiles to ride in, TV and movies to entertain us, luxurious homes to live in, and a million gadgets to serve us, what happens to our souls does not matter. "So what! Laugh, and the world laughs with you; weep, and you weep alone." The apostles of mirth therefore put on their grimacing masks, turn the volume up on their TVs or press down the accelerators on their sports cars, and plunge into their superficial living.

But superficial living will never help us stand against the pressures and problems of life. At the end of the Sermon on the Mount Jesus told the story of two men. One decided to build his house on sand; it would, after all, have been easy to do. The other built his house on rock, although that would have involved more work. Outwardly both houses looked the same. But when the storms and floods came the house built on sand was destroyed. Only the house built on rock withstood the pressures of the flood. "Therefore whosoever heareth these sayings of mine, and doeth them, I will liken him unto a wise man, which built his house upon a rock" (Matthew 7:24). Only when our lives are grounded in the eternal truth of God's Word will they be able to withstand the storms of life. A superficial life which neglects God can never give us a firm foundation for true happiness.

The following comment appeared in an issue of *The London Times:* "The grace of final perseverance is that quality of patience that is always equal to the pressure of the passing moment, because it is rooted in the Eternal over which the passing moment has no power."

Beverly Sills, the former opera star and now a producer, has learned some lessons in adversity. Her first child was born almost totally deaf. The little girl was destined never to hear her mother's beautiful voice lifted in song. Her second child, a son, was born mentally retarded.

So great was the sorrow in Mrs. Sills' life that she took off a year from her demanding profession to work with her daughter and son, trying to make peace with the difficult circumstances. Later, when she was asked how she came to terms with the situation she answered, "The first question you ask is, Why me? Then it changes to Why them? It makes a complete difference in your attitude." Her attitude is the opposite of superficiality.

Now, I am not gunning for TV addicts or movie buffs in particular, but I do strongly contend that life is more than "skin-deep." Look at your popular comedians! Underneath the feigned smirks and the pretended smiles are the furrows and lines of seriousness and sobriety. Although it is their business to make you laugh, they are well aware that life is a solemn business.

Recently a dear friend of ours was told she had cancer. "It is amazing," she said to us, "how one day you can be going along smoothly and the next day one little word from the doctor's lips—'cancer'—radically changes everything. Then you know as you never have before that life is serious, and eternity is only a heartbeat away. Suddenly many of the things that seemed so important just a day ago are no longer very important."

Jesus did not mean "Blessed are the morose, the miserable, or the sullen." The Pharisees made a masquerade of religion, rubbed ashes on their faces to appear religious, but He strongly rebuked them for that. "Be not, as the hypocrites, of a sad countenance," He said (Matthew 6:16).

Who was it that said, "Some people's religion is like a man with a headache—he can't afford to give up his head, but it hurts him to keep it"?

The Meaning of Mourning

What did Jesus mean when He said: "Happy are they that mourn"? Certainly He did not mean to imply that a special blessing is promised to "crybabies," "weeping Willies," or the emotionally upset. This verse was not intended to be a comfort for abnormal psychopathic cases, which have somehow become mentally warped and take a morbid view of life. No, it was addressed to normal, average people for the purpose of showing them how to live happier, fuller, richer lives.

Let us begin with the word *mourning* itself. It means "to feel deep sorrow, to show great concern, or to deplore some existing wrong." It implies that if we are to live life on the higher plane then we are to be sensitive, sympathetic, tenderhearted, and alert to the needs of others and the world.

Perhaps we can see its meaning more clearly by thinking about its opposite. What is the opposite of mourning? Some might say it would be joy—and that is correct to a certain degree. But more than that, *the opposite of mourning is insensitivity, lack of caring, unconcern, callousness, indifference.* When I mourn it is because my heart has been touched by the suffering and heartache of others—or even by my own heartache. When I do not care and am indifferent, then I do not mourn. The person who mourns is a person with a tender and sensitive heart.

Kinds of Mourning

Let's list just six kinds of mourning which I believe were implied in this most significant saying of our Lord. The word here employed by Jesus covers such a wide range of attitudes that five shades of meaning are implied. We should ponder each one of them prayerfully.

First, there is *the mourning of inadequacy.* Jeremiah, the weeping prophet who mourned not in self-pity but for a wayward, lost world, said: "O Lord, I know that the way of man is not in himself: it is not in man that walketh to direct his steps" (10:23).

Now, before I can become strong. I must first realize that I am weak. Before I can become wise, I must first realize that I am foolish. Before I can receive power, I must first confess that I am powerless. I must lament my sins before I can rejoice in a Savior. Mourning, in God's sequence, always comes before exultation. Blessed are those who mourn their unworthiness, their helplessness, and their inadequacy.

Isaiah, the mighty prophet of God, knew by experience that one must bow the knee in mourning before one can lift the voice in jubilation. When his sin appeared ugly and venomous in the bright light of God's holiness, he said: "Woe is me! for I am undone; because I am a man of unclean lips: for mine eyes have seen the King, the Lord of hosts" (Isaiah 6:5).

We cannot be satisfied with our goodness after beholding the holiness of God. But our mourning over our unworthiness and sinfulness should be of short duration, for God has said: "I, even I, am he that blotteth out thy transgressions for mine own sake, and will not remember thy sins" (Isaiah 43:25).

Isaiah had to experience the mourning of inadequacy before he could realize the joy of forgiveness. If I have no sense of sorrow for sin, how can I know the need of repentance?

In God's economy, a person must go down into the valley of grief before he or she can scale the heights of spiritual glory. One must become tired and weary of living without Christ before he or she can seek and find his fellowship. One must come to the end of "self" before one can really begin to live.

The mourning of inadequacy is a weeping that catches the attention of God. The Bible says: "The Lord is nigh unto them that are of a broken heart; and saveth such as be of a contrite spirit" (Psalm 34:18).

We have received hundreds of letters from people who tried desperately to "get hold of themselves," who in their own strength tried to shake off their habits, their sins, and their nasty dispositions—but all in vain. Finally in desperation they came to Christ, and in Him they found strength to be more than conquerors.

Experience reveals that we are inadequate. History proves that we are inadequate. The Bible declares that a person is inadequate to save himself. Christ's coming to the world proves the inadequacy of the race.

The happiest day of my life was the day I realized that my own ability, my own goodness, and my own morality were insufficient in the sight of God and I publicly and openly acknowledged my need of Christ. I am not exaggerating when I say that my mourning was turned to joy and my sighing into singing.

Happy are they who mourn for the inadequacy of self, for they shall be comforted with the sufficiency of God.

The Mourning of Repentance

Another kind of mourning is *the mourning of repentance.*

Following the consciousness that we are inadequate comes the awareness of the reason for our insufficiency—sin. As individuals we have no control over the fact of sin in the universe, but as creatures of choice we are responsible for its presence in our lives. Because "all have sinned, and come short of the glory of God" (Romans 3:23), all need to mourn the fact of sin in their lives.

One technique of modern psychoanalysis is the association of present conflicts with past experiences. Sometimes when patients of psychiatry confess to past sins, they experience a certain release from their feelings of guilt. But since psychiatry is a science of the mind, it can do nothing for the soul. Only Christ is the Physician of the soul.

God has said: "Turn ye even to me with all your heart . . . with weeping, and with mourning" (Joel 2:12).

The mourning of repentance is not the weeping of self-pity; it is not regret over material losses nor remorse that our sins have been found out. It is entirely possible to be deeply sorry because of the devastation which sin has wrought in our lives—and yet not repent. I have had people pour out their hearts to me with tears, because their sins have been discovered and they are in serious trouble. But true repentance is more than being sorry for our sins and regretting the way we have allowed sin to shatter our lives. True repentance is a turning *from sin*—a conscious, deliberate decision to leave sin behind—and a conscious turning *to God* with a commitment to follow His will for our lives. It is a change of direction, an alteration of attitudes, and a yielding of the will. Humanly speaking, it is our small part in the plan of salvation—although even the strength to repent comes from God. But even so, the act of repentance does not win us any merit or make us worthy to be saved—it only conditions our hearts for the grace of God.

The Bible says: "Repent ye therefore, and be converted, that your sins may be blotted out, when the times of refreshing shall come from the presence of the Lord" (Acts 3:19). Our part is repenting. God will do the converting, the transforming, and the forgiving.

It will not be easy to bend our warped, stubborn wills; but once we do, it will be as though a misplaced vertebra has snapped back into place. Instead of the stress and tension of a life out of harmony with God will come the serenity of reconciliation. Our nerves will sense that our minds and hearts are relaxed, and they will send this happy news over their network to every fiber of our bodies: "Old things are passed away; behold all things are become new" (2 Corinthians 5:17).

Just as pain precedes birth, mourning over sin comes before spiritual rebirth. I do not mean to imply that in everyone's experience there will be loud, violent weeping over the sin in one's life—sorrow for sin may come quietly, with little or no emotion. But there will be a sincere sorrow for the evils of one's life and a disposition to turn to God for help and salvation. The Bible says: "For godly sorrow worketh repentance" (2 Corinthians 7:10).

The Mourning of Love

There is yet another aspect of this Beatitude, "Happy are they that mourn." There is, third, *the mourning of love.*

In many of the older cars the fuel gauge used to contain a red liquid, and its level in the gauge corresponded to the level of fuel in the tank. As the liquid was in the gauge, so it was in the tank.

If I would know the measure of my love for God, I must simply observe my love for people around me. My compassion for others is an accurate gauge of my devotion to God.

The Bible puts it this way: "Let us love one another: for love is of God; and every one that loveth is born of God, and knoweth God. . . . And this commandment have we from him, That he who loveth God love his brother also" (1 John 4:7, 21).

Some time ago, with some friends, I went through a museum in San Francisco. Among other things, we saw a collection of instruments of torture which were employed by religious people to force other people to believe as they did. History is largely the record of man's inhumanity to man.

This age in which we live could hardly be described as one in which people are honestly sensitive to the needs of others. We have developed a veneer of sophistication—but also cynicism and hardness. Our popular music talks constantly about love, and yet divorce rates skyrocket, child abuse is rampant, and our world is shaken by wars, violence, and terrorism. Major news magazines feature cover stories on "The 'Me' Generation." This generation, it seems, would rather see a prizefight than fight for a prize. Not only has the song "Rescue the perishing, care for the dying" disappeared from most of our songbooks, its theme has disappeared from our hearts, except for physical famine, victims of oppressive regimes and tidal waves. And these are terribly important. It is just that the spiritually perishing need to hear the gospel.

Several years ago we were visiting India. While we were there a terrible tidal wave hit a fifty-mile section of the coast, killing tens of thousands of people and completely destroying hundreds of villages and towns. Indian officials graciously provided a helicopter and accompanied us to the area, and we were among the first to view the devastation. I will never forget the terrible destruction and the stench of death—as if a thousand atom bombs had gone off at the same time. And yet this terrible disaster rated only a few inches in many American newspapers and only a minute or so on the evening news.

Abraham Lincoln once said, characteristically: "I am sorry for the man who can't feel the whip when it is laid on the other man's back."

Much of the world is callous and indifferent toward mankind's poverty and distress. This is due largely to the fact that for many people there has never been a rebirth. The love of God has never been shed abroad in their hearts.

Many people speak of the social gospel as though it were separate and apart from the redemptive gospel. The truth is: There is only one gospel. Divine love, like a reflected sunbeam, shines down before it radiates out. Unless our hearts are conditioned by the Holy Spirit to receive and reflect the warmth of God's compassion, we cannot love our fellow men as we ought.

Jesus wept tears of compassion at the graveside of a friend. He mourned over Jerusalem because as a city it had lost its appreciation of the things of the spirit. His great heart was sensitive to the needs of others.

To emphasize the importance of people's love for each other, He revised an old commandment to make it read: "Thou shalt love the Lord thy God with all thy heart . . . and thy neighbor as thyself" (Luke 10:27).

St. Francis of Assisi had discovered the secret of happiness when he prayed:

> O Divine Master, grant that I may not so much seek
> To be consoled as to console,
> To be understood as to understand,
> To be loved as to love;
> For it is in giving that we receive;
> It is in pardoning that we are pardoned;
> It is in dying that we are born to eternal life!

This generation is rough and tough. I heard a little boy boasting one day about how tough he was. He said, "On the street I live on, the farther out you go the tougher they get, and I live in the last house."

Tears shed for self are tears of weakness, but tears of love shed for others are a sign of strength. I am not as sensitive as I ought to be until I am able to "weep o'er the erring one and lift up the fallen." And until I have learned the value of compassionately sharing others' sorrow, distress, and misfortune, I cannot know real happiness.

The Mourning of Soul Travail

Another kind of mourning which brings comfort is, fourth, *the mourning of soul travail.*

This may seem cryptic, but it represents a very real and a profitable kind of mourning. The Bible says: "As soon as Zion travailed, she brought forth her children" (Isaiah 66:8).

We don't use this phrase "soul travail" very often, not as much as our spiritual forefathers a generation or so ago. "Travail" means "toil, painful effort, labor." "Travail of soul" therefore means spiritual toil—not necessarily outward labor which others will see, but that which takes place within the secret recesses of our souls. It refers to the continual flow of prayer which rises out of the Christian heart for a world which is spiritually unborn. And don't be under any illusions: this kind of soul travail is difficult and costly, because we are involved in spiritual warfare against Satan, the Enemy of Souls. "Pray without ceasing," the Bible says (1 Thessalonians 5:17).

God has worked in a miraculous way in our crusades down through the years. Thousands of men and women have made their decisions for Christ. Their coming was not the result of one man's work or the efforts of a group of men—it was the product of much prayer by many people around the world. God has said: "If my people . . . pray . . . then will I hear from heaven" (2 Chronicles 7:14).

Before three thousand people were brought into the Church on the day of Pentecost, the disciples had spent fifty days in prayer, fasting, and spiritual travail.

John Knox, with an all-consuming soul-concern for his country, prayed: "Give me Scotland, or I die!" His earnest travail was rewarded with a spiritual rebirth in his land. This is what is termed "praying in the Spirit." It is the manifestation of a deep spiritual concern for others, and it is instilled by the Spirit of God.

The Bible says: "For we know not what we should pray for as we ought: but the Spirit itself maketh intercession for us with groanings which cannot be uttered" (Romans 8:26).

This kind of prayer can span oceans, cross burning deserts, leap over mountains, and penetrate jungles to carry the healing, helping power of the gospel to the objects of our prayer.

This kind of mourning, this quality of concern, is produced by the presence of God's Spirit in our lives. That "the Spirit itself maketh intercession" indicates that it is actually God pleading, praying, and mourning through us. Thus we become co-laborers with God, actual partners with Him: our lives are lifted from the low plane of selfishness to the high plane of creativeness with God.

John Knox travailed in prayer, and the Church in Scotland expanded into new life. John Wesley travailed in prayer, and the Methodist movement was born. Martin Luther travailed, and the Reformation was under way.

God desires that we Christians be concerned and burdened for a lost world. If we pray this kind of prayer, an era of peace may come to the world and hordes of wickedness may be turned back. "As soon as Zion travailed, she brought forth her children" (Isaiah 66:8).

The Mourning of Suffering and Bereavement

Another kind of mourning we shall deal with is, fifth, *the mourning of bereavement.*

Nowhere has God promised anyone, even His children, immunity from sorrow, suffering, and pain. This world is a "vale of tears," and disappointment and heartache are as inevitable as clouds and shadows. Suffering is often the crucible in which our faith is tested. Those who successfully come through the "furnace of affliction" are the ones who emerge "like gold tried in the fire."

The Bible teaches unmistakably that we can triumph over bereavement. The Psalmist said: "Weeping may endure for a night, but joy cometh in the morning" (Psalm 30:5).

Self-pity can bring no enduring comfort. The fact is, it will only add to our misery. And unremitting grief will give us little consolation in itself, for grief begets grief. Ceaseless grieving will only magnify our sorrow. We should not peddle our sorrows and bewail our bad fortune—that will only depress others. Sorrow, or mourning, when it is borne in a Christian way, contains a built-in comfort. "Blessed are they that mourn: for they shall be comforted" (Matthew 5:4).

There is comfort in mourning *because we know that Christ is with us.* He has said: "Lo, I am with you always, even unto the end of the world" (Matthew 28:20). Suffering is endurable if we do not have to bear it alone; and the more compassionate the Presence, the less acute the pain.

How often when a child have you stubbed your toe, bruised a leg, or cut a hand, and, running to the arms of your mother, you there sobbed out your pain? Lovingly caressing you and tenderly kissing the hurt, she imparted the magic of healing; and you went your way half healed and wholly comforted. Love and compassion contain a stronger balm than all the salves and ointments made by man.

Yes, when a loved one dies it is natural for us to feel a sense of loss and even a deep loneliness. That will not necessarily vanish overnight. But even when we feel the pain of bereavement most intensely, we can also know the gracious and loving presence of Christ most closely. Christ—who suffered alone on the cross, and endured death and hell alone for our salvation—knows what it is to suffer and be lonely. And because He knows, He is able to comfort us by His presence. "Blessed be God, even the Father of our Lord Jesus Christ, the Father of mercies, and the God of all comfort; Who comforteth us in all our tribulation, that we may be able to comfort them which are in any trouble, by the comfort wherewith we ourselves are comforted of God" (2 Corinthians 1:3–4).

So, in our lives, there can be a blessedness in the midst of mourning. From suffering and bereavement God can bring into our lives new measures of His strength and love.

Jesus said, "Let not your heart be troubled . . . believe . . . in me" (John 14:1). When faith is strong, troubles become trifles.

There is also comfort in mourning *because in the midst of mourning God gives a song*. God says in Job 30:9: "I am their song." In Job 35:10 Elihu asks, "Where is God my maker, who giveth songs in the night?" His presence in our lives changes our mourning into song, and that song is a song of comfort. Sometimes it must be night to have that song!

This kind of comfort is the kind which enabled a devout Englishman to look at a deep, dark hole in the ground where his home stood before the bombing and say, "I always did want a basement, I did. Now I can jolly well build another house like I always wanted."

This kind of comfort is the kind which enabled a young minister's wife in a church near us to teach her Sunday school class of girls on the very day of her husband's funeral. Her mourning was not the kind which had no hope—it was a mourning of faith in the goodness and wisdom of God; it believed that our Heavenly Father makes no mistakes.

In addition, there can be comfort in mourning *because God can use our sufferings to teach us and make us better people*. Often it takes suffering to make us realize the brevity of life, and the importance of living for Christ. Often God uses suffering to accomplish things in our lives that would otherwise never be achieved.

The Bible puts it succinctly: "Count it all joy, my brethren, when you meet various trials, for you know that the testing of your faith produces steadfastness. And let steadfastness have its full effect, that you may be perfect and complete, lacking in nothing" (James 1:2–4, RSV). Some of the godliest people I have ever known were men and women who had been called upon to endure great suffering—perhaps even being invalids for many years. Many people would have grown bitter and resentful if they had faced such circumstances—and yet because they knew Christ and walked in the joy of His presence every day, God had blessed them and turned them into people who reflected Christ. Often I have gone into a sickroom or hospital room to encourage someone—and have left feeling I was the one who had been encouraged and helped, because God had used their trials to make them more like Christ.

Before the power of the atom was discovered, science had to devise a way to "smash" the atom. The secret of the atom's immeasurable and limitless power was in its being crushed.

Dr. Edward Judson, at the dedication of the Judson Memorial Church in New York City, said, "Suffering and success go together. If you are succeeding without suffering, it is because others before you have suffered; if you are suffering without succeeding, it is that others after you may succeed."

Most of all, there is comfort in mourning *because we know that this life is not all, but we have the hope of Heaven*. Paul said, "If in this life only we have hope in Christ, we are of all men most miserable" (1 Corinthians 15:19). But he knew that our hope was not just in this life, but in Heaven. Our hope is in the resurrected Christ who has opened the door to eternal life for all who put their trust in Him. "O death, where is thy sting? O grave, where is thy victory? . . . thanks be to God, which giveth us the victory through our Lord Jesus Christ" (1 Corinthians 15:55, 57).

I will never forget the last few months of my mother's life, just before she went to be with the Lord. During those months she grew weaker and weaker physically—but her joy and excitement about heaven grew stronger and stronger! Whenever anyone went to visit her they came away marveling at her radiance and sense of expectancy. Yes, when she died there were tears—but in the midst of them, those of us who loved her had a deep sense of joy and comfort because we knew she was with the Lord. "Happy are they that mourn, for they shall be comforted."

This was the apostle Paul's hope—a hope based squarely on the fact of Jesus' resurrection. "We are troubled on every side, yet not distressed. . . . though our outward man perish, yet the inward man is renewed day by day. For our light affliction, which is but for a moment, worketh for us a far more exceeding and eternal weight of glory; While we look not at the things which are seen, but at the things which are not seen; for the things which are seen are temporal; but the things which are not seen are eternal" (2 Corinthians 4:8, 16–18). Jesus declared, "I am the resurrection, and the life: he that believeth in me, though he were dead, yet shall he live: And whosoever liveth and believeth in me shall never die" (John 11:25–26).

Do you have that hope in your heart? Do you know that if you were to die tonight you would go to heaven to be with Christ forever? You can, if you will trust Christ as your personal Savior and Lord. Jesus promised, "I go to prepare a place for you. . . . that where I am, there ye may be also" (John 14:2–3).

"Blessed (happy) are they that mourn." They are happy because they know that their aim, their distress, and their privation are the travail of a new creation, the birth pangs of a better world. They are happy because they are aware that the Master Artist—God—is employing both light and shadow to produce a masterpiece worthy of divine artistry.

They are also made to glory in their infirmities, to smile through their tears, and to sing in the midst of their sorrow because they realize that in God's economy "if we suffer, we shall also reign with him" (2 Timothy 2:12).

The Mourning of Blank Despair

Lastly, there is *the mourning of blank despair.* "I could not think about my own death," says one young AIDS victim. "I wanted to live forever."

The tragedy of AIDS is obvious. But as C. S. Lewis said of war, "War does not increase death. Death is total in every generation." So it could be said of AIDS; it does not increase death; death is total in every generation.

However, in this present grim situation, a merciful God has given people time. A short time perhaps, torn with frustration, anger, bitterness and fear—but still time. Time to think of God, His love for a world gone wrong, the sending of His Son to bear in His own body on the cross, all the sins of mankind. Time to come to Him in childlike repentance and to discover the love of Jesus, His transforming power, and the life everlasting that He promises and has gone to prepare for us.

4

Happiness through Meekness

Blessed are the meek: for they shall inherit the earth. Matthew 5:5

Most of us seek short cuts to happiness. We search for the gold nuggets of spiritual satisfaction on the surface instead of in the depths, where they are found in abundance. It is only natural to follow the line of least resistance, forgetting all the while that heat and light are both products of resistance, a resistance which releases the latent forces of life.

Many of us are like the man out West who had a junk yard. He labored hard and long, buying and selling the old salvage he gathered from the back alleys of the city. But one day he discovered that his junk yard was located on an oil field. He hired a drilling crew, and soon the black gold flowed abundantly from the bosom of the earth. His junk yard was transformed into a veritable mine of wealth which knew no limits.

In these Beatitudes we have a mine of spiritual gold. To many it seems too good to be true, so they go their way, scratching around on the surface of life, picking up salvage in the form of gadgets, gold, and gimmicks. Because they ignore the challenge and the promise of these secrets of happiness, they miss the key to radiant living and remain spiritual paupers, submerged in a misery of their own making.

They forget that what happens *within* them is more important than what happens *to* them. Because they have built no inner fortifications, they fall a prey to the Enemy. They become filled with resentments and are baffled by frustration and depressed by disillusionment.

Would God have bothered to send His Son to the world if we had been able to face life and eternity alone? Christ's coming to the world proved that God was not happy with our unhappiness. He sent Him not only that we might have eternal life but that we might have life here and now, and that we might have it more abundantly—Life with a capital *L!*

Jesus' teaching was unique and different. He took religion out of the theoretical realm and placed it in the practical. He used no qualifying statements or phrases in declaring His way of life. He didn't use such phrases as "I venture to say" or "Perhaps it's this way" or "It is my considered opinion."

He spoke with authority! He spoke with finality! He spoke as though He knew . . . and He did! When the Sermon on the Mount was completed we read that "the people were astonished at his doctrine: for he taught them as one having authority, and not as the scribes" (Matthew 7:28–29).

His was not the soft, empty conjecture of the philosopher who professes to search for truth but readily admits he has never found it. It was more the confident voice of the mathematician who gives his answers unhesitatingly because the proof of the answer can be found within the problem.

He taught with authority because He was more than just another religious teacher—He was God Himself, who had come down in human flesh. His words are true, because He is God and God cannot lie. "God . . . hath in these last days spoken unto us by his Son, whom he hath appointed heir of all things, by whom also he made the worlds" (Hebrews 1:1–2). And because He is God incarnate, we can depend totally and absolutely on the trustworthiness of Him and His Word.

In this third Beatitude we have the words "(Happy) are the meek: for they shall inherit the earth." Has it ever occurred to you that there is happiness in meekness?

Searching for the Meaning of Meekness

To most people today the word "meek" brings to mind a picture of someone who is a weak personality, someone who allows everyone to walk over him. Meekness, in fact, in the popular mind is not seen as a desirable personality trait. Our society says, "Get ahead by intimidation" or "Look out for Number One." In the eyes of many people the only way to get ahead is to disregard other people and shove them out of the way. "I want to climb the ladder of success," one woman was quoted as saying, "and I don't care whose fingers I step on as I climb up the rungs."

But what does Jesus mean when He speaks of meekness? Does He, for example, mean that we are to be cringing before God, fearful of Him and slavishly yielding to His will because of fear of what He might do to us if we fail?

Could it be that Christ wanted His followers to be like the subdued puppy that comes crawling into its master's presence whipped and beaten? Is happiness the result of forced submission? Certainly not!

Jesus is not trying to convey the thought that God is an autocrat whose ego can be satisfied only by coerced yielding. Nothing could be further from the truth. There is no happiness in being compelled to do what you do not wish to do. No employees are more miserable than those who constantly resent their position in life. It would be against God's nature, as well as against man's free moral agency, to demand an allegiance which is not freely offered.

God conducts Himself in keeping with His righteousness. He will never violate our freedom to choose between eternal life and spiritual death, good and evil, right and wrong. His ultimate goal is not only to glorify Himself but also to make a happy relationship with His crowning creation—man. Never will He make any demands which encroach upon our freedom to choose.

Or does the meekness to which Jesus refers mean *weakness?* Does it mean that a special blessing is to be given to the feeble, the frail, or the fragile?

Certainly God has a special concern for those who are weak and powerless in this world. "Like as a father pitieth his children, so the Lord pitieth them that fear him. For he knoweth our frame; he remembereth that we are dust" (Psalm 103:13–14). But this is not what Jesus means by meekness here. The disciples were to be meek, but not weak and vacillating. They were to be disciplined, but not subdued and harmless in the face of evil.

Or does Jesus refer to those who are by nature mild-tempered? Some people are born with nicer dispositions than others. Their mild manner is not so much the product of prayer and spiritual grace as it is a matter of heredity. They are mild because their mother, or father or grandmother was mild-mannered. This is an admirable trait, but Jesus surely didn't refer to these fortunate few who by nature have good dispositions. That would mean that many who have dispositions like buzz saws could never know this happiness to which He refers.

In His characteristic way, Jesus was saying something quite shocking and quite revolutionary to His listeners in these words: "Happy are the meek." He was saying something quite the opposite to our modern concept of the way to happiness.

We say, "Happy are the clever, for they shall inherit the admiration of their friends"; "Happy are the aggressive, for they shall inherit prosperity"; "Happy are the talented, for they shall inherit a career"; "Happy are the rich, for they shall inherit a world of friends and a house full of modern gadgets."

The True Meaning of Meekness

What, then, did Jesus mean? The dictionary says that the word *meek* means "mild, submissive, and compliant." William Barclay points out that the Greek word for "meek" was the word which was often used to describe an animal which had been tamed to obey the command of its master. It might be a strong animal like a horse or ox, able to do a great deal of work. It was not "weak"— but it was "meek," always obedient to the will of its owner. A tame horse contributes much more to life than a wild one. Energy out of control is dangerous; energy under control is powerful.

That is a vivid picture of what Jesus means by "meekness." When we are apart from Christ we are, in a sense, like a wild animal. We live according to our own desires and wishes, obeying our own instincts and ruling our own lives. But when we come to Christ our goal is different. Now we want to live for Him and do His will. This, after all, is God's will for us, for Christ "died for all, that they which live should not henceforth live unto themselves, but unto him which died for them, and rose again" (2 Corinthians 5:15). We are "meek," submissive to the will of our Master and ready to work for Him. And when our lives and hearts are marked by true meekness, we will know true happiness.

Jesus did not say, "Be meek, and you shall inherit the earth." He, more than anyone else, knew that meekness was a gift of God, a result of a rebirth, a new life within.

Moses was meek, but he was not meek by nature. He slew an Egyptian in anger, and on more than one occasion he showed that he was not naturally meek. When he found the children of Israel turning from the Lord and worshiping idols, he became angry and dashed to the ground the tablets of stone upon which were inscribed the Ten Commandments. His meekness quite obviously was contrary to his nature. It was a miracle of God! Numbers 12:3 says, "Now the man Moses was very meek, above all the men which were upon the face of the earth."

Peter was not meek by nature. He became angry and cut off the ear of a guard who had come to arrest Jesus. (And I think we can safely assume he was aiming for his neck!) He swore profusely and angrily when accused of being one of Jesus' disciples. And yet he became one of the meekest of men and one of the strongest, most virile exponents of Christianity. Where did he get his meekness?

Paul, before his conversion, was not meek. Proudly and brutally he apprehended all Christians and sought to destroy them. He was bigoted, selfish, and boastful. But when he wrote his warm and affectionate letter to the churches of Galatia, he said, among other things: "The fruit of the Spirit is . . . gentleness, goodness . . . meekness" (Galatians 5:22, 23). His meekness was something God-given, not something man-made.

It is not our human nature to be meek. On the contrary, it is our nature to be proud and haughty. That is why the new birth is so essential to each of us. That is why Jesus frankly and pointedly said not only to Nicodemus but to every one of us: "Ye must be born again" (John 3:7).

Meekness begins there! You must have a change of nature. Do you want this happiness? Then you must be born again—this is the first step! If you are too proud, stubborn, and willful to take this first step, then you do not qualify to inherit the earth.

When we reject this command of Christ, we automatically forfeit our right to His subsequent promises. We cannot end right when we begin wrong. If there is no rebirth, there can be no imparted meekness. And if there is no meekness, there can be no genuine happiness.

Arrogance has its own built-in misery. Arrogant people may offend others, but they hurt themselves more. My feelings of anger hurt me more than they do the people I'm angry at!

I was once stung by a honeybee. The sting hurt me, but it killed the bee. It died as a result of that thrust, but I didn't. In like manner, I may lash out at someone in anger. Yes, they may be hurt by my action—but like the bee I am the one who is hurt even more.

Muggings, and vigilante attacks in retaliation, have become commonplace; and they are only the tip of the iceberg. Fathers and mothers wrangle and bicker. Abuse of children and the elderly is rampant. Homes are disintegrating. High government officials in Washington engage in name-calling and in heated disputes not at all in keeping with the dignity of their office.

Why and how has all this savagery crept into our social life? It is because we have forgotten Jesus' words: "Happy are the meek: for they shall inherit the earth."

We have glamorized vice and minimized virtue. We have played down gentleness, manners, and morals—while we have played up rudeness, savagery, and vice. We have reverted to the barbaric era of "tooth and claw," "the survival of the fittest," and the philosophy of "might is right." We are rich in knowledge but poor in wisdom; rich in the know-how of war but sadly lacking in gentleness, meekness, and faith. Individually, we are mechanisms of resentment, irritation, bitterness, and frustration!

Meekness Means Gentleness

The word *gentle* was rarely heard of before the Christian era and the word *gentleman* was not known. This high quality of character was a direct by-product of Christian faith.

The Bible says: "The wisdom that is from above is first pure, then peaceable, *gentle*, and easy to be entreated, full of mercy and good fruits, without partiality, and without hypocrisy" (James 3:17).

St. Francis of Sales said: "Nothing is so strong as gentlemen; nothing so gentle as real strength." Charles Dickens wrote: "A man can never be a true gentleman in manner until he is a true gentleman at heart."

I have seen tough, rough, hardened men open their hearts by faith, receive Christ as Savior and become gentle, patient, merciful gentlemen.

I remember, when we were in London, the Ford Motor Company lent us two new Fords and employed two drivers to take our team to their various assignments. One of the chauffeurs was a typical roughneck who had missed little of what this world had to offer. He came to the meetings and looked on the scene perfunctorily with an occupational detachment. But one night he was moved to go to the counseling room and make his decision for Christ. You never saw such a change come over a man! His hardness disappeared; his veneer of sophistication melted away. He was a new creature! He threw away his x-rated literature, began to memorize the New Testament, and took on the true marks of a Christian gentleman. The fruit of the Spirit is ". . . gentleness, goodness . . . *meekness*" (Galatians 5:22, 23).

Of Eric Liddell, the missionary and great runner whose story is told in the film, "Chariots of Fire," someone has said, he was ". . . ridiculously humble in victory, utterly generous in defeat." That's a good definition of what it means to be meek.

Meekness Involves Yieldedness

The word *yield* has two meanings. The first is negative and the second is positive. It means "to relinquish, to abandon"; and also "to give." This is in line with Jesus' words: "He that loseth (or abandoneth) his life . . . shall find it" (Matthew 10:39).

We have heard the modern expression "Don't fight it—it's bigger than both of us." Those who are meek do not fight back at life. They learn the secret of surrender, of yielding to God. He then fights for us!

The Bible says: "For as ye have yielded your members servants to uncleanness and to iniquity . . . even so now yield your members servants to righteousness unto holiness" (Romans 6:19).

Instead of filling your mind with resentments, abusing your body by sinful diversion, and damaging your soul by willfulness, humbly give all over to God. Your conflicts will disappear and your inner tensions will vanish into thin air.

Then your life will begin to count for something. It will begin to yield, to produce, to bear fruit. You will have the feeling of belonging to life. Boredom will melt away, and you will become vibrant with hope and expectation. Because you are meekly yielded, you will begin to "inherit the earth" of good things which God holds in store for those who trust Him with their all.

Even science teaches in unmistakable terms the Christian concept of entire surrender. Thomas Huxley once wrote Charles Kingsley: "Science says to sit down before the facts as a little child, be prepared to give up every preconceived notion, be willing to be led to whatever end Nature will lead you, or you will know nothing." S. I. McMillen said: "Surrendering one's will to the divine will may seem a negative procedure, but it gives positive dividends."

Happy are the meek. Happy are the yielded. Happy are those who trustingly put their lives, their fortunes, and their future in the capable hands of their Creator. Happy are those who "let go and let God."

God does not discipline us to subdue us, but to condition us for a life of usefulness and blessedness. In His wisdom He knows that an uncontrolled life is an unhappy life, so He puts reins upon our wayward souls that they may be directed into the "paths of righteousness." That is what God seeks to do with us: to tame us, to bring us under proper control so we can do His will.

"I beseech you therefore, brethren, by the mercies of God, that ye present your bodies a living sacrifice, holy, acceptable unto God, which is your reasonable service. And be not conformed to this world: but be ye transformed by the renewing of your mind, that ye may prove what is that good, and acceptable, and perfect, will of God" (Romans 12:1–2).

God does in the spiritual realm what science does in the physical realm. Science takes a Niagara River with its violent turbulence and transforms it into electrical energy to illuminate a million homes and to turn the productive wheels of industry.

God took Peter—a zealot, a political reactionary of his day—and diverted his energy and his unbounding enthusiasm to high purposes instead of low, and he helped lead a movement which reshaped the world.

He took Matthew—a suave, tricky politician, who knew the political ropes well enough to keep from dangling from one of them by the neck—and, putting the bridle of grace upon him, changed him into an agent of blessing.

God had to do a job of taming with each of the disciples. Taming was not a matter of doing away with their powers and their energies but of *redirecting* them.

You have a *temper!* There is nothing unique about that. Most people have tempers, in varying degrees of course. God does not ask that you get rid of that temper. But He does say that if you are to be happy, it must be brought under control and rechanneled to proper use. God does not use a person without a temper as well as He does one with a controlled temper. There are too many professed Christians who never get "wrought up" about anything; they never get indignant with injustice, with corruption in high places, or with the godless traffics which barter away the souls and bodies of people. Someone has said, "There are some things that don't improve the longer you keep them. There are others that do. Your temper is one of them!" The Bible warns about an uncontrolled temper, "A wrathful man stirreth up strife: but he that is slow to anger appeaseth strife" (Proverbs 15:18).

You have an *ego*—a consciousness of being an individual! Of course you do, and God does not ask you to get rid of that ego. In fact, it is important for us to have a right understanding of our value and importance—what the psychologists call a healthy self image. But we develop that best when we begin to see ourselves as God sees us—as persons who are so valuable to Him that He wants us to be forgiven and cleansed of sin so we can be His children. But that doesn't mean that you are to worship yourself, to think constantly of yourself, and to live entirely for self. Common sense tells you that your life would be miserable if you followed that course. God is infinitely more concerned about your happiness than you could possibly be. He says, "Deny yourself, and follow Me."

There are people in our mental institutions today who thought excessively about themselves, to the exclusion of God and others. Hypochondriacs who have a fanciful anxiety about their health will never be well regardless of their physical condition. They remind me of the people who have this sign on their desk:

"*I* am planning to have a nervous breakdown. *I* have earned it. *I* deserve it. *I* worked for it and nobody is going to keep me from having it!"

Each of us has a *tongue* and a *voice*. These instruments of speech can be used destructively or employed constructively. I can use my tongue to slander, to gripe, to scold, to nag, and to quarrel; or I can bring it under the control of God's Spirit and make it an instrument of blessing and praise. The Bible says, "The tongue is a little member, and boasteth great things. Behold, how great a matter a little fire kindleth! And the tongue is a fire, a world of iniquity" (James 3:5–6). Only God can control it, as we yield it to Him.

The twentieth-century version of James 3:3 says, "When we put bits into the horses' mouths to make them obey us, we control the rest of their bodies also." Just so, when we submit to the claims of Christ upon our lives, our untamed natures are brought under His control. We become meek, tamed, and "fit for the Master's service."

Meekness Denotes Forbearance

"Forbearance" is a word which has been almost dropped from our modern vocabulary. It means to abstain from condemning others, to refrain from judging the actions and motives of those about us.

The Bible says: "With all lowliness and meekness, with long-suffering, forbearing one another in love" (Ephesians 4:2).

This generation is quick with the deadly thrust but slow with the ointment of healing. The harsh criticism of others and unfair appraisals of those about us may hurt them, but it hurts us more. The unjust condemnation of others has a boomerang effect. I hurl my vindictive indictments with the hope of crippling others, but, alas, I discover that I am hurt more than they are.

Many a person is lonely today because he has driven away by his own bitterness and harsh words the very friends he needed. Many a wife has discovered that scolding and nagging will never win a husband but often results in a divorce situation.

Some people go through their entire lives with a "chip on their shoulder," carrying hurts and resentments over things that were said or done decades ago. Like a poison, their bitterness has made not only their own lives miserable but the lives of those around them. They have never learned the secret of forgiveness and forbearance. The Bible warns us to be on guard "lest any root of bitterness springing up trouble you, and thereby many be defiled" (Hebrews 12:15).

Meekness and forbearance are "musts" if I am to live harmoniously in society and if I want to build a happy family life.

The Bible says: "Speak evil of no man . . .but (be) gentle, showing all meekness unto all men" (Titus 3:2). I cannot be happy as long as I magnify the faults of others and minimize their virtues. This is a good way to frighten away my friends, forfeit my domestic happiness, and fritter away a rosy future.

Here is the Christian answer to neighborhood quarrels, to family fusses, and community feuds: "Forbearing one another, and forgiving one another, if any man have a quarrel against any: even as Christ forgave you, so also do ye" (Colossians 3:13).

There is a story told of a devout old deacon who, goaded apparently beyond endurance by the persistent malice of an enemy, publicly vowed to "kill him." His enemy heard of his intentions and waited sardonically to see what the harmless old saint would do. Actually, instead of rendering evil for evil, the old deacon sought out every opportunity to do his enemy good. This was at first a source of merriment and some slight annoyance, but when at last the deacon rendered an unquestioned sacrificial service to his enemy by risking his life to save the man's wife from drowning, the deadlock between them was broken.

"All right," said his enemy, "you've done what you said you would do. You've killed me—or at least you've killed the man I *was*. Now, what can I do for you?"

This world is not yet impervious to a solid Christian act! What the world needs is not more Christianity but more Christians who practice Christian forbearance and forgiveness.

Meekness Suggests Patience

This is a high-strung, neurotic, impatient age. We hurry when there is no reason to hurry, just to be hurrying. This fast-paced age has produced more problems and less morality than previous generations, and it has given all of us a set of jangled nerves. Thomas à Kempis said: "All men commend patience, although few be willing to practice it." John F. Newton wrote: "Be patient enough to live one day at a time as Jesus taught us, letting yesterday go, and leaving tomorrow till it arrives."

Impatience has produced a new crop of broken homes, a million or more new ulcers, and has set the stage for more world wars. In no area of our lives has it been more damaging than on the domestic scene. This homely little couplet bespeaks the rack and ruin modern life has wrought in our homes:

> Theirs was a "beef stew" marriage,
> And their case was somewhat crude—
> The wife was always "beefing,"
> And the husband, always "stewed."

But the Bible says: "But let patience have her perfect work, that ye may be perfect and entire, wanting nothing" (James 1:4).

I know of a woman—a professed Christian—who, though good in many respects, was very impatient. Her pastor one day spoke to her husband about his soul, and the man replied, "My wife is a good homemaker, but if religion would make me as impatient as she is, I want no part of it."

The minister had a frank talk with the woman, and in tears and humility she confessed that her sin was the sin of impatience. A few days later her husband came in from fishing. As he walked through the living room with rod in hand, he accidentally knocked over a prized vase that went crashing to the floor. His wife ran into the room, and he braced himself for the second crash—a tirade of words from his nervous wife. But instead, she smilingly said, "Think nothing of it, dear, accidents happen in the best of families."

We will not pursue the story any further except to say that a few weeks later he made his decision for Christ and became a staunch worker in the church. He saw Christianity in practice in the life of his wife!

The apostle Peter declared that some husbands "though they do not obey the word, may be won without a word by the behavior of their wives, when they see your reverent and chaste behavior. . . . with the imperishable jewel of a gentle and quiet spirit, which in God's sight is very precious" (1 Peter 3:1–2, RSV).

The world believes that Christianity is a good thing, but Christians have too often failed to "adorn the doctrine" by living meek and patient lives.

"Happy are the meek: for they shall inherit the earth." Only those who are contrite, humble, and submissively dependent upon God can inherit the earth of radiance, joy, and contentment.

Jesus said to Saul: "It is hard for thee to kick against the pricks" (Acts 9:5; 26:14). The pricks He referred to were goads which were in the harness of the oxen to keep them under control. They were not put there to harm the ox but to make him useful, to direct his energies constructively.

Many of you reading these words have been "kicking against the pricks." Your quarrel has not been so much with others, as you thought, as it has been with yourself. God does not want you to live in constant rebellion against life, its seeming injustices, its hurts and its wrongs. He bids you to stop your futile strivings, to surrender your resentments, to yield your will, and to exercise gentleness and patience. Then you will be happy, and others about you will see Christ in you and will be drawn toward Him.

Meekness is not something I can acquire by myself. It is not something I can get in college or in a scientific laboratory. It is not something I inherit. It is God-given! Jesus said: "Take my yoke upon you, and learn of me; for I am meek and lowly in heart: and ye shall find rest unto your souls" (Matthew 11:29).

Happiness and Meekness for You

Go into a television store and notice all the televisions on display. On some of them bright pictures are to be seen, filled with vibrant colors and giving out the sounds of the latest program. But there are others on display which are only sitting there, their screens dark and silent. Your eye naturally goes to the sets that are on; there is nothing particularly interesting about a dark television screen. What is the difference? Only one thing: the dark television sets are not connected to the power. And that can be true of us, if we try to develop true meekness apart from God. We need to have a living relationship with Him.

God is no respecter of persons. Each of us deserves our just share of happiness. Each of us has the same capacity for God. I should not stand back lamenting my bad luck and my bad breaks in life. I should be joined to the source of power. Take Christ's yoke upon you, "and ye shall find rest unto your soul"!

"But I can't live it! I would surely fail in the attempt to be a Christian!" you protest.

Jesus said: "Take My yoke upon you." It is His yoke, and I may rest assured that He will bear the heavy part of the load.

Before He left His disciples, Christ promised that He would send a Comforter to help them in the trials, cares, and temptations of life. This word *comforter* means "one that helps alongside." He is the Holy Spirit, the powerful Third Person of the Trinity. The moment we are born again He takes up residence in our hearts.

We may not emotionally feel Him there, but here again we must exercise faith. Believe it! Accept it as a fact of faith! He is in our hearts to help us to be meek!

We are told that He sheds the love of God abroad in our hearts. He produces the fruit of the Spirit: "love, joy, peace, long-suffering, gentleness, goodness, faith, meekness, temperance" (Galatians 5:22, 23). We cannot possibly manufacture this fruit in our own cannery. It is supernaturally manufactured by the Holy Spirit who lives in our hearts!

I must yield to Him . . . surrender to Him . . . give Him control of my life. Then through the meekness I receive from Him I will find happiness!

5

Happy though Hungry

Blessed are they which do hunger and thirst after righteousness: for they shall be filled. MATTHEW 5:6

"Two VERBS HAVE built two empires," wrote St. Augustine, "the verb *to have* and the verb *to be*. The first is an empire of things, material possessions and power. The second is an empire of the Spirit, things that last."

This fourth Beatitude of Christ expresses a crucial, central truth. When Jesus spoke these words: "Happy are they which do hunger and thirst after righteousness," He addressed them to the multitude. It was not enough to be hungry and thirsty. The important question was, "What were they hungry *for*?"

The multitude on that torrid, sultry day in Palestine symbolizes the great parade of men and women down through the centuries. What He said to them, He says to us and has been saying to all people through the years. Most of the people in that throng were deprived spiritually, socially, and economically. Their hungers were very deep, but none would be more important than their spiritual longings and yearnings. How "righteous" is our society at its core? Perhaps a couple of stories from the daily news will help to answer this question.

A Sick Society

Even the interns at San Francisco General Hospital flinched when they saw the injuries of a young policeman who was carried in on a stretcher. His cheek was bloody from an ugly wound, he was in agony from a savage kick in the groin, and his nose was broken after being stomped on by a teenager's foot. Forty minutes earlier he had tried to arrest two drunken rowdies on Market Street in the heart of downtown San Francisco. A crowd had gathered almost at once.

"The people stood around gawking and laughing at me," the officer said. "When other hoodlums tried to take away my prisoners, numbers of the crowd held my arms. One took my gun, and they let the thugs beat me. Some even joined in the assault. Nobody tried to help me."

More mystified than critical, the officer stared up at the hospital ceiling and asked wonderingly, "What's happened to the people these days? Many of them act as if policemen are their enemies."

This injured officer was the victim of a social malady which is threatening the peace of this nation. There is a growing contempt for authority and for law.

In Los Angeles, two officers arrested two boys who were creating a disturbance in an amusement park. Quickly the police were surrounded by a cursing, jeering mob of several hundred people. Bricks were hurled, bats and jack handles were wielded, and the police cars were overturned.

The attitude toward officers is so menacing in New York City that the Police Commissioner has ordered a special tactical patrol force to disperse the taunting, dangerous mobs which try to interfere with the work of the police.

The hazards of police work are increasing. In New York City alone, nearly fifteen hundred policemen were attacked by bystanders, youths, and passersby, in one recent eight-month period. The Commissioner of Police in New York City says grimly, "The police cannot fight crime and the public at the same time."

There are many contributing causes to the rioting and crime wave in the nation. Certainly one of the contributing elements is poverty. But another contributing element is found in the home.

Much of today's disrespect for authority stems from a disorganized or indifferent family life. Young people reflect the attitudes of their parents. Even though the overwhelming majority of Americans want law, order, peace, and security, an increasingly vocal minority is revolutionary in its attitude. Until the attitude of government, the family, the home, the church, the courts, becomes predominantly "righteous," our democratic form of government is in danger of being overthrown. What is the answer to our problem?

We can give people social and economic freedom, but if their thirst for fellowship with God remains unquenched, they will still behave like animals. Witness the prosperity of Western civilization at this very moment. We have everything a machine age can provide, yet boredom and unhappiness have reached an all-time high and our morals have plunged to an all-time low. The reason: our hunger for God has not been dulled or wiped out by other things. We have dulled our hunger and quenched our thirst with the desire for money, security, fame, and success.

A man and his wife visited an orphanage where they hoped to adopt a child. In an interview with the boy they wanted, they told him in glowing terms about the many things they could give him. To their amazement, the little fellow said, "If you have nothing to offer except a good home, clothes, toys, and the other things that most kids have—why—I would just as soon stay here."

"What on earth could you want besides those things?" the woman asked.

"I just want someone to love me," replied the little boy.

There you have it! Even a little boy knows that "man shall not live by bread alone" (Matthew 4:4; Luke 4:4).

The heart cannot be satisfied with computers and sophisticated video equipment. We were created "a little lower than the angels" (Hebrews 2:7) and our souls can never subsist on the husks of this pleasure-seeking world. Our deeper yearnings and longings can be met only by a renewed fellowship with the One in whose image we were created: God. As St. Augustine said, "Thou hast made us for Thyself and our hearts are restless till they find their rest in Thee."

Happiness in Hunger

"Happy are they which do hunger and thirst after righteousness: for they shall be filled."

We can all understand the metaphor which Jesus employed here—hunger. We have all experienced some time in our lives the gnawing pain, the dizziness, and the faint feeling which accompanies intense hunger. We know what it is to experience the dry parchedness of thirst. We have also seen the haunting pictures on television of painfully thin mothers bending over little children with swollen bellies and vacant eyes, tragic victims of famine in Africa or other parts of the world. So, quite naturally, we come to attention when He says: "Happy are they which do hunger and thirst."

But what happiness is there in hunger and thirst?

Well, to begin with, hunger is a sign of life. Dead men need no food, they crave no water.

The Bible teaches that it is possible through lack of spiritual earnestness to harden one's heart as Pharaoh did long ago. This is one of the most dangerous processes that can take place in the human soul. It is possible through sin to harden our hearts against God so long that we lose all desire for God. Then the Scripture says: "God gave them up" (Psalm 81:12; Romans 1:24).

If I have the slightest bit of hunger in my heart for God and righteousness, then it is a certain sign that it is not too hardened to be receptive to the voice and message of Christ. I am yet alive and sensitive to the Spirit's voice.

Those who have no cravings for God, no longings for Christ, and no thirst for the things of the Spirit are not only dead in trespasses and sins, but they are also insensitive to the Spirit's promptings. They are like the dead and are in danger of remaining in a state of spiritual stupor that will lead eventually to eternal death.

A man once told me that he nearly froze to death in the far north. His hands lost their feeling, his feet became numb, and he was overcome with an impulse to lie down in the snow and go to sleep when it dawned upon him that he was freezing to death. He jumped up and ran vigorously until his circulation was stimulated. If he had not suddenly become conscious that he was dying and acted upon that consciousness, he would have frozen to death.

Happy are those who respond to the Spirit's warnings. They alone have hope of being filled.

A hungry person is a normal person. Those who are sick and abnormally upset refuse nourishment, but the normal person craves food. In that sense there is a blessedness in hunger. It is a natural reaction.

The normal person also possesses a spiritual hunger—although he may not label it as such. He may think he has filled it, but apart from God there is no lasting quenching of his spiritual hunger and thirst. David said: "As the hart panteth after the water brooks, so panteth my soul after thee, O God" (Psalm 42:1).

Isaiah said: "With my soul have I desired thee in the night; yea, with my spirit within me will I seek thee early: for when thy judgments are in the earth, the inhabitants of the earth will learn righteousness" (Isaiah 26:9).

Each of us was created in the image and likeness of God. We were made for God's fellowship, and our hearts can never be satisfied without His communion. Just as iron is attracted to a magnet, the soul in its state of hunger is drawn to God. Though you, like thousands of others, may feel in the state of sin that the world is more alluring and more to your liking, someday—perhaps even now as you read these words—you will acknowledge that there is something deep down inside you which cannot be satisfied by the alloy of earth.

Then with David, the Psalmist (who had sampled the delicacies of sin and had found them unsatisfying), you will say: "O God, thou art my God; early will I seek thee: my soul thirsteth for thee, my flesh longeth for thee in a dry and thirsty land, where no water is" (Psalm 63:1).

The trouble with most of us is that we make happiness our goal instead of aiming at something higher, loftier, and nobler. Unhappiness is like pain—it is only an effect of an underlying cause. Pain cannot be relieved until the cause is removed. Pain and disease go together: disease is the cause, and pain is the effect.

Unhappiness is an effect, and sin is the cause. Sin and unhappiness go together. All was blissful happiness in the Garden of Eden until sin crept in. Then happiness crept out. The two just cannot exist together.

Hunger for Righteousness

What is this righteousness we are to desire? Is this righteousness to which Jesus referred in the fourth Beatitude a religious experience? Is it some mysterious ecstasy which comes to only a few people fraught with cataclysmic emotions and spiritual sensations?

Any kind of religious experience which does not produce righteousness in our lives is a counterfeit and not worth seeking. Today there are all kinds of cults and philosophies which claim to have the power to change our lives for the better—but they cannot live up to their claim because they have no power to change the human heart. At worst, they end up enslaving their adherents. But God's will is that we would be righteous in our living. God is holy, and the whole scheme of redemption has holiness for its goal. The apostle Peter declared that Christ was the one "Who his own self bare our sins in his own body on the tree, that we, being dead to sins, should live unto righteousness" (1 Peter 2:24).

The kind of religious experience which does not produce righteousness in the life is hardly worth seeking. But religious demonstrations that do not create in us better morals and a Christlikeness of character serve no useful purpose and could certainly do more harm than good. God is holy, and the whole scheme of redemption has holiness for its goal.

Nor is this righteousness to which Jesus referred a perfunctory, mechanical performance of religious rites. Jesus taught the futility of holding to religious theory apart from Christian practice when He said: "Except your righteousness shall exceed the righteousness of the scribes and Pharisees, ye shall in no case enter into the kingdom of heaven" (Matthew 5:20).

Neither is righteousness an abstract, speculative morality so prevalent in the world today. Many people condemn sin in high places but fail to recognize it in their own personal lives. They condemn it in the government and society but condone it in their own hearts.

It is just as sinful in God's sight for an individual to break the marriage vow as it is for a nation to break a treaty.

The Nature of Righteousness

What is this righteousness that Jesus exhorts us to hunger for? The Bible teaches that God is holy, righteous, and pure. He cannot tolerate sin in His presence. However, man has chosen to disregard the divine laws and standards. As a result of man's transgressions, he is called a "sinner." Sin immediately breaks his fellowship with God. Man becomes unrighteous, impure, and unholy in the sight of God. A holy God cannot have fellowship with that which is unholy, unrighteous, and unethical. Therefore, sin breaks off friendship with God. Man is called in the Bible an "alien," an "enemy" to God, and a "sinner" against Him. The only way that man can again have fellowship with God and find the happiness that he longs for is to find some way to possess a righteousness and holiness that will commend him to God.

Many have tried to reform to gain favor with God. Some have mutilated their bodies and tortured themselves, thinking thereby to gain favor with God. Others have thought that if they would work hard and live moral lives, they could somehow justify themselves.

But the Bible teaches that all our righteousness—falling short of the divine standard as it does—is as filthy rags in the sight of God. There is absolutely no possibility of our manufacturing a righteousness, holiness, or goodness that will satisfy God. Even the best of us is impure to God.

I remember what happened one day many years ago when my wife was doing the washing. This was before we had a clothes dryer. The clothes looked white and clean in the house, but when she hung them on the line they actually appeared soiled and dirty in contrast to the fresh-fallen snow.

Our own lives may seem at times to be morally good and decent; but, in comparison to the holiness and the purity of God, we are defiled and filthy.

In spite of our sins and moral uncleanness, God loves us. He decided to provide a righteousness for us. This is the reason that He gave His Son, Jesus Christ, to die on the cross.

Have you ever stopped to think why it is the cross has become the symbol of Christianity? It is because at the cross Jesus purchased our redemption and provided a righteousness which we could not ourselves earn. "The gift of God is eternal life through Jesus Christ our Lord" (Romans 6:23). On the ground of faith in the atoning death and resurrection of His Son, God has provided and ascribed righteousness for all who will receive it.

This means that God forgives all past sin and failure. He wipes the slate clean. He takes our sins and buries them in the depths of the sea and removes them as far as the east is from the west.

To use another illustration from the Bible, in our natural state we are clothed with filthy rags because of our sin, and we cannot come into the presence of God our King. But God in Christ takes away our old filthy garments and clothes us instead with new garments—the pure white garments of Christ! As the old hymn declares:

> When He shall come with trumpet sound,
> Oh, may I then in Him be found;
> Dressed in His righteousness alone,
> Faultless to stand before the throne.

Our God Forgets!

The omniscient God has the unique ability that we do not have: He has the ability to forget. The God of grace forgets our sins and wipes them completely from His memory forever! He places us in His sight as though we had never committed one sin.

In theological language, this is called *justification*. The Bible says: "Therefore being justified by faith, we have peace with God through our Lord Jesus Christ" (Romans 5:1).

There is no possibility of true happiness until we have established friendship and fellowship with God. And there is no possibility of establishing this fellowship apart from the cross of His Son, Jesus Christ. God says, "I will forgive you, but I will forgive you only at the foot of the cross." He says, "I will fellowship with you, but I will fellowship with you only at the cross." That is the reason it is necessary for us to come to the cross in repentance of our sin and by faith in His Son to find forgiveness and salvation.

The Goal of Righteousness

As we have noted, when we come to Christ God imparts His righteousness to us. It is almost as if an accounting entry had been made in the books of Heaven, declaring us righteous for Christ's sake!

But when we come to Christ by faith and receive Him as our Savior our "hunger and thirst after righteousness" are not ended. Yes, my sins have been washed away and my salvation is secure in Christ. But I also know that within my soul there still is sin. My motives are not pure; my tongue may not be tamed; my love for others may be dim. It is God's will for this to be changed, however, and for us to exhibit increasingly in our lives the righteousness of Christ. "Let your light so shine before men, that they may see your good works, and glorify your Father which is in heaven" (Matthew 5:16).

Sometimes I have had persons who have not been Christians very long come to me and say that they had decided they must never have been Christians after all. When I have asked them why, they have replied that everything seemed fine for a few weeks after their decision for Christ, but then they found themselves committing sin. They had thought—mistakenly—that if they were Christ's they would never sin again. But that is not true! As long as we are in the flesh we will always be engaged in a continual battle against sin in our lives.

But it is not God's will for us to continue in sin—and in fact, if we are completely indifferent to the presence of sin in our lives the Bible indicates we do not really know Christ. Instead, we are to "hunger and thirst after righteousness"—to pursue righteousness and purity with God's help, so that our lives become increasingly like Christ every day.

Righteousness is something which we do not possess as a natural gift, but it is a God-given gift to be specially received. It is a bit of heaven brought to earth. The righteousness of the God-man is applied to us in justification and in sanctification, so that righteousness is progressively implanted in the believer's heart. It is God's sharing His nature with us. We become partakers of divine life.

Now, God says that only those who hunger after it will receive it. God thrusts this heavenly manna on no one. We must desire it, above everything else. Our yearning for God must supersede all other desires. It must be like a gnawing hunger and a burning thirst.

There are several things that can spoil our appetite for the righteousness of God.

Stumbling Blocks to Righteousness

FIRST: *Sinful pleasure* can ruin our appetite for the things of God.

Paul had a young co-laborer in the gospel named Demas. Because his appetite for the pleasures of the world was greater than his thirst for God, we hear very little of young Demas. Paul wrote his entire history in nine words: "Demas hath forsaken me, having loved this present world" (2 Timothy 4:10).

Many of us have no appetite for spiritual things because we are absorbed in the sinful pleasures of this world. We have been eating too many of the devil's delicacies.

I once heard the story of a man walking down the road to market. A pig followed behind him. All the other farmers were driving their pigs, struggling to get them to market. A friend called to him and asked him how he got the pig to follow him. He said, "It's very simple. Every step I take, I drop a bean, and the pig likes beans."

Satan goes along the road of life dropping his beans, and we are following him to eternal destruction.

Our sins may be very obvious and open, or they may be very respectable or subtle. Perhaps we are preoccupied with material things which, while not wrong in themselves, have wrapped their tentacles around us and are squeezing out our spiritual hunger and thirst for righteousness. We may be preoccupied with our career or our education, or any of hundreds of other things which can dull our appetite for God and His righteousness.

SECOND: *Self-sufficiency* can impair our hunger after God.

No one is so empty as he who thinks he is full. No one is so ill as he who has a fatal disease and yet thinks he is in perfect health. No one is so poor as he who thinks he is rich but is actually bankrupt.

The Bible says: "Thou sayest, I am rich, and increased with goods, and have need of nothing; and knowest not that thou art wretched, and miserable, and poor, and blind, and naked" (Revelation 3:17).

A person who is filled with himself has no room for God in his life. Self-sufficiency can ruin one's appetite for the things of Christ.

THIRD: *Secret sin* can take away our appetite for the righteousness of God.

That secret sin we commit has a price. We may think we've kept our sin a secret, but remorse for it will remain in our hearts. Those evil resentments we harbor in our minds against our neighbor! The failure to forgive those who have wronged us! When the heart is filled with wickedness, there is no room for God. The jealousies, the envies, the prejudices, and the malices will take away our appetite for the things of the Spirit.

Judas was one of the twelves disciples, outwardly a diligent follower of Christ. But in his heart he tolerated greed and evil, and they led him to betray Jesus and eventually commit suicide. King Saul outwardly welcomed the young lad David into his palace, but in his heart he was filled with bitterness and jealousy of him. Eventually those secret sins consumed him and destroyed him.

When our lives are filled with the husks of prejudice and the chaff of resentment, we can have no thirst for righteousness. If we allow our hearts to be filled with Satan's rations, we will have no desire for heaven's manna.

FOURTH: *Neglect of our spiritual life* can take away our appetite for the righteousness of God.

All Christians believe in God, but nominal Christians have little time for God. They are too busy with everyday affairs to be concerned with Bible reading, prayer, and being thoughtful to their fellow men. Many have lost the spirit of a zealous discipleship.

If you ask them if they are Christians, they would probably answer, "I think so," or "I hope so." They may go to church at Easter and Christmas and other special occasions, but otherwise they have little time for God. They have crowded God out of their lives.

The Bible warns us against neglect of our souls. It is possible to harden our hearts and shrivel our souls until we lose our appetite for the things of God. Just like someone who refuses to eat and eventually grows weaker and weaker until he dies, so a person who is "too busy" for God will starve himself and wither away spiritually.

This hunger, then, that we should have is a desire to be always right with God. It is a consciousness that all searching for peace of heart except in Him is in vain. It is an admission of our own futility, our own helplessness, and our complete abandonment to His will.

Like Peter, who stepped out upon the waves of self-sufficiency only to find that they would not bear him up, we cry, "Master, save me, or I perish!"

Like the prodigal son, who sampled the devil's delicacies in the far-off city, we discover that the world's husks fill but do not satisfy. It is then in the knowledge of our real need that we say, "Father, I have sinned against heaven, and before thee.... Make me as one of thy hired servants" (Luke 15:18, 19).

The prodigal son's "come-back" began down in the swine pen when he said, "How many hired servants of my father's have bread enough and to spare, and I perish with hunger!" (Luke 15:17). The very moment that he began to hunger, God began to "set the table" for spiritual reunion. His deepest yearnings and longings were not for food but for being reconciled to his father. The first thing he said was, "Father, I have sinned against heaven, and before thee, and am no more worthy to be called thy son...."

Neither is our goal to be blessings, experiences, or even answers to our prayers, taken by themselves. These are all the accompaniment of being right with our Heavenly Father.

God, like the prodigal's father, says to all of those who hunger and thirst after righteousness, "Son, all that I have is yours."

But the key to spiritual satisfaction is being right with God. When through faith we are in the position of sonship, then God's riches become our riches; God's abundance, our abundance; God's power, our power. When a proper relationship has been restored between us and God, then happiness, contentment, and peace of mind will be a natural outgrowth of that restored relationship.

The Difference Between Believing and Receiving

You ask, "How can I start? What do I have to do?"

Jesus said: "You must be converted." The word *conversion* means to "turn around," to "change your mind," to "turn back," and to "return."

In many ways conversion is a mystery, for from our viewpoint as humans it is both man's work and God's work. Our responsibility is to turn to Christ in faith and repentance, turning from our sins and asking Him to come into our hearts by faith. We express our desire to change the course of our lives, and we acknowledge our helplessness to do this apart from God's help. We commit ourselves to live in accordance with God's will. And when we do, God the Holy Spirit comes to dwell within us. If our commitment is genuine, God works in our hearts to regenerate us. Then we have truly been converted—we have been born again by the Spirit of God!

But many people immediately argue, "I do believe in Christ. I believe in the Church, and I believe in the Bible. Isn't that enough?"

No! We must *receive* Christ.

I may go to the airport. I have a reservation. I have a ticket in my pocket. The plane is on the ramp. It is a big, powerful plane. I am certain that it will take me to my destination. They call the flight three times. I neglect to get on board. They close the door. The plane taxis down the runway and takes off. I am not on the plane. Why? I "believed" in the plane, but I neglected to get on board.

That's just it! A person may believe in God, Christ, the Bible, and the Church—but neglect to actually receive Him in the heart. That kind of belief is impersonal and speculative. It does not involve complete *commitment* to Him.

The moment we receive Him, the Bible says, we are born again. God's nature enters into our own souls, and we become a child of God in full spiritual fellowship.

This is what we might call the "vertical relationship," the perpendicular companionship between God and man. It is absolutely the first step toward happiness. There is no use reading the rest of this book until you are absolutely sure that you have repented of sin, received Christ by faith, and been born again. The vertical relationship must always precede the "horizontal."

Our sustenance, our supply, our power come from above. Man is like a tram or a streetcar. He must be connected vertically (above) before he can move horizontally. Our relationship must be right with God before it can be right with man. And if this be true, then the converse is equally true—if we are wrong with God, we are wrong with man also.

There is a law in musical tone which says, "Two instruments tuned to the same pitch are in tune with each other." A similar rule in mathematics is: "Two quantities equal to the same quantity are equal to each other."

So two people in tune with God are in tune with each other. Two people in love with Christ have love for each other.

The moment I receive Christ as my Lord and Savior, Christ, through the Holy Spirit, comes to live in my heart. The Scripture says: "Christ in you, the hope of glory" (Colossians 1:27). We may not see Him with the natural eye and we may not feel Him with our emotions, but He is there nevertheless. We are to accept Him by faith!

This aspect of righteousness for which we are to hunger is called, in theological language, *sanctification.* Don't let this word frighten you. It actually means "separated" or "clean." In one sense, sanctification is instantaneous. The moment I receive Christ as Savior, the Holy Spirit comes into my heart.

There is also a sense in which sanctification is progressive. I grow in the grace and knowledge of Jesus Christ. Being a Christian is more than just an instantaneous conversion—it is a daily process whereby I grow to be more and more like Christ. When we start out, we begin as a baby does in physical life. We must be fed on the simple things of the Bible, and we learn to walk in our Christian life gradually. In Elizabeth Goudge's delightful book, *The Dean's Watch,* she describes a part of the saintly Miss Montague's spiritual pilgrimage: "Until now she had only read her Bible as a pious exercise, but now she read it as an engineer reads a blueprint and a traveler a map, unemotionally because she was not emotional, but with profound concentration because her life depended on it. Bit by bit over a period of years, that seemed to her long, she began to get her scaffolding in place." At first we fall down and make many mistakes, but we are to continue growing.

The Dangers of Spiritual Staleness

However, there are many people who have stopped growing. They remain spiritual babes all their lives. I am afraid that this experience is all too common today. Perhaps it is yours.

Do you remember the day when you gave your heart and your life to Christ? You were sure of victory. How easy it seemed to be more than conqueror through Christ, who loved you. Under the leadership of a Captain who had never been foiled in battle, how could you dream of defeat?

And yet to many of you, how different has been your real experience! Your victories have been few and fleeting and your defeats many and disastrous. You have not lived as you feel children of God ought to live.

As Mrs. Hannah Whitall-Smith reminds us in her book, *The Christian's Secret of a Happy Life*, "You have had, perhaps, a clear understanding of doctrinal truths, but you have not come into possession of their light and power. In your life Christ is believed in, talked about, and served, but He is not filling you hour by hour. You found Christ as your Savior from the penalty of sin, but you have not found Him as your all-sufficient Savior from its power. The joy and thrill of Christian experience is gone."

There is only a dying ember of what used to be a mighty prairie fire for Christ in your soul. In the very depths of your heart you know that your experience is not the scriptural experience. Down through the years it seems that all you can expect from your Christianity is a life of ultimate failure and defeat—one hour failure, and the next hour repenting and beginning again, only to fail again.

Vigor in the Early Church

We read in the Scriptures that the early church was filled with the Holy Spirit. They had no church buildings, no Bibles, no automobiles, no planes, no trains, no television, no radio. Yet they turned their world "upside down" for Christ. They instituted a spiritual revolution that shook the very foundations of the Roman Empire. They were young, vigorous, virile, powerful. They lived their lives daily for Christ. They suffered persecution and even death gladly for their faith in Christ. What was the secret of their success—even in the face of opposition and death? One reason beyond doubt is that they hungered and thirsted after righteousness. And those with whom they came in contact could not help but be impressed by the quality and purity of their lives and their love.

The reason certain false philosophies and religions are making such inroads in the world today is that somewhere along the line the people who were supposed to live Christian lives failed. We have failed to meet the standards and requirements that Jesus set forth. If we would live for Christ we must be willing to count all else as "nothing but refuse." We must be as dedicated, as committed, and as willing to sacrifice all, as the followers of false religions are.

The great masses of the unbelieving world are confused as they gaze upon the strife within and among religious bodies. Instead of a dynamic, growing, powerful, Christ-centered Church, we see division, strife, pettiness, greed, jealousy, and spiritual laziness—while the world is standing on the brink of disaster.

The great need in Christendom today is for Christians to learn the secret of daily, wholehearted recommitment to Christ.

Paul himself spoke of his struggle. He spoke of desiring to please God, but in himself he found no strength to do so. The things he did not want to do he sometimes did; and the things he wanted to do he did not do. Nearly driven to distraction, Paul shouts out: "Who shall deliver me from the body of this death?" (Romans 7:24).

And in the next verse he records the answer to that all-important, searching, bewildering question when he says: "I thank God through Jesus Christ our Lord" (Romans 7:25).

Christ can be our Deliverer!

Many of us ask the questions: "Why do I, as a Christian, do some of the things I do? Why do I, as a Christian, leave undone the things I ought to have done?"

Many name the Name of Christ, but live in constant defeat. They have unclean hands, unclean lips, unclean tongues, unclean feet, unclean thoughts, unclean hearts—and yet claim to be Christians. They claim Christ, attend church, try to pray—and yet they know there are things in their souls that are not right. There is no joy in their hearts, no love for others. In fact, there is little evidence of the fruit of the Spirit in their lives. The fire in their souls has been quenched.

Yet as we look around, we do know some people who are living different lives. They bear the fruit of the Spirit. But some get only snatches of victory. Once in a while they will have a day that seems to be a victorious day over temptation, but then they slide right back into the same old rut of living, and hunger and long for the righteousness of daily growth.

There are other Christians who have never really learned the biblical truth of separation: separation from unclean thoughts and unclean habits.

There are some Christians who have learned little of a daily devotional life.

Surrender and Devotion

Some time ago a policeman asked me what the secret of victorious living was. I told him that there is no magic formula that can be pronounced. If any word could describe it, I would say *surrender*. The second word I would use would be *devotion*.

Nothing can take the place of a daily devotional life with Christ. The great missionary, Hudson Taylor, said, "Never mind how great the pressure is—only where the pressure lies. Never let it come between you and the Lord, then the *greater* the pressure, the more it *presses* you to His heart!" Our quiet time, our prayer time, the time we spend in the Word is absolutely essential for a happy Christian life. We cannot possibly be happy, dynamic, and powerful Christians apart from a daily walk with Christ.

It is unfortunate that even in Christian circles our conversation is of comparatively small matters. We can quote the batting average of our favorite baseball star, but we are unable to quote a Bible verse other than John 3:16. We are full of talk about our homes, our cars, our television—but we are woefully ignorant of the things of God.

If a sick and dying man should stumble through our door, we would be incapable of guiding him through his problems to Christ the Savior.

Our spiritual intellects have become poverty-stricken; hence the trite verbal interchanges that pass between us. Our daily conversation when we meet each other, whether it be in the office or on the campus or in the shop, should be concerned with the things of God. We should be exchanging spiritual blessings and thoughts that we have received from our daily Bible reading.

It is not enough for us to have been confirmed, or to have made a decision for Christ at an altar, and to hope to walk in the glow of that experience successfully for the rest of our lives. Being human, we have to return and renew our commitment to God. We have to take inventory and get regular spiritual checkups.

Steps to Surrender

Christ is calling Christians today to cleansing, to dedication, to consecration, and to full surrender. It will make the difference between success and failure in our spiritual lives. It will make the difference between being helped and helping others. It will make a difference in our habits, in our prayer life, in our Bible reading, in our giving, in our testimony, and in our church membership. This is the Christian's hour of decision!

But many ask, "How can I begin?" I would like to suggest that you take all of the sins that you are guilty of and make a list of them. Then confess them, and check them off, remembering that Jesus Christ forgives. The Bible says: "If we confess our sins, he is faithful and just to forgive us our sins, and to cleanse us from all unrighteousness" (1 John 1:9).

In addition, ask God to cleanse you from those sins you may not be aware of, and to make you more sensitive to the presence of hidden sins in your life—wrong motives, wrong attitudes, wrong habits, wrong relationships, wrong priorities. It may even be that you will have to make restitution if you have stolen anything, or you may have to seek out someone and ask their forgiveness for a wrong you have committed.

Then, after you have confessed every known sin in your life, yield every area of your life. Yield your girl friend, your boy friend, your family, your business, your career, your ambitions, your soul, the innermost thoughts and depths of your heart; yield them all to Christ. Hold nothing back. As the songwriter says: "Give them all to Jesus."

Take your eyes and your ears and your hands and your feet and your thoughts and your heart: give them completely and unreservedly to Christ. Then by faith believe that God has accepted your surrender.

Paul said: "I am crucified with Christ: nevertheless I live; yet not I, but Christ liveth in me" (Galatians 2:20).

We can reckon ourselves indeed dead unto sin. The Bible says we can be more than conquerors through Him who loved us.

The Secret of Surrender

It has been my privilege to know what it means to walk in the way of Christ. What a thrilling, joyous experience it is to wake up every morning and know His presence in the room! What a thrilling, joyous experience it is to know in the evening, when the sun is setting, the peace of God as you go to bed and to sleep the sleep of only those who know Christ! What a joy it is to walk in the eternal and permanent experience of Christ!

> God is in every tomorrow,
> Therefore I live for today—
> Certain of finding at sunrise
> Guidance and strength for the way.
>
> Power for each moment of
>   weakness,
> Hope for each moment of pain.
> Comfort for every sorrow,
> Sunshine and joy after rain!
>
> *Anonymous*

And I know what it is to fall flat on my face. As Alexander Whyte, the great Scottish clergyman, said at the turn of the century, "Perseverance of the saints consists in ever new beginnings."

Do you hunger for such a walk? Do you long for such joy, peace, contentment, abandonment, and adventure in your own soul? Do you long to produce the fruit of the Spirit, which is "love, joy, peace, long-suffering, gentleness, goodness, faith, meekness, temperance" (Galatians 5:22, 23)? You can if you abide in Christ as the branch abides in the vine.

First, remember that the Christian life is lived by "Christ in you." However, if Christ does not have *all* of us, it is impossible to live a happy Christian experience. When He has all of us, then He fills us to overflowing and He produces in us the fruit of the Spirit. It is absolutely impossible for any person to manufacture, generate, or produce the Christian life apart from the power of the Holy Spirit. He stands at this moment ready to enter our hearts with a floodtide of blessing if we will surrender every area of our personalities and lives to Him. It is our birthright! We must claim it—believe it—accept it! It's ours *now.*

If this is your hunger and desire, then God will do exactly what He has promised to do: He will fill you. "Happy are they that hunger and thirst after righteousness: for they shall be filled." Every promise God has ever made He has kept. He will fill you now if you are hungry enough to surrender.

The Source of Righteousness

Second, God will fill you with His righteousness, because man has no holy longings, no holy cravings that cannot ultimately be satisfied.

We shall *not* be perfect in thought, word, and deed until we are glorified in the world to come, but the breath of that glory, and a godlikeness of character, is the Christian's proper heritage in this earthly walk. We are *Christians*, and the world should sense to its conviction that, wherever we walk in its midst, a heavenly virtue still goes out from whatever truly bears His Name.

People hunger for food, and God sends the sun and rain upon the golden fields of grain. The grain is made into flour and flour into bread, and our physical hunger is satisfied.

People hunger for love; and ideally they are born into a home where their parents love them. Later, perhaps, God ignites the fire of affection in another heart, and two hearts are made complete in the bonds of holy matrimony.

People hunger for knowledge, and God raises up institutions of learning. He calls out committed instructors and puts it into the hearts of the rich to endow these schools, and students are satisfied in their thirst for knowledge.

People hunger for fellowship, and God allows engineers to build cities. Their people can share their industry, their knowledge, and their skills.

Don't tell me that God can supply us with an abundance of everything material and yet will let us starve spiritually!

The Bible says: "Hearken diligently unto me, and eat ye that which is good, and let your soul delight itself in fatness" (Isaiah 55:2).

Again the Bible says: "For the bread of God is he which cometh down from heaven, and giveth life unto the world" (John 6:33).

Satisfaction in Christ

Third, God will satisfy the hunger and thirst of those who desire His righteousness, because He loves the world with an undying affection. He moved heaven and earth to redeem us. Would it seem logical that a father would pay a huge ransom to redeem a son and then forsake him in his hour of hunger? The fact that the initial cost of our salvation was so great helps us know that God certainly does not desire that we shall want for anything. A parent who loves his child will not willingly see him starve.

The Bible says: "But my God shall supply all your need according to his riches in glory by Christ Jesus" (Philippians 4:19).

This promise, "Happy are they which do hunger and thirst after righteousness," is one which makes us responsible to God, and God responsible to us. Our small human part is to hunger and to thirst.

If we have no desire for righteousness, it means only that we have permitted sin and neglect to spoil our desire for fellowship with God. No matter how alluring, attractive, and pleasant the tidbits of the world may seem, they can never satisfy our deeper longings and heart cravings.

We can only know peace of heart and tranquillity of mind when we admit and confess our deeper hungers, when we yield completely to God and when we are willing to turn from the synthetic substitutes of the world and drink in the "water of life."

6

Happiness through Showing Mercy

Blessed are the merciful: for they shall obtain mercy. MATTHEW 5:7

THE BIBLE SAYS, "He that hath pity upon the poor lendeth unto the Lord; and that which he hath given will he pay again" (Proverbs 19:17). A group of businessmen had a hunting lodge. It was their custom to have devotions each evening. One night they called on the godly mountain caretaker to lead in prayer. "O Lord," he prayed, "have mercy on us, 'cause mercy suits our case." In the Bible mercy refers to compassion, to pity for the undeserving and the guilty. Perhaps no more beautiful illustration of it exists in the Bible (apart from God's mercy to us in Christ) than that of Joseph and his undeserving brothers.

You recall how, through jealousy, the brothers sold Joseph into slavery, convincing his father that he had been devoured by wild beasts. In the following years Joseph, through his faithfulness to God and his masters, rose in position in Egypt until he was second in power to Pharaoh himself.

It was famine that drove the unsuspecting brothers down to Egypt to buy food. Read again the incredible story of Joseph recognizing his brothers, his compassionate dealing with them, how he got them to bring his old father and move with their families to Egypt where he could nourish them through the remaining years of famine. Where vengeance and just retribution were certainly justified, Joseph showed only mercy and lovingkindness.

In fact, he says to his apprehensive brothers (in Genesis 50), " . . .you thought evil against me, but God meant it for good. . . .Now therefore fear ye not: I will nourish you and your little ones. And he comforted them, and spake kindly unto them" (vv. 20–21).

What mercy!

So, too, in our lives, we might be prompted to be merciful to those who have wronged us, hurt us, or even done incredibly cruel things to us. If we were submissive and loyal to God we could see behind the unkindness and evil, God's love working for our good and His glory.

We have a contrasting story in the rich young ruler who, when told by Jesus to go and sell all he had and give to the poor, then come and follow Him, "went away sorrowful, for he had great possessions" (Matthew 19:22). Here an opportunity to show mercy was held back by greed.

The rich young ruler thought possessions would bring him happiness—but they didn't. And yet he was unwilling to turn to Christ, the only true source of lasting happiness. He could not show mercy to others because of his selfishness and greed—and so he "went away sorrowful," never experiencing true happiness and fulfillment. "Happy are the merciful."

Jesus knew that one of the real tests of our yieldedness to God is our willingness to share with others. If we have no mercy toward others, that is one proof that we have never experienced God's mercy.

Mercy Is Not Self-centered

To paraphrase this Beatitude we might say, "They which have obtained mercy from God are so happy that they are merciful to others." Our attitude toward our fellow men is a more accurate gauge of our religion than all of our religious rantings.

Alexander Pope prayed:

> Teach me to feel another's woe,
> To hide the fault I see;
> That mercy I to others show,
> That mercy show to me.

Emerson must have been reading the gauge of human mercy when he said: "What you are speaks so loud that I cannot hear what you say."

Jesus summed up the whole matter of genuine Christianity when He said: "If any man thirst, let him come unto me, and drink. He that believeth on me, as the Scripture hath said, out of his inmost soul flow rivers of living water" (John 7:37, 38).

Christianity is, first, a coming to Christ—an inflowing of the Living Water; second, it is a reaching toward others—an outflowing. It is to be shared in love, mercy, and compassion with others.

A body of water which has an inlet but no outlet becomes a stagnant pond. When we think of Christianity as *my* experience, *my* emotions, *my* ecstasy, *my* joy, *my* faith—with no desire to share mercifully with others—we can only boast of stagnation. Not living, vital, flowing Christianity!

The Scripture says: "Defend the poor and fatherless: do justice to the afflicted and needy" (Psalm 82:3). "Whoso stoppeth his ears at the cry of the poor, he also shall cry himself, but shall not be heard" (Proverbs 21:13).

Jesus said: "Give to him that asketh thee, and from him that would borrow of thee turn not thou away" (Matthew 5:42). And: "Give, and it shall be given unto you; good measure, pressed down, and shaken together, and running over, shall men give into your bosom" (Luke 6:38).

In this Beatitude, which we could well term the "out-flowing" Beatitude, Jesus is emphasizing the fact that we are to be unchoked channels through which His love and mercy flow out to other people.

If we have a religion which does not work effectively in everyday life, one which fails to condition our attitudes toward our fellow men and one which makes us spiritual introverts, we may be sure that we do not know the Christ who spoke these Beatitudes!

Satan does not care how much you theorize about Christianity or how much you profess to know Christ. What he opposes vigorously is the way you live Christ—the way you become an instrument of mercy, compassion, and love through which He manifests Himself to the world. If Satan can take the mercy out of Christianity, he has killed its effectiveness. If he can succeed in getting us to talk a good case of religion but to live a poor one, he has robbed us of our power.

If we embrace a spiritual, aesthetic gospel only and disregard our obligation to our fellow men, we annul it all. The gospel of the New Testament can come into full blossom only when the seed of the Spirit is buried in the rich soil of human mercy.

It is first an intaking, and then an outgiving. Jesus said in our outgiving we would find happiness.

Some time ago a lady wrote and said, "I am sixty-five years old. My children are all married, my husband is dead, and I am one of the loneliest people in all the world." It was suggested to her that she find a way of sharing her religious faith and her material goods with those around her. She wrote a few weeks later and said, "I am the happiest woman in town. I have found a new joy and happiness in sharing with others."

That's exactly what Jesus promised!

Mercy in Action

What are some of the areas in today's world toward which we can show mercy?

First: We can show mercy by *caring for the needs of others.* We should look around at our neighbors and see if any are hurting or in need.

Who is my neighbor? He who is closest to me—my husband or wife, child, parent, brother, sister, the person next door, the couple down the street. It is easier to be concerned with the deprived person halfway around the world, and ignore the needs of those closest to me—perhaps only a word of encouragement or appreciation. At the same time, we cannot ignore the needs of our fellow men on a worldwide scale.

When I go to bed tonight, I must remember that over half of the world's population is hungry, poor, and wretched. Most of these are illiterate people who are unable to read or write. Most use farming methods a thousand years old. Many are little better than slaves to the big landlords who own the land. Others live in countries with corrupt or oppressive governments. Their lives are burdened with injustice or prejudice, and they have little opportunity to get ahead. Their lives are marked by hopelessness and despair. They need food, education, clothes, homes, medical care, and—most of all—love. We have a responsibility to these downtrodden peoples of the world.

Did not Jesus feed the multitudes as well as preach the gospel to them? Did He not point out to us the folly of talking religion and failing to put it into action? Did He not say: "Woe unto you, scribes and Pharisees, hypocrites! for ye shut up the kingdom of heaven against men . . . for ye devour widows' houses, and for a pretense make long prayer: therefore ye shall receive the greater damnation" (Matthew 23:13, 14)?

A young man from our community is a skilled helicopter pilot. He undoubtedly could make a very high salary working for a major corporation, but instead he has joined a small Christian mission which uses helicopters to reach remote areas of the world with the gospel and with relief supplies. Much of his work has been in some of the drought-stricken areas of Africa, where millions of people live on the brink of starvation every day. Recently he wrote, "I often feel at a loss of words to describe some of the conditions in places here. Some I don't want to describe—just forget." But then he added, "The rewards are high here in seeing our efforts really helping people." In the midst of terrible, heartbreaking conditions he has discovered the truth of Jesus' words: "Happy are the merciful."

How can we theorize about religion and debate doctrinal matters while the world is dying in misery without the necessities of life and, in many cases, without hope?

What a selfish and ingrown people we have become! Little wonder that there is so much boredom, frustration, and unhappiness. The words of Jesus, "Happy are the merciful," are certainly applicable to us.

The late Dr. Frank Laubach once wrote me, "In my opinion, the United States must make an all-out effort to help the destitute half of the world out of its misery, or we shall find that the world has gone Communist because of our neglect."

Most of us cannot go to these faraway lands, but we can give to missionary and charitable causes that will help build hospitals, educational institutions, and orphanages—and provide the necessities of life to many of these destitute millions.

But let's come closer home. If we only looked, we would find people near us who are in physical need. One Christmas Eve a friend came to my house and said, "Would you like to go out with me distributing Christmas packages up in the mountains?" I was glad to go. And I was in for one of the greatest surprises of my life! I thought everybody in our community had all the necessities of life.

But I was taken back into some little mountain valleys where people did not have enough to wear, enough to eat, and could not even afford soap to wash their bodies. Appalled and humbled, I asked God to forgive me for neglecting the people in my own community. I had not even bothered to look around me to see what people's needs were.

If we will ask God to show us, we will find people in our own communities who need physical help.

There are others in our community who need a friend. There are many lonely people who never know the handclasp of a friend. They never receive a letter. They sit isolated in their loneliness. Having an interested friend willing to write to them and to visit with them would change their entire lives. One of the happiest women in our church lives alone but makes a habit of visiting nursing homes. She reads to the patients, wheels them to the gift shop and cafeteria. When my mother had very few visit her from her church, this dear woman was faithful to her weekly. She is happy in a ministry in nursing homes.

There are others who are lonely and miserable because they perhaps do not have personalities that lend themselves to mixing with other people. I have a friend who went to a social gathering. A harelipped lad with pimples on his face sat over in the corner. No one paid any attention to him. He looked lonely, despondent, and miserable, and completely out of place. My friend went over and spent the evening with him. When he left, the lad was full of smiles. This friend had shown mercy.

There are a thousand little ways that we can be merciful in our daily lives. There may be a hospital nearby which we could visit. There are scores of people on hospital beds who long for someone to call on them, to bring them flowers and a cheery smile. We can show mercy by visiting the sick.

Prejudice—a Barrier to Mercy

SECOND: We can show mercy by *doing away with our prejudices.*

All over the world a new nationalism is rising. Color bars are being broken down while other social barriers are being raised. Prejudice stalks many countries.

I have been privileged across the years to visit many, many countries in every part of the world. However, I have never visited a country which did not have some problem with prejudice. At times it was prejudice against a racial or religious minority within its boundaries. At times it was prejudice against people from other nations. At times it was prejudice or resentment against those who were wealthier or those who were poorer than the average. But prejudice is a universal problem. Why? One reason is because prejudice has its roots in pride— and pride is at the heart of sin. Just as sin is universal, so prejudice is universal as long as our hearts are untouched by God's regenerating power.

The word *prejudice* means "prejudging" or "making an estimate of others without knowing the facts." Prejudice is a mark of weakness, not of strength; it is a tool of the bigot, but never a device of the true Christian. One of our great problems in this complex age continues to grow since modern man has forsaken the pathway of Christian mercy and understanding—and has chosen to walk the road of intolerance and intrigue. Someone has said, "Prejudice is being down on what you're not up on." Lack of awareness along with prejudice stifles mercy.

Edwin Markham referred to the prevailing gentility of yesteryear when he said:

> He drew a circle that shut me out,
> Heretic, rebel, a thing to flout;
> But Love and I had the wit to win,
> We drew a circle that took him in.

Prejudice is measured by computing the distance between our own biased opinions and the real truth. If we would all be perfectly honest before God, there would be no prejudice. But since most of us by nature are possessed of biased minds and perverted hearts, prejudice is widespread in the world.

The late Edward R. Murrow once said, "There is no such thing as an objective reporter. We are all slaves of our environment."

All of us have personal biases and prejudices. Despite our improved educational system, our prejudices have grown in the past few years—so we can conclude that education is not the cure for all prejudice.

Even the great Charles Lamb once said: "I am, in plainer words, a bundle of prejudices, made up of likings and dislikings."

Prejudice is a form of robbery, for it robs its victim of a fair trial in the court of reason. It is also a murderer, because it kills the opportunity of advancement for those who are its prey.

Jesus struck at the very core of it when He said: "And why beholdest thou the mote that is in thy brother's eye, but considerest not the beam that is in thine own eye?" (Matthew 7:3). And then He laid down a specific rule against it when He said: "Judge not, that ye be not judged" (Matthew 7:1).

I seriously doubt if we would be prejudiced against anyone if we had all the facts in hand. We are quick to judge and prone to denounce that which we do not understand or know or experience.

Often prejudice would vanish if we had all the facts in hand. We also would be less quick to judge if we would put ourselves in the place of other people, understanding their background, sensing their problems, sympathizing with their weaknesses. Yes, education can do much to neutralize our prejudices—and yet we often find that when we apparently have conquered one type of prejudice, another type crops up in our hearts which is just as strong. I have known people who were able to overcome prejudices against people of another race—

and yet their hearts were filled with scorn and prejudice against people of their own race who were of a different social class or a different political party.

The Antidote to Prejudice

But how can we get rid of this murderous prejudice? There is only one way we can get rid of prejudice: by the process of spiritual rebirth through faith in Christ. Only then do we discover God's love for all humanity, and only then will we begin to look at others through the eyes of God and see them as He sees them. Only then does God's love begin to take root in our hearts, pushing out the hate and indifference and selfishness that have resided there. In myself I do not have the capacity to love others as I should, but "The fruit of the Spirit is love" (Galatians 5:22). Yes, Christ can give us a love for others we would never have otherwise, "because the love of God is shed abroad in our hearts by the Holy Ghost which is given unto us" (Romans 5:5). This is an operation which only God can perform.

Listen to the words of Saul of Tarsus, once one of the world's most prejudiced men: "Love suffereth long, and is kind; love envieth not; love vaunteth not itself, is not puffed up. . . . Rejoiceth not in iniquity, but rejoiceth in the truth; Beareth all things, believeth all things, hopeth all things, endureth all things" (1 Corinthians 13:4–7).

What the logic of Greece could not do for Saul, the grace of God did. What the culture of Rome could not do, the grace of God accomplished. After his experiences on the Damascus road, Paul found his old prejudices melting away. *Mercy* became the key word of his preaching, the theme of his Epistles, and the pattern for his conduct. "I beseech you therefore . . . by the mercies of God, that ye present your bodies a living sacrifice" (Romans 12:1) was the theme of his pleadings. Having received mercy, he was an exponent of mercy. Having been delivered from his own prejudices, he was eager that all might find release from their destructive power.

How can we be so brazen as to be prejudiced against a person when God in His mercy has been so merciful toward us?

Go with the Gospel

THIRD: We can show mercy by *sharing the gospel of Christ* with others.

Man's spiritual poverty is even more wretched than his physical poverty. His failure to do what he ought to do and be what he ought to be proves that there is something inherently wrong with him.

The Bible puts it this way: "The heart is deceitful above all things, and desperately wicked" (Jeremiah 17:9). All immorality, wantonness, greed, selfishness, prejudice, suffering, hatred, and bigotry stem from one source: the human heart. Nothing in the universe has fallen lower, and yet by the grace of God nothing can rise higher.

Physical poverty, of course, is more visible and apparent to us. We are touched by pictures of those who are starving or who live in rat-infested slums or on the street—and we should be. But spiritual poverty is much more difficult to see, because we only see it as we look at the world through the "spectacles" of God's Word. I have a friend who is extremely near-sighted. Even objects only a few feet away are a blur to him, and if he were to look across a valley, for example, he would be unable to tell you if it had houses or trees on the other side. But when he puts on his glasses it is a different story! Then his vision is almost as sharp as that of an airline pilot. In the same way, the spiritual poverty of the world is not clear or even evident to us until we begin to look at it in the light of God's Word, the Bible. But when we begin to understand God's Word, we realize that the world is lost and under the judgment of God apart from Christ.

Some people have said,"Oh, well, it does not really matter what people believe, just so they are sincere. Somehow all paths lead eventually to God, I guess. And if God is a loving God, then everyone will be saved eventually, whether they are trusting Christ or have rejected Him." But the Bible says otherwise. "Neither is there salvation in any other: for there is none other name under heaven given among men, whereby we must be saved" (Acts 4:12).

The fact that after two thousand years of Christianity more than half of the world's population still knows nothing about the saving, transforming grace of Christ should stir us to a renewed dedication to tell a dying world about the mercy of God.

Jesus said: "Go ye into all the world, and preach the gospel to every creature" (Mark 16:15).

Notice the little word *go*. A little word—but world-wide in its sweep! The apostles first had to *come*, and now Jesus commands them to go!

We have come in this generation and stopped short, but Christ says, "Go." A little word—but wrapped up in this little word is the whole sum and substance of Christ's gospel. "Go" is the first part of the word "gospel." It should be the watchword of every true follower of Christ. It should be emblazoned on the banners of the Church. "Go," says the Master. Nearly two thousand years have dragged their weary lengths down the road of time, and yet millions of people are sitting in spiritual darkness.

Is There Any Other Remedy?

There are two opposing concepts about man's true nature. Some assert that human nature is basically good and may rise to higher and higher levels of excellence apart from God. Humanity's basic problem, according to this view, is simply ignorance or unfavorable social or economic conditions. If people can be educated enough and if their social and economic situation is right, then selfishness and conflict will be eliminated. This makes a powerful appeal to our pride, for we do not want to think that we are unable to rise above ourselves. But human experience has repeatedly shown otherwise. Yes, education is important; God, after all, is the author of all truth, and in Christ "are hid all the treasures of wisdom and knowledge" (Colossians 2:3). But lust, greed, and selfishness remain firmly entrenched in our hearts, no matter how much education we have or how ideal our social conditions may be.

The other concept of human nature is that of the Bible. It holds that man was created in the image of God, and as such was originally perfect—exactly the way God intended him to be. But humanity turned its back on God, choosing to be independent of Him. And when they did, something radical and devastating happened to the human heart.

However, today there are statesmen who assume that better organized human government is the remedy for the world's dilemma. They assume that inasmuch as vice and crime flow from ignorance and poverty, virtue could issue from knowledge and competence. Yet history proves this theory inadequate. Constitutional and statutory law lacks the essential element to purify human nature. The power is not within the province of law, whether human or divine.

The Bible says: "By the deeds of the law there shall no flesh be justified in his sight" (Romans 3:20). Again: "What the law could not do, in that it was weak . . . God sending his own Son in the likeness of sinful flesh . . . condemned sin in the flesh" (Romans 8:3).

All of us agree that one form of government may be better than another, but all forms of government have been inadequate to suppress vice and give universal prevalence to virtue to change human nature. Rome was no more pure under the eloquent Cicero than under the cruel Nero.

History proves that it is impossible to solve the problem of human nature by civil law. That is not to say, of course, that laws against evil are unnecessary or unimportant—quite the opposite. The Bible says in fact that God has given to civil government the authority to punish wrong-doing, and we are to support justice and the common good of society. "For rulers are not a terror to good works, but to the evil" (Romans 13:3). Good government is also to work for the positive good of society.

But all too often we think that some particular form of government will solve all our problems. Some tyrants and dictators will do all they can to impose their type of government or their political philosophy on other nations. by force or subversion if necessary. Yes, some forms of government are certainly better than others—and one reason is that they have a better understanding of the limitations and possibilities of human nature. Government and civil laws are somewhat like the cages in a zoo—they can restrain evil and keep it from getting out of hand, but they cannot change the basic nature of the human heart.

As an American, I rejoice in our liberties and the legal safeguards we have against those who would seek to destroy society.

But our government is certainly going to fall like a rope of sand if unsupported by the moral fabric of God's Word. The moral structure in our country grew from Judeo/Christian roots. When those values are applied, they produce moral fruits. But if that structure disappears, the moral sentiment that shapes our nation's goals will disappear with it.

Then also, there is the person who claims that the remedy for vice is to be found in a universal system of education. His opinion is that man will be made pure and happy by intellectual culture and mental repose.

Suppose that education is the answer to all the problems that man faces. Develop the intellectual to the maximum; yet do you get virtue? Knowledge did not save Solomon from vice or Byron from immorality. Art and education may refine the taste; but they cannot purify the heart, forgive sin, and regenerate the individual. The Holocaust was carried out by educated people, some brilliantly so. It could well be called a demonstration of educated depravity.

A few years ago my wife and I visited the Nazi death camp of Auschwitz, located in southern Poland. Here some six million people—both Jews and non-Jews from throughout Europe—were brutally imprisoned and murdered. We saw the barbed wire, the instruments of torture, the airless punishment cells, the gas chambers and crematorium. Every square foot of that terrible place was a stark and vivid witness to man's inhumanity to man. We laid a memorial wreath and then knelt to pray at a wall in the midst of the camp where 20,000 people had been shot. When I got up and turned around to say a few remarks to those who had gathered with us, my eyes blurred with tears and I almost could not speak. How could such a terrible thing happen—planned and carried out by people who were often highly educated? The problem is the human heart. Jesus declared, "For out of the heart proceed evil thoughts, murders, adulteries, fornications, thefts, false witness, blasphemies" (Matthew 15:19).

It is not simply education in civilization that the world is wanting today, but civilization with enlightened conscience; not simply institutions and airlines and gigantic corporations, but all these entities free from graft and taint of every kind. Yet today an educated, civilized society is turning its face while thousands of unborn babies are being killed. God Himself, if not history, will judge this greater holocaust.

Where is mercy?

I would rather have a world filled with ignorant savages than with civilized sophisticates without morality. Better the wild, unexplored wilderness than the debauched palace of civilized shame. Better the cannibal of the South Seas than the civilized vultures of our cities.

The mathematician can solve problems on paper but can he solve his personal problems? The orthopedic surgeon can set broken bones but what can he do for a broken heart' The engineer can read the blueprints but where is his blueprint for daily living?

Reformed by Regeneration

Should we drive out civilization? you ask. No, we should pray God to *reform* it *by regeneration.* Starve out graft and put in honesty. Drive out prejudice and put in the Golden Rule. Drive out ruthlessness and put in mercy. This can be done only through an acceptance of Jesus Christ as personal Savior on the part of individuals who make up the society of the world.

We can put a public school and a university in the middle of every block of every city in America—but we will never keep America from rotting morally by mere intellectual education. Education cannot be properly called education which neglects the most important aspects of man's nature. Partial education throughout the world is far worse than none at all if we educate the mind but not the soul.

Turn a half-educated man loose upon the world, put him in the community with inexhaustible resources at his command but recognizing no power higher than his own—he is a monstrosity! He is but halfway educated and is far more dangerous than if he were not educated at all. He is a speeding locomotive without an engineer. He is a tossing ship without a compass, pilot, or destiny.

To think of civilizing people without converting them to Christ is about as wise as to think about transforming wolves into lambs merely by washing them and putting on them a fleece of wool.

"Happy are the merciful: for they shall obtain mercy."

The mercy the world needs is the grace, love, and peace of our Lord Jesus Christ. It is His transforming and regenerating power that the world needs more than anything else.

To be sure, we are to use the world's physical resources, but along with them we are to take the regenerating power of Christ. We are to take a cup of cold water in one hand and regeneration in the other and give them to a physically and spiritually starved world. We have thought that man's needs were entirely physical, but we are beginning to realize that they are also spiritual.

The Gifts of the Gospel

The gospel of Christ provides for our *physical being.* Materialism can see nothing in our bodies except laboratory analyses, but the Bible with stern rebuke exclaims: "What? know ye not that your body is the temple of the Holy Spirit?" (1 Corinthians 6:19).

The gospel provides for our *intellect*. It stimulates the intellect to the highest activity. It commands the complete education of all our intellectual powers. The Bible instructs: "Gird up the loins of your mind" (1 Peter 1:13). It opens before a regenerated person a whole universe of truth.

The gospel also provides for our *sensibilities*. "Let not your heart be troubled" (John 14:1). "Blessed are they that mourn: for they shall be comforted," says Jesus. This is what humanity needs. Humanity wants comfort in its sorrow, light in its darkness, peace in its turmoil, rest in its weariness, and healing in its sickness and diseases: the gospel gives all of this to us.

The gospel provides for our *will*. It provides that we may yoke our will to the omnipotent will of God and thereby strengthen our own will.

The gospel also provides for man's *moral nature*. Its code of morals is acknowledged by any man to be above reproach.

The gospel also provides the only satisfaction in the universe for our *spiritual nature*. The gospel recognizes the tremendous fact of sin and proposes an adequate remedy.

It does not evade the age-old question, "What must I do to be saved?" by saying there is no need of salvation. It does not lift us out of the pit by telling us that we are not bad. It does not remove the sting of our conscience by taking away conscience itself. It does not haunt us.

The gospel shows people their wounds and bestows on them love. It shows them their bondage and supplies the hammer to knock away their chains. It shows them their nakedness and provides them the garments of purity. It shows them their poverty and pours into their lives the wealth of heaven. It shows them their sins and points them to the Savior.

This is the message we are to take to a lost, confused, and bewildered world! This is showing mercy!

There are those near us in our communities who need the regenerating power of Christ. We can call them by name. I suggest that each of us make a list and begin by spending time in prayer for these needy people. We should ask God to show us how to witness to them and how to win them. Their lives can be transformed by the message we give them. We are to share this gospel we have received. If Christ has done anything for us, then we *must* share it. In so doing, we are showing mercy!

William Shakespeare wrote:

> The quality of mercy is not strained;
> It droppeth as the gentle rain from heaven
> Upon the place beneath: it is twice blest
> It blesseth him that gives and him that takes:

'Tis mightiest in the mightiest; it becomes
The throned monarch better than his crown.

No, the path to happiness is not found in selfish living and indifference to others. Instead, when we have experienced the mercy of God then we will show mercy to others. Then we will indeed be "twice blest" because we will both make others happy and experience true happiness ourselves. "Happy are the merciful: for they shall obtain mercy."

7

Happiness in Purity

Blessed are the pure in heart: for they shall see God. MATTHEW 5:8

IN THE BIBLE the heart is considered to be something far more complex than a bodily organ. It is called the seat of the emotions. Fear, love, courage, anger, joy, sorrow, and hatred are ascribed to the heart. It has come to stand for the center of the moral, spiritual, and intellectual life of a person. The "heart" is said to be the seat of a person's conscience and life.

Jesus said, "Happy are the pure in heart." Now, we should be able to take that for just what it means. If the heart is the seat of affection, then our love toward God must be pure. If the heart is the center of our motives, then our motives must be pure. If the heart is the residence of our wills, then our wills must be yielded to Christ. We are to be pure in love, pure in motive, and pure in desire.

It might be well to pause at this point to observe just what is meant by being "pure in heart."

The True Meaning of Purity

The word which is translated "pure" here was used in several ways in the original Greek language. For one thing, it was often used to mean something that was unadulterated or unmixed with anything foreign, such as pure gold which has not been mixed with any other metal, or milk which has not been watered down. Or again, it often simply meant "clean," like a dish which had been thoroughly washed or clothes that had been scrubbed.

Now apply those meanings to "pure in heart." If we are truly pure in our hearts, we will have a single-minded devotion to the will of God. Our motives will be unmixed, our thoughts will not be adulterated with those things which are not right. And our hearts will be clean, because we will not tolerate known sin in our hearts and allow it to pollute us. We will take seriously the Bible's promise, "If we say that we have no sin, we deceive ourselves, and the truth is not in us. If we confess our sins, he is faithful and just to forgive us our sins, and to cleanse us from all unrighteousness" (1 John 1:8–9).

There is, however, another dimension to this word "pure." It also sometimes meant something which was purged of wrong so it could be used for right. William Barclay points out that it could be used of an army which had been purged or cleared of soldiers who were cowardly or weak and unable to fight. It would then be a "pure" army, filled with dedicated and trained soldiers ready for battle. This would be like a person's body which is purified of sickness so it is strong and able to work. In the same way, when we are "pure in heart" we are ready to do those good things which God has for us to do.

In other words, purity of heart has both a negative and a positive side. On one hand, our hearts are to be emptied of sin and its dominion over us. On the other hand, we are to be pure in our actions and filled with all that is pure. The Bible illustrates these negative and positive sides to purity: "*Put to death* therefore what is earthly in you: fornication, impurity, passion, evil desire, and covetousness. . . . *put them all away:* anger, wrath, malice, slander, and foul talk. . . . *Put on then,* as God's chosen ones, holy and beloved, compassion, kindness, lowliness, meekness, and patience. . . . And above all these *put on* love" (Colossians 3:5, 8, 12, 14, RSV, emphasis added).

Misconceptions about Purity of Heart

Did Jesus mean that we were to attain a sinless perfection, a spiritual state in which it would be impossible for us to fail again? No.

To be pure in heart does not mean that I must live in a straight jacket, looking pious and retreating periodically into monastic seclusion. Jesus denounced the Pharisees because they had a false conception of heart purity. He said: "Woe unto you, scribes and Pharisees, hypocrites! for ye are like unto whited sepulchers, which indeed appear beautiful outward, but are within full of dead men's bones, and of all uncleanness" (Matthew 23:27).

Jesus' debate with the Pharisees was right at this point. They avowed that the favor of God was gained by making clean the outside of the cup, by observing certain religious rites, and by keeping the letter of the law. In other words, they worked from the "outside in" rather than from the "inside out."

But this was not God's plan. This did not produce purity of heart. This did not bring about happiness of soul.

Their superficial religion was powerless to cleanse their hearts from their moral filth and corruption; hence the Pharisees were not happy men. They were full of resentments, bitternesses, prejudices, and hatreds. Why? Simply because they had lost sight of God's conception of the pure in heart. They thought that as long as they kept the letter of the law, this was enough.

But Jesus taught that God looks deeper than the outside actions of an individual. He searches and ponders the heart. God judges not so much the outside as He does the inside. He looks to the motives, thoughts, and intents of our heart.

We called one of our daughters "Bunny." She was a sweet, loving, cooperative child. At that time, many years ago, she was at the age where she was obsessed with the desire to help Daddy. Whatever I did, she would say, "Daddy, let me help you." Now Bunny meant well, but between you and me, she was seldom of any valuable assistance in a constructive way. If she helped me weed the flowers she pulled up the flowers instead of the weeds. If she helped me unload the groceries, she invariably dropped something of value and broke it. If she helped me clean my study, she made a mess of things in general. But Bunny's motive was good—she really wanted to help. So I tried to encourage this good, though undeveloped, trait, realizing Bunny's motives. Incidentally, she has grown up to be an extraordinarily helpful, caring person.

This is exactly what God does. He does not judge the superficial goodness or the superficial badness of what we do. He goes deeper into the soul and probes as a surgeon! When God is through probing our hearts, he says: "The heart is deceitful above all things, and desperately wicked: who can know it?" (Jeremiah 17:9).

Evil in the Heart

When Jesus had finished probing the hearts of the people with whom He came in contact, He said: "Out of the heart of men proceed evil thoughts, adulteries, fornications, murders, thefts, covetousness, wickedness, deceit, lasciviousness, an evil eye, blasphemy, pride, foolishness" (Mark 7:21, 22). Jesus taught that the human heart was far from God: darkened, unbelieving, blind, proud, rebellious, idolatrous, and stony. He taught that the human heart in its natural state is capable of any wickedness and any crime.

A teenage boy was arrested in New York for having committed one of the most vicious murders of our time. His mother exclaimed, "But he is a good boy!" She had not stopped to realize that an unregenerate human heart is potentially capable of any crime. A certain poet has written:

> Qicken my conscience till it feels
> The loathsomeness of sin.

That is the reason why many of the peace treaties which have been signed in human history have not been kept and war has ensued. These treaties have been signed in good faith, but they were signed on the basis of trusting the motives of the other party. They have been broken time after time and millions have died on the battlefields of the world because the human heart is deceitful and desperately wicked.

Our hearts are impure! As a result, we are filled with inner tension, pride, frustration, confusion, and a thousand and one other spiritual, mental, and physical ills. The very root of our lives is bad. The theologian, William G. T. Shedd, said, "Human character is worthless, in proportion as abhorrence of sin is lacking in it."

Jesus says we will never be completely and supremely happy until our hearts are pure. Samuel Rutherford urged us to "Labor for a strong and lively sense of sin . . . the more sense of sin, the less sin."

The Cure for a Sick Heart

But if we have bad hearts, what can we do about them? "Should we try to reform or improve our hearts in some way?" someone asks.

Man—ever intent to live independently of God and His transforming grace—claims that environment, education, and right mental attitudes can change the heart and make it pure. "Put people in a wholesome atmosphere and they will be good," the humanist argument goes.

Although this may sound perfectly logical—like a good many man-made theories—it simply will not hold water. Put an African baboon in a Boston drawing room, and how long will it take for him to act like a human being? "But that is twisting the argument," our humanist friends will object.

I think not! For we are dealing with the problem of nature as opposed to environment. The nature of an animal is affected by environment but can never be radically and essentially changed by it. An animal trainer may subdue that wild nature to a degree, but the baboon will always have the nature of a baboon, regardless of training and environment. Furthermore, the first crime, Cain's murder of Abel, was committed in a perfect environment!

There are others who say that our mental attitude toward life needs to be changed: "If we *think* right, we *are* right." To them the problem of evil is a psychological one. "Think positively," they say. "As a man thinketh in his heart, so is he."

This is all very good, and I have a great deal of sympathy for those who are trying through psychological means to help bring about better mental attitudes. But this also gives encouragement to the people who say, "Goody, goody! We can help ourselves, just as we had always thought." The "do-it-yourself" rage is spreading everywhere, and people are being told that to be happy all they have to do is to think "happiness thoughts." Such thoughts might cheer us, but they will never change us.

However, God says that our need is deeper-seated than the mind. He did not say, "Blessed are they who think happiness thoughts." He said: "Blessed are the pure in heart: for they shall see God."

This heart purity is not produced by mental suggestion, by environment or by education. It is a miracle wrought by God Himself. God says: "A new heart also will I give you, and a new spirit will I put within you: and I will take away the stony heart out of your flesh" (Ezekiel 36:26).

Purity of heart is a result of a rebirth, a miracle, a new creation. As the Bible says: "Which were born, not of blood, nor of the will of the flesh, nor of the will of man, but of God" (John 1:13).

We need cleansed, forgiven, justified, new hearts! Such can be received only as an act of God on the ground of the death of Christ on the cross.

A Sunday school teacher once told a class of boys and girls that nothing was impossible with God. One little boy objected, saying that he knew one thing God could not do.

"And what could that be?" asked the astonished teacher.

"To see my sins through the blood of Jesus Christ," the youngster wisely answered.

When we have properly confessed and renounced our sins and by faith received Christ into our hearts, then we receive a new heart from God. Only then can we be called "pure in heart." Only then can we know the secret of happiness!

Again, I should like to emphasize that this is not an emotional experience, though emotion may be a factor. I may not "feel" that I have a new heart but I can accept the fact by faith. Faith goes beyond logic, rationalization, and understanding. You may not be able to accept intellectually all that has been said on these pages, but I challenge you to believe and accept by faith that which you cannot understand. There would be no need for faith if we could understand all about God.

Jesus insisted that we must become as little children before we could enter the kingdom of heaven. Each of us must become as a little child and by faith grasp that which we cannot altogether understand. But on the other hand, realize that God can be trusted. Faith is not a blind leap in the dark! It is instead based squarely on what God has done for us in Jesus Christ. Our faith has a firm foundation, because it is not based on speculation or wishful thinking, but upon God and His Word. God can be trusted to keep His promises to us.

Certainly purity of heart is a prerequisite to entering the kingdom of heaven. There is no chance of a person's ever going to heaven until that one has received purity of heart. This purity of heart comes as an act of God after one has renounced sin and received Christ!

Have you received a new heart? If you have, then you stand on the threshold of discovering the secret of happiness!

It is impossible to live pure lives until we have pure hearts. Many people today are trying to put the cart before the horse. They are teaching purity of motives, desires, and actions to old, deceitful hearts! No wonder we have ended up such moral failures in spite of our vaunted knowledge and psychological approaches. Pure motives, desires, and actions stem from pure hearts.

The Nature of the Pure Heart

If we have received a cleansed and pure heart from God, we are expected to live a pure life. Theologically (as we have already seen in the chapter on "Happy though Hungry"), this is called "sanctification."

Pure hearts will be Christlike. It is God's desire that we be conformed to the image of His Son. If Christ lives within us and our bodies become the abode of the Holy Spirit, is it any wonder that we should be like Him? And just what do we mean by Christlike?

The Bible says: "Let this mind be in you, which was also in Christ Jesus" (Philippians 2:5). Jesus had a humble heart. If He abides in us, pride will never dominate our lives. Jesus had a loving heart. If He dwells within us, hatred and bitterness will never rule us. Jesus had a forgiving and understanding heart. If He lives within us, mercy will temper our relationships with our fellow men. Jesus had an unselfish heart. If He lives in us, selfishness will not predominate but service to God and others will come before our selfish interests. But even more, Jesus' one desire was to do His Father's will. This is the essence of Christlikeness—eager obedience to the Father's will.

You say, "That's a big order!" I admit that. It would be impossible if we had to measure up to Him in our own strength and with our own natural hearts.

Paul recognized that he could never attain this heart purity by his own striving. He said: "I can do all things *through* Christ which strengtheneth me" (Philippians 4:13).

God hasn't left us alone, out on a limb! Jesus said to His disciples: "Lo, I am with you alway, even unto the end of the world" (Matthew 28:20). They did what they did because He was with them. They were nothing but a group of rough, unlettered men; but with Christ in their hearts they "turned the world upside down" (Acts 17:6).

Christ provided the possibility of purity by His death on the cross. We have seen that the righteousness and the purity of God are imputed to men who confess their sins and receive Christ into their hearts.

Webster defines purity: "Freedom from foreign admixture or deleterious matter. Cleanness; freedom from foulness or dirt. Freedom from guilt or the defilement of sin; innocence; chastity. Freedom from any sinister or improper motives or views."

Though all of these ideas are embraced in the term *purity*, they do not set up an absolute standard by which to judge what is foreign and what is not, what is sin and what is not. It is best to regard purity in the all-embracing connotation: complete conformity to the holiness of God.

The Scriptures continually ask us to strive after *physical, mental,* and *moral* purity. God says: "Be ye holy; for I am holy" (1 Peter 1:16). Further, the Scripture says that without holiness, "no man shall see the Lord" (Hebrews 12:14). Again the Scripture says: "Who shall ascend into the hill of the Lord? or who shall stand in his holy place? He that hath clean hands, and a pure heart; who hath not lifted up his soul unto vanity, nor sworn deceitfully" (Psalm 24:3, 4). We are actually commanded in Scripture: "Keep thyself pure" (1 Timothy 5:22).

Physical Cleanliness

God wants us *to be pure in body.* This includes *physical cleanliness.*

Caverno says, "When one realizes that by uncleanness of person or property he may endanger the health or life of family or even of society about him—as in keeping conditions that develop typhoid fever—he begins to realize that there is a close tie between cleanliness and morals."

The ancient Jews strove for physical cleanliness on religious grounds; and although many of the Old Testament laws of purification have been abolished as detailed prescriptions for today, others are incorporated into our own way of life. The principle of physical cleanliness is still in force. In the Middle Ages, however, many Christians felt that not bathing was a sign of humility and the dirtier they became, the more holy they were!

Even in the poorest of circumstances a person can afford some soap and water. There is absolutely no excuse for a Christian's being unclean, unkempt, or slovenly. If you have a pure heart, you will also want to have a pure body.

Physical cleanliness means more than just keeping our bodies washed, however. For example, God has given us our bodies and we are to take care of them in every reasonable way we can. The apostle Paul commanded Christians to be pure in body and to take care of their bodies. "What? know ye not that your body is the temple of the Holy Ghost which is in you, which ye have of God, and ye are not your own? For ye are bought with a price: therefore glorify God in your body, and in your spirit, which are God's" (1 Corinthians 6:19–20).

We need to get proper exercise, and we need to eat properly. We need to realize also that there is a close relationship between our physical health and our spiritual, mental and emotional outlook. Science is discovering more and more the truth of what the Bible said centuries ago: "A merry heart maketh a cheerful countenance: but by sorrow of the heart the spirit is broken" (Proverbs 15:13). The Bible also states, "A merry heart doeth good like a medicine: but a broken spirit drieth the bones" (Proverbs 17:22). When David sinned against God he was burdened inside with his guilt, but it also affected him physically. Later he wrote, "When I kept silence, my bones waxed old through my roaring all the day long" (Psalm 32:3).

Moral Cleanliness

Being pure in body also includes *chastity*. Thus Paul says: "This is the will of God, even your sanctification, that ye should abstain from fornication . . ." (1 Thessalonians 4:3).

How often the Scriptures warn against the sins of adultery and fornication. It is significant that in many references Paul mentions "uncleanness" immediately after "fornication."

Our newspapers are filled with stories of immorality in various parts of the nation. In fact, immorality is glorified today. Some of the most popular TV programs are about the decadent rich!

Let me warn you: the Scripture teaches that God hates immorality!

For several centuries our civilization has often been caught in the crosscurrents of a number of different secular philosophies. Often these have gained popular acceptance for a time, and have had a great impact on our institutions, ideas, and values. Some, for example, have taught that there are no firm or absolute moral values by which we are to guide our lives. Instead, morals are relative; we are to do whatever we think is right for us, without worrying about God and His moral law. Such views, however, only lead to moral chaos—and chaos within our society as well. One lawyer told me recently that the vast majority of his clients are not concerned about the fact they have done wrong— all they are interested in is not getting caught!

Many have been convinced that the Bible is not God's revelation, that salvation is to come through man and not through Christ, and that morality is relative and not absolute. As well say rules of the road are relative and not absolute. How would you like to land at an airport where the laws of aviation were relative?

The practical results of this intellectual acceptance of humanism and behaviorism have been a degeneration of morals and the abandonment of religious ideals. The wave of behavioristic psychology that swept our college campuses and permeated the high school classrooms is now ingrained in the way our youth are living. The ideal of purity is scorned, immorality is laughed at in school— "God is old-fashioned!" What else can we expect but that thousands of our young people are growing up to be immoral? The Bible warns time after time that no immoral nation can survive and no immoral individual shall enter the kingdom of God.

One of the Ten Commandments says: "Thou shalt not commit adultery"

(Exodus 20:14). I am keenly aware that this delicate subject is no longer considered taboo by clergymen. The newspapers mention it, pornographic writers make it the theme of their writings, it is the theme of everyday gossip, children talk about it, and almost every magazine has discussions and pictures about it. And beyond all that, the Bible mentions it over and over again as one of the worst sins! So why in the name of all that is just, proper, and holy should not preachers sound the warning against it?

The Bible says time after time: "Thou shalt not commit adultery." What does this word *adultery* mean? It is derived from the same Latin root from which we get our word *adulterate* which means "corrupt; to make impure or to weaken."

Sin is not merely the use of that which is corrupt, but more often the misuse of that which is pure and good. So adultery can apply to many things. This sin was so terrible that under Jewish law it was punishable by death. Under the Roman law it was punishable by death. Under the Greek law it was punishable by death. And under God's law, the Bible says, it is punishable by spiritual death.

The Bible says. "She that liveth in pleasure is dead while she liveth" (1 Timothy 5:6) and "The wages of sin is death" (Romans 6:23). The Bible says we are to keep our bodies pure, we are to abstain from fleshly lust. This sin is a sin not only against the body but against God.

Pure in Our Minds

God also wants us *to be pure in mind.* William Barclay said: "Pure thoughts mean those thoughts which can be examined by the Holy Spirit." Paul said: "Whatsoever things are pure . . . think on these things" (Philippians 4:8).

Returning to the question of chastity, we note that Jesus said: "Ye have heard that it was said . . . Thou shalt not commit adultery: But I say unto you, That whosoever looketh on a woman to lust after her hath committed adultery with her already in his heart" (Matthew 5:27, 28).

You can commit immorality *by evil imaginations.* In Genesis 6:5 we read: "And God saw that the wickedness of man was great in the earth, and that every imagination of the thoughts of his heart was only evil continually." God is concerned with our imaginations, for they in a large measure determine what kind of a persons we are to be.

Solomon said: "As [a man] thinketh in his heart, so is he" (Proverbs 23:7). If our thoughts are evil, then our acts will be evil. If our thoughts are godly, then our lives will be godly.

Robert Browning said: "Thought is the soul of the act." Ralph Waldo Emerson said: "Thought is the seat of action, the ancestor of every action is thought."

If God destroyed the world during Noah's time for its continual evil imaginations, is it not reasonable to believe that all of the sin, lust, and licentiousness rampant today grieves His heart just as it did in that day?

Many people dream of sin, imagine sin, and if granted the opportunity would indulge in sin. All they lack is the occasion to sin. So in the sight of God they are sinners as great as though they had actually committed immorality.

All transgression begins with sinful thinking. We who have come to Christ for a pure heart, must guard against the pictures of lewdness and sensuality which Satan flashes upon the screens of our imaginations. We must select with care the books we read. I must choose discerningly the kind of entertainment I attend, the kind of associates with whom I mingle, and the kind of environment in which I place myself. I should no more allow sinful imaginations to accumulate in my mind and soul than I would let garbage collect in my living room.

Benjamin Franklin said: "It is easier to suppress the first desire than to satisfy all that follow it." St. Augustine said: "Purity of soul cannot be lost without consent." Ask God to cleanse your mind and keep it purified. This can be done through reading the Bible, daily prayer, and association with the right kind of people.

As we have seen, Jesus indicated that one can engage in immorality by a *look.* The Bible places the "lust of the eye" right along with other major sins. Listen: "For all that is in the world, the lust of the flesh, and the lust of the eyes, and the pride of life, is not of the Father, but is of the world" (1 John 2:16).

Peter spoke of having "eyes full of adultery" (2 Peter 2:14). No wonder Job said: "I made a covenant with my eyes; why then should I think upon a maid?" (Job 31:1).

Our eyes see only what our soul allows them to see. If one's heart is out of harmony with God and he has never been born again, the odds are that he will have a perverted, distorted view of life. Like Paul, the scales of lust and animal passion can fall from our eyes when we catch a vision of Christ. At this moment I can make a covenant with my eyes. I can take my eyes and nail them to the cross until I can say, "They have been crucified with Christ, never again to lust."

Immorality can be engaged in by the *tongue.* The Scripture warns about evil communications that corrupt good manners. The psalmist said: "Set a watch, O Lord, before my mouth" (Psalm 141:3). Off-color jokes and dirty stories have no place in the Christian life. Thousands of people are engaging in immorality by the way they talk. Keep your talk pure. Ask God to purify your tongue.

I can engage in immorality by the way I *dress.* If women purposely dress to entice a man to sin, then they are guilty whether the act is committed or not. A girl said one day, "I came forward in your meeting and accepted Christ. A few nights later I was going to a party. I put on my dress. I looked in the mirror, and it seemed as though Jesus were looking at me. I went to my wardrobe and changed my dress. And now I dress as though Jesus were my escort each evening." Dress to please Christ—in all modesty and good taste.

I can engage in immorality while *reading* unclean books and looking at unclean pictures. Our newsstands today are so indecent that a Christian cannot look upon them without blushing, and yet thousands of people are buying unclean books and the wrong type of magazines. The same is true of our movie and TV screens. By feeding our lusts, we are sinning against God.

Many of you who are reading these pages have committed this terrible sin of breaking the Seventh Commandment. You have been unfaithful to your wife or husband, or you young people have yielded to this temptation of illicit sex. You have become impure in regard to chastity. The prophet Malachi wrote:

> Yet ye say, Wherefore? Because the LORD hath been witness between thee and the wife of thy youth, against whom thou hast dealt treacherously: yet *is* she thy companion, and the wife of thy covenant. And did not he make one? Yet had he the residue of the spirit. And wherefore one? That he might seek a godly seed. Therefore take heed to your spirit, and let none deal treacherously against the wife of his youth. For the LORD, the God of Israel, saith that he hateth putting away: for *one* covereth violence with his garment, saith the LORD of hosts: therefore take heed to your spirit, that ye deal not treacherously (2:14–16).

Although the Bible teaches that this sin leads to hell, there is good news! The woman at the well had broken this commandment, but Christ forgave her and met the need of her life. Mary Magdalene had broken this commandment, but Christ wonderfully met the need of her life and cleansed her from sin. The sinful woman who had been taken in adultery was brought to Jesus by the Pharisees, but He said: "Neither do I condemn thee: go, and sin no more" (John 8:11). He did not condone her, but neither did He condemn her, because she had trusted in Him. He sent her away redeemed and forgiven, but commanded her to sin no more. Christ will do the same for you if you will let Him.

Pure in Our Actions

Not only does God want us to be pure in body and pure in mind, but He wants us to be pure in conduct.

Paul says: "Let no corrupt communication proceed out of your mouth, but that which is good to the use of edifying, that it may minister grace unto the hearers" (Ephesians 4:29).

Jesus said to the Pharisees: "Ye generation of vipers, how can ye, being evil, speak good things? for out of the abundance of the heart the mouth speaketh. A good man out of the good treasure of the heart bringeth forth good things: and an evil man out of the evil treasure bringeth forth evil things. But I say unto you, That every idle word that men shall speak, they shall give account thereof in the day of judgment. For by thy words thou shalt be justified, and by thy words thou shalt be condemned" (Matthew 12:34–37).

Cursing, telling smutty stories, smearing the good name of another and referring irreverently to God and the Scriptures may be considered as coming under the expression *corrupt speech*. Our speech is to be clean, pure, and wholesome.

Under this rule of good conduct also come our associations. Paul says that evil companionships corrupt good morals (1 Corinthians 15:33). The Bible warns against being unequally yoked with unbelievers. This condemns all business, social, fraternal, and religious associations in which unchristian principles and practices govern. Concerning the latter, John says: "If there come any unto you, and bring not this doctrine, receive him not into your house, neither bid him Godspeed: For he that biddeth him Godspeed is partaker of his evil deeds" (2 John 10, 11).

Christians who are involved in associations that are evil and corrupt are asked to "come out from among them, and be ye separate, and touch not the unclean thing" (2 Corinthians 6:17). God promises that if we do this, He will receive us into His most intimate fellowship.

The Bible teaches that purity of conduct includes *truthfulness*. God's Word teaches that we should be truthful in our representations of ourselves. With what scorn Christ denounced the hypocrisy of the scribes and Pharisees! In the Sermon on the Mount, He rebuked all hypocritical giving, praying, and fasting.

We should also be truthful in speaking of our past achievements in our particular vocation. God does not ask us to understate the facts—that might even be untruthfulness—but neither does He want us to overrate our achievements or our gifts, either in thought or in speech. In the Septuagint (Greek) version of the Old Testament Proverbs 24:28 says, "Overstate not with thy lips."

Purity in the Marketplace

We are also to be truthful in our business affairs. All misrepresentations of the quality of our merchandise, all false weights and measures, all padding of expense accounts, all forging of checks and other legal papers, and all unjust alterations of accounts are sins of untruthfulness and indicate lack of purity. The farmer who puts his spoiled wheat between two layers of good wheat when he takes it to the market and the fruit grower who puts his best fruit on top in his measure are dishonest. The tourist who misrepresents an article that is subject to duty on entering the country and the taxpayer who does not supply all the desired information are dishonest.

Being pure in conduct also includes *honesty* and *integrity* in dealing with our fellow men. Employers in business are to give proper wages for work done, while employees are to put in a full hour's honest labor for the wages they receive. A Christian should be known in his or her neighborhood or place of business as an honest person—one who can be trusted.

Purity and Happiness Are Possible

Jesus said: "Blessed are the pure in heart."

Do you want to be happy? All right, apply this Beatitude to your heart. Take it to yourself. The pure in heart are the only ones who can know what it means to be supremely happy. Their hearts are pure toward God and, as a result, are pure toward their fellow men.

They are happy because in possessing Him who is All and in All, they envy no one's worldly goods. They are happy because they envy not another person's praise or another person's place in the sun. Because they are the enemy of no one, they regard no one as their enemy. The result is peace with God and the world. Because their sins have been freely forgiven, they freely forgive those who have wronged them. They are thus purged of contemptuous malice.

But the greatest happiness that comes to the pure in heart is not only a proper relationship with others but a sublime relationship with God. "For they shall see God." The gates of Eden swing open once more. God and man walk together once again.

Dying to Dirt

From the old magazine *Hi Call* comes this story:

Visiting in a mining town, a young minister was being escorted through one of the coal mines. In one of the dark, dirty passageways, he spied a beautiful white flower growing out of the black earth of the mine. "How can there be a flower of such purity and beauty in this dirty mine?" the minister asked the miner. "Throw some of the coal dust on it and see," was the reply. The minister did so and was surprised that as fast as the dirt touched those snowy petals, it slid right off to the ground, leaving the flower just as lovely as before. It was so smooth that the dirt could not cling to the flower.

Our hearts can be the same way. We cannot help it that we have to live in a world filled with sin, any more than the flower could change the place where it was growing. But God can keep us so pure and clean that though we touch sin on every side, it will not cling to us. We can stand in the midst of it just as white and beautiful as that flower.

The secret of purity is God! The secret of seeing and knowing God is a pure heart . . . a pure heart comes from God! Get a pure heart, and you can be supremely happy—no matter what the circumstances!

8

Happiness through Peacemaking

Blessed are the peacemakers: for they shall be called the children of God.
MATTHEW 5:9

THE PROBLEM OF human strife is as old as man. It had its beginning on the outskirts of Eden when Cain, driven by envy, murdered his more devout brother, Abel. Men fought then as now: primarily because strife was inherent in their natures.

Jesus spoke prophetically of our times when He said: "And ye shall hear of wars and rumors of wars . . . nation shall rise against nation, and kingdom against kingdom . . ." (Matthew 24:6, 7).

Someone has pointed out that over the past 4,000 years there has been less than 300 years of peace. Yet one wonders, was that universal peace? It is more likely that down through history there has always been a war, or wars, in various parts of the world. Even the most optimistic person is forced to admit that there is something seriously wrong with a world that has such a passion for destruction.

If a man were sent from Mars to report earth's major business, he would in all fairness have to say that war was the earth's chief industry. He would report that the nations of the world were vying with each other in a race to see which could make deadlier weapons and amass bigger nuclear arsenals. He would say that earth's people are too quarrelsome to get along with each other and too selfish to live peacefully together.

Dr. Robert Oppenheimer, who supervised the creation of the first atomic bomb, was asked to appear before a Congressional Committee. They asked him if there was any defense against this awesome new weapon of war. "Certainly," the great physicist replied.

"And that is—" someone asked.

The audience awaited the answer in subdued silence. "Peace," the eminent scientist replied softly.

The Search for Peace

But why is it that after these thousands of years of life on this planet we are no nearer peace than were the warring tribes of ancient history?

The world is desperately searching for peace. There are millions of people who would gladly give their right arms to find it. They would like to have peace—deep, inward, satisfying peace.

They also yearn for peace in our world—freedom from conflict and war, freedom from the hatred and strife which divide families and communities, and freedom from fear of the future, wondering when a computer will malfunction or a maniacal dictator will place his finger on the nuclear or biochemical button and wipe out civilization as we know it.

The world thinks peace would come if everyone made a lot of money, but people haven't found peace in possessions. They have thought the world would have peace if all arms were destroyed. Yet Cain killed Abel without a handgun. It is man's heart that is the problem.

Some thought peace could be found in a bottle, but they didn't find it there. But it was an artificial peace, frequently leading to death. They thought one would find it in getting and accumulating a lot of knowledge, so they got all the degrees they could get, but still didn't find it. Some have searched the religions of the world, even exotic and mind-warping cults, but haven't found peace even there.

There are a thousand ways we've turned, trying to find peace, but we haven't found it. We've escaped from reality for a few moments, for a few hours, and then it's back there—the old burden, the old suffering, the old emptiness, the old monotony, the old grind. Jesus Christ is the only One who can give "the peace that passeth all understanding."

The simple fact is: there can be no real peace in the world until we have peace with God.

The motto of the Apollo II flight was, "We come in peace for all mankind." This motto was on the plaque which was left there on the surface of the moon, where the astronauts landed on the Sea of Tranquillity. Astronauts Neil Armstrong and Buzz Aldrin found themselves in a wonderfully peaceful place there on the moon. Do you know why? There had never been any humans there before!

Not long after the development of the atomic bomb Albert Einstein declared, "The unleashed power of the atom has changed everything except our way of thinking. We shall require a substantially new manner of thinking if mankind is to survive." Later a photographer who had noted the look of immense sadness on Einstein's face asked him, "So you don't believe that there will ever be peace?" "No," the great scientist replied. "As long as there will be man, there will be wars."

Peace is more than a mere cessation of hostilities, a momentary halt in a hot or cold war. Rather, it is something positive. It is a specific relationship with God into which a person is brought. It is a spiritual reality in a human heart which has come into vital contact with the Infinite God.

The Bible says: "But now in Christ Jesus ye who sometimes were far off are made nigh by the blood of Christ. For he is our peace, who hath made both one" (Ephesians 2:13, 14).

A Breach Repaired

I saw a painting in England which showed a soldier who had gone to the front to repair the communications lines. The message which was to flow through those lines meant life to hundreds and perhaps thousands of men. He found a breach in the wires but had nothing with which to repair the break. While the enemy shells were bursting around him, he took one broken cable in his left hand and stretching his right hand grasped the other cable and made the connection. The dramatic picture had a oneword title: "Through."

Christ, in His vicarious death on the cross, repaired the breach between God and man. The Bible says: "He is our peace" (Ephesians 2:14). Those who were afar off are made nigh . . . He has made both one. *Through Him alone* we have peace!

Although God has never been humanity's enemy, we by choice became enemies of God. The revolt began in the Garden of Eden, when Adam revolted against God and allied himself with Satan. It was there that the enmity began. It was there that the abysmal breach was made by humanity, by deliberate choice. Enmity and enemy come from the same root.

The history of man has been the record of a futile effort to live happily and peacefully apart from God. When Israel turned from the worship of Jehovah to the worship of idols, she lost her peace, and either fell a prey to other nations or entered a series of wars. Any step away from the true, living God is a step in the direction of strife.

Hitler felt pretty sure of himself when he denounced the Bible and Christianity and tried to create a "pure Aryan" church with a god who bore a striking resemblance to Thor or Woden, the war gods. We are all acquainted with the record of what happened in Germany. A regime which on the surface looked strong enough to conquer the world crumbled and fell swiftly. Today a new Germany has emerged out of the rubble of World War II. In our tours of Germany we have sensed the heart-hunger of these gifted and virile people for a faith which brings peace and not war.

Jesus said: "Blessed are the peacemakers: for they shall be called the children of God." Notice, He calls for us to be *peacemakers*—not pacifists. There is a world of difference between the two!

Where does peacemaking begin? How can we become peacemakers?

We have pointed out that peace can never come out of war. War is the sire of poverty, depression, suffering, and hatred—it has never given us permanent peace.

Can peace be discovered within ourselves? Psychiatry has told us that peace is but a mental attitude. Cast off our phobias, shed our neuroses, and "voilá!"— we'll have the coveted peace men long for.

Psychiatry Alone Won't Work

I respect psychiatry and psychology for what they can do. One of my sons-in-law is a practicing psychologist and a Christian, and has dedicated his life to helping people who have emotional problems. Many of those problems, he tells me, have a direct relationship to spiritual and moral problems which have caused a person to become insecure and unstable. But emotional stability and peace of mind are no substitute for the lasting inner peace which can only come from God. If psychiatry leaves God out, ultimately we shall see psychiatrists going to each other for treatment. There can be no peace until we find peace with God. The Bible says: "He is our peace" (Ephesians 2:14).

The Bible is not content to leave the nature of the peace Christ purchased for us in doubt. It sketches that peace in the clearest of outlines. Christ made peace by the blood of His cross (Colossians 1:20). He bore the sins of all, so those who know His saviorhood need be troubled by them no longer. He interposed Himself between doomed humanity and the wrath of God. And He stands still between the Holy God and fallen man in his strife, rebellion, and conflict. He is the only hope for peace in the inner spiritual warfare of the soul, and for that reason also is the only hope for social stability.

In a materialistic world which has tried to sever diplomatic relations with God, we have nowhere to retreat except within ourselves. We are like turtles in a traffic jam—the best we can do is to pull our heads back into our shells and shut our eyes. But that's a good way to get the life crushed out of you, as any dead turtle can attest.

Where Does It Begin?

Where does peacemaking begin? How can we become peacemakers in our broken, nervous, frightened, and dangerous world?

If we are to be peacemakers, we first must make our peace with God.

The Bible says: "There is no peace, saith the Lord, unto the wicked" (Isaiah 48:22). The same prophet said: "The way of peace they know not; and there is no judgment in their goings: they have made them crooked paths; whosoever goeth therein shall not know peace" (Isaiah 59:8).

Man's conflict with man has been but an expression on the human level of his conflict against God. Until we find an armistice with God, we cannot know peace among ourselves. Both ancient and modern men have discovered the peace of God. David said: "I will both lay me down in peace, and sleep: for thou, Lord, only makest me dwell in safety" (Psalm 4:8).

A former unbeliever, having recently discovered the peace of God, said to me some years ago, "My wife and I used to wake up in the morning quarreling and go to bed at night bickering—but since we have found peace with God, our home is a heaven on earth."

We can have peace with God! "But how can we discover this peace?" you ask.

A Ceasefire Needed

The first step in finding peace with God is to stop fighting Him. Through the Bible, through the church, through the lives of Christian people, God has been trying to get through to us for years with the message that He wants to give us peace. Christ said to His disciples: "My peace I give unto you" (John 14:27). He is no respecter of persons—He wants to give us peace. But He can't give us His peace as long as we lift high the red flag of rebellion. We must stop resisting God! We must no longer shut Him out of our lives! We must stop fighting! We must give up!

The Solace of Surrender

The second step in finding peace with God is to surrender to Him. We must put down our weapons of war! We must get off the offensive, and stop *being* offensive! The Bible says regarding a people who had no peace with God: "Be ye not stiffnecked, as your fathers were, but yield yourselves unto the Lord" (2 Chronicles 30:8).

When we surrender to a "friendly enemy"—to One who loves us—we are using good sense.

The peace which follows the acceptance of Christ as Savior is more than earthly peace, and it is the greatest of spiritual treasures even though it may not always bring worldly prosperity with it. To know Christ is to have the supremest of riches, a place in the kingdom of God. And men and women who give Him first place find that there is no need for anxiety about this world's goods. "Seek ye first the kingdom of God . . . and all these things shall be added unto you" (Matthew 6:33).

But there is one more aspect of this peace with God. It is not just a passive peace which sits idly under a willow tree strumming a harp. It is a peace of activity and service.

The Secret of Service

The third step in finding peace with God is to serve Him. The Bible told an ancient people who sued for peace not only to yield but to "serve the Lord your God, that the fierceness of his wrath may turn away from you" (2 Chronicles 30:8).

In all of life there is nothing more wonderful than discovering peace with God. Step one to this discovery is realizing God's plan—peace and life. God loves you and wants you to experience peace and life—abundant and eternal.

The Bible says, ". . . We have peace with God through our Lord Jesus Christ" (Romans 5:1). John 3:16 says, "For God so loved the world, that he gave his only begotten Son, that whosoever believeth in him should not perish, but have everlasting life." In John 10:10 Jesus said, ". . . I am come that they might have life, and that they might have it more abundantly."

Since God planned for us to have peace, and the abundant life right now, why are most people not having this experience? Step two is acknowledging man's problem—separation. God created man in his own image and gave him an abundant life. He did not make him as a robot to automatically love and obey him, but gave him a will and freedom of choice. Man chose to disobey God and go his own willful way. Man still makes this choice today. This results in separation from God.

The Bible says, "For all have sinned, and come short of the glory of God" (Romans 3:23). In Romans 6:23 the apostle Paul says, "For the wages of sin is death (separation from God); but the gift of God is eternal life through Jesus Christ our Lord." Man through the ages has tried to bridge this gap in many ways without success.

There is only one remedy for this problem of separation. Step three is recognizing God's remedy—the cross. Jesus Christ is the *only* answer to this problem of separation. When Jesus Christ died on the cross and rose from the grave, He paid the penalty for our sin and bridged the gap from God to man. His *death* and *resurrection* make a new life possible for all who believe.

"God is on one side and all the people on the other side, and Christ Jesus, himself man, is between them to bring them together" (1 Timothy 2:5, *The Living Bible*).

The Bible says, "But God commendeth (showed) his love toward us, in that, while we were yet sinners, Christ died for us" (Romans 5:8). John writes, "Jesus saith unto him, I am the way, the truth, and the life: no man cometh unto the Father, but by me" (14:6). Paul says, "For by grace are ye saved through faith; and that not of yourselves; it is the gift of God: not of works, lest any man should boast" (Ephesians 2:8, 9).

God has provided the only way. . . . Man must make the choice. Step four is for man to make his response to receive Christ. We must trust Jesus Christ and *receive Him* by personal invitation. The Bible says, "Behold, I stand at the door, and knock (Christ is speaking): if any man hear my voice, and open the door, I will come in to him" (Revelation 3:20). "But as many as received him, to them gave he power to become the sons of God, even to them that believe on his name," writes the apostle John (1:12).

Is there any good reason why you cannot receive Jesus Christ right now? You must:

1. Admit your need (I am a sinner).
2. Be willing to turn from your sins (repent).
3. Believe that Jesus Christ died for you on the cross and rose from the grave.
4. Through prayer, invite Jesus Christ to come in and control your life. (Receive Him as Lord and Savior.)

If we take these steps, we have the assurance that ". . . whosoever shall call upon the name of the Lord shall be saved" (Romans 10:13). If we sincerely ask Jesus Christ to come into our lives, we have this promise: "He that hath the Son hath life (right now), and he that hath not the Son of God hath not life. These things have I written unto you that believe on the name of the Son of God; that ye may *know* that ye have eternal life, and that ye may believe on the name of the son of God" (1 John 5:12, 13)

Some time ago a Christian workman was fatally injured when he fell from a high scaffolding on a construction job. A minister was called, and when he saw the serious condition of the man, he said, "My dear man, I'm afraid you're dying. I exhort you, make your peace with God!"

"Make my peace with God, sir!" said the man, "Why, that was made nineteen hundred years ago when my Savior paid all my debt upon the cross. Christ *is* my peace, and I do know God—I *do* know God!"

Every person can experience the peace of God through Christ: "For he is our peace" (Ephesians 2:14).

Becoming Peacemakers

To have peace *with* God and to have the peace *of* God is not enough. This vertical relationship must have a horizontal outworking, or our faith is in vain. Jesus said that we were to love the Lord with all our hearts and our neighbor as ourselves. This dual love for God and others is like the positive and negative poles of a battery—unless both connections are made, we have no power. A personal faith is normally useless unless it has a social application. A notable exception would be the thief on the cross and other similar situations.

I once saw a cartoon of a man rowing a boat toward a golden shore labeled "heaven." All around him were men and women struggling in vain to reach the shore and safety, but he was heedless of their peril. He was singing, "I am bound for heaven, hallelujah!" That is not an adequate picture of the Christian life.

If we have peace with God and the peace *of* God, we will become peacemakers.

We will not only be at peace with our neighbors, but we will be leading them to discover the source of true peace in Christ.

Christianity increases the scope and area of our lives. It takes us from self-centeredness to multi-centeredness. Conversion takes us from introversion to extroversion.

Our lives take on new dimensions when we find peace with God. To explain this in simpler terms, let us visualize a right-angle triangle sitting on its horizontal base. At the apex or highest point in this triangle write the letter "G," representing God. At the point where the perpendicular line meets the base write the letter "Y," representing you. Then, at the opposite end of the horizontal line write the letter "O," which represents others. There, in geometric form, you have a visual diagram of our relationship with God and man. Our lives (which before we found the peace of God were represented by a single dot of self-centeredness) now take in an area in vital contact with two worlds. Peace flows down from God and out to our fellow men. We become merely the conduit through which it flows. But there is peace in being just a "channel."

Being Peacemakers in the Home

There are many areas of our lives where we can be peacemakers. There is no part of our lives which is not affected by this peace of God which we are to share with others.

First: We can be peacemakers in the *home.*

In a complicated, mechanized age, it is no easy matter to keep the domestic life on an even keel. Modern gadgets, modern transportation and modern social changes have all but revolutionized our domestic life. Families are fragmented. The old-fashioned taffy pulls, Sunday afternoon fun times and family altars seem to have gone out with the horse and buggy.

Many homes today have become little more than dormitories, where the members of the family eat and sleep but otherwise have little communication with each other. One woman wrote me and stated, "Our home is a war zone." Major newsmagazines carry stories of "latchkey kids," youngsters who come home from school to an empty house, seldom seeing their parents and growing up with little love or discipline. Our society has said, "Get ahead! Do your own thing! Don't worry about anyone else—run your own life!" But in the process family life disintegrates and children grow up emotionally scarred and insecure because they have never known the stability of a happy family.

The divorce rate has escalated drastically in recent decades. The home—which is the basic unit of our social structure—continues to disintegrate at an alarming rate, even among Christians. The breaking of the marriage vow is having an effect upon our other social institutions. A chain reaction has set in that could ultimately destroy the nation.

In the marriage ceremony, after the vows are said, the minister solemnly and reverently remarks: "What God hath joined together let no man put asunder." Is not God the party of the third part in a marriage? Should He not be taken into account in the marriage and in the home that emerges from that marriage? If God joins the couple together at the outset, should not His Presence be recognized in the home continually from that point on?

Many homes are in trouble today because God has been left out of the domestic picture. With the continual clash of personalities in a domestic pattern, there must be an integrating force, and the Living God is that Force!

He can give love where there has been hate or indifference. He can make a husband sensitive to the needs of his wife, and the wife sensitive to the needs of her husband—instead of two people constantly clamoring and demanding only to have their own needs met. True self-giving love—the kind God has for us, and the kind He can give us for others—is like a beautiful diamond which sends out flashes of light from its many facets. The Bible gives the most profound and concise summary of love's facets in all of literature: "Love is patient and kind; love is not jealous or boastful; it is not arrogant or rude. Love does not insist on its own way; it is not irritable or resentful; it does not rejoice at wrong, but rejoices in the right. Loves bears all things, believes all things, hopes all things, endures all things" (1 Corinthians 13:4–7, RSV).

A gentleman came to me with a serious domestic problem. He and his wife quarreled violently over trifles. Each blamed the other and the domestic stress had built up to the breaking point. I asked him a question to which I already knew the answer, "Do you and your wife go to church, and do you have family prayer?" He answered that they did neither.

"Your trouble in the home, Mr. B," I said, "is the reflection of your lack of peace with God. Get right with God, and you'll be right with your wife!"

The man did just that. In sincere repentance he confessed his sin to God, and I saw his facial expression change as the peace of Christ came into his heart. The light in his face mirrored the new glow in his soul. A few days later he led his wife to Christ. That home is now a happy one, for Christ is its head.

Many couples think that if they have a more luxurious home, get a better job, or live in a different neighborhood their domestic life will be happier. No! The secret of domestic happiness is to let God, the party of the third part in the marriage contract, have His rightful place in the home. Make peace with Him, and then you can be a real peacemaker in the home.

Peace and Our Community

SECOND: We can be peacemakers in the *community*.

Our society is shot through with slander, libel, and gossip. The strife in many communities is almost unbearable. Here again, the basic cause is a faulty relationship with God.

The Bible says: "The works of the flesh are . . . hatred, variance . . . wrath, strife, seditions . . . envyings" (Galatians 5:19–21). True, we find some of these in the first-century community of Christians. Yet "Behold, how they love one another" was the remark of those who observed the unique peace of the Christian society.

How can I be a peacemaker in my community?

The formula is simple: first, I must make my own peace with God, and then I can make peace in the community. The fruit of human nature is discord and bickering; "but the fruit of the Spirit is love, joy, peace, long-suffering, gentleness, goodness, faith, meekness, temperance" (Galatians 5:22, 23).

Our trouble is that we have tried to build a good society without God. In many localities we have taken the Bible out of our schools and God out of our conversation. The result is that decency has disappeared from the community, and bedlam reigns. Peace and decorum will be restored when the individuals in the community give God His proper place once more.

That does not mean it is easy to solve the complex problems that face our communities. But they can be alleviated, and we must not withdraw or refuse to lend our hand in untangling some of the problems and injustices that bring havoc to some communities. Nor must we stand back and let those who peddle evil take over our communities and twist the minds and corrupt the bodies of our young people. Paul spent two years in Ephesus—and the corrupt practices of the magicians and others in that pagan city were reversed. We need more men and women who are willing—for Christ's sake—to become involved in political issues and concerns in their communities, and to be peacemakers in His name.

In regard to racial peace, let me say that for true Christians there is no race problem! The ground is level at the cross and there are no second-rate citizens with God. Admittedly, the problems are great, and will not be solved overnight; but if all people concerned will make sure that they have made their peace with God, it will then be a simpler matter to make peace with each other. If we approach the problem with a vindictive, intolerant, and un-Christian attitude, we are destined to failure and disaster.

Peace in the Church

THIRD: We can be peacemakers in the *church.*

We might as well face it: strife has even infiltrated our church life. It is true enough that the church is now the church militant. But as such its warfare ought to be that of dedication to revealed truth and divine holiness, and not internal bickering and carnal disputes.

We read in the second chapter of Luke that Joseph and Mary lost Jesus one day. Where did they lose Him? They lost Him in the most unlikely place in all the world—in the temple. Strange, I know! But, I have seen many people lose Jesus right in church. I have seen them lose Him in a dispute about who was to be choir director, who was to play the organ, who was to be an elder, or who was to be the minister. Yes, because we are human, though Christian, it is easy to lose sight of Jesus right in the temple!

I know of two deacons who had quarreled over an old line fence, and they had not spoken to each other for a long time. One of them, wanting to make peace, took his Bible and went to visit his neighbor. Handing his Bible to his "old enemy," he said, "John, you read and I'll pray. We must be friends."

But John, fumbling for his glasses, said, "But I can't read. I haven't my spectacles."

"Take mine," said his peace-loving neighbor.

After they had read the Word and prayed together, they arose and embraced each other. John handed back the spectacles to his neighbor and said through his tears, "Jim, that old line fence looks different through your glasses."

When we have the peace of God, we can see things through "the other man's glasses," and by doing that we can make peace.

Working for Peace at Our Work

FOURTH: We can be peacemakers at *work*.

One of the greatest points of tension in our economy is the labor-management relationship. Many industries today are recognizing that disputation is costly on the part of both labor and management and are seeking industrial peace through God and faith in Him.

One minister wrote us the other day and said that he was chaplain in three industrial plants in Indiana. The managers had found that if they sat down with their employees and listened to the Christian message once each day that everyone was in a better frame of mind.

In London, an industrialist gave his heart to Christ. He wrote us that he now conducts a chapel service in his plant and that two hundred attend the service regularly. "Never has there been more peace in our factory," he wrote.

Would you like to be an industrial peacemaker? You can be one—whether manager or laborer—if you make your peace with God first, and then seek by His grace to impart this peace to others.

When an employer and employees really know Christ, the lie is given to the Marxist thesis that an opiate religion is for the common people. To know Christ is to have part in His saviorhood and Lordship of life. Godlier employers and godlier employees will find that the right makes a claim upon every life. Where the employer is Christ's servant and the employee is the employer's spiritual partner, they are linked in an eternal vocation.

Peacemaking in Our World

FIFTH: We need peacemakers on the *international scene,* also.

Many years ago President Eisenhower knelt in a chapel in Geneva before the Big Four Conference and asked God for divine guidance in the deliberations to follow. I believe that God heard and answered, for President Eisenhower during those days displayed the spirit of a true peacemaker on the international level. Kind, considerate of the opposition's viewpoint, and given to intelligent discussion, he emerged the undisputed hero of the Geneva Conference. This was not because he held a "big stick" but because he convinced the others, at least in a measure, that he wanted peace and not war.

Several years ago I was invited to Moscow to attend an international conference of religious leaders to discuss the subject of world peace. It had been called by Patriarch Pimen, the head of the Russian Orthodox Church. At first I was reluctant to go, knowing that my presence might be misunderstood or I might be accused of being naïve or manipulated by Soviet authorities. But after much prayer and thought I went, and one reason was my recollection of Jesus' words: "Happy are the peacemakers." I went as an observer and also as a speaker, delivering an address to the entire conference on "The Biblical Meaning of Peace." Later a leading western political figure told me, "At first I thought you were wrong to go. But you were right. We must take risks for peace, because the world is too dangerous unless we learn to listen and talk to each other."

As I made clear in Moscow, I am not a pacifist, nor am I for unilateral disarmament; nations have the right to defend themselves against aggressors. Nor am I naïve about the very real problems and barriers that exist between nations of different ideologies. But we must do all we can to work for peace, in whatever ways are open to us.

Is it really possible, however, for a single individual to have any impact in a world which often seems out of control? Certainly! First, encourage those who are leaders to seek peace. Second, pray for peace. The Bible commands, "I exhort therefore, that, first of all, supplications, prayers, intercessions, and giving of thanks, be made for all men; For kings, and for all that are in authority; that we may lead a quiet and peaceable life in all godliness and honesty. For this is good and acceptable in the sight of God our Savior" (1 Timothy 2:1–3). The Bible also reminds us, "The effectual fervent prayer of a righteous man availeth much" (James 5:16).

The only corrective measure in establishing peace is for men as individuals to know the peace of God. Though I am not averse to movements which strive in one way or another for world peace, I have a strong conviction that such peace will never come unless there is a spiritual dynamic at the core. I pray for wars to cease just as I pray for crime to stop; but I know that the basic cause of both crime and war is the inherent sinfulness of human nature.

When Jesus told Nicodemus that he "must be born again," He was addressing not only this great Jewish teacher but all of us, for He saw in Nicodemus a typical representative of the race. The world cannot be reborn until men are born again and are at peace with God.

James asked, "From whence come wars and fightings among you? Come they not hence, even of your lusts that war in your members?" (James 4:1).

Peacemaking is a noble vocation. But you can no more make peace in your own strength than a mason can build a wall without a trowel, a carpenter build a house without a hammer or an artist paint a picture without a brush. You must have the proper equipment. To be a peacemaker, you must know the Peace-Giver. To make peace on earth, you must know the peace of heaven. You must know Him who "*is* our peace."

Jesus didn't leave a material inheritance to His disciples. All He had when He died was a robe, which went to the Roman soldiers; His mother, whom He turned over to His brother John; His body, which He gave to Joseph of Arimathea; and His spirit, which returned to His Father.

But Jesus willed His followers something more valuable than gold, more enduring than vast land holdings and more to be desired than palaces of marble—He willed us His peace. He said: "My peace I give unto you: not as the world giveth, give I unto you. Let not your heart be troubled, neither let it be afraid" (John 14:27).

Only as we know Him and the peace He imparts can we be peacemakers . . . and He promised happiness to a maker of peace!

The key is commitment to become peacemakers—to be men and women who actively seek to bring the peace of Christ to others and to our world.

9

Happiness in Spite of Persecution

Blessed are they which are persecuted for righteousness' sake: for theirs is the kingdom of heaven. MATTHEW 5:10

WHO WANTS TO be persecuted? We cannot see happiness in persecution. No one enjoys being maligned. Almost all of us want the good will of our neighbors, and it is difficult to see what blessedness there could be in the enmity of others.

Offhand, it would seem that being a Christian should elicit the admiration and acclaim of those about us. A Christian is usually one who lives his life with kindness, honesty, and unselfishness. Such a person should be blessed, not blasted, it would seem. His peers should stand around him and sing, "For he's a jolly good fellow, which nobody can deny!"

It would seem so! But such is not the case. And it is good that this Beatitude gives us the occasion to sit down and rethink this age-old question: "Why are good people persecuted?" Or as a modern-day author has asked, "Why do bad things happen to good people?"

We Are Not Exempt

A Christian was released from a country that had a hostile regime. He eventually got a job working with Christians. He was asked one day how it had felt to be persecuted for his faith. With a surprised look he said, "We thought it was the normal Christian life."

You may have concluded, as have others, that there is usually something wrong with those who are persecuted for righteousness' sake, that there is some quirk in their disposition, some personality peculiarity or some religious fanaticism which causes others to mistreat them. No, that is not always, or let us say that is not usually, the case.

Nowhere does the Bible teach that Christians are to be exempt from the tribulations and natural disasters that come upon the world. It does teach that the Christian can face tribulation, crisis, calamity and personal suffering with a supernatural power that is not available to the person outside of Christ.

Christiana Tsai, the Christian daughter of a former governor of Kiángšu Province in China, wrote, "Throughout my many years of illness (53), I have never dared to ask God why He allowed me to suffer for so long. I only ask what He wants me to do." St. Augustine wrote, "Better is he that suffereth evil than the jollity of him that doeth evil."

The eagle is the only bird which can lock its wings and wait for the right *wind*. He waits for the updraft and never has to *flap* his wings, *just soar. So as we wait* on God He will help us use the adversities and strong winds to *benefit us!* The Bible says, "They that wait upon the Lord . . . shall mount up with wings as eagles" (Isaiah 40:31).

Christians can rejoice in the midst of persecution because they have eternity's values in view. When the pressures are on, they look beyond their present predicament to the glories of heaven. The thought of the future life with its prerogatives and joys helps to make the trials of the present seem light and transient. ". . . for theirs is the kingdom of heaven."

Christians in the People's Republic of China are an illustration of blessings under persecution. In 1949 when the missionaries were forced to leave, there were approximately 700,000 Christians in China. In the beginning, landowners, the educated and Christians were marked for elimination. Of these three categories, which increased in spite of persecution? Those who were "persecuted for righteousness' sake." Today, reliable estimates range from 30 million to 50 million Christians in China.

The early Christians were able to experience joy in their hearts in the midst of persecution. They counted suffering for Christ not as a burden or misfortune but as a great honor, as evidence that Christ counted them worthy to witness for Him through suffering. They never forgot what Christ Himself had gone through for their salvation, and to suffer for His name's sake was regarded as a gift rather than a cross.

He Made No False Promises

Jesus Christ spoke frankly to His disciples concerning the future. He hid nothing from them. No one could ever accuse Him of deception. No one could accuse Him of securing allegiance by making false promises.

In unmistakable language He told them that discipleship meant a life of self-denial, and the bearing of a cross. He asked them to count the cost carefully, lest they should turn back when they met with suffering and privation.

Jesus told His followers that the world would hate them. They would be "as sheep in the midst of wolves." They would be arrested, scourged, and brought before governors and kings. Even their loved ones would persecute them. As the world hated and persecuted Him, so they would treat His servants. He warned further, "They will put you out of the synagogue: indeed, the hour is coming when whoever kills you will think he is offering service to God" (John 16:2, RSV).

Many of Christ's followers were disappointed in Him, for in spite of His warning they expected Him to subdue their enemies and to set up a world political kingdom. When they came face to face with reality, they "drew back and no longer went about with him" (John 6:66, RSV). But the true disciples of Jesus all suffered for their faith.

Tacitus, a Roman historian, writing of the early Christian martyrs, said, "Mockery of every sort was added to their deaths. Covered with the skins of beasts, they were torn by dogs and perished, or were nailed to crosses, or were doomed to the flames and burnt, to serve as nightly illumination, when daylight had expired. Nero offered his gardens for the spectacle." How true were the words of Paul to the early Christians. "Through many tribulations we must enter the kingdom of God" (Acts 14:22, RSV).

Bathed Hands in the Blaze

We are told that the martyrs went rejoicing to their deaths, as if they were going to a marriage feast. They bathed their hands in the blaze kindled for them, and shouted with gladness. One early historian, witnessing their heroism, wrote, "When the day of victory dawned, the Christians marched in procession from the prison to the arena as if they were marching to heaven, with joyous countenances agitated by gladness rather than fear."

We are not surprised that the early Christians rejoiced in suffering, since they looked at it in the light of eternity. The nearer death, the nearer a life of eternal fellowship with Christ. When Ignatius was about to die for his faith in A.D. 110 he cried out. "Nearer the sword, then nearer to God. In company with wild beasts, in company with God."

The Christians of the early church believed that "the sufferings of this present time are not worth comparing with the glory that is to be revealed to us" (Romans 8:18, RSV). Thus they could regard present difficulties as of little consequence and could endure them with patience and cheerfulness.

In all ages Christians have found it possible to maintain the spirit of joy in the hour of persecution. In circumstances that would have felled most people, they have so completely risen above them that they actually have used the circumstances to serve and glorify Christ. Paul could write from prison at Rome, "I want you to know, brethren, that what has happened to me has really served to advance the gospel" (Philippians 1:12, RSV).

In our day millions of Christians in our world live in very difficult situations. For some, life is difficult because they are only a tiny minority in societies in which non-Christians predominate, and they may find themselves discriminated against or scorned. For others, however, there is active oppression or even persecution from governments that do not tolerate religious freedom. It has been estimated that more Christians have suffered and died for their faith in this century than in all previous centuries combined.

In mainland China, for example, thousands of Christians were killed and their churches destroyed or plundered under the Cultural Revolution. Indeed, many Christians had to go underground to worship. Recent reports indicate these restrictions now seem to have been relaxed, but religious faith is still not encouraged. The same is true in many other parts of the world. The resurgence of some of the major non-Christian religions has brought new waves of oppression and persecution for many Christian believers.

That Christians make the best citizens, the most faithful and reliable workers, has begun to dawn on only a few. Until it does, these atheistic regimes are the ultimate losers. The persecuted Christians are definitely on the winning side, if not in this world, then most definitely in the one to come.

There is no doubt that the Bible teaches that every believer who is faithful to Christ must be prepared to be persecuted at the hands of those who are enemies of the Gospel. "Indeed all who desire to live a godly life in Christ Jesus will be persecuted," said Paul (2 Timothy 3:12, RSV).

Other Kinds of Persecution

Is persecution, however, only confined to physical torture and death? Or are there other kinds of persecution?

Certainly persecution can take many forms—some of them obvious, but many of them very subtle. We need to realize that a godly person—one who serves Christ, and exhibits purity and integrity in his life—is not necessarily welcomed or admired by those who live differently. They may even react in scorn, or refuse to include a Christian in their social gatherings because his very presence is a rebuke to them. I have known families who disowned a member who took a strong stand for Christ. An employee may find his advancement blocked because a supervisor is prejudiced against Christians. A teenage girl may find herself laughed at because she refuses to join in the immorality of her schoolmates, or a young man may find that his refusal to get involved with alcohol or drugs makes him unpopular with those who do.

But whatever form it takes, the Bible tells us not to give in to the pressures we face, nor are we to lash out at those who oppose us. Instead, we are to do all we can to show Christ's love to them. "Bless them which persecute you: bless, and curse not. . . . Recompense to no man evil for evil. . . . If it be possible, as much as lieth in you, live peaceably with all men. Dearly beloved, avenge not yourselves. . . . if thine enemy hunger, feed him; if he thirst, give him drink; for in so doing thou shalt heap coals of fire on his head. Be not overcome of evil, but overcome evil with good" (Romans 12:14, 17, 18–21).

Patience in Persecution

However, Christ told His disciples that they were not to count it a stroke of affliction when they were reviled and persecuted. Rather, they were to count it as a favor and a blessing. They were to "rejoice, and be exceeding glad" (Matthew 5:12). Just as Jesus had overcome the world, so they through His grace and strength would overcome the world. Thus they were to be of good cheer. Here is something to contemplate for those who are persecuted: When the godless plot, God laughs (Psalm 2:4; Psalm 37:12, 13). When the godless prosper, don't fret (Psalm 37:7).

They were to be "more than conquerors" (Romans 8:37). They were to rejoice in tribulation (Romans 5:3). When beaten and threatened with worse treatment if they continued to preach Christ, Peter and John departed, "rejoicing that they were counted worthy to suffer dishonor for the name. And . . . they did not cease teaching and preaching Jesus as the Christ" (Acts 5:41–42, RSV).

As we read the Book of Acts we soon realize that persecution and death intensified the joy of the early Christians. The apostle Paul could write, "With all our affliction, I am overjoyed" (2 Corinthians 7:4, RSV).

In all his sufferings and sorrows Paul experienced a deep, abiding joy. He writes of being "sorrowful, yet always rejoicing" (2 Corinthians 6:10, RSV). With sincerity he declared that for Christ's sake he was "content with weaknesses, insults, hardships, persecutions, and calamities" (2 Corinthians 12:10, RSV).

I have found in my travels that those who keep heaven in view remain serene and cheerful in the darkest day. If the glories of heaven were more real to us, if we lived less for material things and more for things eternal and spiritual, we would be less easily disturbed by this present life.

In these days of darkness and upheaval and uncertainty, the trusting and forward-looking Christian remains optimistic and joyful, knowing that Christ someday must rule, and "if we endure, we shall also reign with him" (2 Timothy 2:12, RSV). As someone has said, "Patience (hupomone) is that quality of endurance that can reach the breaking point and not break."

At the same time I am equally certain that Christians who have spent years at hard labor or in exile, have passed through periods of discouragement—even despair. Those who have had loved ones destroyed have felt deep loss and intense suffering. Victory for such has not come easily or quickly. But eventually the peace of God does come, and with it His joy.

An Upside-Down World

Here is a spiritual law which is as unchangeable as the law of gravity: "All that will live godly in Christ Jesus shall suffer persecution" (2 Timothy 3:12).

We must get this fact firmly fixed in our minds: we live in an upside-down world. People hate when they should love, they quarrel when they should be friendly, they fight when they should be peaceful, they wound when they should heal, they steal when they should share, they do wrong when they should do right.

I once saw a toy clown with a weight in its head. No matter what position you put it in, it invariably assumed an upside-down position. Put it on its feet or on its side, and when you let go it flipped back on its head.

In our unregenerate state we are just like that! Do what you may with us, we always revert to an upside-down position. From childhood to maturity we are always prone to do what we should not do and to refrain from doing what we ought to do. That is our nature. We have too much weight in the head and not enough ballast in our hearts, so we flip upside down when left alone.

That is why the disciples to the world were misfits. To an upside-down man, a right-side-up man seems upside down. To the nonbeliever, the true Christian is an oddity and an abnormality. A Christian's goodness is a rebuke to his wickedness; his being right side up is a reflection upon the worldling's inverted position. So the conflict is a natural one. Persecution is inevitable.

When Christ's disciples began preaching that Jesus was the Christ, the people cried in consternation, "These that have turned the world upside down are come hither also" (Acts 17:6). Herein lies the fundamental reason for Christian persecution. Christ's righteousness is so revolutionary and so contradictory to man's manner of living that it invokes the enmity of the world.

If we could assume that people were basically upright, then it would be the popularly accepted thing to "live godly in Christ Jesus" (2 Timothy 3:12). But as long as Satan is loose in the world and our hearts are dominated by his evil passions, it will never be easy or popular to be a follower of Christ.

The Bible says: "But ye are a chosen generation, a royal priesthood, a holy nation, a peculiar people; that ye should show forth the praises of him who hath called you out of darkness into his marvelous light: which in time past were not a people, but are now the people of God: which had not obtained mercy, but now have obtained mercy. Dearly beloved, I beseech you as strangers and pilgrims . . ." (1 Peter 2:9–11).

Aliens are rarely shown the "welcome mat." They are often accepted only with a tongue-in-cheek attitude. Being aliens, with our citizenship not in the world but in heaven, we as Christ's followers will frequently be treated as "peculiar people" and as strangers.

Our life is not of this world. "Our conversation is in heaven" (Philippians 3:20). Our interests, primarily, are not in this world. Jesus said: "Lay up for yourselves treasures in heaven . . . for where your treasure is, there will your heart be also" (Matthew 6:20, 21). Our hope is not in this world. The Bible says: "We look for the Savior, the Lord Jesus Christ: Who shall change our vile body, that it may be fashioned like unto his glorious body, according to the working whereby he is able even to subdue all things unto himself" (Philippians 3:20, 21).

Hence, in every sense we are an enigma to the world. Like a few right-handed persons among a host of left-handed persons, we comprise a threat to their status quo. We cramp their style. We are labeled as "wet blankets," as kill-joys, and as prudes. Like the enemies of Jesus, the world still inquires contemptuously, "Art not thou also one of his disciples?" (John 18:25).

Called Counterfeit

There will be times when the eyes of suspicion will be upon us, because, with people's hearts as they are, they cannot conceive of anyone wanting to live selflessly. Unbelievers will say we have "something up our sleeve," that we have a motive in being so righteous, that it is all a game, that it is sheer hypocrisy. The cry of "counterfeit!" follows the Christian's sincere efforts.

Still another reason for persecution is that there is a war in progress.

The Word of God indicates this! The Bible says: "Fight the good fight of faith, lay hold on eternal life" (1 Timothy 6:12). Again: "No man that warreth entangleth himself with the affairs of this life; that he may please him who hath chosen him to be a soldier" (2 Timothy 2:4).

War in the World

The world, the flesh, and the devil are our enemies. In times of war one can hardly expect the good will of the enemy's forces. During World War II the American journalist Cecil Brown wrote a cover story on the tragedy of the sinking of two British battleships, namely, the *Prince of Wales* and *Repulse*. He said, "There is always the danger of underestimating the enemy to the point where you are *over confident*. Figure him to be *twice* as *good* and *twice* as *smart*, then make preparations in advance!" Though our weapons are not earthly, the enemy's weapons are earthly, and we can expect Satan to use every tool at his command for our persecution and destruction. War atrocities will be committed. They who live godly in Christ *shall* suffer persecution.

All life is a struggle—that is the nature of things. Even within our physical bodies, doctors tell us, a conflict for supremacy is going on. The bacteria in our bloodstream is waging a constant war against alien germs. The red corpuscles fight the white corpuscles constantly in an effort to maintain life within the body. The recent increasingly rampant epidemic of AIDS tragically illustrates this point.

A battle is also raging in the spiritual realm. The Bible says: "We wrestle not against flesh and blood, but against principalities, against powers, against the rulers of the darkness of this world, against spiritual wickedness in high places" (Ephesians 6:12).

"We fight," the Bible says, "against the rulers of the darkness of this world."
Darkness hates light. The hymn-writer was writing about war when he asked:

> Must I be carried to the skies,
> On flowery beds of ease;
> While others fought to win the prize,
> And sailed through bloody seas?

I once had a dog that would rather have dug up a moldy carcass to chew on
than to have the finest, cleanest meal. He couldn't help it—that was his nature.

People cannot help that it is their nature to respond to the lewd, the sala-
cious, and the vile. They will have difficulty doing otherwise until they are born
again. And until they *are* changed by the power of Christ, they will likely be at
enmity against those who are associated with Christ.

The Cross for Christians

And, finally, Jesus said that a cross is the Christian's lot. "He that taketh not
his cross, and followeth after me, is not worthy of me" (Matthew 10:38).

Does this mean that we are to wear a symbol of the cross around our necks
or on the lapel of our coats? Or does it mean that we are literally to carry a
wooden cross?

No! It means that the reproach of Christ's cross, which He carried when He
was in the world, is ours to carry now. Being at "cross-purposes" with the world
is part and parcel of the Christian life. We should not covet or expect the praise
of ungodly men. On the contrary, we should expect their enmity. The very fact
that they are inclined to persecute us is proof that we are "not of the world,"
that we are "in Christ." All of the persecution, all of the blasphemy, all of
the railing that they would heap on Christ, they hurl against us. He took the
reproach of the cross for us; now, it is ours to take for Him.

The Privilege of Persecution

As Paul said: "God forbid that I should glory, save in the cross of our Lord
Jesus Christ, by whom the world is crucified unto me, and I unto the world"
(Galatians 6:14). This, Paul considered a privilege—the privilege of persecution.
In that he gloried, because in a small way he was allowed to share in the suffer-
ings of Christ.

Now, let us remember that this Beatitude says: "Blessed are they which are
persecuted for righteousness' sake . . . when men shall revile you, and perse-

cute you, and shall say all manner of evil against you falsely . . ." (Matthew 5:10, 11).

Many times we suffer because of our own poor judgment, stupidity and blundering. There is no blessedness in this. I have known professed Christians who were dominated by bad dispositions, snap judgments, and poor manners and thought that people were opposed to them because of their "righteousness." It was not their goodness which people resented—it was their lack of it.

We must be careful not to behave offensively, preach offensively, and dress offensively, and, when people are offended and shun us, blame it on the "offense of the cross." Our personal offensiveness is no credit to the gospel we preach.

Shabby Christians are poor advertisements for Christianity. Paul said: "We . . . suffer reproach, because we trust in the living God . . . but be thou an example of the believers, in word, in conversation, in charity, in spirit, in faith, in purity" (1 Timothy 4:10, 12). The reproach we experience is the natural resentment in the hearts of men toward all that is godly and righteous. This is the cross we are to bear. This is why Christians are often persecuted.

Positive Thoughts on Persecution

We have considered the reasons for Christians being persecuted. Now let us see what happiness and blessedness there is in persecution. As George MacDonald puts it, we become "hearty through hardship."

Our Lord instructs the persecuted to be happy. "Rejoice," He said, "and be exceeding glad: for great is your reward in heaven; for so persecuted they the prophets which were before you" (Matthew 5:12).

The word *joy* has all but disappeared from our current Christian vocabulary. One of the reasons is that we have thought that joy and happiness were found in comfort, ease, and luxury. James did not say, "Count it all joy when you fall into an easy chair," but he said, "Count it all joy when you fall into divers temptations" (James 1:2).

The persecuted are happy because they are being processed for heaven. Persecution is one of the natural consequences of living the Christian life. It is to the Christian what "growing pains" are to the growing child. No pain, no development. No suffering, no glory. No struggle, no victory. No persecution, no reward!

The Bible says: "The God of all grace, who hath called us unto his eternal glory by Christ Jesus, after that ye have suffered a while, make you perfect, stablish, strengthen, settle you" (1 Peter 5:10). It is so easy to forget that "all things work together for good to them that love God" (Romans 8:28).

Jesus, in the Sermon on the Mount, had some commandments for us with regard to our attitude toward persecution. We are to:

1. Rejoice and be exceeding glad	Matthew 5:12
2. Love our enemies	5:44
3. Bless them that curse us	5:44
4. Do good to them that hate us	5:44
5. Pray for them that despitefully use us and persecute us	5:44

I have a friend who lost his job, a fortune, his wife, and his home. But he tenaciously held to his faith—the only thing he had left. One day he stopped to watch some men doing stonework on a huge church. One of them was chiseling a triangular piece of stone.

"What are you going to do with that?" asked my friend.

The workman said, "See that little opening away up there near the spire. Well, I'm shaping this down here so it will fit in up there."

Tears filled my friend's eyes as he walked away, for it seemed that God had spoken through the workman to explain the ordeal through which he was passing, "I'm shaping you down here so you'll fit in up there."

After you have "suffered a while, make you perfect . . . settle you," echo the words from the Bible.

The persecuted for "righteousness' sake" are happy because they are identified with Christ. The enmity of the world is tangible proof that we are on the right side, that we are identified with our blessed Lord. He said that our stand for Him would arouse the wrath of the world. "And ye shall be hated of all men for my name's sake: but he that endureth to the end shall be saved" (Matthew 10:22).

In a sense, Christ is King in exile, and we who are His followers are often looked upon with derision. To be identified with Him here and now quite naturally entails some "loss of face," some persecution; but some day, we are told, we shall be "kings and priests" and shall be active participators in His kingdom.

Paul must have had this fact in mind when he said: "For I reckon that the sufferings of this present time are not worthy to be compared with the glory which shall be revealed in us. For the earnest expectation of the creature waiteth for the manifestation of the sons of God" (Romans 8:18, 19).

Hope Hangs a Halo

If we should be called upon to suffer all our lives, it would not be long compared to eternity. We are in the position of heirs to a large estate who gladly endure a few days of suffering and privation with the hope that we shall soon come into our fabulous inheritance. Such a glorious hope hangs a halo over the drab existence of the here and now.

Life cannot lose its zest when down underneath our present discomfort is the knowledge that we are children of a King. Complaining becomes foolish; behaving in the manner of the world is unworthy; and love, gentleness, and meekness become the hallmark of God's nobility. "All things" are taken in stride; burdens become blessings in disguise; every wound, like good surgery, is for our good; and etched in every cross is the symbol of a crown.

And last, persecution is blessed because it forms a dark backdrop for the radiance of the Christian life.

The Need for Sunshine and Shadow

All the masterpieces of art contain both light and shadow. A happy life is not one filled only with sunshine, but one which uses both light and shadow to produce beauty. The greatest musicians as a rule are those who know how to bring song out of sadness. Fanny Crosby, her spirit aglow with faith in Christ, saw more with her sightless eyes than most of us do with normal vision. She has given us some of the great gospel songs which cheer our hearts and lives. She wrote some 2,000 hymns of which 60 are still in common use.

Paul and Silas sang their song of praise at midnight in a rat-infested jail in Philippi, their feet in stocks, their backs raw from the jailer's whip. But their patience in suffering and persecution led to the conversion of the heathen prison warden. The blood of the martyrs is mixed well into the mortar which holds the stones of civilization together.

The self-sacrifice of God's people through the centuries has contributed immeasurably to our culture, to our ethics, and to our faith. Down deep we know that there are still things worth dying for, that an existence void of faith is still a fate worse than death.

O children of God, despair not at your suffering and persecution. In the words of Thornton Wilder: "Without your wounds, where would your power be that sends your low voice trembling into the hearts of men? The very angels of God in heaven cannot persuade the wretched and blundering children of earth as can one human being broken on the wheels of living. In love's service only wounded soldiers will do."

Messages from the Martyrs

Sanders, the martyr, said, "Welcome the cross of Christ. . . . I feel no more pain in the fire than if I were on a bed of down."

Another martyr said, "The ringing of my chain hath been music in my ears; O what a comforter is a good conscience." Kissing the stake, he said,

"I shall not lose my life but change it for better; instead of coals I shall have pearls."

You may not be called upon to suffer as the martyrs suffered, for this is an hour when Satan employs psychological warfare. Jesus said: "Men shall revile you . . . and shall say all manner of evil against you falsely, for my sake" (Matthew 5:11). The tongue often inflicts a more painful wound than does the sword. To be laughed at can be harder to take than to be flogged.

Some in reading this may feel that because they are not at present being persecuted, they are not living godly lives. That is not necessarily so. While there are countries where today to be an active Christian is to court death and worse, we live in a predominantly Christian country where active persecution is at a minimum.

Our environment, as well as the age in which we live, has much to do with the amount of persecution a Christian will be called upon to bear. I have known certain overly eager Christians who actually courted persecution for fear that otherwise they would not be living godly enough lives.

Remember, not all Christians are called upon to suffer at all times. Even our Lord increased in wisdom and knowledge and in favor with God and man. But the periods of popularity did not last. It ended on a cross. The important thing is to walk with Christ. Live for Christ! Have one consuming passion in life—to please Him! And let the chips fall where they may. I believe it was Samuel Rutherford who said, "Never take one step out of the pathway of duty either to take a cross or to escape one."

W. C. Burns of India wrote, "Oh, to have a martyr's heart if not a martyr's crown!"

Popularity and adulation are far more dangerous for the Christian than persecution. It is easy when all goes smoothly to lose our sense of balance and our perspective. We must learn like Paul "how to abound" and "how to be abased." We must learn in "whatsoever state" we are "therewith to be content" (Philippians 4:11).

As we have said, the important thing is to walk with Christ, to live for Christ, and to have one consuming passion to please Him. Then, whatever happens, we know that He has permitted it to teach us some priceless lesson and to perfect us for His service. He will enrich our circumstances, be they pleasant or disagreeable, by the fact of His presence with us. The tomorrows fill us with dread. John 10:4 says, "He putteth forth his own sheep." Whatever awaits us is *encountered* first by Him—like the oriental shepherd always went ahead of his sheep—therefore any attack on sheep has to *deal first* with the shepherd—all the *tomorrows* of our lives have to pass Him before they get to us!

Three Hebrew children were cast into the burning fiery furnace, but the king said: "Lo, I see *four* men loose, walking in the midst of the fire, and they have no hurt; and the form of the fourth is like the Son of God" (Daniel 3:25). Our God is with us in the persecution of this life!

A comforting story comes from some unknown writer. The first convert of a certain missionary was tortured to death for his faith. Years later, the missionary too died. In heaven he met that first convert and asked him how it felt to be tortured to death for his faith. "You know," the man replied with a shrug and looking a bit bewildered, "I can't even remember."

10

Steps to Happiness

KING GEORGE V wrote on the flyleaf of the Bible of a friend: "The secret of happiness is not to do what you like to do, but to learn to like what you have to do."

Too many think of happiness as some sort of will-o'-the-wisp thing that is discovered by constant and relentless searching. Happiness is not found by seeking. It is not an end in itself. Pots of gold are never found at the end of the rainbow, as we used to think when we were children; gold is mined from the ground or panned laboriously from a mountain stream.

Jesus once told His disciples: "Seek ye first the kingdom of God, and his righteousness; and all these things shall be added unto you" (Matthew 6:33). The "things" He spoke of were the basic needs of life: food, drink, clothes, shelter. He told us not to make these the chief goal of our lives but to "seek the kingdom," and these needs would be automatically supplied. And if for some reason only He knows they should be withheld, know that it is for our good and His glory. There have been occasions when Christians have been deprived of one or all these things. They have died of starvation at times—or of thirst or exposure. It is not because He has broken His promise, but because He has something better for us.

There, if we will take it, is the secret of happiness: "Seek ye first the kingdom of God . . . and all . . . shall be added unto you."

Steps to Abundant Living

In the foregoing pages we have tried to interpret Jesus' formula for happiness. We realize that in many ways the interpretation falls short, both in content and clarity. The more we read this introduction to the Sermon on the Mount, the more wisdom we see hidden in it and the more convinced we are if it is read thoughtfully and prayerfully and applied to life that a richer, fuller happiness will ensue.

In summing up the secret of happiness within the framework of the Beatitudes, we would like to suggest several steps to the abundant life:

We must recognize our spiritual poverty.

Don't let pride say, "I am rich, and increased with goods, and have need of nothing" (Revelation 3:17). Remember that our own righteousness is as filthy rags and that salvation is not of works but is the gift of God. We must keep ever in mind the first Beatitude: "Blessed are the poor in spirit: for theirs is the kingdom of heaven."

God measures people by the small dimension of humility and not by the bigness of their achievements or the size of their capabilities.

We must make sure we have received Christ.

Remember, it is not creeds, culture, or even respectability that saves us. It is Christ. The Bible says: "But as many as received him, to them gave he power to become the sons of God, even to them that believe on his name" (John 1:12).

Let us say that one day you decided to go to Europe on a jet plane. Perhaps you might contact your travel agency and get all kinds of information about flight schedules and the type of plane you would be flying. You might talk with people who had traveled across the Atlantic on that aircraft. You might even have investigated the airline's safety record and become convinced that the pilot and crew were trustworthy and the aircraft would take you safely. You might have said to yourself, *I believe this airplane is able to take me across the Atlantic.* You might even have gotten a ticket and gone to the airport. You might have done all this and still never have crossed the Atlantic. One thing was lacking: you needed to get on the plane—commit yourself to it and trust it to carry you to your destination.

To know about Christ is not enough. To be convinced that He is the Savior of the world is not enough. To affirm our faith in Him, as we do in the Apostles' Creed, is not enough. To believe that He has saved others is not enough. We really don't actively believe in Christ until we make a commitment of our lives to Him and receive Him as our Savior.

We can best demonstrate our faith in a bank by putting our money in it. We can best show our faith in a doctor by trusting him with our physical welfare in times of illness. We can best prove our faith in a boat by getting aboard and going some place on it. We can best demonstrate our faith in Christ by trusting Him with our life and receiving Him unconditionally as our Savior.

We must maintain a contrite spirit.

The Bible says: "A broken and a contrite heart, O God, thou wilt not despise" (Psalm 51:17). Remember it was to Christians that John wrote: "If we confess our sins, he is faithful and just to forgive us our sins, and to cleanse us from all unrighteousness" (1 John 1:9).

A cultured person is quick with a courteous apology when he has done wrong. If a gentleman stumbles over a lady's foot in a drawing room, he doesn't wait a week to say, "I beg your pardon!" He begs forgiveness immediately.

When we break God's law, utter a hasty, bitter word, or even think an evil thought, immediately we should confess this sin to God. And in accordance with His Word, He will forgive and cleanse our hearts and transform us into His likeness.

We must be sensitive to the needs of others.

In the eternal triangle of Christianity, God is first, others are second, and self is last. "Rejoice with them that do rejoice, and weep with them that weep" (Romans 12:15). We should be sympathetic, tolerant, and understanding. Remember the third secret of happiness: "Blessed are they that mourn: for they shall be comforted."

There is no joy in life like the joy of sharing. Don't be content to have too much when millions in the world have too little. I should remember every time I read the Bible that millions have no Bible to read. We should bear in mind when we hear the gospel preached that more than half the world has never heard the gospel story. Let our lives, our means, and our prayers be shared with those millions who at this moment are wondering whether there is any relief from their distress.

Don't be a half-Christian.

There are too many of such in the world already. The world has a profound respect for people who are sincere in their faith.

The Bible tells us that we can't serve God and Mammon, that no man can serve two masters. Too many Christians, so called, are like the little chameleon which adapts its coloration to that of its surroundings. Even a critical world is quick to recognize a real Christian and just as quick to detect a counterfeit.

We must live surrendered lives.

The Bible is explicit at this point. It says: "Know ye not, that to whom ye yield yourselves servants to obey, his servants ye are to whom ye obey; whether of sin unto death, or of obedience unto righteousness?" (Romans 6:16).

A friend of David Livingstone once said: "When I watched Livingstone carry out the 'leave all and follow me' life, I became a Christian in spite of myself." The world knows no greater challenge than the surrendered life.

We should be filled with the Spirit.

People who have moved the world have been Spirit-filled. Filled with the Spirit, the first disciples "turned the world upside down." Filled with the Spirit, the reformers started the spiritual blaze which became the Reformation. Filled with the Spirit, John and Charles Wesley, working out of Oxford University, saved a great nation from moral and political collapse. Filled with the Spirit, Francis Asbury, George Fox, Jonathan Edwards, Charles Finney, and David Brainerd set the mountains and prairies of America aglow with the fires of real Christianity. Filled with the Spirit, D. L. Moody and Ira Sankey shook two continents out of their spiritual lethargy. Corrie Ten Boom and Mother Teresa impacted their world greatly.

The tides of civilization have risen, the courses of nations have been changed and the pages of history have been brightened by people who have been filled with the Spirit of God.

What does it mean to be filled with the Spirit? It is not necessarily an emotional experience, nor will it necessarily bring us some type of spiritual experience that is obvious or open. *To be filled with the Spirit is to be controlled by the Spirit.* It is to be so yielded to Christ that our supreme desire is to do His will. When we come to Christ the Spirit comes to dwell within us—whether we are aware of His presence or not. But as we grow in Christ, our goal is to be controlled by the Spirit. Have you yielded your life to Christ without reserve, asking Him to fill you and use you for His glory?

We should seek to produce the fruit of the Spirit in our lives.

The Bible says: "The fruit of the Spirit is love, joy, peace, long-suffering, gentleness, goodness, faith, meekness, temperance" (Galatians 5:22, 23).

You say, "I am powerless to produce such fruit. It would be utterly impossible for me to do so!"

With that I agree! That is, we can't produce this fruit in our own strength. Remember, the Bible says: "The fruit of the *Spirit* is love, joy, peace, long-suffering, gentleness, goodness, faith, meekness, temperance" (Galatians 5:22, 23). When the Spirit of God dwells in us *He* will produce the fruit. It is ours only to cultivate the soil of our hearts through sincere devotion and yieldedness that He might find favorable ground to produce that which He will.

I might have a fruit tree in my yard; but if the soil isn't enriched and the bugs carefully destroyed, it will not yield a full crop.

As Christians, we have the Spirit of God in us. But ours is the responsibility to keep sin out of our lives so that the Spirit can produce His fruit in us.

We must become grounded in the Bible.

As Christians, we have only one authority, one compass: the Word of God.

In a letter to a friend, Abraham Lincoln said: "I am profitably engaged in reading the Bible. Take all of this Book upon reason that you can and the balance upon faith, and you will live and die a better man."

Coleridge said he believed the Bible to be the Word of God because, as he put it, "It finds me."

"If you want encouragement," John Bunyan wrote, "entertain the promises."

Martin Luther said, "In Scriptures, even the little daisy becomes a meadow."

The Bible is our one sure guide in an unsure world.

Great leaders have made it their chief Book and their reliable guide. Herbert J. Taylor, formerly international president of Rotary, told me that he began each day by reading the Sermon on the Mount aloud. President Ronald Reagan revered the Bible so much that he proclaimed 1984 the "year of the Bible."

We should begin the day with the Book, and as it comes to a close let the Word speak its wisdom to our souls. Let it be the firm foundation upon which our hope is built. Let it be the Staff of Life upon which our spirit is nourished. Let it be the Sword of the Spirit which cuts away the evil of our lives and fashions us in His image and likeness.

We must witness for Christ.

Jesus said to us: "Ye are the light of the world. . . . Let your light so shine before men, that they may see your good works, and glorify your Father which is in heaven" (Matthew 5:14, 16).

One faithful witness is worth a thousand mute professors of religion.

The late Tom Allan, Scotland's famous preacher, was brought to Christ while a black soldier was singing "Were You There When They Crucified My Lord?" He said it was neither the song nor the voice, but the spirit in which that soldier sang—something about his manner, something about his sincerity of expression— that convicted him of his wicked life and turned him to the Savior.

Our faith grows by expression. If we want to keep our faith, we must share it—we must witness!

We must practice the Presence of God.

Jesus said: "Lo, I am with you alway, even unto the end of the world" (Matthew 28:20). Remember, Christ is always near us. We should say nothing that we would not wish to say in His presence. We should do nothing that we would not do in His presence. We should go to no place that we would not go in His presence. But He is not with us just to judge or condemn us; He is near to comfort, protect, guide, encourage, strengthen, cleanse and help. He will not only be with us until the "end of the world," but He will be with us "world without end." He will be with us throughout all eternity.

We must learn the exercise of prayer.

Jesus said: "Men ought always to pray, and not to faint" (Luke 18:1). He said on another occasion: "Pray to thy Father which is in secret; and thy Father which seeth in secret shall reward thee openly" (Matthew 6:6).

Prayer is not just asking. It is listening for God's orders.

The late Frank Laubach said: "Prayer at its highest is a two-way conversation; and for me, the most important part is listening to God's replies."

The world's great Christians have set regular hours for prayer. John Wesley arose at four in the morning and started the day with prayer, followed by an hour's Bible study.

I suggest an established time for communication with God. Make a date with Him and keep it. The Christian will never regret such a practice, for the "fervent prayer of a righteous man availeth much" (James 5:16).

We must develop a taste for spiritual things.

"Happy are they which do hunger and thirst after righteousness: for they shall be filled."

Spiritual tastes, like physical tastes, can be cultivated. I didn't always like yogurt, but they told me that it was good for me, so I kept trying to like it—and now I enjoy it.

It will not perhaps be easy at first to read the Bible, witness, and pray. But after we experience the strength that can come from these means of grace, they will become part of our routine, as much as breathing and eating. These are the things that give strength to the soul.

We must not be critical of others.

Habitual criticism can stifle our spiritual growth. We must not build up ourselves at the expense of others. If I praise others, then others will praise me. But if I condemn others, they in turn will condemn me. Criticism begets criticism, but praise begets praise. As Jesus said: "Happy are the merciful: for they shall obtain mercy."

We must not be envious of others.

Two of the most devastating sins of today are envy and covetousness. Envying others can work havoc in our spiritual lives and sap us of our spiritual strength. It can also ruin our social batting average and weaken our Christian testimony. We must not be enslaved by this ruinous evil! It can destroy our happiness and rob our lives of their sweetness.

We should love everybody.

The Bible says: "Let love be genuine; hate what is evil, hold fast to what is good" (Romans 12:9, RSV). This Scripture says: "*Let* love," as if it were possible for us to hinder love from being all that it should be. The love of Christ, if unhindered and unblocked by our prejudices and our malices, will embrace everyone. Christ in us will go on loving even the unlovely if He is not hindered by our selfishness. We must realize the difference between loving the sinner while hating his sin.

We should stand courageously for the right.

Horace Pitkin, the son of a wealthy merchant, was converted and went to China as a missionary. He wrote to his friends in America, saying: "It will be but a short time till we know definitely whether we can serve Him better above or here." Shortly afterward, a mob stormed the gate of the compound where Pitkin defended the women and children. He was beheaded and his head offered at the shrine of a heathen god, while his body was thrown outside in a pit with the bodies of nine Chinese Christians. Sherwood Eddy, writing about him, said: "Pitkin won more men by his death than he ever could have won by his life." The same could be said of the five courageous Christians who died for Christ in Ecuador.

Christ needs people today who are made of martyr stuff! Dare to take a strong, uncompromising stand for Him.

We should learn to relax in Christ.

I once watched a little baby learning to walk. As long as it kept its eyes on its mother it was relaxed and in perfect balance. But as soon as it looked down at its little wobbly legs, it failed.

Simon Peter found it possible to walk over the waves of Galilee as long as he kept his eyes on Christ—but when he looked away from the Savior he sank.

These are turbulent times in which we live. People are harassed with tensions, fears, and phobias. Nothing can relieve the tensions of life like a valid faith in Christ.

You, too, can learn to relax in *Christ!*

We must not be victims of paranoia.

I am not talking here, of course, about the specific mental illness of paranoia which grips some people and which needs to be treated professionally; I refer here to it in a more general sense. I am talking about an excessive sensitivity to what others say or do about us, which causes us to become overly absorbed in worry and anxiety over what people think about us.

In other words, don't be hypersensitive to criticism or entertain an exaggerated sense of your own importance. This is the secret of unhappiness. Many egocentric people are victims of this terrible disease of the mind. If people never actually criticize them, they at least imagine that they do, and they suffer the agonies of a mental inferno.

Or some people are insecure, lacking in self confidence, and are therefore easily bruised by what other people say. It may not be easy, but such a person needs to develop more self-confidence by seeing himself the way God sees him. If this is your problem, recognize it for what it is and realize the damage it can cause you. Then ask God to help you overcome it in practical ways.

The paranoid sees two acquaintances talking together somewhat seriously, and immediately he imagines that they are discussing his faults. He retreats into the torture chamber of his own mind where he manufactures misery in wholesale lots. Run from paranoia as you would run from a plague.

We must remember we are immortal and will live forever.

To expect absolute, unqualified bliss in this life is expecting a bit too much. Remember, this life is only the dressing room for eternity. In the Beatitudes Jesus said that in this life there are persecution, slander, libel, and deception. But He also said: "Rejoice and be exceeding glad: for great is your reward in heaven" (Matthew 5:12).

He strongly hinted that relative happiness in this life is related to an absolute happiness in the after life. Here we have an "earnest" of our inheritance, a "down payment," but in heaven we come into our full estate of happiness.

Christians think and act within the framework of eternity. They are not embittered when things don't turn out the way they planned. They know that the sufferings of this present world are not worthy to be compared with the glory that shall be revealed hereafter. So rejoice and be exceedingly glad!

In the covered wagon days when gold was discovered in the Old West, the pioneers endured the sufferings of the prairies, the mountains, and the desert, and the savage attacks of the Indians because they knew that beyond those Sierras lay the promise of gold.

When Bill Borden, son of the wealthy Bordens, left for China as a missionary, many of his friends thought he was foolish to "waste his life," as they put it, trying to convert a few heathen to Christianity. But Bill loved Christ and he loved people! On his way to China he contracted a disease and died. At his bedside they found a note that he had written while he was dying. It read: "No reserve, no retreat, and no regrets."

Borden had found more happiness in his few years of sacrificial service than most people find in a lifetime.

Many thousands of rational, cultured citizens of the earth have found happiness in Christ. You can too! But, remember, you will never find it by searching directly for it. As the Lord of happiness said: "Seek ye first the kingdom of God, and his righteousness; and all these things shall be added unto you" (Matthew 6:33).

Answers to Life's Problems

The whole Bible was given to us by inspiration from God and is useful to teach us what is true and to make us realize what is wrong with our lives; it straightens us out and helps us do what is right. 2 TIMOTHY 3:1, TLB

CONTENTS

V. BIBLICAL QUESTIONS

INTRODUCTION

IF TALK IS cheap, advice is free.

Advice columnists, astrologers and books offering tips on how to make money, how to avoid disease, and how to get in physical shape are as plentiful as cars during rush hour in our major cities. But not all advice is good. Much of this advice is based on human wisdom or false hopes or the wrong motives—and many who take such advice are disappointed and disillusioned.

Those who grew up in the troubled 1960s in America were told by the media, the rock music culture, their professors at college, and their friends that the values held by their parents and grandparents were old-fashioned. They threw off what they regarded as encumbrances in favor of "alternate lifestyles" and "doing your own thing." There was widespread cultural support for their ideas and behavior. "Doing your own thing" became the "in" thing to do.

Tragically, a survey published in *Rolling Stone* magazine revealed that those who bought into the '60s counterculture mentality and believed the lies they were told, are now having trouble communicating to their own children the necessity of the values they rejected. The survey reveals that having overdosed on drugs and "free" love (which turned out not to be free at all) the flower children of the '60s now "embrace psychiatry as something to be relied on."

Is there a standard which can be depended on to give good advice and accurate information and answers to questions about ourselves and our lives?

There is. For nearly thirty years I have been writing a newspaper column called "My Answer." Actually, the column has been more than *my* answer to every imaginable question people have sent me. My answers are based on what the Bible says. Though cultures differ and times change, the Word of our God stands forever as an unchanging source of answers to all of life's problems.

President Reagan has correctly stated that the answer to all of life's problems can be found in the Bible, if people would only read it. He is right because every problem known to mankind has a spiritual origin.

Chances are that you will find the answer to one or more of your questions about God, the Bible, interpersonal relationships, job frustrations, the universe, and a host of other subjects in this book. We have documented evidence that these answers have helped thousands. I am convinced that the major reason many of us seem to have so many unresolved problems is that we are ignorant of what God has to say about our problems or we reject His answer out of hand without ever giving it a try.

In more than fifty years as an evangelist I have read many books, consulted many psychologists and other experts in many fields, but I have yet to discover a source of information, practical advice and hope that compares to the wisdom found in the Bible.

My prayer is that you will discover in this book that source of information and, more important, God's plan for your redemption through Jesus Christ.

Billy Graham

I
RELATIONSHIPS

1

Is There Such a Thing As True Love?

I am in my early twenties and I have always had very high moral standards. I date a lot, but frankly I'm very disillusioned about men because all they seem to be interested in is sex. I want someone to love me for myself, but now I'm beginning to wonder if there is such a thing as true love.

There was a popular song a few years ago which contained the lyric, "I was looking for love in all the wrong places." There is a lot of so-called love in our world today which is not really love but is instead based on selfishness and even lust. In fact, I get many letters every day from people who got married because they wanted their own selfish needs satisfied, and have only later come to realize that this does not work.

But there is such a thing as love—honest, selfless love. This is the kind of love the Bible talks about when it speaks of God's love for us. It is also the kind of love that the Bible describes briefly but profoundly in 1 Corinthians 13:4–7: "Love is patient, love is kind. It does not envy, it does not boast, it is not proud. It is not rude, it is not self-seeking, it is not easily angered, it keeps no record of wrongs. Love does not delight in evil but rejoices with the truth. It always protects, always trusts, always hopes, always perseveres."

My prayer is that you will stick to your standards—you will be glad you did in the years ahead. But more than that, I pray that you will commit this whole area of your life—and in fact every area of your life—to Jesus Christ. God wants to teach you what true love is, as you come to experience and understand His love for you. He also has His perfect will for your life—including your future husband, if it is His will for you to be married. Don't be satisfied with anyone less than the one who is God's will for your life's mate, no matter what the pressures might be.

We live in a time when God's standards are often dismissed or scorned as old-fashioned and useless. But God's standards have not changed, and neither have His promises to those who follow Christ. There are many young men who are seeking to honor God in their lives, and you should trust God that He will lead you in the way that is best for your life.

My boyfriend is not perfect and sometimes I wonder if he would make a very thoughtful or sensitive husband, but I am afraid of letting go of him because I wonder if I will ever find another husband. What should I do about him?

I suspect there are many women reading this who would like to write you and say, "Don't feel you have to take the first eligible man who comes along! If he is insensitive and selfish now, he will be insensitive and selfish as a husband. This is what I did, and I have regretted it ever since!"

No husband or wife is going to be perfect, of course; after all, you probably have your faults as well! But seriously, my concern for you is this: more than anything else, you need to learn to trust your future to God and obey Him. This is true for everything in your life, including your marriage.

One of the greatest truths of the Bible is that God loves us. And because He loves us, He wants to give us what is best for us. I firmly believe that if it is God's will for you to be married, then He has already chosen a man who should be your husband. Seek God's will and trust Him, because His will is best. "Which of you," said Jesus, "if his son asks for bread, will give him a stone? . . . If you, then, though you are evil, know how to give good gifts to your children, how much more will your Father in heaven give good gifts to those who ask him!" (Matthew 7:9, 11).

Look for a husband who honors Christ in his life and wants His will. That man will be loving and sensitive, and it will be your joy to be loving and sensitive to his needs in return.

Some time ago I found out that my boyfriend is involved in selling drugs. I guess I ought to stop going with him, but I think I love him and I hope somehow I can reform him. Do you think there is any hope of this?

I know you are concerned for your boyfriend and want to help him, but I seriously doubt if you will be able to make him reform. In addition, marriage is not a reform school. I have met many women who believe that their mothering instincts extend to the men they marry. There is a high probability that instead of you reforming him, he will instead influence you and cause you to become involved in things that are wrong. It may be that breaking off your relationship will be the one thing that will shake him into realizing the seriousness of what he is doing.

What he is doing *is* serious—not only in the eyes of the law but in the eyes of God. The reason is that he is causing others to get involved in drugs, and is therefore affecting countless lives in terrible ways. You need to talk frankly with him about this. You also need to realize that there is probably very little future in this kind of relationship. What if you were to get married some day? What kind of husband and father would he make?

Your boyfriend and you have a deeper need, however—even deeper than the need to stop what he is doing and live a responsible life. You both need to come to Jesus Christ and turn your lives over to Him. Right now you are living for yourselves. But God created you, and He loves you. He wants you to do what is right and to follow Him because He knows that is the only way to true peace and happiness in life. Jesus said, "I have come that they may have life, and have it to the full" (John 10:10).

God has a perfect plan for your life—including His will for your marriage with a man who loves Christ. The road you and your boyfriend are on is wrong and will only lead to disaster. Follow God's way before it is too late.

I feel like I am really in love with a man who works in the same office I do. He doesn't really know my feelings, however, as we have never dated. Should I express them to him? The problem is that he has a wife and family.

Turn the question around. What if you were married to this man and another woman was writing to me asking for a divorce because she was in love with your husband? As strongly as I can, I urge you to put this relationship out of your mind—even if it means changing jobs. Unless you do, there is only pain and heartache ahead. If somehow you were to win him and cause him to leave his family, you would be wrecking the lives of many people. And you would never have a secure marriage for yourself either, because what assurance would you have that he would not turn around and leave you, just as he left his wife? No, the only right thing for you to do is put this idea behind you.

Your letter tells me that you are searching for love. There is nothing wrong in that as long as you pursue your search in the right direction. After all, God made us so we would love others and experience love ourselves. But you need to realize that love—lasting, true love—will elude you if you go about it selfishly and without regard to the consequences for others.

I am concerned, therefore, about your present situation. But even more I am concerned about the whole direction of your life. Your greatest need right now is not just a human companion or love. Your greatest need is to realize that you are God's creature. God loves you and He has a perfect plan for your life. He knows what your true needs are, and if it is His will for you to be married (as it probably is), then He has someone who will be the right husband for you if you will trust Him and let Him lead you. Trust God to lead you to the man He has for your husband—a man who will be a committed Christian and who will love you unselfishly.

I grew up in a one-parent family. I am old enough that it should no longer trouble me, but my problem is that right now I am in love with a young woman who is also from a broken home. Do you think this would in any way influence our happiness in marriage?

All things being equal, it would seem to me that your chances for a happy married life would be very good. Having felt the pain of a broken home, you have probably learned the importance of laying a solid foundation for a home that will remain united and happy. The mistakes of your parents in both instances will serve as warnings for you not to fail in the same way.

In making your plans, I would urge you to be utterly frank and open with each other in all areas so that no misunderstandings arise. Do not base your love on a mutual sympathy because of your unfortunate experiences, but on genuine respect and admiration. Then you should include Christ in your planning. Even though many homes have some degree of marital happiness without Him, there is much that is lacking in any home when Christ is not received and honored.

Have your time of worship together, confessing your faults and praying for each other. This will cement your lives to each other and the happiness you seek will be the result of God's blessing and presence. The Living Bible says: "The man who finds a wife finds a good thing; she is a blessing to him from the Lord" (Proverbs 18:22).

The man who wants to marry me claims to be a Christian. So I could on that basis marry him. But every now and then he lies to me, and it troubles me, for I cannot endure deception. Am I safe in marrying him, seeing that he is a Christian?

Just because a person claims to be a Christian does not necessarily mean that he is one. In fact, when you say this young man uses deception now and then, has it never occurred to you that he may be deceiving you when he makes the claim to a Christian faith?

Truthfulness and honesty are basic in the Christian walk. Jesus once said: "I am the way, the truth and the life" (John 14:6). In another place He said, "I came to bear witness to the truth" (John 1:7). Truth is consistency. If this young man will deceive you in one matter, he may deceive you in many for he lacks respect for the truth.

David once confessed to God in his repentance: "Thou desirest truth in the inward parts" (Psalm 51:6, KJV). You can live with many other faults more easily than with dishonesty. By all means avoid it.

I am in love with a fine young man, but my parents do not approve of him. To what extent is one obligated to parents?

The Bible teaches everywhere that we are to honor our parents, but it does not teach that they have the right to control their adult children. "Honor your father and your mother, that your days may be long in the land which the Lord your God gives you" (Exodus 10:12, RSV). The New Testament says: "Children, obey your parents in all things: for this is well-pleasing to the Lord." There was a period in life when you were directly responsible to them. You were to be obedient in all things. What they have forgotten is that such a relationship does not continue in adulthood. You should still honor them as your parents, but you are not obligated to forego the joy of married life and your own family for them.

But there is another aspect to this problem. We sometimes discover the will of God through giving heed to the counsel of others if they are definitely committed Christians. I am sure you want God's will in the choice of a life partner. Consider carefully their point of view, but then make your decision, seeking the Lord's leading as you do so.

At times I think I am going to die of a broken heart. I had been living with my boyfriend for three years, always hoping we would get married, but last week he told me to get out because he didn't want anything more to do with me. Why has God done this to me, when I really love this man?

Suppose you had an accident and were injured because you decided you would ignore the speed limit and instead travel twice as fast as you should. Who would be to blame for your accident? The person who set the speed limit, or you? I think you know the answer: You would be to blame. Your accident came about because you refused to obey the speed limit.

In the same way, we must never blame God for things which are a result of our own actions—especially when those actions are in direct violation of God's clear law. The Bible warns, "Do not be deceived: God cannot be mocked. A man reaps what he sows" (Galatians 6:7). It was wrong in God's eyes for you to live with this man outside the commitment of marriage, for His Word is clear on this point. You therefore cannot blame Him for the result.

But where do you go from here? In the past you have sought your security in this relationship—a relationship where there was never any lasting commitment. Will you make the same mistake again? I pray not. God loves you, and

He does not want you to drift through life with no anchor. Make Christ your anchor, and He will change you and give you a whole new reason for living.

I am an eighteen-year-old girl, a freshman in college. I have fallen in love with a senior who wants me to marry him now although he has not yet made up his mind what his life's work shall be. Should I give up my college career for him?

The very fact that you are weighing your own career against the uncertainties of marriage makes me feel that you are not yet ready to make this momentous decision. Obviously you have known this young man for only a few months. Also, his own future plans are so indefinite that they give you pause. This all adds up to a strong indication that you should wait. Waiting has two advantages. It will enable you to know your heart and to decide whether it is love or other considerations which have attracted you to each other. Also, it will give both of you time to mature in your thinking and planning. Finally, a Christian has the right and privilege of asking God's guidance in everything. The Bible says, "Seek ye first the kingdom of God; and all these things will be added unto you" (Luke 12:31, KJV).

My boyfriend and I want to be engaged very soon but both of our parents object. Though we are quite young, we are serious but don't intend to get married for at least three years. Should we insist on doing it our way?

Perhaps your parents are objecting on the basis of your age alone. They perhaps think you aren't mature enough to make this all-important decision. There seems to be only one reason why you insist on an engagement: Because you are afraid that one or the other might feel too free otherwise. I would warn you that if you cannot trust each other under the present conditions you are perhaps not genuinely in love.

Then you must always take into account your mutual relationship in Christ. You must not hope for a completely successful marriage if it is done merely on your own. I would suggest, therefore, that you follow the suggestion of your parents. All they object to is the formality of engagement, and that is not the most important part of it. Your mutual commitment of your lives to Christ is all you need. This in addition to your love for each other will make your present friendship become even more meaningful in years to come.

I have been living with my boyfriend for over a year. I know this is wrong, but I get scared whenever I think of leaving him because I'm afraid to be alone. Pray that I'll have wisdom to know what is right.

Yes, I will pray that you will know what is right—but more than that I will be praying that you will *do* what is right. I think you have come to realize that what you are doing is wrong in God's eyes, since you admit that you know it is wrong. But the problem for you is not so much knowing what is wrong, but acting upon that knowledge.

God's Word, the Bible, makes it clear that sex outside of the commitment of marriage is wrong. One of the Ten Commandments declares simply, "You shall not commit adultery" (Exodus 20:14). The reason is because God has given marriage to us for our good, and the sexual relationship is to be confined to marriage. Ultimately if sexual relationships are treated casually, marriage itself—and therefore the family—is endangered. I stress this because I want you to realize that what you are doing is wrong in the eyes of God.

There is no shortcut to doing the right thing. God's will—which is perfect and best for you in the long run—is for you to break off this relationship. It will not be easy, I know, but I pray that you will have the courage to do what is right.

But beyond that, my prayer for you is that you will not only do what is right in this situation, but that you will come to see your own need of God and yield your life totally and without reserve to Jesus Christ. You need God's forgiveness, and you need His guidance in your life every day. You need strength to do what is right, and you need to discover God's perfect will for your life.

Turn to Christ. You are never alone when Christ is with you, and you can experience the joy that comes from knowing that you are a child of God and He is with you every day.

I am living with my boyfriend, who is the father of my baby. I know this is wrong, but I love my boyfriend deeply and just can't imagine life without him. The problem is he seems to be growing more and more distant toward me and now I am afraid he is going to leave me all alone. I just don't know what to do.

There may be someone reading this question right now who is being tempted to do the same thing you have done. My prayer is that your experience will be a warning to them and that they will have the courage to turn their backs on this temptation. The problem—as you have sadly discovered—is that the kind of relationship you have had may have seemed ideal for a time. But when there is no commitment (unlike marriage, which involves a vow of commitment), things eventually become unraveled.

It will not be easy for you to do the right thing, I suspect. But doing the wrong thing will only lead to a deadend of heartache and grief. What is the right thing? The right thing is for you to end this relationship, especially if (as you indicate) your boyfriend shows little evidence of being in love with you and wanting to make a commitment of marriage to you. What you are now doing is morally wrong in God's eyes and continuing in this relationship only increases the problem. Your child needs the example and security of a stable home life.

But I want to point out a very important fact to you. You are fearful about the future and concerned about being alone. But you are not alone—God is with you. You need to turn to Him and find in Him the forgiveness and security you need. And He wants you to come to Him because He loves you.

What you have done is wrong and your life will not necessarily be easy as a single parent. But God cares for you. "The Lord is compassionate and gracious, slow to anger, abounding in love . . . as high as the heavens are above the earth, so great is his love for those who fear him" (Psalm 103:8, 11).

2

Isn't Sex an
Expression of Love?

*My boyfriend and I have talked about sex a lot. We have decided that if two
people really love each other sex before marriage is all right. Don't you think
sex is supposed to be an expression of love?*

Yes, sex is an expression of love—but it also should be combined with deep
commitment. That is one reason why the Bible tells us that the sexual relationship is to be confined to marriage. God has been very clear on this, and I
strongly urge you to reconsider your position and do what He wants you to do.
Let me warn you honestly that it is easy to talk yourself into doing something
that is wrong, and which you will later regret.

God tells us, "Among you there must not be even a hint of sexual immorality, or of any kind of impurity" (Ephesians 5:3). The more I study the Bible and
the more I see the results in the lives of those who disobey God's law, the more
I see that God has actually given this commandment for our own good—physically, emotionally, socially, and spiritually.

We are seeing, for instance, an alarming rise in sexually transmitted diseases because of widespread sexual immorality in our country. The specter
of AIDS hovers over us like a plague. God also knows that we need and want
the security of true commitment in love—a commitment that can only come
when two people pledge themselves to each other alone in the bond of marriage. God has also told us, "You shall not commit adultery" (Exodus 20:14)
to preserve the family, which is the basic essential unit of any society. History does not give us a single example of a civilization that survived once its
families broke up.

My prayer is that you and your friend will give your lives to Christ and discover the joy of having Him lead you every day.

*I have a friend who says sex before marriage is okay, because the Bible only
talks about adultery, which is having sexual relations with someone once you*

are married. Is this true? I need to know because my boyfriend is putting pressure on me about having sex with him.

The Bible makes it clear that sexual relations outside the bond of marriage are wrong in the eyes of God—and you should not take this lightly.

This is true when the marriage bond is broken through adultery. Jesus summed up the Ten Commandments when He said, "Do not murder, do not commit adultery . . ." (Matthew 19:18). But it is equally true for every kind of sexual relationship outside marriage. The Bible commands, "Flee from sexual immorality. All other sins a man commits are outside his body, but he who sins sexually sins against his own body" (1 Corinthians 6:18). The word translated as "sexual immorality" in this verse is actually a general term in the language in which the New Testament was originally written, and it includes not only fornication but adultery, lust, and incest. (Interestingly enough we also get our word "pornography" from this word.)

Although this sin has become common in our society, I urge you to keep yourself pure. God has given sex to us, and His purposes for it can only be fulfilled within the commitment of marriage. You need God's guidance for the future, and you need His strength also to live as you should—particularly in our time, when there are so many pressures on you to turn your back on God's way.

My boyfriend and I are deeply in love and have talked a great deal about marriage. We are compatible in every way, except he has no interest in God or the church. These are very important to me, however. Do you think this will be a problem when we get married?

Yes, I must frankly warn you that this can become a serious problem later on. It is far better for you to face it and deal with it now rather than to wait until even greater harm may be done.

I have met many women who, after years of marriage and attempts to reform their husbands, wish that they had listened to the Bible's advice about a life partner and had married a man who was a committed Christian. How will it be a problem if you marry him? This can happen in several ways. The most obvious is what you will do with your children and their spiritual upbringing. Even if your husband were to agree that they could be active in Sunday school and church (which is not always the case), by his example he is teaching them that he thinks God is unimportant—and that can be a powerful influence on them. Why should they take Christ seriously when He means nothing to someone they respect and love?

But it can affect your marriage in other ways as well. Inevitably a person who is uninterested in God and His will is going to have different priorities, and this will cause tension. Or you have to face the possibility that over the years he will influence you and slowly but surely draw you away from your own commitment to Christ.

The Bible's message is clear: "Do not be yoked together with unbelievers" (2 Corinthians 6:14). Have you definitely made your own commitment to Jesus Christ? Share your convictions honestly with your boyfriend, and pray that God will help him realize his own need of Christ. However, if he continues to have no interest in Christ, trust God to lead you to another He has chosen for you so your family will be united in Christ.

I am a student in a university and was reared in a Christian home. I was shocked to find out that many students live for sex and seem to have no moral restraints. I feel completely out of place here. Should I try to make an adjustment to this way of life?

Some young people still believe that they must "sow their wild oats." What they forget is that "Whatsoever a man soweth, that shall he also reap" (Galatians 6:7, KJV).

By all means, don't conform to those who have been overwhelmed by the tide of immorality sweeping our country! Professor Sorokin of Harvard once said that America is a victim of a sex revolution that could ruin our nation. What will our future be if young people like you, with ideals and convictions, yield to the pressures to be immoral?

Many marital breakdowns can be traced to loose morals of college years. "Wild oats" have a way of hounding people throughout the years, and springing up at the most embarrassing moments.

While there are some who laugh at a person with standards and ideals, most people will admire you. Our nation grew strong in an era when moral standards were emphasized, and it will grow weak when we condone that which we once condemned. Help stem the tide of adultery, divorce, and obscenity in America by standing true to your convictions. You are the kind of young person we most need in America.

My fiancée is of another faith. Now that we are making definite plans for the wedding we are for the first time meeting with innumerable objections. Should we proceed according to plan in spite of these objections?

You had better settle religious questions before the wedding even if it means postponement. Your families no doubt waited until the last minute, thinking that you would not go ahead with your plans. You do see that there's a conflict and that there is no ground where you can stand in agreement. Some would advise that you simply agree to disagree, but that is not practical when two people will live as intimately as husband and wife. To have a happy life together, you must have confidence and respect, and you must have substantial agreement in your faith. The Christian loves Christ as well as believes in Him. It is much more than intellectual assent, it is commitment. Therefore, unless you reach a complete agreement, you will be wiser to cancel your plans. Amos 3:3 asks: "Can two walk together except they be agreed?" This question must always be answered with a firm *no*.

Is it necessary to confess all of the details of a sinful life to one's mate after marriage? If so, should this confession include the names of anyone in sex sins?

It is unfortunate in a marriage if there is an array of sordid memories of past sins on the part of either partner. If young people could only realize that a happy marriage depends not only on the present, but also upon the past, they would be more reluctant to enter into loose, intimate relations with anyone and everyone. Many a marriage has been imperiled by the backlash of past sins which were not just confessed, but "found out."

As to the necessity of confessing past sins to one's mate, I don't think this is always advisable or necessary. I have known of homes that were wrecked by such confessions. The main thing is to confess any past wrongs to God, resolve to be true to your marriage vows, and absolve the black past by a spotless present. The Bible says: "He who conceals his sins does not prosper, but whoever confesses them and renounces them finds mercy" (Proverbs 28:13).

When I was very young I married, but our marriage ended after less than two years. With my second husband I have had two lovely children, but I am troubled all the time about something I heard concerning divorce and remarriage. Am I living in sin because I had a husband and separated from him?

Until we come to Christ, all our lives are sinful and wrong. That is why God has provided a salvation that covers and removes all our sins and makes a new creature out of a sinful and sinning one. Because you have trusted Christ, He has forgiven all your past sins. The Bible speaks of the sin of the people of God, putting away a husband or wife for the express purpose of taking another (Matthew 19:1–10). God's ideal is for permanence in the marriage bond, but the key is your attitude now. Jesus said to the woman at the well, "Go and sin no more." Christ's blood cleanses from *all* sin. "If we confess our sins, he is faithful and just to forgive us our sins, and to cleanse us from *all* unrighteousness" (1 John 1:9, KJV).

My counsel to you is to simply thank God for forgiving your past, and then purpose to live entirely for Him. Be the kind of devoted wife and mother you should be in the light of your present Christian faith. If God has forgiven your sins, why should you continue to refuse to forgive yourself? You are not glorifying God as you should unless you take His forgiveness and the freedom He secures for us (Galatians 5:1).

I grew up thinking that sex was something dirty and shameful, and now that I am married that attitude is still with me and is causing me a problem. How can I change?

Sex is a gift of God which—like any of His other gifts—can become something destructive and twisted when we misuse it or use it selfishly. And when we do misuse it, it can become something dirty and shameful. But when we understand why God gave us this awesome gift of sex, and when we use it in accordance with His will, then it can be a source of great happiness and joy.

Why did God give us sex? The most obvious reason is to continue the human race from one generation to another. God told Adam and Eve, "Be fruitful and increase in number; fill the earth and subdue it" (Genesis 1:28). God also gave us the sexual relationship for our pleasure. There is nothing wrong with this—as long as our passions do not control or dominate us—and God delights in giving us good things. Sex is also an expression of love and unity between husband and wife. It is a sign of their commitment to each other in the bonds of marriage.

This, incidentally, is why the Bible tells us that sex is to be practiced only within marriage. The sexual relationship should be a sign of commitment and love—the kind of commitment that is part of the marriage vow of two people to each other. "Marriage should be honored by all, and the marriage bed kept pure, for God will judge the adulterer and all the sexually immoral" (Hebrews 13:4).

Realize that God did not intend for sex to be dirty but beautiful—when it is used in accordance with His standards. If you need the help of an experienced Christian counselor who can help you work through your attitudes, don't hesitate to seek it. But most of all let the truth of God's Word help you overcome the misconceptions you may have, and pray that God will help you be the best wife you can be to your husband in every way possible.

I know it is supposed to be wrong to have sex before marriage, but I just can't seem to say no to the boys I date. I'm afraid no one will like me if I refuse to give in. Please help me get out of this rut.

You are being treated by your boyfriends like those disposable cans and bottles which, once the contents have been consumed, are tossed in the trash. Sex is not a shortcut to love because it lacks the commitment necessary for genuine love to grow.

Has it ever occurred to you that rather than having people really like you because of what you are doing, they instead probably only lose their respect for you? In addition, you are only hurting yourself because as long as you try to buy friendship in this way, you will never learn what it means to have a lasting, fulfilling, and loving relationship with others.

God did not make a mistake when He commanded, "You shall not commit adultery" (Exodus 20:14). Why did He give us this command? (The command, incidentally, covers all types of sexual immorality.) He gave us this command not because He wanted to restrict us and make us unhappy, but because He loves us. And because He loves us and created us, He knows what is best for us. God has restricted the exercise of His gift of sex to marriage, because it is only within the commitment of marriage that true love can be fully expressed between a man and a woman.

There is no shortcut for your problem. You need to turn away from what you are doing, and you need to turn to God. God loves you—you don't need to buy His love for you. All you need to do is accept it.

I have been keeping company with a man for fifteen years. We have broken the Seventh Commandment many times. I could have married him long ago, but did not want to leave my home. Now we are planning to marry. What chance of happiness do we have?

Yours is not an ideal setting for married happiness, but I sincerely hope you can get your lives straightened out. To begin with, your relationship with this man seems to have been on a purely biological level, and sex is certainly not the only ingredient of marital bliss. In fact, marriages that are based on this alone are doomed to failure. The divorce courts are full of disillusioned people who mistakenly thought that animal magnetism was true love.

Do you love this man, and are you both willing to take God into your marriage partnership? The Bible says: "What God hath joined together let not man put asunder" (Matthew 19:6, KJV). The only really sound marriages are those based on mutual respect. In the light of your continuously breaking the Seventh Commandment, do you two have respect, admiration, and love for each other?

Marriage may ease your conscience a bit, but if I were you two, I would bow before God together and ask Him to forgive you for deliberately breaking His law, and jeopardizing your reputations and your influence in the community. He has said: "Though your sins be as scarlet, they shall be as wool." With God you can be happy.

3

We No Longer
Love Each Other

My husband and I no longer love each other, and there just doesn't seem to be much point in keeping our marriage together any longer. Do you think we are wrong to think like this?

Genuine love is not (or should not be) based on feelings. God doesn't always feel good about what we are doing, but He always loves us. The question is not how you feel about your husband at the moment. The question is, are you *willing* to love him? If you are, then feelings of love will follow. If you are not willing to love him, then you will experience no feelings at all. Our culture puts feelings first, but true love isn't based on feelings. That is why there are so many divorces today. When the early romantic feelings in a marriage do not remain constant as they do during dating, many people believe divorce is the answer. They try to find someone else who can rekindle those good feelings. Some marry many times, in constant search of a "high" that can never be maintained.

My prayer is that you and your husband will do everything possible to restore the joy and happiness that once were central to your marriage. I hope you will do this first of all because marriage is a sacred vow or commitment you both made before God, and it is a very serious matter to break that vow. I also hope you will do it because God gave marriage to us for our happiness, and I believe with His help you can discover what it means to build your lives together on Christ's foundation.

As you look back on your marriage, it would be good for you to think about what has gone wrong. Has there been a slow drifting apart, a slackening in communication and trust? Have other things—a job, money, personal ambitions—come between you and your husband? Have there been little things—a sharp tongue, an unforgiving spirit—that have eaten away at your relationship? One of the hardest things you both may have to do is to face these and say "I'm sorry." And yet it could be the first step in restoring a wonderful relationship.

But I also want to challenge you to add a new element to your marriage that your letter suggests has been lacking. That missing ingredient is God. Elsewhere in your letter (in a part I have not quoted) you acknowledge that God has played almost no part in your lives. But God gave marriage to us, and a solid marriage actually involves three—you, your husband, and God. Let God heal your marriage. It is worth it, and He wants to help you if you will but turn to Him.

I have been married for several years, and I am beginning to worry about our marriage. At first we were deeply in love, but now those feelings of love seem to be fading. How can we get them back?

Some years ago there was a popular song which included the phrase, "I'm hooked on a feeling." And, "If it feels good, do it," was a popular slogan in the 1960s. I have observed, however, that there is a distinction between romance (feelings) and true love. They are often related to each other very closely, but there is a difference. Let me explain.

Romantic love is often very emotional. Two people are attracted to each other, and strong feelings develop between them. This is often what people mean when they say they are in love—they have strong romantic feelings toward another person. There is nothing wrong with this, of course—there is definitely an emotional side to true love.

But the problem with merely romantic love is that it gradually fades as time goes on. Unfortunately, when this happens a couple may decide that there is no longer any hope for love in their relationship and decide to end the marriage.

I hope, however, that this will not be the case with you. It need not be if you will work at establishing your relationship on true love. True love includes romantic love, but it is more than that. True love involves a commitment to each other, and a settled determination to be kind and considerate to the other person instead of selfish.

Love, you see, is more than a feeling—it also is an action. Look at the characteristics of true love that the Bible lists: "Love is patient, love is kind. It does not envy, it does not boast, it is not proud. It is not rude, it is not self-seeking, it is not easily angered, it keeps no record of wrongs. Love does not delight in evil but rejoices with the truth. It always protects, always trusts, always hopes, always perseveres" (1 Corinthians 13:4–7).

This is the kind of love God has for us, and my prayer is that you and your wife will discover His love by giving yourselves to Christ and basing your marriage on Him. Then work on expressing true love to each other. When you do, you will find that the feelings of romance you once had will grow again, and your love will be far deeper and richer than you could ever imagine.

I can't believe this is happening to me. My husband is in his late middle age, and he says he has fallen in love with a girl who is in her early twenties. He says he just can't help it. Please pray for me.

Yes, I will pray for you, and I also will pray for your husband. What he is doing is wrong, and (as you know personally) it is hurting a lot of people. What he may not realize (or at least admit) is that he also is hurting himself.

I have often asked myself why this kind of thing happens. It is, unfortunately, not that uncommon for a man who is middle-aged or older to start acting like a giddy teenager in love and leave his family for a much younger woman. Perhaps one reason is a secret fear of growing older, or at least a refusal to face the fact that he is getting older. Perhaps it is very flattering to his ego to find that he is "not as old as he thought he was," and is attractive to a younger woman. It makes him "feel young again" and diverts his attention from the fact that he is getting older.

Whatever the reason, your husband must come to grips with the fact that he is responsible for his actions. His statement that "he just can't help it" is not true—he is just unwilling to do what is right, break off this relationship, and concentrate on being a good husband and father. The truth is that he is getting older, and rather than try to escape from that inevitable fact he instead needs to come to grips with it and discover that it can be a wonderful time of life.

Your husband needs to repent of this action of his, and there is no shortcut to that. It not only is something which hurts you, but it is wrong in God's eyes as well. Marriage was given to us by God, and when you both took your marriage vows you were making them before God as well as other people. "Therefore what God has joined together, let man not separate" (Matthew 19:6). In the meantime, concentrate on being the best wife you possibly can, letting your husband know that you love him and will forgive him for what he has done.

My husband is breaking my heart because he is involved with another woman. He says he knows it is wrong, but he says God will forgive him anyway so it doesn't really matter. Is this true, or is he just deceiving himself?

The Bible asks, "Shall we go on sinning that grace may increase?" (Romans 6:1). I believe your husband is in a very dangerous position for several reasons, and my prayer is that he will realize the foolishness of what he is doing and turn from it.

God's forgiveness in the Bible is always—without exception—related closely to repentance. Repentance involves a recognition on our part that what we are doing is wrong, and it also involves a deliberate turning from sin as well. It is not enough to know that what we are doing is wrong in God's eyes. We also are commanded to turn from it. Jesus declared, "I have not come to call the righteous, but sinners to repentance" (Luke 5:32). Paul stated that God "now . . . commands all people everywhere to repent" (Acts 17:30). Many other verses could be quoted. We make a mockery of God's forgiveness when we deliberately engage in sin because we think He will forgive it later.

Your husband also is deceiving himself in thinking that he will find true happiness in rejecting God's way for his life and instead is embracing a life of sin. Yes, for a time he may think he has found happiness but it is only an illusion. He will never find lasting happiness or security in this way. The Bible warns, "But the wicked are like the tossing sea, which cannot rest, whose waves cast up mire and mud. 'There is no peace,' says my God, 'for the wicked'" (Isaiah 57:20–21).

Pray for your husband, that God will convict him of the seriousness of his sin and his responsibility to fulfill the vow he took before God when you were married. And pray that God will make you the best wife you possibly can be, so that he will realize that your home can be a place of joy and security.

I feel like I am in a hole that I have dug for myself. I have had several extramarital affairs to get back at my husband, who often treats me unkindly. However, I realize that I have only hurt myself. Can God forgive me and help me, or is it too late to do anything about the mess I have made of things?

I am sorry that for so long you have been deceived into thinking that kind of life would solve anything. As you have discovered, however, there is not only no future in living that way, but it also is destructive. It has not solved your marriage problems nor has it brought you real happiness and security. I mention this because it may be there is someone reading this who is tempted to do what you have done, and your experience will be a warning to that person.

You need God's forgiveness—not only for the sins you have mentioned, but for every other sin you have committed as well. The greatest sin is that you have turned your back on God and tried to live your life without Him. But I want you to know a very important truth. God loves you, in spite of what you have done. He is willing to forgive you and He has done everything possible to make your forgiveness possible by sending His Son into the world to die on the cross for your sins. In Christ "we have redemption through his blood, the forgiveness of sins, in accordance with the riches of God's grace that he lavished on us" (Ephesians 1:7–8).

You need His wisdom and help—and He can help you begin to rebuild your marriage and your life if you will let Him rule in your life.

I need your prayers for my marriage. My husband never shows any love for me, and just gets upset whenever I try to get him to be a better husband.

I am sorry that your marriage has not been happy and filled with love. God's plan for marriage is perfect, and He wants marriage to be a source of great joy and strength.

I don't know the details of your situation, of course, but let me first suggest that you be very careful about slipping into a resentful, complaining, nagging attitude which will only cause your husband to become even more withdrawn and even hostile. The Bible says, "Better to live in a desert than with a quarrelsome and ill-tempered wife" (Proverbs 21:19). Your husband needs to know your feelings and you need to learn to communicate with him—but without angering him or cutting off your communication if at all possible. Will your husband go with you to consult a trained Christian counselor?

This leads me to a second suggestion: I would encourage you to do everything you can to express your love to your husband. The little acts of kindness, the care you take with your appearance around the house, the effort you make to turn your house into a warm, secure home—all these will signal your husband that you care for him. They also will show him that you want your home to be a place of happiness and peace. In time you may find that he will respond. But whether he responds at first or not, your calling as a wife is to be the best wife he could ever ask for.

Your letter, however, suggests to me that neither you nor your husband has ever considered seriously your relationship to God. God created you, and God brought you together as husband and wife when you took a vow together before Him pledging your commitment to each other "till death do us part." Why don't you take your marriage back to the One who made it and let Him fix it? Make God the center and foundation of your lives and your marriage. Seek to live each day as He would have you live. Then pray for your husband, that he too not only will realize his responsibilities as a husband, but will come to see his own need of Christ and seek to do God's will also.

My husband and I have had troubles for years, but finally he has packed his bags and left to go live with another woman. I am angry and depressed, and just don't know what to do. Can you offer me any hope?

I do not know whether or not your husband will ever return to you, although I pray that your marriage will somehow get on the right track and you and your husband will discover the joy that God intended marriage to be. But I can offer you hope of another type—and it may be that God will work in ways you could never imagine to bring healing to your marriage.

God wants to help you in this situation. He wants to help you overcome the bitterness and anger that you feel, and He wants to encourage you. He loves you, and He knows that anger and depression will never help you deal with your problems—they only make them worse. Listen to what the Bible says: "Cast your cares on the Lord and he will sustain you" (Psalm 55:22). Or again, "Cast all your anxiety on him because he cares for you" (1 Peter 5:7). God wants you to take this problem and put it into His hands. He wants you to learn to trust

Him and look to Him for strength. The first step you need to take, therefore, is to admit to God that you are angry and depressed, but that you want to commit this whole situation to Him and seek His will and strength.

I would be less than honest with you if I did not tell you of the possibility that your marriage may never be restored. While God's will is that every marriage will endure, man's sin has poisoned many relationships. You should pray for your husband, but you should also move forward with your own life and with what God might do in and through you.

Then get involved in a church where Christ is preached and you can meet other Christians. You may well find some of them who have a similar background to you, and they can help you deal with the problems and adjustment you face.

What do you think is the biggest problem in marriages? I have heard people say it is finances, but in my experience the biggest problem is in-laws who try to interfere.

There are many practical concerns that can cause serious problems in a marriage, and I think you have mentioned two of them. I get many letters from couples who have allowed money problems to drive a wedge between them, and I also get many letters from people who have some other problem (including in-laws who interfere or try to dominate the lives of a young couple). The real question is not what the biggest problem is in marriages generally—the real question is what is wrong specifically in each marriage that is in difficulty.

But I also believe that there is usually a deeper problem involved in many marriages, whatever the immediate practical problems may seem to be. This is the spiritual problem. Marriage was designed by God. And He meant for it actually to involve three people—the man, the woman, and God. When God is left out of a marriage, that marriage will always be less than God intended it to be, even if it is seemingly a happy one. When God is left out of a marriage, it means you have two individuals who will often be competing with each other instead of loving each other and forgiving each other. But when each partner is seeking God's will, and when each partner is allowing God to take away the natural selfishness of his or her heart and replace it with sacrificial love, then there will be joy and peace.

That is why the Bible stresses that a marriage ideally should be a picture or a reflection of Christ's love for His people. "Husbands, love your wives, just as Christ loved the church and gave himself up for her" (Ephesians 5:25).

As to your experience with interfering in-laws, they need to understand that breaking into a marriage can be like a burglar breaking into a home. It can be a violation of one's privacy and sow seeds of discontent that may actually contribute more to marital stress than to the resolution of problems. You should gently tell them that while you appreciate their concern, you would rather have their prayers, and that if you need more than their prayers you will let them know.

I always had very romantic ideas about marriage, but they have surely been shattered. We had a child in our first year of marriage, and my husband not only works full time, but goes to school full time. It just seems like a rat race and sometimes I feel like just throwing up my hands and walking away. What's so great about marriage anyway?

Yes, I'm afraid many young people today have very romantic ideas about marriage—ideas that do not necessarily reflect the truth. That is not to say that romance is wrong, not at all. But romantic feelings alone are not enough when the problems and strains come—as they inevitably do.

Let me first of all encourage you by telling you that your situation will probably not last forever. I would hope that you and your husband have talked honestly (and not bitterly) about this, and that the time will come when his schooling will be over and the pressures can ease. The only danger, however, is that you both allow this period of time to become a permanent pattern, so that once school is over your husband allows something else to take its place and you both drift farther and farther apart.

But don't wait until some distant time to deal with this problem. You and your husband need to face honestly the pressures upon each of you. He needs to understand the pressures you face and you need to see the ones he faces. You both made a vow to each other—a vow not only before other people but before God. You vowed that you would be faithful and loving to each other, even when circumstances were difficult. Marriage is a big responsibility, and you need to pray that God will give you strength and wisdom to fulfill your responsibilities right now.

God did not intend for marriage to be a rat race. That is why my prayer for you and your husband is that you will both yield your lives to Christ and let Him be Lord of your lives and your marriage. You would gain nothing by running away, and you would hurt deeply the lives of many others. Ask Christ to help you and to show you how you both can discover the joy of marriage, and then take practical steps to make the most use of the time you and your husband have together.

A few weeks ago my husband confessed to me that he had had an affair with a girl who works in his office. He says it is all over, and I believe him, but down inside I wonder if I should really forgive him.

Forgiveness does not come easily to us, especially when someone we have trusted betrays our trust. And yet if we do not learn to forgive, we will discover that we can never really rebuild trust. The fact that your husband confessed his action to you probably indicates his sorrow over what he has done, and his yearning for your forgiveness.

The Bible tells us that we are to forgive others—even when they repeatedly offend us. On one occasion Peter asked Jesus, "Lord, how many times shall I forgive my brother when he sins against me? Up to seven times?" Jesus' reply was that our forgiveness should be limitless: "I tell you, not seven times, but seventy-seven times" (Matthew 18:21–22).

But how is it possible for us to forgive others who have hurt us? I believe it is only possible when we concentrate not on what others have done to us, but on what we have done to God—and how He has forgiven us anyway. Do you realize just how much you have sinned against God? That does not mean you have been a terrible person, as far as human standards go. But God created you, and yet you have left Him out of your life. You have turned your back on Him, and sinned against Him in thought, word, and deed. You do not deserve anything from Him except His judgment—and neither does any one of us.

God, however, loves you and has made it possible for you to be forgiven through Jesus Christ, His Son. That is how we are to forgive others—as God has forgiven us in Christ. "Be kind and compassionate to one another, forgiving each other, just as in Christ God forgave you" (Ephesians 4:32). Then I pray that you and your husband will learn to walk with Christ each day and rebuild your marriage on the solid foundation of Christ.

I guess I am just a very mixed-up person. I separated from my husband a few months ago, then got pregnant by another man. Now my husband wants me back again, and is pressuring me to have an abortion. I just don't know how to sort out my life.

You have two problems, actually—an immediate problem concerning the child growing inside you, and a long-range problem concerning the direction of your life. In a few short paragraphs I can't say everything I would like to say, but I hope you will find someone you can trust (like a pastor) who can help you through these difficulties.

First of all, I hope you will not give in to the pressure to have an abortion. I realize that in some ways that would seem to solve a problem rather easily—but do not add still another wrong to the wrongs you have already done. That little life within you is a child, made in the image of God, and it would be tragic to take that life. It may be that the best choice will be for you to allow the child to be adopted—but that decision should be made only after you have looked carefully at all your options and talked with a counselor who can help you think them through.

Second, I am also very concerned about your future—not just in the next few months, but years from now. So far you have been drifting in life, searching for happiness and yet never really finding it. As long as you keep drifting with no real purpose in life, you will always be subject to tangled problems like you are facing now.

So far in your life God has played no part. You have lived apart from Him, as if He didn't even exist. But God not only exists—He loves you and wants you to become His child. He wants you to learn the joy of walking with Him every day, seeking His will for your life and obeying His guidelines and moral laws.

You may not understand everything about God right now, but He loves you and wants you to turn to Him for forgiveness and new life.

The biggest problem in our marriage can be summed up in one word: Money. It seems like we are fighting more and more, and it almost always boils down to differences about money. I feel we are sliding down a hill out of control and will wreck our marriage, but I don't know what to do.

Not long ago I was talking with a psychologist who deals with many people who have marriage problems. He said that arguments over money were a major part of the problem for most of the people he counseled.

There are at least two levels or dimensions to your problem. The first—and more important—is the whole question of what place money (and all that it represents) has in your life. Right now it seems that money and material things concern you most and dominate you. But the Bible warns us against putting money in first place in our lives. That is a place only God should occupy, and money must never take His rightful place. Money has become your master, but Jesus declared, "No one can serve two masters. Either he will hate the one and love the other, or he will be devoted to the one and despise the other. You cannot serve both God and Money" (Matthew 6:24). We become like the God we worship.

The other dimension of your question is the practical one. If you are heavily in debt or do not know how to make a realistic budget for your finances, get advice from someone who can help you. If you seemingly can't control your use of credit, get rid of the credit cards or the charge accounts. Credit can be like a drug. Many people get "hooked" and can't seem to break away and control their finances. Instead, they are controlled by them. God wants to control your life and if you determine to submit your life (and finances) to Him, He will help you. Find an honest financial adviser who will help you get out of debt and establish a budget for you to live within.

My husband is a slave to things, I have decided. He works all the time, and when I try to get him to slow down and spend time just enjoying life he says he can't afford to do it because he wants to provide us with lots of financial security. I worry about him, particularly since a friend of ours about the same age dropped dead of a heart attack a week ago and the same thing could happen to my husband. What can I do to help him?

It is surprisingly easy for some men (and women) to fall into your husband's trap, without ever really thinking about it or realizing how illogical it is. For example, if you were to ask most of them why they work so diligently to give their families financial security, they would say it is because they love them. But they fail to see that never spending time with their children and spouse (as well as working themselves into an early death) is the most unloving thing they can do.

Your husband needs to readjust his priorities. Yes, he has a responsibility to provide financially for his family. But he also has a God-given responsibility to provide for the emotional and spiritual welfare of his family—and he cannot do that if he is totally preoccupied with money and things. Jesus declared, "Therefore I tell you, do not worry about your life, what you will eat or drink; or about your body, what you will wear. Is not life more important than food, and the body more important than clothes? . . . But seek first his kingdom and his righteousness, and all these things will be given to you as well" (Matthew 6:25, 33).

Pray for your husband—and pray for yourself also—that God will help you make your home a warm and happy place where your husband will discover a new joy in family life together.

I am married to a very wonderful person. In spite of the fact that I respect him very highly, I have fallen in love with another man who shows me the attention I crave, while my husband seems to take me for granted. I feel I can't break off with the one I love, but don't know how to bring the news to my husband. What is the right thing to do?

There should be no question concerning what is right. If you want God's answer, it would be that you forget the passing infatuation and settle down. It is easy for another to show you attention when it only involves periodic favors and demonstrations without all the responsibility of being married. If you still consider your husband a wonderful person and if you respect him, you are playing the part of a foolish child to entertain thoughts of infatuation which belong to high-school-age people.

Often if we will demonstrate our love to our mates, the love we are searching for will be reciprocated. But if we first demand love and affection before showing it ourselves, the other partner in the marriage frequently plays the same game and a high wall is erected between the two. Follow the biblical admonition to be obedient and submissive to your husband, and you may find him much more affectionate than you think. Secondly, this infatuation is a sin in God's sight. Confess it and allow this experience to bring you to a true relationship with Christ and your husband.

I have a fine husband but I have been unfaithful to him. Now I realize how very wrong I have been. What should I do?

The Bible tells us that when David realized he was guilty of a similar sin he cried out to God for forgiveness and he was forgiven. Read Psalm 51 after reading 2 Samuel chapters 11 and 12. Here you will see that conviction of sin, sorrow for sin, and turning to God for forgiveness are the steps to cleansing and pardon. David's sin had been known to many and the prophet Nathan told him he had caused "The enemies of the Lord to blaspheme." In your case public confession of your sin could do more harm than good. You should refuse to again associate with the other guilty parties. Having confessed your sin to God and asked Christ for forgiveness, ask Him also for the strength to live a life for His glory. Show your husband how dearly you love him. Try to be the best wife, homemaker, mother, neighbor, and friend possible. Remember you can never do this in your own strength. Ask God daily for the necessary power to overcome sin and live for Him. Spend time in Bible study and prayer. If you do these things you will find the sordid past will become only an unhappy memory.

I have absolute proof that my husband is being unfaithful to me. We have been married ten years and have three children. What shall I do?

There are three areas you must consider and in all three you must ask God's guidance and help. *First,* your husband's soul is at stake and he needs to recognize his sin and ask God's forgiveness. Ask God to give you the grace and wisdom to face your husband with this sin and let him see that you love him and are concerned over his soul's welfare. It may be that God will use you to resolve this problem and win your husband at the same time.

Second, look at yourself: your heart is heavy and your pride is hurt and you are carrying a great burden. Again you must pray for the love and grace to do the right thing.

You can leave your husband but the problem is still unsolved. If he can be won back, it will be far better. Your husband also needs to know that he cannot continue to behave as he is without serious repercussions. Marriage is a contract, not only between the two people involved, but also with God Himself. In human affairs, when a contract is violated, a person can sue in a court of law. Sometimes a smart lawyer can win an acquittal for his client from the judge. But God is just. Your husband will ultimately pay a severe penalty unless he repents.

Third, you must consider your children. If you separate from your husband your children immediately face the problems of a broken home. This can have serious consequences for them. They need a father, just as you need a husband. Also, despite what he has done, he needs his wife and children. Let me urge you to pray earnestly about this and then act in the wisdom and strength God will give you.

My husband became seriously involved with another woman. He has become a Christian and is thoroughly repentant but we decided to move to another town. Now this woman has followed us to this town. What shall we do?

Not knowing the status of the other woman, I can only advise you in a general way. I feel that you and your husband are to be congratulated on your mutual love and trust for one another. You both have passed through deep waters and God has evidently provided the forgiveness and grace needed. Let me urge you both to stick together as never before and to make all your plans accordingly. I would completely ignore this other woman. If she makes advances, as well she may, be sure that she is given to understand that this affair is finished and her presence is unwelcome. In all this, let me urge you two to pray each day for guidance to meet the problems which may arise. Ask God to give you the wisdom and love and good common sense which will ensure that this difficulty is met in His way. If the woman is a schemer, be particularly careful that she does not maneuver you or your husband into a compromising situation. I appreciate the difficulty and embarrassment of your situation, but you have a source of help and blessing in the Lord Jesus Christ which will certainly see you through. Finally, pray for this woman: ask God to convict her of her sin, as He did your husband. She has an eternal soul for which Christ also died.

When we married my husband was not working, and he said it was because of a temporary layoff in his factory. But it has been five years now and he hasn't held a steady job since then. He always has an excuse of some sort, but I have had to face the fact that he is just lazy and is content to let me support us. Can I do anything about this or should I leave him?

What can you do? First, it may be that your husband's apparent laziness is a symptom of a deeper problem which needs to be dealt with. For example, some people have very little confidence in their abilities and become easily discouraged when things do not go exactly right. They are very fearful of failure, and that fear makes them avoid any challenges in life—including a job. Encourage your husband to seek some vocational counseling; your pastor may be able to point you to an agency in your community that can help him face his problems—even if his real problem is only laziness. Pray for your husband also, that he will realize God commands him to be more responsible, and will give his life to Christ, who can take away his selfish attitude. Talk frankly but lovingly with him about your concerns.

Do everything you can to keep your marriage intact. When you married you took a solemn vow before God that you would be faithful to each other "for better or for worse." Your situation may not be ideal, but with God's help it can change.

My husband has had a lot of problems with depression and other things, and frankly it has been a great strain on me having to take care of him all the time. Now I find myself attracted to a man in my office, and I think a lot about how happy my life would be if I could be married to him. I know this is a fantasy, but is there anything wrong with dreaming like that?

Yes there is, and I urge you to face this and seek God's help to overcome this so you can have the attitude God wants you to have.

Why are these fantasies wrong? For one thing, as long as you allow these fantasies to build you will be more and more resentful of your husband and his situation—instead of realizing that God wants to bless you and make you a blessing right where you are. For another thing, fantasies like this easily lead to action. Every day I get letters from people who have wrecked their lives because they have allowed fantasies to get out of hand and ended up breaking their marriage vows. They never started out intending to do so, and often excused their thoughts as innocent and unimportant—but their thoughts led eventually to action. Jesus said, "For out of the heart come evil thoughts, murder, adultery, sexual immorality" (Matthew 15:19).

I urge you to repent of your sins—not just your fantasies, but every sin you have committed—and ask Christ to forgive you. Then turn your life over to Him, and ask Him to give you strength to avoid temptation and to be an encouragement and help to your husband. Pray for him also, that he too will come to Christ and discover the joy of knowing Christ is with him every hour of the day. "But those who hope in the Lord will renew their strength" (Isaiah 40:31).

On account of my husband's business, I am left alone much of the time. A woman becomes weary just being with other women at times, and I wonder if

*any harm would be done by having an occasional meal with a man friend who
frequently invites me to dine with him.*

Try to have a frank talk with your husband at the next opportunity. Perhaps
some solution can be reached. Make it a spiritual matter, in which together
you take your problem to the Lord in prayer. Someone has rightly said, "More
things are wrought by prayer than this world dreams of." Finally, you had better face the blunt fact that your desire for male friendship in your husband's
absence could well lead to intimacy that you now cannot foresee, but which
happens in many cases.

Perhaps you should consider whether you have too much time on your hands.
Call your pastor, local hospital or community service agency and ask whether
you might be able to volunteer to help others who are in need. You will discover the truth of the Scripture that it really *is* more blessed to give than to
receive. You also will learn that it is in giving to others that we receive back
many times what we have invested.

*My wife is expecting her first baby and her disposition has changed so much
that I hardly know her. Sometimes I feel that she hates me and it is breaking
my heart. What can I do?*

Your question seems to indicate that you do not feel a part of this baby when,
in fact, you are. You speak of the child as "her" instead of "our" baby. Creating
a child involves more than biology. It involves a spiritual and psychological
sharing of both parents.

I believe your physician can explain the problem to you and give you sound
advice which will clear things up for both you and your wife. I am told that
such personality changes may occur at times like this and that they usually
clear up spontaneously after the baby comes. Your wife needs your love now
more than ever and although it may be hard for her to reciprocate she will know
that you are trying to be loving and considerate and it will help. I presume that
you are a Christian, but in any case let me urge you to take Christ fully into
your heart. Thank Him for this new life which is being entrusted to you two
and pray daily that you may be given the wisdom and strength to raise this little
one for Him.

Let me also suggest that there is no married couple who have not encountered problems of adjustment and clashes in personality. These things can all
be met and resolved by exercising the mutual love and consideration which all
Christians should have for one another. Nothing helps more in a home than
the family altar, a time when you and your wife join together in reading a portion from the Bible and praying together. Also, do not neglect worship together:

"And all Judah stood before the Lord, with their little ones, their wives and their children" (2 Chronicles 20:13).

My husband and I have been married a little more than a year. Until I became a Christian we got along very well, but since I received Christ we seem to argue all the time. I am at the point of leaving him but want your counsel.

The apostle Peter had something to say about this. He said: "Wives, fit in with your husband's plans; for then if they refuse to listen when you talk to them about the Lord, they will be won by your respectful, pure behavior. Your godly lives will speak to them better than any words" (1 Peter 3:1, AMP).

This is no easy assignment, but the responsibility is upon you, not on your husband, to live a life that will challenge him to make his own decision. This cannot be done by nagging and lecturing, but by the manifestation of a spirit of meekness and submission that he has not discovered in you before.

The pattern is Jesus Christ who, though He was God, emptied Himself and took on the form of a servant. Christ submitted His human will to His Heavenly Father and that is what I am asking you to do with your husband. While you should never submit to anything that is against the will of God (like staying home from church or Bible study), you will learn that there are many ways in which you can submit to him. God knows your motives and as you pray for your husband, God will deal with him through the power of His Spirit. As you submit to your husband, let your countenance be joyful. This should not be a burden, but a delight, because you are, in fact, submitting to the will of God and your husband will be won over as much by your joy as by your submission.

My husband and I have been married for over twenty years, but we have lost all feeling for each other. We just live in the same house together. Can anything be done about this?

God meant for marriage to be a joyous and supportive relationship, and that is true for *your* marriage as well. I know it is often very difficult to heal a marriage that has almost fallen apart—but God can help you do it, and I pray you will have the courage and patience to rebuild your relationship. In the short term it may seem much easier to just let things continue to drift, but now is the time to decide you will do whatever is necessary to strengthen your marriage. It will be worth it.

What can you do? First, I hope you and your husband can face honestly together your need to strengthen your marriage. It is not easy to restore communication when it has been lacking for so long, but make it your goal to be honest with each other—not in anger, but in a spirit of sincere seeking. But even if your husband is reluctant to face the problem, determine in your heart that you will do your best, no matter what his initial reaction may be.

A good marriage takes three persons: you, your husband, and God. Let Christ be the foundation of your life and your marriage. Christ can give you a new understanding of what it means to love another person. As you begin to understand from the Bible how much He loves you, you will begin to see how we are to love others—selflessly and consistently.

There is much more I could write, but let me close with this simple suggestion: take time for the practical little acts that tell a person you care. Learn to praise instead of criticize. You both need to learn to communicate and do the fun things you used to do. Put forth a special effort to make your house a home. Show him you are willing to make his needs and desires come first, and I believe you will find him responding as time goes along.

My husband has become almost impossible to live with. I don't know whether he's getting senile or what. We are both in our seventies, and life is hard enough without him complaining all the time. Sometimes I think it's more than I can bear.

Your husband may have some medical problems. Be sure that he has a thorough medical examination by your doctor. You should not put this off any longer, and many problems can be treated very successfully. This would help not only your husband but you as well.

But let me also suggest that regardless of what your husband's exact problem may be, God calls you to be the best wife you can possibly be. God is able to help you and give you strength and wisdom whenever you face particularly difficult situations.

God loves you, and He wants you to come to know Him personally. He wants to help you, and He wants you to put Him first in your lives. God has blessed you both by giving you long lives—but some day you both will die and go into eternity. How tragic it would be for you to miss the joy and peace of God's Heaven because you never took time to think about your need of Christ and invite Him into your lives. I urge you to turn to Christ right now. The reason for your husband's attitude may be that he is reassessing life and wondering whether it has been productive or what he might have done differently.

Then, when you do, God Himself comes to dwell within you by His Holy Spirit. No, you may not feel that you can bear the burdens you are facing—but the Spirit can help you as you seek God's help every day. The fruit of the Spirit, the Bible says, is "love, joy, peace, patience, kindness, goodness, faithfulness, gentleness and self-control" (Galatians 5:22–23). You need those qualities, and Christ can give them to you as you turn to Him.

I am into my second marriage, and although we have only been married a year, it seems like my love is beginning to fade already. My husband is a good man, but I find myself thinking about other men. Now I am wondering if I'll ever have a stable marriage.

I cannot help but feel that you have probably confused romantic feelings with true love. There is nothing wrong with romantic feelings, of course, but it is easy for these to fade after a period of time if there is not something deeper. When these romantic feelings begin to fade they can even deceive us into thinking that true love has gone forever.

It is very possible that there is a missing ingredient in your marriage. What is it? It is commitment—a determination on your part that you will remain committed to your husband for the rest of your life, no matter what the future may hold for you. True love, you see, is more than feelings of romance. True love involves a steadfast commitment of two people to each other. When you married this is actually what you vowed, both before those who witnessed your marriage and before God. God is the One who gave marriage to us, and He intended it to be a lifetime commitment. Jesus declared, "Therefore what God has joined together, let man not separate" (Matthew 19:6).

It would, therefore, be very wrong for you to be misled by your feelings and become interested in another man. You can have a stable marriage, however, if you determine in your heart that you are committed to your husband, and that you will do everything possible to make your relationship grow and become stronger.

4

How Can We Discipline
Our Children?

My wife and I do not agree on the matter of disciplining our children. I maintain that a child needs a firm hand and a spanking now and then. My wife says that all they need is love and understanding. Who is right?

Discipline and love are related. They are two sides of the same coin. Correct discipline is an act of love. "The Lord disciplines those he loves," says the Bible (Hebrews 12:6). The purpose of discipline is not only correction. It is to help a child conform to God's standard so that the child will be able to lead a happy and productive life.

But there must be the right kind of discipline and parents must agree on it. A child will sometimes exploit different approaches to discipline by his parents and that could be damaging to your child and to each of you.

I have one child who rarely needs to be disciplined. Even if I spoke to her reprovingly, her heart would be broken. I have another who responds to punitive discipline, and pays little attention to the "soft reproof." I think it is hard to lay down any hard and fast rules because children vary so much. The Bible teaches that discipline should be used when required. But it suggests that discipline and love must go hand in hand. It says: "For whom the Lord loveth he correcteth; even as a father the son in whom he delighteth" (Proverbs 3:12, KJV).

It is much easier on the nerves to just let children go, than to plan and execute the kind of discipline they need. But greater than discipline is the power of a good example. Children are more impressed by conduct they can see than by lectures and spankings. If parents would live the Christian life before them, it would have a tremendous influence upon their children.

My husband and I have been Christians for many years. We have a daughter who is past thirty years of age and is still at home with us. She helps around the house but has no plans for the future. What is our responsibility?

Part of our job as parents in rearing our children is to teach them to take responsibility for their own lives. Your daughter appears to have reached a certain level of maturity and then stopped. Perhaps she lacks self-confidence or has grown so dependent on you that she is afraid of failure if she steps out on her own. An easy transition would be to secure employment away from home for a time and then be completely on her own. She also may be concerned about what you will do without her. Assure her that you can manage. Encourage her to become a part of a group of working single adults at your church. They will serve as role models and can probably help her to come out of her shell and, then, out of your house.

I am a Christian widow and mother of seven children. My daughter has married a man who has been married three times before. I feel that she walked into sin with her eyes open. Can I allow him to come to my house, and should I accept him into my home and heart? How can I do this?

The Bible says that even while we were yet sinners, God sent Christ to die for us, so that we might be acceptable in His sight and be welcomed back into His family from which sin had separated us. Since God, who was the offended party, willingly offered to take us back when we disobeyed Him and went our own ways, can you do any less?

In reaching out to your new son-in-law, you are demonstrating God's love toward him. Your goal ought to be at least twofold: You ought to want to win him to Christ (and your daughter, too, if she has never made that commitment), and you should do all you can to make sure that this marriage works. If you are cold and have an attitude of rejection, your daughter might blame you if the marriage does not work, causing severe damage to your relationship. Submit your anger, disappointment, and pride to God and ask Him to work His marvelous love and power in the lives of your daughter, your son-in-law, and yourself.

Sometimes our little boy refuses to say his prayers. What should we do?

Don't try to force your child to pray. Every night set aside fifteen minutes or half an hour before his bedtime for reading and conversation. Show your child pictures of Jesus, and tell him stories of the Savior. Talk to him of the heavenly Father. Explain to him that God sends the sun and the rain. Tell him it is God who makes the flowers grow, and gives us food.

Let your child hear you pray, using simple words he can understand. Say: "Thank You, God, for the good things You've given me." Do this for a few days. Then some evening when you've finished praying, ask, "Isn't there something you would like to thank God for?" If your child says only a few words, be content.

There is no better way to encourage a boy or girl to pray. Later you'll want to teach your child to ask God to forgive the mistakes he's made, and to pray for strength to do what is right. But don't be impatient, or try to force your little one. Let him hear you pray. Surround him with love. Tell him of Jesus and the heavenly Father. And soon he'll want to express his thoughts in prayer.

I have two grown-up sons. One of my daughters-in-law has a terribly jealous and possessive nature. She resents our son coming to visit us and scarcely ever allows us to see their child. This is a great grief to my husband and myself. What can we do?

You say that your daughter-in-law is jealous when your son visits you and that she does not want their child in your home. You don't say whether your daughter-in-law is invited on these visits. Make every effort to include your daughter-in-law in family gatherings. Invite her to lunch by herself and without your son. Ask her advice about things. Offer to come to their house to babysit so that they might enjoy a night out together. Look for ways to demonstrate unconditional love for your daughter-in-law and when she sees that it is genuine, her attitude toward you and the entire relationship is most likely to change.

I'd like to know what guidelines you would give for raising children. We are about to have our first child, and I think about it a lot when I see some of the problems other families seem to have.

I have honestly hesitated to answer your question in this brief column because there is so much that could be said about this complex topic! I am sure you will spend many years to come trying to find out more about being a parent— particularly because each child is different, and what works for one is not necessarily useful for another. But I am thankful you are concerned about this. God has given parents a great responsibility, and it demands our best with God's help.

But let me suggest three general guidelines that may help you to get started in your thinking. First, surround your child with love. I know that sounds simple, but it is easy to forget sometimes. For example, some parents in their zeal to have their child behave better will constantly criticize their child. A child who constantly is hammered with criticism grows up feeling he is not loved and also that he is not worth very much. Love your child—and don't be afraid to express that love, even when it is difficult or when he has done something that is wrong. Be quick to praise.

Then have clear guidelines about behavior and discipline. The other day I heard a leading psychiatrist say on national television that we need more discipline today, and I agree. We discipline not out of anger (or at least we shouldn't), but out of love, knowing that a child needs to learn he is responsible for his actions. Don't change the rules all the time either, or threaten punishment and then not carry it out.

Most of all, make it your priority to help your child spiritually. Pray with him, and pray for him consistently. Let him see that Christ matters in your life, and teach him about Christ in a way He can understand. We do all we can to protect our children from physical harm. In the same way, do all you can to help him spiritually so that some day he will come to his own commitment to Christ.

My husband left me and my small daughter several years ago. It is very hard being a single parent. Do you have any suggestions to help me?

There is no magic formula that will take away all the problems of being a single parent; in the best of situations, I am sure it is still often a difficult task. But think of it as a challenge you can meet with God's help, and I am thankful you have a desire to be the best parent you can be for your daughter.

First, realize that you can never do this job completely by yourself—you need God's help. He can give you wisdom as you look to Him and seek to do His will. But more than that, God wants you to make Him the foundation of your life. Does God have His rightful place in your life? His rightful place, because He created us and redeemed us in Christ, is at the center of our lives. So I pray that you will give your life to Christ, and that you will seek to teach your young daughter about God's love for her as well.

Let your life also be an example to your young daughter. Surround her with love, and do all you can to minimize the insecurity she may feel because of the lack of a father. A child must have a male role model. It may be a brother, an uncle, a grandfather, or a pastor who can help fill the vacuum left by an absent father.

Although I know you may be faced with heavy financial pressures, I hope you won't let those pressures preoccupy you and keep you from spending as much time as possible with your daughter. Christ can give you the joy and peace that will mean so much to her—as well as to you. Don't be overly protective, but establish reasonable rules and discipline in your home.

Then don't be afraid to ask for help from other people. If you are not active in a church I hope you will find one where Christ is preached, and one which has an active program. You may be surprised to find others there who have a similar background, and they can help you as you learn to live as a single parent.

*Maybe there isn't any answer to this, because I know they didn't have televi-
sion in Bible times, but do you think we ought to control what our children
watch on television? My husband says we shouldn't bother because they need
to know what the world is like anyway, but I am concerned about what the
violence and immorality they see on TV might do to them.*

Not long ago I read about some wells in our part of the country that were contaminated because of a nearby chemical waste dump, and you have probably
read similar stories. Now let me ask you a question: Would you allow your
children to drink water from such a well? Of course not, because you know it
could seriously harm them physically.

The same thing is true with our children's moral and spiritual health. Just as
they are affected physically by the things they eat, so they are affected morally
and spiritually by the things they see and hear—whether on television or elsewhere. Yes, they need to learn what the world is like—but they will learn that
soon enough anyway. I would strongly encourage you, therefore, to control what
your children watch and set forth some clearcut guidelines for their viewing
habits. That is not to say all television is a bad influence, any more than all
wells are poisoned, but you need to exercise discernment. The Bible says, "Listen, my son. . . . Hold on to instruction, do not let it go; guard it well, for it is
your life. Do not set foot on the path of the wicked or walk in the way of evil
men" (Proverbs 4:10, 13–14).

Beyond that, however, ask God to help you make your home a place where
Christ is honored. Your example of love and purity and commitment to Christ
will be the greatest influence on your children.

*I am worried about some of the attitudes and ideas my two grade school chil-
dren are picking up at school. For example, my daughter has one teacher who
is quite open about saying he has no religious beliefs, and that there is no such
thing as right and wrong. I don't want to get my children in trouble, but is
there anything I can do?*

This is a problem millions of parents face today, since public education in many
parts of our country has become secular and is sometimes even prejudiced
against those who have strong religious convictions. Even teachers who have
strong moral and spiritual convictions are often discouraged from voicing them,
and this is a tragedy which is doing incalculable harm to our nation.

What can you do? First, discuss your problem with other parents who would
share your concern. (Parents in your church would be a good place to begin.)
You may find out, for example, that parents in your area have already discovered ways of letting their voices be heard. Do not be afraid of speaking to the
principal of the school, either, particularly if this teacher is making fun of your

children's beliefs and the values they have been taught to respect. Don't be hostile or angry—that seldom does anything but get others angry—but ask God to help you and give you wisdom.

You may also wish to consider a Christian school or even home schooling, if possible. Both movements have grown rapidly in recent years and are producing the attitudes and values in children that the public schools often ignore or reject.

Then do all you can to teach your children what you know is right—both by your words and by your example to them. "These commandments that I give you today are to be upon your hearts. Impress them on your children. Talk about them when you sit at home and when you walk along the road, when you lie down and when you get up" (Deuteronomy 6:6–7). You also may need to tell them candidly that while they should respect their teacher, they also should realize he has ideas which are in conflict with God's Word.

I guess this isn't a spiritual problem or anything, but we are in turmoil because our daughter is marrying a man we honestly do not approve of. Their backgrounds are so different, and he seems to have little direction in life. My husband even thinks we ought to tell her we won't go to the wedding. I know we can't forbid her to marry him, but we don't know what to do.

I assume you have voiced your concerns to your daughter, and if she has chosen to ignore your advice, it is her responsibility and you can do little more. I would urge you, however, not to cut yourself off from her—which is what you would be doing if you refuse to go to the wedding. This would not only be embarrassing for her, but would almost certainly cause a deep split between you. It also is very unlikely that you would change her mind about her marriage by threatening to boycott the wedding. Five or ten or twenty years from now you will deeply regret the hurt you will have caused. The Bible says, "Live in harmony with one another. . . . If it is possible, as far as it depends on you, live at peace with everyone" (Romans 12:16, 18).

God is able to bring good out of what we think is wrong. Right now you see no hope for this marriage—but God can help them make it a successful marriage, if they will commit their lives to Christ and seek to follow Him. Let your daughter know that you are praying she will make the right decision and that she will seek God's will for her marriage.

I work in a home for elderly people, and it makes me angry to see the way the families of some of these people treat them. Some of these people never have anyone visit them or write them a letter. Don't you think this is wrong?

Yes, I certainly do. I sometimes wonder how people who neglect their parents will feel when they too are old, and find that their own children are following their example and have abandoned them.

The Bible gives special emphasis to the responsibilities of parents to children, and children to their parents. In fact, one of the Ten Commandments stressed this: "Honor your father and your mother, so that you may live long in the land the Lord your God is giving you" (Exodus 20:12). This implies that God will bless us when we honor our parents, and that when we fail to honor them His blessing will not be upon us. If we love our parents we will want to do what is best for them—and abandoning them to lives of intense loneliness is not an expression of love or honor.

I hope that your question will make many people stop and think about ways they can honor their parents right now, no matter how old they may be or how far removed they may be in distance. It is far too easy in our busy lives to plan to do something for our parents—even write them a letter or make a phone call— and then never get around to it. They probably did not treat us with such neglect when we were children, and now we should make it one of our priorities to help them and encourage them and express our love to them.

Also, I would like to point out that God has given you a unique opportunity. All around you each day are people who are lonely and discouraged. Encourage them and show them that you care. But more than that, if you know Christ you also have an opportunity to share His message of salvation with them. Let this be a challenge to you, to grow in your own spiritual commitment to Christ and then to share His love and grace with those you see every day.

We were shocked when our son came home from college for a brief visit and said that he had become religious. We have never been very religious but now I'm afraid he might have gotten involved in a cult or something. How can I find out if this is the case?

Don't automatically assume that your son has become involved in a cult (although that is always a possibility). I say that because there are many, many college students today who are turning to Jesus Christ and finding a genuine and living faith in Him. If your son has found Christ, you should rejoice in that because it is the most important decision he will ever make.

Since I do not know the details of your son's religious beliefs it is impossible for me to say if he has sincerely become a follower of Christ or if he has instead become involved in some cult. A pastor who is knowledgeable about such groups can help you.

Your son's experience—whatever its nature—understandably is a matter of concern to you. But I hope that it will also cause you to be concerned about something else which is also extremely important, and that is your own spiritual condition. So far God has meant little to you and your husband—but have you ever asked yourselves if God is real and if He should have a significant place in your lives?

Inside each of us there is a hunger for God. We may not recognize it, but each of us senses emptiness and a hunger for something. I suspect that your son has been looking for something to fill that spiritual void in his life, and if he has found Christ his spiritual emptiness has been met. Now it is your turn, and the greatest thing that could happen to your family would be for all of you to be united together in Christ as you turn in faith to Him.

I don't know what to do about my mother. She only lives a few miles from us, and she is constantly criticizing the way we are raising our children. She even does it in front of them. We don't want to hurt her but how can we handle this?

There is no easy solution to this, but for the sake of your family you probably will have to confront her directly with this and ask her to quit. If you do not, but instead let her continue, it will have a harmful effect on your children and your ability to guide them wisely as parents. Also, I suspect, it will keep you and your husband angry or anxious every time she comes to your house, and that is not good.

I know that you run the risk of hurting her, and you should do everything possible to let her know that you love her and respect her opinions. You should explain to her why you are concerned about this—not because you are stubborn and resent anyone telling you how to handle your family, but because it is causing unnecessary strain and also undermines your authority over your children.

It may be your mother has not adjusted to the fact that you are no longer "her little daughter," but are an adult who has her own family now. You need to be sensitive to her needs. But at the same time you also must be sensitive to the needs of your family. Let her know that you honor her as your parent, but that you are the parents of your children, not she. Also, let her know that if she has ideas that are helpful you want to listen to her and gain from her wisdom.

Pray for your mother. It may be that this is a difficult period of her life, and she needs your encouragement. More than that, show her by your example that Christ's love means much to you and you in turn have learned to love others for His sake.

We have a young child, and my mother-in-law is urging us to do something to teach our child about religion. I have always felt that we would just wait and let the child make his own decisions about religion when he grows up. Should we follow her advice?

Yes, you should. The Bible says, "Train a child in the way he should go, and when he is old he will not turn from it" (Proverbs 22:6). It also commands us to do all we can to help our children understand God's truth.

It is true, of course, that the time must come when a child makes his own decision for Christ. But that does not mean we should neglect to guide and instruct him. After all, you seek to protect your child from physical dangers, and you help him to understand (for example) why it is important to be careful when he crosses the street. You also feed him a balanced diet so he will grow physically. He does not know what is best for him at this age, and part of your responsibility is to help him and keep him from harm.

It is important to guard your child physically—but it also is very important to guard him spiritually as well. He is not just a physical or mental being—God has given him a spiritual nature as well. In fact, the most important decision he will ever make in his life will be whether or not he will trust Christ for his salvation and follow Him in his life. Now is the time to help him understand that God loves him and wants him to be His child.

Your question, however, suggests to me that you and your husband do not give much attention to God in your lives. What will you teach your child—not only by your words, but by your actions? If Christ means little to you, your child will probably grow up thinking Christ doesn't need to be very important in his life. But you need Christ. You need to make Him the foundation of your marriage and your family.

Will you please pray for our son? He burned himself out years ago on the drug LSD, and he still has flashbacks and is unable to work. What can we do for him?

First of all, I am deeply sorry for what has happened to your son, and I pray that some who read this will be alerted to the dangers of drug usage. Some people contend that taking drugs—such as marijuana, cocaine/crack, LSD, or any of the other well-known drugs—is a harmless habit that brings inner happiness. But that is not true.

What can you do for your son? (I assume you have done as much as possible to get him whatever medical help he needs.) The most important thing you can do is to pray for him. At first that may not sound like very much to you—but I put it first because it could be the most significant thing possible to bring encouragement and healing to your son. That does not mean that your son will be automatically restored to complete health once you pray. But God wants to help him and strengthen him, and you should pray that God will work in his life—not only to help him overcome the effects of his drug-taking, but to help him come to a personal faith and trust in Jesus Christ. Often a person becomes involved in drugs because he or she is searching for meaning and purpose in life. But God is the only One who can give us true meaning and inner peace.

Then do all you can to encourage your son and assure him of your love. I also hope you will be able to direct him to other Christian young people (perhaps in your church) who can encourage him. You may be surprised how many young people today have been involved in drugs and then have renounced them and turned to Jesus Christ. They can be a source of real strength to your son. They also can help him gain confidence in himself—something that needs to happen before he will feel able to handle a job. God loves your son, and you can take hope from that fact.

My husband and I just don't know what to do about our son, who is our only child. Since he got married and moved away he and his wife have almost nothing to do with us. They make it clear they don't want us to visit, and never write or call. We even have a new grandson we have never seen. I guess there isn't any answer, but what do you suggest we do?

Whatever his reasons, your son is wrong in cutting himself off so completely from you. Some day when his own children are grown and then follow his example of paying no attention to parents, he may realize just how wrong he has been.

For the present, do what you can—even if it seems useless or of little immediate value—to keep some contact with him. Even if he never writes, write to let him know of happenings in the family, and even call occasionally. Remember occasions like birthdays or other special times with cards or gifts, both for your son and for his wife and son. Don't use your letters or calls, however, as opportunities to complain about their treatment of you; this will only make the gap larger. If you need to apologize for things you have said or done in the past that may have aggravated the problem, don't hesitate to do so. The Bible says, "Do not repay anyone evil for evil. . . . If it is possible, *so far as it depends on you,* live at peace with everyone" (Romans 12:17–18, emphasis added).

Then pray for your son and his family. His desire to be independent of you may be a sign of his spiritual struggle—a struggle to be independent of God. But God can work in his heart to show him his need of Christ, and if he turns to Christ he also will realize his responsibility to show more love toward you.

Don't give up, although it may take time for things to change. As your grandson grows older he will realize that other children have a different and happy relationship with their grandparents and he may persuade his parents to establish closer contact with you.

My husband and I have just become parents of a baby girl. Until now we have never thought of religion, and we would appreciate your help on how to begin.

The first realization of responsibility often makes us realize how much we need divine assistance and guidance. Becoming parents makes you sense your responsibility to another soul. You must give her direction and instruction until she can make her own decisions. I would suggest that you first secure a Bible and begin systematic, thoughtful reading together. Begin with the Gospel of John. As you come to any particular Scripture that calls for a decision or action, accept it and act upon it. Questions of a critical nature can wait. As an example, when you read John 1:12, it says that "As many as received him, to them gave he the right to become children of God." Ask yourselves: "Have we received Christ, and do we have the right to become children of God?" Continue that way of life through a personal faith.

Above all, obey God's Word and always settle each question as you come to it. Problems you can't understand will soon have their solution as you progress in your prayerful search for the truth.

In the school where my children attend, there has been much dishonesty and even some immorality. I don't like to have my children associate with such people, but cannot afford to send them to a private school. Are there any steps I can take to protect my children?

There is a danger of protecting our children too much. That is, we can withdraw them from society as it is until they come to have a Pharisaic attitude. We must face the real situation. These dishonest and immoral children are a normal cross-section of humanity and your children will always have to live in contact with them. The wise course of action is to give your children the spiritual and moral training and example at home that will equip them for working and doing business with such people. They will be more likely to develop strong spiritual powers through opposition than through living in a situation where they never need to make decisions. The important thing is to give them the grounding they need in the Scriptures, let them see sin in its real light, and show them that with Christ as Savior and as their guide, they can face opposition and win. Their small victories will prepare them for the larger battles ahead.

Many modern child psychologists disapprove of spanking a child. What do you think?

You must begin by asking yourself a question. Why would you consider spanking your child? Some people spank only when they are angry and that is the wrong motivation. The purpose of spanking is to produce in the child a willingness to behave properly the next time he or she is tempted to misbehave. The child must grow to realize that there is more to fear than physical punishment from incorrect behavior. What you want your child to learn is that all of life consists of rules and regulations. Those who learn to submit to those rules will prosper in business, in home life and family relationships, and in their relationship with God. If that becomes your motivation for spanking, then when your child is an adult, the chances are good that your child will not depart from the way in which you have trained him.

Our home isn't the same since we bought a TV set. The children leave the table before they've finished eating. My husband cares more about the programs than about me. What can I do?

You didn't say how long you've had your TV set. If only for a few weeks, I'm sure it will not always have the drawing power it does now. But in the meantime, good manners and consideration for others must not be forgotten. The Bible says: "Better is a dry morsel, and quietness therewith, than a house full of sacrifices with strife" (Proverbs 17:1, KJV).

Sit down as a family and discuss not only the use of the TV, but rules you must follow to maintain an orderly, happy home. Let the children know what is expected of them. Don't indulge them today and then scold tomorrow. However, sometimes it may be wise to change the dinner hour to let the children see a good program. Talk this over as a family. Decide, with God's help, what is best for all. Then stick to it.

This will be easier if you begin the day with God. Family devotions are as important as breakfast. Read the Bible and pray together. Ask God for guidance, and He will show you how to use all the good things He has given you. TV, like the family car, can be a disrupting force; or it can bring the members of your family together as you share the best it has to offer.

My ten-year-old son wants to spend all of his spare time playing ball. How can I keep him from wasting his time?

It is possible that he is not wasting his time as much as you think. Young people need the recreation and stimulation to be found in wholesome games. They have much excess energy and playing ball is a good way to channel it into a wholesome activity. This does not mean that he should be permitted to neglect home duties. These should be assigned to him and he should be required to carry them out. But do not make his work a punishment—make it a share of the responsibilities in which all participate. Then let him understand that you want him to have a good time, and I know of no better way than playing ball. It might be a good thing for you to go along some afternoon and watch the game. It means much to our children if they find we are interested in their sports and in their friends. Learn about the game so you can appreciate the plays. This will give him a feeling of your interest and that in turn will make him happy to tell you about his other experiences and friendships. Above all else let your boy know that you love him and are interested in what he is doing. His spiritual welfare must come first and if you prove to him your understanding of his boyish interests you have a stronger bond to help him in spiritual matters.

I hear you speak of family devotions. Is a family altar really practical in this streamlined age?

Family devotions are not only practical, they are essential in the well-adjusted home. I list below seven reasons why I consider family worship important:

1. It unifies the homelife, and puts faith in the place of friction.
2. It brings to the family group a sense of God's presence.
3. It shows the children that God is relevant to everyday living, and not just a Being to be worshiped on Sunday.
4. It gives members of the family an opportunity for self-examination and confession of sin.
5. It strengthens the members of the household for the tasks and responsibilities they are to face during the day.
6. It insulates us against the hurts and misunderstandings which come our way.
7. It supplements the work of the church, and makes of our home a sanctuary where Christ is honored.

The Bible says: "And thou shalt teach them diligently unto thy children, and shalt talk of them when thou sittest in thine house . . ." (Deuteronomy 6:7, KJV). I cannot tell you *how* or *what* your family worship should be, I can only urge you to have a regular time together when you honor God.

My sister and her husband are wonderful Christians. They are kind and loving in the home, and yet one of their daughters completely rebels against the Bible, the church, etc. Why is this?

This is not at all unusual. In the Christian ethic, no one is forced to follow Christ. The Bible says: "Whosoever will, may come." Christianity is an involvement of the will and no one can be coerced into becoming a Christian.

I have observed a number of rebellious children from Christian homes, but this is usually just a stage in the child's development. It is often a sign of strong character in the child. Some children take things for granted, and others will not accept truth until they have examined it carefully. In the end, these types often make outstanding Christians.

We don't want our children to be rubber stamps of what we believe just to please us. We want their faith to be deep-rooted and strong. Don't be discouraged if there is a temporary revolt against Christ and His claims upon life. Some of the strongest Christians I know (including my wife) are people who were slow to accept the truth of Christ in their late teens.

I have been raised in an atmosphere where social drinking has been taken as a matter of course. My daughter is showing signs of becoming addicted to liquor. What is the Christian solution?

Your problem is being reflected in thousands of American homes today. The scourge of alcoholism and the hurt it causes to relatives, friends, and colleagues is growing. It is now being considered as a disease and the emphasis seems to be on teaching people how to drink in moderation. As I see it, under present conditions, there is but one safe and Christian solution—total abstinence. Liquor is not necessary either for health or for so-called gracious living. On the other hand, it is the cause of untold sorrow, suffering, and material loss, not to mention the spiritual implications of drinking.

In the Bible, in the Book of Proverbs, we read these words: "Wine is a mocker, strong drink is raging: and whosoever is deceived thereby is not wise" (20:1, KJV). These words were written nearly three thousand years ago but they describe the situation today. In America it seems to be a peculiar problem—Americans seem unusually lacking in judgment or restraint about liquor. One of our leading officials told me that the gravest danger to America centered in the cocktail lounges in Washington. Liquor loosens tongues and removes inhibitions and can do infinite harm. As to your daughter, ask God to help her and set out on a program immediately whereby you set an example. If you have alcohol in the home, get rid of it. Alcoholics Anonymous is an effective program. Above all, lead her to Christ who will give her the victory over her desire.

I am only a young person, but my faith in Jesus is very real. Neither my father nor mother are Christians, and they won't let me go to the church I like. They would rather have me stay home than go there. Sometimes I sneak out, but then it bothers me. Should I sneak out anyhow to hear God's Word preached?

Talk with the pastor of the church you have been attending and explain your problem to him. He will probably have heard it before. Yours is a common problem. Ask him to speak with your parents, who probably feel threatened by your new faith in Christ. Your parents may be under conviction because of their own sin, but the best witness you can be to them during this time of your life is to be loving, thoughtful, respectful and Christlike in your relationship with them. In doing so, you will be showing them (as well as telling them) about the value of a relationship with Christ. You should not neglect your Bible reading and prayer time. You ought to go to church, but you should not be "sneaky" about it. This is where your pastor comes in. He may be able to work out a compromise and, in the process, minister to your parents.

Our sixteen-year-old is rebellious and we are afraid he will become a problem to us. My husband and I both work. Can you recommend some place where we can send him so he will be properly managed?

There is no substitute for a home for a sixteen-year-old boy. Many of our finest young people are presently rebelling against neglect more than anything else. They need the sense of security that comes from a home where they are loved and wanted. They need the discipline of a well-ordered home to prepare them for social obligations as adults. It would be far better for you to adjust your scale of living to a smaller budget, and have the necessary time to give to your young son. In a short time he will be leaving home. Then you will forever regret that you did not give him the home training for which there is no good substitute. Teach him the basic principles of good character. Teach him eternal values. Help him to find his way to God as he observes your life and your walk with God. You have the solution to your problem within reach. Do not neglect it while you have opportunity. And remember there is no substitute for love.

I am concerned about some of the books my son is having to read in high school. I don't like the language or the philosophy they convey. Do you think I have a right to be concerned about this?

I know this is a common problem facing millions of parents today, and it also is an area of some controversy in the courts. However, if your children are in public schools they probably will confront this issue, and the first thing you should do is be able to talk candidly with your children about this—and listen to them as well.

Yes, you should be concerned about this, and perhaps there are ways in your community that you and other parents can express your concern to the school administration or school board. It especially concerns me that children today often can come away from school with a thorough knowledge of various secular and even anti-religious points of view—and yet cannot pray or read the Bible in the classroom or be taught in any measure the basic beliefs of Christians.

This means that you need to make a special effort to train your son so that he realizes the difference between the truth of God's Word, the Bible, and various philosophies that are being presented through his reading assignments. I am convinced we need to do more to instruct our children in God's standards of right and wrong. When the Law was given to the people of God in the Old Testament, they were commanded, "Love the Lord your God . . . these commandments that I give you today are to be upon your hearts. Impress them on your children. Talk about them when you sit at home and when you walk along the road, when you lie down and when you get up" (Deuteronomy 6:5–7).

Then realize too that God can use the experiences your son is facing to help him understand the way many people today think. If he is a Christian, he should be praying not only that he will not be affected in a wrong way, but that God will help him to reach out to his classmates who are searching for meaning in life.

I'm sure you must get many letters from people like us, but we don't know what to do. Our son has totally rebelled against everything he was taught, and is living a life that is not only wrong but will eventually destroy him, we are afraid. What can we do to help him?

There is no easy answer to this, because each situation is different and each person is different. That is one reason why you need to pray first of all for yourselves—that God will give you wisdom in dealing with this difficult situation. The Bible promises, "If any of you lacks wisdom, he should ask God, who gives generously to all without finding fault, and it will be given to him" (James 1:5).

That verse (and many others in the Bible) reminds us of a very important truth: God loves both you and your son, and God is deeply concerned also about your son's rebellion and its effects. God is "not wanting anyone to perish, but everyone to come to repentance" (2 Peter 3:9). Therefore pray for your son, because only God can convict him of his need to turn from his way of living and turn instead to Christ. I know that it may seem like a small and fruitless thing to pray, but "the prayer of a righteous man is powerful and effective" (James 5:16). Pray that he will see the destructive nature of what he is doing, and most of all pray that he will come to Christ for forgiveness and salvation.

Then take whatever steps you can to maintain contact with your son. You will especially need wisdom at this point. For example, your tendency may be to use the contact you have with him to let him know of your strong disapproval of what he is doing—and at this stage that might only alienate him and drive him further from you. At the same time, there may be times and ways you can use to help him see the outcome of what he is doing (perhaps by questions that lead him to see things for himself rather than giving him all the answers). But most of all let him know that you love him, in spite of what he is doing, and you want to welcome him back some day, just as the father welcomed the prodigal son (Luke 15).

I guess video games and other things like that are harmless, but our teenage son seems to spend almost all his time—and money—on them. So far we haven't said anything to him but I wonder if we are right to ignore this.

You have already answered at least part of your question by questioning whether your son's video game habit is really harmless; it may be more harmful than you realize. Not only is it taking a great deal of his time—which he could be putting to better use (including his homework)—but it is very possible that he also is not learning to develop personal relationships as he should with others. In addition, some psychologists have suggested certain young people may be influenced in a negative way by the violence that is part of many games.

No, you should not ignore this. Instead you need to talk frankly with your son, and then set down some guidelines about the amount of time and money he can spend on his interest. If you love your son, you want what is best for him; and he needs your loving guidance. It may be that you also need to talk with him about the whole subject of how he spends his time, and set down some guidelines about such things as his homework, what time he should be in at night, etc.

But more than this I hope you are encouraging your son spiritually. Your letter does not indicate if you and your family have committed your lives to Christ and are active in a church—but if you have never opened your heart to Christ you need to do so without delay. Your son needs to see that Christ is real to you, and that He can make a difference in his life as well.

Then pray for your son. Encourage him to put Christ first in his life also, and to get involved in a church or interdenominational Christian youth group. The teen years are often difficult, but they are also decisive and you need to do all you can, under God's guidance and wisdom, to help him discover God's will for his life.

My husband is a man of strong opinions, and it seems like every discussion with our teenaged son ends up in a shouting match. This is turning our son against us more and more, but I don't know what to do.

Being a good parent is certainly one of the hardest jobs any of us has to do in life, but unfortunately many of us never give much thought to the way we act as parents and what the long-term effects may be on our children. You and your husband face many decisions as parents and you need God's wisdom—especially during your children's difficult teenage years.

There is another job that is also very hard for many of us—especially those of us who are men—and that is admitting that we don't have all the answers and we sometimes can be wrong. From what you say, your husband sounds like he may need to stop and think through his role as a parent, and how he should relate to your son. The Bible says to parents, "Don't keep on scolding and nagging your children, making them angry and resentful. Rather, bring them up with the loving discipline the Lord himself approves, with suggestions and godly advice" (Ephesians 6:4, TLB). I realize it may not be easy for you to get him to face this, but you should make it a matter of continual prayer and discuss it with him.

What should you and your husband seek to be doing with your son? First of all, you should be seeking to point him to Christ. He should see that Christ is real to you, and that you take seriously your role as parents under God. If you have never actually opened your hearts to Christ and asked Him to rule your lives you need to do that right now. Then encourage your son to seek God's will for his life, and let him know that you love him and want what is best for him.

One reason the teenage years are often so difficult is that a child is seeking to become more independent, and sometimes we as parents resent this. A teenager, however, needs to learn responsibility, and he will never really learn it if we continue to try to make all his decisions for him. He needs guidance, but he also needs a greater amount of freedom, and we need God's wisdom in deciding the balance.

5

I Am a Teenager . . .

Did you ever get the feeling that nobody really cared for you or understood you? I am a teenager, and nobody seems to really understand what I'm going through—not even myself.

I am sure many young people your age go through the same feelings. But remember that every adult around you at one time was a teenager and went through the same problems you are facing. So don't feel that no one understands, even if they may find it difficult to communicate their love and concern to you.

There is one truth, however, which is even more important. In fact, it is the most important thing I could tell you. It is this: no matter how others may seem to misunderstand you or not care, God is not like them. God understands you perfectly—far better than you will ever understand yourself.

He also loves you with a love that is far deeper than anything you can imagine. How do I know that? I know it because God loved you so much that He was willing for His only Son, Jesus Christ, to come down from Heaven and die on the cross for our sins. "This is how God showed his love among us: He sent his one and only Son into the world that we might live through him" (1 John 4:9).

Have you ever realized that God loves you? And have you ever responded to that love? You are at a stage in life when you are making major decisions. But the most important decision you will ever make is this: Who will be Lord of your life? Will you decide to be your own ruler in life, running your own life without God? Or will you let God—who created you and keeps you every day—be Lord of your life and lead you according to His perfect plan?

Then I hope you will seek out the fellowship of other Christians. Get involved in a church where Christ is preached—preferably one that has a number of young people in it your own age. They can help you sort out some of your problems and help you grow spiritually. And they can encourage you so you know you are never alone because you are part of the family of God.

I am fourteen years old, and I have already run away from home several times. My parents have lots of problems, and sometimes I just want to get away. Please help me learn to do what is right.

First of all, I suspect you have already found out that running away from home does not really solve anything. It only creates another set of problems. And you may also have begun to realize that trying to live away from home at your age can be very dangerous, and get you involved in things that will harm you and change you for the worse.

I am sorry you are facing such an unhappy situation at home. I know it is a strain on you, and perhaps your question will help some parents realize what harmful impact their problems can have on their children.

The most important thing I can tell you right now is that God loves you, and He wants to help you in the midst of this situation. He created you, and He wants you to learn to turn to Him for the strength you need to do what is right. He also wants to help you to help your parents by praying for them and perhaps even encouraging them to deal with their problems in the right way.

Do you have a Bible? If so, begin reading in one of the Gospels (John is a good place to start). Notice how Jesus dealt with people, and what His attitude was toward others. Then realize that just as Jesus showed love to others, He also loves you. In fact (as you will discover), He loves you so much that He was willing to die on the cross so you could be forgiven of your sins and have eternal life. What He wants you to do is turn to Him and invite Him into your life as your personal Savior and Lord. Then He wants to help you each day.

Realize also that just as Jesus loved others—even when they were imperfect and hostile—so He wants you to love others, including your parents. Ask God to help you love them as you should. God loves you, and when you discover that great truth it will make all the difference.

I am a teenager, and I get very alarmed when I read the headlines every day about the future. It just looks like there isn't any hope for the future. Is there?

No one knows the future—except God. Yes, there are many dark clouds on the horizon of our world. Some people are even feeling that things are out of control and we are nearing the terrible times of which the Bible speaks toward the end of the world. Whether or not that is true, however, I want to point you to the only sure source of hope and strength as you face the future personally.

No matter what happens in our world, the most important thing you can do is trust God and commit your life to Him. God is ultimately in control of this world—although for a time Satanic powers have great strength. The Christian knows that there will never be perfect peace and happiness on this earth through human efforts alone. No political or economic solution will solve our problems completely. Why? The reason is that our basic problem is a spiritual problem—it is the problem of the human heart. The Bible says, "What causes fights and quarrels among you? Don't they come from your desires that battle within you?" (James 4:1). Only Christ can change the human heart—and He will, when we open our hearts and lives to Him as Savior and Lord.

The headlines each day warn you of the futility of man's efforts to solve his own problems apart from God. And they warn you as well that we need to trust Christ and commit our lives to Him. Have you ever turned your life over to Christ and committed your future to Him? If not, I urge you to do so right now.

Yes, there is hope for the future—hope in God. Some day Christ will come again, and all the sin and evil that infests our world will be taken completely away. That is our hope—and it can be yours as well as you turn to Christ.

I am eighteen years of age, am desperately in love, but my parents don't want me to get married because they say it is too early to know my own mind. They want me to finish my education, but I think love is greater than knowledge. What do you advise?

I have no doubt that you are in love, for love comes to the young as well as the mature. But I think your parents have a point and I think you should pray over this decision which can make or break your life.

The young person who takes a dim view of education is really curtailing his future earning power, and while I have heard of people saying they could live on love, I know of no documented record of anyone ever having done it.

What's wrong with going on to school and staying in love? True love can be a real stimulus to study and a moral balance wheel. After all, it has been the inspiration of some of our great literature, art, and music.

But you must remember that there are two kinds of love. First, there is physical magnetism which is the natural attraction of two people of the opposite sex. Then there is true love which has a spiritual basis. If your love is genuine, it can wait awhile. The Bible says: "Love suffereth long and is kind . . . seeketh not her own." Above all, make sure that you have the mind and will of Christ. Then your decision will be the proper one.

I'm in high school, and I'm afraid I've gotten in with the wrong crowd. I find myself doing lots of things (like drugs) that I never thought I would get involved in. I hate myself for this, but can't seem to get out of it. How can I get back on the right road?

I probably don't need to tell you that you are in a very serious situation, and it would be tragic if you were to ruin your whole life because of what you are doing right now. I pray that will not happen, and I am encouraged that you want to change. That is an important step.

No, you may find it impossible to break away from the life you are living in your own strength—but God wants to help you, if you will let Him. The Bible says, "I can do everything through him who gives me strength" (Philippians 4:13), and that is the key to changing your life—Christ, the One who gives you strength. That is why the first thing you need to do is honestly confess your sins to God, ask His forgiveness, and invite Jesus Christ to come into your heart by faith. You may not understand all the implications of that step of faith, but when Christ comes to dwell within you things will be different. The Bible promises, "If anyone is in Christ, he is a new creation; the old has gone, the new has come!" (2 Corinthians 5:17).

That doesn't mean, however, that suddenly all your temptations will disappear or that you don't need to take steps to fight against temptations. The opposite may be the result for a period of time, in fact, because Satan will do all he can to keep you from living for Christ.

That is why it is imperative for you to make a clean break with your past. If (as you suggest) there are friends who are dragging you down, you will need to find a new set of friends who will honestly help you. Look for other Christians your own age and find your new circle of friends among them. They will help you grow spiritually and become stronger in your faith, and they also will be able to help you when times of temptation come.

You are very important to God—He sent His Son to die for you. Give your life to Christ, and then look to Him each day for the strength and practical wisdom you need to live as you should.

I'm still a teenager, but I have gotten so mixed-up I'm afraid I've really messed up my life—an abortion, flunked out of school, can't get along with anyone, etc. I'd give anything to start all over again, but I don't think it's possible, do you?

Yes, I do believe it is possible for you to start all over again, and I sincerely hope and pray you will take the steps that are necessary. That does not mean it will be easy for you, but I want to assure you it is worth it. Your life is valuable—not only to you but to God—and it would be tragic for you to keep on the same road you are on because it will destroy you and keep you from true happiness.

The reason it is possible for you to start over again is that God can help you. I suspect you already know that you do not have the strength in yourself to change—but God can give it to you. He can give you a new purpose in life, and by His Holy Spirit He will come into your life and help you change your way of living.

Does this mean all your problems will vanish? No, not necessarily. But it does mean you will be headed in the right direction, and Christ will be with you. Each day you can turn to Him and commit that day into His hands. You can seek His guidance about what you should do.

At the same time, I believe there are several practical steps God would have you take. When you come to Christ, get into a church where Christ is preached, because you will need consistent Bible teaching and the fellowship of other Christians. Then take steps to get away from your old habits. The Bible says, "Submit yourselves, then, to God. Resist the devil, and he will flee from you. Come near to God and he will come near to you" (James 4:7–8). If at all possible, get back to school, also. But above all, let Christ's love surround you and change you, so that all you do the rest of your life is in response to His love for you.

I am in high school, and I think the thing that controls me most is my desire to be popular with other people. I have even stolen money to buy clothes and things so I will impress my friends. I know this is wrong, but how do I get out of this trap?

You are at the stage in your life when you are especially likely to be influenced by peer pressure (that is, the pressure to do things others your age do because you want to be accepted by them). But you need to learn to deal with these pressures because they can mold you into the wrong kind of person if you are not careful. In addition, as you have discovered, these "friends" can tempt you into doing things that are wrong.

Have you ever asked yourself why you are so concerned about popularity? I can think of several possible reasons, and maybe you can think of others. For example, right now you are changing in many ways—physically, emotionally, and mentally. This can be a little bit frightening, and you probably feel a need to be reassured that you are normal. You very much want to know that you are a useful person: a psychologist would say, I think, that you want to feel good about yourself and what you are. The approval of others can give you this assurance. In addition, like any normal person you don't like to be lonely.

The problem, of course, is that your desire to have the approval and friendship of others is causing you to do things that are wrong—and which really don't help you feel good about yourself either. My prayer for you is that you would turn your life over to Jesus Christ, because I know that He can help you deal with these things.

Then live each day for Christ. Turn from things you know are wrong, and seek His approval above all else. J. B. Phillips translates Romans 12:2 this way: "Don't let the world around you squeeze you into its own mold, but let God re-make you so that your whole attitude of mind is changed." Take your stand for Christ and seek to do His will, because that is the really important thing in life.

All my mother does is criticize me. She complains about my school work, my friends, my habits—everything. How can I get her off my back?

You are reaching a point in your life when you are naturally seeking to become more and more independent. This is not necessarily bad, because we each need to learn to make our own decisions as the years go by. But this time also can be a very difficult time for you because in your desire to become more and more independent, you can go to an extreme that is dangerous.

What am I suggesting? Simply this. Be on guard against an attitude or emotion in yourself that automatically resists or rejects anything your mother suggests to you, simply because she is your mother and you are trying to become more independent. It is not easy for someone in your position to listen to your parents' advice without getting upset sometimes—but constantly you need to be on guard against this and evaluate carefully what your mother (or father) might be saying. For example, I get letters every day from young people who have gotten involved with "the wrong crowd." This crowd seemed to offer them excitement and adventure, but ended up getting them involved in things that were wrong or harmful. So learn to weigh carefully what your mother says. She may have much to teach you, and because she loves you, she wants you to avoid those things that she knows will harm you.

At the same time, I know parents can sometimes be too critical and never praise a young person, not even realizing what they are doing. They love their teenagers and are anxious to see they make right decisions. Have you honestly—and without getting into a heated argument—discussed your feelings with your mother?

You face many decisions in life right now, and you need Christ to help you and guide you. My prayer is that you will turn your life over to Him.

We are really worried about our daughter. She seems obsessed with keeping her weight down, and even does things that are harmful to her body to lose weight. Please pray for her.

Yes, I will pray for her. You must seek medical (and, if necessary, psychological) help for your daughter. Hers is an increasingly common problem in our society which tells girls, especially, that they have value only if they are thin and beautiful. Many have died from eating too little, hoping to be accepted.

But this also can be a problem that has a spiritual dimension as well. There may be various reasons why someone like your daughter becomes obsessed with keeping her weight down. For example, some people feel no one can ever love them unless they are a certain way physically. They may even feel that they cannot like themselves or have any self-respect unless they conform to our society's idea of an attractive person. But our society often puts far too much emphasis on such things. Yes, we should take care of ourselves physically. After all, the Bible tells us we should take care of our bodies and we are to "honor God with your body" (1 Corinthians 6:20). Our goal should be to please God and honor Him, and not to spend all our time worrying about how other people will see or accept us.

There is something very liberating about realizing that God loves us just as we are. We don't have to wait until we are perfect in God's eyes apart from Christ. "But God demonstrates his own love for us in this: While we were still sinners, Christ died for us" (Romans 5:8).

This is why I hope you will urge your daughter to get the help she needs— and to give her life as well to Jesus Christ, who went to the cross to die for her sins and reconcile her to God. God in His mercy and grace accepts her just as she is and can help her become the person He wants her to be. Pray for your daughter, and pray that God will give you wisdom in dealing with her so she will see the harm she is doing to herself and seek instead to discover the joy of doing God's will every day and walking with Him.

I am a teenager, and I dream constantly about being a famous singer or actress so people will like me. Do you think daydreams like this are harmful?

It is good to think about the future—but in your case, I suspect there is a real danger that your daydreams may keep you from facing realistically the goals and plans you need to make for the future. In addition, you have responsibilities right now that you need to accept, and often daydreaming of this sort will make you neglect the duties you have right now in school and in your family.

There is another thing about your question which frankly concerns me, and that is the idea you seem to have that the most important thing in life is to be popular. Yes, we all want—and need—friends. But you need to be concentrating on ways you can build true friendships right now, not friendships that are based only on some superficial kind of popularity, but relationships where other people accept you for what you are. In addition, it is not good to always want to be the center of attention, or to think that that will really gain you true friends. Some of the most miserable people I have ever met have been people like you mention who are very popular with the public, but down inside are empty and miserable.

The most important thing you need to do right now is to set the right priorities for your life. What should your priorities be? First, you should seek God's will for your life above all else. God loves you, and He created you for a purpose. The greatest joy in life comes when you discover His purpose in life and then do it. Have you committed your life to Jesus Christ? Have you ever invited Him to come into your heart by faith and be your personal Savior and Lord? If not, I urge you to make that step of commitment right now. Then commit your future to Him and ask Him to show you His perfect will.

The Bible says, "The world and its desires pass away, but the man who does the will of God lives forever" (1 John 2:17). Make it your goal to love God and do His will. Then ask God to help you love other people.

My father has just remarried. The problem is that our stepmother treats my brother and me very differently from our own mother (who is divorced from my father and lives some distance from us). Sometimes I even feel like running away from home. How can I get along with her better?

First of all, nothing really would be solved by running away; you would only swap one set of problems for another—which would probably be worse and would definitely cause you much harm in the long run. But I believe with God's help you can work on this problem and things can be better.

You say that your stepmother treats you quite differently from your natural mother. But let me ask you a question: do you also treat her quite differently from your own mother? Rather than expressing any love or concern for her, do you instead constantly put her on the defensive or try to test how much you can get by with? Or are you constantly complaining or even comparing her openly with your natural mother? You see, you and your brother are probably not the only ones who are having a hard time adjusting to a new situation. Your stepmother also is undoubtedly still trying to find her place in the new family, and may feel quite insecure and uncertain in her new role. Sometimes the easiest thing to do in that kind of situation is to be stricter than might be the case otherwise, hoping to establish authority and control.

I want you to pray, therefore, that God will give you a genuine love for your stepmother. Pray also that He will help you express it as well, instead of bickering or trying to gain power. Most of all, pray that Christ will become the foundation of your family—and of your own life, if you have never trusted Him. The Bible says, "Let the peace of Christ rule in your hearts, since as members of one body you were called to peace" (Colossians 3:15).

Divorce brings many problems with it that are very difficult, which is one reason God's perfect plan for marriage does not include divorce. As you grow older pray that God will help you learn so that some day you will have a strong marriage built on Christ.

My husband and I are heartsick because our daughter—who is only seventeen— has just told us she is pregnant. We always thought her boyfriend was a nice young man and never suspected there could be any problem, but now he wants nothing to do with her. What sort of advice can we give her?

Unfortunately, this has become a very common problem today among teenagers. Perhaps your question will alert some parents to the need to talk honestly and clearly with their teenagers about the whole subject of morality and the need to resist the dangerous trend in our society that says premarital sex is not wrong.

This is a difficult time for her—as well as for you and your husband. She needs to know that you do not approve of what she has done, but that you still love her and want to help her. She needs your loving advice and wisdom right now. Claim God's promise that "If any of you lacks wisdom, he should ask God, who gives generously to all without finding fault, and it will be given to him" (James 1:5).

With all my heart I hope you will do all you can to help her resist the pressures she may feel to have an abortion. Some may try to persuade her that it is the easy way out, but it would be the wrong course of action. It would destroy that precious life within her, which would be wrong in God's eyes since that little life bears the image of God. In addition, every day I get letters from those who have had an abortion and now are riddled with guilt and depression over what they have done. There are countless childless families who want to adopt a child if it is not feasible for her to keep the baby after its birth.

God could use this experience in her life to make her realize her need of Christ—His forgiveness, His strength, and His direction. Pray for her, and pray also that God will give you and others natural opportunities to speak clearly to her about her need to commit her life to Christ as Savior and Lord.

We are a family of children whose mother recently died. Now Father is planning to remarry, and we don't believe we can ever get along with a stepmother. Can something be done to help us?

It is unfortunate that the word "stepmother" has fallen into disrepute. Some of the noblest women I know are stepmothers. In some ways the role of stepmother is much more difficult than being a mother. The love of her mate must be divided between many people, and she must do a tedious job of family "wire-walking."

You say that you know you can never get along with a stepmother. It is this preconceived sort of attitude that usually rules out any chances of happiness in a situation like yours.

I am deeply sympathetic with you children, for you have sustained a great loss. I suggest you think of the self-sacrifice of the woman who loves your father enough to share her love with his first wife's children, and who is willing to submerge her own identity, her own desires, and her own freedom in your family situation.

Would you try to tell parents that it is really hard to be a teenager? I don't think they understand what it means to feel like you are being tugged a dozen different ways at the same time, and it is really a confusing time for those of us who are in that stage of life.

Yes, I am sure parents—who were, after all, once teenagers themselves—can sometimes forget just what it was like during that stage of life. But I suspect also that there are often pressures on teenagers today that are more intense than those your parents experienced. For example, there are often enormous pressures on teenagers to experiment with drugs or sex. Parents need to understand these pressures, and do all they can to help their children resist them.

There are two things you especially need to keep before you. First, do all you can to keep the lines of communication open with your parents. They have experienced much in life, and you can profit from their wisdom. Don't just say "They wouldn't understand"—they might understand more than you think they do. But also you need to take time to listen to them and understand them. Communication is a two-way street.

Then I urge you to give your life to Jesus Christ if you have never done so. You need the strength that He gives to help you know what is right and to avoid what is wrong. You also need His guidance as you face the future. Remember: Even if no one else seems to understand, God knows you even better than you know yourself. Furthermore, He knows what is best for you because He made you and He loves you. "Remember your Creator in the days of your youth, before the days of trouble come" (Ecclesiastes 12:1).

Don't let yourself be tugged in directions that are wrong and will harm you. God has a perfect plan for your life, and the greatest joy in life comes from discovering His plan and doing it. Invite Christ into your heart by a simple prayer of faith, and then seek to walk with Him every day as you face the future.

Please pray for my little brother and me. Our parents have just told us they are getting a divorce, and I don't know what we will do. We even feel as if it somehow might be our fault. I am depressed and can't concentrate on my school work or anything, but mainly I just want them to get back together so we can be a family again.

One of the most tragic consequences of divorce is the effect it has on the children of the marriage. I am deeply sorry for the heartache you are experiencing right now. Perhaps your question will make some couple who is considering divorce stop and think about the consequences, and then work to rebuild their marriage with a stronger commitment to each other and to God—who gave marriage to us and intended it to be a life-long commitment.

First of all, it is natural for you and your brother to wonder if somehow you were the cause of this breakup—but you should not feel this way at all. The real problem, you see, is this: since your parents are telling you that they no longer love each other, you wonder if that also means they no longer love you. In the midst of a divorce action your parents may be preoccupied with their immediate problems, but that does not mean their love for you has faded.

Nothing that I can say will completely take away every hurt that you feel right now—but this could be an important time for you and your brother in another way. God loves you, and His love never changes. My prayer is that you and your brother will ask Jesus Christ to come into your lives, and that you will learn to trust Him every day. He understands your heartache and your fears about the future. "Cast all your anxiety on him because he cares for you" (1 Peter 5:7).

Then pray for your parents. It is a confusing time for them also, and the best thing that could happen to them would be to see that Christ makes a difference in your life and can make a difference in their lives as well if they will open their hearts to Him. And let them know that you love them both, and will continue to love them even in the midst of this tragedy.

Life in our small town is very dull. Any activity we get involved in is regarded as wild by the older people, and they say it isn't Christian. We kids get bored. Do you think that having a good time is wrong?

One of the reasons young people are bored is that there is not enough activity to consume their energy. If you are a normal young person, you want to give yourself to something and spend your energy on it. Many older people forget that they once were young, and that is why they fail to understand your desire for activity.

Plan some creative activity that will challenge the other young people. There are many wholesome games of competition that are enjoyable and clean. No, having a good time is not wrong. It is when we abuse and misuse what God has given us that it becomes evil. The Bible says that "God . . . richly provides us with everything for our enjoyment" (1 Timothy 6:17).

These gifts of God are for our use. To discern the true gifts of God, apply this standard to all activity: "Whatever is true, whatever is noble, whatever is right, whatever is pure, whatever is lovely, whatever is admirable . . ." (Philippians 4:8). These are the things the Christian should accept and enjoy to the glory of God.

How can I be a Christian and not be accused of being peculiar by the other kids in high school?

If you will keep the two things clearly separated you will find your problem so much easier. Being a Christian is the important thing and it involves a commitment of your life to Him as Savior and Lord. To be a true Christian means that we live by the ideals Christ would give us as the pattern for our lives. This means an attitude toward and a way of daily living that must be distinct from the world and those who do not know Christ. While some will think you "peculiar," do not let this disturb you, for just as many others will secretly admire you for your stand. But be sure that you do not assume a sanctimonious attitude toward others, or an attitude that you are better than they. Always remember that a Christian is only a sinner saved by grace and that we have no possible cause for boasting or pride. It is very possible that you will be persecuted by jokes and be misunderstood by some. If you accept this with patience and in a spirit of love, God can use this very thing to help you win some of your friends. Try at all times to show the joy and happiness in your life which a Christian should have. Actually, we are the only people in the world who have a right to be happy for we know where we are now, who is our Savior, and where we are going. Pray for your friends and love them. God will bless and use you to win them.

I have committed a horrible sin and I want to know if it means that I must go to hell. I am only fifteen years old but have committed adultery with a married man. Is it possible for God to forgive me when I really don't repent of my sins?

The reason that adultery is such a serious sin is that marriage is a picture of the relationship between God the Father, God the Son, and God the Holy Spirit. When we commit adultery, we are breaking our marital vow to "forsake all others until death do us part" and causing a rupture in a human relationship which God ordained. We also cause severe damage to many other people. Adultery, like all sin, is forgivable if placed at the cross of Christ. But you should know that even with forgiveness, the scars of this act may remain for a lifetime!

Many times adultery is condemned in the Bible, and this is the Christian standard. Under the law of Moses its punishment was death (Leviticus 20:10; Deuteronomy 22:22–24). As serious as this sin may be, God can forgive it. Read John 8:3–11, but do not forget that without repentance, there is no hope of forgiveness. Repentance will mean more than sorrow for sin. It will mean that with God's help you renounce it once and for all.

I was recently elected president of my class in high school. Many of the traditional activities I cannot take part in as a Christian. Do you think it wise for me to resign or continue in office?

You will have to make your own decisions all through life concerning doubtful practices. The office itself does not entail an activity of which you disapprove.

It does put you in a place where you can bear a most effective witness to Christ. You are never responsible for activities the rest call for, for you have chosen to preside and guide but not to require them to do certain things. As long as you are able, take a clear position without compromise; let the office be a vantage point from which to proclaim the gospel with tact and force. Jesus said that the apostles should be "wise as serpents and harmless as doves." Do your work well and gain the admiration and respect of your class, and they in turn will accept your Christian influence. As the "salt of the earth" we must go everywhere with the message of Christ.

My mother is always getting after me because of the music I listen to. I guess some of it is kind of loud, but all my other friends listen to it so I don't see why she should be so upset.

I always get a lot of mail whenever I attempt to answer a question like this, because young people and their parents often have strongly differing opinions about modern music! Nevertheless, there are several things you ought to keep in mind.

Why do you suppose your mother sometimes gets so disturbed about the music you prefer? Yes, some of it may be because your music is different than what she knew when she was your age (although I suspect the music she listened to as a teenager might have gotten on her mother's nerves also!). But there may be other reasons that you need to listen to carefully. For one thing, she may be concerned because you may be inconsiderate of others, and play your music too loud or at the wrong time of day. You need to learn to be sensitive to others, not only when you play your music but in every other area of your life as well. Courtesy is not old-fashioned—it is something which should be part of our lives every day. Jesus said, "In everything, do to others what you would have them do to you" (Matthew 7:12).

Your mother also may be concerned, however, because she senses that some popular music can have a harmful effect on its listeners. For example, the words of some songs today glamorize immorality or drug experiences, and some even speak of Satanic themes. These ideas can mold your thinking and turn your heart from God's truth, and you should avoid music which by its words or rhythm intentionally stimulates wrong thoughts or actions.

The writer of Proverbs had some words of wisdom for young people: "Listen, my son, to your father's instruction and do not forsake your mother's teaching. They will be a garland to grace your head and a chain to adorn your neck. . . . For the Lord gives wisdom, and from his mouth come knowledge and understanding. . . . he is a shield to those whose walk is blameless, for he guards the course of the just and protects the way of his faithful ones" (Proverbs 1:8–9; 2:6–8).

6

Can God Help Me in My Job?

I am a nurse, and I get very discouraged and depressed because of all the suffering I see. For the first time in my life I am beginning to think about God. Do you think He can help me in my job?

I can understand why you become discouraged and depressed as you deal with suffering and death each day. Frankly, if I were not a Christian I too would get depressed because there would seem to be little hope in the world.

There is much we may not fully understand about suffering and why God allows it. The Bible speaks of evil as a "mystery" (2 Thessalonians 2:7). But there are several important truths I want you to know about. First, God loves us and He understands what it is like when we suffer. How do I know this? I know it because Jesus Christ suffered and died on the cross. Christ is God, come in human flesh to win our salvation. And Christ knows what it is to suffer. In fact, He suffered far more than we could ever suffer, because He took upon Himself the punishment and burden of our sins.

Then I want you to know that death is not the end, but the beginning of a new dimension of life—eternal life. Yes, there is hope for life beyond the grave, because Christ made it possible. By His death He made it possible for us to go to Heaven if we will turn to Him in trust and faith. By His resurrection from the dead He demonstrated beyond doubt that there is life after death.

Christ also is able to strengthen you and help you every day. He wants you to become His child, and He wants you to be a blessing to other people, including those you work with every day.

I am deeply in love with a man who works where I do. He is quite a bit older than I am, and is married with several children. He claims that he loves me, but I am beginning to wonder because he is refusing to get a divorce. How can I tell if he really cares for me?

Let me be perfectly honest with you: your problem is that you are asking the wrong question. Instead of asking how you can find out if he loves you, you ought to be asking instead whether it is right of you even to be involved in this kind of relationship.

That leads me to this comment: it was wrong for you to get involved in this relationship and it is my sincere prayer that you will have the courage to break it off immediately. There are several reasons I say this. For one thing, it looks to me like this man is merely using you and does not really love you. I strongly suspect that if you were to marry him some day your marriage would be unstable and unhappy. (After all, if he is unfaithful to his present wife, what assurance would you have that he would not be unfaithful to you?)

But more than that, it would be morally wrong for you to continue that relationship and attempt to break up this man's family. The Bible tells us that God places a very high value on the marriage vow. God created the family, and "what God has joined together, let man not separate" (Matthew 19:6). The Bible also teaches that any sexual relationship outside of marriage is wrong.

Your letter suggests to me that you are searching—almost desperately searching, in fact—for love. But you are in serious danger of searching in the wrong place or the wrong ways for love, and ending up with only a cheap substitute which will never bring you happiness. How can you avoid this? First, by turning your life over to God, who loves you and wants to help you. Then, learn to walk each day with Him, committing every detail of your life into His hands, including your relationship with members of the opposite sex.

I have been unemployed for eight months and it's terrible to feel so useless. I have looked and looked, but there just aren't any jobs available. How can I deal with this?

Certainly one of the tragedies of our time (or any other time of economic distress) is the widespread unemployment in many nations. We should all pray for our world and its leaders, that they will have wisdom to find solutions to this distressing problem. God did not intend for us to be idle and unproductive, and there is dignity in work.

Let me suggest several things to help you right now. First, I hope you will not give in to despair and become depressed. Pray that God will help you use this time in the best possible way. The Bible tells us to "Be very careful, then, how you live—not as unwise but as wise, making the most of every opportunity, because the days are evil" (Ephesians 5:15–16). Yes, it may be hard for you to see it this way at first, but the time you have right now can be an opportunity, and you have a God-given responsibility to make the most of it as He wants you to do.

Let me suggest first of all that this could be a time of spiritual growth in your own life. Your letter does not indicate if you have ever given your life to Jesus Christ. If not, perhaps He has let this happen to you to show you your need of Him. Open your heart to Christ, and learn to walk with Him every day. If you know Christ, ask Him to help you grow through this experience. Spend time reading and studying the Bible, mediating on its meaning for your life. Spend time in prayer—not just for your own needs, but for the needs of others as well.

Then realize that you can use this time to help others on a volunteer basis. I don't know what opportunities there may be in your church and your community, but pray that God will lead you to ways you can help others. Often volunteer work leads to employment.

My biggest problem is the people I have to deal with at work. Some of them seem like they will do anything to get ahead—even if it means stepping on someone else. How should I react to these kinds of people?

It would be tempting for you to treat them exactly the same way they treat you and other people. The Bible says, "Do not repay anyone evil for evil. Be careful to do what is right in the eyes of everybody. . . . Do not take revenge, my friends, but leave room for God's wrath, for it is written: 'It is mine to avenge; I will repay,' says the Lord" (Romans 12:17, 19).

There are actually several principles indicated in these verses. First, the Bible teaches that those who selfishly step on others to get ahead will eventually find they have taken the wrong path. The reason is that any time we turn our back on God and do wrong, God will judge us for this action. Perhaps He will bring unhappiness to those who have done everything they could to be successful— only to find that once they were successful, their lives were empty and unhappy.

But another principle is that when we do good—even when others are doing wrong—God will bless us. That does not mean God will always bless us in material ways, although at times that is the case. (Your boss, for example, might be led to promote you because he saw you were a person of integrity who could be trusted.) But that is not always the case. God will bless you spiritually for your faithfulness.

If you know Christ and have committed your life to Him, let your life reflect His love for those around you. "Let your light shine before men, that they may see your good deeds and praise your Father in heaven" (Matthew 5:16). By your actions and your words you will be a witness to those you work with every day, and God will honor your witness for Him.

I just can't understand this person who works with me. She claims to be religious, but she has a bad reputation and even has shown up at work drunk once or twice. Frankly I get disgusted with her, although I guess I ought to try to help her.

Jesus said that "not everyone who calls me, 'Lord, Lord' will enter the kingdom of heaven." Many people think they are Christian because they were "born
into a Christian family" or had their names placed on a church cradle roll at
birth or have done good works or have not committed a crime. Your co-worker
may not be a Christian at all in which case you should lovingly seek to share
the gospel of Christ with her.

Your co-worker may, in fact, have received Christ at an early age and drifted
from close fellowship with Him in recent years. This could have led to her "bad
reputation" and drinking bouts.

My advice would be to try to get to know her better without judging her behavior. Find out first what she means when she says she is a Christian. Show
her what Jesus said in John 3, that unless a person is born again, he or she cannot enter the Kingdom of Heaven or be declared a Christian. Next, find out
whether she is having personal problems which have led to her drinking and
other activities which have contributed to her bad reputation.

Only after you have done these things and demonstrated your care and concern for her as a person will you be able to point her to Christ's forgiveness and
restoration. Most of all, pray for her and ask fellow Christians to do the same—
and for you that you might be used of God to help her transform her life.

*I am worried about my husband because he has lost his job and now he feels
like he is totally useless and will never find work again. He is becoming more
and more depressed, even though he is a very able person. How can I help
him?*

Losing a job can be a very traumatic experience. Often our self-esteem is tied
to our work and when someone like your husband is laid off or fired, it can have
a serious psychological effect.

In our culture, men and women often define themselves by the jobs they hold.
Often I have heard people introduced by their name, followed closely by their
job description. This usually happens when their work is in a field that is highly
visible or exciting.

But a person's job tells you nothing about a person's character or value. Let
your husband know that you consider him just as valuable, just as lovable, and
just as much a man as when he held his job.

I have known many people who have lost one job only to find that this was
God's way of redirecting their lives. You and your husband should ask God not
only for his continued provision for you, but also for His direction to another
job and, possibly, a new career.

This can be an important time for spiritual growth for both of you. Instead of
focusing on your own vulnerability, focus on God's ability and strength. If your
husband is not a Christian, this could be God's way of getting his attention and

humbling him that he might consider his need for salvation and for God's direction in his life.

I have recently been fired after several years on my job. The boss said I didn't get along with people like I should, but I think he just had it in for me. I am angry because it was so unfair. There just doesn't seem to be any justice in the world.

I do not know the full circumstances of your case and cannot make a judgment about the fairness of what has happened to you. But when something like this comes into our lives, there are two things especially that I believe God would have us do.

First, you need to examine yourself as honestly as you can to see if there is any basis for your boss's claim that you were not able to get along with people very well. This is not an easy thing to do, because often a person who has difficulty getting along with others tends to blame them for the problem instead of facing the truth about his own difficulties. None of us likes to admit we may have been at fault. I would encourage you to pray that God will help you see areas of your life that need improvement, including the way you get along with other people. If, for example, you always have the attitude that "I am right, and others ought to do things my way," you need to step back and realize that this can be offensive to others and that you need to learn to listen and be more flexible. The Bible says, "If it is possible, as far as it depends on you, live at peace with everyone" (Romans 12:18).

I also believe you need to be on guard against bitterness and anger. They will only destroy you. "See to it that . . . no bitter root grows up to cause trouble" (Hebrews 12:15). Even if you have been treated unfairly, don't let resentment turn you into a bitter person.

But most of all, use this as a time in your life when you re-examine your relationship with Jesus Christ. And don't forget to look for another job!

I am a fireman and have recently accepted Christ as my Savior. Some of my fellow firemen make fun of me, but others have congratulated me for taking a stand for Christ. What should I say to those who laugh at the reality of religion?

The first thing you must remember is that Jesus predicted we would be persecuted. He said that if they persecuted Him they would persecute us, too. They are really persecuting Christ in you, which is one of the proofs that Christ does, in fact, live in you.

Your example is Christ Himself. When He was ridiculed, He did not respond in kind. Neither should you. Your co-workers will be impressed that you do not respond as other men when mocked or challenged. They will soon wonder why you are different and you will have an opportunity to tell them with words what they have witnessed with their eyes.

As a fireman, you are called to rescue the helpless whose lives are in danger. This is a picture of what God has done for us. When we were lost and in danger of perishing in the fires of Hell, God sent His Son, Jesus Christ, to rescue us so that we would not have to face a fiery eternity. If someone in a burning home refuses your help, he will die. It is the same with God's offer of help. Perhaps this analogy will be useful to you as you make a stand for Christ in the fire station. Pray for Christ's patience under persecution and He will give it to you along with the power to witness to your co-workers.

Will God get me a job? I have been out of work for over a year, and before that I never worked much because jobs in my area demand more experience or training than I have. It gets very discouraging and I have almost given up trying to find anything, although I need to work.

One of the greatest truths of the Bible is that God is concerned about every area of our lives—including our jobs. He loves you, and He has a plan for you. That is why the Bible urges you to "Cast all your anxiety on him because he cares for you" (1 Peter 5:7).

The Bible tells us, "Trust in the Lord with all your heart and lean not on your own understanding; in all your ways acknowledge him, and he will make your paths straight" (Proverbs 3:5, 6). It may be, for example, that God wants you to get some new training; many communities offer a wide variety of opportunities for job retraining. Don't close the door on this possibility; these programs were designed for people in your situation. Federal and state governments and local colleges and universities have grant money and low-interest loans available for people who wish to improve their skills by taking classes for credit or for audit. You should consult your local, state or federal government education agency. Career counselors at your local college or university can help. Call them and ask for an appointment.

In the meantime I encourage you to make the best use of the time you have, and commit it to the Lord also. Perhaps you can help others who have special needs through one of the volunteer agencies in your community or through your church, for example. Let this be a time also when you draw closer to God through prayer and the study of the Bible, which is God's Word to us.

I am a Christian, a trained computer operator, and have a good job. My problem is that all day long I hear and talk about things that are either suggestive or downright vulgar. What should I do?

Make this a matter of definite prayer. God knows the situation and He loves all those people who are now indulging in vulgar talk. Tell Him you are willing to do whatever He leads you to do, then ask Him to show you what it is. It may be that God will give you the wisdom to talk to these people, not in a prudish way but by saying there are so many good and lovely things to talk about and by helping you to change the general habits of conversation in the office. Let those around you realize that their talk distresses you, but be sure you do this with both tact and patience. I know of instances where this very thing has transformed an entire office. Once it happened in a shop where one Christian man was used to change the entire atmosphere of the place. As a Christian, remember that you are both light and salt. Let your light shine and be sure that your life gives forth the savor of salt which is good. If you do this, your witness will certainly be blessed—to a few, or possibly to a large number. Consider also that God may not want you in this particular job. Trained computer operators should be able to find work.

I am a student nurse in a very large hospital. Most of the doctors treat all of us with respect and consideration but one of the most famous surgeons curses before us and makes vile jokes about the nurses working with him. I am a Christian and willing to take anything I should but this seems too much.

My advice would be for you to seek out the counsel of a senior nurse who is either a Christian or who shares your concern. Perhaps the two of you could then ask the doctor to discuss a matter of importance. Tell the doctor how much you respect him as a surgeon. Tell him you believe that in order to perform your task to the fullest and be of help to him, it is necessary for you to feel you have his respect as well. Tell him that as a professional, you know he would not knowingly say or do anything offensive to his support staff. Perhaps he is not aware of the injury he is causing you by cursing and making crude jokes about the nurses.

If he rejects your entreaty and continues cursing and making vile jokes, ask your nursing superior to intervene with the hospital administrator. While all Christians will suffer some persecution, there are regulations which protect people from this form of verbal harassment and the hospital ought to enforce them. Pray that your spirit in this will be a sweet one and that your ultimate goal might be to win this doctor to Christ.

I am interested in going into a small business for myself. If I do so, I will sometimes be involved in Sunday work. I would like to have your opinion on the use of Sunday for business purposes.

I wish it would be possible for all of us to reserve Sunday as the Lord's Day and as a true Christian Sabbath. This would give free opportunity for everyone to engage in Christian worship and activity. Nothing hinders the progress of the gospel in and through the church more than the increasing secular use of the Lord's day. If you can do so, you should reserve the one day in seven for unhampered worship and service for Him.

On the other hand, Christians are in constant danger of a legalistic attitude toward Sunday and toward other Christian observances. Jesus said that the sabbath was made for man, not man for the sabbath. We must not submit to a legalistic Christianity that is encumbered with commands and prohibitions. Our first and greatest commandment is to love God and to love our neighbor as ourselves. Therefore, you must make the final decision in this matter. You will ultimately be required to answer to God for the use you make of your money and of your time. Just remember, don't allow your proposed business ever to become an obstacle to your devotion and service to Christ.

I am a Christian and a worker in the church. I want my life to be an example for the Lord. I work as an accountant for a large business firm. Recently, I was approached by the owner of a large night club and gambling house to become their accountant. I would have the same work I now have with a greatly increased salary. Would you advise such a change?

The question is really whether you think Christ would feel comfortable in an environment where men and women are consuming alcoholic beverages, gambling away their money, and engaging in conversation that is often filled with the baser things of life. It is a relevant question for, as a Christian, Christ lives in you and you carry Him wherever you go. The Bible tells us to "come out from them and be separate" (2 Corinthians 6:17). While separation does not mean disengagement from the world, there are certain activities and places that God clearly wants us to avoid not only to protect ourselves from spiritual harm but so that the witness we have will not be tarnished. Suppose other Christians see you working in such an establishment? Won't it then be easier for them to rationalize doing something similar or even worse? If you are in need of a higher income, ask God to supply your needs according to His will for your life.

Can a Christian be a member of a labor organization? I have been advised not to join, but unless I do I will continue to be out of work.

The Bible does forbid our being unequally yoked together with unbelievers, but only where that yoke forces us to partake in their wickedness. A labor union as such is not evil. In fact, some have had definitely beneficial effects on the entire history of labor and industry.

Today, some unions have fallen into the hands of unprincipled and unscrupulous men who have brought disrepute on the entire organization. In unions, as in politics, this has happened because men with high standards and Christian convictions have withdrawn and turned the entire movement over to the forces of evil.

Now, at last, many good Christians are aware of their former errors and are taking places of responsibility in the world, not willing that wicked men should have the control. Take your place and accept responsibility, but never with the intent of compromise or participation in the evil practices. Commit yourself to Jesus Christ, and then go on to extend the gospel and Christian standards. Remember that Jesus said: "Ye are the salt of the earth," and also that "Ye are the light of the world." We cannot do our duty unless we invade the world for Christ.

I am a Christian businessman, but somehow I never prosper as many others do who are not Christians. In fact, God seems to overlook their wickedness and prosper them. This troubles me, though I don't intend to forsake my faith because of it. Is there any explanation that will put my mind at rest in the matter?

There have been others who have had the same dilemma. One who spoke with authority, David the Psalmist, was confronted with the problem and it troubled him for a long time. Not until he got a vision of the final judgment did he see the issue. What you are doing is looking at the matter without any perspective.

When David finally got the right point of view, he wrote it down for our help and said: "Behold, these are the ungodly, who prosper in the world; they increase in riches. Verily I have cleansed my heart in vain." In other words, he felt for a moment that righteousness did not pay. Then he said, "When I thought to know this, it was too painful for me; until I went into the Sanctuary of God; then understood I their end" (Psalm 73:12–13, 16–17, KJV).

God's standards of justice and economics are frequently at odds with our own. Jesus said, "In the world you will have tribulation. But be of good cheer, I have overcome the world." He was speaking to those who believe in Him.

Many of the wicked are receiving their wages now. Many Christians who may not be succeeding according to the world's standards now, will reap great rewards in Heaven if they remain faithful to Christ and "store up treasure in Heaven where moth and rust cannot corrupt and thieves cannot break through and steal."

While things may seem unfair now, ultimately God's economy and justice will prevail.

7

Do I Really
Need the Church?

I have a friend who laughs at religion, because he says it is only for weak people. He says if you are intelligent and mentally balanced you won't need to have a crutch like religion, because you will be able to make it through life on your own. How can I answer him?

In a sense, your friend is right. We are all weak in that we have all sinned and fallen short of the glory of God. None of us can get to Heaven on our own and that is why, even while we were yet weakened by sin, God sent His Son to die for us. Tell your friend that as long as we think we are strong our true weakness will never be revealed and, as a result, our greatest need for forgiveness of sin and a home in Heaven will never be met. Ask your friend whether he has ever tried to lift an object only to find out he was not strong enough to do it. Tell him that sin is such a weight (and thinking we have not sinned is part of that weight) that we can never lift it ourselves. Then pray for your friend and ask him how he came to believe as he does. Has he ever considered what God has to say or has he reached his conclusion without evidence? Then give him the names of some of the most famous men and women in history who have been Christians (beginning in the Bible and through modern times) and ask him if he thinks they are weak. Remember what the Lord said to Paul: "My power is made perfect in weakness" (2 Corinthians 12:9).

I wish you would urge churches to pay more attention to older people. There are several of us who are senior citizens in our church and no one seems to pay us any attention.

I think it would be good for you and others who are in your situation to talk frankly with your pastor about your concern. I suspect he is probably not aware of this, and would very much appreciate your honesty. As you talk with him, don't just complain because you feel that you are left out. Instead, tell him that you want to help in whatever ways you can so that the church can have a more effective ministry with older people.

Then it would be important for you to reach out to other older people in the church and see what you can do together to help each other and have fellowship with each other. In other words, don't just leave everything to the initiative of others—think about what you can do on your own as well. I suspect there are many people in your church who are lonely—and not just older people. Be sure you are friendly and reaching out to others.

Above all, remember that you have much to give your church, and it is unfortunate that those who are younger tend to forget this. Some of the greatest saints I have ever known were those who had walked with Christ for many, many years and were therefore a great inspiration to others. Do you show by your love and your cheerfulness that Christ is your Lord? If not, the first step you need to take is to recommit your life to Christ in a fresh way, asking Him to draw you nearer to God and make you more and more like Christ.

God bless you and make you a living example of Christlike living to others.

Not long ago two people came to our door to talk to us about their religious beliefs. They almost talked us into joining their church, but how can I know their beliefs are true?

There are several cults that specialize in this type of approach, and I think you should be very cautious about being convinced by what they say. (There are also, of course, churches in your community which may seek to make contact with people in this way, and whose beliefs are in line with the historic Christian faith.)

There is only one ultimate guideline for religious truth, and that is God's Word, the Bible. The problem, however, is that you may not know what the Bible teaches, and groups like this (if these people are from one of the cults with which I am familiar) often claim to believe the Bible and act as if they knew its teachings thoroughly.

Let me give you three key questions that will be helpful in determining whether the group is biblical or not. First, what do they think of the Bible? Very often non-Christian sects will claim to believe the Bible, but they also emphasize the writings of someone else as well, such as their founder. Or they may have their own translation of the Bible which they claim is more accurate—although it is not recognized by any other group or by recognized Bible scholars. The Bible, and the Bible alone, is God's Word, and no additional so-called Scripture is necessary to understand it or add to it. It is God's complete and final revelation of Himself to us.

Then, what do they think of Christ? This is ultimately the real issue both for them and for each one of us. Do they see Him as a great religious teacher only, or somehow divine but not fully God? The Bible stresses repeatedly that Jesus Christ is God Himself, come down from Heaven in human form. Our cry should be that of Thomas when he saw Christ after the resurrection: "My Lord and my God!" (John 20:28).

Finally, what do they teach about salvation? Salvation comes to us as a gift of God's grace through faith in Christ. It is never through Christ and anything else—it is Christ alone who saves us. And that is what you can discover for yourself.

Our church is a large one, and sometimes I just feel lost in the crowd. I'm very lonely, but sometimes no one even says hello to me after the service. Should I change churches?

I do not know your situation completely, but I would hope you do not change churches until you have tried several things that might very well overcome this problem you feel.

Yes, a large church can sometimes be intimidating or cold to someone when that person first comes into it. But did it ever occur to you that maybe there are people sitting next to you who are also waiting for someone to take the initiative? Thus you can make it a point to speak to others. And if your church has the custom of having the pastor stand at the door after the service, or at the front of the church, take the initiative to speak to him and let him know of your concern.

Also, I strongly suspect that this church has many, many activities in addition to the regular Sunday morning service, and you need to get involved in some of them. There probably is a Sunday school class, for instance, that is made up of people who have a similar background to yours in terms of age, etc. Often it is in this kind of situation that you really get to know people. Again, you may find there are people there who are also lonely and yet are afraid to reach out to others.

I hope, however, that the church you attend—whether this one or a new one—will be one where you can not only have friends but where you can grow spiritually. In church we come together with other believers to worship God, but we also come together to learn more about God and His Word.

We need the fellowship of other believers. That is why the Bible urges us, "Let us consider how we may spur one another on toward love and good deeds. Let us not give up meeting together as some are in the habit of doing, but let us encourage one another" (Hebrews 10:24–25).

I grew up in a church, but when I reached my teenage years I dropped out. Now that I am married and have a family I wonder if maybe I ought to give the church another try. What do you think?

You are probably realizing that you have many responsibilities you never had before, and now you sense your need for God's help. In addition, the other members of your family also need the help and guidance of God.

By all means I hope you will return to church. But more than that, I want you to realize that your real need is to come to know God personally—and you can know Him. In other words, there is nothing magical about going to church, if your church-going becomes merely a habit that you perform. The message of the church should be centered in Christ, and without Him your church-going can easily become a dull routine.

The Bible says that God loves you and created you, and the most important thing you can do in life is to come to Him and turn your life over to Him. He wants to forgive you of your sins, and He wants to make you part of His family. He wants to be part of your life every day—in fact, He wants to be the foundation of your life (and the lives of your family as well). You have a responsibility to your children, to help them know what is right and wrong, and most of all to teach them about God's love for them so they will want to seek His will for their lives.

How can you come to Christ? First, confess to God that you have left Him out of your life—although He has been taking care of you all these years. Then open your heart to Christ and invite Him to come into your life by faith.

Then seek to live each day for Christ. An important part of that is growing in your relationship to Christ by having fellowship with other believers and hearing His Word taught, which is why the church is important.

Recently a man in our church has been accused of some illegal or question-able actions in connection with a large business deal. People in our church feel that we should not have anything to do with him, while others feel we ought to try to help him in some way. What is your opinion?

I do not know all the facts, of course, but in general the Bible clearly stresses that we need to reach out to people who are in need. This man is hurting, I strongly suspect, and he needs the love and support of those who are his fellow believers. The Bible says, "Carry each other's burdens, and in this way you will fulfill the law of Christ" (Galatians 6:2).

Even if this individual has done something wrong—which has apparently not been proven at this point—you have a responsibility to help him see the seriousness of what he has done and encourage him to repent of it. In 1 Corinthians, Paul had to deal with a man who had committed an open, blatant sin—and who apparently felt no sorrow for it. Only then did Paul instruct the church to remove him from its fellowship. Later, when he repented, Paul urged that he be restored to fellowship at once (1 Corinthians 5:1–7; 2 Corinthians 2:5–10). The Bible commands, "Brothers, if someone is caught in a sin, you who are spiri-

tual should restore him gently. But watch yourself, or you also may be tempted"
(Galatians 6:1).

I cannot help but feel that there may be some in your church who are more
concerned about the public reputation of the church than they are about the
man who needs your love and support and wisdom. Certainly we should be
careful, so that outsiders have no legitimate reason for thinking we are not
concerned about purity of life. But Christ was known as a friend of sinners
(Matthew 11:19), because He went out of His way to demonstrate His love for
those who have sinned. We should be thankful for this, because we have all
sinned and we all need His grace.

I would hope that your church would not only seek what is right in this situation, but that it might cause each Christian in your fellowship to think more
deeply about the love Christ calls us to demonstrate to others. "All men will
know that you are my disciples if you love one another" (John 13:35).

*I feel like an oddball in our church, because I am almost the only single per-
son around. I don't feel like I have much in common with all of the married
couples my own age. What do you think I should do?*

First, you can accept your situation and work to improve it so that your church
begins to reach out to other singles, and you can take steps also to establish
firmer friendships with those in the church who are married. Or second, you
can seek out a church where you feel more comfortable because of its ministry
to singles.

I cannot tell you which choice is right for you; you certainly should make it
a matter of prayer and seek God's will about it. But look at each of these choices:
you could work to improve the situation in your church—and this is probably
the way you should go if at all possible. For one thing, you should talk frankly
with your pastor about your concern. You may be surprised to find that he is
very sympathetic to your feelings and will appreciate your willingness to mention the problem to him. He may in fact ask you for suggestions on ways the
church can help—so be prepared with some specific suggestions! Many churches
today are beginning to reach out to singles, and you actually may have an excellent opportunity to be used of God in your church to reach out to single people
who need Christ. In addition, he may be able to suggest ways in which you
can be of service in the church, and this is often an excellent way to establish
friendships.

It may be you will come to the conclusion you would be happier, and would
grow spiritually in a great way in a church which has others who are single.
But remember most of all that you need other Christians and you need to grow
in your relationship to Christ. Even if your present church is not ideal according to your wishes, ask God if He has a ministry for you there and if you can

grow spiritually there. "But grow in the grace and knowledge of our Lord and Savior Jesus Christ" (2 Peter 3:18).

There is a woman in our community who runs around openly with a married man. She is forty and he is thirty. On Sunday she goes to church and pretends to be the best one there. People are getting tired of the way she acts. Don't you think someone should talk to her?

The Bible prescribes a formula for dealing with the situation you describe. First, someone who is a member of the church should go to her and confront her in private with her sin. Then, if she does not repent, two or three others are to confront her in private. If she will still not repent, she is to be taken before the entire congregation and if she still refuses to repent, she is to be put out of the church.

The emphasis is on repentance, not judgment, except as a last resort—and even then God still cares about her redemption and restoration. I would be especially careful that you and your fellow church members do not exhibit a "holier than thou" attitude. This could be destructive to her and to you as well, for there but for God's grace go you and every other church member. Most of all, pray for this woman and the man she has been seeing (and his wife and family) that they might acknowledge their sin and be cleansed by the blood of Christ.

I have so often wondered if all the different denominations are pleasing to God. When Jesus left this world didn't He command that His apostles carry on His work? In John 17 He prayed that the disciples might be one. Has this prayer of Jesus been in vain?

Some time ago, one of the perceptive leaders of Latin America said to me: "I have been reading that there is a movement afoot in America to bring all Protestant churches into one great church." He went on to say: "I think there is something wholesome in people worshiping God according to the dictates of their own conscience. I hope the time will never come when everybody will be 'rubberstamped' into one ecclesiastical body."

In the first century, the church became divided over trivial differences. Paul and Barnabas were loyal friends and faithful co-laborers in Christ. But they had a dispute because Barnabas insisted on taking Mark with them. The Bible says: "The contention was so sharp, that they departed asunder one from the other." This has been going on throughout the centuries. Perhaps it is God's way of keeping the stream of Christianity from becoming polluted and stagnated.

We must remember that there is a difference between unity and union. I have found a great unity and spirit of Christian cooperation among the churches of the world. They believe, essentially, the same. Though they are not united in name, most of them are unified in spirit. We have seen this as many different denominations work side by side for the glory of God. No, I don't think Christ's prayer for unity was prayed in vain.

Why do you find such difference of opinion and such strong feelings on the part of some Christians about some matters of faith and church procedures?

The Christian faith is so great in its implications that it is difficult for man to see it all. It is something like a diamond with many facets and we see only a part of the diamond at one time. Another reason is that there are times when we magnify some particular point beyond its significance. There are things about the Christian faith which are essential; there are others which are important in varying degrees but which have no bearing on one's personal salvation.

Then too the frailty and perversities of human nature may cause us to interpret certain truths from a purely human viewpoint, thereby losing their spiritual significance. While your question is interesting, let me suggest that you will be wise to look, not at the differences in the church but at the things on which historic Christianity has always agreed; the deity of our Lord, His death for our sins, His resurrection, and His coming again among them. If we agree on the things about which the Bible is very clear, we can agree to disagree on many minor points.

Why do you always say that a new Christian should immediately unite with a church?

Why should a newborn baby have a home? It is as simple as that. A child can be born outside the home, and a person can become a Christian outside the church, but nurture and care is essential to the development of both. These can best be provided in the home in the case of the child, and in the church in the case of a Christian.

Only the church provides the nurture for spiritual growth. Here we are taught to grow in the Word, and here we have the help of other Christians when we are tempted to stumble. The church is a storehouse of spiritual food whereby the inner man is fed, nourished, and developed into maturity. If it fails, it is not fulfilling its purpose as a church.

Years ago someone in my church hurt me very much and I left. I haven't been back to church since. I know this is wrong, but don't you think it is possible to be a good Christian and not attend church?

You need to deal with the hurt you feel. No matter what the facts of the case, you need to forgive the person who hurt you. That is never an easy step to take when we feel someone has wronged us, but the Bible is clear: "Bear with each other and forgive whatever grievances you may have against one another. Forgive as the Lord forgave you" (Colossians 3:13).

The verse I have just quoted gives the key to forgiving others. It says you should forgive in the same way the Lord forgave you. How has Christ forgiven you? He forgave you totally and completely out of His grace and mercy. He did not forgive you half-way, nor did He forgive you because somehow you were able to earn His forgiveness. He forgave you because of His love for you, and in turn you are to forgive others—whether they deserve it or not in your eyes.

Then get back in church. You need the fellowship of other believers, and you need to take your stand publicly for Christ. You need the encouragement of other believers, and God does not want you to be a spiritual infant all your life. Take seriously what God has commanded for us: "Let us not give up meeting together, as some are in the habit of doing, but let us encourage one another" (Hebrews 10:25).

Not having been a Christian for long, I wonder if you can tell me how to choose a church? I don't want to get into one that does not preach the gospel faithfully.

As you say, I would select a church which preaches the gospel faithfully. However, sound theology, as fundamental as it is, is only the first step. I would also choose a church that endeavors to practice what it preaches, and translates its beliefs into everyday life. I would choose a church where there is a degree of love and acceptance toward other Christians. I would choose a church that opens its arms to everyone with a spiritual need, regardless of their social standing, and that has a concern for the social sins of the community. I would choose a church which has a missionary vision and spirit, one which is willing to cooperate in every worthwhile effort to bring Christ to the world. And last, I would choose a church that is worthy of my tithes and offerings, and where I could find opportunity to use my talents and capabilities for the glory of God.

Some time ago I made a pledge to the church for missions. I made it large, mainly to impress people, and now I can't pay it. What are the legal problems involved? Can I be made to pay or what should be my course of action?

I am quite confident that no church group, however spiritually dead, would attempt to force collection of such a promise. But you still must answer to God. Actually your promise was supposedly made to Him. What do you intend to do about it? I see only one course of action now. Either you must make a public statement of your false intentions when you made the pledge or ask for time to honor it. If you did this, you would have a clear conscience toward men, if not toward God. Then you should in repentance turn to God, asking forgiveness in Jesus' name, and He who forgives every sin will also forgive you.

My friends claim I am not a Christian because I do not attend church. Can one be just as religious and good if he is not a member of a church?

I suppose it could be said that going to church will not make one a Christian. But of this we are even more sure: refusing to fellowship with believers will not make you one either.

You could subscribe to the principles of the Rotary Club without being a Rotarian. But it seems to me that if you sincerely wanted to be a good Rotarian or a good Christian you would do well to fellowship with those who have kindred goals and motives.

The church is the family of believers. Christ died, not only for the individual but for the church. The Bible says: "He loved the church, and gave Himself for it." If Christ loved the church enough to die for it, we should love it enough to associate ourselves with it.

By joining a good spiritual church, we are letting the world know where our loyalties are. Even you admit that your friends say you are not a Christian because you do not belong to church. If we really believe in Christ, the least we can do is to identify ourselves with others who believe. In this way your faith is strengthened, and your witness is buttressed.

Our church is so well organized that there seems to be no place for the freshness of spontaneity, or individual expression. Sometimes I feel that I can't see Christ for the trimmings. Am I wrong in feeling this way?

No, I don't feel that you are wrong. I think perhaps you have a point. I'm sure your pastor would welcome any constructive suggestions you may have along this line.

Most ministers regret that their membership does not participate more actively in the life of the church, and I am sure your minister would be for any sanctified "spontaneity" you may bring to the life of the church.

I hope the day will never come when the church abandons the "class meeting" and the prayer service. In these services everyone who so desires should have an opportunity for expression. The old-fashioned "testimony" meeting should be revived, for through this medium we can share with others our faith and our triumphs as well as our needs and mistakes.

But this is important: although opportunities for expression may be limited within the church walls, there is plenty of opportunity to witness to your neighbors and friends to the saving power of Christ. In fact, it is much more effective to witness to those who need Christ, rather than to those who already know Him. More power to you! Be spontaneous and expressive in your Christian witness.

Our church is planning a building program that I think is beyond our financial ability. My friends are enthusiastic. Should I stand in opposition and still work in the church or should I leave as a matter of conscience?

As Christians we do not always find ourselves in total agreement in matters of policy. As long as there is no denial of the essentials of our faith, and as long as your friends do not cease to be your friends simply because you disagree, I would continue to work with them. There is no moral deviation here, but a matter of business judgment. We need to be able to disagree in love and still work together to bring men to Jesus Christ. State your objections and continue to work with them as friends and as brothers and sisters in Christ. Time will show who was right. You will have your friends and your church.

I was raised in a family with very strong church ties. Now I am married and living in a community where there are no congenial churches. Do you think that my husband and I should try to start a new church?

Most of the major denominations have basically the same Christian doctrines. It is true that some are much closer to their original beliefs than others and for that reason congregations and ministers differ greatly. I would suggest that you make a study of the basic beliefs of the churches in your community and then join the one you feel most closely resembles your ideal. Remember that there is no perfect church and no perfect congregation. It can well be that God is opening up for you a new opportunity to serve Him through a church which needs your witness and help. Remember, also, that we sometimes confuse our prejudices with our beliefs. In any case you should join a church where you find spiritual help and strength each week and where you can join in the program of the church in reaching out to the unchurched in your community. It is impossible for me to answer your question in more than broad generalities because there are many details I know nothing of and also because this is a personal problem and God alone can lead you to a final decision which is right. If you and your husband make this a matter of prayer and be sure to follow God's leading in the matter, you will make no mistake.

We have recently moved into a new community where there is no church of our denomination. There is a church here with which we can agree with few reservations. Should we drive a great distance to a church of our own denomination, or could we serve where we are? They have asked me to teach a Sunday school class.

I believe in denominational loyalty, but I also believe that Christians should witness where they live. Unless you show an interest and love for those in your community, people might suspect that you are religious snobs—which of course you are not.

You say that you agree with the doctrine of the local church with few reservations. I have found that nonessentials separate people more often than essentials. In reading the history of denominations, it is interesting to note that the great divisions have always resulted from somewhat minor differences. It is more important to maintain a church attitude in spite of the differences between us. Some people call that "compromise"—others see it as Christian charity.

I have made up my mind to fellowship with all those who love Jesus Christ with all their heart, and are seeking to win men to Him.

I have sometimes been criticized for doing this, but I would rather lose a few friends than the blessing and favor of my Lord. If you feel that you can be a blessing to these people who don't see quite eye to eye with you on every point, by all means serve where you will be the greatest blessing.

Some time ago I served as treasurer of our church. From time to time I took small sums of money, intending to repay it as soon as possible. Now another man has been elected to the office and I am ashamed to tell him what I did, but I must repay the amount to balance the record. Can you help me with a suggestion?

I would suggest that you take the pastor of the church into your confidence. Your problem is certainly one that has some spiritual implications, and you can probably be sure that he will not betray your confidence.

There is no question about what must be done. It is merely a matter of procedure, and it would be the proper policy to confide in your pastor. He should be the kind of person you need to include in such a problem. In fact, he has much at stake in every such problem. The Bible tells us that we should submit to those who have such responsibility: "They keep watch over you as men who must give an account. Obey them so that their work will be a joy, not a burden, for that would be of no advantage to you" (Hebrews 13:17).

I get tired of preachers always begging for money for their pet projects. Our pastor has been preaching about it a lot, and it seems like many of the preach-

ers I see on television take a lot of time to urge people to give money. What do you think of this?

While it is true that some ministers may seem to constantly plead for money, particularly on television, it is also true that many others do not. When Jesus told us that it is more blessed to give than to receive, He was making an important point. God does not need our money. He owns everything, including "our" money. What He wants to discover is where our central focus of worship lies. Is that focus on God or is it on our money? Some people use a preacher's request for funds as an excuse not to give because such persons really worship their bank account more than they do God. Make sure that is not your attitude.

The Bible indicates that God is more interested in our attitude when it comes to giving. We should give wisely, making sure that the recipient is a good steward of God's money. Ask for a financial statement so you can make sure that the money is being used for the intended purpose. Then talk with your pastor about your concerns. Jesus said, "Give, and it will be given to you. A good measure, pressed down, shaken together and running over, will be poured into your lap . . ." (Luke 6:38).

I hate to admit it but I find church and sermons boring. I try to pay attention, but it just doesn't work. I know I ought to go to church, but why bother if I am not getting anything out of it? Is there something wrong with me?

There may be several reasons for your problem—which unfortunately is shared by many people. But the gospel should never be dull, for it is the most exciting and relevant news we could ever receive. When we find it dull, it is a warning sign that something is going on inside us and we need to take action to correct it.

Some problems may be on a practical level. For example, many of us are so used to the fast pace of television that we find it hard to concentrate on a longer message, such as a sermon. To overcome this, let me urge you first of all to pray before each service, asking God to speak to you and keep you alert. Then be sure you get enough rest; some people work so hard at their weekend recreation that they have little energy left for the Lord's Day! In addition, take notes on your pastor's sermons, jotting down the main points. This will help you concentrate and also will help you remember the sermon's teaching during the week.

There may be a spiritual problem behind this also. If you are just going to church out of habit instead of from a personal commitment to Christ, it is not surprising you find church boring. Have you ever committed your life to Jesus Christ, deliberately and consciously turning your life over to Him and determining to follow Him as His disciple? The true child of God will have a hunger for worship and God's Word. "I will praise you with an upright heart as I learn your righteous laws" (Psalm 119:7).

I live in one of our large cities, and I have become very concerned because there are so many people in our city who don't even have enough food to eat. Do you think churches ought to do more about this project?

Yes, churches and individual Christians should certainly be concerned about this problem, and should be doing all they can to help alleviate it. Jesus stated that His true followers would be those who care for the hungry and others in need (see Matthew 25:31–46). The Bible also says, "Suppose a brother or sister is without clothes and daily food. If one of you says to him, 'Go, I wish you well; keep warm and well fed,' but does nothing about his physical needs, what good is it?" (James 2:15–16).

I would encourage you to find out more about programs in your community to help those who are hungry or homeless; you may discover many churches are already deeply involved in some of them. Recently I have been in several of our major cities and have visited a number of church-sponsored programs for feeding the hungry. In many of our crusades in recent years we have collected truckloads of food for the hungry.

If God leads you to become personally involved in a church-sponsored program to help those who are hungry in your community, pray that He will use you not only to meet the physical needs of people but to minister to their spiritual needs as well. Jesus fed the hungry, but He also declared, "I am the bread of life. He who comes to me will never go hungry" (John 6:35).

II
SPIRITUAL CONCERNS

8

I'm Afraid My
Life Is Ruined

I am afraid my life is ruined. I think I have herpes. Why would God punish me so much just for being sexually active?

Your doctor can advise you about the seriousness of your condition and exactly what you can expect in terms of its damage to your health.

Although God has allowed this to happen to you, I want you to realize that you are the one who is responsible, and not God. I believe venereal disease (and there are many forms of it, including other new strains that defy medical treatment) is one way God warns us about the seriousness of sexual license. Sex is not given to us by God for our own selfish pleasure or gratification. It was instead given to us by Him as a sign or symbol of the oneness that should characterize married love. Any sexual act outside marriage is wrong—not because God wants to destroy our happiness, but because He knows that sex only reaches its highest joys within marriage. Love without commitment is not true love. We defile one of God's greatest gifts when we treat sex as something casual. "Marriage should be honored by all, and the marriage bed kept pure, for God will judge the adulterer and all the sexually immoral" (Hebrews 13:4).

I am not in a position to advise you medically, of course, although at present there is no medical cure known for the venereal disease you mention, Herpes Simplex II. It is a disease that has swept our country, however, and I believe this is an indication of the widespread moral laxity we have seen in our country in recent years.

Therefore I urge you to turn to Christ. By a simple prayer of faith you can invite Him into your heart, and then each day you can learn the joy of walking with Him and seeking to do His will.

I have recently become fascinated with the subject of predicting the future, and have bought several books on fortune-telling. Do you think it is possible for someone to know what the future holds?

Only God knows the future, and you should not allow yourself to get involved in any scheme or teaching which claims to have accurate knowledge of the future. (I am not talking about projections which some social scientists or others might make based on present trends, but about those who claim to have supernatural abilities to predict the future precisely.) At best, such schemes are mere guesswork; at worst, they may be involved in dangerous occult practices. The Bible clearly warns against such things (e.g., Deuteronomy 18:9–13).

Have you asked yourself why you have become interested in this subject? I cannot help but feel you are searching for certainty about the future, and about your own life as well. Use your fascinations to find out what Christ has to say about the future.

The greatest discovery we can ever make in life is not some supposed "truth" about the future, but the joy of peace with God. God loves you, and He wants to come into your life and establish a personal relationship with you if you will but open your heart to Him.

Then learn to trust the future to Christ. We may not know everything God has in store for us, but when we know Christ we know that God is in ultimate control and we need not fear the future. "If God is for us, who can be against us? ... For I am convinced that neither death nor life, neither angels nor demons, neither the present nor the future ... will be able to separate us from the love of God that is in Christ Jesus our Lord" (Romans 8:31, 38–39).

I have just been through my sixth surgery in the last year, and all I seem to have ahead of me is more pain and sickness. I have always felt that God was good to us, but now I am beginning to wonder if God really cares. Why must I suffer?

There is no easy answer to the question of suffering and why some people seem to have especially heavy burdens of pain to bear. Some day—in Heaven—we will understand everything fully. "Now we see but a poor reflection; then we shall see face to face. Now I know in part; then I shall know fully, even as I am fully known" (1 Corinthians 13:12).

God cares because He knows what it is like to suffer. God came down on this earth in the person of His Son, Jesus Christ, and He suffered the horror of a cruel death on a cross. His death was even more terrible because He was perfect and did not deserve to die. The Bible says, "He was despised and rejected by men, a man of sorrows, and familiar with suffering" (Isaiah 53:3). His suffering was more intense than anything you and I could ever know, because the sins of the whole world were being placed on Him. He did this willingly, because He loves us and wanted to do everything possible to bring us forgiveness.

God is with you in the midst of your suffering. He has not abandoned you, because "God has said, 'Never will I leave you; never will I forsake you'"

(Hebrews 13:5). Do you remember Job in the Old Testament? It seemed that virtually everything that could go wrong did go wrong for him. He lost his children, his possessions, and his health. And yet he knew that God could be trusted even in the midst of his circumstances.

Perhaps God can use you in another life—one who is suffering. Turn your eyes away from your situation, and by faith turn to Christ. Open your heart to Him, and thank Him that He loved you enough to die on the cross for you. Then you will join the countless millions throughout the ages who have discovered that "You will even be able to thank God in the midst of pain and distress because you are privileged to share the lot of those who are living in the light" (Colossians 1:11–12, Phillips Translation).

How can I believe God loves me when He destroyed our entire crop?

When a ship's carpenter needed timber to make a mat for a sailing vessel he did not cut it in the valley, but up on the mountainside where the trees had been buffeted by the winds. These trees, he knew, were the strongest of all. Hardship is not our choice, but if we face it bravely it can toughen the fiber of our souls.

Even if you can't understand why your crop was destroyed you can still trust God. From disaster He can bring victory. A fire sweeps over a hillside, burning the pines like matchsticks; but God has planted spruce seeds there, and in the sunlight they push up, making a new forest. A tornado destroys a community. Then men and women arise to meet the challenge, building a more beautiful city. History has proved that God can build upon the ruins. But He needs the hands of consecrated men and women. Christ did not promise His followers ease or comfort. He said again and again: "Take up the cross and follow me."

This experience could be your steppingstone to finding Christ as your Lord and Savior. That could be why it happened. When I was in Korea following the war there a young GI who had lost both eyes said to me: "I'm glad I came to Korea, because losing my eyesight brought me to Christ!" He had found Christ better than eyesight!

I have been trying to be a Christian, but I'm not having much success. I will do well for a while, then suddenly I will give in to temptation and be right back where I started. Do you have any secret on how I can be a better Christian?

Be clear about what a Christian really is—and then be sure you are one. What is a Christian? Many people think a Christian is a person who lives a moral life and tries to follow the Ten Commandments and the moral teachings of Jesus. Certainly a Christian will want to live like this—but simply trying to live a good life does not make a person a Christian. Instead, the Bible says a Christian is a person who has committed his life to Jesus Christ, and is trusting Him alone (and not his good deeds) for salvation. Have you realized you are a sinner and cannot save yourself by your own good deeds? Have you realized that Christ died on the cross for you, and He offers you His salvation as a free gift, if you will only receive it? If you have never opened your heart and invited Jesus Christ to come into your life, do so today.

Then be clear on what God has given you to grow spiritually. Just as God has given us food so we can grow physically, so He has given us spiritual "food" so we can be strengthened spiritually. What is that "food"? First, it is the Bible, which is His Word. Are you spending time reading and thinking about His Word? He also has given us prayer, and fellowship with other Christians. Make use of these each day, and He will strengthen you spiritually.

Can God forgive an unwed mother?

Not only can God forgive an unwed mother, He can also forgive an unwed father as well as married and single persons, whether they are parents or not. But His forgiveness does not come cheaply. It cost Him the life of His Son, Jesus Christ. The wonderful news is that God's forgiveness is available to all who ask for it. But you must ask.

God does not forgive everyone automatically. That would devalue the sacrifice of Christ on the cross for your sins and mine. Before asking for God's forgiveness there is something important you must do. You must repent, that is, turn from the behavior and lifestyle which led you to become an unwed mother. Then God will forgive you and give you the strength you need for you and your child to face the future with Him.

I have a brother who has some brain damage because he got involved in some heavy drugs. I know you believe that Jesus Christ came to take away the consequences of sins that we commit. Do you think if he invited Christ into his life that God would take away that damage?

First of all, the Bible does not promise that all of the consequences of sins we have committed in the past will automatically vanish. Sin is a terrible and destructive thing, and sometimes we have to pay the consequences for our foolishness and our refusal to obey God. King David in the Bible sinned greatly when he committed adultery with another man's wife. God forgave him when he truly repented and asked God for forgiveness—but the child born of that illicit union still died as an act of God's judgment on David.

I therefore do not want to hold out a false hope to your brother, promising that if he invites Christ into his life all of the results of his drug habit will definitely vanish. At the same time, I know that God "is able to do immeasurably more than all we ask or imagine, according to his power" (Ephesians 3:20). There are times when God works in ways that are beyond our human understanding to bring healing and restoration, although none of us can predict when this will be the case. This much is certain: your brother needs Christ.

Your brother needs forgiveness for what he has done, and he needs strength that Christ can give him every day. He needs hope for the future. God has graciously spared him, and God can use him if he opens his life to Christ.

Encourage your brother to come to Christ. It is the most important decision any of us will ever make. What has happened to your brother is tragic, but God wants to help him and make him His child through faith in Christ.

I know God is mad at me because of the way I have been living. How can I get Him back on my side? My life is on a deadend road unless I change, I know, but how can I win God's approval when I have so many bad things against me?

Suppose you owed someone a very large sum of money. What could you do? One possibility would be to pay them back. But what if you did not have the money, and had no prospect of ever getting it? Then your only possibilities would be to undergo bankruptcy and suffer the loss of everything you had, or else to go to him and ask to have the debt forgiven. But in human experience that kind of forgiveness is very rare.

But that is what God offers you—free and full forgiveness for your sins! You see, you cannot "buy" God's favor, nor can you somehow do enough good deeds to balance off your bad deeds. Why? Because God is holy, and even one sin is an offense to Him. "Your eyes are too pure to look on evil; you cannot tolerate wrong" (Habakkuk 1:13). No, the only hope is if God will forgive you. But is that possible? Yes! It is possible because Jesus Christ, the righteous Son of God, took upon Himself the punishment you and I deserved for our sins. "God made him who had no sin to be sin for us, so that in him we might become the righteousness of God" (2 Corinthians 5:21).

Don't turn your back on God's forgiveness any longer. Instead, realize that your only hope is in Christ and open your heart to Him by faith. "For the wages of sin is death, but the gift of God is eternal life in Christ Jesus our Lord" (Romans 6:23). How can you receive Christ? Simply tell Him that you know you are a sinner, and you need His forgiveness. Then turn from your old way of living and with God's help begin to follow Christ every day.

God is on your side. God is not mad at you, but at your sin. You don't need to win God's approval. Christ did that on the cross.

I am the mother of one illegitimate child and am expecting the second one. Recently I was converted. When can I begin the new life and how can I leave the old life behind with two children born in sin?

When a group of pharisees brought a woman to Jesus who had been taken in the act of adultery, Jesus asked them to cast a stone at her, whoever was without sin (John 8:1–11, KJV). When it appeared that there was no sinless one to cast the first stone, they departed. Then Jesus said to the woman, "Neither do I condemn thee: go and sin no more." Repentance and faith are genuine and valid when the sinner enters a new way of life. There may be the reminders of the past with you, but you can have this assurance that there is no sin that cannot be forgiven to those who desire the new life that comes about through our faith in Jesus Christ. Begin by being the best mother you know how to be, praying for your children and bringing them up in the knowledge of Christ. The time will come when they will recognize the transformation wrought in your life.

Would it be wrong for me to pray that God would take my life? I am tired of living, because no one cares for me, including God. My ex-husband abused me mentally and physically for years, and I feel worthless and useless. I yearn to be happy, but I know now it will never happen.

Yes, it would be wrong for you to ask God to take your life—because He wants to help you discover there can be happiness and joy in life for you, if you will turn to Him.

You have been painfully scarred emotionally by your past, and God knows that and understands your feelings. Those experiences have taught you to believe that you are worthless and no one cares—but they have not told you the truth! In spite of what has happened to you, God loves you and you are very important in His eyes. Although elsewhere in your letter you indicate you have never given much thought to God, you have never been far from His thoughts, and He has a plan for your life. God says in His Word, "'For I know the plans I have for you,' declares the Lord, 'plans to prosper you and not to harm you, plans to give you hope and a future. Then you will call upon me and come and pray to me, and I will listen to you. You will seek me and find me when you seek me with all your heart'" (Jeremiah 29:11–13).

By faith accept God's love by inviting Jesus Christ to come into your life. You can do this by a simple prayer, telling God you know you need Him and that you want to turn your life over to Him. You might also consider getting into a support group for abused women. Then take time each day to read the Bible to discover how much God loves you. "This is love: not that we loved God, but that he loved us and sent his Son as an atoning sacrifice for our sins" (1 John 4:10). Knowing God cares will make all the difference.

I feel so lonely that sometimes I just want to end it all. I yearn to have close friends—I am in high school—but it is impossible. You see, my parents are divorced and my mother is an alcoholic, and friends would just laugh at me if I took them home. Would God forgive me if I just ended my life?

My heart goes out to you, and I know you have been carrying a heavy burden. However, I urge you as strongly as possible not to be tempted by the thought of suicide. There are people who care for you and want to help you, and your situation—although it is not easy—is not impossible. With God's help you cannot only come through this but you can become a strong and joyful person.

God understands your situation, and He understands your feelings as well. Perhaps the most important thing I can tell you is that God loves you, and He wants to come into your heart and help you. The Bible promises, "Cast your cares on the Lord and he will sustain you; he will never let the righteous fall" (Psalm 55:22). You see, Jesus Christ came into this world to take away our sins and to restore us to God. As we commit our lives to Him, God accepts us and adopts us into His family, and He becomes our daily companion and friend. Ask Christ to come into your life today by a simple prayer of faith.

Then I would encourage you to step out and make friends. Find a church which has an active program for young people; there may also be a Christian group like Campus Life or Young Life in your school. There you will not only meet people who will be genuine friends, but you will find spiritual encouragement. Share your burden also with an adult, such as a church youth leader. With Christ there is hope for the future.

I am old and virtually alone now. I have a number of relatives, but they don't pay any attention to me because we never got along. Pray for me, because I am unhappy and the future is not very hopeful either.

Loneliness is certainly one of the most common and serious problems in our society, and yet God made us with the plan that we would find happiness in our relationships. Yes, I will pray for you, and I encourage you to be praying also for yourself.

One thing you should be praying for is wisdom about ways you can overcome your loneliness. For example, your letter does not say why you never got along with your family. Can you honestly say it was all their fault? Or did you contribute to these problems by stubbornly insisting on your own way when you should have been more willing to adjust to others? Has an unforgiving spirit on your part kept those splits alive? Pray that God will help you face those questions honestly, and then deal with them by seeking His forgiveness and the forgiveness of any you have hurt across the years. Even if your forgiveness does not heal the split, you still need to get rid of any bitterness or resentment you have in your heart. "Be kind and compassionate to one another, forgiving each other, just as in Christ God forgave you" (Ephesians 4:32).

Then do what you can to reach out to others around you. Don't let self-pity paralyze you, but realize there are probably people all around you who are also lonely and yearn for someone who will be a friend to them and care for them. Most of all, realize that Christ is with you if you have committed your life to Him, and you are never alone or without hope when you know Christ.

I believe I am a Christian, but I always seem to be faced with strong temptation. Is there any way to overcome such temptation?

God never promised to remove temptation from us for even Christ was subject to it. The Bible says that He was tempted in all points like we are, yet without sin (Hebrews 4:15). There is really no good reason why you should seek to escape, for such times of testing have beneficial effects: "Tribulation worketh patience; and patience experience; and experience hope; and hope maketh not ashamed. . . ." There is a sense of achievement and assurance that results from victory over temptation that cannot come to us otherwise. Temptation really shows others what kind of people we are. It does not make us Christian or un-Christian. It does make the Christian stronger and cause him to discover resources of power. It also makes evident the false profession and hypocrisy of the non-Christian. You can benefit from what might be tragedy if you will only discover that in just such a time of temptation, Christ can become more real to you than ever, and His salvation will become more meaningful.

I thought I was off drugs but I'm not. I went through a rehabilitation program, but two weeks after my release I am back in the same old habits. I think I could have made it if I hadn't gone back to my old friends, who have dragged me down. Please warn people about this, because I know my habits are going to destroy me.

One reason I have reprinted your letter is that it might serve as a warning to someone who is facing a similar situation. Peer pressure—the pressure from one's "friends" to act the way they want you to act—can be very strong and harmful. The Bible warns, "Do not set foot on the path of the wicked or walk in the way of evil men. Avoid it, do not travel on it; turn from it and go on your way. For they cannot sleep till they do evil; they are robbed of slumber till they make someone fall" (Proverbs 4:14–16).

But don't give up or assume there is no hope for you. Yes, you have fallen—but with God's help you can get back on the right path and get free of the drugs and other habits that threaten to destroy you. I do not promise that it will be easy, but God wants to help you, and He will if you will let Him.

What must you do? First, admit that you cannot lick this problem by yourself, and ask Christ to come into your life to help you. God loves you, and Christ died on the cross to take away your sins. He also rose from the dead and sends His Holy Spirit to live within us so we can receive His power. Then make a clear and definite break with the past, including your "friends" who are dragging you down. Seek a fellowship of Christians where you can find new friends who will encourage you and help you spiritually. Some of them, you may find, have been through the same struggles you are facing.

I am facing surgery next week and I am scared to death. The doctor suspects there might be cancer. I have hardly been sick a day in my life, but suddenly I am faced with the possibility of losing my health. Can you give me any words of encouragement?

Death is something every one of us must face sooner or later. It is frightening.

Have you ever thanked God for the years of good health He has given you? Perhaps you have taken good health for granted, but it has been a gift from God. Perhaps you have even taken God for granted, or thought very little about Him and the place He should have in your life. But just as He has been with you in the past, so He is with you now as you face this situation.

Let this be a time, therefore, when you discover God's love and nearness. Let this also be a time when you realize—perhaps for the first time—that life for every one of us is short, and the most important thing you can do is to prepare for eternity. The Bible reminds us, "There is a time for everything, and a season for every activity under heaven: a time to be born and a time to die . . . God does it, so men will revere him" (Ecclesiastes 3:1–2, 14). The Bible also promises, "Because of the Lord's great love we are not consumed, for his compassions never fail. They are new every morning; great is your faithfulness" (Lamentations 3:22–23).

Give your life to Jesus Christ. He died on the cross for you, and He offers you forgiveness and eternal life if you will trust Him as your personal Lord and Savior. No, you do not know what the immediate future holds (nor do any of us, no matter how healthy we seem to be). But when you have committed your life to Christ, you know He is with you every moment of the day. Don't let another day go by without turning your life over to Him.

I don't have any problem feeling close to God when things are going smoothly in my life, but when things get rough then God seems far away. Is this a common problem?

Yes, it is a common problem—in fact I am sure almost every believer has experienced it. But God does not change just because circumstances change, and we need to learn to trust Him in every situation.

Do you remember the incident of Jesus' life when He had stayed behind to pray while His disciples went on in a boat across the Sea of Galilee? During their journey a storm arose and they were very afraid. Suddenly Jesus came to them, miraculously walking on the water toward their boat. Then we read that Peter, in a burst of faith and in obedience to Jesus' command, "got down out of the boat and walked on the water to Jesus. But when he saw the wind, he was afraid and, beginning to sink, cried out, 'Lord, save me!'" (Matthew 13:29–30). Peter was all right as long as he kept his eyes on Christ, but when he turned away and concentrated on the storm then he was in trouble.

We are often like Peter. As long as things are smooth in life we have no trouble, but when the storms come we take our eyes off God and become filled with doubts and fears. But notice that Peter knew what to do when he had failed— he turned back to Christ and began to trust Him again.

You need Christ every day, and in every circumstance. And He can be trusted no matter what happens. He is God, and He knows what is best for us in every situation. Like a child who turns to his father when he is afraid, so we need to turn to Christ when we have times of need.

God can be trusted—and that is the basic issue. If you can trust Christ for your eternal salvation, can't you also trust Him in the midst of life's problems? Of course you can! "If God is for us, who can be against us? He who did not spare his own Son, but gave him up for us all—how will he not also, along with him, graciously give us all things?" (Romans 8:31–32). Trust God and the promise of His Word, because He is worthy of your trust.

I just feel like I am a total failure. My husband has left me (and my three children) for another woman. I just don't feel like there is anything left for me and sometimes I even think I ought to end it all.

I know you feel that there is little hope for the future, but this is not true. Don't let your emotions mislead you into doing something that would be so final. Certainly if you were to decide to "end it all" you would have chosen the wrong path, and my prayer is that you will find in God the strength you need to bring you through this experience. Think of your children! How tragic it would be for them to have neither a father nor a mother.

It is important for you to be honest in dealing with your feelings of failure. You feel rejected right now, and you feel that somehow there must have been something wrong with you to have caused your husband to abandon you. But your husband is the one who has to bear responsibility for what he has done, and that has nothing to do with your value. I know that you may be thinking of things you wish you could have done differently during your marriage. Learn from those experiences—but don't believe that they make you worthless. God says you are valuable. You are valuable to your children, and you are valuable to God. God loves you, and the proof of your value to Him is that He was willing to send His only Son into the world to die on the cross for you.

Then you need to begin to look to the future and not concentrate on the past. I know that may not be easy, and you may even shrink from it because you feel the future is bleak. But listen! You are not alone as you face the future—God is with you. God has a plan for your life, and the greatest thing you can do is discover His plan and commit yourself to Christ. The Bible says, "You have made known to me the path of life; you will fill me with joy in your presence, with eternal pleasures at your right hand" (Psalm 16:11). Begin afresh by committing your life to Christ and He will help your life each day with the joy of His presence.

I wish I had time and space to tell you all the harm that has been done in my family because of one relative who seems to spend her time gossiping about other family members—and usually without knowing the full facts. Does the Bible condemn gossiping?

Yes, the Bible has some strong things to say against gossiping. The Old Testament commands, "Do not go about spreading slander among your people" (Leviticus 19:16). Among the sinful actions condemned in the New Testament are hatred, discord, dissensions, and factions (Galatians 5:19–20)—all of which are a result of malicious gossip. Those who seek to follow Christ are commanded instead to "rid yourselves of all malice and all deceit, hypocrisy, envy, and slander of every kind" (1 Peter 2:1). Among the seven sins which are said to be "detestable" to God are "a lying tongue . . . a false witness who pours out lies and a man who stirs up dissension among brothers" (Proverbs 6:16–19).

Gossiping is certainly one of the most common sins—so common, in fact, that most people do not take it as seriously as they should and instead tolerate it in their lives. But you have put your finger on one of the reasons gossiping is wrong: it destroys relationships between people. "Consider what a great forest is set on fire by a small spark. The tongue also is a fire, a world of evil among the parts of the body. It corrupts the whole person, sets the whole course of his life on fire, and is itself set on fire by hell" (James 3:5–6).

The practical problem you face, however, is how to deal with this relative of yours. Pray for her. This is a spiritual problem most of all, and she needs to yield her whole life—including her tongue and her thoughts—to Jesus Christ as Lord. Then pray that God will give you both wisdom and an opportunity to confront her—lovingly but firmly—with the facts about her gossiping and the damage she is doing. She may not even be aware of how serious a matter this really is. This will not be easy, but in the long run it is far better to do this than allow her to continue to destroy the reputation of others. You may actually find that she will appreciate your honesty and your concern for her, and will—with God's help—come to grips with this problem.

Many years ago I did a very foolish thing. I left my first husband and married another man who was much older than I. I hurt an awful lot of people, and now that I am elderly I am very, very lonely, with no one who really cares about me. I wish you would warn young people about the cost of doing foolish things like this.

I am sorry that you have had to learn through experience that when you break God's laws you end up instead being broken by them. You are—as you know—paying the bitter price for your foolishness and disobedience. My prayer is that your testimony will perhaps touch someone who right now is being tempted to take a similar path. As the Bible says, "Sin pays its servants: the wage is death" (Romans 6:23, Phillips Translation). There is a terrible price to be paid for following the temptations of Satan, both in this life and in eternity.

But I want to say something else very important to you. It is not possible to go back and change the past; what is done is done. But has it ever occurred to you that God still loves you, in spite of what you have done? You may feel that God is just like all the people you have hurt, and that He really could not care for you or love you because of what you have done. But that is not true! You have committed many sins—but every one of those sins was placed on the back of Jesus when He died on the cross. He endured the loneliness of the cross so that you could be forgiven of your sins and reconciled to God. Wouldn't it be wonderful to be able to look yourself in the mirror each day and know that you are completely forgiven, and you are a child of God? Wouldn't it be wonderful as you approach the end of your life, to know that you have the hope of eternal life in Heaven because of what Jesus Christ has done for you?

It is not too late to open your heart to Jesus Christ, and my prayer is that you will make that commitment today. Christ died for sinners—including you. Accept Jesus' invitation: "Come to me, all you who are weary and burdened, and . . . you will find rest for your souls" (Matthew 11:28–29).

I have a friend who used to be very active in church, but now she has turned her back on that and says she doesn't believe in anything. She is a very miserable person and I would like to help her, but she gets very agitated whenever I begin to bring up the subject. How can I help her?

I firmly believe that your friend knows in her heart what she has done and she is trying with all her might to flee from God. But she cannot flee from Him. The Bible says, "Whither shall I go from thy spirit? or whither shall I flee from thy presence? If I ascend up into heaven, thou art there: if I make my bed in hell, behold, thou art there" (Psalm 139:7–8, KJV).

Furthermore, I am encouraged by the fact that she is miserable—because that shows she is under conviction by God and is sensitive to Him, even though she is trying to flee from Him. The person who is in the most serious spiritual condition is the person who has become totally insensitive to God and can no longer hear the voice of God calling him back to repentance and faith.

You can help your friend first of all by praying for her. She needs to realize in a new way that God loves her, and although she has sinned by deliberately turning her back on God, He wants to forgive her and welcome her into His family. You should also pray that God will help you talk with her in a loving and gentle way that does not make her defensive or angry. She needs to know that you really care for her, and that you want to help her. She needs to sense in your life something of the peace and joy that Christ gives to those who follow Him.

I cannot help but feel that your friend also may have substituted religious activity—like going to church—for a sincere and genuine personal commitment to Jesus Christ. Without a personal commitment to Christ, being active in church can become empty and meaningless. Your personal example of faith and trust in Christ may be the most important way you can help your friend turn to God.

9

I Feel So Empty Inside

I don't understand myself. I have everything I ever thought I wanted, but down inside I am just existing. I am bored with life and feel empty inside. What is wrong with me? How do I get out of this feeling?

We not only have a body and a mind but we have a spiritual side to us as well, because God created us with a soul. Most people spend their lives feeding their bodies and their minds—and yet starve their souls. When they do, their lives are incomplete and empty, no matter how prosperous they may be outwardly.

But what does your soul yearn for? It yearns for God—and only God can satisfy that inner longing. You see, God created us originally so we could have a personal relationship with Him. But when we leave Him out of our lives, there is a blank space in our hearts that will not go away, because only He can fill it. As St. Augustine said centuries ago, "You have made us for Yourself, O God, and our hearts are restless until they find their rest in You."

Not only do we need God, but God actually wants us to come to know Him. He wants to enter our lives and fill them, and He wants us to know the joy of His presence. That is why Christ came into the world. "For Christ died for sins once for all, the righteous for the unrighteous, to bring you to God" (1 Peter 3:18).

What must you do? First, turn to God and confess your sins to Him—including your sin of leaving Him out of your life. Then ask Christ to come into your heart by faith. He has promised, "I stand at the door (of your heart) and knock. If anyone hears my voice and opens the door, I will go in and eat with him, and he with me" (Revelation 3:20). You can know God's presence right now if you will open your heart to Christ.

Last year I was going through a painful divorce. This man in my office was going through the same experience, and naturally we were drawn to each other. Well, one thing led to another and he asked me to move in with him, promising we would get married when the divorces were finalized. But now he only laughs at the idea of getting married, saying he isn't ready. Now I realize I made a mistake, but I don't know how to get out of it. I don't know where to turn.

We live at a time when divorce no longer has the social stigma it once had. It used to be that no one could be elected president if he had been divorced. That is no longer true. Regardless of what our society thinks of divorce, God's opinion has not changed. God says He "hates" divorce.

It is understandable that you would be lonely and wish to reach out to someone else for comfort and assurance that you are a valuable person. But just as it was not God's intention for you or this other man to be divorced, you should also realize that your decision to live with him merely compounded an already serious situation. This man's lack of commitment to his wife has led him to think that he need not be committed to anyone. In your own pain you are now finding that the happiness you sought has eluded you. It is because you have been searching for it in the wrong place.

The Bible is very clear about how we should live. It says "Flee from sexual immorality" (1 Corinthians 6:18). But God does not want you to keep on living this way, without any secure foundation in life. He loves you and He wants you to get on the right road in life—which is His way of living. The Bible warns, "There is a way that seems right to a man, but in the end it leads to death" (Proverbs 14:12).

Now is the time for you to face your need of Christ and turn to Him for forgiveness and new life. By faith ask Him to come into your life as your Lord and Savior. Then with His help turn from sin—including this relationship. It may not be easy, but God will bless you if you will put Him first.

How do you deal with a person who says their church is the only one which is right, and if you do not belong to it you cannot get to Heaven? I have a friend at work like this, and it has made things difficult because she is constantly trying to get others to come to her church (although it is a small group that I think may even be a cult).

The Bible teaches there is only one thing that saves us and gives us eternal life, and that is our relationship to Jesus Christ. We are not saved by our church membership (important as that is to our spiritual growth), nor are we saved by our own good deeds or religious actions. Only Christ can save us, as we turn to Him in faith and trust Him as our Lord and Savior. The Bible says, "Salvation is found in no one else, for there is no other name under heaven given to men by which we must be saved" (Acts 4:12).

Pray for your friend. Down inside she has a deep insecurity and a spiritual hunger for God—a hunger that cannot be satisfied in a lasting way by church activity alone. Then ask God to give you opportunities to talk with her about

Christ and encourage her to read the New Testament on her own. (Many cults claim to believe the Bible, but in fact they distort its clear message and discourage people from reading it on their own.)

Most important, be sure of your own relationship with Christ. Are you trusting Him for your salvation, and have you committed your life (and your eternal salvation) into His hands? If you are unsure of your own relationship to God, turn to Christ in faith and trust without delay. "For God so loved the world that he gave his one and only Son, that whoever believes in him shall not perish but have eternal life" (John 3:16).

Is there any difference between pride in one's accomplishments and personal pride, such as one's appearance? According to the Bible it seems to be sin; but without pride there seems to be no reason for careful grooming, good housekeeping, etc.

Nowhere in the Bible do I read that God puts a premium on slovenliness. However, the Bible places the emphasis on spiritual slovenliness, rather than physical. It is possible for a person to be impeccable in his attire and person, and yet be slovenly in his morals and conduct. On the other hand, a person of modest means may not be put on the "best-dressed" list but his or her character can be irreproachable. God says, ". . . man looketh on the outward appearance, but the Lord looketh on the heart" (1 Samuel 16:7, KJV). But at the same time, I believe that a neat, clean, well-groomed Christian is more impressive than a slovenly one. It would be poor policy to keep the inside of our houses immaculately clean, but let tin cans and garbage accumulate in the yard. By the same token, if Christ has cleansed our hearts, the least that we can do to keep our bodies, which are the temples of the Spirit, clean, neat, and presentable.

I do want to do right but sometimes I am too weak to overcome temptation. What hope is there for me?

You are exactly where all of the rest of us are. None of us is strong enough to overcome temptations, regardless of how good our motives may be. That is the reason God sent His Son into the World—to take away the guilt and penalty of our sins and to give us the strength to overcome temptation. May I suggest that your trouble is probably too much looking inside at self and not enough looking outward and upward to Christ who wants to help you? The Bible says: "There hath no temptation taken you but such as is common to man; but God is faithful, who will not suffer you to be tempted above that ye are able; but will with the temptation also make a way of escape, that ye may be able to bear it" (1 Corinthians 10:13, KJV). When temptations come let me suggest that you ask God for strength and also to show you the way He has prepared for your escape.

One other word of counsel: be very sure that you do not deliberately place yourself in a position to be tempted. All of us are not subjected to the same weaknesses and temptations. To one, alcohol may be the temptation; to another it may be impure thoughts and acts; to another greed and covetousness; to another criticism and an unloving attitude. Regardless of what it may be, be sure that Satan will tempt you at your weak point, not the strong. Our Lord has given us an example of how to overcome the devil's temptations. When He was tempted in the wilderness He defeated Satan every time by the use of Scripture. The psalmist tells us how to do this when he says: "Thy word have I hid in mine heart, that I might not sin against thee" (Psalm 119:11, kjv).

A few months ago I think I became a Christian. I'm not really sure though, because the decision didn't solve any of my problems. In fact, I have had more trouble since then. Isn't Christianity supposed to solve problems for you?

The Bible does not promise that God will get us out of trouble or solve all of our problems. What it does promise is that God will give us the power to overcome our problems and will sustain us in our troubles. In 2 Corinthians 12:9 God says to Paul, "My grace is sufficient for thee, for my strength is made perfect in weakness."

Faith in Jesus Christ solves the problem of sin. This is really man's greatest problem, and from sin come all the other problems. Salvation is not like aspirin, dulling the nerves to feeling. Salvation goes to the root of the problem and makes a new person out of you. "God made him who had no sin to be sin for us so that in him we might become the righteousness of God" (2 Corinthians 5:21).

I'm crippled with arthritis and I'm useless. What's the good of living?

Christ died for you—that makes you worth a great deal. God doesn't think you're useless. He needs all kinds of people to do His work. He needs the quick and the slow. He needs the strong and the weak. I know a boy without any arms who paints with his toes. The lad's courage has inspired many to forget their handicaps. If you are cheerful and patient when in pain, you are witnessing for Christ.

A retired minister spends three hours each day writing friendly notes to those in trouble. His message brings courage and comfort to thousands every year.

God has something special for you to do. Ask Him to show you how you can serve Him, and He will.

We can't understand why illness comes, but when we suffer we must still trust our Heavenly Father. Then we have more time for prayer than ever before. Pray for others as well as yourself. Pray for those in positions of authority.

Pray for peace and justice. Even when lying flat on your back, you can pray. This is one way you can now labor for Christ and His kingdom.

I was involved in a religious cult until a few months ago. I have broken free of it but now I am still confused about God. I would like to know God personally, but I don't know where to look.

The Bible promises you, "Ask and it will be given you; seek and you will find; knock and the door will be opened to you. For everyone who asks receives; he who seeks finds; and to him who knocks, the door will be opened" (Matthew 7:7–8). The One who spoke those words was Jesus Christ, and He wants you to discover the truth. Where can you find God? You can find God in only one way and that is through Jesus Christ. He is the One to whom you must look. Why is this true? Because Jesus Christ is God Himself. He came down on this earth in human form so we could know what God is like. And He showed us that God loves us, because He went to the cross and died for our sins. He proved that He was God's only Son who is worthy of our worship and our lives, because He rose again from the dead.

Jesus declared, "I am the way and the truth and the life. No one comes to the Father except through me" (John 14:6). That is a staggering claim—but millions of Christians throughout the ages have discovered it to be true. God "wants all men to be saved and to come to a knowledge of the truth. For there is one God and one mediator between God and men, the man Christ Jesus, who gave himself as a ransom for all men" (1 Timothy 2:4–6).

The rising number of religious cults (which claim to have the truth about God but actually do not and enslave a person in their doctrines) is one of the most alarming signs of our time. They and their leaders remind me of those about whom Paul warned Timothy: "They are the kind who worm their way into homes—never able to acknowledge the truth . . . men of depraved minds, who, as far as the faith is concerned, are rejected" (2 Timothy 3:6–8). I am thankful you have broken free of this group, because you would not find God and His will for your life through its teachings.

Yes, you can know God personally by turning to Christ and accepting Him in faith as your Lord and Savior. Then get into the Word of God, the Bible, and get help from other Christians so you can grow spiritually.

Our oldest son was killed in an automobile accident just a few months before graduating from college. It all seems so senseless, and frankly it has even shaken my faith in God. Can you help me understand this?

Whenever I receive a letter like yours I always wish I had an easy explanation I could give that would cover all situations and answer all questions. But we do not always understand completely why things happen to us that are seemingly so senseless or evil. The Bible talks about "the mystery of iniquity" (2 Thessalonians 2:7, KJV), suggesting that there is indeed a mystery to some of the things that happen to us.

At the same time, we need to remember that we live in a world badly stained and twisted by sin. The world was not this way when God created it; instead, "God saw all that he had made, and it was very good" (Genesis 1:31). But then sin entered the world when the human race turned its back on God and chose instead to go its own way. And although we cannot fully understand it now, that rebellion has had terrible consequences for the human race, bringing heartache and death in its wake.

The loss of a child is very painful and God allows us a grieving process so we can withstand that pain. He knows your pain and your hurt and anger.

As you consider this, I also want to remind you of something else very important. You are deeply hurt, but I want to assure you that God knows exactly how you feel. How do I know this? I know it because God's only Son, Jesus Christ, also died. He suffered and died on a cross, so you and I could be reconciled to God. God understands your heartache—and He wants to surround you with His love if you will let Him.

There is a verse in the Bible that says "Whatsoever is born of God doth not commit sin." I used to think of myself as a Christian, but I know that I have sinned. Does that mean that I am not a child of God?

You are probably referring to the Scripture found in 1 John 3:9. Many people are confused by the verse. What it actually means is that whatsoever is begotten of God does not sin as a way of life or he does not continually practice sin.

Don't let your failures or your weaknesses discourage you. If in your heart you desire to live in fellowship with God, and if you have confessed Christ as your Savior, you have the assurance that His blood does cleanse from all sin. I like the way The Living Bible cites this verse: "The person who has been born into God's family does not make a practice of sinning, because now God's life is in him; so he can't keep on sinning, for this new life has been born into him and controls him—he has been born again."

I have been a Christian for several years. Although I still love Jesus and feel sure that I am His child, I know I am not making any definite progress. I seem always to be treading water or marking time. Is there any simple answer to this problem that you can give?

No complete answer to so complicated a problem can be given, but I can offer some specific suggestions.

1. Never forget that the real source of all spiritual growth and progress is the Bible. Unless you systematically study the Bible, you cannot hope to make any true progress.

2. Prayer is important. It is a vital part of your life with God. Prayer is your true desire, expressed or hidden. If you desire what is promised in the Bible, then there is communication with God.

3. Obedience is the key to Bible knowledge. You don't read the Bible to satisfy curiosity but to find the practical answer to a real problem, and when you find the answer, you act decisively upon it.

4. Praise is essential. For every known blessing, give praise to God both privately and when fitting, publicly. Praise is the action that puts you before others as an example. Do not avoid this public display of your love for God.

If one is a Christian and God directs and allows everything that happens to you, what takes place between God and you when you sin?

I believe your question can best be answered by a rather simple illustration. I ask you this question: What happens to the father-son relationship in everyday life when the son does something that is displeasing to the father?

The Bible does not tell us that we are going to live free from sin as long as we are in this body. The Bible says: "If we claim to be without sin, we deceive ourselves and the truth is not in us" (1 John 1:8).

Actually what will happen is that there is a rupture that takes place in our fellowship, and this fellowship is not completely restored until confession of that sin is made. In other words, we may still be sons of God without enjoying the fellowship that sons rightfully should have. There are thousands of Christians who do not have the joy and peace that fellowship with God brings. There is no joy or ecstasy quite like that of daily fellowship with God. Try it!

I am a very old man and have lived a wicked life. I would like to turn to God now but am afraid He won't accept me at this late hour. Besides, I am no longer able to do anything to merit His favor. Can you help me?

Don't you know that the desire to know the Lord indicates the Spirit of God is now speaking to you? If He were not, you would not have this desire. Your age is not the most important consideration in this matter so long as there is the desire. I recently heard of a 94-year-old lady who came to Christ.

Jesus once gave a parable to show that it makes no difference providing you respond to the invitation when it is given. That parable is found in Matthew 20:1–16 and ends with the familiar verse: "So the last will be first, and the first will be last."

There is a good reason why this is so. Salvation does not depend on your personal merit but on the merit of Jesus Christ. In a lifetime we could not store up sufficient merit to enter heaven. Concerning this Paul once wrote: "Where, then, is the boasting? It is excluded. On what principle? On that of observing the law? No: but on that of faith" (Romans 3:27). I encourage you, then, to respond to the urge to trust Christ, for He is able to save all who come unto God by Him.

I don't agree with you when you make such general statements about everybody being a sinner. There are many wonderful people in the world who certainly aren't that bad.

The Bible says so: "All have sinned and fall short of the glory of God" (Romans 3:23). If there were no other reason, that in itself would be sufficient. But there is a second reason also. Human nature is best explained when you accept this view. The wonderful and good people you mention are without a doubt as good as you say when judged by human standards. It is when we make the comparison with the holiness of God that we realize the truth of this statement. Any person who is not fully as good as Jesus Christ is a sinner. He alone is the world's only example of One who was without sin. Other people, even the good and wonderful ones you may have in mind, have their weak moments when they fall below their own faulty standards. That is why we all need a sinless Savior. Of Jesus, the Bible says: "God made him who had no sin to be sin for us, so that in him we might become the righteousness of God" (2 Corinthians 5:21).

I was reared in a Christian home where the Bible was clearly taught and believed. Since I have grown up I have seen older people converted and how they rejoiced. I have never had this kind of feeling. Is it because I have been taught about Jesus and "good" all my life?

There are perhaps two reasons why you have never experienced this "joy" you have observed in other people.

First, if you accepted Christ in early life, the transition from innocent childhood to a believing Christian was not nearly so noticeable as it is in a mature person whose conscience has been weighed down with years of accumulated guilt. To illustrate: let us say that a farmer and his son were walking home from the cornfield. The boy carries a few ears in his hands, but the father bends beneath the weight of a hundred-pound sack of corn. Now suppose a friend comes down the road with a wagon and offers to carry father and son home. He carries the load of each, but it is obvious that the father would be the more relieved and grateful of the two. The child coming to Christ, because his burden of sin is light, may not experience the overwhelrning joy of the confirmed sinner who finds relief from his guilt through Christ. His load was greater—thus his joy is greater.

The other reason could well be that you have trusted in your good upbringing rather than in the person of Christ. Only you can decide which applies to your case.

How can a person know for sure if he is a Christian?

The Bible suggests ways in which we can have the assurance of our salvation.

We know because of a change that takes place. The Bible says: "Therefore if anyone is in Christ, he is a new creation; the old has gone, the new has come" (2 Corinthians 5:17).

We know by the presence of God's Spirit in our lives. "Hereby know we that we dwell in him, and he in us, because he hath given us of his Spirit" (1 John 4:13, KJV).

We know we are Christians if love is the dominating force in our lives. "Beloved, let us love one another: for love is of God; and every one that loveth is born of God, and knoweth God . . . for God is love" (1 John 4:7, 8, KJV).

We know we are Christians when we find it in our hearts to obey God. "And hereby we do know that we know him, if we keep his commandments" (1 John 2:3, KJV).

And last but not least, we know because we receive Christ. "As many as received him, to them gave he power to become the sons of God, even to them that believe on his name" (John 1:12, KJV).

I hear people talking about inner peace, and that is certainly what I wish I could have. I even go to church sometimes but I still feel like I am missing something. Is it really possible to have peace in our hearts?

Yes, it is possible to have peace in our hearts. Christ promised His disciples, "Peace I leave with you; my peace I give you. I do not give to you as the world gives. Do not let your hearts be troubled and do not be afraid" (John 14:27).

How does Christ's peace come to our hearts? Notice that Jesus did *not* say that He will necessarily give us peace by taking away all our problems and difficulties; in fact, He spoke those words to His disciples just a few hours before He was to be arrested and put to death on the cross. Instead, Christ can give us peace even in the midst of the storms of life. Let me suggest three kinds of peace that Christ gives to us when we open our hearts to Him and trust Him.

First, there is the peace of forgiveness. We have sinned against God, and although we may try to hide it, we feel guilty and know we deserve only God's judgment. But Christ came to give us peace with God. "Therefore, since we have been justified through faith, we have peace with God through our Lord Jesus Christ" (Romans 5:1).

Second, there is the peace of Christ's presence. When we come to Christ, God the Holy Spirit takes up residence in our lives. Think of it! God Himself comes to dwell within us. Even when we do not feel His presence He is still there, and by faith we can be certain of that fact. Jesus promised, "Surely I will be with you always, to the very end of the age" (Matthew 28:20).

Third, there is the peace of God's strength. We can't live as we should—but God will help us when we turn to Him for strength. The apostle Paul knew Christ's strength, as have Christians throughout the ages: "I can do everything through him who gives me strength" (Philippians 4:13).

How can you know God's peace? By opening your life to Christ by faith and yielding your life to Him as Savior and Lord. As you take that step and learn to trust His Word, the Bible, every day, you will know the joy of His peace.

Outwardly I suppose I am a good person, but I would die of embarrassment if anyone could read my thoughts. I admit I have bad thoughts about other people—anger and things like that. I don't like this but I can't seem to control them. Do you have any answer for this? Or is everyone like this down inside?

I suspect we all have felt like you do from time to time—and with good reason, because our thoughts are the most reliable indication of what we are really like. And when we face our thoughts and our motives honestly, we have to admit we are not as good as we would like other people to believe.

One of the greatest truths of the Bible is that God wants to change us—not only our outward actions, but our innermost thoughts. One reason is this: He knows that when we do wrong it is because we have first allowed evil thoughts to control us. Jesus said, "For out of the overflow of the heart the mouth speaks. The good man brings things out of the good stored up in him, and the evil man brings evil things out of the evil stored up in him" (Matthew 12:34-35). And God can change us—both outside and inside—if we turn our lives over to Christ and allow Him to work in our hearts.

Begin by giving your life to Jesus Christ and asking Him to come into your heart and mind. Then learn each day to walk with Him and allow Him to fill your life. Have you ever seen a bucket filled with stagnant, smelly water? The only solution is to empty it and clean it—and then fill it with fresh water. That is what Christ will do if we commit our lives to Him and let His Word, the Bible, fill our hearts. "Do not conform any longer to the pattern of this world, but be transformed by the renewing of your mind" (Romans 12:2).

How can I feel close to God? I have a friend who is constantly talking about how real God is to her, and I wish that was true for me, but it isn't. Is there a secret to knowing God, or is it just something you have to hope will happen to you?

Have you ever thought about the way a friendship develops between two people? First they have to be introduced to each other; you can't be a friend to someone you have never met! Then you have to spend time with each other and talk to each other. Without time together a relationship can never become deeper.

It is the same way in our relationship with God. God loves us, and He wants to be our friend—in a far deeper way than any human friend. Have you ever been "introduced" to Him, by turning to Him and asking His Son, Jesus Christ, to come into your heart and take away your sins? If not, open your life to Him and commit yourself to Him. Then learn to spend time with God and talk with Him every day. How do you do that? You do it through the Bible, which is God's Word and is His way of speaking to us. Then pray to Him, thanking God for all He does for you and sharing your burdens and concerns with Him. Jesus said, "I have called you friends, for everything that I learned from my Father I have made known to you" (John 15:15).

Each day spend time alone with God. It may only be a few minutes at first, but as you realize His love for you and come to understand that He is with you every moment, then your closeness to Him will grow and you will realize you can turn to Him at any moment. Even when you may not feel His presence, by faith you know that He is still with you for He has promised, "Never will I leave you; never will I forsake you" (Hebrews 13:5).

Somewhere along the line I feel like we have missed the boat. My husband and I are middle-aged, and we have been very successful materially. Every one of our children has gotten into some kind of difficulty (like drugs), and we are empty inside. Where do you think we went wrong?

The Bible gives us a formula for training our children but it also gives them a free will to make the choice between following the ways of men or the way of God. From your question it appears that you may have set the pursuit of material gain ahead of pursuing God's will and way for your lives and that of your children.

I would suggest that you first earnestly seek God's forgiveness for your failure to be the kind of parents God wanted you to be. Then, go to your children individually and confess to them. Tell them you are sorry for putting material things ahead of them and ask their forgiveness. Do not expect it immediately, for there is much healing that will need to take place.

Then, determine that Christ will be at the center of your life and marriage from this day forward. If you must relinquish some of your lifestyle in order to make things right with God and with your children, do so. You have again proved the Scripture which says, "What shall it profit a man if he gains the whole world and loses his own soul?"

Above all, keep in mind that nothing is too hard for God, including the redemption of yourselves and your children.

What exactly is an atheist? Is it a person who doesn't know whether or not God exists? If so, I guess I am one because I have a lot of doubts and wonder if we can really know anything about God. I would like to know God is real, but I don't.

The term "agnostic" would more accurately describe you. An atheist does not believe in God; an agnostic is not sure whether or not God exists. The word literally means "one who is without knowledge"—that is, a person who says he does not know whether or not God is real.

But can you come to know about God? Yes! And not only can you know that God exists, but you can come to know Him by having a personal relationship with Him. You see, God has not left us to wander around guessing whether or not He exists or what He is like. Instead—and this is very important for you to understand—God has shown Himself to us. How has He done this? He has done it in a way that staggers our minds. He did it by actually taking upon Himself human flesh and becoming a human being. Do you want to know what God is like? Examine Jesus Christ, because Christ was God in human flesh. "He is the image of the invisible God. . . . For God was pleased to have all his fullness dwell in him" (Colossians 1:15, 19). Christ confirmed that He was the Son of God by rising from the dead after His death on the cross.

I invite you to look with an open mind and heart at Christ as He is found in the New Testament. When you do, you will discover that God loves you, and He has done everything possible to remove the barriers between God and humanity. Then commit your life to Christ and discover for yourself that "to those who believed in his name, he gave the right to become children of God" (John 1:12).

I know preachers talk a lot about repenting of sin, but what exactly do you mean by that? I know there are a lot of things wrong in my life, but if I have to wait until I get rid of all of them before God will love me, then I guess I don't have a chance.

The word "repent" is used frequently in the New Testament, and it literally means "to have a change of mind" about the way we are living. Jesus said, "I have not come to call the righteous, but sinners to repentance" (Luke 5:32).

In other words, to repent is to face the fact that we are sinners and the way we have been living is wrong in God's eyes. It means we also have a new attitude toward sin—no longer loving it or excusing it, but realizing that it is wrong and displeases God. When we truly repent we actually want to turn from sin, and with God's help we will turn from it. Repentance is not merely feeling guilty for our sins, or sorry because we know we have done wrong. Repentance means we actually turn from sin as best we know how, seeking God's forgiveness and strength.

But repentance is only one side of the coin. Yes, we are to repent. But the good news of the gospel is that God will forgive us when we repent! God loves us, and Christ died on the cross to take away our sins. "The blood of Jesus, his Son, purifies us from all sin" (1 John 1:7). When we repent and then accept Christ into our lives by faith, God forgives us and makes us His children. He receives us just as we are.

Have you realized your own need of repentance and faith in Christ? Don't let pride get in the way. Instead, confess to God that you know you are a sinner and you are sorry for your sins and repent of them, and then ask Christ to come into your life as your Lord and Savior.

Do you know exactly when you became a Christian? I have friends who say they do, and that everyone should be able to remember it, but it makes me feel strange because I can't. Does this mean I'm not really a Christian? I grew up in a Christian home and as long as I can remember I have felt that God loved me and I trusted Christ for my salvation.

Yes, I can recall very vividly the night I made my decision to follow Christ. I was seventeen at the time, and a visiting evangelist was holding a series of meetings in my home town of Charlotte. After a time of spiritual struggle I went forward and made a public commitment to follow Christ.

My wife, on the other hand, cannot recall a time when she did not believe in Christ and trust Him for her salvation. Her parents were godly missionaries in China, and from her earliest years they had taught her about Christ and the way He loves us and died for our sins. Her experience was somewhat like that of Paul's young helper Timothy: "From infancy you have known the holy Scriptures, which are able to make you wise for salvation through faith in Christ Jesus" (2 Timothy 3:15).

The point is that people come to Christ in different ways. The central question is not how or when we came to Christ, but that we are sure to have come, and that we are trusting Him alone for our salvation. Tragically, many people grow up in a religious background and go to church all their lives, and yet their religion is only a habit and they are not truly trusting Christ alone for their salvation. Thank God for your background and your trust in Christ, who died on the cross for you. And be sure you are continuing to grow in your relationship with Him through His Word and prayer every day.

Some time ago I read one of your answers concerning evil thoughts. I, too, am troubled over this because the more I try to dismiss them from my mind, the more they trouble me. In fact, the problem grows worse as I try to overcome it. I am a Christian and wish to please God. Is there any answer to this problem?

It is known that we cannot always control the thoughts we have. In fact, you will find that your desperate attempt to dismiss them from your mind is exactly the thing that keeps them active. It is just like most spiritual struggles.

They are not overcome by our own self-will and determination. The best resolution will not overcome the enemy. Only when we admit our helplessness, and call upon God to deliver us, will we find deliverance. As long as you try by your own strength, you will fail, but when you draw upon the resources of His strength, you will find relief.

You are worried about the wickedness of these thoughts. As long as you disapprove of them, you are well, but when the time comes that you approve of them and affirm them with your will, then you are certainly in a low spiritual condition. Paul once wrote: "Finally, brethren, whatsoever things are true, whatsoever things are honest, whatsoever things are just, whatsoever things are pure, whatsoever things are lovely, whatsoever things are of good report; if there be any virtue, and if there be any praise, think on these things" (Philippians 4:8, KJV).

I watched you the other night on television as you spoke about loneliness. I guess that is my biggest problem. I have a good job and everything, but I just about go crazy when I come home to the four walls of my apartment. Please pray for me.

I believe loneliness is one of the most critical problems in our nation today. There are some things in our society—such as the fast pace of city living—that truly make many people lonely in the midst of a crowd.

There are two things I especially want to tell you. First, no matter what your situation may be, God is always with you. You are never completely alone when you know Christ. The Bible promises, "God has said, 'Never will I leave you; never will I forsake you'" (Hebrews 13:5). No matter where you go or what you do, God is there and by faith you can reach out to Him. This is one reason I am convinced the first step in solving your problem is for you to ask Jesus Christ to come into your heart by faith. Jesus stands at the door of our hearts and promises, "If anyone hears my voice and opens the door, I will come in and eat with him, and he with me" (Revelation 3:20).

The second thing I want to urge you to do is to take definite, practical steps to establish friendships with others. Church is an excellent place to do this—not only in Sunday morning worship, but especially in the many other activities most churches have. (You also need the fellowship of other Christians to grow spiritually.) Ask God to lead you to a church where Christ is preached and where you can find friends.

Also take other steps to reach out to others. Are there others at work who are also lonely? Are there others in your apartment building who seem to have few friends? It may not be easy for you at first, but learn to be a friend to others. A good way to start is to do something practical for someone else who has a need.

I am an entertainer and work at night. I do feel my need of God, but lately I have taken to drink. I sometimes feel that life is so futile and empty. Is there any help for me?

You are right to be concerned about the direction of your life and my first advice to you would be not to seek solace in alcohol. Alcohol obscures good judgment and leaves you unable to think clearly or understand what God is trying to say to you.

The fact that you are reaching out indicates that you are troubled about where your life might lead. Life *is* futile and empty without Christ. God made us to have a relationship with Him and we try to fill the void God wants to fill with Himself, with success, fame, money, lust, and all sorts of other false gods that never satisfy.

The Bible says "Him that cometh unto me I will in no wise cast out" (John 6:37, KJV). What you must first do is come to God. Confess your sin to Him and receive Jesus Christ as your Savior. Then consider the kind of "entertaining" you have been doing and ask yourself whether this is God's will for your life. Find others who desire to live for God and begin spending time with them and reading God's Word.

10

Does Prayer Really Make a Difference?

Do you think prayer really makes any difference about how things turn out?

Yes, I am convinced that prayer makes a difference. Let the Bible answer your question: "The prayer of a righteous man is powerful and effective" (James 5:16). God always answers prayer—not sometimes, but all the time.

We may not always understand how God answers our prayers—at times He says "yes," while at other times He answers "no" or "wait." But one of the greatest privileges of the child of God is the privilege of coming directly to God in prayer. This is possible because Jesus Christ has reconciled us to God through His death on the cross. We are separated from God, but Christ took away our sins and when we come to Christ by faith we are united with God. "Therefore, since we have been justified through faith, we have peace with God through our Lord Jesus Christ, through whom we have gained access by faith into this grace in which we now stand" (Romans 5:1–2). Yes, we have access to God through Jesus Christ.

Does that mean we can ask God for anything at all—no matter how selfish it might be—and He will automatically give us our request? No, what we should seek when we pray is God's will, not our own. (That does not mean, of course, that we are not to bring our own concerns to God in prayer—quite the opposite. But our desire is to see God work in accordance with His perfect will.) The Bible says, "This is the assurance we have in approaching God: that if we ask anything according to His will, He hears us. And if we know that He hears us—whatever we ask—we know that we have what we asked of him" (1 John 5:14–15).

Is prayer a central part of your life? Pray for your own needs. Pray for the needs of others. Praise God in prayer, and pray for His guidance in your life. "Devote yourselves to prayer, being watchful and thankful" (Colossians 4:2). Remember, Christ prayed repeatedly, and if He—the sinless Son of God—needed to pray, how much more should we learn to "pray continually" (1 Thessalonians 5:17).

What do people mean when they end a prayer "in Jesus' name"? I have never really understood this.

In order to understand the meaning of this you have to know something about the meaning and importance of a name in the ancient world.

To people in Jesus' time, a person's name was very important. (This was true in Old Testament times as well.) The reason is that a person's name was seen as summarizing or indicating a person's true character or nature. You could almost say that a person's name gave a picture of his personality. A name was not simply a sound or a word—it had meaning. (We have lost that idea today, but at one time it was true in English also; e.g., someone named "Armstrong" had strong arms.)

Let me give an example from the Old Testament to show you what I mean. On one occasion, David had difficulty with a man named Nabal. The word "Nabal" in the original Hebrew language means "fool"—and that was exactly what this man was. He refused to help David although David had helped him. Nabal's wife, however, urged David not to harm her husband in spite of his mistreatment of David. She said, "Pay no attention to that wicked man Nabal. He is just like his name—his name is Fool, and folly goes with him" (1 Samuel 25:25). His name—fool—indicated the whole character or personality of the man.

Now think about the name of Jesus. "Jesus" in the original language of the New Testament means "The Lord Saves." Its full meaning is given by the angel to Joseph: "You are to give him the name of Jesus, because he will save his people from their sins" (Matthew 1:21).

Therefore, when we pray "in the name of Jesus" we are recalling who Jesus is and what He has done for us through His death and resurrection. We are recalling that He has made our prayers possible because He has saved us, reconciled us to God, and is our mediator. We cannot come before God in our own merit, because we are sinners. But Christ has taken away our sins and made forgiveness possible. To pray in Jesus' name—as we should—is to acknowledge our need of Christ and our desire to seek His glory and His will alone in our prayers.

Do you think it is possible for God to get angry with us because we pray too much about a particular problem we have? I worry about bothering Him too much with my problems.

No, the Bible tells us to persist in prayer and to pray about everything. God does not always answer the *way* we think He should, or *when* we think He should. (We should be grateful for this—He knows far better than we do what is best!) But, the Bible tells us to "always keep on praying" (1 Thessalonians 5:17, TLB). Jesus, in fact, told a parable about a persistent widow who constantly begged a judge to act on her case, which He eventually did. (You can read it in Luke 18:1–8.) One reason Jesus told this parable was to encourage us to pray frequently.

There are, however, two things I would like to add as footnotes, so to speak. First, be sure that you are not trying to change God's mind about something which He has already answered. In other words, it is possible that God will answer a prayer of ours with a "no" rather than a "yes." Are we willing to accept His will? Remember that God answers prayer in one of three ways as far as time is concerned; yes, no, and wait. In prayer we seek above all else to have God's will done, and when He has acted we must not second-guess Him or try to get Him to change His perfect will.

Second, remember that there are times when we ourselves are to act as well as pray. That is, we become the answer to our own prayers. For example, on one occasion Jesus told his disciples to "Ask the Lord of the harvest, therefore, to send out workers into his harvest field." In the very next verses we find that the disciples themselves were sent out to do God's work. They became the answer to their own prayers! (See Matthew 9:38, 10:1.)

Prayer is one of the privileges of the child of God, made possible because Jesus Christ has opened up the way to our Father. God loves you, and He wants you to "not be anxious about anything, but in everything, by prayer and petition, with thanksgiving, present your request to God" (Philippians 4:6).

I have a friend who tells me that if I just pray and read my Bible every day my problems will work out. I'm not so sure it's that simple, are you?

No, the Bible does not promise that if we are committed to Jesus Christ all of our problems will vanish. We should commit our lives to Christ because He is "the way and the truth and the life" (John 14:6), and not because we hope to escape all the problems of this life. Yes, when we come to Christ many of our problems are solved. For example, if we truly understand what Christ has done for us on the cross we do not need to be burdened with a load of guilt any longer, because He has washed away our sins. But we may find new pressures that come because we are seeking to be faithful to Christ.

Look at the example of the apostle Paul, the greatest follower of Jesus Christ the world has ever known. And yet His life was often marked by difficulties and circumstances that were far from pleasant. (You can read about some of his troubles in 2 Corinthians 11:23–33.)

That does not mean, of course, that it makes no difference whether or not we believe in Christ—not at all! Yes, you may face problems in your life just as other people do, but there is a difference—Christ is with you! He can strengthen you in the midst of difficulties you have in your life, and He can give you wisdom in dealing with them. He also gives you hope, because you know that this world is not the end of everything. Some day we will go to be with Christ in

Heaven, where "There will be no more death or mourning or crying or pain, for the old order of things has passed away" (Revelation 21:4).

In one way, therefore, your friend is pointing you in the right direction. God will not necessarily remove all your problems when you give your life to Christ, but through praying to Him and through studying the Bible every day (and trusting its promises) you will grow closer to Christ and know in a fuller way "the peace of God, which transcends all understanding" (Philippians 4:7)—no matter what circumstances you face.

For months I have been praying that God would change me and make me a better person. Nothing seems to happen however. What do you think is wrong?

I cannot help but wonder if you feel somehow that God should reach into your life and miraculously change you all at once. Almost like a bolt of lightning striking you. But that is not the way God usually works. Think of it this way— it took a while for you to become what you are. It will take a while for God to change you.

Indeed, you need to realize that God also expects us to do our part. I do not know what specific problems you face in your life that you want God to change. But let's say, for example, that you have a particular problem with your tongue. Perhaps you say things that hurt others and cause them to resent you, or you have problems because you gossip easily about others. How do you think God will deal with that problem?

First, God will want you to see the seriousness of this problem. He wants you to know that a sharp or undisciplined tongue is a sin which not only hurts your relationships with other people but is wrong in His eyes. "The tongue also is a fire, a world of evil among the parts of the body. It corrupts the whole person, sets the whole course of his life on fire, and is itself set on fire by hell" (James 3:6).

Then God wants you to commit this problem to Him, repenting of it and admitting that you need His strength to combat it. "Repentance" means that you deliberately turn from it and with God's strength fight it in your life. It means you will avoid situations where you know you will be tempted to fail— and this requires discipline on your part. It also means that you will seek to use your tongue to honor Him as well as to refrain from evil. In addition, God has given you the Bible, and your daily study and application of its teaching to your life is crucial.

How can I get close to God? Praying to Him sometimes feels like praying to a brick wall; and although countless prayers of mine have been answered, it seems that my prayers just slide into the blackness of I-don't-know-where. Do you think you could possibly help me?

I'm afraid you are trying to use God as a genie, as a kind of Aladdin's lamp. You say that countless prayers of yours have been answered. That seems to me like a pretty good average. God answers all our prayers, but in His wisdom, He sometimes answers them with a "no."

Prayer is not our using God; it is more often employed to get us in a position where God can use us.

I watched the deckhands on the great liner, *United States,* as they docked that ship in New York Harbor. First, they threw out a rope to the men on the dock. Then inside the boat the great motors went to work and pulled on that great cable. But oddly enough, the pier wasn't pulled out to the ship; instead, the ship was pulled snugly up to the pier.

Prayer is the rope that pulls God and man together. But it doesn't pull God down to us: it pulls us up to Him. We must learn to say with Christ, the Master of the art of prayer: "Not my will, but thine, be done" (Luke 22:42, KJV).

Is it always necessary to pray for long periods of time to maintain a spiritual outlook?

It is not the length of the prayer that is important. Do you think God is persuaded by long prayers or by the earnestness with which we pray? Put it on the level of the human: What makes the strongest impression on you? Is it the long but indifferent request or the terse but earnest plea of one who has a strong desire? I am sure you can see that it is the condition of the heart and the definiteness of the request that makes the difference. Jesus said, "When ye pray, use not vain repetitions, as the heathen do" (Matthew 6:7, KJV). The simple and direct request in Jesus' name will accomplish far more than millions of half-hearted and indefinite words. Finally, pray expectantly. God knows when you pray without hope of an answer. You cannot pray unless you pray with hope.

It is interesting to note that Jesus often prayed all night in private but His public prayers were very brief.

Is it more meaningful to kneel while you pray? Is it just an expression of humbleness, or are one's prayers more likely to be heard when kneeling?

It is not the posture of the body, but the attitude of the heart that counts when we pray. The Bible speaks of bowing in prayer, kneeling on one's face before God, standing, sitting, and walking. The important thing is not the position of the body but the condition of the soul. If the heart is attuned to God, one can pray in any posture imaginable.

Jesus prayed sitting, standing, kneeling, and in a prone position. Moses often fell on his face to pray. Daniel frequently kneeled. The disciples were sitting in the upper room when the Holy Spirit descended upon them in answer to prayer. Ahab prayed with his face between his knees.

There are times when I like to kneel in prayer. There are other times when it seems more natural to sit or stand. I don't believe there is any special virtue in any particular posture. God doesn't look upon the outward appearance, but upon the heart.

My problem is that I cannot concentrate when I pray. In other matters I am quite able to keep my mind from wandering but not when I kneel to pray. Is there something wrong with me?

There is not necessarily anything wrong with you. This was the problem the disciples had in the Garden of Gethsemane. They went to sleep when they had been commanded to "watch and pray." Of all the activity of the Christian life, prayer is the most difficult. The Bible even points this out, saying that "We know not how to pray as we ought."

Someone has said: "Satan trembles when he sees the weakest saint upon his knees." When we get to Heaven, I am convinced we will be amazed at our prayerlessness. Prayer can move mountains. Thus Satan will do all in his power to distract you. You may never be entirely free from distraction in prayer, but you can improve your concentration by quoting psalms and using prayer helps. Remember also that prayer is a two-way conversation. Be still and listen for the voice of God. Most of us want to do too much talking in prayer. God has promised special help in the matter of prayer: "In the same way, the Spirit helps us in our weakness. We do not know what we ought to pray, but the Spirit himself intercedes for us with groans that words cannot express" (Romans 8:26). No matter what your problem, don't get discouraged. Continue to pray.

I have a lot of problems I would like to see solved. Is it really true that if you have enough faith then all your prayers will be answered? How can I get that kind of faith?

Being a Christian does not guarantee us a trouble-free life. Jesus "was despised and rejected by men, a man of sorrows, and familiar with suffering" (Isaiah 53:3). The apostle Paul frequently encountered troubles and difficulties as he worked for Christ.

But God does promise several important things. He promises that in the midst of troubles He will be with us to help us and strengthen us. He may give us special wisdom to deal with a situation. He may give us a special measure of spiritual courage and strength. "Fear not, for I have redeemed you; I have called you by name; you are mine. When you pass through waters, I will be with you; and when you pass through rivers, they will not sweep over you. . . . Do not be afraid, for I am with you" (Isaiah 43:1–2, 5).

Then He promises to give us peace in the midst of life's storms. When we learn to trust the future into His hands, then we know that we do not need to be anxious and worried about the outcome. "Do not be anxious about anything, but in everything, by prayer and petition, with thanksgiving, present your requests to God. And the peace of God, which transcends all understanding, will guard your hearts and your minds in Christ Jesus" (Philippians 4:6–7). God hears our prayers, and we can have confidence that He will answer in the right way.

Finally, God gives us hope for the future. Even when our lives seem to be engulfed with troubles, we know there is a bright future ahead in Heaven for all those who know Christ. Then there will be no more pain or troubles, and we will be with Christ forever.

I know you urge people to take time each day and spend it in prayer and Bible study, but somehow I just can't seem to get going on it. Why do you think it is important? I do go to church several times a week and feel I am getting closer to God through the Bible teaching I get there.

It is good you are gaining spiritually from Bible teaching in your church. But God also wants to bless you spiritually as you meet with Him every day. This need not be a complicated or lengthy time, but each of us can profit from time alone with God. Let me suggest four guidelines that might help you get started.

First, have a purpose. Many people don't take time—even just a few minutes—for prayer and Bible reading each day because they don't see its importance. Such a practice, however, can strengthen you spiritually. It also can help others as you take time to pray for them. Remember too that God wants our fellowship.

Second, have a time. I have found unless I deliberately plan a definite time for Bible study and prayer, other things all too easily intervene and crowd it out. We can always find time for things we think are really important. Set aside a time when you are alert and will not be disturbed, even if it is only a few minutes at first, and discipline yourself to give it priority.

Third, have a plan. Spend a few minutes in prayer—thanking God for His blessings, bringing your needs to Him and remembering the needs of others. Many find it helpful to keep a list of the people for whom they are praying. Then spend time in reading the Bible. Don't feel that you necessarily have to read a long section—it is far better to read a few verses and get their meaning than to read a larger section and not get much out of it. Start in a book (such as the Gospel of John) and move through it day by day.

Finally, understand and apply. What is this Bible passage saying about God, or about how we should live? And in what ways should my life be different as a result of what God has shown me here?

Yes, it is important to talk to God each day, and allow Him to talk to us through His Word. And when we know Christ we can have fellowship with Him at any time.

11

I Want to Know
God's Will

I am a new Christian and I honestly want to know and do God's will, but how can I know what His will for me really is?

There are many ways by which God leads us but it is only when we have minds and hearts surrendered to Him that we sometimes hear His voice. God speaks to us through the Holy Spirit, sometimes while we are praying. I know a man who was faced with a very difficult problem. He was an earnest Christian and he prayed about this particular problem and while he was praying he had a clear sense of the answer, so much so that he got up from his knees and wrote it down. Later in the day, during a conference in which the problem was under discussion, he read this statement. Immediately the entire group, although they had differed sharply one with the other, felt this was the answer and unanimously agreed. As a result, an issue which had divided Christians for months was resolved in absolute harmony.

God sometimes leads men through the words or acts of other people. He often gives direct leading as we pray about it and read our Bibles. There are times when a group of individuals may come to a conclusion which indicates how one of them should act. The important thing is to be willing to do God's will. When that is true, God will surely make it known. Many Christians have experienced the fulfillment of the words of the prophet Isaiah: "And thine ears shall hear a word behind thee, saying, 'This is the way, walk ye in it, when ye turn to the right hand, and when ye turn to the left'" (30:21, KJV). Another promise is found in Proverbs 3:5–6: "Trust in the Lord with all thine heart; and lean not unto thine own understanding. In all thy ways acknowledge him, and he shall direct thy paths" (KJV).

I have no patience with people who get intoxicated, but do you think a little social drinking to promote good fellowship does any harm?

Of course it does. Can you be blind to the fact that one drink often leads to another? In every city I visit someone asks me to pray for a husband, or wife, or son who started as a social drinker and now has become an alcoholic. Today you think you have perfect self-control. But if you make a habit of drinking what will you do when you face anxiety or disappointment?

You also have some responsibility for the welfare of your neighbor. Your example may lead him into a habit he cannot break. If you encourage him to do anything which brings about his downfall you are guilty. And don't forget that alcohol is the cause of many of our traffic accidents (estimates of alcohol-related highway fatalities hover at around 50 percent). A man who commits murder on the highway because his responses are slow, or he doesn't see where he's going, is guilty in the sight of God.

Our bodies are the temples of our souls. We must treat them with respect. The Bible says: "Whether therefore ye eat, or drink, or whatsoever ye do, do all to the glory of God" (1 Corinthians 10:31, KJV). This is a command no Christian should ignore.

My wife and I are having an argument about something and I wonder what your opinion is. She says that watching some of the shows on television that have a lot of violence or sex can be harmful, but I'm not sure it really makes much difference, since those shows are just fictional stories.

The fact that the shows are fictional does not mean they cannot excite our imaginations or stir our desires—sometimes in a wrong way. We need to be careful therefore, what we allow to enter our minds.

The Bible makes it clear that what we see and what we think about can have a powerful influence on our lives. That is why the Bible urges us to turn our minds away from things that feed our hearts in a wrong way and instead turn our attention to those things which are good. "Set your minds on things above, not on earthly things. . . . Put to death, therefore, whatever belongs to your earthly nature: sexual immorality, impurity, lust, evil desires and greed" (Colossians 3:2, 5). The reason for this is that God's will is for us to be pure, and to be guided by Him.

Your question makes me wonder, however, if you have ever honestly examined your own life and asked yourself if your priorities are right. Are you honestly concerned about God's will for your life, or are you somehow seeking to keep Him at arms' length so you can run your own life without Him? God created you, and He sent His only Son to die on the cross so you can be forgiven of your sins and become His child forever. If you have never committed your life to Christ, turn to Him and invite Him to come into your heart as your Lord and Savior. Make Him Lord of every area of your life—including your time, your imagination, and your marriage.

Then seek God's will for the way you spend your time. Yes, we all need times of relaxation—but these should become times that strengthen us spiritually as well as physically, rather than tear us down. Remember the Bible's command: "Do not conform any longer to the pattern of this world, but be transformed by the renewing of your mind" (Romans 12:2).

I feel very much like I would honestly like to do God's will in my life—if only I knew what it was. It seems like it would be far more worthwhile to do God's will rather than do things that don't make any difference, but how can I know what His will is?

I am thankful that you realize the most important thing in life is doing the will of God. It would be tragic to look back over our lives and realize that nothing we ever did had any truly eternal significance. But we can know the will of God, because He has a perfect will for each of us and He wants to show it to us.

How does one discover the will of God for his life? First of all, God has revealed His will to us in the Bible. That does not mean the Bible will necessarily give precise, detailed guidance for each day—but it gives something very important: principles by which our lives are to be lived. And every day of your life you will know the will of God in many, many situations because you know the truth of God's Word.

For example, perhaps there is someone near you (such as a neighbor or a relative) who is facing some particular problem right now. Is it God's will for you to try to help that person? Yes, it probably is, because God's Word tells us that we are to "Love your neighbor as yourself" (Matthew 22:39, RSV). The Bible also teaches us that we are to demonstrate our love for others through our actions. "If anyone has material possessions and sees his brother in need but has no pity on him, how can the love of God be in him? Dear children, let us not love with words or tongue but with actions and in truth" (1 John 3:17–18).

I could give many other examples, but the important thing is that you allow your life to be saturated with the teaching of God's Word. I heard someone say long ago that if we are ignorant of God's Word we will also be ignorant of God's will, and that is true. At the same time, when we are open to His will we find He also will direct us through circumstances and through the inner promptings of the Holy Spirit. But that directing is never in conflict with the written Word of God.

In science class at school, all living things are classified as animals. Are human beings actually animals, or does God classify them differently?

Biologically, man is an animal. That is to say, he does not make his own food by photosynthesis. He is thus distinguished from plant life. But he is more than an animal. He has three attributes which four-footed animals do not have: reason, conscience, and will. Animals are motivated by instinct. Their behavior patterns are instinctive, not intelligent. Since their responses are instinctive, they have no conscience. A dog probably feels no more remorse after biting a man, than he does when chewing a bone. Then again, an animal's decisions are not volitional, but instinctive. He has no will but acts instinctively, according to set, inner urges.

Why is man different than the other animals? Because he was created in the image of God. He was directed with three attributes as we have said. The first man, Adam, used all three of these attributes. First, he reasoned that his own judgment was as good as God's, and he ate the forbidden fruit. In that act, the will of man came into play, for he could have decided either way. Then, after he broke God's command, he felt conscience-stricken and ran away to hide in the garden. Strangely, this man-animal has been following that same pattern through the centuries. Within these God-given attributes are life or death, happiness or sorrow, and peace or conflict. If he dissipates the powers which God has given him, he is of all creatures most miserable. But if he uses them properly, he can make of his world a paradise.

What Christian grace in my heart can make me a better Christian and a better witness for Christ?

The greatest Christian grace is love—not the sentimental feeling often called love today but that deep regard for the welfare of others which will prompt us to help them when they need help; to be sympathetic when sympathy is needed; to make us say kind things about people instead of being critical; to make us long to win them to Christ if they are not Christians.

Love is at the very heart of everything that comes from God, for He is love. It was love which prompted the sending of His Son into the world to die for our sins. It is love which is mentioned first when the apostle Paul enumerates the fruits of the Spirit (Galatians 5:22). It is love which must characterize our attitude to God and man, if we are to fulfill His law. In Matthew 22:37–38 we read: "Thou shalt love the Lord thy God with all thy heart, and with all thy soul, and with all thy mind. This is the first and great commandment." Following this, Christ said: "The second is like unto it, Thou shalt love thy neighbor as thyself" (Matthew 22:39, kjv). After that, Christ tells us: "On these commandments hang all the law and the prophets." It is God's love which should constrain us. The Bible says: "This is love: not that we loved God, but that he loved us, and sent his Son as an atoning sacrifice for our sins" (1 John 4:10). If you have a loving heart, you will bear fruitful witness for Christ.

For the benefit of those who are confused, would you explain your position on tithing? Should we give a tenth of our gross income or a tenth of what we have left after expenses are paid?

I can only tell you my personal convictions in the matter. If I were to wait until all expenses were paid before I tithed my income, there would be none left for the Lord. Income means, "what comes in," and if we give one tenth of our income to kingdom work, then we must give a tithe of our gross.

The trouble with too many of us is that we try to see how little we can get by with rather than how much we can do for God. Even the federal government recognizes tithing and charitable giving as a citizen's duty and allows such to be deducted from income tax. I have had many people tell me that nine tenths of their income went farther with God's blessing on it than ten tenths of it did without His blessing. We have found that true in our own experience. Did not God say, "Bring ye all the tithes into the storehouse . . . and prove me now herewith, saith the Lord of hosts, if I will not open you the windows of heaven, and pour you out a blessing, that there shall not be room enough to receive it" (Malachi 3:10, KJV)?

I worry about the attitudes that our children seem to have toward money and possessions. We were always taught in my generation to work hard and save all we could—I still have memories as a child of the Great Depression. But our children seem to want all the possessions they can get and even go deeply into debt to get them, and this worries us. I guess this doesn't sound like a spiritual problem, but I wonder what you think?

Our attitude toward money is very often a sign of what we really think is important in life. Your question does, therefore, deal with a spiritual problem because it touches the whole question of what you and your children consider central in life.

Look carefully at something Jesus said in the Sermon on the Mount. He declared, "Do not store up for yourself treasures on earth, where moth and rust destroy, and where thieves break in and steal. But store up for yourselves treasures in heaven, where moth and rust do not destroy, and where thieves do not break in and steal. For where your treasure is, there your heart will be also" (Matthew 6:19–21).

Was Jesus saying we should never work hard or save money? No, this was not His point; the Bible commends such things as honest work and thrift, and warns us of the dangers of debt. His point instead was that money and things can easily take the place of God in our lives. We begin to think that our real security in life comes from our bank account, and we turn away from trusting God. Jesus was also warning against a spirit of materialism which puts things and the pleasures of life in place of God. The Bible teaches as well that we would use our money not only for ourselves but to help others.

How do your children observe your attitudes toward money? Do you tithe to your church? Are you frugal, but not stingy, with the money God has made it possible for you to have? A generous spirit on your part will serve as an example to your children, and while they are responsible for their own attitudes about money, you can help shape those attitudes by the way you live.

Immediately after graduating from college I went into the Army and am due to be discharged in a few months. I honestly want to serve God but I don't know what He wants me to do.

I am convinced that anyone who honestly wants to know God's will for his life will be led to a clear understanding of God's plan for him. This has its foundation in a personal faith in Jesus Christ as Savior. In the Irish Channel there are a series of lights which the pilot of a ship must line up before entering one of the harbors. In determining God's will for our lives, once we have given our hearts to Christ, there are certain factors which converge in giving us spiritual leading. First, there is the inward impulse coming from the leading of the Holy Spirit. Then there is the Bible which corroborates our sense of divine guidance. Finally, God often uses a trend of circumstances through which He indicates His leading. In this connection Proverbs 3:5–6 is a wonderful promise. "Trust in the Lord with all thine heart; and lean not unto thine own understanding. In all thy ways acknowledge him, and he shall direct thy paths" (KJV). Here is a definite promise. Believe it and act on it. God will not fail you.

I have a brother who is on drugs, and I am afraid he is going to just get in deeper and deeper if somebody doesn't help him. I would like to help him, but I don't know how. What do you suggest?

The first thing you need to do is to pray that God will give you (and others in your family and among his friends) wisdom in dealing with this. Remember the promise of God: "If any of you lacks wisdom, he should ask God, who gives generously to all without finding fault, and it will be given to him" (James 1:5).

At some time your brother needs to be confronted in a loving way with the problem he is facing. Often a person in his situation may think his habits are hidden from others, and he may try to deny that he is having a problem with drugs. But if you are certain of this, you owe it to him and let your concern be known in an open and frank way. Before he will seek the help that he needs, he has to face the fact that he has a problem. He also needs to sense that he has the support of those who love him. Simply condemning him for his actions will probably only alienate him. He needs to know you love him so much that you will not stand by and allow him to destroy himself.

Get professional help. You do not indicate your brother's living situation, but if he is still at home I believe your parents should insist on his getting help. Your pastor may be able to help you at this point and you and your parents should seek his counsel and the counsel of others who might be able to help.

Most of all, pray for your brother. Pray that he will find strength to fight this problem, and pray that he will come to grips with his need for God. God will not only help him, but Christ can give him the meaning and sense of direction in life that he will never find through drugs.

Is it wrong to have questions about God and religion? I have a lot of questions about things I don't understand, but I wonder if maybe I ought to just try to put them out of mind.

Our minds are limited, and we will never fully grasp the greatness of God. Only in Heaven will we receive the answers to some of the questions we have now. "Now we see but a poor reflection; then we shall see face to face. Now I know in part; then I shall know fully" (1 Corinthians 13:12).

But that does not mean you should try to bury your questions or not seek answers to problems that are keeping you from a full relationship with Christ. Faith does not mean that we have no understanding. We can't know everything, but that doesn't mean we can't know some things about God. Even more important, we can come to know God in a personal way.

I know it may seem hard for you at first, but the most important step you can take is to open your heart to Jesus Christ and let Him come into your life by faith. You may reply that it is hard to take that step when you have so many questions. But let me stress one very important thing: God can be trusted. God does not lie, for He is perfect and holy. And He has said that if we turn to Him in faith He will accept and forgive us. If anyone in the universe can be trusted, it is God! Let your prayer be the cry of one man who came to Jesus but was nevertheless still plagued by some doubts: "I do believe; help me overcome my unbelief" (Mark 9:24).

Then seek answers to the questions you have. The most important resource for you—or anyone else—is God's Word, the Bible. Get into the Bible on a regular basis and ask God to help you understand it and apply it to your life—not just to answer your questions but to help you become the person God wants you to be. Then don't hesitate to ask other believers about questions you have and books they would recommend. But when you come to Christ, I suspect many of your questions will fade because you will come to realize the greatness and love of God.

I recently met a girl in one of my college classes who claims she is a witch, but she denies she has anything to do with the worship of Satan or anything evil. This seems weird, but I am fascinated and wonder what you think.

I know that someone like this girl would claim there are various kinds of occult practices, and that she is involved in practices which have nothing to do with satanism. But the Bible—as well as the history of occult practices—shows this is not true. Ultimately all occult practices have their origin in Satan rather than God. They are a false substitute for the worship and service of God, and as such they are wrong.

That is one reason why the Bible constantly tells us we should avoid any type of occult practices. This could include not only the type of thing this girl is involved in, but any type of fortune telling, sorcery, charms, spiritism, or any other occult practice or belief. These were all common in the ancient world, but God's people were commanded not to have anything to do with them. "Let no one be found among you . . . who practices divination or sorcery, interprets omens, engages in witchcraft, or casts spells, or who is a medium or spiritist or who consults the dead" (Deuteronomy 18:10–11). When those who were involved in occult practices in Ephesus turned to Christ, they immediately burned their occult books (see Acts 19:19).

We have seen a great upsurge of interest in the occult in recent years. I have asked myself why that is the case, and I am convinced it is because of a deep spiritual hunger on the part of many people. I suspect you are like this, and that down inside you are searching for the meaning of life. But you will not find the true meaning of life in this way. You will find it only in Jesus Christ, the Son of God, who loves you and wants to come into your life.

Don't get fascinated by practices which you think will lead you to God. Instead, you can know God personally by giving your life to Jesus Christ.

III
PSYCHOLOGICAL
PROBLEMS

12

I Feel So Guilty

I used to go to church a lot, but I have done something very wrong and now I don't go to church because it just makes me feel guilty over what I have done. Can you understand why I react this way?

Yes, I can understand why you react this way—but I want to point out a very important fact. You are not solving your real problem; you are only avoiding it. What you need to do is face this problem and deal with it.

What is your real problem? The problem is not your guilt feelings, although they are kind of like a medical thermometer that tells you something is wrong. The problem is that you have done something wrong and you need God's forgiveness. No matter how much you hide or suppress your guilt feelings, you still are guilty of wrongdoing and you need to deal with the fact of that guilt.

But here is the most important truth you can know: you don't need to carry the burden of your guilt any longer! The reason is that God wants to forgive you and lift the burden from you. Can that be possible? Yes! It is possible because God loves you, and in His love He sent His only Son into the world to die as a perfect sacrifice for your sins. On the cross Christ took upon Himself the burden you are now carrying—the burden of sin and shame and guilt (not just for this one sin that you have done, but for every other sin you have ever committed). The Bible says, "He himself bore our sins in his body on the tree, so that we might die to sins and live for righteousness; by his wounds you have been healed" (1 Peter 2:24).

God's salvation is a free gift, offered to you in Jesus Christ. You could never take your own sins away—but Christ could, and He did. There is no reason for you to bear the burden of guilt any longer. Turn to Christ in repentance and faith, and accept His forgiveness as you invite Jesus Christ into your heart. There is no greater joy than knowing your sins are forgiven, and that can be your experience right now through Christ.

Years ago I was "the other woman." My husband was married to another woman, and he left her for me. We have a good marriage, but now I find myself feeling very guilty over what I did. I realize now I have messed up the lives of a lot of people. What can I do?

One of the greatest tragedies of a marriage breakup is what it does to other people—children, close relatives, etc. I am afraid people today tend to overlook that dimension, and seek only their own selfish desires without regard to the hurt they bring to others. Perhaps your letter will make someone who is in the position you once were to stop and think.

You cannot undo the past. But the most important thing you can do is to seek God's forgiveness for what you have done. When David sinned by committing adultery with another man's wife—something clearly forbidden by the Ten Commandments—he tried (like you) to avoid facing his responsibility. But the time came when he was confronted with his sin. He knew he had greatly wronged many people, but he also knew that his greatest sin was against God. That is why he confessed, "Against you, you only, have I sinned and done what is evil in your sight. . . . Surely I have been a sinner from birth" (Psalm 51:4–5).

Yes, you have sinned—against others and against God. That is why you feel guilty. But I want to tell you something very important: God loves you in spite of what you have done, and He sent His only Son Jesus Christ into the world to die in your place. By turning to Him in repentance and faith, you can be forgiven by God and you can become His child. Open your heart to Him as your Savior and Lord. Then you can say with David, "Blessed is he whose transgressions are forgiven" (Psalm 32:1).

Then I suggest you think of some practical ways you can seek the forgiveness of others you have wronged. It will not be easy, but it might be you should write some letters, for example, telling others that you have wronged them, and not only have you sought God's forgiveness for this but you seek theirs as well.

About a year ago I had an abortion. It was against everything I believed in, and since then I am filled with guilt and hatred for myself. How can I expect God to forgive me when I can't even forgive myself?

God's forgiveness for us is not conditional on our forgiving ourselves. The Bible says that "While we were still sinners, Christ died for us" (Romans 5:8). This means that even before we were interested in repenting and asking God to forgive us of our sins, God had already taken the initiative.

I want you to know that the child you aborted is with God in Heaven at this moment. Now God wants to forgive you if you will ask Him to do so. I know of many young women in your situation who believed the lie that the baby they carried was nothing more than an inconsequential piece of tissue and who came to realize the truth too late. Many are now active in telling other women in similar circumstances about their experience and helping others not to make their mistake. Perhaps this is what God has in mind for you.

I was raised in a Christian home and my parents always tried to teach me what was right. But when I got older and left home I left all that behind me and decided I didn't need it. Now I realize I was wrong to do this, and I feel very guilty over it. But is it too late? I think it is, and that He has turned His back on me, just as I have done to Him.

Think for a moment how wonderful you would feel if you could go to bed tonight and know beyond doubt that God has forgiven every sin you had ever committed. And that can be your experience, because God loves you and is ready to receive you back to Himself.

Jesus Christ has already done everything that is necessary to bring you complete forgiveness. When He died on the cross He took upon Himself your sins and my sins. No, He did not deserve to die, for as God's Son He was sinless. But Christ willingly took your sins upon Himself, and He willingly took upon Himself the punishment you deserved for those sins. The debt that you owe God has already been paid by Christ! "In him we have redemption through his blood, the forgiveness of sins, in accordance with the riches of God's grace that he lavished on us . . ." (Ephesians 1:7–8). If you had been the only person in the world who needed forgiveness, Christ would still have been willing to go to the cross for you. God loves you that much.

God has promised, "If we confess our sins, he is faithful and just and will forgive us our sins and purify us from all unrighteousness" (1 John 1:9). That promise is to you, no matter what you have done in the past. Don't let the past keep you from Christ any longer, but get on your knees, confess your sins to Him, and then receive Christ and His gift of forgiveness today.

I admit I haven't been a perfect person by a long shot, and down inside I have a lot of guilt over things I have done that I know are wrong. How can I know God will forgive me? I want to make a new start in life, but I am afraid I will only fail.

God has given you feelings of guilt to persuade you to change your way of living, and to seek the relief of His forgiveness. And His forgiveness is real; God would not have given these feelings to you if He did not also offer you forgiveness.

How can you know God's forgiveness? You have already taken the first step by facing honestly your sin and your inability to do anything about it. Now turn to Christ for forgiveness. You see, Christ came to take away our sins. As God's Son He was perfect and without sin, but He willingly took upon Himself the sin and the punishment you and I deserve when He died on the cross. He died in your place, so that you might be forgiven. "Here is a trustworthy saying that deserves full acceptance: Christ Jesus came into the world to save sinners" (1 Timothy 1:15). Why did God do this? He did it because He loves you.

Christ has done everything necessary to bring you forgiveness, and He offers it to you as a free gift. What must you do? Like any other gift, God's gift of salvation must be received.

This may seem like a simple question, but why do I feel guilty when I do something I know is wrong? I don't claim to be a very religious person, although I believe in God, but I can't get away from feelings of guilt when I do wrong. Is this just a psychological thing, as some of my friends suggest, or is there more to it?

The reason we feel guilty is that we *are* guilty. You see, God has made this world so that some things are morally right and other things are wrong—and when we go against His rules for living we are guilty of breaking His laws. Furthermore, God has made us with a conscience, so that when we do wrong we know it and are sensitive to it. This is one of the things that makes us different from plants and animals.

But let me pursue this just a bit more. Why did God make us so we would have feelings of guilt when we disobeyed Him? One reason is so that we would realize our need of Him. When you put your hand on a hot stove you immediately feel pain. God gave you the ability to experience that pain, and He did it for a purpose—so you would move your hand and not hurt yourself. Now guilt is something like that. It is a kind of "pain" that God gives us when we sin, so we will realize what we are doing not only is wrong but will hurt us. Its purpose is to drive us from sin and help us realize we need God.

Have you ever honestly faced your own need of God? You need His forgiveness for your sins, and you need His help every day. More than that, you need the eternal life He alone can give. "God has given us eternal life, and this life is in His son. He who has the Son has life; he who does not have the Son of God does not have life" (1 John 5:11–12). Open your heart to Christ today.

13

I'm Angry

I know it will probably offend you, but I am angry at God. I have just lost my wife to cancer, and I find myself overwhelmed with resentment and bitterness—even though she was a fine Christian and I know she is in Heaven.

Be thankful that your wife knew Christ and is now in Heaven with Him—where pain and death will never touch her again. Be thankful that God is with you right now, and that He loves you and wants to help you. God is still in control—even if you do not understand all that happens in this sin-scarred world. Like Paul we can be "sorrowful, yet always rejoicing" (2 Corinthians 6:10).

Then confess to God how you really feel. He already knows it, of course, but you need to be honest with Him and face your own need of repentance and healing. You need to admit your need of His comfort for your grief. Remember that Christ died on the cross for you—and that means God knows what it is to grieve. Christ is "a man of sorrows, and familiar with suffering" (Isaiah 53:3). Open your life in a fresh way to Christ by faith, for He wants to help you.

This is not an easy time for you—but you can come through this experience with a deeper sense of God's love. Christ came "to comfort all who mourn . . . to bestow on them a crown of beauty instead of ashes, the oil of gladness instead of mourning, and a garment of praise instead of a spirit of despair" (Isaiah 61:2–3).

I am of a different racial background than most of the people where we live. Frankly, I have seen a lot of prejudice and while I try to overlook it it is hard not to be angry. Can you understand how I feel?

Yes, I certainly can. One reason is because I have seen far too much prejudice in my lifetime. Early in my ministry I determined that our crusades would not be segregated. I also have been in foreign countries where I was no longer of the same race as most people, and at times I have sensed that hostility some have against my own race. Racial prejudice, I have come to realize, is found in many parts of the world—and is sometimes very intense.

A Christian who is seeking to live as Christ wants him to live will realize that racial prejudice and hatred are wrong. The apostle Paul had grown up being very proud of his racial heritage, but when Christ came into his life he began to see people differently. He began to look at them the same way God looks at people, and reached the point where he could say, "So from now on we regard no one from a worldly point of view. . . . All this is from God, who reconciled us to himself through Christ and gave us the ministry of reconciliation" (2 Corinthians 5:16, 18). God had given him a new love for others, and Paul became the great apostle to people who were not of his race.

At its heart, racial hatred is a spiritual problem caused by sin. We would support laws and other measures that promote racial harmony, but at the same time the deeper problem of hatred is a spiritual one which can only be fully solved by God. Christ can change a person's heart, replacing hatred with love and indifference with compassion.

Don't let hatred control you, no matter what others do that causes you to get angry. You would only become guilty of the same sin that afflicts them, and nothing would be solved. Instead, open your life to Christ and let Him give you a new love for others. Let Him show you ways you can help bridge the gap between peoples, and let Him help you in every area of your life to live for Him.

Three months ago I was in an auto accident, and it has left me with a physical handicap that will be with me all my life. I don't understand why God let this happen to me. I am in college and this has wrecked my plans for the future. I admit I am angry at God, and I can't help it, although I know you would say that is wrong.

Have you ever stopped to ask why you were spared—when so many people die each year in automobile accidents? And have you ever actually thanked God for sparing your life?

I do not know why God allowed this accident to happen to you—any more than I know why He spared you. But I do know this: God cares for you, and He wants to help you in the future. You can go through life constantly asking "Why?"—but what good will that do? It will only twist you and hurt you, and cut you off from those around you. The Bible warns, "Resentment kills a fool and envy slays the simple" (Job 5:2).

Don't cut yourself off from God's help. Instead, open your heart to Jesus Christ and ask Him to come into your life and help you. Some of the finest people I have ever met have been those who were handicapped, and yet they had discovered the secret of walking with Christ every day and knowing His strength and joy. This can be your experience as well, if you will commit your life and future into His hands. "I can do everything through him who gives me strength" (Philippians 4:13).

I have so many problems that I just feel like God has turned His back on me. I know that is not supposed to be true, but it's hard for me not to be angry at Him.

I know it is often hard for us to face problems in our lives that are very difficult and not ask why God has allowed them. It is only a step from that to anger and bitterness, feeling somehow that God has abandoned us or is punishing us unjustly. But that is not true, and we need to learn to look beyond the immediate problems we face to God Himself, learning to trust Him in every situation.

Let me give an example from the Bible. There came a time during Jeremiah's day when his nation was devastated by a foreign invader. In many ways the nation was not innocent, for the people had turned their backs on God. But it still came as a shock to Jeremiah, seeing the nation and its beautiful capital city of Jerusalem destroyed. Yet in the midst of the pain he felt, he learned to look to God because he knew that God still loved His people and was near to them. Listen to what Jeremiah wrote: "Yet this I call to mind and therefore I have hope: Because of the Lord's great love we are not consumed, for his compassions never fail. They are new every morning; great is your faithfulness" (Lamentations 3:21–23).

God loves you, in spite of the problems you may not be able to understand. And He has not abandoned you. How do I know He loves you? I know it because He was willing to let His only Son go to the cross and die as a sacrifice for your sins and mine. If He did not love you, Christ would never have died to make it possible for you to know God and go to Heaven when you die. But He loves you, and the greatest thing that could happen to you right now would be for you to reach out in faith and accept God's love in Jesus Christ.

You may not understand why some things happen to you—but you can learn to face each day with the certainty that Christ is with you even in the midst of the storms of life.

I know we are supposed to love other people, but it is hard for me not to be angry at my husband's brother and sister. His mother is quite elderly and lives with us because she has a lot of health problems. But they never come to visit her or offer to help in any way. We can afford to care for her, but in principle I think they ought to be more thoughtful, don't you?

Yes, they should be more thoughtful. After all, when they were children she took care of them for many years, and it is sad that they do not do more to express gratitude for all she did for them. Some day they also will probably be elderly and less able to take care of themselves. How will they feel when their children—who are undoubtedly observing them and noting the way they treat their mother—pay no attention to them in their time of need?

The Bible says much about our responsibility toward our parents. One of the Ten Commandments declares, "Honor your father and your mother" (Exodus 20:12). The Bible also states, "If anyone does not provide for his relatives, and especially for his immediate family, he has denied the faith and is worse than an unbeliever" (1 Timothy 5:8).

This kind of thoughtlessness and ingratitude points to a spiritual issue. When we are selfish and treat others selfishly, it indicates that we have not allowed God's love to touch us and control us. When we have no regard for our parents, it is a sign that we also have no regard for God, our heavenly Father. Pray for your relatives, not only that they will show more love for others but that they will come to know Christ and experience His love and forgiveness.

At the same time, do not let bitterness or anger destroy you. Perhaps you need to take the initiative and invite your relatives over to your house from time to time not to argue, but to let them know they are welcome. "Do not repay anyone evil for evil. Be careful to do what is right in the eyes of everybody. If it is possible, as far as it depends on you, live at peace with everyone" (Romans 12:17–18).

Recently my husband took a new job in another city. I have always been close to my family where we used to live, and now that we have moved to a new city I am depressed and angry at him for doing this to me. Do you think I would be justified in telling him we either move back or else I leave and go back without him?

You have a responsibility to be the best possible wife you can for your husband. When you were married you took a vow—not only before others but before God—to be committed to each other, no matter what circumstances might come your way.

God wants to use this time to help you grow spiritually and emotionally. Have you ever thought about this and asked God to help you? You need to ask Him not only to help you adjust to your new situation, but also to learn whatever lessons He wants to teach you during this time. Do you remember the story of Abraham in the Old Testament? He had a very successful and happy life in the city where he grew up, but the time came when God called Abraham to leave that city and go to a new place. The Bible says, "By faith Abraham, when called to go to a place he would later receive as his inheritance, obeyed and went, even though he did not know where he was going" (Hebrews 11:8). Abraham learned to trust God, and God rewarded his trust.

If you have never given your life to Christ, now is the time for you to make that important decision. Then ask God to show you practical ways you can overcome your feelings and become adjusted to your new neighborhood. Get involved in a church where Christ is preached—it will do much to help you overcome your loneliness. Paul said, "I have learned the secret of being content in any and every situation . . . I can do everything through him who gives me strength" (Philippians 4:12–13). This can be your experience as you yield your life to Christ and grow closer to Him each day.

I find it hard not to be angry at God. I lost both my sister and my mother to cancer during the last year, and I miss them very much. Why did God let this happen to them? They both had faith that God would heal them but He didn't, and I don't understand that.

I know this is a difficult time for you and inevitably you ask the question, "Why?" We are limited as human beings, and we don't always understand fully why some things happen to us. We often presume that this is a better place and a better life than what God has in store for us in Heaven where there is no pain, no suffering, and no more death. If you can focus more on what Heaven must be like and on a God who loves your sister and mother so much that He brought them home to be with Him, rather than see them suffer, you will begin to feel much better about God's graciousness toward them and toward you.

The Bible teaches that God is a loving God, and he also is in ultimate control of this universe. The Bible also teaches that evil is real, and calls death an "enemy" (1 Corinthians 15:26). These things are true—even if I cannot fully understand them or reconcile them.

You can have one of two reactions to what has happened, and I want you to think about them carefully and not let your emotions cloud the truth. On one hand, you can react against God, blaming Him for what has happened and becoming bitter and angry. If you do this, you will be saying that God is unloving and unfair, and is even wrong in what He does.

On the other hand, this event can bring you closer to God. How can this happen? It can happen if you realize that you need God right now. You need His love and compassion, and you need His hope for the future. You need the inner peace that He alone can bring—and will bring to you if you learn the secret of trusting Him.

Look beyond your present grief to Jesus Christ. God knows what it is like to suffer and even experience death—because His Son died on the cross. He did this so you could have forgiveness and eternal life. Do you want to know—really know—that God loves you? Look at Christ. "This is how we know what love is: Jesus Christ laid down his life for us" (1 John 3:16). Your mother and sister were evidently women of great faith, and right now they are with Christ in Heaven, completely free of the pain and sorrow of this life. Don't let bitterness grow and poison your life, but turn to Christ and renew your commitment to Him.

I admit I am angry at God, because I have had a physical handicap since birth and it has always cut me off from normal life. Why did God do this to me? I'll never be able to hold down the kind of job I would like or anything. You can't begin to understand how frustrating it is to be stuck in a wheelchair most of the time.

Most of us who have never faced the difficulties you face cannot fully understand the frustration you feel; one reason I have printed part of your letter is to encourage all of us to be more sensitive to those who have any kind of handicap.

One of the most striking things about Jesus was the way He demonstrated His concern for those who were sick or handicapped. "People brought to him all who were ill with various diseases, those suffering severe pain, the demon-possessed, the epileptics and the paralytics, and he healed them" (Matthew 4:24). And I encourage you to bring your own personal burdens and hurts to Christ, for He loves you and He wants to help you. We may not fully understand why God allows suffering and handicaps. You can allow anger and bitterness to control you the rest of your life, or you can accept your limitations. We are all limited in some way, but with God's help we can discover the joy of living life to its fullest potential.

Anger and bitterness will distort and destroy you; in their own ways, they will make you even more handicapped than you are. But Christ wants to take all that away, and He will help you adjust and gain victory over the things that will hold you back.

14

I'm Getting More
and More Depressed

Please help me, because I am getting more and more depressed. I have been in love with a man who is much older than I. He has a family, but always claimed that he loved me. Now he has turned his back on me and I just don't know what to do.

I hope you will not think that I am insensitive to your emotions, but very frankly you should be thankful this has happened to you. You have been spared even greater heartache down the road, I strongly suspect, because if you had eventually married this man you would probably not have had a secure and happy relationship. After all, if he was willing to sneak away from his family and his wife for you, what guarantee would you have that he would not do the same thing to you?

There is only one right thing to do, and that is to leave this behind you and get your feet on the right path. What you have done is wrong in God's eyes, because marriage is a very sacred thing to God. It would have been a terrible thing for you to be responsible for breaking up this man's family—terrible for them, and terrible in the eyes of God.

Your question suggests to me that you have never really considered your own need of Christ in your life. Down inside you are looking for love and happiness—but you will never find it in this way. However, God loves you, and He wants to come into your life and give you a joy and peace that you could never experience any other way. Jesus said, "Peace I leave with you; my peace I give you" (John 14:27).

God created you, and God loves you. His only Son, Jesus Christ, loved you so much that He gave His life on the cross so you could be saved from your sins and become a child of God. When you accept Christ into your life, something wonderful and supernatural happens. God Himself comes to dwell within you! You become part of His family, and you can know the joy of His presence every day. You can commit every area of your life to Him, because He has a perfect plan for your life. Get on your knees right now and invite Jesus Christ into your heart. It will be the most important decision you will ever make, and will get you on the right path.

I am haunted by my past. I was a soldier in Viet Nam, and like a lot of others who were there I will never get over the memory of some of the things I saw. I also got into some things (like drugs) that have been hard for me to shake. I have been involved in several rehabilitation programs that have helped me some, but once again I have become so depressed I can't even hold a job or anything. Please pray that God will help me somehow.

God has an amazing way of taking things that are painful or even wrong in our backgrounds, and helping us overcome them so that we are no longer slaves to them. I pray that this will be your experience.

That is why I encourage you to turn to Christ for the help and forgiveness you need. What can God do for you? First, He can bring you freedom from guilt, for He alone can forgive you of your sins—and one thing that is haunting you from the past is your sins. You see, sin separates us from God. But God loves us, and He wants to forgive us and bring us back to Himself. And He has done everything necessary to make our forgiveness possible, by sending His only Son, Jesus Christ, to die on the cross in our place. The Bible promises that in Christ we have "the forgiveness of sins, in accordance with the riches of God's grace" (Ephesians 1:7).

Then God also wants to give you a new purpose and strength for living. He wants you to find His will for your life—and there is no more exciting adventure than knowing God and following His will. He can also guide you to some practical programs that can help you deal with your problems. When we know Christ, we have an anchor that will keep us secure no matter what storms come our way.

Our son has a slight physical disability, and we are worried because he is very self-conscious about it and is getting more and more withdrawn. The problem is his classmates make fun of him because he is different and can't do all the things they do. Should we be concerned about this or will he grow out of this attitude, do you think?

Yes, you should be concerned and should do all you can to help him overcome it. Otherwise he is in danger of developing negative attitudes about himself and about others that could handicap him the rest of his life. Modern psychology is discovering a truth the Bible taught long ago—that the early years of a child's life are extremely important in shaping his character and direction.

Talk frankly with your son's teachers about this problem; they are probably unaware of it, and will want to do all they can to help your son. They also need to help his classmates be more sensitive—not just toward your son, but toward all who are handicapped in our society. In addition, do all you can to encourage your son and let him know that you love him just as he is.

Beyond this, however, encourage your son to commit his life to Jesus Christ. One of the most important truths any of us can discover is that we are important and valuable to God—no matter what other people may think about us or what other problems we may face. "Fear not, for I have redeemed you; I have called you by name; you are mine. When you pass through the waters, I will be with you" (Isaiah 43:1–2). How do we know this is true? We know it because Jesus Christ was willing to go to the cross and die on our behalf. Pray for your son, that he will realize he is never alone if he knows Christ.

I've always believed in God, but since our precious baby lived only a week, I'm despondent. I can't seem to pray any more. How can I find courage to go on?

I wish I could sit down and talk to you and give a full hour to answering your question. A situation like yours puts Christianity to the supreme test. Don't imagine that you are the only one who has had moments of spiritual darkness. Even the saints had their dark days. But they found God again. You can too. Do these four things:

1. Each morning kneel and thank God for all the joy He has brought through the years. Surrender your day to Him. Ask Christ to guide and direct you. Then all through the day think of Him as walking by your side.

2. Read your Bible. There you find words of wisdom and comfort, as "For now we see through a glass, darkly; but then face to face: now I know in part; but then shall I know even as also I am known" (1 Corinthians 13:12, KJV).

3. Seek opportunities to help those in need. There is someone who needs your love and care. Ask God to show you who it is.

4. Hold fast to your belief in Eternal Life. Death is not the end, but the doorway into Heaven.

This is a difficult hour for you. Remember that Jesus did not promise that His followers would escape suffering and heartache. No, He promised instead that they would have peace in the midst of pain, and be given a divine strength to support them in hours of weakness. The Bible says: "This is the victory that overcometh the world, even our faith" (1 John 5:4, KJV).

My wife is going through chemotherapy as a follow-up to the cancer surgery she had several months ago. The whole process has been difficult for her physi-

cally, but the surprising thing is that her spirits are very high—while I have been getting more and more depressed. I try to hide it from her, but it is only getting worse. Maybe her faith has something to do with her attitude, but whatever it is I wish I had what she has.

From what you say elsewhere it is clear that your wife has a strong faith in Christ, and God has given her an extra measure of strength for this difficult time. My prayer is that you also will come to know Christ so you can share together the joy of belonging to Him.

Why is your wife's faith making the difference? One reason is that when we know Christ we know we are never alone, no matter what problems or suffering we face. "Where can I go from your Spirit? Where can I flee from your presence? . . . if I make my bed in the depths, you are there . . . even there your hand will guide me, your right hand will hold me fast" (Psalm 139:7, 8, 10). Another reason is this: she knows this life is not all, and that some day she will go to be with God in Heaven throughout eternity. And she knows in Heaven "There will be no more death or mourning or crying or pain, for the old order of things has passed away" (Revelation 21:4).

Right now God is seeking to get your attention. Don't turn your back on Him. Instead, confess to God that you know you are a sinner and need His forgiveness, and then ask Jesus Christ to come into your life as your Savior and Lord. When you do, you will begin to see life (and death) in a new light, and Christ will replace your despair with hope and the light of His presence.

I guess I would have to say I have never been happy at any time in my life. My father was always too busy making money and my mother always nagged me. My marriage has not been happy, and I find myself getting increasingly depressed. Maybe if I tried God it would help.

I am sorry your life has been filled with so much unhappiness. Some of your feelings, I suspect you know, probably come from your childhood experiences, and parents need to realize how much their behavior affects the lives of their children for years to come.

Yes, God can help you in this situation, and He wants to help you because He loves you. Throughout your life you have felt that people did not really love you—and whether you realize it or not, you probably have felt down inside that you were not worth loving and that life was hardly worth living. But I want to tell you good news—God loves you! How do I know that He loves you? I know it because Jesus Christ, God's only Son, was willing to die for your sin so that you could become part of His family. If you had been the only person with sin in the whole world, Christ still would have gone to the cross as a sacrifice for your sins. That's how much He loves you!

This is why one of the most important things you can do is to begin to see yourself the way God sees you. You cannot be the same once you realize God's love is focused on you. "How great is the love the Father has lavished on us, that we should be called children of God! And that is what we are!" (1 John 3:1).

Yes, God has done everything possible to wash away your sins and bring you into a personal relationship with Himself. But you must respond to His love. How can you do that? By accepting Jesus Christ into your heart by faith, asking Him to come into your life and become Lord of your life. God is only a prayer away, and He stands ready to receive you. Then get into the Scriptures, and see what they say about God's love for you. God wants to change you and give you an inner peace you have never known—and He will, as you turn in faith to Him.

A couple of months ago I took an overdose of pills because I was very depressed. I am better now, but lurking in the back of my mind is the fear that I will lose control and try to do it again. How can I get over this fear?

As I am sure you have discovered, there are many causes of depression. From a medical point of view I am sure your doctor would strongly urge you to seek professional help immediately if you find your depression is returning. But I also believe you can receive help from God to deliver you from your fears and strengthen you spiritually and emotionally.

This is why the most important thing I can tell you is to learn to trust God in every circumstance, and to keep your eyes on Him. On one occasion, the great prophet Elijah got so discouraged that he even asked God to take away his life. (You can read of his struggle in 1 Kings 19.) There were probably many things that contributed to Elijah's depression—physical weariness, hunger, a sense of defeat because he felt he had not been successful, fear of the future, and even fear that his enemies would kill him. But the heart of the matter was that Elijah was concentrating on his circumstances rather than on God. God's answer was to meet his physical needs by giving him rest and food—but more than that God gave him a new vision of the glory and power and love of God. Elijah went on to do many great things for God.

God loves you, and He wants you to know that He is with you in every situation. Christ can take away your fears, and He can give you strength to live each day. The Bible promises, "Fear not, for I have redeemed you; I have called you by name; you are mine. When you pass through the waters, I will be with you; and when you pass through the rivers, they will not sweep over you" (Isaiah 43:1–2). This can be your experience as you walk with Christ each day.

I have just been released from a mental hospital where I was treated for severe depression. I am much better now but in the back of my mind there is always the fear that it will return. For the first time in my life I am thinking about my need of God, although one of my friends says religion is just a crutch and I should learn to stand on my own two feet.

It is not a sign of weakness to admit that you need God. In fact, I would suggest that your friend is the one who is actually weak, because he is unwilling or too proud to be honest with himself and admit that he also needs God. Don't let his remarks keep you from the most important decision you can make in life—your decision to follow Christ.

We all need God, whether we admit it or not. We need Him first of all for forgiveness, because only God can truly forgive us for all the sins we have ever committed. We also need Him because He alone knows what is best for our lives, and we need His guidance if we are to live as we should. We need Him as well for strength—strength to resist temptation, strength to do what is right, and strength for daily living. And we need God because He alone can give us true hope for the future, both in this life and for the life after death.

Yes, we need God—and the wonderful thing is that God loves us and wants us to come to Him. He loves you. He knows all about your problems and your fears, and He wants you to trust all of those into His hands. How do we know this is true? We know it because God sent His Son to this earth to die on the cross for our sins.

God has promised to make you His child if you will simply ask Him to. The Bible says, "To all who received him, to those who believed in his name, he gave the right to become children of God" (John 1:12). You can go to bed tonight knowing Christ is with you, and He will never leave you no matter what the future holds for you.

I have just been told by the doctor that I have a form of cancer. He claims that it can probably be cured, but sometimes I wonder if it is even worth trying. Why does God let things like this happen?

It is understandable that you feel depressed over this news and wonder if it is even worth the effort to try to combat it. But I pray you will not give in to your despair. Your doctor undoubtedly has good reason for saying you have a good chance of being cured (although you may want to get a second opinion on this also). There have been remarkable advances in the fight against cancer in recent years, and it would be wrong for you to turn your back on these possibilities. In addition, you should remember that there are others who love you and depend on you, and for their sake you should seek the right answer to this problem.

We do not always know all the reasons why God allows things like this to happen to us. But I want to tell you something that I have heard time after time from people who have faced similar difficulties—and which I have also experienced. It is this: God can use even the painful experiences in our lives to draw us closer to Himself and accomplish His purposes. The Bible reminds us, "No discipline seems pleasant at the time, but painful. Later on, however, it produces a harvest of righteousness and peace for those who have been trained by it" (Hebrews 12:11).

Therefore, whatever the eventual outcome of your illness may be, I pray that you will constantly be open to whatever God wants to teach you. Perhaps, for example, God wants to teach you about the importance of putting Him first in your life. Perhaps He is teaching you to trust Him more and more in every situation. Perhaps He is teaching you that the things of eternity are more important than the things of time. Don't let bitterness or anger overcome you, but use this time to discover more of God's love and mercy in your life.

What does the Bible say about suicide? Would I be forgiven if I committed suicide?

Normally I do not answer anonymous letters, but I have made an exception in your case because I sense that you are a deeply troubled person who is on the verge of doing the most serious and final thing you can do—taking your own life. With all my heart I pray that you will not take that step, for I am convinced it would be wrong. Yes, God knows our hearts, and He can forgive our sins. But that must never, never be an excuse for doing what is wrong. And if you do not know Christ, I must tell you frankly that death would not end your problems. You would instead have an eternity ahead of you of sorrow and loneliness, separated forever from God and Heaven. In other words, I want to impress upon you the seriousness of the step I sense you are about to take.

But I especially want to impress you with another great truth, and that is that God loves you and wants to come into your life right now to take away your despair and give you hope and peace. Perhaps you think that is not possible—but it is, because God is more powerful than your problems, whatever they may be.

Listen to what Jesus says to you: "Come to me, all you who are weary and burdened, and I will give you rest. Take my yoke upon you and learn from me, for I am gentle and humble in heart, and you will find rest for your souls. For my yoke is easy and my burden is light" (Matthew 11:28–30). Countless people throughout the ages have discovered this is true—and you can discover it as well as you cast your burdens on Christ. Don't give in to depression and despair—God has a plan for your life, and the most important thing you can do is to discover Him and invite Christ into your heart by faith.

A friend told us you said in a column that God would not save a person who committed suicide, no matter what the circumstances were. Our son suffered from a terrible mental problem for years and eventually committed suicide, although I really believe he knew God. What is the basis of your position?

This is not my position. Either your friend misunderstood something in the column or—as sometimes happens because of space limitations—your newspaper omitted part of the column. I regret very much this misunderstanding.

I receive many letters every week from people who are thinking about suicide. I always try to be very careful in answering them, because suicide is a terribly serious matter and I would never want someone to use something I might say as an excuse for committing this terrible act. Life is given to us by God, and He alone has the right to take it away. Furthermore, even in the midst of very difficult circumstances God is with us when we know Christ, and He can help us gain victory over them. On one hand, therefore, I must stress the fact that suicide is wrong and not part of God's plan.

But there also are situations when a person may not understand what he is doing because of mental disability, as in the case of your son. God understands such situations—even when we don't. "As a father has compassion on his children, so the Lord has compassion on those who fear him; for he knows how we are formed, he remembers that we are dust" (Psalm 103:13–14). The Bible also promises "that neither death nor life . . . nor anything else in all creation, will be able to separate us from the love of God that is in Christ Jesus our Lord" (Romans 8:38–39).

Only one thing will keep us from Heaven, and that is our refusal to turn to Christ in faith and trust. We are never saved by our good works, because we can never be good enough to earn God's favor. God saves us by His grace alone as we trust Christ. We must never presume on God's grace or think that it means we can do anything we want without paying the consequences. But take comfort in God's grace as you remember your son—and seek to live for Christ every day.

Why is it that some of the most glamorous people in life also seem to be so miserable? I think of some of the movie stars, for example, who can't seem to find a happy marriage and even end up committing suicide.

The Bible tells us that we were made for God, and when we refuse to give Him His rightful place in our lives then things go wrong and our lives become distorted. I have discovered that often people who seemingly have everything in terms of fame and fortune believe that somehow they will eventually find happiness by pursuing those things even more. But it is a dead-end road, for lasting happiness and peace can only come from God.

This is what King Solomon discovered. During his reign, Israel had peace and was very wealthy. Solomon could have had anything money could buy, and in search for happiness he tried everything imaginable—wealth, sex, power, pleasure, alcohol, even religion (although it was only a dead and formal kind of religion for him). "I denied myself nothing my eyes desired; I refused my heart no pleasure!" (Ecclesiastes 2:10). But what was the result of Solomon's search? "Yet when I surveyed all that my hand had done and what I had toiled to achieve, everything was meaningless, a chasing after the wind" (Ecclesiastes 2:11). Finally he realized that lasting happiness and meaning in life could only be found in God.

These things should be warnings to us, to be sure that we do not seek to fill the emptiness in our lives through things that can never satisfy our hearts. Only God can do that—and He will if we will open our hearts to Jesus Christ. Jesus said, "I have come that they may have life, and have it to the full" (John 10:10). This has been the experience of Christians throughout the ages, and it can be your experience as well as you open your heart and invite Jesus Christ into your life.

Centuries ago, God, through the prophet Isaiah, declared, "Why spend . . . your labor on what does not satisfy? . . . Give ear and come to me; hear me, that your soul may live" (Isaiah 55:2, 3). This is His invitation today as well, inviting you to come to Christ and find the true meaning of life.

I hear a lot of talk these days about the so-called "mid-life crisis." Does the Bible say anything about this?

This term is, of course, just a few years old but I think there are probably some good examples of it in the Bible. As I understand it, those who speak about a "mid-life crisis" are referring to the fact that many people (especially, I believe, men) undergo a time of crisis in their middle-age years as they think about their goals and what they have (and have not) accomplished. For some people this "crisis" causes them to flee from their responsibilities or strive to be young again—often in foolish ways, such as a middle-aged man who suddenly leaves his wife and falls in "love" with a teen-aged girl.

I wonder if in some ways King David had something of a similar experience when he reached his middle years. You may recall that one time he was supposed to be in battle with his troops, but for some reason he had grown slack and stayed instead at the palace. There he saw a beautiful woman named Bathsheba. She was another man's wife, but David committed the sin of adultery with her. It was a dark time in the life of a man who otherwise had tried to obey God, and for some months David lived out of fellowship with God. (You can read about this in 2 Samuel 11.)

But eventually David faced his sin and realized the foolishness—and the evil— of what he had done. One of the most eloquent prayers of repentance in the whole Bible is found in Psalm 51. "Have mercy on me, O God, according to your unfailing love; . . . Wash away all my iniquity and cleanse me from my sin" (Psalm 51:1, 2).

If you sense that you are facing this kind of crisis—or any other kind—realize that the most important thing in life is to yield your life to Christ and then seek to do His will. If we know we are in the will of God, there need not be moments of self-doubt and crisis. As David said elsewhere, "You have made known to me the path of life; you will fill me with joy in your presence, with eternal pleasures at your right hand" (Psalm 16:11). You can know this also as you follow Christ as your Lord.

I guess I am going through sort of a mid-life crisis, because suddenly I have realized I am getting older and I have wasted so much time. I have always acted as if I would always be young and able to do anything I wanted, but now I know it isn't true. I don't know why I am writing you, but somehow I feel as if I need to rethink my life and where I am heading.

I am thankful you are facing these questions; one of the saddest things I know of is to see persons who come to the end of life and have never asked who they are or why they were here.

You are not here by chance; God put you here. He put you here for a purpose, and the most important thing you can do is discover that purpose and to commit yourself to it. What is God's purpose for you? First of all, God wants you to come to know Him personally by giving your life to Jesus Christ. Then He wants you to discover in your daily life what it means to live for Him and follow His will. The Bible says, "But seek first his kingdom and his righteousness" (Matthew 6:33).

What have you been living for? Money? Pleasure? Security? Happiness? Success? Whatever it has been, it can never give you lasting happiness or security. You were made for a relationship with God, and you will only find true meaning and purpose in Christ. So far you have made yourself the center of your life. Now make Christ the center of your life by asking Him to come into your heart as your Lord and Savior. Then you can say of God with the Psalmist, "You have made known to me the path of life" (Psalm 16:11).

I have read a lot recently about mid-life crisis, and I think it fits my husband exactly. He has always worked very hard and been successful, but now he says he is fed up with everything and wants a new career and a new family. Our heart is broken, but he has left us for his girl friend, who is much younger. Is there anything I can do!

I know a lot has been written in recent years about the so-called mid-life crisis—a time when some people become disillusioned with their lives and decide to strike out in radically different ways. Whatever the cause, decisions such as the one your husband has made inevitably bring heartache and unhappiness—not only to those around him, but eventually to the person himself.

Pray for your husband. As did the prodigal son in the story which Jesus told (Luke 15:11–32), your husband has deceived himself into thinking that he will find happiness by fleeing his responsibilities and disobeying God's moral law. Only God can awaken him to the tragedy and foolishness of what he is doing. Pray that God will break through the moral blindness which has gripped him, and convict him of his sin. Pray also that your husband will realize his need of repentance, and that he will turn to Christ for forgiveness.

Then in whatever ways are open to you let your husband know that you still love him and want to forgive him. The time may come when he (like the prodigal son) will sink so low that he will come to his senses and realize the only right thing to do is to return home. The father of the prodigal son welcomed him, and you should let your husband know you will welcome him if he will turn from his wrongdoing. Let him know also that you are willing to make adjustments if they are necessary—adopting a more relaxed lifestyle, for example, so he does not feel trapped by a constant push for success.

Finally, do all you can to help your children right now. It is a difficult time, but seek God's wisdom and strength to carry on and help your children mature. If Christ has never been the foundation of your family before this, turn to Him and make it your goal to help your children understand that God never fails us—even when our human fathers may fail.

I understand that the Bible tells us to forgive our enemies many times. Although I have tried to forgive a certain person for a wrong done deliberately, I simply cannot. I have no other enemies. Do you think God will judge me for having just this one person whom I cannot forgive?

Even the non-Christian has friends and loved ones, but he loves them because they love him in return. Here is the distinctiveness of the Christian life. Jesus said: "Love your enemies, and pray for those who persecute you" (Matthew 5:44). On another occasion He said that we should forgive until seventy times seven. God can and will give a forgiving spirit when we accept His forgiveness through Jesus Christ. When you do, you will realize that He has forgiven you so much that you will desire to forgive any wrong. In the world, a policy of getting even with the other fellow is generally accepted. We Christians, on the other hand, should follow the policy of enduring wrong for the sake of Christ and forgiving that men might through us discover the grace of God in forgiving the sinner.

15

Why Do I Act
the Way I Do?

*I don't understand why I act the way I do. I grew up with an alcoholic father,
and I always hated it and swore I would never be like him. Well, now I find I
can't control my drinking either, and secretly I fear ending up the same old
way he did. Why am I this way?*

Children of alcoholics often end up on the same road as their parents—in spite
of the destruction they have seen.

There may be several reasons for this. Some recent research, for example,
suggests some people are physically very susceptible to alcoholism, and that
this tendency may even be inherited. But it also is clear that for many people
alcohol becomes an easy "solution" to escape from their problems (although it
is never a real or lasting solution). In other words, possibly you have been scarred
and hurt emotionally by your background—and in spite of your better judgment,
you had turned to alcohol to try to take away some of that hurt.

But whatever the reasons may be, the important thing is for you to face it
and get the help you need. Don't assume you can deal with this on your own;
alcoholism can destroy you. The Bible warns, "Who has woe? Who has sorrow?
Who has strife? . . . Those who linger over wine . . . In the end it bites like a
snake and poisons like a viper" (Proverbs 23:29, 30, 32). There are organizations
in your community that can help you. Share your problem honestly with your
pastor and/or doctor and let him help you get the help you need.

Above all you are very important to God and He does not want you to allow
yourself to be destroyed. He loves you, and He wants to help you. Commit your
life to Christ and ask Him to guide you to the help you need.

*My home life was chaotic when I was growing up—alcoholic father, mother
who ran around a lot, eventual divorce, running away from home, foster homes,
etc. My aunt always told me I was to blame for all the troubles my parents
had because I was just a problem to them. Now that I am an adult I find those*

accusations still haunt me and I feel like I am worth nothing. What ideas do you have about overcoming these feelings?

Feelings like this which have their roots in long-lasting childhood experiences are not easily overcome. It may even be helpful for you to seek out a counselor (a trained psychologist or psychiatrist) who can help you work through these things and understand them better; your pastor can perhaps suggest someone if this is necessary.

However, the greatest thing you can do is discover the great truth of how God feels about you. You feel very negative about yourself, but have you ever thought about how God looks at you? Listen: He loves you, and you are very valuable to Him. This is a *fact*, no matter what your *feelings* may tell you. Our feelings, you see, can deceive us. They can actually trick us into believing something which is not true. There are reasons why your feelings are the way they are—but they still are not telling the truth, because God says you are very precious to Him.

Ask Christ to come into your life by a simple prayer of faith. Then read the Bible on a daily basis. Start with the Gospel of John or the little book of 1 John and note what is said repeatedly about God's love for us. The Bible says, "Perfect love drives out fear" (1 John 4:18)—and God's perfect love can drive out your fear that you are worthless, as you realize the wonderful truth of His love for you.

I am always getting excited about projects of various sorts, and throw myself into them with all my energy. But then I lose interest and it seems like I never finish anything I start out to do. I wonder why I can't seem to overcome this. I guess this isn't a spiritual problem, but maybe you have some ideas.

Every problem has a spiritual side to it and yours is no exception. Let me assure you also that God is concerned about the problems we face in life, and He wants to help us deal with them.

Have you ever really asked yourself why you back away from projects and never seem to complete them? I do not know the answer, and there may be several reasons—but I would encourage you to examine this. For example, some people never finish a task because down inside they are afraid of failure—and the easiest way to avoid failure is to avoid doing the project in the first place. But we should not let fear of failure or embarrassment keep us from doing things in life; God, after all, accepts us just as we are. I suspect you would begin to overcome this problem if you would stay with one project all the way (perhaps asking others to help you stick to it)—and discover you really can do it.

But let me point you to a far more important question: Have you let this attitude spill over into your spiritual life? Has there been a time in your life when you got excited about following Christ and doing God's will—and then you drifted away? Or have you ever faced your own need of God and given your life to Christ? Commit your life to Him, and then with His help "run with perseverance the race marked out for us. Let us fix our eyes on Jesus . . . so that you will not grow weary and lose heart" (Hebrews 12:1–3).

Both my brother and sister are very gifted. I am just ordinary. They get many chances to do work in our church while I only get a few. This makes me feel very discouraged, for I feel the Lord can't use me as He does them. How can I avoid getting so discouraged?

The Bible is full of ordinary people. As a matter of fact, God uses ordinary people far more often than He does the rich, the powerful, the famous, and the influential. Jesus chose ordinary people as His disciples. Moses had grave doubts about his abilities.

God uses the humble, not the proud, to achieve His objectives. You say that your brother and sister are very gifted, but so are you. When God gives the gift, it is valuable, no matter what it may be. God's greatest gift to man is salvation and it is the greatest gift we can give to others.

The Bible says that God has chosen the foolish (or ordinary) things of this world to confound the wise. You are very valuable to God because He made you just as you are. Ask God to show you His plan for your life. When you discover God's plan for your life and act on it, you will begin to see yourself as God already sees you: as an extraordinary person whom God loves and needs.

I have just completed a prison sentence of three years. Upon returning home, I find that I am not accepted in society anymore. I have no work and almost no friends. Do you think I am wrong to be resentful toward people who will have little to do with me? I want to go straight, but it seems that people want to push me back down where I was.

Yours is one of the problems common to every person who has violated the law and been imprisoned. Your problem is not new. What you must realize is that you have given people a reason to distrust you, and now it is up to you to give society a reason to accept you. It won't be easy, and it is one of the aspects of your punishment. I would suggest two things for you to do.

The burden is upon you, first of all, to convince society of your intention to go straight. This will take time and will be painful for you, but it will be worth the effort.

Second, discover a power that will hold you true to the purpose you have set before you. You cannot go the road alone, for you too are a social creature.

Remember that to begin with, God made you to have fellowship with others. Even though society cannot forget quickly your crime, God will forgive your sins the moment you take Jesus Christ as your Savior.

You have already gone halfway in repentance in being sorry for your sin. Why not go the other half of the way and turn to God who right now is seeking for your heart and for your faith? Then find a fellowship of Christians who will accept you. There are some, even though you do not think so now. If you do that, God will sustain you through the days of readjustment, and even more, He will keep you to the end of life in fellowship that is more precious than the best friend can provide.

I think I must be addicted to television soap operas. I know I spend too much time watching them, but I get hooked on them and just can't seem to break the habit. Do you think there's anything harmful in this?

I suspect that you know the answer to your own question, because I detect a sense of guilt in your letter and a feeling that you know you should be using your time in a more productive way. Yes, I think you need to reexamine the way you spend your time.

There are at least two reasons I say this. First, I suspect there is a good chance you are spending so much time watching television (from what you say) that you are neglecting other things that you ought to be doing. Time is a very precious thing—once a minute is lost, it is lost forever. The Bible tells us to "redeem the time" (Colossians 4:5, KJV). There is a legitimate place for relaxation and recreation. But we also have been given responsibilities by God—within our family, our job, etc.

Second, you need to ask yourself if your time can be used to better advantage or profit, and even if this sort of activity could be harmful to you. (We should ask this about anything that threatens to absorb our interest and I don't mean to single out soap operas any more than any other activity.) The Bible gives a general principle which should guide our thinking and our activities: "Whatever is true, whatever is noble, whatever is right, whatever is pure, whatever is lovely, whatever is admirable—if anything is excellent or praiseworthy—think about such things" (Philippians 4:8). By this standard I am afraid many of our activities (including, frankly, much that appears in the media today) do not measure up.

I have been urging you not to escape from your responsibilities. But I would include especially your spiritual responsibilities in this. Have you ever thought seriously about your own relationship with God? Are you spending time each day in prayer and Bible study, seeking to learn more about God's will for your life?

My husband has been a fine man in many ways, but our home is being wrecked because he is obsessed with gambling. He is always hoping his luck will change. He says he doesn't see anything morally wrong with it, but I wonder what your opinion is.

What your husband is doing is wrong for several reasons, and I hope he will have the courage to face this, turn from what he is doing, and get help. It may not be easy, I know; some people are so compulsive about gambling that it becomes almost like an addictive drug. But there are organizations that can help such people—and most of all God wants to help you and your husband deal with this and get your home back on a solid foundation.

Let me mention two reasons why your husband's compulsive gambling is wrong. First, it is wrong because of the motive behind it. Greed can easily take over someone who is deeply involved in gambling, and even if such a person wins he will often keep on gambling hoping to win even more—which usually doesn't happen. The Bible wisely says, "Whoever loves money never has money enough; whoever loves wealth is never satisfied with his income" (Ecclesiastes 5:10). One of the Ten Commandments declares, "You shall not covet" (Exodus 20:17). Why does the Bible warn us against covetousness and greed? Because God knows that when greed consumes us it pushes out of our lives things that should be there, and makes us do things that are wrong.

Second, it also is wrong because of its effects. Your letter indicates that your husband has incurred some serious debts because of his gambling. In addition, he is spending time and energy on his gambling habit and is neglecting his responsibilities as a husband and father. The Bible rightly says, "A greedy man brings trouble to his family" (Proverbs 15:27).

Pray for your husband, and seek to talk frankly—but not in anger with him. If he is honest he will realize he needs to turn from his habit, and seek the help and strength that God wants to give him.

Do you think God is concerned about how we take care of our bodies? I have never taken very good care of it and I'm seriously overweight, although I am still in my twenties.

God is concerned about our bodies. He gave them to us, and it is wrong for us to abuse them. But if you know Jesus Christ as your Lord and Savior, there is a further reason to take care of your body, and that is because God the Holy Spirit now lives within you.

This is why the Bible says, "Do you not know that your body is a temple of the Holy Spirit, who is in you, whom you have received from God? You are not your own; you were bought at a price. Therefore honor God with your body" (1 Corinthians 6:19–20). Note that the Bible here teaches that one reason Jesus

Christ died for you on the cross was to make you His own, including your body. You no longer "own" it—it is God's. You therefore are to be a good steward or guardian of it, and not abuse it or use it for purposes that dishonor God. Instead, the way you treat your body should be a sign of how you treat God. We can abuse our bodies in many ways—overeating, drugs and alcohol, lack of proper exercise, etc. Of course we also can become overly concerned about our bodies, so that we spend all our time and money trying to impress others with our beauty or strength. Either extreme—neglect, or overindulgence—is wrong.

But this leads me to ask you a very direct question. Have you ever seriously considered the fact that you need to offer your whole life—not just your body, but everything else, including your mind and your future—to Jesus Christ? God is not only concerned about your body, He is concerned about you. He wants to come into your life as Lord. He loves you and wants you to experience His love every day.

There may be many reasons why you have not taken care of yourself as you should. Perhaps you do not really see yourself as a person who is worth something, for example. But God says you are worth something! And He wants to take your life and turn you into the person He created you to be.

I am a married man, with a good wife, and seven healthy, happy children. I work hard, and can barely make ends meet. But my neighbors who have no children get a new car every year, are able to go on trips, and eat much better than we do. I must confess I am a little envious of them. How can I keep from envying them?

I wouldn't be surprised to find out that your neighbors envy you more than you envy them. By almost every measure, you are a rich man. Happily married, a good wife, seven happy, healthy children, and able to work. You are one of the wealthiest persons in town.

The Bible says: "Better is a dinner of herbs where love is, than a stalled ox and hatred therewith" (Proverbs 15:17, KJV). If you could stand back and look at yourself objectively, you would see that you have every reason to be happy.

Perhaps you lack just one thing. The Bible says: "Better is a little with the fear (reverence) of the Lord than great treasure and trouble therewith" (Proverbs 15:16, KJV). Your display of envy shows that you have a spiritual need. Slip to your knees tonight and say: "Dear God, forgive me for being envious of my neighbor who in reality has much less than I. Help me to reverence You and to live for You." See if this doesn't help you.

All my friends think I am a very happy person, but on the inside I know it is not so. I really feel empty inside, and I don't know what to do about it, do you?

Where do you suppose that empty place in your heart came from? The Bible says that it came from God. You see, you were created to have fellowship with God, and to have Him at the center of your life. That is true for all of us. But when we leave God out of our lives, it leaves a blank or empty space that nothing can fully fill. No matter how hard we try or what means we use—material possessions, money, pleasure, drugs, or whatever—the emptiness is still there.

There is only one lasting solution to this problem. If the void or empty place in our hearts is there because we have left God out of our lives, the only solution is to let Him come back into our lives and assume His rightful place.

Is this possible? Yes, it certainly is, and I have seen it happen to countless people of every background. I have experienced it in my own life. Apart from Christ, the Bible tells us, we are "harassed and helpless, like sheep without a shepherd" (Matthew 9:36). But God loves us, and one reason He has allowed you to have this feeling of emptiness in your heart is that He loves you and wants you to seek Him. He wants to enter your life and take up residence there. Jesus says to you today, "Here I am! I stand at the door and knock. If anyone hears my voice and opens the door, I will come in and eat with him, and he with me" (Revelation 3:20). Christ stands at the door of your heart, asking to come in, and promising to enter your life and have fellowship with you if you will turn your life over to Him.

How can you do this? Imagine that someone offered you a lovely gift. This person has paid for it—all you had to do was reach out and take it. Christ has already paid the price for your salvation—the shedding of His blood on the cross. All you have to do is reach out by faith and accept it. Then you can know the peace of Christ in your heart.

I just don't understand what is wrong with me. I don't have any problems in my marriage and our children are all grown up and are successful. I have a lot of friends and more than enough money. However, somehow I feel completely empty inside. What is wrong?

I believe that your question could be echoed by many people in our society. We are the richest society that has ever lived. Yet we have discovered that it takes more than wealth or leisure or pleasure to satisfy the deepest longings of the human heart.

Why is this? The reason is that God created us for a purpose, but as long as we turn our backs on Him and decide to run our own lives without Him we will always be unfulfilled. Many centuries ago King Solomon of Israel accumulated great wealth—in fact, he was apparently the wealthiest man of his time. But his heart was empty, so he began to search for ways to fill it. He tried everything—from even greater wealth to pleasure to alcohol. But in the end, he realized that only God could fill the emptiness of his life. (You can read of his search in the Old Testament book of Ecclesiastes.)

Let Christ come into your life and give you meaning and purpose. Let Him fill the empty space you sense is there. Let Him become the center of your life, instead of all the substitutes you have tried to use to give happiness to you. You need Christ, and you need to discover the amazing truth that God loves you. Jesus said, "I have come that they may have life, and have it to the full" (John 10:10). Invite Christ to come into your life by faith right now—there is no reason to delay.

Then learn to walk with Him each day. He is as near as a prayer. He is as near as your Bible—which you should turn to each day to understand more of what God has done for you and what He wants you to do. "Why spend money on . . . what does not satisfy? . . . Give ear and come to me; hear me, that your soul may live" (Isaiah 55:2, 3). How good God has been to you in a day when many families are falling apart.

I have always been a nervous and high-strung person, but recently it has become worse and I am constantly worrying and anxious about the future. Do you suppose some people are just this way, or can I do anything about it?

People have different temperaments and personalities, and some individuals undoubtedly have a tendency toward excessive worrying. But God wants to help us at the exact places where we are weak, and He wants to help you overcome this problem.

The key is to realize that nothing—not a single thing—takes God by surprise, because He knows all about the future. And when we are in His hands, then we need not fear the future either, because we know He is with us every step of the way. "So do not fear, for I am with you; do not be dismayed, for I am your God. I will strengthen you and help you; I will uphold you with my righteous right hand" (Isaiah 41:10).

What should you do? First, commit your life to Jesus Christ by asking Him to come into your heart as your personal Lord and Savior. Then turn to Him each day, and in prayer commit every day and every problem into His hands. Let His Word, the Bible, also be part of your life every day, and learn to trust the promises God has given you in it. God knows your weaknesses and your fears, but He will strengthen you as you learn to trust Him and thank Him. "Rejoice in the Lord always. . . . Do not be anxious about anything, but in everything, by prayer and petition, with thanksgiving, present your requests to God. And the peace of God, which transcends all understanding, will guard your hearts and your minds in Christ Jesus" (Philippians 4:4, 6–7). Let this be your experience as you trust every detail of your future into His loving hands.

16

I Worry about
the Future

I am retired, and I am consumed with worry about the future. It seems like every time I open the newspaper they are talking about the terrible state of the economy, and I wonder if I'm going to have enough to live on in my old age. I know I shouldn't worry so much, but I can't seem to help it.

As long as you look only at the situation in the world today, it will be very hard for you, I think, to overcome your worries because it is true that there are many problems and the future is unknown to us. I'm sure that as a retired person you find much of what is happening in the world to be frightening.

But I want you to lift your eyes beyond your circumstances and learn instead to trust God and His goodness. You can't see the future, no matter how hard you try. It may bring problems—or it may not. (And worrying about it won't change anything, of course, although it is easy for us to forget that.) Jesus said, "Who of you by worrying can add a single hour to his life?" (Matthew 6:27). But note this very carefully: you don't know the future, but God does. And even more important, God is in control of the future. And because He loves us and is in control of the future, He can be trusted to take care of us and watch over us.

Let me suggest two phrases that should constantly be in your heart as you think about the future. They are "Give thanks" and "Trust God." First, learn to give thanks to God for what you have, and for the ways He has blessed you. Even when life may be difficult, we should thank God for all He does for us—which we do not deserve. We should be "always giving thanks to God the Father for everything, in the name of our Lord Jesus Christ" (Ephesians 5:20). Most of all, we should thank God for what He has done for us in Jesus Christ. Have you ever done that, and have you accepted Jesus Christ into your heart by faith so that you know you will go to be with Him in Heaven? Your relationship to Christ is the most important thing you should be thinking about right now, and you can settle it once and for all by turning to Christ in faith and trust.

And when you come to Christ, then you realize you can trust God for your future—both now and eternally. Read what Jesus had to say about worry in Matthew 6:25–34, and look to Him to supply all your needs.

I am seventy-two years old. I have a depressed and hopeless feeling. I have no living relatives. Is there anything left in life for a man of my age? If so, how can I find it?

A very old man—much older than you—when he lay dying, said, "I have found that all the sugar is at the bottom of the cup." Life can grow sweeter and more rewarding as we grow older if we possess the presence of Christ. Sunsets are always glorious. It is Christ who adds colors, glory, and beauty to man's sunsets. Try to find one person a day whom you can tell about your new joy in Christ.

I am a very old man now. I have been very wicked all my life. Just recently I found Jesus through one of your radio broadcasts. Is there any way I can redeem the years I have lost?

Sin makes an indelible impression on us in this life. You will never get over the regret of having lived for the devil all these years. But God can do the impossible. God can do more with a few days of your time if given completely to Him, than He can with a whole life characterized by a half-hearted service. The lukewarm Christian can accomplish nothing with a whole life in which to do it. If you have lived for sin and self these many years, your witness will have telling effect on all who have known you. They will see the change and will be deeply impressed by God's power in your life. Take every advantage to let everyone know the change that has been brought about in you through your faith in Christ. God can, through your yieldedness, accomplish much in a short time. Now is not the time for discouragement, but for a song of triumph and victory. Let everyone know of God's grace toward you.

I have passed the proverbial "three score years and ten," have been pensioned by my company, and in general seem quite useless. Actually, I feel very well and would like to be doing things, but nobody wants my help.

You can have some of your most useful and happy years before you. With no responsibilities in employment you can devote your time, strength, and wisdom gained from experience to help in very worthwhile projects in your church and community. Your busy pastor has many tasks that are really important in themselves to which he can assign you. There are shut-ins to visit and widows and orphans to advise, the discouraged to cheer, the young men to counsel. With an old head and a young heart you can be a source of real strength to the many who need your cheer and encouragement.

In your community you will find tasks that should be done, but are overlooked or neglected by busy people in the prime of life, and which you can do very satisfactorily. If you seem to be "on the shelf" make sure that you are on a shelf so low that your friends and neighbors can reach you easily and enlist you to help them do the things for which you are much better qualified than they are. Just do not sit in the corner and look inward; rather, be on the corner to respond to the challenge—and above all make sure you have made preparation for the inevitable by accepting Christ as your personal Lord and Savior. Life does not begin at forty but with God.

17

Do I Need a Psychiatrist?

I have some emotional problems, and my family doctor says that I need to see a psychiatrist. A friend of mine, however, says that if I just have enough faith these problems will go away. What do you think?

I would be the first to say that faith in God is very, very important. It is essential for our eternal salvation, and it is crucial for our everyday lives as well. But at the same time I do not agree with your friend, because God may choose to use an able psychiatrist to help you with some of the problems you are facing.

You see, when you have faith in God, you are actually trusting a problem into His hands. You are saying, in effect, "Lord, I don't know how to deal with this problem, but I have faith that You do. I trust You to lead me and give me wisdom, so I will know what is right. I trust You to show me the right answer to this situation." Faith, in other words, does not necessarily mean that we sit back and fold our hands, assuming that God will work without ever using any human tools.

Do you remember the incident when Jesus healed a man who had been blind since birth? (You can read about it in Chapter 9 of John's Gospel.) Jesus could have simply pronounced the man healed. But instead He used some mud which He put on the man's eyes, and then told him to go and wash it off in a certain pool of water. I believe one reason Jesus did this was to show us that at times He uses earthly tools or instruments to bring healing.

Therefore you should not feel that you are wrong in seeking the help of a psychiatrist or trained psychologist if that will help you deal with some deep-seated emotional problems. Seek one who will not discourage you in your faith in God. (Your pastor can perhaps suggest a Christian psychiatrist in your area.) And at the same time ask God to help you grow in your faith in Him. I am convinced that many emotional problems today are caused by spiritual concerns. Some people, for example, are beset with deep feelings of guilt that they cannot shake. Christ, however, is the only ultimate answer to guilt because He alone can offer us full forgiveness. God bless you as you seek help to overcome these problems.

I am a homosexual. I have tried to conquer it and have prayed to God time after time, but nothing changes. I desperately want to deal with it, but I don't know what to do. Please help me.

God wants to help you with this problem, and I am thankful you are facing it honestly and not excusing it (as the tendency is in some circles today). Homosexual behavior is wrong in God's eyes, but He still loves you and can guide you as you seek to deal honestly with your situation.

There are steps that are crucial for you to follow if you are ever to conquer this. First, if you have never asked Christ to come into your life I urge you to do so without delay. Christ took all your sins upon Himself when He died on the cross. You need the forgiveness only Christ can bring, and when you turn to Him He freely forgives you by His grace. Right now you are burdened with the knowledge you have sinned but Christ can lift that burden if you will trust Him as your Lord and Savior.

Then get help from others for your problem. Don't be afraid to seek help or to share your problem in confidence with someone you can trust who also can help you. There may be many complex reasons for your homosexual tendencies, and a skilled pastor can probably point you to a Christian psychologist or psychiatrist who has had experience in dealing with others who have been in your situation. Such a person can help you understand yourself and why you have become the person you are, and will also help you—both emotionally and spiritually—to leave your old way of living and become the person Christ wants you to be.

Finally, several people who have dealt with persons such as yourself have stressed how important it is for you to remove yourself from every type of temptation. This has a strong grip on you, and that grip will only become stronger if you do not separate yourself from those persons and surroundings that have entrapped you in the past. God bless you as you turn your life over to Christ and take practical steps to overcome this.

Why do you so often suggest that religion is a cure-all, when modern psychiatry has done so much for mentally disturbed persons?

Religion is not a cure-all but the gospel of Christ certainly is the only answer to the sin problem. If the problem is one that is related to sin and its consequences, then Christ is the answer, and not psychiatry. If the disturbance is purely a mental one, then a competent psychiatrist might give satisfactory help. It would call for a psychiatrist with real spiritual insight to be able to tell the difference between the purely mental problem and the spiritual one. Let it be known that Christianity is not opposed to everything modern but only such claims that are not totally true and that do injustice to the claims of the gospel.

I wish every mentally disturbed person might be counseled by one who knows the functioning of the human mind and knows equally well the message of deliverance through Jesus Christ.

I have difficulty sleeping at night without sleeping tablets. Is it wrong to use artificial aids for sleep?

Physicians say that millions of Americans must take sleeping tablets in order to sleep. I heard of one man who set his alarm clock for 2 A.M. to wake himself up, so he could take another pill!

Sleeplessness is caused by a number of things: tension, worry, and the lack of proper work or exercise. The Bible suggests another reason for sleeplessness: "But the wicked are like the tossing sea, which cannot rest, whose waves cast up mire and dirt" (Isaiah 57:20). Though I would not go so far as to say that believing Christians are never troubled with insomnia, I do believe that much sleeplessness is caused by a troubled conscience. I used to have sleepless nights when thoughts of my critics raced through my mind. But as I dropped on my knees and asked God to fill my heart with His love, I have found peace—and rest.

Try repeating this verse from Isaiah over and over in your mind when you can't sleep: "Thou wilt keep him in perfect peace, whose mind is stayed on thee" (26:3, KJV). Let thoughts of God's love, holiness, and majesty fill your mind, and I believe it will help you to find rest and relaxation.

My mother committed suicide some time ago. I have since been obsessed with the fear that I would do the same thing sometime. Can you tell me how to overcome such a fear?

Apart from any religious meaning, I believe you are suffering from a kind of identification with your mother, which is a common thing. No doubt you cared for your mother and also believe that you might have some of the same potential within yourself. You must recognize the fact that there is no reason why you should be compelled to do the same, unless it is a result of concentrating on it. You must divert your mind and begin to think on something else.

Your problem is not only psychological but also spiritual. If you have given yourself completely to Christ and are absolutely surrendered to His control, there can be no thought of suicide. The apostle Paul once said: "Don't worry about anything; instead, pray about everything; tell God your needs and don't forget to thank him for his answers. If you do this, you will experience God's peace, which is far more wonderful than the human mind can understand. His peace will keep your hearts quiet and at rest as you trust in Christ Jesus"

(Philippians 4:6–7, TLB). The apostle again said: "Fix your thoughts on what is right and pure and good . . ." (Philippians 4:8, TLB). Christ can so completely change your nature and control your mind that you can find complete relief and joy in serving Him. I would suggest that you see your minister and have a frank discussion with him.

I cannot forget the abortion that was performed on me. Can you help me find peace of mind?

You did not give any details about your case. Assuming that the termination of your pregnancy was for selfish reasons, other than to save your own life, it is clear that you have sinned, as did those who had a part in it. God gives life, and we have no right to take it. But we are not to assume that this sin is unforgivable. Moses once killed a man, but found forgiveness, and went on to become one of history's great emancipators. Saul of Tarsus had participated in the execution of Stephen, but he had an encounter with Christ on the Damascus Road, and became the first and perhaps greatest Christian missionary. This does not excuse abortion, nor should women seek an abortion simply because God can forgive a truly repentant heart, but to despair over the magnitude of your sin will only make matters worse. My suggestion is that you come to Him who said: "Come unto me, all ye that labor and are heavy laden, and I will give you rest" (Matthew 11:28, KJV). No person, regardless of the extent of his sin, ever responded to this call without finding rest of soul. Don't delay any longer. God is ready, able, and willing to forgive you and give you His peace.

I worry constantly. At the present time I am almost on the point of a break-down. I know this is not fitting for a Christian. All those with whom I have counseled tell me there is nothing to be concerned about, but I believe there is much to worry about. With a sick husband, a boy in the Army, an uncertain job, and a few other things, I can't help it. Do you have any suggestions?

You certainly seem to have much to worry about. Your problems are great and without God's help, you cannot bear them. You are entitled to worry unless you believe God. Faith and worry are mutually exclusive. I would not tell you that there is nothing to be concerned about. But what I would tell you is that there is Someone who loves you and cares for you. There is Someone who knows your problem, and still better, He can take your cares. Peter tells us: "Cast all your anxiety on him because he cares for you" (1 Peter 5:7). So, although you have much to worry about, let Jesus take that worry. If He can carry the load of your sin and the sin of the world, He can also bear your present burden, lift the load, and give you inner resources that will enable you to live victoriously.

Although I am a Christian and do trust the Lord, I find I am becoming very nervous and irritable—often about quite trifling things. I feel I have just about reached the breaking point and cannot cope any longer. What do you think is wrong with me?

More than one thing may be wrong, but it sounds as though you are physically rundown and have got into a state of nervous exhaustion. In that case you need to relax a bit more, to find time for some recreation, and if possible to get away for a few days' holiday.

Remember that as a Christian it is your duty to keep yourself as fit as possible, spiritually *and* physically. You cannot be the best for God if you drive yourself to the point where you are practically dropping with fatigue and something within you is about to snap.

When the apostles returned from their first preaching tour the Lord Jesus said to them, "Come ye yourselves apart . . . and rest awhile" (Mark 6:31, KJV). He recognized that they had bodies as well as souls. He knew their need of rest if they were to be of further service to Him.

There is something else I would ask you to remember. When Jesus called those apostles to come apart and rest awhile, He was inviting them to spend time in communion with Him. I wonder how that applies to you? Are you finding time each day for fellowship with the Lord?

Nothing so restores mental equilibrium as regular, daily prayer. Try the apostolic formula: "Do not be anxious about anything, but in everything by prayer and petition, with thanksgiving, present your requests to God. And the peace of God . . . will guard your hearts and your minds in Christ Jesus" (Philippians 4:6–7).

I have a chronic intestinal trouble which the doctor says is caused by worry. He tells me to relax, but how can I when the success of my business and the employment of thousands of people depends upon me?

Your question indicates that you believe your work is important. If that is true, it is God's work. He has given it to you. And He will help you do it, if you ask Him.

Begin each day by saying the Lord's Prayer. When you come to the words, "Give us this day our daily bread," remember that Jesus told us to ask only for the needs of one day. Most of our worries come from being too concerned about the future. When Christ was in Galilee He gave Himself entirely to the work there. He didn't wear Himself out by worrying about what would happen to Him in Jerusalem when it was time for Him to go there. He knew that when future trials came, He could meet them with the Father's help.

In the life of Christ we find our example. Trust in God. Each morning ask

Him to guide you in the decisions you must make that day. Every hour take time to send a minute prayer to Heaven. You may have felt like a deep-sea diver who is suffocating for want of air. Prayer is the lifeline that brings divine oxygen to your lungs.

Then when you go from your place of business, leave all thoughts of your work behind. Enjoy your family and friends. Take time to read the Bible daily. Take some recreation each week.

Jesus said: "Take no thought for the morrow: for the morrow shall take thought for the things of itself" (Matthew 6:34). Do this. Live one day at a time, trusting in God, and you'll find no need to worry.

18

Is There Life after Death?

I would give anything to know—really know—that there was a God and that there was life after death. But I have almost given up, because it seems like everyone has a different opinion on this subject.

How do you suppose we could know beyond doubt that God existed and that there was indeed life after death? If you think about those two questions, I believe you will agree that we could know that God existed only if He revealed Himself to us. And we could only know for certain that there was life after death if someone clearly came back from the dead.

And this is exactly what has happened! We are not left to guess or grope around for the truth—because God has shown us the truth. The Bible tells us something that is almost beyond our comprehension: God Himself has come down and walked on the planet. He did this by becoming a man, and He did it not only so we could know that God existed, but so we could know Him and have a personal relationship with Him. You can know God right now by committing your life to Jesus Christ. God loves you, and just as surely as you could have known Jesus Christ almost two thousand years ago, you can still know Him because He is alive in Heaven and wants to come into your heart.

But we also know that there is life after death because Jesus Christ died and then rose again to life. Christ died on the cross as a sacrifice for our sins, and He rose again to show us we can be forgiven and can have eternal life with God in Heaven. Some day all those who know Christ will be raised again and given new and glorious bodies, and we will be with Christ forever.

You can know—really know—God, and you can know the joy of eternal life right now by receiving the gift of God's Son into your life and committing your life to Him. "For God so loved the world that he gave his one and only Son, that whoever believes in him shall not perish but have eternal life. For God did not send his Son into the world to condemn the world, but to save the world through him. Whoever believes in him is not condemned" (John 3:16–18).

What do you think about these stories of people who have supposedly died and then been revived on the operating table, and experienced the sensation of feeling like they were being welcomed by a divine being clothed in light? Don't these prove there is life after death?

Recently I wrote a book on the subject of death and life after death, and in the course of my research I investigated a number of these alleged incidents (which are, incidentally, relatively rare). Various explanations have been given for them—from the influence of chemicals on the brain to demonic hallucinations. Whatever the cause, however, they are not a conclusive proof of life after death. There are certainly other cases (including that of my own mother) when a dying person may be given a glimpse of Heaven.

We do not need to look to such experiences for proof of life after death, however. For the Christian there is one supreme reason for knowing there is life after death, and that is the resurrection of Jesus Christ. Christ died on the cross for our salvation, and God raised Him from the dead to demonstrate beyond doubt that there is hope beyond the grave. "Praise be to the God and Father of our Lord Jesus Christ! In his great mercy he has given us new birth into a living hope through the resurrection of Jesus Christ from the dead, and into an inheritance that can never perish, spoil or fade—kept in heaven for you" (1 Peter 1:3–4).

Do you have this hope today? If you were to die tonight, do you know—beyond doubt—that you would go to be with God in Heaven forever? You can have the certainty, if you will confess your sins to God and trust Christ alone for your salvation. Give your life into His hands without delay.

I have never admitted this to very many people, but I think about death a great deal and worry about it because I don't know what will happen when I die. Right now I look on death as just the end of the road with nothing beyond, but I would give anything to know there is hope for life after death.

One of the greatest tragedies in life today is that countless people refuse to think about the fact of death—although there is nothing so certain as the fact that one day every one of us will come to the end of our lives.

Death is not the end of the road—it is merely a gateway to eternal life beyond the grave. The Bible teaches that every one of us will continue some type of existence after death—either in Heaven or in hell. The most important decision you will ever make is the decision you make about eternity.

How do I know death is not the end? I know it because Jesus Christ came back from the grave. His resurrection demonstrated once for all that there is life after death, and it also demonstrated that He alone can save us and bring us to Heaven. You see, the one thing that will keep us out of Heaven is our sin.

But God loves us, and Jesus Christ came to take upon Himself the punishment we deserve for our sins. Christ died in our place, and by faith and trust in Him we can know our sins are forgiven and we are going to go to be with Him in Heaven forever.

Commit your life to Christ and trust Him for your salvation. He is alive, and you can know Him personally by turning to Him in faith. Put your hope and trust in Him, for the Bible says that Christ "has appeared once for all at the end of the ages to do away with sin by the sacrifice of himself" (Hebrews 9:26).

Then let Christ be your guide and ruler every day. Christ wants to give you hope for the future—but He also wants to help you right now and change you into the person God created you to be. He wants you to learn what it means to walk with Him every day, and He also wants to use you to tell others about His glorious salvation. When you come to Christ, God gives you eternal life—which begins right now as you open your heart to Him.

The doctor has just told me I must have triple by-pass surgery on my heart and I am frankly frightened. I have never thought about death much, and I am not sure I can get up enough courage to go through with this operation, although I know I will probably die without it. Help me deal with my fears.

Your fear is not just of the operation, but of death. The most important thing I can tell you is that we do not need to fear death if we have Christ in our hearts and belong to Him. Yes, death is a reality, and you are right to be fearful of it because apart from Christ you would have no hope of eternal life in Heaven. You would only face eternity alone, separated from God forever in hell. But Jesus Christ came to give us eternal life, and you can have that hope in your heart if you turn to Christ.

You see, the problem we all face is the problem of sin. We have sinned against God, and the Bible says "the wages of sin is death" (Romans 6:23). Our greatest need is forgiveness, and God has made that possible by sending His Son to die on the cross for our sins. We deserved to die because of our sins, but Christ died in our place. When we trust Christ for our salvation, then death simply becomes a transition between this world and the next—like walking through a doorway from one room to another.

The most important decision you will ever make is your decision about Christ. Some day you will die—whether you like to think about it or not—and then it will be too late. Accept God's offer of salvation right now, by asking Jesus Christ to come into your heart by faith and trusting your life into His hands. Then you will know that "neither death nor life . . . neither the present nor the future . . . nor anything else in all creation, will be able to separate us from the love of God that is in Christ Jesus our Lord" (Romans 8:38–39).

A friend of mine recently lost her husband. Although she has been a fine Christian, she seems to have lost interest in everything. What help or counsel should I give her?

The husband-wife relationship is the closest of all earthly relationships, and it is not to be wondered at that the death of one will come as a blow to the other. It does not mean that the bereaved is without faith. The Bible teaches that on the occasion of death "we sorrow" (1 Thessalonians 4:13). Abraham, who is cited as an example of faith, wept and sorrowed at the death of his wife, Sarah (Genesis 23:2). But the Christian does not sorrow as do those who are without hope. He looks forward to the time of the resurrection and reunion. Point out these wonderful truths to your bereaved friend, and pray for her that the Lord will use His Word to afford her comfort in a time of deep sorrow and loss. Show her that the loss is her loved one's gain, and at worse is only temporary.

I am afraid to die. I have tried to get over this fear, but cannot. Is there anything one can do to overcome it?

The fear of death is something that all people have sometime. With many, this fear is greatly aggravated. You did not tell me if you were a believer in Christ or not, but that makes a great difference. Christ has removed forever the fear of death for those who believe in Him. He has brought life and immortality to light through the gospel. Man, by nature, fears death because death is always associated with judgment and with the unknown. We fear it because we do not know what lies ahead. But Christ has made the way for us through His own death. He provides eternal life and has promised His presence in all of life's experiences, and even in death. "Yea, though I walk through the valley of the shadow of death I will fear no evil," said the Psalmist. You, too, can lose that fear when you commit your whole self to Christ. Trust Him for salvation from sin, and He will remove the sting of death, which is sin.

Last night I dreamed I was dying and woke up in an agony of fear. Today I know I am not ready to die. What can I do?

God may have permitted you to have this dream to make you realize that you have neglected the most important thing in this life and in the next. You can have peace in your heart and the assurance of salvation if you will humbly acknowledge yourself as a sinner in God's sight, ask His forgiveness and cleansing, and trust in Jesus Christ, God's Son, as your Savior from sin. Christ died on the Cross to do just this very thing for you. Let me urge you to get a Bible and read, or ask someone to help you read, the following verses: Romans 3:12,

Romans 3:23, 2 Timothy 3:5, Romans 3:19, Ephesians 2:8, Luke 19:10, Romans 5:8, Hebrews 7:25, Romans 10:13, and Romans 10:9, 10.

These are not magic verses. They simply tell us about our need and how to find that need met in Jesus Christ. You do not have to do some wonderful thing to be saved. All you have to do is accept the wonderful thing Christ has done for you. After you have this assurance in your heart, tell other people about it. Also, show by your daily life that Christ has changed it for His own glory.

Recently, some friends and I were discussing whether we go immediately to Heaven when we die. Can you answer this question?

The Bible clearly teaches that when a believer in Christ dies, he goes to be with the Lord. "Absent from the body . . . present with the Lord" is what Paul said about it (2 Corinthians 5:8, KJV). Also, in one of His parables Jesus told of the rich man and Lazarus who were already at their destination. But the Bible also teaches that there is a day of resurrection and judgment which is yet future (2 Timothy 2:18). Here reference to a past resurrection is misleading and in error. It is the coming event when Jesus comes again. The Bible says: "For if we believe that Jesus died and rose again, even so them also which sleep in Jesus will God bring with him. . . . the dead in Christ shall rise first; then we which are alive and remain shall be caught up together with them . . . to meet the Lord in the air" (1 Thessalonians 4:14–17, KJV). The answer seems to be that there is an intermediate state when we are with the Lord, but have not yet received the glorious body of the resurrection.

I am almost overcome with grief because of my husband's death several months ago. I just don't see how I can ever get over this. However, I think it would be easier to bear if I knew that my husband and I will recognize each other in Heaven. Does the Bible teach this?

Yes, we will recognize our loved ones in Heaven, and they will recognize us. Furthermore, the Bible indicates that we will know them in a far deeper and closer way than was ever possible on earth—and without the imperfections and sins that mar our human relationships on earth. "Now we see but a poor reflection; then we shall see face to face. Now I know in part; then I shall know fully, even as I am fully known" (1 Corinthians 13:12).

The fact that we will know our loved ones who have died and gone to Heaven before us is clear from several passages of Scripture. For example, in 1 Thessalonians 4 Paul tells us that we are not to grieve "like the rest of men, who have no hope" (v. 13). He then goes on to say that those who have died in Christ will some day return with Him when He comes again. "After that, we who are still alive and are left will be caught up with them in the clouds to meet the Lord in the air. And so we will be with the Lord forever" (1 Thessalonians 4:17). Here it is clear that we will be with all those who have died and gone to Heaven before us—including our loved ones.

I know this is a difficult time for you, and I pray that you will take courage from the many promises of God's Word—not just about the fact that you will see your husband again some day, but that when we know Christ we have the certain hope of Heaven. Rejoice that your husband knew Christ, and that now he is safely beyond the touch of pain and suffering and death.

But you also should be praying that God would help you right now not only to get over your grief, but to grow closer to Christ and to serve Him more each day. God still has a purpose in your being on this earth—to glorify Him in all you do. Seek above all else to do His will in your life.

Do you think there is anything in the Bible that would forbid me donating some of my bodily organs (such as my kidneys or my eyes) after my death?

No, I find nothing in the Bible that would forbid this, and in fact it could be a very loving act on your part because it might give the gift of sight or even life to someone else after you have gone. Some day, the Bible teaches, we who are in Christ will be given new and perfect bodies by God in eternity, and He is not dependent on the elements of our old bodies to accomplish this miracle.

I am thankful you are thinking about ways you can help others—but I want to use your question to challenge you also. It is good to want to help people in this way (as long as you or your immediate family have no objections), but have you given much thought to ways you should be helping others right now, while you are still alive? If you know Christ as your Lord and Savior, the greatest treasure you can give to another is not merely the gift of physical help, but pointing them to Jesus Christ. It is important to help people who are in physical need—but it is even more important to help those who have spiritual needs. Are you praying that God will use you in the lives of other people, to encourage them and make them see their own need of Jesus Christ?

Your question also reminds me of what Jesus Christ has done for us through His death on the cross. You want to give the gift of life to others through your death—and in a far greater way, that is what Christ did for us. He took upon Himself our sin and our guilt, and in their place He offers us forgiveness, new life, and eternal salvation. "But God demonstrates his own love for us in this: While we were still sinners, Christ died for us" (Romans 5:8).

Life is brief, and no matter who we are it will soon be over. If ever we are going to trust in Christ and live for Him it must be now. May God encourage you and challenge you to live for Him as you yield your life to Him.

Do you believe there is really any proof that there is life after death? If so, do you think it is possible for a person to know what life after death is like?

Yes, there is life after death, and in fact the experience of death is but a gateway to an eternity of conscious life after death.

I want you to think a moment about how we might come to know beyond doubt that there is life after death. I believe you will agree with me that the only ultimate proof would be if someone were to die and then come back to life again and tell us if there was life beyond the grave. To make the test valid, the person would have to really die—not just be on the border of death for a few minutes—and then have his restoration to life witnessed by a large number of people.

Has this ever happened? Yes! It has happened only once, when Jesus Christ died, was placed in the tomb for several days, and then came back to life. The Bible tells us that over 500 people were witnesses to His resurrection (1 Corinthians 15:6). The resurrection of Jesus Christ is one of the best-attested facts of history, and demonstrates that there is life beyond the grave.

But the resurrection of Christ is important for several other reasons also, and they are all important for your question. For example, the resurrection shows that Jesus Christ was in fact who He claimed to be—the eternal Son of God, come down from Heaven to die as a sacrifice for our sins. The resurrection of Jesus also shows that He has conquered sin and death, and that we need not fear the grave if we belong to Him.

I said that there is life after death, but there is one other thing I must stress. The Bible teaches that for some people life beyond the grave will be joyous, because they will be in Heaven with God. For others, however, life beyond the grave will be "darkness, where there will be weeping and gnashing of teeth" (Matthew 25:30). That is why it is so important for you to come to Christ right now and accept Him as Lord and Savior of your life. Then you can know beyond doubt that Christ is your Savior and there is a joyous eternity ahead of you.

My husband has terminal cancer with only a few months to live. He smoked for over fifty years and he is dying with lung cancer. Do you think churches should say more about smoking?

God is concerned about the way we treat our bodies, and you are right—the church should be concerned about everything (including smoking, overeating, alcohol and drug abuse, and other harmful practices) that dulls our senses or hurts our bodies. The Bible says, "Do you not know what that your body is a temple of the Holy Spirit, who is in you, whom you have received from God? You are not your own; you were bought at a price. Therefore honor God with your body" (1 Corinthians 6:19-20).

There is, of course, a lot of interest in our society in physical fitness, and much of that is good. People need to be made aware of the dangers of abusing their bodies, and of the benefits of taking care of them. At the same time, however, we must never forget that the Bible places special emphasis on another type of fitness—spiritual fitness. The Bible declares, "Physical training is of some value, but godliness has value for all things, holding promise for both the present life and the life to come" (1 Timothy 4:8).

I pray that the next few months will be special months for you and your husband. I pray especially that there will be times when you and your husband sense in a wonderful way the presence of God in your lives. Do you and your husband know beyond doubt that you have committed your lives to Christ, and that no matter what the future holds, you both will go to be with Christ in Heaven when you die? You can make sure, by yielding your lives without reserve, trusting Him alone for your salvation.

It is never easy (humanly speaking) for us to face death—either our own, or that of a loved one. But Christ came to take away the sting of death. May you both come to know that in a richer way during these months.

I know this may seem silly to you, but recently my dog had to be put to sleep and it has made me grieve deeply. Do you think I will see my pet in Heaven?

I do not believe Scripture gives us any direct answer about this, although many Bible scholars believe the evidence suggests there will be animals in Heaven. The difference will be that they will no longer fight and kill, because in the heavenly kingdom all will be peace. "The wolf will live with the lamb, the leopard will lie down with the goat. . . . They will neither harm nor destroy on all my holy mountain" (Isaiah 11:6, 9).

There is one thing you can be certain of, however. God loves us, and He knows what our needs are. He also wants us to be completely happy in Heaven—and we will be. Therefore, if God knows we will be happier because there will be animals with us in Heaven, then you can be assured He will do what is best for us. Remember that our happiness and joy in Heaven will be based especially on the fact that we will be with Christ, and we will worship Him and serve Him there. "No longer will there be any curse. The throne of God and of the Lamb will be in the city, and his servants will serve him" (Revelation 22:3).

I realize that you may be very sad over the loss of this pet, but I want to challenge you to use this time to think more carefully about what you can do in the future to serve God more fully. For example, all around you are people who have never thought much about Heaven or about their relationship to Christ. There also are people around you who are facing many problems and heartaches. Are you praying for them, and are you seeking to share Christ's love for them as

God gives you opportunity? And are you growing spiritually yourself, learning to trust God more and more each day and learning more about Him through His Word, the Bible? The most important thing in life should be our relationship to Christ, and my prayer is that He will have first place in your life.

Do you believe God will give people a second chance after they die to believe in Him and go to Heaven?

The Bible does not teach this. In fact, it teaches the opposite. It stresses that the time to decide for Christ is now, because once we die it will be too late. As the author of the book of Hebrews in the New Testament declared, "Man is destined to die once, and after that to face judgment" (Hebrews 9:27). This verse also, incidentally, shows us clearly that there is no such thing as reincarnation—the idea that our souls return again and again to this earth.

The important thing for every one of us to realize is that God has done everything possible to bring salvation to us, and there is no reason for us to delay accepting His plan for our lives. God sent His only Son, Jesus Christ, into the world to die for our sins on the cross. This was something that no one else could ever do, because only Christ was without sin and could therefore be a perfect sacrifice for our sins. All we must do is turn our sins over to Christ, and trust Him for our salvation by faith. God's salvation is a wonderful gift to us that we can never earn. All we have to do is receive it.

I have often asked myself why many people who know what Christ has done for them still delay coming to Him for forgiveness. I suspect some people delay because secretly they hope that somehow there will be another chance for them after they die. That is one reason I have wanted to answer your question, because it would be tragic for them to miss out on God's greatest gift—salvation throughout all eternity in the joy of Heaven—because they mistakenly thought somehow they would have another chance. I am sure many people also delay turning to Christ because they think somehow that being a follower of Christ will be dull and unexciting, or because they want to continue in their sins as long as possible.

But none of these reasons is valid, and my challenge to you is to invite Christ into your life, if you have never done so, without delay. "I tell you, now is the time of God's favor, now is the day of salvation" (2 Corinthians 6:2).

I know you believe in life after death, and so do I. But I don't believe a loving God would send anyone to hell. In fact I don't think there is such a thing and I believe everyone will go to Heaven when they die. I find great comfort in this, because I know I am not perfect.

It is a very sobering thought to realize that hell is real and not everyone will go to Heaven. But the Word of God makes it clear that hell is just as real as Heaven.

Let me point out two things you may not have thought of. First, if there is no hell then there is no judgment for evil—and we therefore live in an unjust universe. Do you honestly believe the Hitlers of this world will never be judged for their crimes, but will be allowed to spend eternity with God in spite of the fact they fought against God and broke every moral law He gave us?

Second, if there is no hell then Christ is a liar—because He repeatedly warned us about its reality. "The Son of Man will send out his angels, and they will weed out of his kingdom everything that causes sin and all who do evil. They will throw them into the fiery furnace, where there will be weeping and gnashing of teeth" (Matthew 13: 41–42). But if Christ did not tell the truth about this, how do you know you can trust what He said about anything—including His death for our eternal salvation? But Christ can be trusted because He is God—and God does not lie.

The good news, however, is that you do not have to face hell. Why? Because Jesus Christ took upon Himself the punishment you and I deserve when He died on the cross for our sins. Don't deceive yourself, but turn to Christ and trust Him for your salvation.

What is your opinion with regard to the soul after death? Does it lie in the grave until the resurrection or does it go straight to God?

It is unwise to speculate beyond those things clearly stated in the Bible. To the repentant thief on the cross, Jesus said: "Today shalt thou be with me in paradise." This would indicate that the soul of a Christian at death goes immediately to be with the Lord in glory. At the same time, that is not the final state of the believer for at the resurrection, the bodies and souls of believers will be reunited and will be given a glorified body which will live forever in God's presence. In the first book of Thessalonians we are told: "For the Lord himself shall descend from heaven with a shout, with the voice of the archangel, and with the trump of God; and the dead in Christ shall rise first: then we which are alive and remain shall be caught up together with them in the clouds, to meet the Lord in the air: and so shall we ever be with the Lord" (4:17). There are many mysteries that have been withheld from our knowledge. But this we can affirm: the person who puts his trust in Jesus Christ and what He has done for us is immediately changed from death to life; and he has been born again and physical death can never separate him from God. If you believe in Christ, you have eternal life now and death is but a transition into His presence.

In the afterlife, will a man and woman who have been married remain married? When a person dies, will he remain the same age throughout eternity?

The marriage contract terminates at death. "Until death do us part" is the clause we repeat when we are wed. Legally, and in the sight of God, all marriages are dissolved when one or the other of the partners enters eternity.

The Sadducees asked Jesus this same question and He said: "The people of this age marry and are given in marriage. But those who are considered worthy of taking part in that age and in the resurrection from the dead will neither marry, nor be given in marriage" (Luke 20:34–35).

Yet I am certain that in Heaven everything we need for our complete happiness will be there. I am equally certain that married couples will know and love each other in the after-life—though the relationship will be no longer physical but spiritual.

As to remaining the same age throughout eternity, Heaven has no clocks or calendars, and "time will be no more." The thing with which we should be most concerned is preparing for eternity, and though we may find the answer to every mystery, but fail to prepare to meet God, we will be in hopeless straits in the world to come.

After a person has died and gone to another life, does he know or realize what he did while on this earth?

While it is not given us to know all of the details about the afterlife, we are given some insights into some aspects of it.

In the parable of the rich man and Lazarus, Christ indicated that the rich man could recall many of the events of earth. Particularly did he remember the sins of omission. He remembered that he had ignored the need of the beggar Lazarus. He remembered his five brothers and feared that they might also end up in hell, and asked that a messenger might be sent to earth to warn them.

There are evidences that we will remember many of the events of life. In the light of eternity, we will see that the things we thought so important were unimportant, and that the things we considered unimportant were really the things we should have attended to. Part of hell's torments will be the suffering of remorse, and of regretful memory.

For the saved, there will be the joys of having been faithful, and the thrill of unfolding knowledge throughout eternity. The Bible says: "Now we see but a poor reflection; but then we shall see face to face. Now I know in part. I shall then know fully, even as I am fully known" (1 Corinthians 13:12).

IV
ETHICAL ISSUES

19

Why Doesn't God Do Something about the Evil in the World?

Why doesn't God do something about all the evil in the world? For example, today's paper tells about all the suffering in Ethiopia because of the new famine, and how hundreds of thousands could die as a result. Why doesn't God wipe out all the evil, if He really cares about us?

We do not know all the reasons why God permits evil. We need to remember, however, that He is not the cause of evil in this world and we should therefore not blame Him for it. Remember that God did not create evil, as some believe. God created the world perfect. Man chose to defy God and go his own way, and it is man's fault that evil entered the world. Even so, God has provided the ultimate triumph of good over evil in Jesus Christ, who on the cross, defeated Satan and those who follow him. Christ is coming back and when He does, all evil will be ended forever and righteousness and justice will prevail.

Have you ever thought about what would happen if God suddenly eliminated all the evil in this world? Not one person would be left, because we are all guilty of sin. "If you, O Lord, kept a record of sins, O Lord, who could stand?" (Psalm 130:3). As the Bible says, "Because of the Lord's great love we are not consumed, for his compassions never fail" (Lamentations 3:22). Or again, have you thought about how many evils in this world are caused by human greed and lust? For example, isn't it ironic (and tragic) that the bestseller lists are filled with books on dieting—while millions starve in other parts of the world? Man—not God—must bear the responsibility.

Evil is a reality—but God's whole purpose is to eliminate it, and in fact that is why Christ came and died on the cross for our sins. "The reason the Son of God appeared was to destroy the devil's work" (1 John 3:8). Have you asked Christ to take away the sin in your life—and then to use you as His instrument to combat sin in the world?

I guess some people would consider me old-fashioned, but I am appalled at many of the things that are on television today—sex, violence, alcohol, drug abuse. Do you think there is anything we can do about this?

I suspect there are many people who feel as you do, because the tendency to ignore—or even laugh at—moral values in the media today is very strong. In part this is a reflection of the drift away from moral values in our society today. But this also encourages even greater levels of immorality within our society, and that trend will have tragic consequences if it is not reversed.

You need to remember that in our nation, television, radio, magazines, and other aspects of the media are all supported by advertising. Companies purchase advertising on a program because they believe people will be receptive to their message and eventually buy their products. But if advertisers become aware of the fact that many people are offended by the programs they are sponsoring, and are therefore not going to purchase the products they sell, then those advertisers will put pressure on the programmers to come up with programs that are acceptable.

Do you, therefore, have a way to let your voice be heard? Certainly! If a program offends you because of its language or subject matter, take down the names of the sponsors and write them directly. Tell them you do not believe they should be sponsoring that type of program. Write the television station also, and even the network. I have had several people in that industry tell me that only a few negative letters can have a strong impact. Don't be angry in your letters, but let your views be known clearly.

Whether or not such things do change, remember that those of us who claim to belong to Christ must not give in to the pressures in our society that would call us to forget God's standards. "What kind of people ought you to be? You ought to live holy and godly lives as you look forward to the day of God" (2 Peter 3:11–12).

Why do people seem to be so rude today? I grew up in a small town where people were courteous to each other and cared for each other, but I have moved to a large city and it seems that no one shows even a little bit of courtesy. I even find myself becoming indifferent to others. Does the Bible say anything about good manners, or do they vary from culture to culture?

Although many social customs differ from one culture to another, the Bible makes it clear that such things as courtesy and thoughtfulness should be part of our lives, no matter where we live. It is perhaps best summed up in the words of Jesus (which have come to be called "The Golden Rule"): "In everything, do to others what you would have them do to you, for this sums up the Law and the Prophets" (Matthew 7:12). Notice that this is a positive command; that is, we are not simply to refrain from doing evil to others, but we are to go out of our way to do what is good. Courtesy and kindness are part of this.

Why does courtesy seem to be declining in our society? One reason is that we have lost sight of the Bible's teachings about how we should live and act toward others. We also live in a society which has encouraged selfishness—the "me first" attitude—and that destroys common courtesy and kindness.

Yes, I wish there were more kindness in the world. But the real problem is a spiritual problem, because we have left God out of our lives.

Do you think it really pays to be good in today's world? It seems like the only way to get ahead is to live for yourself and bend the rules a bit.

I know that this often seems to be the case, but there are several things I want you to think about before you decide that this is the way you want to live.

It is not always true that this is the way to get ahead in the world. Some of the most successful people I know have been people who had strong moral principles and stuck to them regardless of the situation. Their reputation for honesty and hard work has won the respect of other people, and they have often found that people preferred to deal with them because they could be trusted. The Bible constantly exhorts us to be honest, because it is right in God's eyes and we are accountable to Him.

Think about the fact that those who "bend the rules a bit" often end up in great difficulty. It may be that they eventually do something illegal and are caught, bringing great heartache to their families and punishment to themselves. There is a strict biblical principle which declares that eventually our wrong deeds will create havoc in our lives. The Bible declares, "Do not be deceived: God cannot be mocked. A man reaps what he sows. The one who sows to please his sinful nature, from that nature will reap destruction" (Galatians 6:7–8).

That is why I want you seriously to consider the claims of Jesus Christ on your life. He calls you to follow Him. It is not always easy, and most people may not think it is worthwhile. But doing the will of God is the most important thing in life—and the most rewarding as well.

How do you account for the fact that in some places (like Lebanon and Northern Ireland) people who claim to be Christians are constantly fighting and killing?

There have been far too many instances in history when people and groups who claimed to be Christian have acted in ways that were not in accordance with the teachings of Jesus.

The real problem is that the word "Christian" has lost much of its original meaning. Today it often does not refer to a true follower of Jesus Christ, but simply to someone (or to some movement or group) that only claims to be Christian or has a vague Christian heritage. We should remember the sober warning of Jesus: "A good tree cannot bear bad fruit, and a bad tree cannot bear good fruit. . . . Not everyone who says to me, 'Lord, Lord' will enter the kingdom of heaven, but only he who does the will of my Father who is in heaven" (Matthew 7:18, 21).

What is a Christian? The first occurrence of the word "Christian" in the Bible is in Acts 11:26, which says "The disciples were first called Christians at Antioch." The word meant "one who follows Christ," and you will note that the Bible applies the term to those who were disciples, or active followers, of Christ. Jesus said, "If you hold to my teaching, you are really my disciples" (John 8:31). In other words, a Christian is one who has committed himself to Jesus Christ as Savior and Lord, and is actively seeking to follow Him and His teachings in his everyday life.

Do not be distracted by people who may claim to be Christians but are not following Christ as they should. Instead, make it your goal to follow Christ yourself, and look to Him every day. He is worthy of your trust and our faith.

Does the Bible say anything about smoking marijuana? My boyfriend says it doesn't and it is therefore okay to smoke it, but I'm not sure.

The Bible strictly commands us not to do anything which would dull our minds or make us lose control of our moral judgment. This is clearly seen, for example, in the statements of the Bible against drunkenness. "Do not get drunk on wine, which leads to debauchery. Instead, be filled with the Spirit" (Ephesians 5:18).

Therefore, although the Bible does not mention marijuana by name (since it was apparently unknown to the biblical writers), the Bible makes it clear that any drug which can distort our judgment is wrong. (You should remember that alcohol is actually a drug.) The medical consequences of marijuana are still being studied, but there can be no doubt that it—along with other drugs, such as cocaine—influences the mind. I know there are some people who substitute their drug experiences for an experience of God, and this is tragic because it keeps them from knowing the joy and peace and forgiveness that God alone can bring to our hearts.

I hope you and your boyfriend will honestly reconsider your involvement in drugs—no matter how popular they may be with some of your friends. But more than that, my prayer is that you will both reconsider with an open mind your need of God. God created you, and He has a perfect plan for your lives. He wants you to come to know Him and follow Him. He wants you to learn what it means to love Him and to love others for His sake.

There is no greater joy in life than having Jesus Christ as your Lord and Savior, living in your heart and giving you hope for the future. No drug experience—

or any other kind of experience—can really do this for you. Open your heart to Christ right now by faith and commit yourself to follow Him every day as you walk with Him in the light of His Word.

Why do you think we ought to be so concerned about things like world hunger? It seems to me we have a lot of people in our own country who need all the help we can give them.

Yes, we need to be concerned about people in our own country who face needs of various kinds, particularly during a time of economic recession. But we also need to be concerned about the pressing needs of people in other parts of the world, millions of whom will die as a direct result of malnutrition and starvation.

God is concerned about the whole world, and He commands us to be concerned about the whole world also. This is true in evangelism; those of us who have come to know Jesus Christ have been commanded to "go and make disciples of all nations" (Matthew 28:19). But it is equally true for our concern about the physical needs of others as well, because God is concerned about the whole person—body, mind, and spirit. Man's greatest need is spiritual because the human race is lost and apart from God, but our love for others includes a concern and compassion for their physical needs as well.

Consider the example of Jesus, who healed the sick and fed the hungry during His ministry on earth, as well as preached the Gospel of salvation. Jesus warned His disciples that they would be judged for their failure to help those who were in need, wherever they might be found. "Depart from me, you who are cursed, into the eternal fire prepared for the devil and his angels. For I was hungry and you gave me nothing to eat, I was thirsty and you gave me nothing to drink . . . whatever you did not do for one of the least of these, you did not do for me" (Matthew 25:41–42, 45).

Ask God to give you love for others, even if they are very different from you. Ask Him to help you find practical ways to help them. This is part of our responsibility.

Do you think that the Bible teaches that the world is going to end in a nuclear war? If so, doesn't that mean that we may be nearing the end of time?

Some of the descriptions in the Bible which portray the end of history as we know it are very vivid, and some Bible scholars have pointed out that they could be describing the type of thing that would happen in an all-out nuclear war. No one can say, however, that that is exactly what the Bible is picturing for us.

It is not so important for us to try to figure out exactly what will happen at the end of time when Christ returns to establish His kingdom. More important is the fact that some day God will intervene and the world as we know it will come to an end. The Bible stresses that "No one knows about that day or hour, not even the angels in heaven, or the Son, but only the Father" (Matthew 24:36). Some day the sin and evil of this world will be completely conquered, and Christ will reign in righteousness. "But in keeping with his promise we are looking forward to a new heaven and a new earth, the home of righteousness" (2 Peter 3:13).

Christ could come today, or His coming might be delayed for another thousand years. Certainly there are many signs that His coming may be near, and we need to take them seriously. But the real question is, are we ready for His coming? "Therefore keep watch, because you do not know on what day your Lord will come" (Matthew 24:42). The end of the world as we know it and the establishment of Christ's kingdom should not lead us to laziness or complacency—quite the opposite. We should instead be busy doing the Lord's work and living for Him. We should do all we can to tell others about Christ's salvation, for "Night is coming, when no one can work" (John 9:4).

Make it your goal, therefore, to live for Christ, no matter what the future may hold. God is not finished with His plans for this world, and we should seek to live for Him every day of our lives.

Should a Christian participate in defense measures of war involving the use of weapons, considering that this purpose is to kill other children of God?

The purpose of war is not to kill other children of God. If they are killed through the ravages of war, it is because they are members of a warring society and incidentally Christians. War is one of the consequences of living in a fallen world in which sinful men and women are unable to settle differences between each other by peaceful means.

I believe there are just wars, World War Two, for example, in which a tyrant sought to take over the world while at the same time eradicating an entire race of people. Only war put a stop to his bloodshed and enslavement of others. But war is certainly not the Christian way to settle either individual or global problems.

We must accept our responsibility as citizens. A man may protest against war and criticize his government for becoming involved in war, but as a citizen accepting the privileges and benefits of his government, he must also accept certain responsibilities. If we are in entire disagreement with our government, we can always elect to take our citizenship elsewhere. John the Baptist said one time when soldiers inquired of him concerning their duty: "Extort from no man by violence, neither accuse any one wrongfully; and be content with your wages." But he did not tell them that they must cease being soldiers.

A Christian would find it hard to be a loyal citizen in a nation that promoted warfare. We can thank God that we are part of a nation that seeks to solve all problems by peaceful means.

I read a lot in the newspapers about trying to control nuclear weapons and the arms race, and I know you have said that you think we should try to do something about the arms race. But do you really think there is any hope of eliminating war?

No, I do not believe that war will be completely eliminated from the earth until Jesus Christ returns to establish His Kingdom. At that time He will rule with complete justice and authority, and the ancient prophecy of Isaiah will be fulfilled: "He will judge between the nations and will settle disputes for many peoples. They will beat their swords into plowshares and their spears into pruning hooks. Nation will not take up sword against nation, nor will they train for war anymore" (Isaiah 2:4).

This does not mean we should be cynical about efforts for peace, because nations can from time to time come to agreements that give a temporary measure of peace. The catastrophic consequences of a possible nuclear war must also cause us to be alarmed, because in a nuclear holocaust hundreds of millions of people could die. If we suddenly discovered a hundred million people were going to die of starvation in some distant country I suspect we would do all we could to help them. I am not a pacifist nor do I believe in unilateral disarmament, but we should encourage the leaders of the world's great nations to work for peace and avoid a disaster.

War comes from the human heart, which Christ alone can change, and as long as there are sinful men on this earth there will be war. But God can restrain evil and we should be diligent in praying that He will guide our leaders. The Bible declares, "I urge, then, first of all, that requests, prayers, intercession and thanksgiving be made for everyone—for kings and all those in authority, that we may live peaceful and quiet lives in all godliness and holiness. This is good, and pleases God our Savior" (1 Timothy 2:1–3). This gives us a clear command which we should obey every day. At times we may feel like we can do very little to influence world events. But God is at work, and the most important thing we can do is pray for our world and its leaders.

Why don't you ever say anything about drunk driving? We recently lost our only daughter to a drunk driver, and the judge let the driver off with almost no penalty.

I have actually spoken out frequently against drunk driving, as well as other automobile-related safety matters—but perhaps not as frequently as I should. Drunk driving is clearly one of the most serious social problems we face in our nation. Probably well over half of the fatal car accidents in our nation are alcohol-related—a terrible toll of tens of thousands of lives each year.

Certainly you have put your finger on one of the problems we have in combating this critical issue. Undoubtedly there has been a tendency by our legal system to treat drunk driving as a minor offense instead of the serious matter it is. If someone walked into a crowded shopping mall waving a loaded pistol and threatening to shoot anyone who got in his way, I suspect the police and the law courts would treat it very seriously. If someone gets on an airplane and threatens to blow it up, it is treated as a very serious offense. But a drunk driver on the loose on the roads is every bit as dangerous, and we must support much stronger penalties for this offense. (Some countries in Europe have done this, and have much less a problem with drunk drivers.)

Drunk driving is only one part of the larger problem of alcoholism that plagues our nation today. Right now there may be someone reading this who knows that alcohol has taken possession of him, or that person may even have refused to face the fact that they have gotten hooked on alcohol (or some other drug). If that is your situation, my prayer for you is not only that you would never, never drive while drunk, but that you would face your need honestly. The first step to take—and the most important step in life for any of us—is to open your heart to Christ and ask Him to help you fight this problem. It may not be easy, but you need God's help and He wants to help you if you will turn to Him in faith and trust.

In an hour when it appears as if Russia might dominate us, can we not rely on the fact that this nation is better than Russia, and therefore God will not allow that wicked nation to overcome a good one?

I wish I could have such confidence, but unhappily it is not according to God's pattern or His Word. Many good nations have been overrun by those who were wicked. That is because there are so many hidden elements involved in judgment. We see only the surface appearance. But you have also raised a question concerning goodness. Are we really a good people? If taking the lead among the nations for crime is goodness and if exalting the sensuous is goodness, then we are. But if it is otherwise, then we may be lagging in basic integrity and morality.

Even if we are better than some other nations, God might still chasten us under the hand of another nation to bring us back to a place of fearing and loving Him.

One of the prophets complained, "For the wicked surround the righteous, so justice goes forth perverted" (Habakkuk 1:4). But God corrected his error and told him that "I am working a work in your days, that you would not believe if told" (Habakkuk 1:5). In an age such as this one, the people of God were counseled to live by faith, and not to judge by appearance of the moment. That is what we must do in ours.

In college I have been studying a course in ethics. I find that quite often a higher standard of ethics is held by secular thinkers than I experience in my contact with religious people. Is there any explanation for this?

There is an explanation for this. You must understand that culture and training have a great influence upon conduct. In the study of ethics, you are dealing with the highest ideal of human conduct that man is capable of expressing. Such expressions of conduct are theoretical, and the Bible clearly tells us that "Indeed, when Gentiles, who do not have the law, do by nature things required by the law, they are a law for themselves, even though they do not have the law, since they show that the requirements of the law are written on their hearts . . ." (Romans 2:14, 15). Most people know in theory what is right. What secular ethics does not and cannot provide is the motivation for right action. There is a great difference between the theory a man holds of conduct and the conduct itself.

You must also remember that the Christian is subjected to many temptations that are not common to those who are not Christians. On the average, you will find that the ethical and moral level of true Christians is now and always has been the highest. Only Christianity provides both the ethical standards and the adequate motivation.

My husband and I would like to have children, but it seems to me that the world is in such terrible shape that we worry about what might happen to our children in the future. Do you think it is right to think this way?

If you were to pick up a book which surveyed the history of the world, I doubt if you could find a single time throughout human history when conditions were ideal or the future was not clouded with uncertainty and threats of war. Even when social and political circumstances have been reasonably good, the world has been ravaged by natural disasters and plagues.

That is not to dismiss the fact that the world is in bad shape right now. We do live in a time of great uncertainty, and if, on the one hand, modern medicine has removed many of the things which threatened life only a generation or two ago, on the other hand, modern technology has developed weapons of mass destruction that can wipe out entire civilizations in a few hours. And new diseases such as AIDS rise up to threaten our survival.

But God is in control of the future. "The Lord reigns, let the earth be glad" (Psalm 97:1). I think of the time of the prophet Jeremiah in the Old Testament. It was a terrible time in many ways, with the Jewish people being carried away into captivity in Babylon and facing a very uncertain future. I am sure many of them must have asked the same question you have asked, but Jeremiah told them, "Marry and have sons and daughters. . . . For I know the plans I have for you, plans to give you hope and a future" (Jeremiah 29:6, 11).

Jeremiah could say this because he knew that God was Lord over the future as well as the past and present. It does not mean everything will be easy for our children. But our responsibility is clear: if God gives children to us, we should do whatever we can to strengthen them spiritually so that they too can face the future with a confident hope in God.

20

How Can We Know
What Is Right and Wrong?

How can we know what is right and what is wrong? There are so many conflicting ideas, and one becomes confused. Is there really any rule to go by?

"If any man's will is to do his will, he shall know whether the teaching is from God" (John 7:17, RSV). I think before one can know what is right and wrong, he must first align himself with God. Only then is he in a position to do right.

J. Wilbur Chapman once said: "The rule that governs my life is this: Anything that dims my vision of Christ, or takes away my taste for Bible study, or cramps my prayer life, or makes Christian work difficult, is wrong for me, and I must, as a Christian, turn away from it."

When I have a problem of deciding right from wrong I always give it three tests. First, I give it the common-sense test, and ask if it is reasonable. Then, I give it the prayer test. I ask God if it is good and edifying. Then, I give it the Scripture test. I see if the Bible has anything to say for or against it. Then, I may add a fourth: the conscience test. But the most important thing is to follow Jesus' suggestion: "If any man will do his will he shall *know* . . ." (John 7:17, KJV).

I have heard that you oppose abortion. I don't agree with this, since I think a woman ought to have a right to do whatever she wants to with her own body.

I know this is a very sensitive and emotional issue—I always get a great deal of mail whenever I deal with it. It has become a political issue today, but my concern is not political but moral and spiritual.

Yes, I oppose abortion (except in rare situations such as when the mother's life is clearly in danger and abortion becomes the lesser of two evils). The central question we have to face is this: is the little life within the womb just a piece of human tissue, or is it more than that—a human being—even when it is very young and could not sustain itself outside the womb? It is at this point that emotions tend to get in the way and people attempt to answer the question in a way that will agree with their own desires. But we need to look at this as reasonably as possible.

As a Christian my ultimate standard is the Bible, because I believe it to be God's Word which reveals absolute truth to us. I may have opinions about various things, but if God has spoken on a subject then I must submit my opinions to the rule of Scripture. Does the Bible, therefore, give any answer to the question of whether or not a fetus is a human being in God's eyes?

Yes, it does, giving us several illustrations to indicate that a fetus is a human being. God told Jeremiah, for example, "Before I formed you in the womb I knew you, before you were born I set you apart; I appointed you as a prophet to the nations" (Jeremiah 1:5). Or take the case of John the Baptist. When Mary, the mother of Jesus, became pregnant by the Holy Spirit she went immediately to visit her cousin Elizabeth, who was pregnant with John the Baptist. John's mother declared, "As soon as the sound of your greeting reached my ears, the baby in my womb leaped for joy" (Luke 1:44)—implying that the fetus was fully human.

I hope you will reconsider your stand—but I also hope you will study the Bible for yourself, not just on this issue but on your own need of Christ.

There are two further things I would like to say about this subject. First, the widespread acceptance of abortion is a symbol or sign of something deeper within our society that should also concern us greatly. This is the tendency today to decide moral issues or questions only on the basis of whether or not they are convenient or bring pleasure to a person. For example, many people today have discarded the Bible's clear teaching on sexual relations outside of marriage, simply because they are absorbed only in their own pleasures and desires. The tragedy, however, is that we never break God's laws without paying for it. The Bible declares, "Do not be deceived: God cannot be mocked. A man reaps what he sows. The one who sows to please his sinful nature, from that nature will reap destruction" (Galatians 6:7–8). That can be true of nations as well. "It is a dreadful thing to fall into the hands of the living God" (Hebrews 10:31).

But the other thing I would like to say is that God loves us, and He is willing to forgive us of our sins. He has made it possible by sending His only Son to die on the cross as a sacrifice for our sins. If you, or a person you know, has been guilty of this serious sin, know that God still loves and wants to forgive all who come to Him in sincere repentance and faith in Christ.

I had four abortions before I got married, and now I have discovered I am unable to have children at all. Do you think God is punishing me for the things I did in the past?

Several doctors have told me that abortion can be a difficult (and even dangerous) surgical procedure which can have permanently damaging effects on the

woman. It is not just a simple procedure that can be carried out without consequences—quite apart from the moral issues involved.

I cannot say whether or not God is using this directly as punishment in your
life, although the Bible clearly teaches that when we turn our backs on God
and choose to disregard His moral laws there are inevitable consequences.
Furthermore it is not God who is to blame for the consequences, but the person who has broken His law. Let me use an illustration from physical laws.
Suppose that you decided you would jump out of a second-story window. No
matter how much you might wish it, the law of gravity is not going to be sus-
pended when you jump. In a sense, the law of gravity is responsible for the bones
you would probably break—but actually you are responsible, because you dis-
regarded the law of gravity. Just as there are physical laws which we cannot
break without harming ourselves, so there are spiritual laws as well.

But the important question at this stage is, where do you go from here? God
loves you, and you need Him. You need His forgiveness for what you have done
in the past. Also you need His guidance and help in your life every day. So far
in your life you have neglected Him, and all it has brought you is heartache
and trouble. Now I pray that you will face honestly your need of Him, and you
will invite Christ into your heart by faith.

Then seek God's will for your future. God wants you to be the best wife you
can possibly be with His strength. He has a plan for your life, if you will turn to
Him and seek to follow Jesus Christ.

*I know people like you are always talking out against abortion, but I think
you are looking at things the wrong way. After all, as a woman I have rights,
including the right to do with my body anything I want to do with it, and no
one is going to tell me differently.*

There are certainly many things I could say to you about this issue, and why I
do not agree with your position because of the Bible's teaching. But in all honesty I suspect that you have heard all of the arguments before, and (as your last
comment says) you aren't really open to them. Therefore I will deal frankly with
the deeper issue you are facing—but may never have realized.

The real issue with you is not just abortion and whether or not you have a
right to terminate the life of a child who is growing within you. The real issue
is whether or not you will insist on running your own life according to your
own standards, or whether you will instead let God run your life. You have made
your declaration of independence, as it were—independence from anyone else's
ideas of how you should live, and most of all independence from God. By doing
so, you are saying that you know better than God does what is best for you.
You also are saying that you do not need God.

But this is wrong. God created you, and furthermore He loves you. And because He loves you, He knows what is best for you and wants you to be fulfilled as a person by doing His will. Right now you are a slave—a slave to yourself and your own limitations, whether you like to admit it or not. But Christ wants to free you. He wants to help you discover the excitement and joy of knowing why you are here and where you are going in God's plan.

Don't be afraid of God, and don't be afraid of opening your heart to His Son, Jesus Christ, as your Savior and Lord. You need Christ, and you will never find the joy and inner peace you are seeking apart from Him. He was willing to die for you on the cross because of His great love for you. The way you are going right now is a dead-end road—but Christ's way is "the road that leads to life" (Matthew 7:14).

For some time I have been stealing small amounts of money from the company that employs me. Now that I have come to know Christ, I feel that I must do something about this. I'm afraid to tell my employer lest I lose my position, yet I cannot live with my conscience troubling me as it now does. What would you suggest?

I think you will find that your employer will respect you for making an honest confession. Even though your life up until this time has been one of deception, yet the confession will convince him more than ever that something has taken place in your life. It is even possible that he will come to regard you as one of the most dependable workers he has. There is something even more important than clearing your own conscience, however. It is the thing you should do in order to give you the best possible opportunity to tell what God can do in the life of one who turns to Him. Having done what is pleasing to God, you can always leave the results to Him. We will pray that you will have courage to do what you know is the right thing.

I have always been a very proud person, but recently I have had a lot of financial reverses. Now I have lost my job and it looks as if I may have to go on some type of public welfare in order to survive. Do you think there is anything morally wrong with doing this?

Our society has a system of social welfare or assistance which is meant for people who are in genuine need. Yes, I know there are probably those who abuse it or use it as an excuse to avoid working—but the abuses of the few should not make you think that there is something wrong with the system as a whole. If you sincerely need the kind of help that our nation's welfare system is meant to bring to people, then you should not let your pride stand in the way. The ancient society of Israel had definite ways to assist those who were poor, and that is true of virtually any modern society today. The Bible says, "The righteous care about justice for the poor, but the wicked have no such concern" (Proverbs 29:7).

There are two other things I would like to mention concerning your question. First, although I know we live in difficult times economically, I hope you will continue to seek employment. Over the past several years the job market has been continually improving.

The other thing has to do with your reference to your pride. Elsewhere in your letter you indicate that you have never really had very much to do with the church or with God. I wonder if perhaps your pride has been a major reason for this—believing that you did not really need God because you were able to run your life quite satisfactorily without Him.

But you need God. You need Him right now in the midst of the problems you are facing, and you need Him for the future—both for the rest of your life and for eternity. Sometimes the hardest thing for someone like you to admit is that you need God—and sometimes God allows things to happen to us that show us we are not nearly as able to run things as we thought we were.

That is why this difficult time you are facing could be the best time of your life, if you were to face your need of Christ and turn to Him in repentance and faith. Don't let your pride keep you from the greatest gift in the universe—the gift of salvation which God offers you in Christ.

I have always loved rock music a great deal, but recently I began to listen to the words of some of the songs on my records. Do you think it is wrong to listen to that kind of music?

You need to remember that your mind is molded in many different ways—often in ways we are not aware of at the time. I am convinced that many things—the films we watch, the television we see, the music we listen to, the books we read—have a great effect on us.

Furthermore, you need to realize that if you belong to Jesus Christ you are called to live a life of purity and holiness. God wants your mind to be shaped by Him so that your thoughts and goals reflect Christ. That is why the Bible often places a high value on our minds and stresses the importance of what goes into them. The Bible tells us that we are not to live as unbelievers do "in the futility of their thinking. . . . You were taught, with regard to your former way of life, to put off your old self, which is being corrupted by its deceitful desires; to be made new in the attitude of your minds" (Ephesians 4:17, 22–23).

It is important, therefore, for you to pay attention to the words of the music you mention. Much modern music has strong sexual overtones in the words (and some people feel even in the rhythm). Some music today speaks favorably about drug experiences, or suggests that certain patterns of life are best—patterns which are wrong to a Christian who is seeking to please God. When this is the case with your music, then it is time to turn from it.

But beyond this is a deeper question—the question of what your goal is in life. Are you seeking to live for Christ, wanting to please Him in all you do? My prayer for you is that you will commit yourself to Him and put Him first in your life. Then you will want everything you do to honor Him.

What is your definition of greed? I admit I like nice things and comfortable living and I think about money a lot because I know I have a responsibility to my family, but that isn't necessarily wrong, is it?

Greed is an unreasonable or all-absorbing desire to acquire things or wealth. It can take all kinds of forms (including a grasping desire for money, possessions, luxury, food, power, or any number of other things).

One test of greed is that it is never satisfied. The prophet Isaiah said of the greedy of his own day, "They are dogs with mighty appetites; they never have enough" (Isaiah 56:11). Another test is that the greedy person has little or no regard for the needs of others, and may think nothing of hurting others or taking advantage of others in order to get more. His life is dominated by selfishness.

Greed is repeatedly condemned in the Bible. One of the Ten Commandments declares, "You shall not covet your neighbor's house . . . or anything that belongs to your neighbor" (Exodus 20:17). Why is this true? One reason is that a greedy person is only concerned about himself—and is therefore not concerned with God and His will. One of the writers of Proverbs prayed, "Give me neither poverty nor riches, but give me only my daily bread. Otherwise, I may have too much and disown you and say, 'Who is the Lord?'" (Proverbs 30:8–9).

It is not wrong to want to work and earn a decent living; in fact, God has given work to us. But this legitimate desire can very easily cross the line into greed—especially in our materialistic society. We need to be on guard against greed, therefore. But above all we need to make sure our lives are centered in Christ and not things. Have you committed your life to Him?

I am a clerk in a small-town bank. I have reason to believe that the cashier is dishonest. I am afraid to report him lest I lose my position, yet I believe it should be checked on. What is my responsibility in a case like this?

Your report would never need to be made known. The bank examiners would appreciate any information and it would be kept in strictest confidence. You have a higher responsibility than to a dishonest employer. You are a servant of the community and you have a responsibility to them. To remain silent would be to participate in the crime just as much as we sin when we give assent to the misdeeds of others. The Christian has a great obligation to be ethical and honest in all things, even sometimes at personal hazard. It is in the difficult situation that the qualities of a Christian are seen. They may go without notice in normal conditions, but when the crisis comes, then the distinctive qualities of the Christian are clearly seen.

I have a job in an office which is so large and in which there is so little supervision that some of the women do practically nothing all day long. They say they are "riding the gravy train" and get mad when I say they are stealing. What is right?

Accepting pay for which a corresponding service is not rendered is dishonest. From what you write, I think that you are correct in saying these girls are stealing. But I am not sure you have approached the problem in a helpful way. If you are a Christian, your first obligation is to see that you yourself give a full day's work for your wages. Then, as opportunity presents itself, you can wisely bring up the discussion of what is right and what is wrong. If such a discussion is started in a proper spirit, some of these women may be led to be more faithful in their work.

If all tactful methods fail, it would not be unethical to suggest to the head of the office force that some system of supervision be set up to ensure more effective work by all. One of the Ten Commandments is "Thou shalt not steal." There are many ways of taking that which is not our own. Many of us have been guilty of failing to do all that we could to earn what we are paid. Make this problem a matter of prayer. See if there are not other Christian women in the office and ask them to join in praying about it. Above all do not assume a holier-than-thou attitude. Be sure you are living as a Christian, not only in relation to your office work but also in other ways.

I am a partner in a small manufacturing concern. Due to business reverses we have been forced into bankruptcy. When the people of my church learned that I had filed bankruptcy, they insisted upon dropping me from the membership. Was my action so wrong that I can no longer have the fellowship with Christians?

That depends entirely upon the reasons and upon the motives of bankruptcy. Personal bankruptcy in order to avoid the payment of just debts is certainly not honest and not Christian. However, even men in the world of business recognize that there is a legitimate cause for bankruptcy when it is intended to avert law suits and litigation, in order to give you opportunity to make good on debts that have been honestly incurred. People unfamiliar with the procedure of business are not able to detect what your motives are. You will, however, have to give an answer to the Lord. Our prayer for you will be that your reason was to glorify Christ by being honest in all your relations and this was merely a method to accomplish that in the shortest possible time. Meanwhile, do not condemn the people of your church for their action. They simply did not understand your reasons and acted most likely according to the best light they had.

Is it always right to tell the truth, especially when you know it will hurt someone? If I tell the truth about my business affairs, it will ruin chances for the happiness of my family.

I would rather answer you by stating the matter in quite another way. It is always wrong to be dishonest. Dishonesty is never justified. God will never approve, and even your own conscience will rise up to condemn you sooner or later. I have not known of a single instance when a man has been ruined or his family injured because of his basic honesty. It may not always be either wise or expedient to publicly announce all your personal affairs, but to conceal the truth from persons involved is never the right course of action.

If you had been sure of the matter you would never have raised the question. Romans 14:23 says: "But the man who doubts is condemned if he eats, because his eating is not from faith; and everything which does not come of faith is sin." Do nothing until all the doubts are removed. This is a fairly safe procedure in all matters.

I am associated in business with a man who is active in his church on Sunday but who cheats his customers during the week. This has disgusted me with Christianity.

Some of your customers may possibly pay you with a ten-dollar bill which proves to be a counterfeit. Will you stop accepting ten-dollar bills because of a counterfeit? If your business associate is a hypocrite, it is he who is wrong, not Christianity. One can but wonder how you are working out the proceeds of the cheating you mention. If you are profiting by it, you are just as guilty as he. To be perfectly frank, one must wonder if your so-called disgust with Christianity is not really an excuse for not being a Christian. You know that all of us need Christ. He alone can change our hearts and give us the grace and strength to live as Christians should live. You evidently have high ideals in your own life. You are probably right in your disgust with your associate. Let me urge you to give your heart to Christ so that you can set the right example before him. If you do this, both of you will honor the name of the Christ you profess.

*Since becoming a Christian I have the problem of being in business with a man
who is not one, and who does not conduct our business on Christian principles.
My life's investment is in the business, so I can't very well leave without tremendous loss. What shall I do to make him change?*

Your problem is a complex one for it also involves the matter of your Christian
stewardship. You want to live your life and conduct your affairs as a Christian,
and at the same time you must be custodian of your earnings and regard them
as a stewardship. Many prosperous men make the mistake that is warned against
in the Bible saying: "My power and the might of my hand hath gotten me this
wealth." We have the right to say only that it is the Lord who "giveth thee power
to get wealth" (Deuteronomy 8:17, 18, KJV).

But your partner has a conscience even if he is not a Christian. He will recognize the merit and rightness of the "Christian way" even though he may not
accept the redemption provided in Christ for sinners. Get him to conduct the
business on Christian principles as a trial and then depend upon God to change
his heart.

*I am studying the psychology of religion in college. My professor tells me that
conversion is nothing more than a psychological phenomenon experienced by
most religions. Right now I am plenty worried about things I learned in my
home church, for they seem to be slipping away from me. Do you think my
conversion was real?*

Certainly your conversion was real, if when you were converted you came from
darkness to the light of the gospel. If you received Jesus Christ as your Lord and
Savior, then and there you became a new creature. I wouldn't take anything for
granted, not even a religious experience. You see, your professor is right when
he says conversions are experienced as a part of most religions. But don't allow
that to disturb you, for although all men may have some kind of religious experience, only the ones who receive Jesus Christ in a moment of repentance and
faith are born again.

The fact that others have similar religious emotions and conversions merely
shows that God so made man that he is capable of being converted. How tragic
it is when a man is converted falsely! This is what I would suggest. To overcome your fears and intellectual dilemma, just give as much time to the study
of what God has to say about it as your professor does. Don't argue with him,
but test everything he says in the light of God's Word. You need not fear then,
for the Bible can stand the onslaught of any enemy.

I am a freshman in college and am greatly confused because we are being told that science has disproved much of the Bible and that I will have to "rethink" my faith if I expect to have any faith.

When you are told that science has disproved the Bible, ask specifically where such is the case. True science and a true understanding of the Bible are never at variance. Furthermore, at many points where it was thought a few years ago that science was disproving the Scripture, records have since been cleared up and the Bible is now admittedly correct. Of course, if one is definitely antagonistic to the Christian faith and the Scriptures, he is prone to back his position by supposed inaccuracies in the Bible. But the best answer to such people is to insist on a statement on their part of just what the inaccuracies are. In most cases they are not forthcoming. In others, if you do not have an explanation yourself you will be wise to ask your pastor or some biblical scholar who can give you the answer. In truly scientific circles today there is much less antagonism toward the Christian faith and to the Bible than was true a few years ago. This is due to the fact that scientific discoveries (not theories) are found more and more to fit into the record God has given us in His Word. Before you "rethink" your faith it may be wise to examine the critics of the Bible. In the end your faith will be even stronger.

In my college class in advanced astronomy, the question has been raised whether the explosion theory of the origin of the universe permits the possibility of divine creation. What do you think?

I do not feel competent to speak on the various theories held by scientists with reference to the origin of the universe. But this one thing I am very sure of—any theory which leaves the Sovereign God out of His own universe is a very poor one. For the creature to ignore the Creator is utter folly. To think that this universe, so vast that even now its limits are unknown, is the product of self-contained and self-directed matter seems hardly worthy of consideration.

In our own world there are evidences on every hand that in all of nature there is a perfection and a controlling and directing hand which must be infinite and divine. Should we find a watch by the side of the road, and, had we never seen a watch before, we would be led to believe in some being capable of thought and design who made that watch. How much more do we have evidence on every hand of God and of His creative power and wisdom! Psalm 19 tells us that the heavens and the earth show forth the glory of God. In the first chapter of Paul's letter to the Romans we read: "For the invisible things of him from the creation of the world are clearly seen, being understood by the things that are made" (v. 20). Any theory of the universe that does not take into account the God and Creator of the universe is not worthy of serious consideration.

Since coming to the university, I find that unless I join a sorority I am just left out of the social life here. Still I can't approve the program sponsored by those I know about. Is compromise the only answer in this world, or do I have to be on the outside?

Many times the Christian feels at odds with the world, and if we are to depend upon the words of the Savior, it will continue to be that way. Jesus once said: "Behold, I send you forth as sheep among wolves." Although it may not appear that unconverted people are fitting that description, it certainly shows that there is no good way to effect a reconciliation unless they are reconciled to God first. In answer to your question about compromise, it will have to be said that when you do, only you are the loser. The very ones whose social pressure caused you to compromise will despise you for it. They probably respect your convictions and many of them wish they had the moral stamina to stand alone. May the Lord give you added courage to be a witness for Him, even in a hard place.

Don't be a prude, or snobbish, but let your life "glow" for Christ. We are lamps shining in the darkness. Be attractive and winsome, but do not compromise your convictions for the sake of popularity.

21

What about the Christian and Politics?

Do you think the church ought to get involved in political issues? That seems to be all our preacher ever talks about.

The church of Jesus Christ has been given a distinctive and unique task in our world by God, and that is to proclaim the gospel of Jesus Christ. When we fail to do that, we are not doing what God wants us to do. We are under orders: "Therefore go and make disciples of all nations, baptizing them in the name of the Father and of the Son and of the Holy Spirit, and teaching them to obey everything I have commanded you" (Matthew 28:19–20). Those orders have never been changed.

This is why—generally speaking—I do not feel the church as an organization should become involved in political matters. There are times, however, when political issues also have moral and spiritual dimensions and when this is the case we have a responsibility to speak for the truth. I believe things like abortion are morally wrong, for example, and we have a responsibility to take a stand. At the same time, this must not be our primary task. This is not an easy question, but the greatest need of our hour is for Christians and the church to proclaim the gospel. Only Christ can change the human heart, and this is the basic cause of our problems today. On the other hand, if an individual Christian feels the call to become active in politics, I am all for such activity.

Pray for your preacher, and don't be afraid of letting him know of your concern. Be thankful for the sensitivity he demonstrates about some of the moral and spiritual problems that infect our world—but encourage him also to teach and preach the full message of the Bible. After a ministry of several years in Ephesus the apostle Paul could say, "I have declared to both Jews and Greeks that they must turn to God in repentance and have faith in our Lord Jesus. . . . I have not hesitated to proclaim to you the whole will of God" (Acts 20:21, 27). Proclaiming "the whole will of God" should be the goal—and the joy—of every church and every preacher.

Don't you think that Christians should stay out of politics? Doesn't the Bible warn us "not to be entangled again with the yoke of bondage"?

I certainly do not think that Christians should be disinterested in the affairs of our government. Christ said: "Give to Caesar what is Caesar's and to God, God's" (Mark 12:17).

Nothing would please the racketeers, gangsters, and the underworld more than for all church people to stay away from the polls and to be uninformed about what is happening in Washington and in their own states and cities.

I would urge every Christian to vote and to show a keen interest in the politics of his community. I would even encourage him, if he felt so called, to take an active part in politics and to crusade for clean, honest, and upright handling of community affairs through good government.

The cliché, "Politics is dirty," is plainly untrue. I know men and women who are in government who have high principles, fine motives, and unquestioned integrity. They have dedicated themselves to a life of public service because they sincerely want to serve their fellowmen. While it is true that politics seems to attract some people of questionable principle, that fact makes it all the more imperative that good people everywhere cast their vote for the best candidates.

Recently I heard a preacher, while referring to politics during a sermon, make the statement that corrupt conditions in politics is the reason he has never registered or voted. Don't you think that Christians should vote?

Personally, I don't think people who are not even interested enough in what is going on in our country to register or vote are qualified to speak authoritatively on government. I know a great number of fine, upstanding Christian statesmen. Perhaps there are some who are unethical and ulterior in their motives. That gives even more reason why every Christian should vote. The ballot is part of our great American heritage and freedom. It is our only means of keeping government clean and proper. I think that it is not only the right, but the duty of every American to use his voting franchise, prayerfully and thoughtfully.

Russia is an example of a country which was indifferent to corrupt politics, and when the Communists took over, they destroyed the partisan system, and subsequently, the right of free franchise. Let us hope that the indifference of our people toward the importance of voting will not lead to a similar situation here in the years to come.

I find that there is still much racial prejudice in our country. What can we Christians do about it?

I think Christ was quite definite as to the position that every true Christian should take. He said: "Thou shalt love thy neighbor as thyself." We must approach our racial problems with love, tolerance, and a spirit of give and take, no matter what the conditions. There is no excuse for any Christian to participate in acts of violence against a person because of race. Proverbs 10:12 says: "Hatred stirs up dissension, but love covers over all wrongs." Again the apostle John says in 1 John 2:9: "Anyone who claims to be in the light but hates his brother is still in the darkness." A true Christian will have love, tenderness, compassion, and understanding when he approaches this problem that threatens to divide the country.

In Acts 4 we see the disciples selling all and putting their money in a common treasury, and all sharing alike. What is the difference between this and the Communistic belief?

There is a great difference. The "having all things common" of the early Christians was based entirely on love. There was no force or coercion. There were no police to enforce the will of authorities. In fact there were no authorities; it was entirely a matter of the heart.

At the time in Jerusalem there was much poverty and the disciples were just fresh from being filled with the Holy Spirit. They felt an inner compulsion to share with others; they were full of the new gospel "Love thy neighbor as thyself," and it spilled over into their social life.

If we spent more time with the Lord and were filled with the Holy Spirit, we too would be compelled to share both our goods and our faith with others. We would not only give of our means, but of our goods, our time, and our talents that others might discover the joy we know.

V

BIBLICAL QUESTIONS

22

Prove the Existence of God!

I dare you to prove the existence of God. I want to be a scientist when I go to college, and I won't believe anything unless it can be proved. I don't see what room there is for religious belief in a scientific age like ours. Religion to me is just an outdated superstition.

Just a few days ago I came across a lengthy article which dealt with the religious views of a number of scientists. They came from various institutions (including Princeton and Stanford), and many of them are working on the frontiers of scientific research in such areas as physics and genetics.

They are, in other words, some of the finest scientific minds in our country—and without exception they were giving witness to their personal faith in God and their commitment to Jesus Christ. Far from being an "outdated superstition," Christianity is for them the very foundation of their lives and their understanding of the universe. One common thread in their thinking is that their research has pointed them to God. The world is so complex, they have realized, that the only logical explanation is that God created it. They also have realized that science has limits. For example, science can describe the world, but it cannot say where it came from or why we are here.

Let me challenge you therefore not to have a closed mind. Have you, for example, ever read the New Testament for yourself, seeking to discover what it really says? You see, the Bible says we can know God, because He has made Himself known to us. "No one has ever seen God, but God the only Son, who is at the Father's side, has made him known" (John 1:18). The most important discovery you will ever make is that God loves you and you can know Him personally by committing your life to Jesus Christ.

Did Jesus ever claim to be God? I have heard that He never did, but that the idea of Jesus being divine was thought up by His disciples later on. I would be interested to hear how you would answer this.

You cannot read the New Testament without realizing that Jesus claimed—frequently and clearly—that He was the divine Son of God, sent from Heaven to save us from our sins. It is also clear from the Gospel accounts that His disciples did not believe His claims at first, but only gradually came to understand and accept them (particularly after the resurrection, which proved beyond doubt that He was who He claimed to be).

His claim to be God is seen in many passages of Scripture. To His disciples He declared, "I and the Father are one . . . Anyone who has seen me has seen the Father" (John 10:30; 14:9). When Thomas (a disciple who doubted that Jesus had been raised from the dead) met Christ after the resurrection, he exclaimed, "My Lord and my God!"—and Jesus accepted his praise (John 20:28). Even the enemies of Jesus knew of His claim to divinity. On one occasion, for example, they picked up stones to try to kill Him "for blasphemy, because you, a mere man, claim to be God" (John 10:33).

Anyone could claim to be divine, of course, but did Jesus do anything to back up His claim? Yes! His miracles, which were witnessed by thousands, were an evidence of His unique nature. His resurrection verified His claim. But why is this important? It is important because only a divine Savior could truly save us from our sins. If Christ were just a great religious teacher, He would have no power to bring us forgiveness. But because He was God's only Son, He could die as a perfect and final sacrifice for our sins. Have you accepted the gift of forgiveness He offers you?

How can you say that there is such a thing as hell, if God is really a God of love?

Let me say at the beginning that God does not want us to go to hell; instead, He wants us to live with Him eternally in Heaven. The Bible says, "He is patient with you, not wanting anyone to perish, but everyone to come to repentance" (2 Peter 3:9). At the same time, the Bible also makes it very clear that hell is a reality, and it would be foolish for you to turn your back on that fact.

How can God, who loves us, also allow hell to exist? That is not an easy question to answer, but perhaps the right place to begin is to realize that God is not only a God of love, but a God of justice as well. He is holy and perfect, and He is also completely just in all He does. The Bible says, "The Lord is righteous in all his ways and loving toward all he has made" (Psalm 145:17). Let me put it this way: God has made this world in such a way that some things are right, and some things are wrong. It is always wrong to murder someone, for example, or to steal from someone.

But imagine what kind of world it would be if God did not ever judge evil. Imagine if the Hitlers of this world, who oppress and kill others, never had to give account for their sins or be judged. But that is not the way it is! "For God will bring every deed into judgment, including every hidden thing, whether it is good or evil" (Ecclesiastes 12:14).

You have, in other words, two great truths: God judges sin because He is righteous; God also loves us. And yet if we are honest we must admit that we have sinned against God and we only deserve to be judged. We have not followed His will and have turned our backs on Him. But now I want you to see a very important truth: God in His love has made it possible for us to escape His judgment—because Christ was sent from God to take upon Himself the judgment that we deserved. God loves you, and that is why "he gave his one and only Son, that whoever believes in him shall not perish but have eternal life" (John 3:16).

Do you think that the gospel of the first century as stated in the Bible is relevant for our present time?

The Bible says that the grass withers and the flowers fade, but the Word of our God stands forever. It also says that Jesus Christ is the same yesterday, today, and forever. Ideas, books, and people come and go, but the Bible and the truth it contains is for all time. That is why the Bible is a living Book and can be trusted for its advice and direction and knowledge of God at the end of the twentieth century just as much as it could be trusted by first-century Christians. God has given us a message that is not only for past times and this time, but for all time.

I know you place a lot of emphasis on the Bible. But does it really have anything to say about our practical modern-day problems, since it was written so long ago?

Yes, I place a great deal of emphasis of the Bible—and one reason I do so is precisely because it is so practical and deals with problems we all face in our everyday lives.

Why is this the case? It is true because first of all it is God's Word to us. It is not a book of human ideas and advice—it is God's Word, given to us by Him to teach us how to live. "All Scripture is God-breathed and is useful for teaching, rebuking, correcting and training in righteousness, so that the man of God may be thoroughly equipped for every good work" (2 Timothy 3:16–17). God knows what we are like—far better than we know ourselves—and He knows what we need if we are to live as we should.

It also is true because man does not change. Yes, we live in a world which is much different from that of the biblical writers. But man is the same. Our greatest need is to be reconciled to God, who created us, and in the Bible we discover the wonderful truth that this is possible through faith in Jesus Christ.

We also need to know how to live. We need to know what is right and wrong, and we need to know how to love others and get along with others. The Bible shows us the way. "Your word is a lamp to my feet and a light for my path" (Psalm 119:105).

I invite you to discover the Bible for yourself. (A good place to start would be with the Book of Proverbs in the Old Testament and the Gospel of John in the New Testament.) Read it every day, and ask God to show you its truth for your life. If you do, you will not only discover that it will guide you in your daily living, but you will discover the wonderful truth that God—the Bible's author—loves you and wants you to be His child through faith in Jesus Christ.

I suppose this may sound like a dumb question to you, but where are the Ten Commandments found? Does God still expect us to follow them? It seems like I never hear any sermons on them.

Don't apologize for asking what you think is a "dumb question"! Tragically, many people never get around to asking the really important questions of life (such as "how can we be saved?") because they are afraid someone will laugh at them. But it is far better to know God's truth than to be ignorant of it.

The Ten Commandments are found in two places in the Bible. The first is in the Old Testament Book of Exodus, chapter 20, verses 1-17; the second is in the Book of Deuteronomy, chapter 5, verses 6-21. In both places it is stressed that the Ten Commandments are given to us by God, and they tell us what God expects of us. If you look carefully at them you will notice that the first four commandments especially concern our relationship to God, telling us that we are to love God and serve Him above all else. The second set of commandments (the last six) tell us how we are to act in our relationships with other people.

The Ten Commandments are just as valid today as they were when God gave them to Moses. They reflect the moral character of God, and they also provide the foundation of right living with others. God's character does not change, and neither does His moral will for us. You will find that the New Testament has much to say about these commandments.

But there is one central truth you also need to remember. The Ten Commandments reveal God's standard for us—but if we are honest, we know that none of us are able to keep them completely. None of us have ever loved God completely and perfectly. None of us have ever avoided completely the sin of coveting what was someone else's possession. In other words, we can never be saved by keeping the Ten Commandments, because none of us can keep them perfectly. But Christ did! And by faith in Him we can be forgiven of our sins and know the joy of following Him every day.

I have been in college now for a few weeks, and it seems like I am questioning everything I have ever believed. I even am beginning to wonder if God is real, or if He is just a product of our imagination or wishes. Can you help me?

It is not uncommon for someone like yourself to go away to college and suddenly find that things you have believed are questioned by others who appear smarter or more experienced than you. Then doubt begins to creep in and can easily overtake you if you do not take steps to combat it.

There are three things I would like to tell you. First, there are answers to the questions you may be having—good, solid answers. You are not the first person in history to wonder about whatever questions are bothering you right now. There have been many highly intelligent men and women who have been (and are) faithful followers of Christ. Perhaps your pastor or a Christian worker on your campus can direct you to books that deal with these questions.

Then you need to seek the encouragement and strength of other Christians. On your campus there are undoubtedly many sincere Christians, and you should pray that God will guide you to them. (There are several interdenominational groups, for example, that work especially on college campuses, such as Inter-Varsity, Navigators, or Campus Crusade.) Not only will you find others who have worked through the same questions you are facing, but you will be strengthened by the regular fellowship of other believers.

In addition, you need to spend time alone with God each day. There is no substitute for a personal walk with God through systematic Bible reading and prayer. In this way you can get to know God better and be able to face the temptations and doubts Satan wants to throw at you. You also will be able to help others who are struggling with questions about God. "Always be prepared to give an answer to everyone who asks you to give the reason for the hope that you have" (1 Peter 3:15). And if you have never really given your life to Jesus Christ, this is a time to learn more about Him and His claim on your life.

23

How Should We
Read the Bible?

*I am ninety years old and in the last fifty years I have read the New Testa-
ment through over two hundred times. I find something new in it every time
I read it. I wish you would encourage people to read the Bible more.*

Thank you for the testimony about the importance of the Bible. Yes, I find something new in the Bible every time I read it also, and that can be the experience
of everyone who comes to it wanting to discover more of God's truth.

Your words point out several things about Bible reading that I think are important to stress—things you have learned by personal experience across the
years. You give us a good idea about how we should read the Bible.

How should we come to the Bible? First, we should come expectantly. The
Bible is not just another book—it is the Word of God, given to us by God to
help us and instruct us. The Psalmist declared, "Your word is a lamp to my
feet and a light for my path" (Psalm 119:105). Therefore, when we come to the
Bible we should come expectantly—expecting God to teach us and show us new
truths about Himself and His will for our lives. That is one reason why we should
always pray when we open the Bible and ask the Holy Spirit (who inspired the
writers of the Bible) to illumine or make clear its meaning for our lives. It means
we also should read it carefully, not just hurrying through a passage or reading
it without understanding.

Second, we should read the Bible systematically. I am thrilled by your testimony of reading the New Testament more than two hundred times during the
last fifty years—an average of once every three months! I'm sure there were
many times you were very busy and could have found other uses for your time,
but you discovered the value of systematic and disciplined reading.

Finally, we should read the Bible obediently—ready to obey the truth that
God has for us. God gave the Bible to us "for teaching, rebuking, correcting and
training in righteousness" (2 Timothy 3:16), and the Bible can change our lives
as we read it and obey its teachings every day.

I'm beginning to read the Bible for myself. Are there any particular study methods I should observe?

Very definitely there are. To begin with, you must read the Bible with a desire to know and to accept any truth you discover. You can be critical but you must be fair and open-minded. Then, you must read systematically, and not just at random. The Bible will yield the richest blessing in the long run to those who study systematically. Begin regular reading of the Bible from beginning to end in your morning Bible-reading time, and concentrate on a specific book in your evening time. I would suggest the Gospel of John and then the Book of Romans.

In addition, you must study prayerfully, relying upon God to enlighten your mind and enable you to understand what you read. Pray frequently as you read and you will discover a fellowship with God that is both intimate and satisfying. Finally, make use of dependable helps but do not rely upon them. Many helps are actually a hindrance. Make sure you are learning the Bible and not the views of some individual. You may be in perfect agreement but there is a blessing in knowing you got it from God.

I would like to have a better understanding of the Christian religion, but never seem to get much out of the Bible when I read it. Can you tell me of some book or commentary that will answer the question in a more simple way?

No book ever takes the place of the Bible. It is its own best commentary. I would urge you to go on studying the text of the Bible itself. Only when you find it in the Bible are you sure it is Scriptural truth. As a help, I would make a few simple suggestions.

Be open-minded. If you begin with a prejudice, you will be blind, or else you will read into the Bible what is not really there.

Act upon the basis of what you discover. The Bible is a guidebook, leading men to God in a personal faith. Like a map or guidebook, it will show you the way, but you must take it one step at a time.

Ask God to enlighten your mind. In other words, read it prayerfully. The sound of the words will not help, for you must understand what you read. God provides enlightenment for those who wish it.

Finally, *continue your study.* Be patient, for the knowledge of God comes gradually and slowly. The fact that God is infinite makes the study of His word a lifetime occupation. The Bible is to your soul what bread is to your body. You need it daily. One good meal does not suffice for a lifetime.

I have recently begun to read the New Testament. Now I am told that the church existed before the New Testament, and therefore is in possession of more authority than the Bible itself. Can you explain this problem to me so that I can study with restored confidence?

Historically, the church was in existence before the New Testament. That does not place it in authority above it, for you will notice that the writers always appeal to the existing Old Testament as authority. Also, you will notice that God approved the genuineness of the work and the dependability of the writer, by miraculous demonstration and by general consent of the body of believers in every place. The books we call canonical were able by the weight of their contents to separate themselves from all spurious and pseudo books. The evidence is in the books themselves, not alone because of the power of their combined message. The vitality the Bible exhibits in every generation causes this work to commend itself to you as being superior to continuing organizations or conflicting voices in any age. Its power to transform lives is its best apologetic.

My friend says the Bible doesn't say anything about drugs. Is that true? I used to feel guilty when I first started experimenting with them, but now I know drugs can help me and make me much more creative. I know some drugs can harm you, but if you know what you are doing they help you.

It is not true that the Bible is silent about such things. The Bible condemns the use of any substance which alters or distorts our thinking (including alcohol, which was the most common drug in ancient times). It may interest you to know that the Greek word used in the New Testament to designate a sorcerer or a person who practiced occult magic is "pharmakeus," or one who mixed drugs and used them to induce spells. (We get modern words like "pharmacy" from this ancient Greek word.) Such practices are included in the list of "acts of the sinful nature" in Galatians 5:19–21 that God will judge.

Your letter concerns me greatly, however, because it is clear you have allowed yourself to be deceived and enslaved by drugs. One of the characteristics of some drugs (such as cocaine) is that they make a person feel strong and alert—when in fact the opposite is the case. Don't allow yourself to be deceived. You are on a dead-end road, in spite of what you tell yourself, and my prayer is that you will realize it and turn back before it is too late.

The Bible says, "Be self-controlled and alert. Your enemy the devil prowls around like a roaring lion looking for someone to devour. Resist him" (1 Peter 5:8–9). How can you resist the temptation to escape from life through drugs? First, admit your helplessness and turn to Christ for forgiveness and strength. Then surround yourself with His Word and with His people who can help you fight this problem.

If the Bible is the Word of God, as you constantly say, why are there so many off-color stories in it?

Because there are so many sinners in the world. The Bible is not an idealistic fairy story. Rather it is a record of God's dealing with mankind and of many individual men and women. There is nothing which indicates the inspiration of the Scriptures more than the factual and faithful record of men and their failures. For instance, one of the greatest men in the Bible is King David. And yet, the Bible tells us he was guilty of both adultery and murder. But it also tells us of his repentance and turning back to God. All of these records are for our warning and instruction. They show us how sinful man needs God and His redemptive work in Christ and they tell us of many who accepted this love and were transformed. There is one thing about the stories in the Bible where sinful acts are mentioned: they do not glorify sin, nor do they make people want to go out and copy them. The Bible always shows sin up for what it really is, an offense against God and something to be repented of and turned from. Try studying the Bible with that attitude and you will find out for yourself.

Some people say we should not take a critical attitude toward the Bible. How can one be intellectually honest and not do so? Are we to swallow the whole thing without examining it?

The answer to your question centers in part on the meaning of the word "critical." In the ordinary usage of the word this means to be fault-finding or censorious. There are, of course, other meanings of the word. However, in the study of the Bible the word means to evaluate, analyze, and also to study the historic, cultural, and linguistic backgrounds of the times during which the Bible was written. Such a critical study of the Bible has produced a tremendous volume of information, has clarified the meaning of many passages, and has made it possible for us to understand far more clearly the messages God would give us.

On the other hand there is a form of biblical criticism which starts with certain preconceived ideas and which seeks to interpret the Bible in the light of these presuppositions. For instance, if one rejects the miraculous and the supernatural, one will reject these elements of the whole written revelation from God. One can approach the Bible with a cold rationalistic attitude or one can do so with reverence and the desire to hear God speak. I have a friend, a physician, who says there is a difference between the attitude of a scientist dissecting a dead body in a dissecting hall and that of a surgeon who operates on a living person in the operating room. The Bible should be approached with the assurance that here we have God-breathed literature and that it is our privilege and joy to find out what He has to say. Paul tells Timothy: "All Scripture is

God-breathed and is useful for teaching, rebuking, correcting and training in righteousness, so that the man of God may be thoroughly equipped for every good work" (2 Timothy 3:16–17). That is the attitude with which we should approach the Bible.

Almost all of my family and acquaintances are Christians. They keep telling me to read the Bible and find out how to live the Christian life. Honestly, I get bored when I sit down to read it and when I try to pray I keep thinking of a thousand other things. Is there something wrong with me?

I don't think there is anything wrong with you that is not typical of most young people. Having grown up in a religious atmosphere, you are right now passing through a period of revolt. You want to be on your own and make your own decisions without your family's influence.

There is another fact you should know. One of the devil's methods is to attack everyone, old and young, in this matter. He knows that the Word of God is powerful, and he will try to keep you from it. That means you are involved in a spiritual warfare.

If you would stop for a moment and think as a mature person, you would realize that your parents are trying to get you to do what is for your good. Don't rebel, but give God the opportunity to change your life and help you over the problems of youth, for they are many. Solomon once said: "Remember your creator in the days of your youth" (Ecclesiastes 12:1), and this is what you should do to find the greatest joy.

I find it helpful to read my Bible on the train on my way to work each morning. Some of my friends tell me I ought not to do this, as it is flaunting my religion in the face of others and probably makes them feel uncomfortable. What do you advise?

If I were you I would not worry too much about what other people say or think in a matter of this kind. If you bother unduly about the opinions of others you will never do anything at all!

By all means read your Bible on the train if you find this helpful. While those around you are filling their minds with the bad news about man in their daily papers, steep yourself in the good news about God in His precious Word!

Of course, I will admit that a crowded railway car is not the best place for reading the Bible, for it is not easy to concentrate in such circumstances; and real Bible study requires concentration. Nevertheless, it is well to use every moment of the day to the best advantage, and no doubt a great deal of time is wasted on such journeys that could be employed in a much better way.

I do not quite understand why the fact of your reading the Bible in public should make others feel uncomfortable—unless they are non-Christians or backsliders. And in that case they have no right to be comfortable! They need to be aroused out of their comfortable indifference and reminded of the claims of God's Word; and it may be that your example will serve to remind them of the Book they have neglected.

24

Does the Bible Say Anything about Life on Other Planets?

I am fascinated by space travel and things like that, and if there is intelligent life on other planets maybe we could learn things from them—like how to have world peace, for instance.

No, the Bible is silent about the possibility of life on other planets. At the same time the Bible does not explicitly say there is no life on other planets; it is simply silent on the question.

While it is interesting to speculate about such questions, let me point out that God has already given us a blueprint for peace. Have you ever asked yourself why we do not have peace in the world—in spite of the fact the yearning for peace is universal? The problem is not that we lack knowledge. The problem is the human heart, which by nature is self-centered. The Bible says, "What causes fights and quarrels among you? Don't they come from your desires that battle within you? You want something but don't get it. You kill and covet, but you cannot have what you want. You quarrel and fight" (James 4:1–2).

Our greatest need is for the human heart to be changed. But how can that happen? Education is not enough. Peace treaties or more just economic or political systems are not enough. No, the only answer is God, for He alone can change our hearts. In fact that is one reason Jesus Christ came—to reconcile us to God so we could have peace with Him, and then to reconcile us to each other. "We love because he first loved us" (1 John 4:19). Have you come to know God's peace in your own heart, by turning to Christ and asking Him to come into your life? Don't put your hope in speculations about life on other planets, but put your hope in Christ alone.

I am a student of the physical sciences. Some of my associates are inclined to believe that there is life on other planets. If there are people who inhabit these planets, what does that do to our faith in the gospel? Can it be that God is primarily interested in this planet?

From my studies in the Scriptures I can find nothing that would change our essential faith in the gospel if we did discover life on other planets. Our Bible is clearly designed for this particular planet with its particular problem of man's sin. When we observe this fact we are on safe ground. It is not a part of the Bible's message to inform us of what God has done elsewhere. Its message is concerned with earth dwellers, their origin, the reason for their existence, the cause of their misery, and the plan of redemption for a fallen race. I am sure that if there are dwellers on other planets, they are either not involved in the sin problem, or else God has made satisfactory provision for them. The God of the Universe is the God of our Lord Jesus Christ. He is entirely able to support all of creation and is able to govern it in righteousness.

What is your opinion of current experiments in space? Will they interfere with the planets in any way, such as the power of the sun, or the disarrangement of the earth or moon? If so, can the Lord stop these adventures into space?

Though I am a minister and not a scientist, I have no qualms about the experiments in space upsetting the order of the universe. It would be just as logical to get upset at children casting stones into the ocean, fearing that their childish actions might upset the rhythm of the tides. God's universe is so vast and limitless that man's probing into space is less expansive than a minute pinprick in the outer skin of an onion. Our solar system is just one of billions in God's colossal creation. No, I don't think you need to fear that the rocket experiments are endangering the universe.

Perhaps all this is to beckon our attention to the greatness and majesty of God. The Bible says: "When I consider thy heavens, the work of thy fingers, the moon and the stars, which thou hast ordained: What is man, that thou art mindful of him? . . . O Lord, how excellent is thy name in all the earth" (Psalm 8:3–4, 9, KJV).

25

Is Jesus Coming Back?

On what grounds do you base your statement that Jesus Christ is coming back?
Did not Christ say, "Lo, I am with you always, even unto the end of the world"?

We look for the return of the Lord because He said many times that He would come—and because it is one of the most frequently mentioned subjects in the Bible. Christ is with us today through His Holy Spirit, and He will be with Christians and with the church down to the end of the age. When He ascended up into heaven, the disciples were told by two angels standing by that He would return again as they were now seeing Him go (see Acts 1:11).

This climactic event of history is yet in the future. It will be sudden and final—the culmination of the ages. It will take the unbelieving world by surprise, and people will try to hide from His holy presence. At the return of Christ the resurrection of believers will take place. They will be gathered together to be with the Lord forever. We can only speculate about the exact details of His return. The important thing is that He is coming again and that we yet have time to trust in Him as our Savior and Lord. The Bible says all people must face Him at that time—as either Savior or Judge: "When the Son of Man comes in his glory . . . he will sit on his throne in heavenly glory" (Matthew 25:31).

Do you believe that Jesus Christ is going to make a visible, physical return to this earth?

Yes, I believe this with all my heart, not because of the opinions of others, but based solely on what the Bible plainly teaches. In the Old Testament there are prophecies which can be fulfilled only by our Lord's return. In the New Testament we find more than three hundred references to the Second Coming. For instance, Christ Himself said again and again that He is coming back: "I am going . . . to prepare a place for you. And if I go . . . I will come back and take you to be with me that you also may be where I am" (John 14:2–3). He also said:

"They will see the Son of man coming on the clouds of the sky, with power and great glory" (Matthew 24:30).

In 1 Thessalonians 4:16 Paul said: "For the Lord himself will come down from heaven, with a loud command, with the voice of the archangel and with the trumpet call of God. . . ."

His coming will be visible: ". . . he is coming with the clouds, and every eye will see him . . ." (Revelation 1:7). When our Lord ascended up into heaven, two men suddenly stood by the disciples and asked, "Men of Galilee . . . why do you stand here looking into the sky? This same Jesus, who has been taken from you into heaven, will come back in the same way you have seen him go into heaven" (Acts 1:11). In Revelation 1:8 Jesus said: "I am the Alpha and the Omega . . . who is, and who was, and who is to come, the Almighty." The fact that Christ is going to return is both a glorious hope and a stern warning: ". . . now is the time of God's favor, now is the day of salvation" (2 Corinthians 6:2).

I have heard people talk about someone or something called the antichrist, which I believe is mentioned in the Bible. Who or what is this? Or is it just a term used to describe anyone who tries to do things against the Christian message?

The term "antichrist" is found several times in the Bible, and refers to a person who will come in the days just before Christ returns to establish His Kingdom. "You have heard that the antichrist is coming" (1 John 2:18).

This person is not Satan, but will use every evil device of Satan to oppose the work of God. The apostle Paul uses the term "the man of lawlessness" or "the lawless one" to speak of this individual (2 Thessalonians 2:3, 8). He will be the embodiment of evil, and will have great power to deceive those who choose to follow him. "The coming of the lawless one will be in accordance with the work of Satan displayed in all kinds of counterfeit miracles, signs and wonders, and in every sort of evil that deceives those who are perishing" (2 Thessalonians 2:9–10). The time will come, therefore, when someone who is totally opposed to Christ will achieve great influence. However, in the end, he will be defeated by Christ.

At the same time the Bible warns us there are many in the world who have the same spirit as the antichrist and oppose the work of God. "Even now many antichrists have come" (1 John 2:18). This means we need to be discerning and not be misled by those who oppose God's truth. How can we avoid being led astray into falsehood? The most important thing is to yield our lives to Jesus Christ, and then to know more and more the truth God has given us in His Word, the Bible.

Do you really believe that this world will come to an end?

Yes, I believe that this world, as we know it, will come to an end. When, I do not know, but all history is pointing toward a climactic event when everything now seen will be purified by fire. This is not fanciful imagination but the clear and repeated testimony of the Bible. In both the Old and New Testaments we have this climax foretold. Our Lord Himself said such would take place. A study of this universe, in which this world is but an infinitesimal speck, shows that any one of a number of factors could bring about this physical cataclysm.

The Bible says: "But the day of the Lord will come like a thief. The heavens will disappear with a roar; the elements will be destroyed by fire, and the earth and everything in it will be laid bare" (2 Peter 3:10). This same Bible says: "Believe in the Lord Jesus Christ and you will be saved—you and your household" (Acts 16:31).

I agree that Christianity has some good ideas, but I think that we ought to look at all the religions of the world and get the best from each of them. What do you find wrong with that idea? What does the Bible say?

I suspect many people would agree with your ideas—although few actually would begin to search seriously through the major religions of the world. If they did, they might come to realize more fully how contradictory some of them are and how impossible it is to take the various ideas they have and draw them together into an intelligent system.

There are two problems I want to point out concerning your plan. First, how will you judge or know whether the ideas you are taking from each religion are really true? Unless you have some kind of standard, you are as likely to take ideas which are false as you are to take ideas that are true.

There is a still more important fact to be noted, however. There are many religions in the world, and they have developed because various people have had various ideas about God. But Christianity makes a unique claim. Christians claim that we do not need to grope after God or guess what He is like. We can know what He is like—and in fact we can know God personally. Why is this possible? It is possible because God Himself has come down to us in human form in the person of His Son, Jesus Christ. Do you want to know what God is like? Then look at Christ. "No one has ever seen God, but God the only Son, who is at the Father's side, has made him known" (John 1:18). If this is true—and it is—then you need not search the religions of the world for truth, because Christ is "the way and the truth and the life" (John 14:6).

God is not an object to be studied and analyzed, like a butterfly or a chemical solution. He is our Father, who created us and loves us. Commit your life to Jesus Christ, and you will not only know the truth about God but you will come to know God personally.

Commitment Page

A FRIEND OF mine once asked me, "Billy, if I become a true believer in Christ, will all of my problems go away?"

My answer was, "No, but you can have the power to deal with them."

We live in a fallen world. It is not the world that God designed, which was perfect, without pain, without suffering and without death. When our first parents, Adam and Eve, decided they knew better than God what was best for them, sin, with all of its terrible consequences for the human race, entered the world.

That is why I believe most problems have a spiritual answer. We often want our own way, not God's way. We often seek to please ourselves first, instead of God. What is interesting is that when we seek to please God first, very often we discover that we end up far more pleased than we did when we put ourselves first.

In order to begin to find solutions to our problems we must first change our attitude. How do we do that? By exchanging our old, selfish nature for God's selfless nature.

And how do we do that?

The Bible tells us that each of us is born with a propensity to sin. We know that we behave the way we do because of that nature. Have you noticed that children do not have to be taught to be selfish or jealous? It comes to them naturally and that is because as David, the great king of Israel said, "I was born in sin. . . ."

In order to begin to really solve our problems, we need a *new* nature. How do we acquire a new nature? By giving up our old one and accepting God's new nature through Jesus Christ.

The apostle Paul wrote, "If any man be in Christ, he is a new creation. Old things are passed away; behold, all things have become new."

There is no adequate human analogy to this spiritual truth. All I know is that I have seen it work tens of thousands of times and in the same way with everyone who has accepted the promise that God has made.

When you accept Christ as your Savior and make Him your Lord, He gives you the Holy Spirit. The Holy Spirit is given to guide and lead you so that as you read the Bible and desire to serve God instead of yourself, you develop a new attitude, a new perspective on your life and the problems you face.

It does not happen overnight. Your problems will not instantly disappear in most cases. But your problem of not having a relationship with God will immediately disappear and He will give you the power to deal with your problems and to sustain you in them and see you through them that is not available anywhere else.

God loves you with a perfect love no human being can fully understand. Human love is conditional. God's love is unconditional. It is so unconditional that the Bible says even while we were yet sinners, God sent His Son, Jesus Christ, to die in our place, to pay the sin debt that we owed to God. How many people do you know who would be willing to pay all of *your* debts, particularly when you were rebelling against them and had no desire to be their friend?

God has paid the greatest debt you will ever incur and once you understand the incredible sacrifice He has made just for you, you will feel compelled to turn to God and to accept Jesus Christ into your heart.

Will you accept what God has done for you today? It is so simple. Just pray a prayer something like this: "Dear God, I confess to You that I am a sinner and have tried to do everything my own way. Please forgive me. I now invite Jesus Christ into my heart and life and ask Him to save me from my sins. Please help me to get to know You and please give me the power to deal with the problems in my life. In Jesus' name, Amen."

If you prayed that prayer, or one like it, and sincerely meant it from your heart, God has done what He promised He would do. He has come into your heart and life, perhaps for the first time, or to renew your spirit.

I urge you to immediately locate a church near you where the Bible is taught as the Word of God and to begin attending every Sunday. You should also become involved in a Bible study so that you might discover the wonderful riches God has to pour out on your life.

It is important that you have your own personal quiet time with God every day, reading from His Word and praying to Him. Like a good diet and proper exercise helps the body, a good spiritual diet requires "digesting" the Word of God and "exercising" your spiritual muscles through prayer.

I hope you will write me about your decision. The address is: Billy Graham, Box 779, Minneapolis, Minnesota 55403. I would like to send you some literature that will help get you started in your new walk with Christ, who is the *real* answer to every problem that confronts us.